TOMBSTONES

OF

SUSSEX COUNTY

DELAWARE

VOLUME ONE

Downstate Delaware Genealogical Society

Heritage Books

2024

HERITAGE BOOKS

AN IMPRINT OF HERITAGE BOOKS, INC.

Books, CDs, and more—Worldwide

For our listing of thousands of titles see our website
at
www.HeritageBooks.com

Published 2024 by
HERITAGE BOOKS, INC.
Publishing Division
5810 Ruatan Street
Berwyn Heights, MD 20740

Originally published by
Downstate Delaware Genealogical Society
Dover, Delaware

Heritage Books by the author:
Tombstones of Sussex County, Delaware, Volume One
Tombstones of Sussex County, Delaware, Volume Three

International Standard Book Number
Paperbound: 978-0-7884-2744-2

INTRODUCTION

This volume is the first in a series that the Downstate Delaware Genealogical Society hopes to publish in order that professional and amateur genealogists may have a readily available and up-to-date source of information from the gravestones of Sussex County, Delaware.

Should any item of information in this or later volumes become primary evidence of a birth, death, marriage or other fact, it is strongly recommended that a personal examination be made of the stone to confirm that data. The recorders have performed their tasks in a diligent manner but have worked under adverse conditions at times and are, therefore, subject to making an occasional mistake. This Society assumes no responsibility for errors or omissions.

At the outset of this project we were aware that some stones were two hundred or more years of age and in spite of using various methods of causing letters and numbers to be more distinct some would remain questionable. To assist in deciphering the data as well as to include information from stones now lost, buried, stolen or otherwise not available, we decided to utilize information contained in the Hudson Tombstone Book at the Delaware Public Archives, Dover, Delaware. This book contains tombstone information collected in 1930 by Sussex County residents employed by Millard F. Hudson of Brookmont, Virginia. This book is not a complete record of all cemeteries because some Hudson records were destroyedd by fire before publication and because it does not appear that African-American and Native-American cemeteries were included in the project. However, six hundred (600) cemeteries were included and the recordings appear to be accurate. Therefore, in any instance when the Hudson Book contains information from a tombstone which readers of this project did not find, the information from the Hudson Book was added to ours under a separate heading at the end of each cemetery listing.

All data on stones was recorded except verses and religious inscriptions. Misspellings and other apparent errors were recorded exactly as on the stones. The recorders made no decisions as to accuracy of data. If a date of birth was not shown and the decedent's age was shown in years, months and days, the recorder did not attempt to mathematically compute the date of birth. Relationships with other persons were always recorded if shown on the stone, but when severalnames appeared and the relationship was stated, the recorder made no assumptions as to the relationship. However, after each of these names we added "SSW" and gave the name of the other individuals. For these purposes the abbreviation "SSW" means "same stone with." This method enabled us to arrange all names alphabetically but still show that relationship existed with certain other persons.

Each cemetery has been assigned two identification numbers. The first is our number which has two letters and three numbers. For example BC-030 means that this was the thirtieth cemetery from Broad Creek Hundred. The second identification always begins with HU, which is an abbreviation for Hudson, and the number which follows is the number assigned to that cemetery in the Hudson Book. If the second identification number is HU-NR, it was not recorded by Hudson.

The Hundreds of Sussex County are taxable subdivisions and their names and abbreviations are as follows:

HUNDRED	ABBREVIATION
Baltimore	BA
Broad Creek	BC
Broadkill	BK
Cedar Creek	CC
Dagsboro	DA
Georgetown	GN
Gumboro	GU
Indian River	IR
Lewes & Rehoboth	LR
Little Creek	LC
Nanticoke	NA
Northwest Fork	NF
Seaford	SE

The location of each cemetery is shown as being in a town or lying in a specific direction from a town. The only towns used were those having a postal zip code (except Gumboro), and names of crossroads, hamlets and residential subdivisions were disregarded. An exception, however, was made for Gumboro because of the large number of cemeteries in that area.

In plotting the cemetery locations, US route numbers, Delaware route numbers, Sussex County road numbers, and road names recently assigned to routes and roads by the County were used. There now exists a process whereby a route or road name may be changed if requested by a specific number of residents, and this process may be invoked once per year; therefore, if difficulty is experienced in locating a cemetery, it may be because the route or road has been renamed, in which case the use of route or road numbers in locating cemeteries is used.

The majority of the cemeteries of Sussex County are located on private property. Some are in wooded areas, some on tilled land, some by the edge of a road, and some even on a lawn of a private residence. The Downstate Delaware Genealogical Society requests that you consider the privacy of the property owners and obtain their permission before trespassing upon their property.

Harold J. Maloney
Cemetery Committee

Dover, Delaware
December 1999

TABLE OF CONTENTS

BALTIMORE HUNDRED

BROAD CREEK

BROADKILL

CEDAR CREEK

NANTICOKE

(BA-001 & HU-25) BLACKWATER PRESBYTERIAN CHURCH CEMETERY

Located West of Clarksville on the S. E. side of Omar Rd. (CR-54) at the intersection with Blackwater Road (Rd. 374)
Recorded: December 19, 1953

AYDELOTTE, Maria C., b. 08/07/1831, d. 01/11/1923
AYDELOTTE, Stephen C., b. 10/05/1823, d. 09/05/1901
CHAMBERLAIN, Elizabeth B. Tunnell, w/o G. W., b. 11/17/1829, d. 03/26/1904
CHAMBERLAIN, G. W., b. 10/30/1839, d. 09/26/1909
HARPER, Bessie M., ssw-George C., b. 08/22//1907, d. 01/13/1988
HARPER, Elizabeth E., ssw-Myrtle, b. 09/08/1914, d. N/D
HARPER, Frank H., ssw-Elizabeth E., b. 12/26/1910, d. 05/26/1987
HARPER, George C., ssw-Bessie M., b. 08/28/1909, d. 03/24/1988
HARPER, Ida M., ssw-John E., b. 1875, d. 1933
HARPER, John E., ssw-Ida M., b. 1885, d. 1941
HARPER, John Ian, b. 05/21/1976, d. 02/01/1990
HARPER, Lewis W., ssw-Myrtle, b. 1914, d. 1969
HARPER, Myrtle, ssw-Lewis W., b. 02/21/1921, d. N/D
HELM, Herschel N., ssw-Sarah E., b. 1882, d 1967
HELM, Sarah E., ssww-Herschel N., b. 1888, d. 1990
HILL, Elizabeth, w/o Henry E., Age 75, b. N/D, d. 10/01/1878
HILL, H. E., Age 73, b. N/D, d. 04/13/1872
HILL, James B., Age 30y, b. N/D, d. 05/17/1838
LAYFIELD, Dellie E., ssw-Robbie L., Isabelle J. & Robert H., b. 1878, d 1879
LAYFIELD, Isabelle J., ssw-Robert H., Dellie E. & Robbie L., b. 1857, d. 1934
LAYFIELD, Robbie L., ssw-Robert H., Dellie E., & Isabelle J., b. 1884, d. 1884
LAYFIELD, Robert H., ssw-Dellie E., Isabelle J. & Robbie L., b. 1850, d. 1907
LITTLETON, Horace, ssw-Sallie, b. 1920, d. N/D
LITTLETON, Sallie, ssw-Horace, b. 1930, d. N/D
LONG, Fredrick, Inf. s/o Robert S. & Mary Tunnell, b. N/D, d. N/D
LONG, Keturah P., ssw-William S., b. 1848, d. 1938
LONG, Malvena Holloway, b. 06/25/1884, d. 10/18/1957
LONG, Mary A., w/o Robert S. & d/o Jas. M. Tunnell, Age 23-6-0, b. N/D, d. 11/07/1850
LONG, Robert Schofield, b. 01/18/1914, d. 03/04/1955
LONG, Robert Schofield, M.D., b. 09/18/1882, d. 03/15/1928
LONG, William S., ssw-Keturah P., b. 1847, d. 1922
MORRIS, Chester R., ssw-Edna R., b. 06/20/1908, d. N/D
MORRIS, Edna R., ssw-Chester R., b. 10/21/1907, d. 03/03/1986
SMITH, Daniel R., ssw-Estella C., b. 1869, d. 1939
SMITH, Estella C., ssw-Daniel R., b. 1871, d. N/D
TOWNSEND, Ann C., w/o Littleton, b. 11/25/1807, d. 11/02/1894
TOWNSEND, Annie Lizzie, d/o Littleton & Ann C., b. 09/12/1843, d. 09/26/1843
TOWNSEND, George A., s/o Littleton & Ann C., b. 03/07/1848, d. 10/17/1849
TOWNSEND, Littleton, b. 06/21/1810, d. 05/10/1848
TRIMBLE, George R., ssw-Louise R., b. 1875, d. 1949
TRIMBLE, George R., Jr., ssw-Marguerite W., b. 10/07/1912, d. 08/25/1991
TRIMBLE, Louise R., ssw-George R., b. 1880, d. 1967

TRIMBLE, Marguerite W., ssw-George R., Jr., b. 03/28/1913, d. N/D
TUNNELL, Charles E., b. 03/27/1843, d. 10/06/1920
TUNNELL, Elizabeth M., w/o Charles E., b. 10//02/1834, d. 08/04/1905
TUNNELL, Henry M., ssw-Rhoda E., b. 11/25/1831, d. 02/03/1904
TUNNELL, Hetty, w/o James M. & d/o Harry Maull, born in Lewes, Age 40y 5m 23d, b. N/D,
      d. 05/03/1847
TUNNELL, Isaac E., s/o James & Hetty, Age 24y 9m 24d, b. N/D, d. 06/28/1863
TUNNELL, James Elisha, s/o James M. & Sarah Ethel, b. 12/13/1908, d. 05/26/1909
TUNNELL, James H., Capt., b. 1829, d. 1907
TUNNELL, James M., Age 77y 1m 18d, b. 01/16/1794, d. 03/04/1871
TUNNELL, James M., ssw-Sarah Ethel, b. 1879, d. 1957
TUNNELL, James Miller, Jr., s/o Sarah Ethel Dukes & James Miller, b. 06/17/1910, d. 06/06/1986
TUNNELL, John M., b. 06/24/1869, d. 05/31/1914
TUNNELL, John M., Capt., b. 03/24/1834, d. 01/08/1886
TUNNELL, Kate J., w/o James H., b. 07/03/1840, d. 05/21/1919
TUNNELL, Martha A., w/o John M., Age 32y 11m 1d, b. N/D, d. 08/13/1877
TUNNELL, Mildred South, w/o James Miller, Jr. & d/o Anna Cooper & Frank E. South, b. 05/10/1912,
      d. 07/10/1984
TUNNELL, Rhoda E., ssw-Henry M., b. 02/06/1836, d. 02/19/1903
TUNNELL, Sarah Ethel, ssw-James M., b. 1885, d. 1956
TURNER, Anna M., w/o Henry C., ssw-Henry C., b. 11/13/1852, d. 05/10/1928
TURNER, Elizabeth H., w/o James, Age 75y 180d, b. N/D, d. 12/14/1880
TURNER, Elmer J., ssw-Nancy R., b. 1885, d. 1936
TURNER, Henry C., ssw-Anna M., b. 10/04/1842, d. 09/16/1914
TURNER, Henry E., s/o E. J. & N. R., b. 01/06/1917, d. 06/14/1980
TURNER, James, Age 79y 22d, b. N/D, d. 02/02/1878
TURNER, Lester B., b. 01/26/1921, d. 03/24/1977
TURNER, Nancy R., ssw-Elmer J., b. 1887, d. 1980
WATSON, Henrietta M. (Etta Layfield), b. 1890, d. 1957
WATSON, William C. (Presbyterian Minister), b. 1878, d. 19—

(BC-001 & HU-315) OLD CHRIST CHURCH CEMETERY
Located East of Laurel, on the North East side of Chipmans Pond Rd. (Rd. 465) at the intersection with
Christ Church Rd. (Rd. 465A). Recorded: October 11, 1997.

STATE OF DELAWARE MARKER
(OLD CHRIST CHURCH)

Established on Broad Creek in 1770 as a "Chapel of Ease" of Stepney Parish, Maryland on land purchased
by a levy of 80,000 pounds of tobacco. Building completed by Robert Holsten in 1772 at a cost of 510
pounds.

(NATHANIEL MITCHELL)

STATE OF DELAWARE MARKER
(1752 – 1813)

This Federalist served as the Governor of Delaware between 1805-1808. He was born in Laurel in 1752, attended Old Christ Church and is buried in this Churchyard. Mitchell was commissioned as adjutant of militia in 1775, promoted to Captain in 1776 and appointed Brigade Major in 1779. He was delegate to the Continental Congress between 1786-1788 and was a member of Delaware's General Assembly between 1808-1812.

ALLEN, Mary V., d/o Wm. D. & Hester Allen, Age 8y 8m 23d, b. N/D, d. 06/02/1887
ALLEN, Sallie F., d/o Wm. D. & Hester Allen, Age 19y, b. N/D, d. 1885
ALLEN, Eliza, d/o Wm. D. & Hester Allen, Age 22y, b. N/D, d. 04/23/1884
BARR, Richard Spencer, s/o Vera M. & William S. Barr, b. 12/09/1957, d. 12/14/1957
BELL, Hamilton, Rev., Age 29, b. N/D, d. 11/26/1811
BELL, Levenia, Age abt. 71y, b. N/D, d. 05/05/1866
BELL, Levin A., Age 26y, b. N/D, d. 02/19/1845
BELL, William S., Age 61y 6m 5d, b. N/D, d. 10/15/1871
CANNON, Purtyman, Age 45y, b. N/D, d. 03/29/1829
COLBOURN, John H., b. 05/20/1856, d. 12/08/1924
COLBOURN, Sarah A., b. 08/06/1832, d. 11/12/1909
CULVER, Almond V., s/o Wilbert M. & Dellie Culver, Age 8m 10d, b. N/D, d. 10/05/1884
CULVER, Hiran G., s/o Hiran C. & Patience Culver, Age 23y 5m 29d, b. N/D, d. 10/09/1888
DAVIS, Mary E., b. 06/30/1865, d. 03/18/1951
DAVIS, Raymond, s/o Mary Davis, b. 04/21/1890, d. 02/16/1904
HASTINGS, Herman D., b. 07/27/1861, d. 05/13/1907
HASTINGS, Irving W., b. 07/28/1859, d. 07/07/1909
HASTINGS, Juliann, w/o Asbury Hastings, Age 59y 5m 27d, b. 05/23/1825, d. 11/19/1884
HASTINGS, Kesson A., Age 68y 4m 7d, b. N/D, d. 06/04/1888
HEARN, Michael W., Age 63y 21d, b. 03/28/1827, d. 04/19/1890
HEARN, Sarah J., w/o Michael W., b. 08/13/1837, d. 01/19/1910
HITCHENS, Josiah R., b. 11/03/1860, d. 09/28/1946
MITCHELL, Nathaniel, Major, Governor, Age 61y, b. N/D, d. 02/21/1813
POLK, John, Age 52y 2m, b. N/D, d. 10/14/1842
PUSEY, George S., Age 75y 11m 7d, b. 03/09/1815, d. 02/16/1891
PUSEY, George W. of A., ssw-Martha L., b. 1842, d. 1913
PUSEY, Martha L., ssw-George W. of A., b. 1850, d. 1891
SKELLY, Sarah, Age 60y, b. N/D, d. 06/28/1830
SKELLY, William, Rev., Age 50y, b. N/D, d. 01/25/1808
TOWNSEND, Mary, w/o Thomas Townsend, Age in 33y, b. N/D, d. 01/10/1822
VAUGHAN, Joseph, Age 79y 10d, b. 07/24/1817, d. 08/04/1896
WINDSOR, Sallie A., w/o Samuel D., Age 73y 3m 11d, b. N/D, d. 02/06/1904
WINDSOR, Samuel D., Age 72y 4m 8d, b. 08/14/1837, d. 12/22/1909

(BK-001 & HU-NR) BETTS FAMILY CEMETERY
Located East of Milton on the North side of Broadkill Rd. (Rt. 16) 1.6 miles S. W. of Coastal Highway (Rt. 1).
Recorded: January 12, 1996

ATKINS, Baby, b. N/D, d. N/D
ATKINS, Emma, b. 1883, d. 1883
BAKER, Fannie M., ssw-Joseph J. Betts, Daughter, b. 1867, d. 1897

BAKER, Franklin H., s/o Fannie M., b. 1890, d. 1941

BAKER, Georgia Betts Thornton, ssw-Jane Shea O'Donnell, b. 1926, d. N/D

BAKER, Gladys G., ssw-Joseph B., b. 07/01/1907, d. N/D

BAKER, Jane Shae O'Donnell, ssw-Georgia Betts Thornton, b. 1923, d. 1981

BAKER, Joseph B., ssw-Gladys G., b. 12/14/1892, d. 11/30/1968

BAKER, Nora M., w/o Franklin H., b. 1887, d. 1962

BANDO, Emma P., b. 10/21/1887, d. 05/10/1971

BETTS, Addie M., ssw-Alfred S., b. 02/26/1818, d. 09/26/1968

BETTS, Alfred Ray, s/o Alfred S. & Maggie, b. 02/17/1901, d. 05/05/1901

BETTS, Alfred S., ssw-Addie M., b. 03/10/1878, d. 10/27/1960

BETTS, Alice E., b. 10/23/1859, d. 07/27/1918

BETTS, David H., b. 05/24/1851, d. 11/05/1914

BETTS, David M., b. 08/23/1907, d. 08/03/1992

BETTS, Elizabeth, w/o David, Age 18y 7m 22d, b. N/D, d. 10/27/1874

BETTS, Emeline, w/o Joseph, ssw-Joseph J., Mother, b. 1831, d. 1914

BETTS, Emeline, w/o R. W., ssw-Robert, Age 69y, b. N/D, d. 09/15/1885

BETTS, Estella B., b. 1889, d. 1931

BETTS, Franklin S., b. 04/25/1904, d. 07/10/1979

BETTS, George H., ssw-Winnie H., b. 1856, d. 1933

BETTS, Greensbury W., b. 03/01/1856, d. 04/12/1916

BETTS, Halstead P., ssw-Joseph J., Son, b. 1872, d. 1917

BETTS, Ida P., b. 01/06/1857, d. 10/28/1897

BETTS, Isaac S., s/o Robert & Emeline, Age 13y 5m 20d, b. N/D, d. 07/31/1886

BETTS, James C., b. 1885, d. 1922

BETTS, Joda A., b. 1855, d. 1877

BETTS, Joseph J., ssw-Emeline, Father, b. 1828, d. 1884

BETTS, Joseph L. Reed, s/o David H. & Ida, b. 09/28/1881, d. 09/02/1886

BETTS, Leah, w/o Jules J., Age 76y 4m, b. N/D, d. 09/26/1859

BETTS, Leah J., d/o Robert & Emeline, Age 11d, b. N/D, d. 11/17/1850

BETTS, Leighton, b. 1899, d. 1941

BETTS, Lydia H., d/o Robert & Emeline, Age 9d, b. N/D, d. 11/15/1850

BETTS, Maggie Millman, w/o Alfred S., b. 07/19/1880, d. 07/26/1905

BETTS, Mary E., d/o /Robert W. & Emeline, Age 32y 3m 16d, b. 01/10/1849, d. 04/16/1881

BETTS, Naioma H., w/o William C., ssw-Preston, b. 07/14/1878, d. 06/06/1915

BETTS, Preston, s/o William C. & Naioma H., ssw-Naioma H., b. 06/05/1915, d. 08/23/1915

BETTS, Reedy, b. 08/24/1887, d. 04/11/1915

BETTS, Robert J., s/o Isaac S. & Sarah T., Age 4m 26d, b. N/D, d. 06/26/1854

BETTS, Robert W., ssw-Emeline, Age 67y 11d, b. 10/01/1815, d. 10/12/1882

BETTS, Rose Mae (Baby), b. 1906, d. 1907

BETTS, Samuel of Jas., Age 68y 11m 27d, b. 01/22/1798, d. 01/19/1867

BETTS, William C., b. 07/12/1878, d. 09/28/1958

BETTS, Winnie H., ssw-George H., b. 1858, d. 1885

EHRIE, Clara T., b. 1859, d. 1888

EHRIE, George, b. 02/24/1883, d. 03/19/1883

HARRIMAN, Fannie C., b. 1878, d. 1952

HUFF, Harry A., Sr., Beloved h/o Jennie M. Lofland, b. 1878, d. 1952

HUFF, Jennie M. Lofland, Beloved w/o Harry A., Sr., b. 1876, d. 1957

JOHNSON, Delphine, d/o B. W. & H. J., Age 1y 11m 23d, b. N/D, d. 09/08/1859

JONES, Charles C., ssw-Delema S., b. 03/18/1901, d. 11/09/1963
JONES, Delema S., ssw-Charles C., b. 03/30/1906, d. 03/06/1985
JONES, Emeline, ssw-Willard S., b. 1872, d. 1949
JONES, Willard Frank, b. 10/07/1898, d. 09/05/1976
JONES, Willard S., ssw-Emeline, b. 1862, d. 1933
LOFLAND, Alfred H., Sr., ssw-Annie E., b. 04/25/1873, d. 05/27/1958
LOFLAND, Annie E., ssw-Alfred H., Sr., b. 07/20/1888, d. 11/04/1970
LOFLAND, Blanch P., d/o James H. & Susan M., b. 01/29/1882, d. 09/03/1910
LOFLAND, Carlton S., b. 08/22/1917, d. 01/10/1989
LOFLAND, Henry C., Father, b. 12/21/1862, d. 04/27/1907
LOFLAND, Inf. d/o Alfred H. & Annie E., b. N/D, d. 06/21/1909
LOFLAND, James B., (Our Son), b. 10/07/1894, d. 05/29/1902
LOFLAND, James H., Father, b. 05/30/1838, d. 02/01/1918
LOFLAND, Joanna, b. 1884, d. 1920
LOFLAND, Julia C., Mother, b. 02/13/1860, d. 12/05/1908
LOFLAND, Mark H., b. 04/24/1886, d. 02/14/1959
LOFLAND, Susan M., w/o James H., Mother, b. 09/25/1842, d. 09/25/1907
LOFLAND, Trusten Polk, b. 03/01/1868, d. 02/19/1952
REED, Alfred B., ssw-Eliza A., b. 1839, d. 1893
REED, Betty A., ssw-Carl H., b. 04/19/1917, d 08/11/1984
REED, Carl H., ssw-Betty A., b. 12/13/1914, d. 07/13/1992
REED, Clarence B., b. 04/17/1882, d. 02/09/1951
REED, Eliza A., ssw-Alfred B., b. 1844, d. 1918
REED, George, Capt., b. 02/10/1864, d. 03/14/1948
REED, Laura, b. 1876, d. 1881
REED, Robert B., s/o Alfred B. & Eliza A., b. 03/10/1862, d. 01/15/1890
REYNOLDS, Sadie Betts, b. 1890, d. 1937
ROBINSON, Benjamin W., ssw-Sallie V., b. 1870, d. 1935
ROBINSON, George B., s/o James & Sallie, b. 1906, d. 1915
ROBINSON, Sallie V., w/o Benjamin W., ssw-Benjamin W., b. 1868, d. 1927

(BK-002 & HU-NR) FIRST CONGREGATIONAL UNITED CHURCH OF CHRIST CEMETERY

Located in Milton on the South side of Milton-Ellendale Highway (Rt. 16) between Mulberry & Union Streets
Recorded: January 12, 1996

ABERNATHY, Sallie, Mother, b. 01/18/1925, d. 01/15/1984
ALLEN, Margaret, b. 07/06/1946, d. 11/11/1976
BANKS, Carolee V., b. 01/09/1907, d. 12/14/1986
BANKS, Charles W., Tech5, USA, WW II, b. 10/04/1909, d. 08/27/1985
BEST, George, b. 1919, d. 1989
CLARK, Bessie M., b. 10/24/1896, d. 02/09/1985
CLARK, John W., Jr., ssw-Lulu R., b. 05/13/1894, d. 10/05/1964
CLARK, John W., Sr., ssw-Maggie S., b. 01/16/1875, d. 03/24/1963
CLARK, Lulu R., ssw-John W., Jr., b. 07/30/1897, d. 11/21/1988
CLARK, Maggie S., ssw-John W., Sr., b. 08/20/1876, d. 02/18/1967
CLARK, Ray W., b. 04/03/1931, d. 08/17/1988

CLARKS, Leroy, ssw-Virginia C., b. 06/24/1899, d. 12/29/1991
CLARKS, Virginia C., ssw-Leroy, b. 11/21/1900, d. 04/16/1984
DAVIS, Herschel E., ssw-Wilhelmina E., b. 1941, d. N/D
DRAIN, Herschel, ssw-Minnie V., b. 04/07/1900, d. 06/20/1984
DRAIN, Minnie V., ssw-Herschel, b. 01/24/1898, d. 09/23/1993
ELEY, Emma Mary, b. 02/11/1933, d. 05/12/1982
HANZER, Harold, b. 1925, d. 1981
HANZER, Lester, b. 1911, d. 1984
HARMON, Elmer, b. 03/25/1890, d. 11/08/1962
HARMON, Rufus P., Jr., Del. Cpl 103 Fld Art Bn., b. 04/21/1928, d. 10/02/1969
HARMON, Winona, Mother, b. 02/06/1917, d. 12/04/1974
HARRIS, Daniel J., b. 12/08/1916, d. 06/09/1977
HAZZARD, Elizabeth N., b. 10/24/1900, d. 11/03/1968
HAZZARD, Eric L., b. 11/10/1896, d. 07/06/1952
HAZZARD, Keith W., ssw-Tina M., b. 04/07/1972, d. 04/07/1972
HAZZARD, Tina M., ssw-Keith W., b. 05/07/1960, d. N/D
HENRY, Hattie B., ssw-Hurley C., b. 07/13/1895, d. 10/10/1973
HENRY, Hurley C., ssw-Hattie B., b. 05/25/1889, d. 11/25/1985
INGRAM, Larry, b. 01/01/1875, d. 01/21/1965
KEYS, Henry, b. 1913, d. 1982
LINGO, Lydia H., b. 03/04/1890, d. 03/03/1961
LUCAS, Boyd D., b. 10/20/1911, d. 11/22/1981
LUCAS, Daisey, b. 02/28/1913, d. 02/18/1968
MOSLEY, Sallie E., b. 10/17/1889, d. 10/04/1962
NOCHO, Gertrude, b. 1889, d. N/D
NOCHO, Maurice E., DE, Cpl. 9th Field Signal Battalion, WWI, b. 04/07/1892, d. 11/16/1966
PERKINS, Reese, b. 1948, d. 1979
PETTYJOHN, Carl D., b. 1932, d. 1984
PETTYJOHN, Eleanor M., ssw-William A., b. 1902, d. 1994
PETTYJOHN, William A., ssw-Eleanor M., b. 1900, d. 1971
PINDER, Mary F. Hicks, b. 10/01/1894, d. 10/31/1972
PIPER, Arthur, ssw-Viola W., b. 09/14/1905, d. 1991
PIPER, Viola W., ssw-Arthur, b. 10/11/1907, d. 02/05/1989
PRICE, Aron, Sr., ssw-Letha M., m. 9/7/1950, b. 10/23/1930, d. 10/10/1993
PRICE, Letha M., ssw-Aron, Sr., m. 9/7/1950, b. 08/08/1930, d. N/D
RICKS, Helen, b. 1891, d. 1963
SAMUELS, Ernest, STM1, USN, WWII, b. 1918, d. 1982
SEARLES, Mammie, b. 1888, d. 1970
SOCKUM, Ira, b. 04/02/1894, d. 08/17/1968
TAYLOR, Alice H., b. 04/08/1923, d. 05/22/1989
TOLSON, Mary Ailene Morris, ssw-Thomas A. & Richard L., b. 1933, d. 1989
TOLSON, Richard L., ssw-Thomas A. & Mary Ailene Morris, b. 1956, d. 1975
TOLSON, Thomas A., ssw-Mary Ailene Morris & Richard L., b. 1929, d. 1981
WAPLES, Elizabeth H., b. 1892, d. 1964
WAPLES, Joseph C., b. 1888, d. 1965
WATSON, Callie Hicks, b. 03/01/1897, d. 03/21/1970
WATSON, Marie E., Mother, b. 12/25/1925, d. 11/29/1981
WRIGHT, Robert J., b. 1873, d. 1955

(BK-003 & HU-NR) BETHEL A. M. E. CHURCH CEMETERY

Located N. E. of Milton on the S. W. corner of Broadkill Rd. (Rt. 16) and County Rd. (Rd. 22-A).
Recorded: June 12, 1996

BARROW, Merdis A., b. 11/15/1908, d. 03/01/1937

BELL, John H., ssw-Mary A., b. 1858, d. 1933

BELL, Mary A., ssw-John H., b. 1871, d. 1932

BELL, Robert, Illinois Corp. 370 inf. 95 Div., b. N/D, d. 06/07/1941

BRADLEY, Wilma A., b. 1943, d. 1988

BRINKLEY, Inez, b. 1915, d. 1995

BROWN, John, b. 02/27/1910, d. 02/08/1946

BURTON, Charles Lain, ssw-Jeremiah, David H., Lydia H. & Mary E., b. 1900, d. 1934

BURTON, David H., ssw-Charles Lain, Jeremiah, Lydia H. & Mary E., b. 1873, d. 1874

BURTON, Herman, b. 1914, d. 1985

BURTON, Jeremiah, ssw-Lydia H., Charles Lain, Jeremiah, David H. & Mary E., b. 1850, d. 1926

BURTON, Lena P., b. 05/08/1895, d. 08/25/1950

BURTON, Lydia H., w/o Jeremiah, ssw-Jeremiah, Charles Lain, David H. & Mary E., b. 1848, d. N/D

BURTON, Mary E., ssw-Jeremiah, Charles Lain, David H. & Mary E., b. 1876, d 1924

BURTON, William H., DE Co. F, 808 Pioneer Inf., WWI, b. 11/29/1891, d. 12/30/1950

BURTON, William H., DE Tech 4, Co. C, 619 Engr. CBN, WWII, b. 02/17/1917, d. 10/28/1952

CIRWITHAN, James H., b. 1934, d. 1977

COLEMAN, Lillian E., b. 1914, d. 1995

DAVIS, Virginia M., b. 12/29/1936, d. 05/31/1978

DOWNING, M. Violet, b. 1917, d. 1938

DURHAM, Oscar, b. 06/27/1880, d. 09/17/1959

ELMER, William, b. 07/31/1874, d. 02/21/1922

FAMBRO, Roosevelt A., b. 1955, d. 1993

FRAME, Winnoa L., b. 1911, d. 1975

HARMON, A. Elizabeth Ingram, b. 06/15/1909, d. 06/02/1991

HARMON, Arzelia W., ssw-Levi W., b. 1899, d. 1968

HARMON, Della M., ssw-John L., b. 1901, d 1992

HARMON, Elwood, b. 05/18/1879, d. 09/11/1916

HARMON, Golia, DE, Pvt. 543 Serv. Bat. Engr. C., WWI, b. 07/02/1894, d. 05/21/1959

HARMON, John L., ssw-Della M., b. 1897, d. 1978

HARMON, Leona W., b. 11/02/1914, d. 08/13/1941

HARMON, Levi W., ssw-Arzelia W., b. 1891, d. 1965

HARMON, Mary L., w/o Robert M., ssw-Robert M., b. 1866, d. 1934

HARMON, Melvin, b. 1916, d. 1981

HARMON, Robert M., ssw-Mary L., b. 1861, d. 1951

HARMON, Victoria, w/o Maurice, Age 48y 7m 13d, b. 03/06/1862, d. 10/19/1910

HARMON, Virginia, b. 1903, d. 1988

HEAVELOW, C. J., ssw-J. E., b. 1841, d. 1908

HEAVELOW, J. E., ssw-C. J., b. 1884, d. 1939

HOPKINS, Dorothy M., b. 12/20/1936, d. 07/07/1994

INGRAM, Leonzo, ssw-S. Gladys, b. 1897, d. 1968

INGRAM, S. Gladys, ssw-Leonzo, b. 1911, d. N/D

JACKSON, Mollie (Evangelist), b. 1896, d. 1973

LOPER, Juanita Piper, b. 06/07/1959, d. 07/14/1991

MASON, Ethel C., ssw-John J., b. 07/05/1914, d. N/D
MASON, John J., ssw-Ethel C., b. 06/27/1910, d. 12/28/1990
MASSEY, Andrew, Rev., b. N/D, d. 05/12/1865
MIFFLIN, Elizabeth E. W. (Wingie), b. 09/09/1936, d. 02/02/1958
MIFFLIN, Norman H., DE. Pfc. 8th Pioneer Inf., b. N/D, d. 10/04/1959
MOSLEY, Levi, b. 12/14/1830, d. 11/22/1914
PEAKERS, Agnes, b. 1916, d. 1995
PETTYJOHN, Garnet, USA, Korea, b. 10/18/1930, d. 12/18/1987
PIPER, Albert, b. 10/28/1902, d. 07/04/1993
PIPER, Alice, b. 08/10/1903, d. 12/29/1994
PIPER, Frances M., ssw-Herman D., b. 04/26/1920, d. N/D
PIPER, Herman D., ssw-Frances M., b. 07/16/1906, d. 10/13/1978
PIPER, Marshall, b. 05/14/1962, d. 08/20/1978
PIPER, Martha Ann, Mother, b. 11/20/1870, d. 08/06/1962
PIPER, Mary Ann, b. 09/17/1952, d. 12/05/1978
RICHARDSON, Walter A. R., b. 11/25/1872, d. 02/26/1938
SOCKOM, Henry, Husband, b. 04/09/1863, d. 12/20/1949
SOCKOM, John P., ssw-Lear C., b. 07/16/1861, d. N/D
SOCKOM, Lear C., ssw-John P., Wife, b. 01/08/1870, d. 12/20/1924
SOCKOM, Mary J., ssw-Stephen & Mary L., b. 1857, d. 1898
SOCKOM, Mary L., ssw-Stephen & Mary J., b. 1853, d. 1925
SOCKOM, Stephen, ssw-Mary J. & Mary L., b. 1854, d. 1942
SOMERS, George, b. 03/01/1836, d. 05/25/1892
TACARR, No other information
THOMPSON, Elizabeth H., ssw-Fred R., b. 05/22/1890, d. 03/03/1962
THOMPSON, Fred R., ssw-Elizabeth H., b. 05/25/1884, d. 10/20/1969
TOLSON, Earl, b. 1905, d. 1983
TOLSON, Grace E., b. 03/06/1910, d. 08/11/1978
VAN, Hannah M., w/o Harris, Age 40y 2m 9d, b. 05/10/1863, d. 07/1903
WAPLES, Clara E., d/o Ellen & James, Age 12y 11m 23d, b. N/D, d. 07/28/1898
WAPLES, Ellen, ssw-James, Mother, Age 44y, b. N/D, d. 03/08/1908
WAPLES, James, ssw-Ellen, Father, Age 62y, b. N/D, d. 11/26/1917
WAPLES, Oliver J., Private, 8th Pioneer Inf., Age 26y 9m 19d, b. 12/18/1891, d. 10/02/1918
WAPLES, Ossie O. Perry, w/o Leon S., b. 01/09/1912, d. 12/22/1951
WARREN, Clarence Percy, ssw-Minnie Alverta, b. 1888, d. 1957
WARREN, Minnie Alverta, ssw-Clarence Percy, b. 1888, d. 1971
WATSON, Carrie, ssw-James, b. 1900, d. 1981
WATSON, Gladys, b. 1905, d. 1994
WATSON, James, ssw-Carrie, b. 1902, d. N/D
WHITE, Carter Carlton, b. 1912, d. 1982
WHITE Gertrude, ssw-Louis, b. 1894, d. 1983
WHITE, Joanna H., ssw-Samuel R., b. 08/28/1892, d. 04/14/1984
WHITE, Louis, ssw-Gertrude, b. 1880, d. 1968
WHITE, Samuel R., ssw-Joanna H., b. 08/11/1886, d. 12/25/1953
WRIGHT, Annie M., w/o William H., Age 76y, b. N/D, d. 10/20/1914
WRIGHT, Edgar, b. 1902, d. 1996
WRIGHT, Elizabeth, w/o Robert W., Age 39y, b. N/D, d. 06/23/1875
WRIGHT, Leah, Age 62y, b. N/D, d. 09/19/1869

WRIGHT, Nicholas M., b. 10/13/1903, d. 04/01/1961
WRIGHT, Robert Wells, Rev., b. 1861, d. 1931
WRIGHT, Walter R., ssw-Wilford D., Brothers, b. 04/12/1914, d. N/D
WRIGHT, Wilford, ssw-Walter R., Brothers, b. 01/24/1912, d. 09/15/1951
WRIGHT, William H., Age 67y 3m 28d, b. 12/12/1836, d. 04/10/1904
YOUNG, Clarence Henry, DE, Cpl., USA, WWI, b. 12/22/1896, d. 01/15/1962
YOUNG, Romania E., ssw-Theodore R., b. 09/11/1908, d. 08/18/1980
YOUNG, Sarah J., w/o Alexander, Age 38y, b. N/D, d. 04/15/1939
YOUNG, Theodore R., ssw-Romania E., b. 03/04/1904, d. 06/28/1949

(BK-004 & HU-526) ODD FELLOWS CEMETERY
Located in Milton on the E. side of Union Street opposite Tobin Street.
Recorded: May 22 – June 12, 1996

ABBOTT, Ida W., b. 1860, d. 1941
ABBOTT, Willard H., b. 1859, d. 1927
ADAMS, Calvin C., ssw-Shirley J., b. 07/17/1926, d. N/D
ADAMS, Shirley J., ssw-Calvin C., b. 08/23/1933, d. 01/09/1989
ALEXANDER, M. Jeannette, b. 09/07/1925, d. 06/14/1994
ANDRIE, Edward, ssw-Ida, b. 1887, d. 1964
ANDRIE, Ida, w/o Edward, ssw-Edward, b. 1886, d. 1945
ANDRIE, William H., b. 1914, d. 1995
ANTON, James Lewis, SSgt, USMC, WWII, b. 05/16/1914, d. 04/26/1980
ARGO, Annie K., b. 07/27/1876, d. 11/03/1938
ARGO, Beatrice L., ssw-Milton P., b. 01/26/1910, d. 05/22/1987
ARGO, David H., ssw-Eliza A., b. 02/25/1848, d. 02/12/1919
ARGO, Eliza A., ssw-David H., b. 03/25/1854, d. 01/11/1918
ARGO, Everett F., ssw-Mary K., Sgt, HQ + HQ Co, Fort Dix, N. J., b. 10/22/1910, d. 07/01/1989
ARGO, Harry H., b. 07/11/1874, d. 01/22/1951
ARGO, Harry V., ssw-Norma M., b. 1903, d. 1960
ARGO, Lillie G., ssw-Walter E., b. 06/18/1881, d. 10/18/1955
ARGO, Mary K., ssw-Everett F., b. 08/31/1908, d. 01/02/1991
ARGO, Milton P., ssw-Beatrice L., b. 04/27/1907, d. 11/08/1969
ARGO, Norma M., ssw-Harry V., b. 1906, d. N/D
ARGO, Walter E., ssw-Lillie G., b. 10/29/1877, d. 03/23/1964
ARIAS, Antonio Ruiz, b. 01/17/1922, d. 07/20/1993
ARIAS, Maria, Age 75y, b. N/D, d. 06/08/1996
ATHERHOLT, Gertrude M., b. 09/12/1900, d. 10/01/1988
ATKINS, Allen R., b. 1839, d. 1928
ATKINS, George B., ssw-Lulu M., b. 10/22/1875, d. 12/12/1950
ATKINS, Lulu M., ssw-George B., b. 08/17/1878, d. 11/14/1963
BAILEY, Anna C., b. 01/29/1879, d. 10/18/1963
BAILEY, Cecil H., ssw-Hazel E., m. 7/29/1955, b. 11/05/1934, d. 10/10/1981
BAILEY, Hazel E., ssw-Cecil H., m. 7/29/1955, b. 01/10/1939, d. N/D
BAILEY, Helen L., b. 1945, d. 1966
BAILEY, Howard F., ssw-Melba L., Father, b. 04/28/1906, d. 10/15/1982
BAILEY, James Vernon, ssw-L. Michael, DE, SN, USN, b. 03/11/1937, d. 04/04/1965

BAILEY, L. Michael, ssw-James Vernon, b. 10/18/1958, d. 03/29/1987
BAILEY, Melba L., ssw-Howard F., Mother, b. 11/07/1910, d. 09/15/1968
BAKER, Helen M. Roach, w/o Ralph, b. 01/12/1912, d. 04/15/1994
BAKER, Larry J., b. 03/19/1887, d. 02/11/1965
BAKER, Marietta D., ssw-W. Paul, b.09/03/1915, d. N/D
BAKER, Verda L., b. 04/11/1905, d. 08/10/1967
BAKER, W. Paul, ssw-Marietta D., b. 10/21/1916, d. 03/25/1990
BAKER, William P., Sr., "Bake," b. 04/11/1943, d. 03/06/1992
BANNING, Homer, ssw-Huldah, b. 07/06/1902, d. 12/31/1966
BANNING, Huldah, ssw-Homer, b. 09/10/1906, d. 008/09/1985
BANNING, Pauline, ssw-Vinal, b. 1908, d. 1977
BANNING, Vinal, ssw-Pauline, b. 1907, d. 1967
BARKER, Charles S., ssw-Helen N., b. 1898, d. 1962
BARKER, Helen N., ssw-Charles S., b. 1899, d. 1983
BARKER, Howard B., ssw-Margaret M., b. 03/13/1903, d. 11/05/1965
BARKER, Margaret M., ssw-Howard B., b. 09/18/1905, d. 01/07/1993
BEHELER, Allen V., ssw-Elizabeth A., Tec4, USA, WWII, b. 12/03/1918, d. 12/03/1980
BEHELER, Elizabeth A., ssw-Allen V., b. 05/20/1920, d. 11/21/1987
BEHELER, Jerry A., ssw-Susan G., b. 09/05/1949, d. 12/03/1990
BEHELER, Susan G., ssw-Jerry A., b. 10/13/1950, d. N/D
BETTS, Aida C., ssw-Oscar S. Betts and Emma Betts Mason, b. 1903, d. 1905
BETTS, Anita L., ssw-Milton W., Sr., b. 1938, d. N/D
BETTS, Annie M., ssw-Harry F., b. 11/29/1901, d. 01/30/1991
BETTS, Arthur M., ssw-Camille A., b. 06/14/1928, d. 02/17/1991
BETTS, Camille A., ssw-Arthur M., b. 08/01/1926, d. N/D
BETTS, Catherine D., ssw-Oscar Clyde, b. 08/28/1908, d. 05/21/1986
BETTS, Charles W., b. 07/31/1925, d. 06/10/1926
BETTS, Elmeda E., b. 10/03/1927, d. N/D
BETTS, Elsie Smith, b. 02/15/1895, d. 06/04/1982
BETTS, George H., ssw-Naomi L., Pfc. USA, WWII, b. 02/08/1913, d. 05/27/1988
BETTS, Gove, Jr., "Spruce," b. 06/07/1926, d. 05/15/1988
BETTS, Harry F., ssw-Annie M., b. 01/03/1901, d. 11/27/1982
BETTS, James Alfred, b. 03/29/1851, d. 05/16/1930
BETTS, Leah W., ssw-Nelson F., b. 11/19/1932, d. N/D
BETTS, Lolita, b. 01/13/1879, d. 07/27/1955
BETTS, Margaret Ellen, b. 02/26/1853, d. 02/23/1933
BETTS, Milton W., Sr., ssw-Anita L., b. 1907, d. 1995
BETTS, Naomi L., ssw-George H., b. 01/30/1924, d. N/D
BETTS, Nelson F., ssw-Leah W., b. 09/11/1930, d. 08/24/1992
BETTS, Oscar Clyde, ssw-Catherine D., b. 05/30/1906, d. 02/16/1974
BETTS, Oscar S., ssw-Aida C. Betts and Emma Betts Mason, b. 1876, d. 1925
BETTS, William F., USA, WWII, b. 10/28/1910, d. 08/22/1988
BLAKELEY, M. Catherine, b. 1923, d. 1994
BLANDON, Ethel B., 04/12/1930, d. 08/10/1991
BLANDON, John T., III, b. 02/23/1950, d. N/D
BLANDON, John T., Jr., b. 08/12/1928, d. N/D
BLIZZARD, Albert C., b. 07/05/1887, d. 02/17/1920
BLIZZARD, Charles E., Pfc. USA, WWII, b. 10/01/1918, d. 05/19/1993

BLIZZARD, Delema A., ssw-William E., b. 01/11/1897, d. 12/27/1956

BLIZZARD, George A., s/o W. G. & Lillie E., b. 05/01/1909, d. 01/09/1914

BLIZZARD, James E., ssw-Matilda, b. 1857, d. 1947

BLIZZARD, James Edward, USA, WWII, b. 03/03/1921, d. 09/05/1988

BLIZZARD, John J., b. 02/19/1925, d. N/D

BLIZZARD, Lillie E., w/o Walter G., b. 09/14/1887, d. 02/25/1974

BLIZZARD, Matilda, ssw-James E., b. 1861, d. 1934

BLIZZARD, Myrtle, d/o W. G. & Lillie E., b. 02/07/1914, d. 08/08/1914

BLIZZARD, Russell, b. 08/15/1928, d. 04/27/1993

BLIZZARD, Walter G., b. 10/16/1886, d. 03/01/1920

BLIZZARD, Walter Gardner, Tech5, USA, WWII, b. 05/27/1920, d. 05/15/1985

BLIZZARD, William E., ssw-Delema A., b. 05/21/1894, d. 11/23/1951

BOWDEN, B. Ruth, ssw-Lester F., b. 09/19/1922, d. N/D

BOWDEN, Lester F., ssw-B. Ruth, Tech5, USA, WWII, b. 12/18/1912, d. 03/03/1991

BOWER, Mary Manship, ssw-Frank & F. Murray Manship, b. 1877, d. 1948

BOWERS, Albert F., Pvt., USA, b. 08/15/1896, d. 11/27/1974

BOWERS, Alice D., ssw-Frank, b. 1894, d. 1985

BOWERS, Frank, ssw-Alice D., b. 1896, d. 1974

BOYCE, Arthur R., ssw-Elva F., b. 1903, d. 1974

BOYCE, Elva F., ssw-Arthur R., b. 1913, d. 1983

BOYLE, Florence E., b. 11/08/1900, d. 09/15/1952

BRADLEY, James D., b. 1964, d. 1980

BRADLEY, Samuel E., b. 04/01/1941, d. 12/23/1981

BRASURE, Edna Gray, b. 1892, d. 1969

BRASURE, George C., b. 1892, d. 1941

BRITTINGHAM, Calvin L., Sr., ssw-Deborah A., Wed. 6-12-1971, b. 08/21/1936, d. 04/23/1994

BRITTINGHAM, Deborah A., ssw-Calvin L., Sr., Wed. 6-12-1971, b. 02/04/1947, d. N/D

BRITTINGHAM, Emma C., ssw-Joseph S., b. 10/20/1886, d. 09/19/1923

BRITTINGHAM, John, b. 04/19/1857, d. 03/25/1947

BRITTINGHAM, Joseph S., ssw-Emma C., b. 1880, d. 1942

BRITTINGHAM, Julia, w/o John, b. 08/12/1857, d. 07/05/1907

BRITTINGHAM, Loleta, w/o Thos. E., b. 06/14/1888, d. 12/06/1914

BRITTINGHAM, Nancy, ssw-Emma C., b. 1891, d. 19—

BRITTINGHAM, Preston, ssw-Ruth M., b. 04/01/1916, d. 04/30/1973

BRITTINGHAM, Ruth M., ssw-Preston, b. 06/12/1925, d. N/D

BULLOCK, Fred, b. 04/05/1928, d. 05/08/1993

BULLOCK, John Perry, b. 1896, d. 1970

BURNHAM, Claude L., ssw-Margaret E., 1st Lt. Med. C., WWII, b. 09/12/1921, d. 06/18/1970

BURNHAM, Dorsey V., "Jack," ssw-Sarah W., b. 09/28/1930, d. 10/13/1991

BURNHAM, Dorsey Virgil, FL., Mus3, CL 4, Inf., WWI, b. 02/22/1896, d. 01/22/1957

BURNHAM, Margaret E., ssw-Claude L., b. 06/23/1922, d. 01/27/1989

BURNHAM, Nellie B., b. 03/12/1890, d. 05/20/1973

BURNHAM, Sarah W., ssw-Dorsey V., b. 08/15/1929, d. N/D

BURROUGHS, Ada M., ssw-J. Fillmore, b. 02/11/1899, d. 02/03/1995

BURROUGHS, J. Fillmore, ssw-Ada M., b. 09/14/1903, d. 06/02/1977

BURTON, Mamie L., ssw-Robert W., b. 1900, d. 1992

BURTON, Robert W., ssw-Mamie L., b. 1898, d. 1979

BUSHEY, Iva M., ssw-Norman F., b. 09/08/1913, d. 05/13/1980

BUSHEY, Norman F., ssw-Iva M., b. 04/02/1910, d. 06/27/1976
CALHOON, Bertha M., b. 12/08/1899, d. 03/10/1950
CALHOUN, Elizabeth, ssw-James E., b. 1942, d. 1946
CALHOUN, Emma H., w/o Robert, ssw-Robert, b. 10/13/1853, d. 02/15/1928
CALHOUN, Everett B., Pvt. USA, WWII, b. 01/21/1895, d. 10/08/1982
CALHOUN, Gaynell, b. 02/19/1927, d. 07/31/1991
CALHOUN, James E., ssw-Leroy, b. 1943, d. 1944
CALHOUN, John G., s/o Robert & Emma, Age 7y 8m 14d, b. N/D, d. 05/24/1891
CALHOUN, Leroy, ssw-James E., b. 1944, d. 1946
CALHOUN, Robert, ssw-Emma H., b. 04/19/1856, d. 09/03/1932
CAMEAN, William P., b. 1909, d. 1938
CAMPBELL, Asher C., ssw-Ethel M., b. 1904, d. 1989
CAMPBELL, David R., (Buddy,) b. 09/11/1935, d. 07/23/1956
CAMPBELL, E. Grice, ssw-Meta W., b. 10/19/1893, d. 05/26/1928
CAMPBELL, Ethel M., ssw-Asher C., b. 1910, d. 1949
CAMPBELL, Harry T., ssw-Nora B., b. 08/15/1893, d. 09/10/1943
CAMPBELL, Hattie J., ssw-Wm. J., b. 10/26/1870, d. 03/06/1920
CAMPBELL, Mamie W., ssw-Walter L. & Ruth Eleanor, b. 1902, d. 1981
CAMPBELL, Meta W., w/o E. Grice, ssw-E. Grice, b. 09/29/1896, d. 01/06/1975
CAMPBELL, Nora B., ssw-Harry T., b. 03/30/1894, d. 03/30/1988
CAMPBELL, Ruth Eleanor, ssw-Walter L. & Mamie W., b. 1923, d. 1929
CAMPBELL, Walter L., ssw-Mamie W. & Ruth Eleanor, DE, Pvt. Co. D, 312 Inf., 78 D, WWI, b. 02/01/1895,
        d. 06/05/1959
CAMPBELL, Willie S., b. 1892, d. 1970
CAMPBELL, Wm. J., ssw-Hattie J., b. 07/15/1860, d. 04/03/1955
CANFIELD, B. E., b. 1871, d. 1961
CANNON, Charles J., Dr., ssw-Ruth C., m. 9-16-1950, b. 12/09/1928, d. 01/10/1996
CANNON, George T., b. 03/21/1920, d. 08/20/1975
CANNON, Ruth C., ssw-Charles J., m. 9-16-1950, b. 08/08/1930, d. N/D
CAREY, Alice S., b. 05/25/1903, d. 04/04/1982
CAREY, Arthur L., DE, Pfc. Co. 1, 108 Inf., WWI, b. 06/07/1887, d. 02/14/1955
CAREY, Bertha M., ssw-James C., b. 06/21/1887, d. 11/16/1940
CAREY, Christopher M., b. 08/05/1973, d. N/D
CAREY, Dessie E., ssw-Roscoe C., b. 03/27/1918, d. N/D
CAREY, Eliza A., ssw-James Rhodes, b. 11/19/1852, d. 10/26/1933
CAREY, F. Hazel, ssw-J. Arthur, b. 1911, d. N/D
CAREY, Frank E., b. 10/09/1873, d. 08/12/1950
CAREY, Harold R., b. 12/11/1910, d. 06/27/1946
CAREY, J. Arthur, ssw-F. Hazel, b. 1908, d. N/D
CAREY, James C., ssw-Bertha M., b. 08/18/1882, d. 04/12/1960
CAREY, James Rhodes, ssw-Eliza A., b. 05/04/1840, d. 01/26/1911
CAREY, Mattie Roach, b. 11/20/1879, d. 06/08/1973
CAREY, Roscoe C., ssw-Dessie E., b. 12/13/1916, d. 10/11/1989
CAROW, Frances L., b. 07/06/1892, d. 03/19/1976
CARPENTER, Edgar D., ssw-William H., b. 1909, d. 1993
CARPENTER, Helen E., ssw- William H., b. 1911, d. 1968
CARPENTER, Ida Mae, b. 09/11/1908, d. N/D
CARPENTER, James Henry, Jr., b. 09/06/1906, d. 04/15/1977

CARPENTER, William H., ssw-Helen E., b. 1931, d. 1949
CARTER, Joseph D., ssw-Lillian B., Cpt. USMC, WWII, b. 07/25/1924, d. 08/21/1989
CARTER, Lillian B., ssw-Joseph D., b. 10/13/1924, d. 06/01/1976
CHALOVPKA, Bertha, ssw-Frank, b. 1898, d. 1967
CHALOVPKA, Frank, ssw-Bertha, d. 1899, d. 1984
CHALOVPKA, Frank J., b. 1924, d. 1994
CHALOVPKA, Joseph, b. 1905, d. 1970
CHANDLER, Addison E., b. 01/18/1876, d. 01/07/1956
CHANDLER, Isabelle M., ssw-Preston H., b. 10/20/1922, d. N/D
CHANDLER, Jimmy L., b. 1935, d. 1939
CHANDLER, Nellie G., b. 07/24/1908, d. 09/18/1988
CHANDLER, Preston, b. 04/28/1905, d. 04/07/1993
CHANDLER, Preston H., ssw-Isabelle M., Pfc. USA, WWII, b. 11/25/1924, d. 12/07/1980
CHANDLER, Robert W., b. 1838, d. 1970
CHANEY, George G., ssw-Mabel T., Sgt., USAAC, WWII, b. 03/12/1919, d. 05/04/1989
CHANEY, Mabel T., ssw-George G., b. 02/04/1924, d. 04/20/1979
CIABATTONE, Hugh Angelo, b. 1902, d. 1973
CLARK, Mary W., ssw-William C., b. 02/25/1881, d. 05/12/1965
CLARK, Stacy L., b. 01/22/1976, d. 01/22/1976
CLARK, William C., ssw-Mary W., b. 07/21/1879, d. 06/08/1961
CLENDANIEL, Anna L., ssw-Charles L., b. 1888, d. 1973
CLENDANIEL, Charles L., ssw-Anna L., b. 1890, d. 1968
CLENDANIEL, Clarence, ssw-Elizabeth E., b. 1887, d. 1959
CLENDANIEL, David L., ssw-Jennie E., b. 1880, d. 1949
CLENDANIEL, Edward J., ssw-Sadie L., b. 1886, d. 1961
CLENDANIEL, Eliza W., ssw-Henry D., b. 08/24/1897, d. 08/26/1976
CLENDANIEL, Elizabeth E., ssw-Clarence, b. 1891, d. 1968
CLENDANIEL, Emma B., ssw-James A., b. 1881, d. 1953
CLENDANIEL, Harold L., b. 07/16/1913, d. 11/06/1994
CLENDANIEL, Henry D., ssw-Eliza W., b. 06/13/1896, d. 01/24/1956
CLENDANIEL, James A., Emma B., b. 1880, d. 1955
CLENDANIEL, James C., 2nd, b. 09/30/1947, d. 03/25/1969
CLENDANIEL, Jennie E., ssw-David L., b. 1865, d. 1937
CLENDANIEL, Lester E., ssw-Viola C., b. 06/10/1897, d. 07/03/1981
CLENDANIEL, Lester W., ssw-Mattie M., b. 1893, d. 1968
CLENDANIEL, Lester W., Jr., b. 10/10/1921, d. 09/08/1929
CLENDANIEL, Louis P., b. 1882, d. 1938
CLENDANIEL, Mattie M., ssw-Lester W., b. 1893, d. 1949
CLENDANIEL, Sadie L., ssw-Edward J., b. 1885, d. 1974
CLENDANIEL, Viola C., ssw-Lester E., b. 12/29/1904, d. 10/22/1996
CLENDANIEL, William S., b. 01/27/1885, d. 11/27/1960
CLIFTON, Betty L., ssw-Chester C., b. 04/16/1926, d. N/D
CLIFTON, Chester C., ssw-Betty L., USA, WWII, b. 06/10/1923, d. N/D
CLIFTON, Delberta P., ssw-Howard G., b. 04/18/1913, d. 01/21/1991
CLIFTON, Ella L., ssw-Fred E., b. 1885, d. 1971
CLIFTON, Ethel P., ssw-Norman E., b. 07/16/1921, d. 10/22/1988
CLIFTON, Fred E., ssw-Ella L., b. 1886, d. 1967
CLIFTON, Howard G., ssw-Delberta P., b. 12/31/1903, d. 09/25/1970

CLIFTON, John O., ssw-Lucy J., b. 04/13/1883, b. 01/12/1946

CLIFTON, Lucy J., ssw-John O., b. 09/29/1883, d. 09/18/1938

CLIFTON, Mary E., ssw-Willard S., b. 1882, d. 1969

CLIFTON, Norman E., ssw-Ethel P., b. 02/14/1916, d. N/D

CLIFTON, Willard S., ssw-Mary E., b. 1883, d. 1960

COFFIN, No names or dates

COLLINS, Comfort W., w/o E. Lamden, ssw-E. Lamden, b. 1837, d. 1928

COLLINS, George, b. 01/20/1878, d. 02/25/1970

COLLINS, Maggie E., ssw-Robert M., b. 1872, d. 1957

COLLINS, Myrtis V., ssw-Benjamin N. Palmer, b. 1897, d. 1993

COLLINS, Perry J., b. 1934, d. 1991

COLLINS, Robert M., ssw-Maggie E., b. 1872, d. 1931

COLLINS, E. Lamben, ssw-Comfort W., b. 1836, d. 1933

CONAWAY, Joanna B., w/o Andrew, b. 10/07/1869, d. 01/05/1915

CONNARD, Doris R., ssw-George H., b. 01/28/1932, d. 01/17/1992

CONNARD, George H., ssw-Doris R., b. 01/26/1926, d. N/D

CONNER, Charles A., b. N/D, d. 09/16/1941

CONNER, Lillie M., b. N/D, d. 01/31/1956

CONNER, Virginia L., b. 1884, d. 1919

CONNER, William W., b. 1877, d. 1929

CONRAD, Beth, d/o George & Doris, b. 04/26/1972, d. 04/26/1972

CONRAD, Edward J., ssw-Virginia M., b. 06/21/1908, d. 08/12/1873

CONRAD, Edward James, DE. Capt. 18th ATS, AF, b. 08/11/1933, d. 10/23/1962

CONRAD, Ethel Rae., ssw-Edward J., b. 11/22/1941, d. 06/17/1995

CONRAD, Virginia M., ssw-Edward J., b. 09/13/1908, d. 10/09/1991

CONWELL, Arthur C., ssw-Susan E., b. 1867, d. 1943

CONWELL, Bessie M., b. 03/30/1881, d. 01/08/1948

CONWELL, Elena Burton, ssw-Tinley Clarke, b. 03/04/1910, d. N/D

CONWELL, John Clowes, DE. CPL, USA, WWII, b. 07/30/1914, d. 10/17/1970

CONWELL, Susan E., ssw-Arthur C., b. 1869, d. 1942

CONWELL, Tinley Clarke, ssw-Elena Burton, Capt. USN, WWII, b. 11/01/1903, d. 02/22/1990

CONWELL, William W., b. 07/29/1878, d. 01/21/1947

CONWELL, William Y., s/o Wm. W. & Bessie M., Lost at sea to enemy action, North Atlantic, b. 11/23/1912, d. 05/11/1942

CONWELL, William Yeates, USMM, WWII, b. 11/23/1912, d. 04/23/1942

COPE, Cecil H., DE. 1st Sgt. CMP, WWII, b. 06/13/1908, d. 04/21/1950

CORDREY, Lois C., b. 07/07/1949, d. 02/06/1983

COULTER, Ella P., b. 1857, d. 1948

COULTER, John W., b. 1859, d. 1933

COX, Charles E., DE. Co. D 68 Engineer TNG, WWII, b. 05/16/1920, d. 09/26/1969

COX, Elizabeth Vent, b. 04/19/1916, d. N/D

CRAGGS, Betty L., ssw-Robert L., b. 02/09/1930, d. 10/08/1995

CRAGGS, Robert L., ssw-Betty L., b. N/D, d. N/D

CROUCH, Amanda M., ssw-William M., b. 1896, d. 1984

CROUCH, Anna G., ssw-Walter W., b. 03/21/1896, d. 09/25/1980

CROUCH, Daniel M., ssw-Maxine, b. 09/04/1927, d. 09/14/1995

CROUCH, Maxine, ssw-Daniel M., b. 09/29/1927, d. N/D

CROUCH, Walter W., ssw-Anna G., b. 10/09/1874, d. 11/06/1966

CROUCH, William Anthony, b. 02/09/1970, d. 02/10/1970
CROUCH, William M., ssw-Amanda M., b. 1881, d. 1936
DARBY, Charles E., Capt., ssw-Lulu W., b. 1875, d. 1950
DARBY, Emma E., ssw-Lucius C., b. 1881, d. 1941
DARBY, James P., ssw-Margaret K., b. 06/04/1871, d. 10/23/1943
DARBY, Jean E., b. 03/31/1927, d. 02/27/1989
DARBY, Lucius C., Capt., ssw-Emma E., b. 1876, d. 1950
DARBY, Lulu W., ssw-Charles E., b. 1882, d. 1960
DARBY, Margaret K., ssw-James P., b. 08/15/1876, d. 04/10/1946
DAVIDSON, Esther E., ssw-Hammon M., b. 1912, d. 1993
DAVIDSON, Hamilton C., ssw-Margaret L., b. 01/05/1882, d. 10/10/1948
DAVIDSON, Hammon M., ssw-Esther E., b. 01/19/1898, d. 04/24/1981
DAVIDSON, James Edward, s/o William W. & Janie B., b. 01/27/1920, d. 11/28/1920
DAVIDSON, Margaret L., ssw-Hamilton C., b. 04/30/1884, d. 09/23/1977
DAVIS, Elsie F., ssw-Owen L., b. 01/03/1906, d. N/D
DAVIS, Owen L., ssw-Elsie F., b. 11/15/1903, d. 10/30/1972
DECKER, Frederick F., b. 12/22/1878, d. 01/04/1956
DECKER, Margaret S., b. 10/12/1877, d. 11/20/1962
DERRICKSON, Joseph H., ssw-Virgie R., b. 05/25/1895, d. 01/03/1968
DERRICKSON, Virgie R., ssw-Joseph H., b. 11/05/1897, d. N/D
DICKERSON, Alice, ssw-Otto, b. 1900, d. 1988
DICKERSON, Alma V., b. 1914, d. 1914
DICKERSON, Althea B., ssw-Woodrow W., b. 1917, d. 11/29/1996
DICKERSON, Baby, b. 1911, d. 1911
DICKERSON, Carrie H., ssw-Charles B., Lina A., Charles H., Edna M. & Hazel E., b. 1874, d. 1963
DICKERSON, Charles, ssw-Jennie, DE, Cook, Co. D., Pioneer Inf., WWI, b. 11/12/1888, d. 12/26/1963
DICKERSON, Charles A., ssw-Eliza A., b. 04/13/1847, d. 06/11/1925
DICKERSON, Charles B., ssw-Lina A., Carrie H., Charles H., Edna M. & Hazel E., b. 1870, d. 1960
DICKERSON, Charles H., ssw-Charles B., Lina A., Carrie H., Edna M. & Hazel E., b. 1895, d. 1895
DICKERSON, Chester W., ssw-Fannie T., b. 1903, d. 1978
DICKERSON, Clarence A., b. 1874, d. 1944
DICKERSON, Edna M., ssw-Charles B., Lina A., Carrie H., Charles H. & Hazel E., b. 1902, d. 1902
DICKERSON, Eliza A., w/o Charles A., ssw-Charles A., b. 08/15/1853, d. 02/28/1939
DICKERSON, Elsie M., ssw-Eulen, b. 1903, d. 1991
DICKERSON, Eulen, ssw-Elsie M., 1898, d. 1975
DICKERSON, Fannie T., ssw-Chester W., b. 1908, d. 1984
DICKERSON, Hazel E., ssw-Charles B., Lina A., Carrie H., Charles H. & Edna M., b. 1917, d. 1917
DICKERSON, Howard W., ssw-Reba M., Sgt., USA, WWII, b. 05/27/1919, d. 03/12/1982
DICKERSON, Jennie, ssw-Charles, b. 1900, d. 1942
DICKERSON, John, ssw-Maggie, b. 03/03/1897, d. 01/31/1969
DICKERSON, John C., b. 1872, d. 1957
DICKERSON, L. Pearl, b. 1888, d. 1963
DICKERSON, Lina A., ssw-Charles B., Carrie H., Charles H., Edna M. & Hazel E., b. 1878, d. 1907
DICKERSON, Mabel L., b. 12/1904, d. 12/1980
DICKERSON, Maggie, ssw-John, b. 04/24/1896, d. 03/26/1968
DICKERSON, Otto, ssw-Alice, b. 1887, d. 1977
DICKERSON, Reba M., ssw-Howard W., b. 02/15/1922, d. N/D
DICKERSON, Robert W., b. 1918, d. 1918

DICKERSON, Ruth E., ssw-Thomas L., b. 1924, d. N/D
DICKERSON, Ruth L., ssw-Walton M., b. 01/28/1907, d. 08/03/1989
DICKERSON, Sallie E., b. 1873, d. 1946
DICKERSON, Thomas Lee, ssw-Ruth E., b. 1922, d. 11/07/1996
DICKERSON, Walton M., ssw-Ruth L., b. 06/27/1905, d. 05/18/1973
DICKERSON, Woodrow W., ssw-Althea B., Pvt., USA, WWII, b. 06/07/1913, d. 11/04/1983
DICUS, Murrill G., b. 1915, d. 1980
DODD, Amanda J., ssw-Warren, b. 01/08/1902, d. 09/08/1984
DODD, Arthur B., ssw-Elizabeth R., b. 1885, d. 1959
DODD, Elizabeth R., ssw-Arthur B., b. 1892, d. 1956
DODD, Hazel E., ssw-Hershel H., b. 10/25/1908, d. 01/29/1962
DODD, Hershel H., ssw-Hazel E., b. 09/02/1902, d. 02/09/1987
DODD, Richard A., ssw-Elizabeth R., b. 1914, d. 1915
DODD, Warren, ssw-Amanda J., b. 06/25/1896, d. 10/31/1978
DONAHOO, Annie, b. 1860, d. 1932
DONAHOO, Edna V., b. 1879, d. 1959
DONAHOO, James T., b. 1855, d. 1931
DONAHOO, John H., b. 1878, d. 1945
DONOHUE, Glenn Allan, b. 09/02/1964, d. 12/27/1964
DONOHUE, Robert E., b. 1900, d. 1958
DONOVAN, Alberta Emma, b. 10/25/1923, d. 10/15/1969
DONOVAN, Amy P., ssw-Arthur B., b. 08/21/1893, d. 04/21/1973
DONOVAN, Arthur B., ssw-Amy P., b. 04/04/1893, d. 08/27/1981
DONOVAN, Bessie M., ssw-Charlie C., b. 1886, d. 1914
DONOVAN, Caroline C., ssw-Cheryl L., b. 10/09/1935, d. N/D
DONOVAN, Charles Montiwell, ssw-Clara Fields, b. 10/21/1857, d. 12/06/1937
DONOVAN, Charlie C., ssw-Bessie M., b. 1886, d. 1974
DONOVAN, Cheryl L., ssw-Caroline C., b. 05/18/1960, d. 11/20/1980
DONOVAN, Christine, ssw-John P., b. 10/04/1908, d. 03/16/1965
DONOVAN, Clara Fields, ssw-Charles Montiwell, b. 08/10/1871, d. 01/17/1976
DONOVAN, Daniel S., ssw-Mary H., b. 1904, d. 1980
DONOVAN, Eldridge W., ssw-Mildred E., b. 12/19/1900, d. 04/25/1974
DONOVAN, George Alfred, b. 11/08/1917, d. 12/30/1974
DONOVAN, John G., ssw-Lillie J., b. 1867, d. 1955
DONOVAN, John P., ssw-Christine, b. 10/23/1905, d. 06/15/1986
DONOVAN, Lillie J., ssw-John G., b. 1880, d. 1947
DONOVAN, Mary H., ssw-Daniel S., b. 1912, d. 1990
DONOVAN, Mildred E., ssw-Eldridge W., b. 02/06/1906, d. N/D
DONOVAN, Norman L., ssw-Caroline C., b. 04/21/1933, d. N/D
DONOVAN, Robert L., Sr., ssw-Shirley Alice, b. 01/21/1950, d. N/D
DONOVAN, Shirley Alice, ssw-Robert L., Sr., b. 08/29/1952, d. 05/02/1992
DONOVAN, Stella M., ssw-Bessie M., b. 1892, d. 1961
DONOVAN, Reuben, S1, USNR, WWII, b. 05/24/1915, d. 04/06/1945
DORMAN, Arthur R., ssw-Mildred N., b. 07/30/1916, d. 05/21/1994
DORMAN, Harry B., ssw-Virgie M., b. 1895, d. 1956
DORMAN, Mildred N., ssw-Arthur R., b. 11/14/1919, d. N/D
DORMAN, Virgie M., ssw-Harry B., b. 1895, d. 1986
DOUGLAS, Alice G., b. 1919, d. 1984

DOUGLAS, J. Kenneth, b. 1920, d. 1984

DOUGLASS, Baby, b. N/D, d. N/D

DOUGLASS, Elizabeth E., b. 1884, d. 1949

DOUGLASS, Ethel, b. 1887, d. 1888

DOUGLASS, Eugenia W., b. 1856, d. 1929

DOUGLASS, Leighton C., b. 1889, d. 1966

DOUGLASS, Thomas H., b. 1857, d. 1933

DOUGLASS, Wm. E., Dr., b. 1885, d. 1961

DRAPPER, Emily Hazzard, ssw-Richard Ross, b. 09/23/1915, d. N/D

DRAPPER, Richard Ross, ssw-Emily Hazzard, b.10/14/1906, d. 11/07/1975

DUDLEY, Newell E., ssw-Ruth B., b. 06/13/1906, d. 04/20/1995

DUDLEY, Ruth B., ssw-Newell E., b. N/D, d. N/D

DUTTON, David T., Capt., b. 04/16/1867, d. 05/20/1938

DUTTON, David W., b. 04/29/1922, d. 12/01/1968

DUTTON, Eliza J., b. 09/15/1883, d. 05/29/1970

DUTTON, Layton P., ssw-Lillian A., b. 1901, d. 1964

DUTTON, Lillian A., ssw-Layton P., b. 1913, d. N/D

DUTTON, Ora E., d/o David T. & Eliza J., b. 10/22/1916, d. 07/28/1918

EKSTROM, Ruth, ssw-Thure W. F., b. 02/17/1901, d. 05/13/1976

EKSTROM, Thure W. F., ssw-Ruth, b. 03/07/1901, d. 07/07/1977

ELLINGSWORTH, Alice A., ssw-D. Louis, b. 12/28/1842, d. 06/06/1917

ELLINGSWORTH, D. Louis, ssw-Alice A., b. 1875, d. 1942

ELLINGSWORTH, Emma, ssw-Fred, b. 12/11/1853, d. 03/13/1923

ELLINGSWORTH, Fred, ssw-Emma, b. 03/24/1852, d. 01/26/1931

ELLINGSWORTH, George W., ssw-Pauline M. & Verna, b. 1889, d. 1971

ELLINGSWORTH, James P., ssw-Alice A., b. 11/19/1844, d. 07/27/1913

ELLINGSWORTH, Pauline M., ssw-George W. & Verna, b. 1890, d. 1923

ELLINGSWORTH, Verna, Baby, ssw-Pauline M. & George W., b. N/D, d. N/D

EMMERT, Betty M., b. 08/05/1932, d. 01/06/1992

ESPERON, Frances M. B., b. 04/26/1933, d. N/D

FARIES, Irvin, Tec4, USA, WWII, b. 1907, d. 1981

FARRINGTON, C. Max, ssw-Lydia Wilson, b. 01/07/1904, d. 03/04/1986

FARRINGTON, Lydia Wilson, ssw-C. Max, b. 07/08/1907, d. 07/29/1967

FIORITTI, Rita H., b. 09/09/1921, d. 09/14/1981

FISHER, Alvin H., b. 1891, d. 1948

FISHER, Carrie W., ssw-John H., b. 1873, d. 1939

FISHER, Edith R., b. 1921, d. 1923

FISHER, Elizabeth, w/o Thomas, Esq., Age 31y 1m 5d, b. N/D, d. 03/11/1806

FISHER, John H., ssw-Carrie W., b. 1875, d. 1953

FISHER, John, DE. Pvt. Co. 1, 113 Inf., WWI, b. 07/01/1892, d. 11/13/1955

FISHER, Mabel V., b. 10/16/1900, d. 04/01/1978

FISHER, Naomi R., b. 1895, d. 1976

FITHEN, George E., KS, Ensign, USNRF, WWI, b. 11/01/1890, d. 06/10/1964

FITHEN, John David, b. 01/27/1931, d. 04/06/1946

FLETCHER, Hope Elaine, ssw-Joan A., b. 01/24/1972, d. 01/24/1972

FLETCHER, Joan A., ssw-Wade R., Wed. 8-25-1962, b. 03/04/1941, d. N/D

FLETCHER, Wade R., ssw-Joan A., Wed. 8-25-1962, b. 08/29/1938, d. 02/07/1995

FORST, David W., b. 1948, d. 1952

FORST, Evelyn A., b. 1923, d. N/D
FORST, Frances M., b. 1946, d. N/D
FORST, William J., b. 1912, d. 1985
FOSQUE, Emma J., ssw-William H., b. 1856, d. 1924
FOSQUE, William H., ssw-Emma J., b. 1842, d. 1920
FOWLER, D., b. N/D, d. 02/21/1941
FOWLER, Elizabeth K., ssw-George G., b. 06/12/1888, d. 12/01/1986
FOWLER, George G., ssw-Elizabeth K., b. 01/15/1883, d. 09/29/1953
FOWLER, James, b. 1854, d. 1930
FOWLER, Joseph A., b. 1880, d. 1893
FOWLER, Kline, b. N/D, d. 02/19/1904
FOWLER, Mammie A., b. N/D, d. 09/12/1950
FOWLER, Margaret S., b. 1857, d. 1938
FRAZIER, Elizabeth I., b. 07/25/1898, d. 07/23/1980
FURROUGHS, Jeanette D., b. 07/12/1932, d. 03/01/1972
GEYER, Helen, b. N/D, d. 08/30/1945
GILBERT, Franklin, DE. Pvt., 311 Inf., 78 Inf. Div., WWII, b. 12/23/1925, d. 12/13/1944
GIOVANNOZZI, Frank V., S1, USN, WWII, b. 06/10/1921, d. 06/26/1988
GIOVANNOZZI, M. F., b. 12/23/1923, d. N/D
GOODHART, Catherine L., ssw-George E., b. 09/16/1918, d. N/D
GOODHART, George E., ssw-Catherine L., b. 02/24/1916, d. 11/03/1982
GOODWIN, Elizabeth M., b. 1879, d. 1969
GOODWIN, George A., b. 1909, d. 1958
GOODWIN, George A., Capt., b. 1857, d. 1927
GORDY, Walter J., b. 02/12/1913, d. 08/17/1982
GRAVES, Elsie W., b. 1901, d. 1993
GRAVES, Milton T., b. 02/06/1900, d. 12/12/1953
GRAY, Ana Bell Derrickson, ssw-Benjamin Franklin, b. 1862, d. 1929
GRAY, Benjamin Franklin, ssw-Ana Bell Derrickson, b. 1856, d. 1940
GRAY, David L. A., b. 01/12/1987, d. 07/25/1989
GRAY, Joshua Benjamin, b. N/D, d. 03/27/1961
GREEN, Dolly M., ssw-George L., b. 1921, d. 1973
GREEN, George L., ssw-Dolly M., b. 1916, d. 1990
GREEN, John W., b. 09/16/1846, d. 09/20/1923
GREEN, Leah J., w/o John W., b. 11/03/1848, d. 10/19//1898
GREEN, Mary H., ssw-William H., b. 12/27/1884, d. 06/09/1976
GREEN, William H., ssw-Mary H., b. 03/05/1883, d. 01/11/1961
HAINES, Mary Jane D. Hanna, ssw-Raymond T., Sr., b. 1930, d. N/D
HAINES, Raymond T., Sr., ssw-Mary Jane D. Hanna, b. 1923, d. 1996
HART, Allice B., ssw-Clemente F., Clarence J. & Sallie C., b. 1868, d. 1896
HART, Clarence J., ssw-Clemente F., Allice B. & Sallie C., b. 1875, d. 1879
HART, Clemente F., ssw-Allice B., Clarence J. & Sallie C., b. 12/04/1844, d. 03/18/1919
HART, Sallie C., ssw-Clemente F., Allice B. & Clarence J., b. 08/30/1846, d. 12/11/1930
HASTINGS, Annie M., ssw-William H., b. 07/11/1891, d. 11/10/1962
HASTINGS, Carl J., ssw-Joshua J., b. 1928, d. 1928
HASTINGS, Clara P., ssw-Joshua J., b. 1897, d. 1979
HASTINGS, Doris L., b. 1919, d. 1993
HASTINGS, Elmer J., b. 1917, d. 1990

HASTINGS, Estella E., ssw-Joshua J., b. 1921, d. 1921
HASTINGS, Joshua J., ssw-Clara P., b. 1886, d. 1937
HASTINGS, Minnie G., b. 1909, d. 1909
HASTINGS, Sallie A., ssw-William C., b. 1863, d. 1942
HASTINGS, William C., ssw-Sallie A., b. 1857, d. 1931
HASTINGS, William H., ssw-Annie M., b. 11/04/1885, d. 12/04/1961
HAVELKA, Ann M., b. 1905, d. 1992
HAVELKA, Anna, b. 1871, d. 1942
HAVELKA, Joseph, Sr., b. 1871, d. 1935
HAZZARD, E. Virginia, b. 09/26/1876, d. 03/02/1945
HAZZARD, Emma E., ssw-William R., b. 02/13/1854, d. 02/24/1935
HAZZARD, J. Oliver, b. 08/05/1882, d. 01/29/1946
HAZZARD, J. Oliver, Jr., b. 07/27/1912, d. 02/13/1932
HAZZARD, Marian B., b. 06/30/1914, d. N/D
HAZZARD, Mary E., b. 07/15/1886, d. 03/18/1957
HAZZARD, Mary Virginia, d/o J. Oliver & Mary E., b. 12/29/1909, d. 12/18/1910
HAZZARD, Mollie M., b. 07/07/1880, d. 12/06/1969
HAZZARD, William R., ssw-Emma E., b. 10/03/1846, d. 12/19/1897
HICKMAN, Charles B., b. 1898, d. 1899
HICKMAN, Emma E., b. 12/21/1905, d. 02/03/1936
HICKMAN, Jack G., b. 03/25/1931, d. 12/31/1931
HICKMAN, James G., b. 1881, d. 1958
HICKMAN, John A., b. 06/01/1903, d. 10/24/1983
HICKMAN, John A., b. 1858, d. 1925
HICKMAN, Laura S., b. 1859, d. 1932
HICKMAN, Olivia M., b. 1886, d. 1938
HICKMAN, Preston A., Pvt. USA, WWII, b. 06/16/1916, d. 06/11/1977
HILDEBRAND, Mary, b. 10/14/1877, d. 06/20/1980
HILL, William Orville, b. 06/19/1914, d. 10/15/1996
HITCHENS, Annie R., ssw-Francis B., b. 1877, d. 1973
HITCHENS, Bertha H., ssw-Joshua L., b. 1896, d. 1950
HITCHENS, Charles W., ssw-Ella M., b. 07/09/1888, d. 11/29/1978
HITCHENS, Ella M., ssw-Charles W., b. 04/10/1894, d. 05/24/1976
HITCHENS, Francis B., ssw-Annie R., b. 1875, d. 1954
HITCHENS, Grace W., ssw-Norman C., b. 02/26/1914, d. 04/10/1976
HITCHENS, Hessie E., b. 06/05/1905, d. 05/02/1943
HITCHENS, Joshua L., ssw-Bertha H., b. 1894, d. 1954
HITCHENS, Norman C., ssw-Grace W., b. 01/07/1914, d. 01/06/1996
HITCHENS, Robert J., b. 1879, d. 1954
HOLLINGSWORTH, Charles K., ssw-Marie M., b. 09/25/1906, d. 09/29/1980
HOLLINGSWORTH, Marie M., ssw-Charles K., b. 11/22/1913, d. N/D
HOLLOWAY, Alonzo S., ssw-Florence M., b. 05/26/1885, d. 10/31/1915
HOLLOWAY, Florence M., ssw-Alonzo S., b. 12/18/1878, d. 02/18/1962
HOLSTON, Betty A., ssw-Howard B. & Roger A., b. 12/07/1929, d. N/D
HOLSTON, Howard B., ssw-Roger A. & Betty A., b. 10/01/1926, d. 09/09/1983
HOLSTON, Roger A., ssw-Betty A. & Howard B., b. 06/07/1964, d. 11/05/1982
HOOD, Carrie LeCompte, b. 1881, d. 1938
HOOD, Clara M., ssw-John H., b. 1882, d. 1928

HOOD, John H., ssw-Clara M., b. 1875, d. 1932

HOOD, Nathaniel H., b. 09/06/1855, d. 10/28/1915

HOOD, Sarah J., w/o Nathaniel, Age 68, b. N/D, d. 01/27/1912

HOOD, William Thomas, b. 1878. D. 1936

HOPKINS, Alice M., ssw-George E., b. 11/11/1928, d. N/D

HOPKINS, Emma C. Prettyman, b. 11/12/1872, d. 06/26/1946

HOPKINS, George E., ssw-Alice M., b. 11/09/1928, d. N/D

HOPKINS, Merritt F., s/o Theo S. & Emma C., b. 04/04/1898, d. 02/19/1976

HOPKINS, Sandra Lee, b. 08/29/1948, d. 04/27/1950

HOPKINS, Shirley L., b. 1939, d. 1939

HOPKINS, Theodore Samuel, b. 02/24/1873, d. 11/14/1941

HUDSON, Anna Bell, b. 1873, d. 1947

HUDSON, Asher, b. 05/05/1889, d. 05/02/1952

HUDSON, Dorothy A., ssw-Harry T., Sr., b. 07/04/1921, d. 07/14/1981

HUDSON, Harry T., Sr., ssw-Dorothy A., Pfc. USA, WWII, b. 10/13/1920, d. 12/25/1981

HUDSON, James Ruben, b. 11/25/1928, d. 05/12/1989

HUDSON, John F., b. 1873, d. 1944

HUDSON, Mary Elizabeth, b. 08/12/1869, d. 12/09/1934

HUDSON, Samuel, b. 1856, d. 1940

HUDSON, Wilmer R., Jr., DE. Corp., USA, WWII, b. 12/12/1922, d. 03/13/1974

HUGHES, Andrew T., b. 1849, d. 1934

HUGHES, George H., b. 1900, d. 1941

HUGHES, George H., Sr., Cox, USN, WWII, b. 01/25/1925, d. 10/12/1985

HUGHES, Ida C., b. 1862, d. 1944

HUGHEY, George F., Pfc., USA, b. 03/22/1910, d. 08/29/1978

HUGHEY, Virginia M., b. 1919, d. 1970

HURLEY, Adaline D., ssw-Floyd, b. 1889, d. 1978

HURLEY, Charles N., ssw-Robert W. Burton, b. 1916, d. N/D

HURLEY, Elizabeth H., d/o Floyd & Adaline H., b. 02/22/1914, d. 04/01/1914

HURLEY, Floyd, ssw-Adaline D., b. 1889, d. 1970

HURLEY, Pearl N., ssw-Robert W. Burton, b. 1919, d. 1981

HUTCHINS, Clifton, ssw-Eulahlee, b. 07/29/1921, d. 01/29/1968

HUTCHINS, Eulahlee, ssw-Clifton, b. 01/14/1925, d. N/D

INGRAM, Alice P., b. 05/30/1878, d. 02/26/1959

INGRAM, Annie T., w/o Thomas R., ssw-Thomas R., b. 08/28/1844, d. 11/06/1929

INGRAM, Ethel M., b. 04/23/1899, d. 03/01/1974

INGRAM, Riley H., b. 08/31/1902, d. 07/30/1986

INGRAM, Thomas R., ssw-Annie T., b. 05/29/1836, d. 02/26/1915

INGRAM, William R., b. 03/20/1870, d. 06/29/1949

JARMAN, Bessie Lois, ssw-Raymond W., b. 09/16/1915, d. 12/10/1987

JARMAN, Raymond W., ssw-Bessie Lois, b. 11/04/1919, d. N/D

JARMAN, Richard H., b. 1931, d. 1932

JEFFERSON, A. Webster, ssw-Lena. Z., b. 08/02/1904, d. 07/06/1972

JEFFERSON, Arthur Ellis, ssw-Estella Dickerson, Thelma May & James Alfred Jefferson and Linda D.
          Schmierer, b. 1876, d. 1940

JEFFERSON, Berth E., b. 1922, d. 1923

JEFFERSON, Carey R., b. 1923, d. 1923

JEFFERSON, Charles D., b. 1928, d. 1928

JEFFERSON, Clara May, b. 1924, d. 1925

JEFFERSON, David E., ssw-Sallie E., b. 1863, d. 1937

JEFFERSON, David E., Jr., ssw-Priscilla D., b. 1891, d. 1971

JEFFERSON, Delmer W., b. 1898, d. 1978

JEFFERSON, Dorothy E., ssw-William H., b. 12/28/1904, d. N/D

JEFFERSON, Edith M., b. 06/08/1888, d. 10/31/1963

JEFFERSON, Ernest M., b. 06/21/1888, d. 05/16/1982

JEFFERSON, Gladys C., b. 1902, d. 1971

JEFFERSON, Gladys Jones, b. 1908, d. 1984

JEFFERSON, Glendolia J. Campbell, ssw-James H., b. 1905, d. 1946

JEFFERSON, James Alfred, ssw-Arthur Ellis, Estella Dickerson & Thelma May Jefferson and Linda D. Schmierer, b. 1906, d. 1907

JEFFERSON, James H., ssw-Glendolia J. Campbell, b. 1890, d. 1942

JEFFERSON, Kendall D., b. 1918, d. 1927

JEFFERSON, Lena Z., ssw-A. Webster, b. 06/13/1908, d. 10/05/1980

JEFFERSON, Priscilla D., ssw-David E., Jr., b. 1892, d. 1954

JEFFERSON, Sallie E., ssw-David E., b. 1866, d. 1939

JEFFERSON, Sara J., ssw-Wilbert B., b. 09/11/1913, d. N/D

JEFFERSON, Thelma May, ssw-Arthur Ellis, Estella Dickerson & James Alfred Jefferson and Linda D. Schmierer, b. 1917, d. 1918

JEFFERSON, Wilbert B., "Dave," ssw-Sara J., b. 08/03/1913, d. 07/17/1990

JEFFERSON, William H., ssw-Dorothy E., b. 04/13/1900, d. 11/03/1977

JEFFERSON, Estella Dickerson, ssw-Arthur Ellis, James Alfred & Thelma May Jefferson and Linda D. Schmierer, b. 1878, d. 1929

JENNINGS, Mabel E., b. 1923, d. 1975

JENSEN, Ella Z., ssw-Fred K., b. 06/15/1879, d. 03/28/1963

JENSEN, Fred K., ssw-Ella Z., b. 01/01/1880, d. 02/28/1950

JENSEN, John H., ssw-Naomi D., b. 11/05/1904, d. N/D

JENSEN, Naomi D., ssw-John H., b. 07/27/1906, d. 02/23/1990

JERMAN, Matilda, ssw-Thomas E., b. 1896, d. 1970

JERMAN, Thomas E., ssw-Matilda, b. 1896, d. 1962

JESTER, Aubrey, ssw-Estella M., b. 1933, d. 1974

JESTER, Estella M., ssw-Aubrey, b. 1934, d. N/D

JESTER, Frances M., ssw-James I., b. 06/16/1916, d. N/D

JESTER, Hettie A., ssw-William John, b. 1903, d. 1986

JESTER, James I., ssw-Frances M., b. 09/14/1903, d. 03/29/1986

JESTER, William John, ssw-Hettie A., Pvt. USA, WWI, b. 1894, d. 1979

JOHNSON, Alma J., b. 1893, d. 1986

JOHNSON, Annie L., ssw-Maggie C. & J. Hunter, Their Daughter, b. 1892, d. 1965

JOHNSON, Ava W., ssw-Fred M., b. 1910, d. 1995

JOHNSON, Baby, b. N/D, d. N/D

JOHNSON, Benj. B., ssw-Lydia J. & Melvin R., b. 1852, d. 1921

JOHNSON, Benj. T., ssw-Malissa, b. 07/01/1854, d. 12/20/1924

JOHNSON, Bertha A., ssw-J. Edward, b. 10/22/1896, d. N/D

JOHNSON, Betty A., ssw-Robert H., b. 12/02/1930, d. N/D

JOHNSON, Blanche T., b. 1888, d. 1948

JOHNSON, Clara, d/o Wm. H. & Annie E. Mears & w/o Theodore J., b. N/D, d. 01/28/1919

JOHNSON, Clarence, Jr., DE. Pfc. 433 Fighter Sqd. AAA, WWII, b. 05/10/1924, d. 07/07/1962

JOHNSON, Clifford L., ssw-Lillie M., b. 1896, d. 1957
JOHNSON, E., b. 1872, d. 1947
JOHNSON, Edward W., ssw-Eva L., b. 1889, d. 1955
JOHNSON, Elizabeth, ssw-Lemuel, b. 1880, d. 1940
JOHNSON, Emma S., b. 1887, d. 1943
JOHNSON, Eva L., ssw-Edward W., b. 1883, d. 1873
JOHNSON, F. E., b. 1875, d. 1940
JOHNSON, Fred M., ssw-Ava W., b. 1913, d. 1975
JOHNSON, Fred S., b. 1882, d. 1938
JOHNSON, G. Harry, b. 10/02/1879, d. 10/07/1958
JOHNSON, Hannah S., b. 07/03/1915, d. 11/06/1986
JOHNSON, J. Edward, ssw-Bertha A., b. 02/07/1894, d. 05/28/1977
JOHNSON, J. Hunter, ssw-Maggie C. & Annie L., b. 1868, d. 1933
JOHNSON, J. Thomas, ssw-Mollie, b. 1898, d. 1970
JOHNSON, James T., b. 1900, d. 1969
JOHNSON, Lemuel, ssw-Elizabeth, b. 1872, d. 1947
JOHNSON, Lillie M., ssw-Clifford L., b. 1897, d. 1965
JOHNSON, Lydia H., b. 1876, d. 1934
JOHNSON, Lydia J., ssw-Benj. B. & Melvin R., b. 1854, d. 1923
JOHNSON, Lydia J., ssw-William H., b. 1859, d. 1944
JOHNSON, Maggie C., ssw-J. Hunter & Annie L., b. 1871, d. 1949
JOHNSON, Malissa, ssw-Benj. T., b. 07/16/1852, d. 08/22/1938
JOHNSON, Mary Hessie, w/o G. Harry, b. 12/26/1881, d. 06/06/1910
JOHNSON, Mary R., w/o G. Harry, b. 09/06/1880, d. 05/24/1971
JOHNSON, Mary Reba, b. 1900, d. 1943
JOHNSON, Melvin R., ssw-Lydia J. & Benj. B., b. 06/16/1889, d. 07/24/1913
JOHNSON, Mollie, ssw-J. Thomas, b. 1903, d. N/D
JOHNSON, Richard T., "Dickie," b. 03/10/1950, d. 02/24/1978
JOHNSON, Robert D., "Bobby," b. 07/09/1951, d. 01/09/1995
JOHNSON, Robert H., ssw-Betty A., b. 01/16/1923, d. N/D
JOHNSON, William H., ssw-Lydia J., b. 1855, d. 1922
JOHNSON, William P., b. 1881, d. 1961
JONES, Dorothy B., ssw-Sewell P., b. 05/31/1918, d. N/D
JONES, Frederick W., ssw-Margaret M., b. 1902, d. N/D
JONES, Gertrude L., b. 1876, d. 1935
JONES, Herbert W., ssw-Hilda C., b. 1906, d. 1973
JONES, Hilda C., ssw-Herbert W., b. 1909, d. 1972
JONES, James P., b. 1854, d. 1941
JONES, James P., Jr., b. 1913, d. 1943
JONES, Lester E., b. 1903, d. 1945
JONES, Margaret M., ssw-Frederick W., b. 1902, d. 1990
JONES, Sewell P., ssw-Dorothy B., b. 02/15/1901, d. 11/03/1978
JOSEPH, Carlton G., b. 1934, d. 1967
JOSEPH, Everett Burton, b. 08/15/1921, d. 004/13/1995
JOSEPH, Florence Burton, w/o Will, b. 11/12/1890, d. 11/09/1990
JOSEPH, William D., b. 1894, d. 1963
KERIA, Vergie G., ssw-William J., b. 1907, d. N/D
KERIA, William J., ssw-Vergie G., b. 1899, d. 1988

KETTERER, Laura B., ssw-Leroy F., b. 06/16/1909, d. N/D

KETTERER, Leroy F., ssw-Laura B., b. 06/20/1907, d. 05/30/1973

KING, Bertha L., b. 06/18/1878, d. 08/28/1969

KING, Emma J., b. 1890, d. 1956

KING, Irvin Cornelius, Sr., b. 08/20/1877, d. 08/20/1947

KING, James A., DE Pvt. 1st Class 52 Coast Arty., b. N/D, d. 10/31/1943

KING, Joseph S., ssw-Sarah E., b. 01/04/1848, d. 11/23/1913

KING, Roy C., b. 1887, d. 1955

KING, Sarah E., ssw-Joseph S., b. 09/14/1856, d. 04/14/1920

KOHLENBERG, Anna P., ssw-Charles, b. 1867, Phila., d. 1939, DE

KOHLENBERG, Charles, ssw-Anna P., b. 1862, Phila., d. 1933, DE

KRING, Iona M., ssw-William W., b. 1907, d. 1964

KRING, William W., ssw-Iona M., b. 1910, d. 1982

LAMBDEN, Arthur, ssw-Lillie M., b. 1875, d. 1946

LAMBDEN, Lillie M., ssw-Arthur, b. 1879, d. 1965

LANE, Gloria E., b. 07/05/1928, d. 09/04/1987

LANK, Elsie C., b. 02/20/1898, d. 10/13/1982

LAWSON, Lester P., ssw-Sarah E., b. 1902, d. 1975

LAWSON, Lester Paul, b. 06/13/1937, d. 10/25/1952

LAWSON, Phyllis A., ssw-William J., b. 03/29/1941, d. 12/11/1980

LAWSON, Sarah E., ssw-Lester P., b. 1902, d. 1982

LAWSON, William J., ssw-Phyllis A., b. 09/24/1924, d. N/D

LEE, Charles S., ssw-Pauline L., Sgt. USAC, WWII, b. 1908, d. 1963

LEE, Pauline L., ssw-Charles S., b. 1908, d. 1974

LEGATES, Doris C., b. 1926, d. N/D

LEGATES, Thomas Clifford, Cpl. USA, AC, WWII, b. 09/16/1919, d. 07/20/1988

LEHMANN, Fredrick A., b. 1917, d. 1991

LEHMANN, Martha B., b. 1917, d. 1991

LEITHMANN, Frances, ssw-Fritz & Fritz, Jr., b. 03/29/1889, d. 03/17/1979

LEITHMANN, Fritz, ssw-Frances & Fritz, Jr., b. 04/21/1884, d. 11/07/1965

LEITHMANN, Fritz, Jr., ssw-Frances & Fritz, b. 02/02/1913, d. 07/15/1913

LEKITES, Alfred H., Capt., ssw-Laura A. Betts, b. 02/14/1863, d. 06/14/1940

LEKITES, Ella Mae, ssw-Walter G., Sr., b. 10/06/1889, d. 10/17/1975

LEKITES, Laura A. Betts, ssw-Alfred H., b. 05/02/1864, d. 02/26/1920

LEKITES, Pearl, ssw-Raymond A., b. 06/25/1909, d. 10/02/1985

LEKITES, Raymond A., ssw-Pearl, b. 08/01/1908, d. 04/23/1953

LEKITES, Walter G., Sr., ssw-Ella Mae, b. 09/04/1889, d. 02/10/1977

LEONARD, George H., ssw-Nettie F., b. 1878, d. 19—

LEONARD, Nettie F., ssw-George H., b. 1880, d. 1958

LEVERAGE, Carrie H., ssw-John R., b. 1905, d. N/D

LEVERAGE, Della, w/o W. Frank, ssw-W. Frank, b. 04/27/1875, d. 05/30//1929

LEVERAGE, John R., ssw-Carrie H., Pvt. USA, b. 02/12/1899, d. 08/05/1974

LEVERAGE, W. Frank, ssw-Della, b. 07/20/1872, d. 08/15/1958

LEWIS, Anna M., b. 1880, d. 1965

LEWIS, Clara E., b. 1909, d. N/D

LEWIS, Harmon L., b. 1873, d. 1931

LEWIS, Harmon L., Jr., b. 1903, d. 1983

LEWIS, Ida F., b. 08/16/1872, d. 08/14/1940

LINDALE, Charles H., Sgt. USA, WWII, b. 12/21/1914, d. 02/19/1978
LINDSAY, Jean Havelka, b. 1897, d. 1980
LIPPINCOTT, Ann Gray, ssw-Benjamin Franklin Gray, b. 1897, d. 1966
LITTLETON, Alfred I., ssw-Jennie R., b. 09/10/1874, d. 02/19/1940
LITTLETON, Jennie R., ssw-Alfred I., b. 01/13/1885, d. 08/21/1961
LOCKWOOD, Howard G., ssw-Sarah E., b. 1917, d. 1993
LOCKWOOD, Sarah E., ssw-Howard G., b. 1915, d. 1981
LOFLAND, Alberta Mae, b. 09/24/1920, d. 12/13/1984
LOFLAND, Alfred H., III, b. 03/27/1945, d. 11/13/1965
LOFLAND, Arthur H., Jr., ssw-Madaline V., b. 07/12/1914, d. 07/27/1989
LOFLAND, Charles A., ssw-Estella N., b. 1872, d. 1958
LOFLAND, Clarence W., b. 08/22/1904, d. 04/03/1968
LOFLAND, Estella N., ssw-Charles A., b. 1884, d. 1972
LOFLAND, Madaline V., ssw-Arthur H., Jr., b. 08/08/1915, d. N/D
LOFLAND, Mary F., b. 05/12/1914, d. 06/10/1970
LOFLAND, Warren J., b. 08/28/1947, d. 03/25/1969
LONG, Alton W., ssw-Pearl C., b. 02/18/1908, d. 08/15/1991
LONG, Dorothy Helen, b. 10/16/1913, d. 11/11/1928
LONG, Elwood W., b. 04/02/1933, d. 09/26/1987
LONG, Fernando, "Junior," b. 09/16/1980, d. 05/10/1988
LONG, Lulu M., ssw-Oliver H., b. 07/24/1884, d. 12/24/1968
LONG, Oliver H., ssw-Lulu M., b. 06/09/1886, d. 04/07/1950
LONG, Pearl C., ssw-Alton W., b. 01/16/1912, d. N/D
LOPEZ, Francisco J. Ruiz, Jr., b. 11/28/1975, d. 08/14/1994
LOVENGUTH, M. Elizabeth Littleton, w/o Edward, b. 1905, d. 1930
LYNCH, Leroy, ssw-Ora A., b. 09/04/1885, d. 06/29/1972
LYNCH, Ora A., ssw-Leroy, b. 04/23/1888, d. 11/28/1966
LYNCH, Royal A., Sgt., USA, Korea, b. 09/22/1931, d. 09/25/1993
MACATEE, Nellie Gray, w/o Henry C., b. 1882, d. 1955
MADJAROSY, Charles A., DE Pvt., 8 Inf., 4 Inf. Div., WWII, Killed in action in Germany, b. 07/25/1924,
        d. 12/05/1944
MADJAROSY, Frank, b. 04/19/1890, d. 03/29/1967
MADJAROSY, Mary, b. 04/16/1892, d. 10/22/1956
MALCOM, May Welch, b. 06/25/1886, d. 05/26/1969
MANSHIP, F. Murray, ssw-Frank Manship and Mary Manship Bower, b. N/D, d. N/D
MANSHIP, Frank, ssw-F. Murray Manship and Mary Manship Bower, b. 1877, d. 1915
MARKER, Anie, b. 1860, d. 1946
MARKER, James P., b. 1857, d. 1926
MARKERT, William, b. N/D, d. 11/11/1955
MARTIN, Charles Virden, s/o Harry K., b. 07/27/1912, d. 12/23/1912
MARTIN, Dorothy Ann, b. 1953, d. 1954
MARTIN, Franklin W., ssw-Dorothy E., b. 03/23/1933, d. 05/03/1982
MARTIN, Harry K., ssw-Virgie P., b. 1887, d. 1967
MARTIN, Hettie J., ssw-James A., b. 1858, d. 1952
MARTIN, James A., ssw-Hettie J., b. 1859, d. 1945
MARTIN, Virgie P., ssw-Harry K., b. 1890, d. 1968
MARVEL, Albert S., ssw-Minnie, b. 05/21/1898, d. 03/06/1976
MARVEL, Alice S., b. 09/07/1932, d. N/D

MARVEL, Blanche E., ssw-Edgar T., b. 11/19/1902, d. 11/20/1989
MARVEL, Dorthea Ava, b. 09/18/1925, d. 03/04/1926
MARVEL, Edgar T., ssw-Blanche E., b. 08/11/1900, d. 01/09/1985
MARVEL, Elsie M., ssw-Granville T., b. 1902, d. 1976
MARVEL, George C., ssw-Ruth E., b. 09/29/1898, d. 10/30/1960
MARVEL, Glenn, b. 04/07/1904, d. 06/19/1989
MARVEL, Granville T., ssw-Elsie M., b. 1904, d. 1967
MARVEL, Helen P., b. 07/18/1914, d. 08/05/1985
MARVEL, John R., ssw-Mary W., b. 09/23/1890, d. 07/02/1966
MARVEL, Mary W., ssw-John R., b. 01/26/1893, d. 06/06/1985
MARVEL, Minnie, ssw-Albert S., b. 04/06/1899, d. 02/08/1972
MARVEL, Ralph J., DCGS3, USN, Korea, b. 06/11/1931, d. 12/23/1989
MARVEL, Raymond, USN, b. 03/05/1930, d. 04/22/1990
MARVEL, Robert R., b. 01/03/1942, d. 03/24/1959
MARVEL, Ruth E., ssw-George C., b. 04/07/1900, d. 10/26/1985
MARVEL, Wilbur H., b. 09/29/1923, d. 05/13/1924
MARVEL, William S., Pvt. 53 ARD Inf., WWII, b. 02/26/1924, d. 07/30/1944
MASON, Addie P., b. 1858, d. 1925
MASON, Emma Betts, ssw-Oscar S. & Aida C. Betts, b. 1875, d. 1958
MASON, Eugene C., b. 1880, d. 1937
MASON, Mary P., b. 1882, d. 1960
MASON, William W., b. 1858, d. 1929
MASSEY, John D., Pfc. USA, WWII, b. 1913, d. 1983
MASSEY, Joshua J., b. 1886, d. 1940
MASSEY, Nora M., b. 1888, d. 1966
MAULL, Anna V., ssw-Charlie C., b. 1879, d. 1951
MAULL, Charlie C., ssw-Anna V., b. 1873, d. 1966
MAULL, Ella M., ssw-William A., b. 05/16/1887, d. 09/26/1969
MAULL, Emily, b. 1908, d. 1929
MAULL, Georgia V., b. 06/18/1885, d. 09/08/1917
MAULL, William A., ssw-Ella M., b. 12/17/1885, d. 08/27/1958
MAXWELL, Charles, ssw-Violet, b. 1904, d.N/D
MAXWELL, Violet, ssw-Charles, b. 1904, d. 1990
MCALLISTER, Emma L., b. 1862, d. 1934
MCALLISTER, Henry C., b. 1869, d. 1951
MCATEE, Eugene, ssw-Grace, b. 1902, d. 1982
MCATEE, Grace, ssw-Eugene, b. 1881, d. 1975
MCGEE, Bernice E., ssw-Lloyd R.., b. 10/12/1910, d. 10/08/1993
MCGEE, Dorothy E., ssw-Julian R., b. 07/12/1928, d. 05/27/1985
MCGEE, Julian R., ssw-Dorothy E., b. 04/15/1928, d. 05/18/1982
MCGEE, Lloyd R., ssw-Bernice E., b. 04/21/1905, d. 09/22/1975
MCGINNIS, Betty M., b. 05/05/1932, d. 04/11/1958
MCGRATH, Elizabeth A., ssw-Joseph R., b. 1934, d. 1992
MCGRATH, Joseph R., ssw-Elizabeth A., b. 1932, d. 1996
MEARS, Annie E., b. N/D, d. 01/03/1935
MEARS, James A., s/o John E. & Winnie M., b. 08/18/1912, d. 01/08/1914
MEARS, John E., b. 08/28/1882, d. 01/13/1944
MEARS, William H., b. N/D, d. 07/01/1938

MEARS, Winnie M., b. 05/10/1878, d. 06/04/1965

MEGEE, Anna, w/o Capt. Ralph D., b. 08/11/1884, d. 09/25/1908

MEGEE, Betty J., b. 05/03/1932, d. N/D

MEGEE, Charles, ssw-Harry, Jr., b. 1929, d. 1953

MEGEE, Harry, Jr., ssw-Charles, b. 1927, d. 1953

MEGEE, Howard William, b. 02/14/1902, d. 08/26/1985

MEGEE, J. Howard, b. 10/02/1879, d. 09/22/1941

MEGEE, John R., Jr., b. 11/25/1950, d. N/D

MEGEE, John R., Sr., b. 07/02/1930, d. N/D

MEGEE, Lillie J., w/o J. Howard, b. 03/27/1878, d. 02/06/1963

MEGEE, Lucile Kwilus, w/o Howard, b. 08/13/1907, d. 05/13/1985

MEGEE, Lula E., b. 1902, d. 1949

MEGEE, Sharon L., b. 06/07/1952, d. 05/12/1952

MEGEE, William S., b. 1859, d. 1940

MENTZINGER, Irene Collins, b. 1862, d. 1955

MEREDITH, Leonard D., b. 1907, d. 1948

MEREIDER, Anna T., ssw-Robert J. & John F., b. 08/20/1911, d. N/D

MEREIDER, John F., ssw-Anna T. & Robert J., b. 09/21/1903, d. N/D

MEREIDER, Robert J., ssw-Anna T. & John F., DE Pfc. USMC, Vietnam, b. 01/16/1948, d. 01/28/1968

MESSICK, Baby, b. 1981, d. 1981

MESSICK, Florence H., ssw-Vera L., b. 1906, d. 1992

MESSICK, Vera L., ssw-Florence H., b. 1928, d. 1992

MILLER, Frances M., b. 05/05/1887, d. 12/03/1955

MILLER, Gloria K., ssw-Robert J., b. 02/28/1935, d. N/D

MILLER, Jessie L., b. 11/27/1860, d. 10/11/1952

MILLER, Robert J., ssw-Gloria K., b. 04/06/1932, d. N/D

MILLMAN, Clara E., ssw-Joseph B., b. 1900, d. 1919

MILLMAN, Elizabeth N., w/o Jesse M., "Betty," Age 69y, b. N/D, d. 06/08/1996

MILLMAN, Harvey E., ssw-Joseph B., b. 1914, d. 1924

MILLMAN, Howard I., ssw-Joseph B., b. 1919, d. 1924

MILLMAN, Joseph B., ssw-Sallie C., b. 04/22/1874, d. 10/04/1946

MILLMAN, Sallie C., ssw-Joseph B., b. 06/09/1879, d. 02/16/1963

MILLS, Bessie E., ssw-Granville W., b. 1893, d. 1969

MILLS, Earnest Leon, Sr., BM2, USN, b. 05/11/1905, d. 09/22/1977

MILLS, Grace C., b. 03/16/1902, d. 01/31/1980

MILLS, Granville W., ssw-Bessie E., b. 1896, d. 1979

MITCHELL, Cora E., ssw-James H., b. 01/09/1908, d. 05/20/1980

MITCHELL, Fred E., ssw-Olivia H., DE Pfc., 33 Co., 153 Depot Brig, WWI, b. 07/29/1899, d. 08/11/1968

MITCHELL, Fred R., b. 08/09/1933, d. 09/30/1991

MITCHELL, Harriet E., b. 06/24/1919, d. 09/21/1968

MITCHELL, James H., ssw-Cora E., b. 09/27/1904, d. 11/13/1948

MITCHELL, Marshall M., b. 07/16/1977, d. 07/16/1977

MITCHELL, Olivia H., ssw-Fred E., b. 07/24/1900, d. 09/22/1989

MITCHELL, Richard A., "Dickie," b. 12/09/1957, d. 10/08/1973

MOORE, Charles T., ssw-Virginia C., b. 1909, d. 1976

MOORE, Clarence, ssw-Margaret S., b. 1902, d. 1984

MOORE, Elsie E., b. 09/15/1952, d. 01/13/1968

MOORE, Eugene J., ssw-Madge M. & Eugene J., Jr., b. 06/09/1907, d. 12/27/1973

MOORE, Eugene J., Jr., ssw-Madge M. & Eugene J., b. 07/14/1931, d. 02/13/1947

MOORE, Haddie C., ssw-Harold J., b. 04/30/1906, d. 02/01/1991

MOORE, Harold J., ssw-Haddie C., b. 04/18/1902, d. 07/20/1974

MOORE, Harry M., b. 02/09/1942, d. 02/11/1973

MOORE, James E., b. 12/18/1916, d. 10/04/1974

MOORE, Lester S., ssw-Madalene W., b. 11/26/1911, d. N/D

MOORE, Lina M., ssw-Roland W., b. 11/22/1885, d. 05/22/1975

MOORE, Madalene W., ssw-Lester S., b. 12/02/1917, d. N/D

MOORE, Madge M., ssw-Eugene J. & Eugene J., Jr., b. 06/02/1906, d. N/D

MOORE, Margaret M., b. 12/07/1924, d. 04/06/1951

MOORE, Margaret S., ssw-Clarence, b. 1907, d. 1980

MOORE, Martha E., ssw-Robert L., b. 03/19/1934, d. N/D

MOORE, Matilda, ssw-Samuel E., b. 05/14/1917, d. N/D

MOORE, Robert L., ssw-Martha E., b. 03/10/1930, d. 11/10/1985

MOORE, Roland W., ssw-Lina M., b. 11/05/1884, d. 01/18/1951

MOORE, Samuel E., ssw-Matilda, b. 09/16/1912, d. N/D

MOORE, Virginia C., ssw-Charles T., b. 1916, d. 1974

MORGAN, Benjamin P., ssw-Mary P., b. 03/20/1844, d. 12/28/1913

MORGAN, Henrietta B., b. 1895, d. 1955

MORGAN, James Henry, Tec5, USA, WWII, b. 01/10/1907, d. 10/03/1979

MORGAN, Mary K., b. 11/20/1908, d. N/D

MORGAN, Mary P., ssw-Benjamin P., b. 11/19/1855, d. 05/03/1917

MORRIS, Baby, b. N/D, d. N/D

MORRIS, Bessie M., ssw-Gove R., b. 1893, d. 1964

MORRIS, Clara W., b. 1871, d. 1935

MORRIS, Gove R., ssw-Bessie M., b. 1893, d. 1972

MORRIS, Pennelphia C., b. 02/01/1858, d. 08/24/1949

MORRIS, William A., b. 1866, d. 1942

MURRAY, Cleora M., b. 1912, d. 1939

MURRAY, Ellen A., ssw-Leroy J., b. 05/21/1904, d. N/D

MURRAY, Leroy J., ssw-Ellen A., b. 04/03/1906, d. 12/31/1987

MUSTARD, Clarence H., ssw-Sally M., b. 02/06/1891, d. 11/21/1977

MUSTARD, Emma S., b. 1879, d. 1945

MUSTARD, George M., DE Sgt., 334 Fighter Sq., AAF, WWII, b. 01/06/1909, d. 08/28/1970

MUSTARD, James R., b. 1903, d. 1933

MUSTARD, Jannetta H., ssw-Louis L., b. 05/25/1868, d. 05/10/1955

MUSTARD, John B., b. 1858, d. 1932

MUSTARD, Louis L., ssw-Jannetta H., b. 12/10/1865, d. 10/27/1950

MUSTARD, Sally M., ssw-Clarence H., b. 07/27/1891, d. 08/11/1973

NAPOLETANO, Florence W., b. 1881, d. 1950

NEAL, Mary H., b. 1856, d. 1930

NEAL, Theo. E., b. 1856, d. 1937

NEAL, William E., Pvt. USA, WWI, b. 1887, d. 1982

NEARGAROT, Grace L., ssw-Henry A., b. 06/18/1890, d. 10/11/1956

NEARGAROT, Henry A., ssw-Grace L., b. 06/22/1880, d. 06/07/1951

NEEDLES, H. Vernon, ssw-Irma W., b. 03/28/1910, d. 09/11/1993

NEEDLES, Irma W., ssw-H. Vernon, b. 09/06/1912, d. 04/22/1993

NESS, Ethel Johnson, w/o P. E. Ness, b. 1910, d. 1927

NIELSEN, Ethel M., ssw-Julius P., b. 11/13/1921, d. 05/10/1973
NIELSEN, Julius P., ssw-Ethel M., b. 07/04/1904, d. 05/29/1985
NIELSEN, Pauline C. S., ssw-Peter J., b. 12/11/1880, d. 07/18/1953
NIELSEN, Peter J., ssw-Pauline C. S., b. 04/15/1873, d. 02/05/1952
O'NEIL, Barbara Snyder, b. 1935, d. 1968
OLDHAM, Lillian E., b. 1939, d. N/D
OLDHAM, Paul W., Ssgt., USAF, b. 08/05/1936, d. 08/27/1974
ONDRAKO, Irma M., ssw-William E., b. 08/14/1917, d. 11/12/1993
ONDRAKO, William E., ssw-Irma M., b. 08/27/2925, d. N/D
OTT, Bessie M., ssw-William H., Wife, b. 1884, d. 1967
OTT, Charlie M., ssw-Pearl E., Son, b. 1907, d. 1908
OTT, Jennie, b. 11/10/1877, d. 12/25/1969
OTT, Pearl E., ssw-Charlie M., Daughter, b. 1910, d. 1911
OTT, William H., ssw-Pearl E., Husband, b. 1884, d. 1953
OUTTEN, Delema W., ssw-Hiram J., b. 1887, d. 1978
OUTTEN, Hiram J., ssw-Delema W., b. 1884, d. 1952
OWENS, A. L., ssw-J. R., b. 06/24/1973, d. 06/24/1973
OWENS, Goldie W., ssw-Harry L., b. 01/25/1885, d. 03/18/1978
OWENS, Harry L., ssw-Goldie W., b. 09/20/1882, d. 11/14/1912
OWENS, J. R., ssw-A. L., b. 06/24/1973, d. 06/24/1973
PALMER, Adolphus L., b. 1873, d. 1955
PALMER, Alice E., b. 01/01/1858, d. 12/23/1955
PALMER, Alice R., ssw-Robert H., b. 1881, d. 1964
PALMER, Benjamin N., ssw-Mary E., b. 1868, d. 1961
PALMER, Deborah, ssw-James H., b. 1869, d. 1940
PALMER, Elizabeth E., ssw-Robert W., b. 12/22/1916, d. 07/11/1971
PALMER, Elsie E., ssw-T. Harold, b. 09/29/1906, d. 05/05/1993
PALMER, George R., DE Pvt., USA, WWI, b. 02/07/1897, d. 07/25/1973
PALMER, Gladys A., ssw-J. Smedley, b. 02/22/1904, d. 03/01/1975
PALMER, Glenwood W., b. 1921, d. 1939
PALMER, J. Carey, ssw-Stella, b. 1872, d. 1934
PALMER, J. Smedley, ssw-Gladys A., b. 03/26/1904, d. 07/22/1977
PALMER, James H., ssw-Deborah, b. 1856, d. 1945
PALMER, Margaret W., b. 1896, d. 1976
PALMER, Mary E., ssw-Benjamin N., b. 1878, d. 1964
PALMER, Robert H., ssw-Alice R., b. 1881, d. 1955
PALMER, Robert W., ssw-Elizabeth E., b. 09/14/1911, d. 12/29/1974
PALMER, Stella, ssw-J. Carey, b. 1874, d. 1957
PALMER, Susanna S., b. 1871, d. 1956
PALMER, T. Harold, ssw-Elsie E., b. 04/15/1909, d. 05/16/1965
PALSGROVE, Catherine M., b. 03/07/1909, d. 05/31/1987
PANUSKA, Anna M., ssw-Frank, b. 08/18/1885, d. 06/16/1956
PANUSKA, Frank, ssw-Anna M., b. 12/06/1878, d. 07/13/1960
PANUSKA, Frank L., ssw-Hulda T., b. 1909, d.1976
PANUSKA, Hulda, ssw-Frank L., b. 1907, d. N/D
PARKHILL, Morria A., DE MSgt., 394 Signal Co., WWII, b. 12/31/1919, d. 03/09/1969
PARKHILL, Winfred M., b. 07/25/1926, d. N/D
PARSONS, Debra N., b. 09/13/1956, d. 02/28/1992

PARSONS, James B., ssw-Mattie, b. 04/10/1905, d. 07/15/1989

PARSONS, Mattie, ssw-James B., b. 09/07/1900, d. 02/24/1968

PASSWATERS, Barbara C., "Tootsie," ssw-Donald J., b. 03/02/1942, d. 07/16/1993

PASSWATERS, Donald J., ssw-Barbara C., b. 07/20/1938, d. N/D

PEPPER, Charles, ssw- Fred W., b. 1914, d. 1914

PEPPER, Edith E., ssw-Foster H., b. 05/08/1914, d. N/D

PEPPER, Foster H., ssw-Edith E., b. 10/17/1915, d. 07/19/1972

PEPPER, Foster H., inf. s/o Frederick H. & Diane H., ssw-Joseph H., b. 02/17/1976, d. N/D

PEPPER, Fred W., ssw-Nancy & Laura M., b. 1874, d. 1953

PEPPER, Hannah R., ssw-Uhland T., b. 06/20/1907, d. 08/31/1990

PEPPER, Joseph H., inf. s/o Frederick H. & Diane H., ssw-Foster H., b. 09/08/1979, d. N/D

PEPPER, Laura M., ssw-Fred W. & Nancy, b. 1884, d. 1963

PEPPER, Nancy, ssw-Fred W. & Laura M., b. 1882, d. 1911

PEPPER, Russel, ssw-Fred W., b. 1906, d. 1906

PEPPER, Uhland T., ssw-Hannah R., b. 02/23/1906, d. 10/07/1984

PETTYJOHN, Abel J., ssw-Sarah J., b. 10/11/1836, d. 10/25/1907

PETTYJOHN, Carrie L., b. 07/25/1878, d. 04/25/1911

PETTYJOHN, Clara E., w/o Capt. Wm., ssw-Wm. T., b. 04/10/1870, d. 01/09/1922

PETTYJOHN, Ebenezer, b. 08/22/1852, d. 02/18/1903

PETTYJOHN, Fannie M., ssw-James C., b. 1876, d. 1940

PETTYJOHN, James C., ssw-Fannie M., b. 1873, d. 1934

PETTYJOHN, Luther, ssw-Willard, b. 1880, d. 1927

PETTYJOHN, Sarah J., ssw-Abel J., b. 01/01/1842, d. 05/21/1938

PETTYJOHN, Willard, ssw-Luther, b. 1888, d. 1914

PETTYJOHN, William E., Pvt. Co. A., 73 Eng., WWI, b. 03/01/1897, d. 01/17/1967

PETTYJOHN, Wm. T., Capt., ssw-Clara E., b. 04/15/1865, d. 06/19/1944

PHILLIPS, Eva, ssw-R. Brice, b. 1956, d. N/D

PHILLIPS, James E., ssw-Mildred A., b. 1903, d. 1976

PHILLIPS, Jane G., ssw-John Denney, b. N/D, d. N/D

PHILLIPS, John Denney, ssw-Jane G., USA, WWII, b. 04/03/1921, d. 03/27/1992

PHILLIPS, Mildred A., ssw-James E., b. 1908, d. 1966

PHILLIPS, R. Brice, ssw-Eva, b. 1954, d. 1993

PLUMMER, Herbert H., HM3, USN, Korea, b. 04/30/1930, d. 09/07/1993

PORTER, Audrey Davis, Age 85y, b. N/D, d. 06/01/1996

PORTER, Calvin, b. 01/04/1866, d. 08/16/1918

PORTER, Dorman B., ssw-Huldah, b. 1881, d. 1939

PORTER, George C., DE Sgt., 584 Bomb Sq., AAF, WWII, b. 05/26/1910, d. 09/07/1959

PORTER, George C., ssw-Mary E., b. 12/03/1842, d. 06/10/1904

PORTER, Huldah, ssw-Dorman B., b. 1882, d. 1951

PORTER, Mary E., w/o George C., ssw-George C., b. 03/30/1847, d. 01/02/1917

PORTER, William R., b. 07/30/1910, d. 12/09/1991

POSTLES, Barbara Ann, b. 10/26/1933, d. 10/26/1993

POSTLES, David, ssw-Laura, b. 01/20/1851, d. 01/01/1924

POSTLES, Ermon, ssw-Verna, b. 1900, d. 1987

POSTLES, Ethel G., ssw-George E., b. 03/08/1882, d. 04/16/1958

POSTLES, George E., ssw-Ethel G., b. 01/11/1879, d. 04/21/1975

POSTLES, Laura, ssw-David, b. 09/09/1852, d. 04/10/1940

POSTLES, Linden R., b. 12/28/1893, d. 06/25/1964

POSTLES, Verna, ssw-Ermon, b. 1902, d. 1990
POTTER, Hattie, w/o Henry D., ssw-Henry D., b. 1902, d. 1990
POTTER, Henry D., ssw-Hattie, b. 1858, d. 1928
POWERS, Baby, ssw-William M., b. 1962, d. 1962
POWERS, John E., b. 1904, d. 1946
POWERS, William M., ssw-Baby, b. 1931, d. 1964
PRIDE, Geraldine J., ssw-Robert W., b. 07/05/1950, d. N/D
PRIDE, Lillian H., b. 12/04/1894, d. 04/04/1960
PRIDE, Robert W., ssw-Geraldine J., b. 11/18/1949, d. 06/26/1970
PRIDE, William A., b. 08/13/1896, d. 10/06/1979
PRITCHETT, Clarence B., b. 1886, d. 1968
PRITCHETT, Emily J., b. 1892, d. 1963
PRITCHETT, Helen C., b. 1892, d. 1969
QUIG, Mary C., b. 1888, d. 1961
QUIG, Wm. D., b. 1865, d. 1944
QUILLEN, Amy A., ssw-Charles E., b. 10/21/1924, d. N/D
QUILLEN, Charles E., ssw-Amy A., b. 07/17/1920, d. 12/10/1990
REED, Amanda H., b. 02/06/1870, d. 05/17/1949
REED, Amanda K., b. 1881, d. 1964
REED, Annie, ssw-William J., b. 09/13/1876, d. 08/15/1955
REED, Carlyn M., b. 1908, d. 1973
REED, Catherine Jeanette, ssw-Hall D., b. 12/20/1939, d. N/D
REED, Clara P., b. 09/06/1887, d. 07/28/1967
REED, Clarence T., b. 1905, d. 1954
REED, Cleveland, b. 1884, d. 1967
REED, David H., ssw-Pearl V., b. 1900, d. 1977
REED, Earl M., ssw-Mary L., b. 09/02/1886, d. 05/08/1966
REED, Edward P., ssw-Effie O., b. 1895, d. 1968
REED, Effie O., ssw-Edward P., b. 1896, d. 1978
REED, Eldora, b. 1897, d. 1990
REED, Ella E., b. 04/24/1882, d. 05/13/1944
REED, Francis S., ssw-Ralph M., b. N/D, d. N/D
REED, Frederick E., b. 10/03/1887, d. 03/06/1937
REED, George P., b. 06/28/1884, d. 02/13/1957
REED, Hall D., Jr., "Sonny," ssw-Catherine Jeanette, b. 06/28/1937, d. N/D
REED, James R., b. 10/01/1911, d. 11/15/1964
REED, Jane, b. 03/09/1938, d. 04/08/1938
REED, John P., ssw-Mary S., b. 12/15/1913, d. N/D
REED, Lora J., b. 11/28/1959, d. 01/06/1988
REED, M. Ethel, ssw-Walter E., b. 11/22/1890, d. 01/29/1973
REED, Margaret C., ssw-William F., b. 07/14/1909, d. 07/24/1987
REED, Mary L., ssw-Earl M., b. 05/07/1892, d. 11/01/1966
REED, Mary M., b. 05/05/1902, d. 08/30/1979
REED, Mary M., ssw-Rufus M., b. 12/04/1882, d. 12/06/1966
REED, Mary S., ssw-John P., b. 10/22/1910, d. 03/21/1993
REED, Minnie, b. 1869, d. 1945
REED, Pearl V., ssw-David H., b. 1905, d. 1977
REED, R. Allan, b. 03/15/1941, d. 10/17/1987

REED, Ralph M., ssw-Francis S., b. 07/24/1910, d. 01/22/1980

REED, Rena, b. 1887, d. 1954

REED, Richard K., b. 1945, d. 1945

REED, Rufus M., Capt., ssw-Mary M., b. 09/18/1875, d. 03/26/1951

REED, Theodore W., b. 1882, d. 1958

REED, W. Layton, b. 1900, d. 1947

REED, Walter E., ssw-M. Ethel, b. 09/22/1890, d. 02/05/1946

REED, William F., ssw-Margaret C., b. 03/08/1909, d. 01/19/1955

REED, William J., ssw-Annie, b. 12/25/1864, d. 11/19/1948

REED, William R., b. 08/14/1856, d. 12/18/1922

REED, William W., b. 1868, d. 1949

REYNOLDS, B. Marshall, Sr., ssw-Ethel A., m. 12-12-1931, b. 09/11/1911, d. 06/18/1989

REYNOLDS, Brian, Baby, b. 11/03/1972, d. 11/03/1972

REYNOLDS, Elizabeth V., Baby, b. 01/09/1934, d. 01/09/1934

REYNOLDS, Estella M., b. 1883, d. 1930

REYNOLDS, Ethel A., ssw-B. Marshall, Sr., m. 12-12-1931, b. 12/25/1914, d. 04/09/1986

REYNOLDS, Frank L., b. 1874, d. 1944

REYNOLDS, Gerald Lee, ssw-Sandra Elizabeth, m. 7-24-1959, b. 01/03/1939, d. N/D

REYNOLDS, Gove E., ssw-Roberta N., b. 12/29/1896, d. 05/28/1982

REYNOLDS, Nicole Marie, ssw-Randall Lee, Children, b. N/D, d. N/D

REYNOLDS, Randall Lee, ssw-Rocklan Lee, Children, b. N/D, d. N/D

REYNOLDS, Roberta N., ssw-Gove E., b. 09/19/1900, d. 06/14/1964

REYNOLDS, Rocklan Lee, ssw-Randall Lee, Children, b. N/D, d. N/D

REYNOLDS, Sandra Elizabeth, ssw-Gerald Lee, m. 7-24-1959, b. 02/19/1941, d. 04/19/1995

RHODES, Arthur C., ssw-Sallie M., b. 1873, d. 1929

RHODES, Sallie M., w/o Arthur C., ssw-Arthur C., b. 1872, d. 1956

RICE, Mamie L., b. 11/13/1899, d. N/D

RICHARDS, Alice, b. 11/05/1882, d. 06/25/1965

RICHARDS, Grace B., b. 09/30/1915, d. 08/18/1969

RICHARDS, Leighton, b. 06/19/1908, d. N/D

RICHARDS, William, b. 06/27/1878, d. 03/08/1952

RIDINGTON, Howard F., ssw-Irma B., b. 02/09/1908, d. 04/14/1989

RIDINGTON, Irma B., ssw-Howard F., b. 07/02/1909, d. N/D

RILLET, Josephine, b. 1889, d. 1953

RIVERA, Rafael, Jr., b. 08/12/1965, d. 08/29/1974

ROACH, Alfred E., b. 01/08/1906, d. 01/14/1961

ROACH, Barbara A., ssw-Dallas G., b. 01/10/1927, d. 10/04/1995

ROACH, Clara, ssw-Edward, b. 01/02/1888, d. 05/19/1970

ROACH, Dallas G., ssw-Barbara A., b. 01/11/1928, d. N/D

ROACH, Edward, ssw-Clara, b. 10/18/1889, d. 06/26/1963

ROACH, Henry B., b. 09/04/1874, d. 01/04/1941

ROACH, Maurice W., b. 11/22/1854, d. 01/20/1917

ROBBINS, Eliza D., b. 1888, d. 1973

ROBBINS, John M., b. 1847, d. 1931

ROBBINS, Josiah D., b. 1888, d. 1979

ROBBINS, L. Margaret, b. 1853, d. 1940

ROBBINS, Orpha P., b. 1849, d. 1919

ROBBINS, Sarah Eliza., w/o William C., b. 12/25/1856, d. 02/16/1941

ROBBINS, Walter S., DE. Pvt., USA, WWI, b. 11/05/1889, d. 05/07/1967
ROBERTS, Emma Mustard, ssw-Harry D., b. 02/01/1917, d. N/D
ROBERTS, Harry D., ssw-Emma Mustard, Ltcdr, USN, b. 05/05/1912, d. 06/16/1986
ROBERTS, John Grove, s/o Harry D. & Emma Mustard, b. 08/01/1942, d. 01/11/1980
ROBINSON, Emma B., ssw-John A., b. 1882, d. 1954
ROBINSON, Joanna, b. 1862, d. 1938
ROBINSON, John A., ssw-Emma B., b. 1873, d. 1945
ROBINSON, Maggie G., ssw-W. W., b. 08/10/1847, d. 11/26/1925
ROBINSON, Mary A., w/o William, b. 12/16/1839, d. 02/26/1915
ROBINSON, W. W., ssw-Maggie G., b. 08/07/1846, d. 03/17/1938
RODENHEISER, Jennie B., b. 03/20/1917, d. 09/11/1994
ROGERS, Daniel C., Jr., b. 01/21/1966, d. 07/06/1985
ROGERS, Duane R., b. 04/17/1917, d. 09/03/1980
ROGERS, Emma C., ssw-William N., b. 1899, d.1946
ROGERS, William N., ssw-Emma C., b. 1896, d. 1937
ROSE, John H., ssw-Ruth, b. 07/21/1909, d. N/D
ROSE, Ruth, ssw-John H., b. 10/02/1911, d. 10/02/1993
ROTHERGATTER, William F., b. 12/21/1913, d. N/D
ROUSH, Esther M., ssw-George E., b. 09/23/1924, d. 11/21/1982
ROUSH, George E., ssw-Esther M., Tech5, USA, WWII, b. 02/18/1922, d. 04/28/1992
RUARK, Baby Boy, b. 05/2/1976, d. 05/25/1976
RUSSELL, Agnes, b. 04/18/1882, d. 01/23/1975
RUSSELL, Hettie J., b. 1867, d. 1942
RUSSELL, Jean D., ssw-R. Pierce, b. 1923, d. N/D
RUSSELL, Lillie M., ssw-Plaford T., b. 1898, d. 1995
RUSSELL, Plaford T., ssw-Lillie M., b. 1896, d. 1979
RUSSELL, R. Pierce, ssw-Jean D., b. 1919, d. N/D
RUSSELL, Willard E., b. 1863, d. 1948
RUST, Clifford E., ssw-M. Amanda, b. 12/04/1920, d. S05/06/1986
RUST, M. Amanda, ssw-Clifford E., b. 03/17/1921, d. N/D
SANGER, Arthur H., ssw-Sharon E., wed. 3-25/1983, b. 05/08/1956, d. 02/05/1989
SANGER, Sharon E., ssw-Arthur H., wed. 3-25-1983, b. 08/21/1953, d. N/D
SAPP, Lewis W., ssw-Marie Dodd, b. 10/14/1916, d. N/D
SAPP, Marie Dodd, ssw-Lewis W., b. 06/22/1917, d. N/D
SAVAGE, Clarence, ssw-Edna, b. 01/14/1902, d. 04/17/1950
SAVAGE, Edna, ssw-Clarence, b. 05/31/1906, d. 08/28/1957
SAVAGE, Ociola J., b. 1890, d. 1976
SCHIRMER, Carl F., ssw-Ruth D., b. 1921, d. 1992
SCHIRMER, Gladys W., ssw-Harold A., b. 12/03/1919, d. N/D
SCHIRMER, Harold A., ssw-Gladys W., b. 12/17/1917, d. 11/24/1986
SCHIRMER, Ruth D., ssw-Carl F., b. 1929, d. 1955
SCHMIERER, Linda D., ssw-James Alfred, Thelma May & Arthur Ellis Jefferson, b. 1899, d. 1942
SCHOCKLEY, Howard J., b. 10/05/1902, d. 11/06/1964
SCHUNK, Bea, ssw-Raymond, b. 06/10/1929, d. N/D
SCHUNK, Raymond, ssw-Bea, Sgt., USA, WWII, b. 10/09/1923, d. 01/25/1992
SCOTT, Andrew B., ssw-Lora M., b. 1897, d. 1947
SCOTT, Edward M., III, Cpt., USA, WWII, b. 12/31/1924, d. 02/23/1985
SCOTT, Lora M., ssw-Andrew B., b. 1902, d. 1978

SCULL, James B., b. 03/10/1842, d. 06/08/1927
SHARP, Absalom R., ssw-Jannett B., b. 12/16/1829, d. 01/12/1903
SHARP, George W., b. 1861, d. 1933
SHARP, Jannett B., ssw-Absalom R., b. 05/12/1835, d. 12/18/1903
SHEPHERD, Margaret M., ssw-Wesley N., b. 04/27/1917, d. 01/19/1985
SHEPHERD, Wesley N., ssw-Margaret M., b. 02/27/1912, d. 04/12/1993
SHOCKLEY, Helen Mae, b. 05/01/1932, d. 08/31/1932
SHOCKLEY, Laura G., ssw-W. Daniel, b. 01/21/1886, d. 02/10/1939
SHOCKLEY, W. Daniel, ssw-Laura G., b. 01/15/1947, d. N/D
SHORT, Annie L., ssw-Joshua E., b. 1862, d. 1954
SHORT, Gloria T., ssw-William M., Sr., b. 07/31/1925, d. N/D
SHORT, Irene, ssw-William Gilpin, b. 1915, d. 1966
SHORT, Joshua E., ssw-Annie L., b. 10/31/1852, d. 06/09/1913
SHORT, Ward H., ssw-Joshua E., b. 1887, d. 1953
SHORT, William Gilpin, ssw-Irene, Pfc. USMC, WWII, b. 11/23/1910, d. 01/12/1988
SHORT, William M., Sr., ssw-Gloria T., b. 12/22/1923, d. N/D
SIMMONS, Eldora R., ssw-Paul E., b. 02/11/1923, d. N/D
SIMMONS, Paul E., ssw-Eldora R., b. 01/02/1914, d. 11/10/1989
SLAW, Mary Johnson, b. 07/23/1922, d. 07/27/1994
SMIDTH, Louis, b. 1885, d. 1953
SMITH, Albert L., b. 1910, d. 1911
SMITH, Alfred Lee, b. 08/15/1886, d. 04/04/1970
SMITH, Alma E., b. 1918, d. 1925
SMITH, Amanda Ellen, ssw-William J., b. 04/28/1853, d. 04/10/1937
SMITH, Amy T., ssw-John D., b. 1888, d. 1984
SMITH, Annie Laura Martin, w/o Alfred Lee, b. 12/20/1886, d. 10/29/1962
SMITH, Arrilla, b. N/D, d. 11/09/1899
SMITH, Baby, b. 06/24/1948, d. 06/24/1948
SMITH, Charles H., ssw-Sallie S., b. 1861, d. 1940
SMITH, Charles P., b. 1889, d. 1951
SMITH, Daniel B., b. 1892, d. 1966
SMITH, Daniel R., b. 1918, d. 1918
SMITH, Elmer B., Sr., ssw-Ruth C., b. 11/17/1930, d. 01/03/1995
SMITH, Emma Pettyjohn, w/o William F., ssw-William F., b. 1858, d. 1944
SMITH, Eva Emely, d/o Lee & Laura, b. 09/29/1921, d. 01/05/1922
SMITH, Eva K., ssw-William J., b. 02/15/1876, d. 08/17/1946
SMITH, F. Jeannette, ssw-Julian M., b. 11/04/1930, d. N/D
SMITH, Frances B., b. 10/26/1927, d. 09/16/1992
SMITH, George H., ssw-William J., b. 01/18/1878, d. 11/30/1881
SMITH, Herbert B., ssw-Iva S., b. 1921, d. 1995
SMITH, Iva S., ssw-Herbert B., b. 1922, d. 1992
SMITH, J. Byron, b. 1908, d. 1935
SMITH, James W., b. 1889, d. 1965
SMITH, John B., b. 1920, d. 1932
SMITH, John D., ssw-Amy T., b. 1881, d. 1960
SMITH, Julian M., ssw-F. Jeannette, b. 07/30/1925, d. N/D
SMITH, Laura C., b. 1897, d. 1983
SMITH, Leila H., b. 1889, d. 1960

SMITH, Leon J., b. 1925, d. 1937
SMITH, Louie L., ssw-W. Harry, b. 1880, d. 1970
SMITH, Mabel B., b. 04/05/1881, d. 10/08/1973
SMITH, Mary S., b. 01/24/1910, d. 11/21/1934
SMITH, Mattie E., b. 09/20/1896, d. 05/22/1985
SMITH, Ruth C., ssw-Elmer B., Sr., b. 08/25/1931, d. N/D
SMITH, Sallie M., d/o Charles H. & Sallie S., b. 04/06/1907, d. 09/06/1917
SMITH, Sallie S., ssw-Charles H., b. 1864, d. 1940
SMITH, W. Harry, ssw-Louie L., b. 1883, d. 1953
SMITH, William F., ssw-Emma Pettyjohn, b. 1865, d. 1936
SMITH, William J., ssw-Amanda Ellen, b. 11/05/1846, d. 05/07/1917
SNYDER, Estella M., b. 1912, d. 1976
SNYDER, Francis B., b. 08/08/1919, d. 11/29/1974
SNYDER, Russell, b. 1907, d. 1967
SPENCER, Arzie B., ssw-Louis V., b. 1904, d. 1981
SPENCER, Barry L., b. 02/28/1960, d. 12/29/1992
SPENCER, D. Allen, b. 02/11/1938, d. 01/16/1957
SPENCER, Doris E., b. 10/16/1935, d. 02/16/1954
SPENCER, John, Jr., b. 05/18/1918, d. 03/27/1972
SPENCER, Louis V., ssw-Arzie B., b. 1901, d. 1996
SPENCER, Lulua J., ssw-T. Raymond, b. 01/11/1899, d. 04/16/1983
SPENCER, Pearl M., ssw-William W., b. 02/07/1914, d. 05/05/1992
SPENCER, Raymond L., b. 05/31/1949, d. 06/11/1972
SPENCER, T. Raymond, ssw-Lulua J., b. 04/13/1892, d. 11/09/1960
SPENCER, William W., ssw-Pearl M., b. 02/26/1899, d. 01/27/1991
STAIB, Mary E., ssw-William C. & Robert K., b. 04/07/1897, d. 04/14/1970
STAIB, Robert K., ssw-Mary E. & William C., b. 03/23/1894, d. 10/14/1972
STAIB, William C., ssw-Mary E. & Robert K., b. 03/10/1898, d. 09/19/1968
STEELE, Catherine L., ssw-Samuel B., b. 03/19/1914, d. 12/24/1967
STEELE, Samuel B., ssw-Catherine L., b. 08/04/1916, d. 04/26/1963
STEELMAN, Annie B., b. 1860, d. 1948
STEELMAN, Jerry, Age 64y, b. N/D, d. 01/06/1908
STENGER, John R., Dr., ssw-Margaret E., b. 10/17/1926, d. N/D
STENGER, Margaret E., ssw-John R., b. 02/22/1927, d. 02/02/1993
STEPHENS, Clara H., ssw-William H., b. 1859, d. 1941
STEPHENS, William H., ssw-Clara H., b. 1859, d. 1936
STEVENSON, Elwood, b. 1890, d. 1956
STEVENSON, Lulu L., b. 1895, d. 1950
STEVENSON, Richard E., b. 11/01/1919, d. 03/11/1954
STOETZEL, Clemens A., ssw-Lauretta V., b. 10/31/1908, d. N/D
STOETZEL, Lauretta V., ssw-Clemens A., b. 06/24/1914, d. 06/22/1976
STUCHLIK, Charles, b. 1876, d. 1961
STUCHLIK, Charles F., b. 01/29/1909, d. 06/08/1982
STUCHLIK, Margaret M., b. 11/05/1912, d. N/D
STUCHLIK, Mary, b. 1889, d. 1940
STUCHLIK, William, s/o Chas. & Mary, b. 08/14/1910, d. 08/11/1914
SUPPLES, Theodora M., b. 12/27/1910, d. 01/20/1989
SWEET, Bertha M., b. 1907, d. 1953

SWEET, Gertrude M., ssw-Martin E., b. 1901, d. 1976
SWEET, Martin E., ssw-Gertrude M., b. 1900, d. 1970
THACKERY, Charles E., b. 1882, d. 1940
THACKERY, John M., b. 11/26/1840, d. 02/07/1910
THACKERY, Melvina, b. 1889, d. 1958
THACKERY, Susan C., b. 1847, d. 1916
THARP, James E., b. 04/30/1952, d. 12/31/1969
THOMAS, Catherine E., ssw-Harry F., b. 07/31/1923, d. 03/17/1943
THOMAS, Elizabeth R., d/o Iona, b. 1927, d. 1986
THOMAS, Harry F., ssw-Catherine E., b. 03/30/1917, d. N/D
THOMAS, John, Jr., Pfc, USA, WWII, b. 1903, d. 1984
THOMAS, Lydia A., ssw-Paris, b. 04/09/1903, d. 11/29/1978
THOMAS, Paris, ssw-Lydia A., b. 06/17/1898, d. 05/29/1966
TOBIN, Thomas Joseph, DE, Capt., Med. C., WWII, b. 05/30/1918, d. 12/26/1964
TODD, Norma Reed, b. 1910, d. 1964
TRUITT, Annie B., ssw-Miles K., b. 05/13/1884, d. 04/25/1968
TRUITT, Miles K., ssw-Annie B., b. 04/12/1876, d. 11/07/1957
TUGGLE, Danielle Grace, Sp5, USA, b. 03/11/1958, d. 06/18/1982
TURNER, Frances K., d/o J. Ray & Alice G., b. 06/29/1917, d. 10/31/1917
TYNDALL, Lloyd M., Jr., ssw-Ruth L., b. 06/03/1936, d. 12/19/1995
TYNDALL, Ruth L., ssw-Lloyd M., Jr., b. 11/11/1936, d. N/D
UNKNOWN, Herman, b. N/D, d. N/D
UNKNOWN, Robbie, b. N/D, d. N/D
VENT, Clara B., ssw-Clarence W., b. 10/28/1964, d. 1945
VENT, Clarence W., ssw-Ella, b. 1892, d. 1941
VENT, Ella, w/o Clarence W., ssw-Clarence W., b. 1883, d. 1946
VENT, Nancy M., b. 11/04/1923, d. N/D
VENT, William A., b. 05/01/1918, d. 05/01/1973
VENT, William A., ssw-Clarence W., b. 03/10/1856, d. 1944
VERNON, Arthur L., ssw-Sarah L., b. 06/19/1895, d. 01/23/1986
VERNON, Sarah L., ssw-Arthur L., b. 08/17/1898, d. 09/10/1987
VICKERS, Charles Callie, Jr., b. 03/27/1965, d. 03/27/1965
VICKERS, Myrtle Mae, b. 05/03/1921, d. 08/26/1993
WAGAMON, Anne B., b. 09/28/1917, d. 06/29/1991
WAGAMON, Arthur W., DE, Capt., 49 Bomb Sq., AF, WWII, b. 03/07/1917, d. 01/30/1953
WAGAMON, Daniel, ssw-Elsie K., b. 10/09/1892, d. 03/16/1965
WAGAMON, Daniel, ssw-Lillie A., b. 1862, d. 1946
WAGAMON, Elsie K., ssw-Daniel, b. 02/07/1891, d. 06/20/1988
WAGAMON, Emma E., ssw-Henry C., b. 1886, d. 1958
WAGAMON, Frances Shipley, b. 05/18/1917, d. 05/05/1992
WAGAMON, George A., b. 1923, d. 1931
WAGAMON, Henry C., ssw-Emma E., b. 1886, d. 1974
WAGAMON, Lillie A., ssw-Daniel, b. 1867, d. 1946
WAGAMON, Lottie Welch, b. 09/02/1888, d. 04/07/1977
WAGAMON, William B., Sr., b. 08/13/1887, d. 11/04/1969
WALDO, Lydia E., ssw-Wayne M., b. 1922, d. N/D
WALDO, Wayne M., ssw-Lydia E., b. 1924, d. 1987
WALKER, Charles E., ssw-Evelyn M., b. 04/09/1898, d. 11/26/1972

WALKER, Evelyn M., ssw-Charles E., b. 09/14/1913, d. 09/24/1977
WALKER, J. Harrison, b. 03/30/1891, d. 09/30/1918
WALLS, Benjamin F., ssw-Hannah E., b. 02/10/1861, d. 08/29/1921
WALLS, Benjamin Franklin, Jr., b. 10/11/1894, d. 5/08/1921
WALLS, Bernice M., ssw-John S., b. 12/14/1920, d. 01/16/1983
WALLS, Blanche B., b. 08/09/1919, d. 09/29/1991
WALLS, Charles, Jr., b. 1924, d. 1926
WALLS, Charles H., ssw-Minnie H., b. 1887, d. 1955
WALLS, Clarence B., b. 05/02/1907, d. 12/30/1968
WALLS, Ella, ssw-Harvey Gibson, b. 1912, d. 1963
WALLS, Hannah E., ssw-Benjamin F., b. 09/29/1859, d. 03/29/1923
WALLS, Harvey Gibson, ssw-Ella, DE, 76 AAFG, WWII, b. 11/24/1912, d. 12/12/1963
WALLS, John S., ssw-Bernice M., b. 06/30/1920, d. N/D
WALLS, L. Russell, ssw-Roberta D., b. 10/17/1908, d. 02/12/1981
WALLS, Maggie, ssw-Millard, b. 06/16/1885, d. 11/06/1932
WALLS, Millard, ssw-Maggie, b. 10/29/1884, d. 04/09/1941
WALLS, Minnie H., ssw-Charles H., b. 1888, d. 1941
WALLS, Nemiah E., ssw-Rhoda A., b. 1879, d. 1944
WALLS, Rhoda A., ssw-Nemiah E., b. 1882, d. 1942
WALLS, Robert B., Jr., Age 85y, b. 01/27/1905, d. 11/19/1990
WALLS, Robert B., Sr., b. 05/10/1882, d. 02/23/1966
WALLS, Roberta D., ssw-L. Russell, b. 02/22/1914, d. N/D
WALLS, Ronald Lee, b. 01/25/1948, d. 11/18/1953
WALLS, Ura C., b. 09/20/1917, d. N/D
WALLS, Virginia M., b. 09/07/1882, d. 08/26/1962
WALTERS, Ann W., ssw-Donald W., b. 1911, d. 1992
WALTERS, Donald W., ssw-Ann W., b. 1913, d. N/D
WAPLES, Ethel May, b. 08/10/1897, d. 12/08/1907
WAPLES, George H., b. 04/04/1873, d. 10/12/1944
WAPLES, Mary Ellen, b. 06/26/1875, d. 04/27/1953
WARDWELL, Brice F., ssw-Mildred A., m. 6-23-1972, b. 1951, d. 1988
WARDWELL, Mildred A., ssw-Brice F., m. 6-23-1972, b. 1954, d. N/D
WARREN, Henry C., b. 06/04/1844, d. 12/08/1914
WARREN, John Steven, ssw-Regina R., DE, Tec5, USA, WWII, b. 02/17/1918, d. 11/04/1971
WARREN, Regina R., ssw-John Steven, b. 08/09/1924, d. 09/12/1993
WARRINGTON, Bertha E., b. 1886, d. 1925
WARRINGTON, Dela M., b. 1915, d. 1932
WARRINGTON, Della M., b. 1886, d. 1963
WARRINGTON, Edgar R., ssw-Thelma G., b. 1907, d. 1966
WARRINGTON, Elsie E., ssw-Mary E., b. 1905, d. 1908
WARRINGTON, Harry S., b. 1913, d. N/D
WARRINGTON, Joseph H., ssw-Martha E., b. 1858, d. 1925
WARRINGTON, Mabel, b. 1907, d. 1965
WARRINGTON, Martha E., w/o Joseph H., b. 06/05/1858, d. 01/05/1917
WARRINGTON, Mary C., ssw-Walter T., b. 1903, d. 1937
WARRINGTON, Mary E., ssw-Elsie E., b. 1881, d. 1918
WARRINGTON, Mildred E., b. 1910, d. 1930
WARRINGTON, Raymond H., ssw-Virginia M., b. 05/15/1895, d. 10/22/1957

WARRINGTON, Thelma G., ssw-Edgar R., b. 1909, d. 1957

WARRINGTON, Virginia M., ssw-Raymond H., b. 04/29/1888, d. 09/22/1928

WARRINGTON, Walter T., ssw-Mary C., b. 1901, d. 1941

WARRINGTON, Wm. C., b. 1878, d. 1968

WEBB, Harry H., b. 07/10/1889, d. 04/16/1968

WEBB, Leah E., b. 09/16/1895, d. 08/30/1990

WEBB, Nelson D., b. 08/03/1915, d. 01/21/1947

WEBB, Ralton P., ssw-Sara E., b. 07/05/1913, d. 12/01/1975

WEBB, Sara E., ssw-Ralton P., b. 07/06/1912, d. N/D

WELCH, Aileen S., w/o Walter C., ssw-Walter C., b. 03/27/1901, d. 01/03/1992

WELCH, Edgar M., ssw-Mary Jane, DE, 1M12, USNR, WWII, b. 10/19/1923, d. 01/17/1964

WELCH, Edgar Milton, DE, CMM, USNR, WWI, b. 05/24/1895, d. 01/06/1960

WELCH, Edna H., b. 01/15/1904, d. 10/21/1989

WELCH, Frederick B., ssw-Lora H., b. 1874, d. 1949

WELCH, John B., b. 06/07/1883, d. 12/10/1971

WELCH, Lora H., ssw-Frederick B., b. 1880, d. 1951

WELCH, Mary Jane, ssw-Edgar M., b. 1918, d. 1970

WELCH, Ollie P., b. 11/08/1888, d. 02/17/1986

WELCH, Walter C., ssw-Aileen S., b. 10/12/1892, d. 03/19/1964

WELLS, Alberta M., ssw-John, b. 1907, d. N/D

WELLS, J. Nailor, ssw-Ruth R., b. 11/19/1915, d. N/D

WELLS, John, ssw-Alberta M., b. 1898, d. 1934

WELLS, Joseph S., ssw-Lillian N., b. 11/27/1890, d. 07/23/1981

WELLS, Lillian N., w/o Joseph S., ssw-Joseph S., b. 02/17/1893, d. 09/24/1951

WELLS, Ruth R., ssw-J. Nailor, b. 01/23/1917, d. N/D

WELSH, Ann M., b. 1913, d. N/D

WELSH, Dorothea R., ssw-Neal M., b. 1914, d. N/D

WELSH, Ida M., b. 1888, d. 1962

WELSH, Neal M., ssw-Dorothea R., LTJG, USN, WWII, b. 01/29/1913, d. 06/02/1986

WELSH, William H., b. 1871, d. 1954

WELSH, William H., 2nd, Tec4, USA, WWII, b. 11/26/1907, d. 04/22/1990

WEST, Charlotte C., ssw-Fannie M., b. 1934, d. 1936

WEST, Fannie M., w/o James W., ssw-James W., b. 04/25/1895, d. 04/02/1990

WEST, Godwin W., ssw-Fannie M., b. 1925, d. 1925

WEST, James W., ssw-Fannie M., b. 1888, d. 1968

WHITE, Alfred Robert, ssw-William F., b. 09/04/1877, d. 12/06/1945

WHITE, Anna R., b. 09/15/1891, d. 05/20/1971

WHITE, Annie F., d/o W. F. & Ida B., ssw-William F., b. 01/30/1879, d. 11/21/1894

WHITE, Ellen P., b. 1915, d. 1952

WHITE, Ida B., ssw-William F., b. 07/28/1859, d. 01/12/1920

WHITE, Wilford C., b. 09/17/1889, d. 07/31/1958

WHITE, William F., ssw-Ida B., b. 05/23/1858, d. 11/26/1894

WIERS, Tamara R., "Tammy," Age 27y, b. N/D, d. 06/08/1996

WILERSON, Isabelle, b. 1922, d. 1979

WIKINSON, Priscilla H., b.1905, d. 1995

WILKERSON, Edna M., ssw-Harold V., b. 03/25/1918, d. 05/01/1976

WILKERSON, Elisha W., ssw-Naomi R., b. 05/03/1917, d. 08/21/1973

WILKERSON, Harold V., ssw-Edna M., Pfc, USA, WWII, b. 12/26/1908, d. 02/25/1986

WILKERSON, Helen Lee, ssw-Reuben J., b. 02/14/1919, d. 08/29/1985

WILKERSON, Naomi R., ssw-Elisha W., b. 04/02/1922, d. N/D

WILKERSON, Reuben J., ssw-Helen Lee, b. 04/12/1905, d. 06/26/1990

WILKINS, Annie E., ssw-William M., b. 10/09/1874, d. 11/08/1941

WILKINS, Charles T., b. 1899, d. 1947

WILKINS, Edith, ssw-Francis, b. 04/09/1900, d. 11/10/1983

WILKINS, Francis, ssw-Edith, b. 10/18/1895, d. 07/21/1967

WILKINS, Gladys M., b. 04/10/1929, d. N/D

WILKINS, Harry B., b. 01/10/1910, d. 03/05/1928

WILKINS, Mary R., ssw-William R., b. 12/27/1876, d. 05/21/1960

WILKINS, Nora, b. 1900, d. 1973

WILKINS, Norman F., Tec5, USA, WWII, b. 09/08/1914, d. 10/28/1985

WILKINS, William M., ssw-Annie E., b. 05/20/1872, d. 11/28/1956

WILKINS, William R., ssw-Mary R., b. 10/08/1876, d. 07/21/1949

WILLEY, Alton, b. 1908, d. 1994

WILLEY, Anthony C., ssw-Dori M., b. 02/26/1960, d. 09/09/1982

WILLEY, Catherine Virginia, ssw-Robert Alton, b. 08/25/1938, d. N/D

WILLEY, Clara H., ssw-Homer L., b. 1902, d. 1974

WILLEY, Dori M., ssw-Anthony C., b. 06/15/1962, d. N/D

WILLEY, Dorothy M., b. 01/26/1917, d. 01/09/1984

WILLEY, Elizabeth E., b. 05/23/1874, d. 09/14/1942

WILLEY, Elsie F., b. 1915, d. N/D

WILLEY, Geneva R., b. 1914, d. N/D

WILLEY, Homer L., ssw-Clara H., b. 1897, d. 1969

WILLEY, John Franklin, b. 03/27/1943, d. 05/23/1991

WILLEY, Lawrence J., b. 1906, d. 1974

WILLEY, Robert Alton, ssw-Catherine Virginia, b. 12/15/1932, d. N/D

WILLEY, Robert J., b. 08/26/1875, d. 09/02/1951

WILLIAMS, George C., ssw-Helen R., b. 05/22/1896, d. 11/22/1994

WILLIAMS, George R., b. 08/23/1903, d. 11/03/1976

WILLIAMS, Harry T., ssw-Ida D., b. 1876, d. 1936

WILLIAMS, Helen R., ssw-George C., b. 06/25/1900, d. 11/01/1981

WILLIAMS, Ida D., ssw-Harry T., b. 1875, d. 1958

WILLIAMS, James C., b. 1903, d. 1965

WILLIAMS, Samuel Robert, Tech5, USA, WWII, b. 09/30/1904, d. 02/13/1990

WILLIAMS, Sarah M., b. 1902, d. N/D

WILLIS, Dorothy P., b. 1912, d. 1951

WILLISTON, Edward J., DE, CM2, USN, WWI, b. 04/29/1886, d. 04/04//1971

WILSON, Alma R., ssw-Ernest T., b. 1906, d. N/D

WILSON, Carrie L., ssw-Jesse D., b. 09/23/1891, d. 02/06/1919

WILSON, Charlotte L., ssw-Edith A., b. 1864, d. 1942

WILSON, Clara E., b. 1888, d. 1963

WILSON, Clara F. Waples, w/o C. Marshall, b. 01/09/1996, d. 04/30/1914

WILSON, Cornelius W., b. 04/07/1914, d. 05/15/1919

WILSON, Edith A., ssw-Charlotte L., b. 1888, d. 1975

WILSON, Ernest T., ssw-Alma R., b. 1909, d. 1955

WILSON, George A., b. 1863, d. 1945

WILSON, Harriet M., Jr., b. N/D, d. N/D

WILSON, Harriet Marvel, ssw-C. Max Farrington, b. 12/06/1869, d. 02/03/1963

WILSON, Horace W., ssw-Maggie M., b. 1894, d. 1963

WILSON, Jesse D., ssw-Carrie L., b. 10/22/1886, d. 01/31/1919

WILSON, Luther F., b. 1886, d. 1945

WILSON, Lydia, w/o Thomas R., ssw-Riley Cement, b. 11/20/1817, d. 01/07/1902

WILSON, Maggie M., ssw-Horace W., b. 1894, d. 1963

WILSON, Margaret P., b. 1868, d. 1938

WILSON, Marshall F., b. 04/07/1914, d. 02/06/1923

WILSON, Marvel, Twin o/Riley Houston, entombed in Grier Chapel, Milford, OF Cemetery, b. N/D, d. N/D

WILSON, Preston A., SSgt, Paratroopers, b. 01/19/1941, d. 07/11/1980

WILSON, Riley Clement, s/o Thomas R. & Lydia Houston, ssw-Thomas R., b. 08/15/1846, d. 11/30/1916

WILSON, Riley Houston, s/o Thomas R. & Harriet Marvel, ssw-Thomas Rickards, Jr., b. 05/26/1898, d. 01/23/1907

WILSON, Thomas R., ssw-C. Max Farrington, b. 01/24/1854, d. 01/05/1937

WILSON, Thomas R., ssw-Riley Clement, b. 08/28/1818, d. 01/11/1894

WILSON, Thomas Rickards, Jr., s/o Thomas R. & Harriet Marvel, ssw-Riley Houston, Age 21y 5m 20d, b. 02/02/1896, d. 07/11/1917

WILSON, Vannie Alfred, Jr., S1, USN, WWII, b. 09/19/1919, d. 12/14/1978

WILSON, Vannie W., Son, b. 03/26/1945, d. 02/21/1986

WOOTERS, Nelson C., b. 01/29/1935, d. 06/09/1989

WORKMAN, Alwida Jefferson, b. 12/25/1871, d. 09/20/1924

WORKMAN, David B., ssw-Dorothy M., b. 04/26/1918, d. 08/20/1994

WORKMAN, Dorothy M., ssw-David B., b. 08/02/1919, d. N/D

WORKMAN, Ethel T., b. 1886, d. 1907

WORKMAN, F. C., b. 1874, d. 1954

WORKMAN, Fannie E., b. 1883, d. 1905

WORKMAN, John Wesley, ssw-Sarah Adaline, b. 1845, d. 1917

WORKMAN, Robert H., ssw-Virgie, b. 1874, d. 1955

WORKMAN, Sarah Adaline, w/o John Wesley, ssw-John Wesley, b. 1848, d. 1930

WORKMAN, Virgie, ssw-Robert H., b. 1884, d. 1969

WRIGHT, David Wayne, b. 06/02/1946, d. 11/13/1965

WRIGHT, Hilda Michael, ssw-Samuel McMurray, b. 01/04/1907, d. 07/05/1988

WRIGHT, Samuel McMurray, ssw-Hilda Michael, b. 12/06/1905, d. 03/13/1975

WYATT, Anna, ssw-James T., b. 11/18/1882, d. 12/06/1946

WYATT, April Lynn, b. 05/30/1965, d. 05/31/1965

WYATT, Carroll W., ssw-Edna M. & Willard E., b. 05/30/1946, d. 03/19/1947

WYATT, Edna M., ssw-Carroll W. & Willard E., b. 11/02/1942, d. 12/26/1947

WYATT, James T., ssw-Anna, b. 11/17/1891, d. 01/29/1967

WYATT, June Ann Vent, b. 06/30/1947, d. 07/13/1966

WYATT, Willard E., ssw-Carroll W. & Edna M., b. 12/25/1943, d. 12/26/1947

ZELLERS, Melvin A., ssw-Stella May, b. 1892, d. 1954

ZELLERS, Stella May, ssw-Melvin A., b. 1886, d. 1943

ZVOLNEK, John W., ssw-Mary, b. 1871, d. 1947

ZVOLNEK, Mary, ssw-John W., b. 1884, d. 1954

The following stones were recorded by the Hudson Survey but are now missing or unreadable:

ARGO, Delma May, d/o F. G. & L. W., b. 06/20/1913, d. 12/14/1918

DICKERSON, Carrie, b. 1874, d. N/D
DICKERSON, Charles B., b. 1870, d. N/D
REED, Sarah L. S., b. 1908, d. 1922

(BK-005 & HU-NR) HENLOPEN MEMORIAL PARK CEMETERY
Located East of Milton on the Northeast side of Coastal Highway (Rt. 1) and the South side of the
Broadkill River.
Recorded: September 4, 1996

ABBOTT, Laura M., b. 1922, d. N/D
ACETO, Dante A., ssw-Susan B., b. 1936, d. 1989
ACETO, Susan B., ssw-Dante A., b. 1948, d. N/D
ACKO, Catherine M., ssw-Vincent M., b. 01/26/1918, d. 02/17/1991
ACKO, Vincent M., ssw-Catherine M., b. 11/22/1911, d. N/D
ADAMS, Charles E., SC3, USN, WWII, b. 05/02/1918, d. 01/30/1991
ADAMS, Lois B., b. 11/24/1920, d. N/D
AGNEW, Anthony A., ssw-Edna H., b. 1908, d. 1992
AGNEW, Edna H., ssw-Anthony A., b. 1923, d. N/D
AGNOLI, William C., Maj., USA, WWII, b. 10/03/1916, d. 01/15/1980
AHERN, Dorothy H., b. 1926, d. N/D
AILES, Charles C., b. 1931, d. 1995
ALLARD, Catherine B., ssw-Franklin G., b. 1916, d. N/D
ALLARD, Franklin G., ssw-Catherine B., Tec5, USA, WWII, b. 06/01/1918, d. 11/15/1992
ALLOWAY, Jack R., ssw-Natalie S., b. 1922, d. N/D
ALLOWAY, Natalie S., ssw-Jack R., b. 1925, d. N/D
ALTHOFF, Marie A., b. 1919, d. N/D
ALTON, Jerry J., ssw-Pauline D., Cpt., USA, b. 1923, d. 1990
ALTON, Pauline D., ssw-Jerry J., b. 1927, d. N/D
ANNETTE, Mae E., ssw-Robert W., b. 1921, d. 1968
ANNETTE, Robert W., ssw-Mae E., b. 1932, d. N/D
ARMSTRONG, Harry E., Sr., b. 08/25/1912, d. 05/26/1984
ARNETT, Erma L., ssw-Noah L., b. 1902, d. 1975
ARNETT, Noah L., ssw-Erma L., b. 1895, d. 1975
ATTMORE, Gladys E., ssw-Robert G., b. 1922, d. N/D
ATTMORE, Robert G., ssw-Gladys E., b. 1921, d. 1987
ATWELL, Bert J., ssw-Irene N., b. 1905, d. 1987
ATWELL, Irene N., ssw-Bert J., b. 1910, d. N/D
AVERY, David Rowland, b. 08/16/1959, d. 12/27/1993
AVERY, Hildegard E., ssw-Rowland G., b. 01/08/1926, d. N/D
AVERY, Rowland G., ssw-Hildegard E., Maj., USA, WWII, Korea, b. 08/19/1918, d. 01/08/1992
BAER, Evelyn H., b. 05/06/1922, d. N/D
BAILEY, Carolyn S., ssw-Ivan M., b. 1944, d. N/D
BAILEY, Ivan M., ssw-Carolyn S., b. 1904, d. N/D
BAKER, Ira R., ssw-Iva J., b. 1939, d. 1987
BAKER, Iva J., ssw-Ira R., b. 1942, d. N/D
BAKER, James L., b. 1936, d. 1994
BAKER, Paul W., ssw-Sadie M., b. 1908, d. 1995

BAKER, Sadie M., ssw-Paul W., b. 1910, d. 1971
BARKER, Doris Ellen, b. 09/02/1924, d. 01/12/1992
BARR, Carl R., ssw-Janet W., b. 1915, d. N/D
BARR, Janet W., ssw-Carl R., b. 1920, d. N/D
BASSOLS, Arturo Luis, Jr., b. 01/25/1955, d. 09/05/1977
BASSOLS, Evlyn Erdman, b. 11/07/1932, d. 11/29/1991
BATTAGLINO, Margaret, ssw-Ralph, b. 03/01/16, d. N/D
BATTAGLINO, Ralph, ssw-Margaret, b. 07/04/14, d. 08/28/88
BATTEN, Grace R., Rev., b. 1943, d. N/D
BATURA, Ann, ssw-John C., b. 1941, d. N/D
BATURA, John C., ssw-Ann, b. 1942, d. N/D
BAUERNSCHUB, Charles S., b. 1913, d. 1990
BAUERNSCHUB, Eleanor E., b. 1916, d. N/D
BAYER, Bettina Stamm, b. 03/21/1921, d. N/D
BEARDSLEY, Jean E., b. 1927, d. N/D
BEEBE, Susan D., b. 1957, d. 1972
BEIDEMAN, Alvin W., ssw-Lydia A., b. 09/29/1913, d. 06/18/1966
BEIDEMAN, Lydia A., ssw-Alvin W., b. 11/09/1913, d. N/D
BELL, Audrey J., ssw-Howard R., b. 1933, d. N/D
BELL, Emily F., ssw-George W., b. 1906, d. N/D
BELL, George W., ssw-Emily F., b. 1898, d. 1978
BELL, Howard R., ssw-Audrey J., b. 1918, d. 1989
BENDER, Harold M., ssw-Ruth V., S2, USN, WWII, b. 06/11/1925, d. 03/21/1991
BENDER, Ruth V., ssw-Harold M., b. 07/21/1930, d. N/D
BENNETT, Caren R., ssw-Gloria L. Malitzski, b. 1958, d. N/D
BENNETT, William W., ssw-Gloria L. Malitzski, b. 1958, d. N/D
BERINGER, Mae S., ssw-Walter F., b. 10/10/1890, d. 10/05/1982
BERINGER, Walter F., ssw-Mae S., b. 01/27/1893, d. 01/08/1985
BERNHART, Eleanor M., ssw-Paul T., b. 1920, d. 1995
BERNHART, Paul T., ssw-Eleanor M., b. 1916, d. N/D
BERNHEIMER, Joseph Zachary, b. 08/12/1993, d. 11/19/1993
BESENFELDER, John W., ssw-Mildred T., b. 1910, d. N/D
BESENFELDER, Mildred T., ssw-John W., b. 1911, d. 1974
BETTS, Dixie C., ssw-William F., b. 1939, d. N/D
BETTS, Doris R., ssw-William C., b. 1931, d. N/D
BETTS, Hilda M., b. 08/12/1927, d. N/D
BETTS, Pauline C., b. 1911, d. 1971
BETTS, William C., ssw-Doris R., b. 1927, d. N/D
BETTS, William F., ssw-Dixie C., b. 1938, d. N/D
BEUTER, James C., ssw-Jane N., b. 1918, d. N/D
BEUTER, Jane N., ssw-James C., b. 1923, d. N/D
BICKELHAUPT, Barbara L., ssw-Thomas E., b. 05/06/1950, d. N/D
BICKELHAUPT, Thomas E., ssw-Barbara L., USN, Korea, b. 01/27/1932, d. 09/06/1994
BIGLEY, Lulu, b. 02/22/1893, d. 03/02/1977
BILLINGS, William Drake, b. 08/14/84, d. 10/19/84
BINYON, Elizabeth N., ssw-Alexandria N. Fraser, b. 1896, d. 1968
BIRD, Donald A., b. 1924, d. 1994
BIRD, Dorothy J., b. 1929, d. 1993

BISTER, Lisa D., ssw-Wayne S., b. 1964 d. N/D

BISTER, Wayne S., ssw-Lisa D., b. 1963, d. N/D

BLACK, Alvin J., b. 10/09/1911, d. 01/28/1964

BLAINE, Raymond C., Mst. Sgt., USA, WWII, Korea, b. 05/23/1913, d. 01/30/1996

BLAKE, Barbara C., b. 1960, d. 1992

BLAKE, David W., b. 06/14/1954, d. 04/04/1994

BLOTH, George, b. 1901, d. 1956

BOLTZ, Milton R., b. 1940, d. N/D

BOSTON, Catherine E., ssw-Walter L., Jr., b. 1925, d. N/D

BOSTON, Walter L.,,, Jr., ssw-Catherine E., b. 1927, d. 1987

BOUNDS, James W., DE TSGT, 570 Fld. Arty Bn., WWII, b. 02/01/1916, d. 10/25/1970

BOUNDS, Marguerite R., b. 06/13/1916, d. N/D

BOWDEN, Allen R., ssw-Maggie M., b. 1939, d. N/D

BOWDEN, Maggie M., ssw-Allen R., b. 1944, d. N/D

BOWSER, Esther F., ssw-George C., Sr., b. 1914, d. 1988

BOWSER, George C., Sr., ssw-Esther F., b. 1913, d. N/D

BOYCE, Howard C., ssw-Mildred H., b. 1899, d. 1971

BOYCE, Mildred H., ssw-Howard C., b. 1901, d. 1963

BOYLEN, Elizabeth L., b. 07/28/1938, d. N/D

BOYLEN, William P., Jr., USA, b. 1934, d. 1987

BREZINA, Vincent J., USA, WWII, b. 01/04/1923, d. 02/24/1994

BRILLANTE, Philomena S., b. 1919, d. N/D

BRITTINGHAM, Elizabeth A., ssw-Herman O., b. 1899, d. 1982

BRITTINGHAM, Gladys A., ssw-Linden R., b. 12/28/1921, d. N/D

BRITTINGHAM, Herman O., ssw-Elizabeth A., b. 1896, d. 1977

BRITTINGHAM, Joann O., b. 1946, d. 1990

BRITTINGHAM, John R., ssw-Theresa N., b. 1906, d. 1977

BRITTINGHAM, Linden R., ssw-Gladys A., b. 10/11/1920, d. 04/29/1991

BRITTINGHAM, Linden W., DE, L Cpl., 1 AA, Co. 11, MAR 1, MAR Div., Vietnam, PH, b. 03/06/1948,
     d. 03/01/1968

BRITTINGHAM, Theresa N., ssw-John R., b. 1909, d. 1975

BROCKMAN, Emily N., ssw-Vilmar B., b. 1919, d. N/D

BROCKMAN, Vilmar B., ssw-Emily N., b. 1916, d. N/D

BROCKWAY, Dorothy E., ssw-Leonard, b. 1916, d. N/D

BROCKWAY, Leonard, ssw-Dorothy E., b. 1892, d. 1972

BROOKS, Diane M., b. 1949, d. N/D

BROOKS, George W., Pfc., USMC, WWII, b. 10//13/1925, d. 03/01/1988

BROWN, Knoulton, Sr., b. 1904, d. 1961

BROWN, Margaret R., b. 1923, d. N/D

BROWN, Mary E., b. 1911, d. 1986

BROWN, Roger J., b. 1904, d. 1991

BROWN, Ruth, b. 1923, d. N/D

BRYAN, Doris S., ssw-Ransford H., b. 1915, d. 1984

BRYAN, Elma M. Spicer, b. 1909, d. N/D

BRYAN, G. Wilson, ssw-Gwendolyn Leppo, Father, b. 1913, d. 1994

BRYAN, George H., ssw-Gertrude E., b. 1898, d. N/D

BRYAN, Gertrude E., ssw-George H., b. 1906, d. 1976

BRYAN, Ransford H., ssw-Doris S., b. 1907, d. 1978

BUCK, Mary A., b. 1901, d. 1981

BUCKLEY, Gilbert A., ssw-Pearl C., b. 1923, d. 1991

BUCKLEY, Mary F., ssw-Raymond W., b. 1931, d. N/D

BUCKLEY, Pearl C., ssw-Gilbert A., b. 1925, d. 1982

BUCKLEY, Raymond W., ssw-Mary F., b. 1928, d. N/D

BUCKLEY, Raymond Wayne, Sp4, USA, Vietnam, b. 02/06/1949, d. 09/29/1978

BULINSKI, Edith E., b. 08/19/1922, d. N/D

BUNTING, Florence M., ssw-Raymond A., b. 03/18/1892, d. 09/07/1975

BUNTING, Ray, b. 1927, d. N/D

BUNTING, Raymond A., ssw-Florence M., b. 02/10/1906, d. 04/18/1976

BUNTING, Wilford, Pfc., USA, WWII, b. 08/08/1917, d. 01/08/1976

BURBANK, Marion B., b. 1908, d. N/D

BURBANK, William E., b. 1905, d. 1974

BURCIK, Sophie M., b. 11/01/1915, d. 07/25/1988

BURKHART, Jean, b. 1919, d. 1992

BURNELL, Clarence O., ssw-Mary D., b. 1915, d. 1958

BURNELL, Mary D., ssw-Clarence O., b. 1918, d. N/D

BURRIS, Betty L., b. 12/18/1926, d. N/D

BURRIS, Willis O., SC, USN, WWII, b. 12/26/1925, d. 03/13/1978

BUSH, Charles H., Jr., ssw-Etta M., b. 1926, d. N/D

BUSH, Ethel M., ssw-Howard R., Sr., b. 1920, d. N/D

BUSH, Etta M., ssw-Charles H., Jr., b. 1927, d. N/D

BUSH, Florence E., ssw-William B., b. 1924, d. 1992

BUSH, Grace R., b. 1935, d. N/D

BUSH, Howard R., Sr., ssw-Ethel M., b. 1928, d. N/D

BUSH, Leroy O., ssw-Mary E., m. 04/27/1946, b. 1923, d. N/D

BUSH, Lisa Marie, b. 07/18/1966, d. 02/06/1967

BUSH, Mary E., ssw-Leroy W., b. 1923, d. N/D

BUSH, Mary H., b. 1911, d. 1985

BUSH, Raymond A., Son, b. 10/28/1955, d. 03/31/1981

BUSH, William B., ssw-Florence E., b. 1922, d. N/D

BUSHEY, Cloyd F., ssw-Margaret V., b. 1936, d. N/D

BUSHEY, Margaret V., ssw-Cloyd F., b. 1934, d. N/D

BUTLER, Arnold B., ssw-Jean A., b. 1916, d. 1971

BUTLER, Jean A., ssw-Arnold B., b. 1923, d. N/D

CAGLE, Mary B., b. 04/23/1920, d. N/D

CALHOUN, Delbert R., ssw-Doris M., b. 1913, d. 1994

CALHOUN, Dianne M., ssw-Howard J., b. N/D, d. N/D

CALHOUN, Doris M., ssw-Delbert R., b. 1914, d. 1984

CALHOUN, Ella M., b. 1893, d. 1972

CALHOUN, Howard J., ssw-Dianne M., b. N/D, d. N/D

CALHOUN, Idalee, b. 1926, d. 1989

CALHOUN, William, b. 1926, d. 1989

CAMPBELL, Clarence J., ssw-Ruth A., b. 1915, d. 1995

CAMPBELL, Emma J., ssw-Hiram S., b. 1911, d. N/D

CAMPBELL, George W., ssw-Maude A., b. 1914, d. N/D

CAMPBELL, Glenn Douglas, "Dougie," b. 12/06/1949, d. 12/03/1958

CAMPBELL, Hiram S., ssw-Emma J., b. 1903, d. 1983

CAMPBELL, Maude A., ssw-George W., b. 1912, d. 1987
CAMPBELL, Ruth A., ssw-Clarence J., b. 1919, d. 1988
CAPEHART, Elsie H., b. 10/01/1917, d. 12/14/1979
CAPEHART, Henry H., b. 04/17/1912, d. 12/16/1983
CAPEHART, Robert H., b. 11/05/1955, d. 07/25/1980
CAREY, Jane Lynn, b. 1954, d. N/D
CARMEAN, Alvin V., ssw-Patricia R., M Sgt., USAF, WWII, b. 11/21/1924, d. 08/11/1990
CARMEAN, Patricia R., ssw-Alvin V., b. 11/11/1924, d. N/D
CARPENTER, Edith B., b. 1927, d. N/D
CARPENTER, Edward J., ssw-Gladys G., b. 1913, d. 1995
CARPENTER, Gladys G., ssw-Edward J., b. 1923, d. N/D
CARPENTER, Shirley A., b. 1935, d. N/D
CARROLL, Clarence H., b. 1906, d. 1975
CARROLL, Oscar R., ssw-Sylvia M., b. 1929, d. N/D
CARROLL, Sylvia M., ssw-Oscar R., b. 1930, d. 1985
CARTER, Arthur E., ssw-Edna V., b. 1886, d. 1974
CARTER, E. Leonard, DE, Tec4, USA, WWII, Korea & Vietnam, b. 10/01/1917, d. 08/21/1973
CARTER, Edna V., ssw-Arthur E., b. 1894, d. 1985
CARTER, Mary Frances Stevenson, b. 09/18/1919, d. 08/11/1989
CHALABALA, Anna, ssw-Karl V., b. 1925, d. N/D
CHALABALA, Karl V., ssw-Anna, b. 1924, d. N/D
CHAMBERS, Ann, b. 06/27/1929, d. N/D
CHANDLER, Nellie F., ssw-Thomas B., b. 1931, d. N/D
CHANDLER, Thomas B., ssw-Nellie F., b. 1943, d. 1994
CISLER, Edward T., ssw-Joseph H. LaSalle, b. N/D, d. 1989
CLARK, Alice, ssw-Henry S., b. 12/07/1915, d. N/D
CLARK, Conchita Mae, Nanticoke Indian Tribe, b. 12/26/1938, d. N/D
CLARK, Eliza E., ssw-Preston T., b. 09/08/1915, d. 03/07/1993
CLARK, Henry S., ssw-Alice, b. 12/25/1912, d. 10/27/1964
CLARK, Preston T., ssw-Eliza E., b. 02/09/1916, d. 06/16/1982
CLARK, Robert E., ssw-Vivian Gibson, Cpl., USAAC, WWII, b. 05/25/1925, d. 01/17/1993
CLARK, Vivian Gibson, ssw-Robert E., b. 02/05/1931, d. N/D
CLENDANIEL, Evelyn L. M., ssw-Ralph S., b. 1917, d. N/D
CLENDANIEL, Ralph S., ssw-Evelyn L. M., WWII, b. 1913, d. 1987
CLYMER, Charles S., Sr., "Whitey," ssw-Patricia A., b. 03/06/34, d. 02/30/94
CLYMER, Patricia A., ssw-Charles S., Sr., b. 03/14/43, d. N/D
COCHRANE, Estella L., ssw-John, b. 1907, d. 1988
COCHRANE, John, ssw-Estella L., b. 1901, d. 1967
COFFIN, George, Jr., Baby, b. 1995, d. 1995
COLATRIANO, Lea B., ssw-Paul V., b. 1921, d. N/D
COLATRIANO, Paul V., ssw-Lea B., b. 1918, d. 1993
COLE, Walter C., Sr., A3C, USAF, Korea, b. 09/19/1931, d. 02/27/1991
COLLINS, Gilbert H., Jr., ssw-Joyce A., b. 09/07/1932, d. N/D
COLLINS, Joyce A., ssw-Gilbert H., Jr., b. 12/04/1929, d. N/D
CONAWAY, Carolyn S., b. 1939, d. N/D
CONAWAY, Catharine L., ssw-Elwood J., b. 1917, d. N/D
CONAWAY, Elwood J., ssw-Catharine L., b. 1915, d. 1982
CONAWAY, Janet E., b. 06/29/1921, d. 08/21/1981

CONAWAY, Melloy T., b. 12/27/1918, d. 11/14/1976
COOKE, Dorothy E., ssw-Theodore P., b. 01/18/1894, d. 05/25/1969
COOKE, Theodore P., ssw-Dorothy E., CM1, USN, WWII, b. 11/09/1895, d. 02/07/1981
COOMBES, Harold B., USA, WWII, b. 09/02/1917, d. 11/05/1986
COOPER, Elsie M., ssw-John M., b. 1916, d. N/D
COOPER, Eva B., b. 1918, d. N/D
COOPER, John M., Rev., ssw-Elsie M., b. 1911, d. N/D
COOPER, Russell L., DE, Tec 5, Btry. D., 109 AAA Gun Bn., WWII, b. 07/31/1919, d. 05/19/1966
CORDREY, Albert J., ssw-Alline E., b. 1915, d. 1986
CORDREY, Alline E., ssw-Albert J., b. 1919, d. N/D
CORDREY, Eleanor P., ssw-Robert E., b. 1930, d. N/D
CORDREY, G. Norman, ssw-Margaret P., b. 10/06/1907, d. 05/04/1974
CORDREY, George R., ssw-Rhoda B., b. 11/15/1919, d. 01/25/1977
CORDREY, Margaret P., ssw-G. Norman, b. 12/08/1908, d. 12/15/1974
CORDREY, Rhoda B., ssw-George R., b. 01/17/1921, d. 09/09/1976
CORDREY, Robert E., ssw-Eleanor P., b. 1940, d. N/D
CORDREY, Sarah D., b. 1894, d. 1964
CORDREY, Thomas H., b. 1891, d. 1958
CORKERY, Thomas E., SN, USCG, Korea, b. 05/17/1933, d. 08/10/1994
COUCH, Donald F., ssw-Kathryn E., b. 1906, d. 1966
COUCH, Kathryn E., ssw-Donald F., b. 1909, d. 1993
COUCHMAN, C. Joseph, Pvt., USAF, b. 09/14/1931, d. 03/10/1984
COUCHMAN, Delphine B., ssw-Henry C., b. 1898, d. 1974
COUCHMAN, Henry C., ssw-Delphine B., b. 1898, d. 1986
COUGHLIN, Gregg, ssw-Marie D., b. 1913, d. 1988
COUGHLIN, Marie D., ssw-Gregg, b. 1917, d. N/D
COULTER, Clara L., ssw-R. Lee, Jr., b. 1898, d. 1986
COULTER, Drena C., b. 07/25/1949, d. N/D
COULTER, R. Lee, Jr., ssw-Clara L., b. 1895, d. 1978
COURTNEY, William B., Jr., b. 04/26/1912, d. 01/07/1981
COVERDALE, Brenda L., b. 08/30/1952, d. N/D
COVERDALE, Charles D., ssw-Elma B., b. 1922, d. 1991
COVERDALE, Dorothy W., ssw-Wm. Martin, b. 1936, d. N/D
COVERDALE, Elma B., ssw-Charles D., b. 1926, d. 1994
COVERDALE, Wm. Martin, ssw-Dorothy W., b. 1930, d. 1992
COX, Elwood J., ssw-Katherine N. Lutz, b. 1921, d. 1992
COX, Evelyn V., b. 04/23/1915, d. 11/01/1993
COX, Harry E., ssw-C. Donald Dibbble, Pfc., USA, WWII, b. 03/17/1908, d. 02/03/1994
CRAIG, Kathryn H., ssw-William H., Sr., b. 06/16/1921, d. N/D
CRAIG, William W., Sr., ssw-Kathryn H., 1st Lt., USA, WWII, b. 04/21/1917, d. 03/12/1986
CRAIN, Cleda H., ssw-F. Glenn, b. 1917, d. 1980
CRAIN F. Glenn, ssw-Cleda H., b. 1916, d. 1980
CREIGHTON, Audrey J., b. 1929, d. N/D
CROPPER, Denver W., ssw-Maxine, b. 03/09/1912, d. 07/17/1968
CROPPER, Maxine, ssw-Denver W., b. 08/12/1918, d. N/D
CURRIE, Mae, b. 08/12/1921, d. 03/06/1960
CUTSLER, Homer B., ssw-Vivian R., USA, WWII, b. 1920, d. 1988
CUTSLER, Vivian R., ssw-Homer B., b. 07/07/1921, d. N/D

DAINO, Lawrence J., b. 07/23/1902, d. 05/27/1976

DANGERFIELD, Della, ssw-Judy Rockwell, b. 10/29/1932, d. N/D

DANGERFIELD, Dennis V., ssw-Judy Rockwell, Cpl., USA, WWII, b. 01/25/1920, d. 06/22/1993

DANIELS, Archie John, TSgt4, USA, WWII, b. 09/13/1917, d. 09/22/1983

DARBY, C. Virginia Setman, ssw-Lucius Atkins, b. 07/27/1907, d. N/D

DARBY, Lucius Atkins, ssw-C. Virginia Setman, SK1, USN, WWII, b. 12/28/1907, d. 10/09/1994

DAVIDSON, Albert J., ssw-Mildred I., b. 1913, d. N/D

DAVIDSON, Alexander C., ssw-Jessica B., b. 1900, d. 1979

DAVIDSON, Clarence L., ssw-Lillian A., b. 1917, d. N/D

DAVIDSON, Jessica B., ssw-Alexander C., b. 1914, d. N/D

DAVIDSON, Leroy, ssw-Margaret E., b. 1905, d. 1990

DAVIDSON, Lillian A., ssw-Clarence L., b. 1923, d. N/D

DAVIDSON, Margaret E., ssw-Leroy, b. 1907, d. N/D

DAVIDSON, Mildred I., ssw-Albert J., b. 1908, d. 1978

DAVIES, Carl Leonard, PHM3, USN, WWII, b. 07/31/1925, d. 08/23/1991

DAVIES, Claire L., b. 12/12/1920, d. N/D

DAVIS, Grace C., ssw-Robert L., m. 1958, b. 1939, d. N/D

DAVIS, Mary H., ssw-Wilber D., b. 1893, d. 1985

DAVIS, Robert L., ssw-Grace C., m. 1958, b. 1937, d. N/D

DAVIS, Wilber D., ssw-Mary H., b. 1890, d. 1961

DAVISON, Virginia L., ssw-William A., b. 1922, d. N/D

DAVISON, William A., ssw-Virginia L., b. 1912, d. N/D

DEAN, Dorothy E., ssw-Ralph V., b. 10/12/1925, d. 09/05/1994

DEAN, Ralph V., ssw-Dorothy E., Pfc., Army, WWII, b. 08/22/1926, d. 01/13/1984

DEAR, George W., Jr., b. 1951, d. 1972

DEAR, George W., Sr., ssw-Pauline A., b. 1924, d. 1989

DEAR, Pauline A., ssw-George W., Sr., b. 1928, d. 1993

DEES, James H., ssw-Mary E., b. 1911, d. N/D

DEES, Mary E., ssw-James H., b. 1912, d. 1968

DEGRAFFENREID, Jerry D., M Sgt., USAF, WWII, Korea, Vietnam, b. 1928, d. 1975

DELOACH, John, ssw-Ruth, b. 1919, d. N/D

DELOACH, Ruth, ssw-John, b. 1921, d. N/D

DENNIS, Burbage E., ssw-Maude L., b. 1929, d. 1982

DENNIS, Maude L., ssw-Burbage E., b. 1920, d. N/D

DENNIS, Olin W., MD, Pfc., 39 Inf. Div., Co. C., WWII, BSM-PH, b. 04/21/1918, d. 02/27/1968

DENTINO, Anthony J., ssw-Margaret E., b. 1898, d. N/D

DENTINO, Margaret E., ssw-Anthony J., b. 1899, d. 1963

DEPUTY, Georgia S., ssw-Herman B., b. 1918, d. 1984

DEPUTY, Herman B., ssw-Georgia S., b. 1907, d. 1989

DESIMONE, Carlo J., ssw-Louise M., Tec5, USAAC, WWII, b. 03/05/1920, d. 08/19/1986

DESIMONE, Louise M., ssw-Carlo J., b. 02/09/1925, d. 01/15/1989

DETURCK, Bertha T., b. 1897, d. 1987

DEUTSCH, Carolyn E., b. 1928, d. N/D

DIAMOND, Curtis A., DE, F1, USN, WWI, b. 07/02/1893, d. 10/02/1958

DIAMOND, Isabella E., b. 11/13/1905, d. 10/18/1965

DIBBLE, C. Donald, Rev., ssw-Harry E. Cox, b. 1907, d. 1992

DIBBLE, Grace, ssw-Harry E. Cox, b. 1906, d. N/D

DICKERSON, Betty Pase, b. 11/11/1925, d. 03/25/1960

DICKERSON, Edward E., ssw-Lavenia, b. 1893, d. 1971
DICKERSON, Elizabeth J., ssw-Frank T., b. 1906, d. 1968
DICKERSON, Frank T., ssw-Elizabeth J., b. 1899, d. 1984
DICKERSON, George H., b. 1900, d. 1969
DICKERSON, Lavenia, ssw-Edward E., b. 1894, d. 1966
DICKERSON, Marian Novotny, b. 1895, d. 1969
DICKERSON, William F., ssw-William C. Thompson, b. 1929, d. 1995
DIGGINS, Dorothy R., ssw-James Louis, b. 12/30/1923, d. 12/29/1993
DIGGINS, James Louis, ssw-Dorothy R., AVN Cadet, USAAC, WWII, b. 03/20/1924, d. 06/24/1986
DILL, Thelma V., ssw-Walter Graham, Jr., b. 1915, d. 1991
DILL, Walter Graham, Jr., ssw-Thelma V., b. 1912, d. 1980
DIMEGLIO, Irene F., b. 1924, d. N/D
DITTO, John Scott, ssw-Richard S., b. 1961, d. N/D
DITTO, Richard S., ssw-John Scott, 1st Lt., USA, WWII, b. 09/17/1924, d. 06/24/1992
DOERINGER, Mary Jane, b. 11/25/1931, d. N/D
DOHERTY, Edith M., "Edie," b. 1926, d. 1992
DOLBOW, Robert R., b. 1929, d. 1958
DONAHUE, Dolores L., ssw-Gordon A., b. 1937, d. N/D
DONAHUE, Gordon A., ssw-Dolores L., b. 1933, d. 1995
DONOHUE, Eleanor M., ssw-Thomas M., b. 1910, d. N/D
DONOHUE, Thomas M., ssw-Eleanor M., b. 1903, d. 1972
DONOVAN, Albert E., b. 1945, d. N/D
DONOVAN, Annie E., ssw-William E., b. 04/17/1909, d. 06/19/1984
DONOVAN, Clarence O., ssw-Dorothy J., SSgt., USAF, WWII, b. 12/12/1921, d. 01/21/1994
DONOVAN, David W., ssw-Martha L., b. 1906, d. 1984
DONOVAN, Dorothy J., ssw-Clarence O., b. 1926, d. N/D
DONOVAN, Georgia E., ssw-Leighton E., b. 1922, d. N/D
DONOVAN, Helen M., b. 1924, d. N/D
DONOVAN, Howard L., ssw-Mary E., b. 1909, d. 1977
DONOVAN, Leighton E., ssw-Georgia E., b. 1919, d. N/D
DONOVAN, Martha L., ssw-David W., b. 1907, d. N/D
DONOVAN, Mary E., ssw-Howard L., b. 1911, d. N/D
DONOVAN, William E., ssw-Annie E., b. 04/03/1907, d. 08/18/1993
DOOLITTLE, Catherine J., ssw-Ruth E. Lawrie, Sisters, b. 1905, d. N/D
DORRELL, Kathryn G., b. 06/07/1920, d. 08/21/1981
DOTTERER, Joan M., ssw-Iona M. Vanness, b. 1948, d. N/D
DOUGHTY, Mervin A., ssw-Minnie K., b. 1926, d. N/D
DOUGHTY, Minnie K., ssw-Mervin A., b. 1924, d. N/D
DOWNS, No other information
DRONEY, Christopher P., USN, b. 09/29/1966, d. 04/13/1988
DUDDY, Edna E., ssw-William S., b. 1949, d. N/D
DUDDY, William S., ssw-Edna E., b. 1933, d. 1987
DUDLEY, Shirley M., b. 1925, d. N/D
DUGGAN, Francis J., b. 04/26/1907, d. 10/29/1969
DUGGAN, Mary L., b. 10/29/1911, d. 04/26/1980
DUKES, Leona C., ssw-Oakley M., m. 04/28/1932, b. 1909, d. 1993
DUKES, Oakley M., ssw-Leona C., m. 04/28/1932, d. 1912, d. 1984
DUNLAP, Cloyd, ssw-Jennie G., b. 1893, d. 1966

DUNLAP, Jennie G., ssw-Cloyd, b. 1899, d. 1975
DUNMON, Sydney Burton, b. 03/24/1941, d. N/D
DURHAM, Norman K., 3rd, b. 02/04/1965, d. 02/04/1965
EASOM, Norma S., b. 1926, d. N/D
ECKHOFF, Elsie E., b. 1909, d. 1985
EDGENS, Ruth Alice, b. 12/30/1922, d. 07/22/1995
EFFINGER, Joseph C., ssw-Mabel W., b. 1900, d. 1975
EFFINGER, Mabel W., ssw-Joseph C., b. 1908, d. 1981
ELKINS, Beatrice M., ssw-Thomas J., Jr., b. 01/15/1919, d. N/D
ELKINS, Thomas J., Jr., ssw-Beatrice M., Sgt., USA, WWII, b. 10/26/1916, d. 12/01/1986
ELLIOTT, Annie M., ssw-Philip B., b. 04/29/1906, d. 01/20/1989
ELLIOTT, Mary A., ssw-Reese B., b. 1924, d. 1990
ELLIOTT, Philip B., ssw-Annie M., b. 06/25/1894, d. 06/02/1973
ELLIOTT, Reese B., ssw-Mary A., b. 1926, d. N/D
EMICK, Rose A., b. 1927, d. N/D
ERICKSON, Ruth M., b. 07/22/1926, d. N/D
EVANS, Brooke A., ssw-Leona A., b. 1911, d. N/D
EVANS, Ida L., b. 1926, d. 1995
EVANS, Leona A., ssw-Brooke A., b. 1916, d. N/D
EYE, J. Garnet, b. 1892, d. 1960
EYE, Mildred P., b. 1899, d. 1960
FAILOR, Joan I., b. 1935, d. N/D
FARRELL, Clifford B., ssw-Janet L., b. 1936, d. N/D
FARRELL, James E., Sr., b. 12/26/1901, d. 12/02/1980
FARRELL, Janet L., ssw-Clifford B., b. 1947, d. 1988
FARRELL, Mary E., b. 02/02/1911, d. N/D
FARROW, Faith G., b. 1913, d. N/D
FAUST, Anna S., ssw-Howard B., b. 1919, d. 1984
FAUST, Howard B., ssw-Anna S., b. 1919, d. N/D
FENTERS, Betty J., ssw-Richard D., Sr., b. 1930, d. N/D
FENTERS, Richard D., Sr., ssw-Betty J., b. 1931, d. N/D
FERGUSON, Evelyn S., b. 10/15/1928, d. N/D
FERGUSON, Basil E., Tec 5, USA, WWII, b. 06/30/1920, d. 05/05/1991
FERGUSON, James Clive, EM1, USN, WWII, b. 04/21/1914, d. 11/23/1985
FINK, Clara M., ssw-Francis E., Jr., b. 1916, d. N/D
FINK, Francis E., Jr., ssw-Clara M., SHC, USN, Korea, Vietnam, b. 01/15/1935, d. 05/07/1979
FISHER, Betty V., ssw-William Edward, b. 04/22/1928, d. N/D
FISHER, Edith Aline, ssw-Robert B., b. 07/04/1925, d. N/D
FISHER, Elva M., ssw-W. Bryan, b. 1900, d. 1996
FISHER, Jean H. M., b. 1923, d. N/D
FISHER, Kenneth F., b. 01/09/1939, d. 01/20/1993
FISHER, Robert B., ssw-Edith Aline, USA, b. 02/19/1929, d. 04/04/1994
FISHER, W. Bryan, ssw-Elva M., b. 1900, d. 1961
FISHER, William Edward, ssw-Betty V., S1, USN, WWII, b. 12/15/1922, d. 05/03/1991
FITCH, Clyde W., b. 03/05/1905, d. 03/28/1977
FITCH, Horace Samuel, ssw-Winnie L., Pvt., USA, WWII, b. 09/28/1903, d. 01/06/1988
FITCH, Mildred Reed, b. 1907, d. 1991
FITCH, Winnie L., ssw-Horace Samuel, b. 07/03/1908, d. 03/31/1996

FITZCHARLES, Florence M., ssw-Howard M., b. 1885, d. 1969

FITZCHARLES, Howard M., ssw-Florence M., b. 1888, d. 1966

FLOUNDERS, Anthea, ssw-Thomas E., Sr., b. 1886, d. 1974

FLOUNDERS, Thomas E., Sr., ssw-Anthea, b. 1888, d. 1965

FOLTZ, Catherine M., ssw-Earl K., b. 1929, d. 1989

FOLTZ, Earl K., ssw-Catherine M., b. 1919, d. 1990

FORAKER, Grace H., ssw-James D., b. 1920, d. N/D

FORAKER, James D., ssw-Grace H., b. 1919, d. N/D

FORDYCE, Cless Y., Dr., b. 1901, d. 1976

FORDYCE, Dorothy V., b. 1906, d. 1990

FOSKEY, Preston J., Sgt., USA, WWII, b. 02/27/1916, d. 09/15/1984

FOSKEY, Verna B., b. 04/02/1914, d. 09/13/1985

FOSTER, Bonnie S., ssw-Vernon J., b. 1920, d. N/D

FOSTER, Jo Ann, ssw-Laura E., b. 1946, d. N/D

FOSTER, Laura E., ssw-Jo Ann, b. 1920, d. 1986

FOSTER, Vernon J., ssw-Bonnie S., b. 1919, d. N/D

FOUNTAIN, Charles F., ssw-Margaret, USA, WWII, b. 12/02/1921, d. 06/28/1995

FOUNTAIN, Margaret, ssw-Charles F., b. 1926, d. N/D

FOX, Peggy J., b. 04/21/1933, d. 12/26/1990

FRAESDORF, Tillie, b. 1890, d. 1974

FRASER, Alexandria N., ssw-Elizabeth N. Binyon, b. 1892, d. 1977

FREEMAN, Catherine T., ssw-John, b. 06/16/1906, d. N/D

FREEMAN, John, ssw-Catherine T., b. 03/20/1904, d. 12/06/1974

FREISCHMIDT, Albert C., MM2, USN, WWII, b. 06/24/1921, d. 05/13/1985

FREUND, Barbara J., b. 11/29/1925, d. N/D

FRIED, Dale K., ssw-Shirley S., b. 1934, d. 1985

FRIED, Milton K., ssw-Ruth E., b. 1910, d. 1993

FRIED, Ruth E., ssw-Milton K., b. 1910, d. 1978

FRIED, Shirley S., ssw-Dale K., b. 1934, d. N/D

FRIEND, Carrie B., ssw-Ocran F., b. 07/14/1896, d. 10/061964

FRIEND, Ocran F., ssw-Carrie B., b. 08/26/1896, d. 04/08/1991

FRIEND, Steven John, Jr., b. 09/10/1973, d. 09/10/1973

FRYE, Geneva E., ssw-Warren E., b. 1920, d. N/D

FRYE, Warren E., ssw-Geneva E., b. 1918, d. N/D

FULLER, Constance H., b. 1897, d. 1974

GAGE, Elinor M.., b. 1889, d. 1974

GALBRAITH, Elmer C., ssw-Mary N., Sgt., USA, WWII, b. 06/21/1916, d. 05/29/1989

GALBRAITH, Mary B., b. 1943, d. N/D

GALBRAITH, Mary N., ssw-Elmer C., b. 12/16/1914, d. N/D

GALLANT, Cecil Thomas, ssw-Elizabeth L., SSgt., USA, WWII, b. 1916, d. 1986

GALLANT, Elizabeth L., ssw-Cecil Thomas, b. 05/08/1912, d. N/D

GALLO, Francis, ssw-Sandra L., b. 1923, d. N/D

GALLO, Sandra L., ssw-Francis, b. 1936, d. N/D

GARY, Nita, b. 1933, d. N/D

GASSER, Marie H., b. 08/08/1902, d. 12/31/1985

GASVODA, Martin B., DE, Pfc., 224 Co., MPC, WWI, b. 04/27/1891, d. 05/27/1966

GEISE, Ellis Walton, PA, MSgt., 1327 Ser. Unit, WWII, b. 01/15/1904, d. 10/27/1961

GEISE, Woodrow Wilson, b. 05/13/1913, d. 01/01/1989

GEYER, Baby Girl, ssw-Mildred L., b. 07/20/1971, d. 07/21/1971
GEYER, John H., ssw-Louise H., b. 1879, d. 1937
GEYER, John H., Jr., b. 06/28/1910, d. 03/26/1988
GEYER, Louise H., ssw-John H., b. 1878, d. 1963
GEYER, Mildred L., ssw-Baby Girl, b. 03/22/1913, d. 12/21/1970
GIBBONS, Edith C., b. 1928, d. N/D
GIBBONS, John H., b. 1924, d. 1991
GIBBS, Margaret D., b. 05/11/1919, d. N/D
GIES, Doris, b. 1920, d. N/D
GIESS, Alfred A., b. 1905, d. 1987
GILGORE, Walter E., S1, USN, Korea, b. 11/07/1934, d. 06/28/1986
GLADYSZ, Sandra J., b. 1959, d. N/D
GOEPEL, Charles, ssw-Lois H., b. 1926, d. N/D
GOEPEL, John R., Sr., b. 1952, d. 19966
GOEPEL, Lois H., ssw-Charles, b. 1930, d. N/D
GOFF, Janet L., b. 02/22/1932, d. N/D
GOLDEN, Nancy M., b. 1911, d. 1984
GOLDEN, Rollo T., b. 1907, d. 1974
GOOD, Robert G., Cpt., USMC, b. 07/03/1932, d. 07/27/1983
GOODWIN, William L., b. 1916, d. 1987
GORDON, Dorothy C., ssw-Peter Frank, Jr., b. 1922, d. N/D
GORDON, Peter Frank, Jr., ssw-Dorothy C., Cox, USN, b. 09/26/1923, d. 06/25/1990
GORECKI, Joseph J., b. 1926, d. N/D
GORECKI, Patricia A., b. 1936, d. N/D
GOUGE, Laura Greenwood, b. 1921, d. N/D
GRAHAM, Catherine E., b. 04/05/1980, d. N/D
GREEN, Charles O., ssw-Mildred C., b. 1903, d. 1969
GREEN, D. Maxine, ssw-J. Phillip, Sr., b. 1919, d. 1986
GREEN, Doris R., S1, USN, WWII, b. 04/13/1925, d. 09/29/1993
GREEN, J. Phillip, Sr., ssw-D. Maxine, b. 1911, d. 1976
GREEN, Mildred C., ssw-Charles O., b. 1905, d. N/D
GREENLEE, Evelyn T., ssw-L. Paul, b. 02/01/1918, d. 05/29/1987
GREENLEE, L. Paul, ssw-Evelyn T., b. 11/29/1911, d. 02/15/1996
GREENLEE, William E., Pfc., USA, WWII, b. 1921, d. 1988
GRIESBACK, Max, b. 1889, d. 1975
GRIESBACK, Minnie J., b. 1886, d. 1964
GRIFFITH, Donald H., ssw-Marie R., b. 03/23/1928, d. 11/17/1994
GRIFFITH, Donald H., Jr., b. 07/17/1954, d. 11/14/1992
GRIFFITH, Marie R., ssw-Donald H., b. 01/20/1928, d. 02/01/1990
GROLLER, Dolly E., b. 1917, d. N/D
GROSH, Harold A., ssw-Rose C., b. 1911, d. 1977
GROSH, Rose C., ssw-Harold A., b. 1914, d. 1962
GVERIN, Fred J., DE, DM1, USCG, WWII, b. 09/17/1898, d. 10/25/1966
GVERIN, Mary E., b. 01/24/1909, d. 12/17/1967
HAAS, Jean, b. 1930, d. N/D
HAAS, John R., Jr., Pfc., USMC, WWII, b. 01/04/1921, d. 01/14/1993
HACKETT, Richard W., b. 1914, d. 1985
HAEHNLE, Stella C., b. 1920, d. N/D

HALL, Vera M., b. 1910, d. N/D
HAMILTON, Marjorie B., b. 1928, d. N/D
HAMILTON, Richard L., b. 1927, d. N/D
HAMMOND, Lester W., b. 10/17/1953, d. 06/22/1982
HAMMOND, Lester W., DE, S2, USN, WWII, b. 03/13/1920, d. 04/29/1965
HAMMOND, Mary Lou, b. 03/15/1933, d. 03/05/1994
HANDLEY, Kathleen L., ssw-Walter E., b. 1949, d. N/D
HANDLEY, Walter E., "Skip," ssw-Kathleen L., b. 1949, d. N/D
HANLEY, Donald C., ssw-Julia F., b. 1921, d. N/D
HANLEY, Julia F., ssw-Donald C., b. 1920, d. N/D
HARIG, Kathleen E., ssw-Robert N., b. 12/11/1940, d. N/D
HARIG, Robert N., ssw-Kathleen E., Cpl., USA, Korea, b. 11/09/1931, d. 01/10/1995
HARLEY, Gladys H., b. 01/19/1923, d. N/D
HARMON, Rosa E., b. 1917, d. N/D
HARMON, Willis E., b. 1912, d. 1989
HARPER, James L., b. 1924, d. N/D
HARPSTER, Emma E., ssw-William H., b. 1903, d. 1981
HARPSTER, William H., ssw-Emma E., b. 1901, d. 1983
HASSEMER, Elsie P., ssw-Herman J., b. 1904, d. 1988
HASSEMER, Herman J., ssw-Elsie P., b. 1904, d. 1996
HASTINGS, Elmer, DE, Pvt., USA, WWI, b. 06/05/1891, d. 06/08/1967
HASTINGS, Flossie, ssw-Holda, b. 1897, d. 1975
HASTINGS, Helen E., b. 1920, d. N/D
HASTINGS, Holda, ssw-Flossie, b. 1893, d. 1960
HASTINGS, John Wesley, CM2, USN, WWII, b. 01/27/1919, d. 02/16/1977
HASTINGS, Sallie L., b. 08/13/1888, d. 11/30/1970
HATCH, Bertha I., ssw-Lester Albert, b. 1916, d. 1973
HATCH, Lester Albert, ssw-Bertha I., DE, Cpl., USA, WWI, b. 02/10/1898, d. 09/08/1972
HAUGHEY, Robert G., PA., Pvt., USA, b. 03/15/1891, d. 11/21/1959
HAYES, Charles G., Jr., b. 1952, d. N/D
HAYES, James E., ssw-Margaret J., b. 1925, d. N/D
HAYES, Margaret J., ssw-James E., b. 1933, d. N/D
HAZZARD, Joy K., b. 1933, d. 1982
HEATH, Florence V., b. 1925, d. N/D
HEATH, Pearl R., ssw-Wilbur E., b. 1906, d. 1990
HEATH, Wilbur E., ssw-Pearl R., b. 1906, d. 1985
HEIKEL, John Bernard, ssw-Martha E., EN1, USCG, WWII, b. 03/09/1925, d. 10/05/1991
HEIKEL, Martha E., ssw-John Bernard, b. 08/12/1930, d. N/D
HELLMANN, Francis J., ssw-Virginia W., b. 1906, d. 1988
HELLMANN, Virginia W., ssw-Francis J., b. 1906, d. 1988
HENDERLONG, Jeannette, DE, Cpl., WAC, WWII, b. 06/10/1923, d. 02/03/1973
HENKEL, Beverly J., ssw-William W., Sr., b. 1930, d. N/D
HENKEL, William W., Sr., ssw-Beverly J., USN, WWII, b. 1927, d. N/D
HENRY, Hayes T., ssw-Jean A., b. 1912, d. 1995
HENRY, James C., "Jug," b. 01/24/1907, d. 06/24/1965
HENRY, Jean A., ssw-Hayes T., b. 1923, d. N/D
HERHOLDT, Earl Nelson, DE, Capt., 402 Field Art. Gr., WWII, b. 07/25/1917, d. 09/28/1962
HERHOLDT, Elisabeth Satterfield, b. 04/14/1913, d. 02/06/1994

HERHOLDT, John Fredrik, b. 10/28/1912, d. 04/29/1978
HERMICKE, Ernest P., ssw-Hilda R., b. 1908, d. 1983
HERMICKE, Hilda R., ssw-Ernest P., b. 1912, d. N/D
HERRITY, Isabel M., b. 05/21/1918, d. N/D
HESS, Paul Earl, b. 1913, d. 1956
HICKMAN, Harriet W., ssw-Ross E., b. 1926, d. N/D
HICKMAN, Ross E., ssw-Harriet W., b. 1924, d. 1989
HILL, Dallas, USA, b. 09/04/1924, d. 05/06/1993
HILL, Evelyn G., ssw-John R., b. 1917, d. N/D
HILL, John R., ssw-Evelyn G., b. 1908, d. N/D
HITCHENS, Frances M., b. 1918, d. N/D
HOBBS, Margaret N., ssw-Robert G., b. 04/24/1910, d. 12/01/1989
HOBBS, Robert G., ssw-Margaret N., b. 07/20/1897, d. 08/07/1981
HOLDING, Elizabeth C., ssw-Franklin T., b. 07/29/1934, d. N/D
HOLDING, Franklin T., ssw-Elizabeth C., b. 01/28/1934, d. N/D
HOLDING, Franklin T., Jr., b. 1955, d. 1989
HOLLAND, Anne O'C., b. 12/16/1902, d. 03/08/1977
HOLLAND, Dewey B., b. 1899, d. 1966
HOLLEGER, Jean C., b. 1935, d. N/D
HOLLINGER, Lynn A., ssw-Philips, b. 1956, d. N/D
HOLLINGER, Philips, ssw-Lynn A., Sp4, USA, 1st Air Cav., Vietnam, b. 1950, d. N/D
HOLLOWAY, Luzetta, b. 1923, d. N/D
HOLLOWAY, Thomas H., Tec4, USA, WWII, b. 07/07/1910, d. 10/23/1979
HOLLOWELL, Doris M., ssw-Marion F., b. 1902, d. 1970
HOLLOWELL, Marion F., ssw-Doris M., b. 1896, d. 1980
HOLMES, Agnes B., ssw-Robert M., b. 1879, d. 1972
HOLMES, Robert M., ssw-Agnes B., b. 1884, d. 1963
HOOK, Kathleen D., ssw-Leonard E., b. 12/08/1903, d. 05/02/1959
HOOK, Leonard E., ssw-Kathleen D., DE, Tec5, Co. C., 759 MP. BN., WWII, b. 08/10/1903, d. 01/03/1966
HORNECK, Nancy Boise, b. 10/03/1929, d. N/D
HOUSE, Clyde F., MOMM1, USCG, WWII, b. 11/18/1916, d. 10/11/1975
HOUSEMAN, Anna E., ssw-Ellwood O., b. 1918, d. N/D
HOUSEMAN, Ellwood O., ssw-Anna E., b. 1914, d. N/D
HOWELL, Dewitt C., b. 1882, d. 1968
HOWELL, Evelyn M., b. 1911, d. 1975
HOWELL, Harry R., b. 1913, d. 1980
HOWELL, Lucenia C., b. 1891, d. 1979
HROMCHO, Andrew J., b. 1912, d. N/D
HUDECZ, Marie R., ssw-Rudolph, b. 1914, d. 1960
HUDECZ, Rudolph, ssw-Marie R., b. 1883, d. 1960
HUDSON, Anna B., ssw-John R., b. 1896, d. 1984
HUDSON, Dorothy L., ssw-Preston J., b. 1921, d. N/D
HUDSON, Edna L., ssw-William A., b. 1921, d.N/D
HUDSON, Faye W., b. 09/03/1929, d. 04/12/1983
HUDSON, Gertrude L., b. 1923, d. N/D
HUDSON, John R., ssw-Anna B., b. 1893, d. 1972
HUDSON, Preston J., ssw-Dorothy L., b. 1923, d. N/D
HUDSON, Wansel I., Pfc., USA, b. 10/27/1920, d. 07/18/1975

HUDSON, William A., ssw-Edna L., b. 1922, d. N/D
HUGHES, Blanche Mary V., b. 1926, d. 1974
HUGHES, Frederick A., Sr., b. 1916, d. 1994
HUGHES, Thomas A., MM2, USN, WWII, b. 08/31/1920, d. 03/05/1982
HUGHES, Thomas S., Jr., SSgt., USA, WWII, b. 1919, d. 1984
HUMPHREY, Kathleen R., b. 01/15/1946, d. N/D
HUMPHREYS, Edith O., ssw-T. Roland, b. 05/15/1902, d. N/D
HUMPHREYS, T. Roland, ssw-Edith O., b. 01/15/1903, d. N/D
HUNNICUTT, Frances S., b. 1935, d. N/D
HUNNICUTT, Frank S., Jr., b. 1935, d. N/D
HURD, Edna M., b. 1930, d. N/D
HURST, Helen M., ssw-William J., b. 1911, d. N/D
HURST, William J., ssw-Helen M., b. 1909, d. 1987
INGRAM, Carlton W., USA, WWII, b. 07/19/1925, d. 01/20/1995
INGRAM, Charlotte, ssw-Taylor, b. 1924, d. N/D
INGRAM, Taylor, ssw-Charlotte, b. 1932, d. N/D
IRELAN, David W., b. 1963, d. 1977
ISDELL, Gussie, ssw-Richard T., b. 1940, d. N/D
ISDELL, John T., ssw-Karen R., b. 1959, d. 1987
ISDELL, Karen R., ssw-John T., b. 1960, d. N/D
ISDELL, Richard T., ssw-Gussie, b. 1932, d. N/D
JACKSON, Frank A., b. 1904, d. 1965
JACKSON, Louie M., ssw-Norman C., Sr., b. 1930, d. 1994
JACKSON, Norman C., Sr., ssw-Louie M., b. 1928, d. N/D
JAMES, Henry Allen, HM1, USN, WWII, b. 03/21/1927, d. 08/21/1980
JAMES, Margaret T., ssw-Melvin C., Sr., b. 08/03/1902, d. 05/05/1969
JAMES, Margaret Wilkerson, ssw-Everett M. Wilkerson, b. 04/17/1921, d. 06/15/1985
JAMES, Melvin C., Sr., ssw-Margaret T., b. 02/15/1899, d. 08/02/1967
JAQUETTE, Robert T., ssw-Ruth B., b. 04/06/1906, d. 09/24/1967
JAQUETTE, Ruth B., ssw-Robert T., b. 06/23/1910, d. N/D
JEFFERSON, Florence, ssw-Thomas P., b.07/07/1892, d. 08/23/1989
JEFFERSON, Thomas P., ssw-Florence, b. 07/20/1889, d. 10/12/1964
JENSEN, Aage R., ssw-Norma D., TSgt., USAF, WWII, b. 04/12/1927, d. 06/26/1994
JENSEN, Arlyne M., ssw-Emma J. Keenan, b. 1927, d. N/D
JENSEN, Norma D., ssw-Aage R., b. 1933, d. N/D
JERMAN, Etzel B., ssw-Harold E., b. 1921, d. N/D
JERMAN, Harold E., ssw-Etzel B., b. 1921, d. 1979
JESSEN, George Wm., III, b. 02/06/1971, d. 06/11/1972
JESTER, Reese, ssw-Ruth R., b. 1915, d. 1972
JESTER, Ruth R., ssw-Reese, b. 1914, d. 1978
JEWELL, Francis W., ssw-Pauline L., b. 1904, d. N/D
JEWELL, Pauline L., ssw-Francis W., b. 1911, d. 1970
JOHNSON, Anna C., ssw-George H., b. 02/23/1925, d. N/D
JOHNSON, Asa S., b. 1871, d. 1956
JOHNSON, Cheryl A., b. 1957, d. 1994
JOHNSON, Chrissie Jackson, b. 1904, d. 1990
JOHNSON, George H., ssw-Anna C., DE, SM2, USNR, WWII, b. 04/09/1922, d. 05/01/1966
JOHNSON, Guada G. M., ssw-Steve, b. 1958, d. N/D

JOHNSON, Samuel Andrew, ssw-Shirley A., USN, Korea, b. 03/16/1931, d. 09/23/1994
JOHNSON, Shirley A., ssw-Samuel Andrew, b. 03/10/1939, d. N/D
JOHNSON, Steve, ssw-Guada G. M., b. 1954, d. N/D
JOHNSTON, William C., b. 08/01/1888, d. 07/31/1955
JONES, Adele Ora., b. 1950, d. N/D
JONES, Anna Mae, ssw-Crystal G., b. 1921, d. 1996
JONES, Crystal G., ssw-Anna Mae, b. 1962, d. N/D
JONES, John Herbert, ETM2, USN, WWII, b. 11/26/1926, d. 02/06/1983
JONES, Leona B., b. 1935, d. 1990
JONES, Sally Gledhill, b. 1928, d. N/D
JOPLING, Marilla, b. 1901, d. 1994
JOSEPH, Anita B., ssw-Ronnie M., b. 1950, d. N/D
JOSEPH, James F., b. 1955, d. 1976
JOSEPH, Jessie M., ssw-Lawrence, b. 1916, d. 1978
JOSEPH, Lawrence, ssw-Jessie M., b. 1920, d. 1975
JOSEPH, Ronnie M., ssw-Anita B., b. 1949, d. N/D
KABELKA, Otto, DE, Cpl., 6 Eng. Train, WWI, b. 04/04/1892, d. 09/15/1960
KALIOUS, Delores F., b. 05/29/1928, d. N/D
KALVINSKY, Edward G., ssw-Esther G., b. 1934, d. N/D
KALVINSKY, Esther G., ssw-Edward G., b. 1927, d. N/D
KANE, Loretto D., b. 1904, d. 1988
KARL, Hedwig M., b. 04/03/1897, d. 01/09/1979
KARL, Ralph E., b. 12/23/1902, d. 01/06/1977
KAUFFMAN, Clare H., b. 08/15/1925, d. N/D
KAY, Jean C., ssw-Walter S., b. 1917, d. N/D
KAY, Walter S., ssw-Jean C., b. 1912, d. N/D
KEENAN, Emma J., ssw-Arlyne M. Jensen, b. 1895, d. 1992
KELLAM, Harvey, b. 1903, d. 1993
KELLERMAN, Alta M., ssw-Raymond E., b. 1894, d. 1976
KELLERMAN, Raymond E., ssw-Alta M., b. 1883, d. 1967
KELLEY, Ella B., ssw-Norman J., b. 1914, d. 1992
KELLEY, Norman J., ssw-Ella B., b. 1917, d. 1979
KELTNER, Carl A., ssw-Evelyn L., Pfc., USMC, WWII, b. 03/04/1926, d. 03/17/1992
KELTNER, Evelyn L., ssw-Carl A., b. 07/02/1927, d. N/D
KENNEDY, Florence M., ssw-Robert F., b. 1914, d. 1978
KENNEDY, Robert F., ssw-Florence M., b. 1912, d. 1983
KEPLINGER, Gertrude D., ssw-Wesley J., b. 11/28/1906, d. N/D
KEPLINGER, Wesley J., ssw-Gertrude D., b. 09/19/1900, d. N/D
KERPER, Ruth E., ssw-Vernon A., Sr., b. 1919, d. N/D
KERPER, Vernon A., Sr., ssw-Ruth E., Pvt., USA, WWII, b. 08/16/1917, d. 05/02/1995
KERSTIER, Carolyn C., ssw-Ray F., b. 08/20/1917, d. 08/21/1995
KERSTIER, Ray F., ssw-Carolyn C., b. 01/01/1911, d. 04/17/1987
KIDD, Ann C., ssw-Raymond H., b. 1917, d. N/D
KIDD, Raymond H., ssw-Ann C., b. 1918, d. N/D
KILLEN, George Edward, ssw-Thelma K., b. 1913, d. 1988
KILLEN, Thelma K., ssw-George Edward, b. 1914, d. 1980
KILLIAN, Amy E., b. 1938, d. N/D
KING, Carrie E., ssw-Charles H., b. 1895, d. 1988

KING, Charles H., ssw-Carrie E., b. 1893, d. 1975

KING, Clarence E., b. 1886, d. 1957

KING, Donroe W., Pfc., USA, WWII, b. 03/07/1923, d. 06/19/1981

KING, Jennie T., b. 1892, d. 1967

KING, Leona Conaway, b. 10/31/1911, d. N/D

KING, Martin H., ssw-Rose P., b. 1927, d. 1956

KING, Rose P., ssw-Martin H., b. 1928, d. N/D

KIRKPATRICK, Clarence H., D.C., Lt. Col., USA Ret., WWII, Korea, b. 10/08/1911, d. 08/17/1973

KIRKPATRICK, May Augusta, b. 07/01/1913, d. 05/03/1986

KIRKPATRICK, Terrence L., b. 03/18/1940, d. 03/31/1996

KLINE, Alice R., ssw-Paul W., b. 1920, d. N/D

KLINE, Edith C., b. 10/20/1921, d. N/D

KLINE, Paul W., ssw-Alice R., b. 1913, d. N/D

KLINE, Wayne W., Maj., USA, WWII, b. 1918, d. 1985

KLINGER, Charlotte B., ssw-Raymond M., b. 05/23/1920, d. N/D

KLINGER, Raymond M., ssw-Charlotte B., Sgt., USA, WWII, b. 06/11/1919, d. 04/28/1992

KOHEL, Corinne Clogg, b. 03/18/1927, d. N/D

KOHR, Betty J., ssw-Granville H., b. 1921, d. N/D

KOHR, Granville H., ssw-Betty J., S1 (FC), USN, R., b. 1920, d. N/D

KRAJEWSKI, Alexander J., USA, WWII, b. 12/09/1917, d. 08/12/1982

KRAJEWSKI, Vivian I., b. 1926, d. 1986

KRAMER, Glenn H., ssw-Miriam B., b. 1913, d. 1985

KRAMER, Miriam B., ssw-Glenn H., b. 1915, d. N/D

KRILOWICZ, Steven Todd, USN, b. 1962, d. 1995

KUVIK, Anna M., b. 1889, d. 1969

KUVIK, Thomas S., b. 1880, d. 1959

KUYWESKI, Edward J., ssw-Jean M., USA, WWII, b. 1922, d. 1988

KUYWESKI, Jean M., ssw-Edward J., b. 1923, d. N/D

KWACZ, Joseph F., ssw-Veronica D., b. 1913, d. 1996

KWACZ, Veronica D., ssw-Joseph F., b. 1917, d. N/D

LACEY, Nora Augusta, b. 1879, d. 1961

LAMBERT, James K., ssw-Sallie W., b. 1876, d. 1962

LAMBERT, Sallie W., ssw-James K., b. 1874, d. 1960

LANE, Gary Allen, b. 01/29/1967, d. 08/10/1992

LANE, Marion H., ssw-Raymond W., b. 1922, d. N/D

LANE, Raymond W., ssw-Marion H., 1st Lt., USA, WWII, b. 12/14/1913, d. 01/06/1996

LANK, Bertha M., ssw-Walter H., b. 05/14/1891, d. 03/13/1984

LANK, Jo Anne, b. 1947, d. N/D

LANK, Laura E., ssw-Raymond M., b. 1897, d. 1976

LANK, Raymond M., ssw-Laura E., b. 1892, d. 1969

LANK, Walter H., ssw-Bertha M., b. 01/16/1891, d. 08/03/1958

LAPINE, E. Carolyn, b. 1922, d. N/D

LARE, Katherine L., b. 10/22/1915, d. 10/08/1962

LARIMORE, Boyce D., ssw-Charlotte S., b. 1910, d. 1985

LARIMORE, Charlotte S., ssw-Boyce D., b. 1921, d. 1983

LASALLE, Joseph A., ssw-Edward T. Cisler, b. N/D, d. 1984

LAWRIE, Ruth E., ssw-Catherine J. Doolittle, Sisters, b. 1915, d. N/D

LAWSON, Marie T., ssw-Norman Selby, b. 06/18/1921, d. N/D

LAWSON, Norman Selby, ssw-Marie T., DE. SSgt., 828 Ca. Btry., WWII, b. 05/10/1917, d. 09/28/1926
LAWTON, Judith Ann, b. 05/02/1940
LAYTON, Caesar Rodney, USN, WWII, b. 09/03/1926, d. 12/18/1992
LAYTON, Katherine, ssw-Lanny, b. 1925, d. 1976
LAYTON, Lanny, ssw-Katherine, b. 1923, d. N/D
LAYTON, Lorraine L., ssw-Anna M. Morengo, b. 1927, d. N/D
LEACH, Carol L., b. 1944, d. N/D
LECATES, Evelyn B., b. 1923, d. N/D
LECOMPTE, Howard L., ssw-Lillian I., b. 1919, d. 1985
LECOMPTE, Lillian I., ssw-Howard L., b. 1914, d. 1983
LEE, Helen S., b. 03/10/1917, d. 01/28/1995
LEFFLER, Jeanette A., b. 1892, d. 1989
LEGATES, Anna, b. 1918, d. N/D
LEGATES, Dallas B., b. 1916, d. 1993
LEGATES, Norma Lee, b. 01/03/1940, d. 11/01/1980
LEGATES, Rebecca P., b. 1919, d. 1983
LEITTON, Kathleen R., b. 1923, d. N/D
LEMAIRE, Arny C., ssw-May P., b. 1901, d. 1981
LEMAIRE, May P., ssw-Arny C., b. 1901, d. 1984
LEPPO, Gwendolyn, ssw-G. Wilson Bryan, Daughter, b. 1941, d. N/D
LEPPO, Kathryne A. M., ssw-LeRoy F., b. 1912, d. N/D
LEPPO, LeRoy F., ssw-Kathryne A. M., b. 1909, d. 1979
LEPPO, Sara, b. 1944, d. N/D
LEUTHAUSER, Kenneth A., DE, AA, USN, b. 12/15/1946, d. 03/09/1967
LINDSAY, Ann B., b. 11/28/1889, d. 07/10/1959
LITTELL, Grace, ssw-Jack, b. 1927, d. 1987
LITTELL, Jack, ssw-Grace, b. 1923, d. 1995
LITTLEFIELD, George H., ssw-Marie E., Pfc., USA, WWII, b. 01/24/1922, d. 04/23/1994
LITTLEFIELD, Marie E., ssw-George H., b. 04/07/1900, d. N/D
LITTLETON, Bertha E., ssw-Daniel T., b. 1944, d. N/D
LITTLETON, Daniel T., ssw-Bertha E., b. 1920, d. N/D
LLOYD, Florence M., ssw-John Leon, b. 12/16/1923, d. N/D
LLOYD, John E., Tec4, USA, WWII, b. 04/11/1920, d. 09/30/1993
LLOYD, John Leon, ssw-Florence M., BM1, USN, WWII, b. 12/14/1910, d. 01/21/1992
LOCKERMAN, Leighton L., ssw-Lola M., m. 9-12-28, b. 1908, d. 1988
LOCKERMAN, Lola M., ssw-Leighton L., m. 9-12-28, b. 1909, d. N/D
LOWERY, Virginia May, b. 09/14/1915, d. 12/14/1989
LOWRY, Sandra Lee, b. 1946, d. 1971
LUCIEN, Ann H., b. 1915, d. N/D
LUCKHURST, Donna J., ssw-George T., b. 1939, d. N/D
LUCKHURST, George T., ssw-Donna J., b. 1921, d. N/D
LUTZ, Katherine N., ssw-Elwood J. Cox, b. 1916, d. 1992
LUZIER, Dorsey D., ssw-Pearl, b. 1892, d. 1960
LUZIER, Pearl, ssw-Dorsey D., b. 1897, d. 1981
LYNCH, Ernest R., ssw-Leora B., b. 1919, d. N/D
LYNCH, Leora B., ssw-Ernest R., b. 1921, d. N/D
LYONS, Doreen, ssw-John J., b. 1924, d. N/D
LYONS, John J., ssw-Doreen, b. 1919, d. 1994

LYONS, Kathleen T., b. 05/16/1930, d. N/D
MACKENZIE, Alice B., b. 12/29/1937, d. 01/25/1981
MADDEN, Laura M., b. 1899, d. 1972
MADJAROSY, Francesca D., b. N/D, d. N/D
MADJAROSY, Frank, Jr., Sgt., USA, WWII, b. 09/06/1916, d. 04/16/1987
MAGEE, Joann Adele, b. 07/09/1955, d. 08/20/1976
MAGINLEY, Jane W., ssw-Robert T., b. 1923, d. N/D
MAGINLEY, Robert T., ssw-Jane W., Cpl., USA, WWII, b. 01/29/1917, d. 02/16/1994
MAINON, Charles J., Pfc., USMC, WWII, b. 12/09/1928, d. 02/09/1995
MALITZSKI, Gloria L., ssw-William W. Bennett, b. 1932, d. N/D
MALLOY, Shirley M., b. 1931, d. N/D
MALONEY, Horace A., b. 1904, d. 1968
MANAWAY, James Edgar, ssw-Pauline Springs, b. 1917, d. 1991
MANAWAY, Pauline Springs, ssw-James Edgar, b. 1915, d. N/D
MARINGOLA, Jenaro, ssw-Tessie, b. 1896, d. 1968
MARINGOLA, Tessie, b. Jenaro, b. 1896, d. 1972
MAROWSKI, Joseph E., ssw-Loretta E., b. 1911, d. 1985
MAROWSKI, Loretta E., ssw-Joseph E., b. 1918, d. N/D
MARQUES, Lorraine C., ssw-Robert A., b. 1925, d. N/D
MARQUES, Robert A., ssw-Lorraine C., b. 1923, d. N/D
MARSHALL, Elizabeth L., ssw-William J., b. 1922, d. N/D
MARSHALL, Jobe D., ssw-Virginia A., b. 1924, d. N/D
MARSHALL, Virginia A., ssw-Jobe D., b. 1932, d. N/D
MARSHALL, William J., ssw-Elizabeth L., b. 1907, d. 1980
MARTIN, Charles F., ssw-Janet H., b. 1939, d. N/D
MARTIN, Doris E., b. 04/06/1918, d. 02/14/1981
MARTIN, Janet H., ssw-Charles F., b. 1940, d. N/D
MARTIN, Lawrence J., Jr., ssw-Marie H., USN, b. 1922, d. 1988
MARTIN, Marie H., ssw-Lawrence J., Jr., b. 08/06/1923, d. ND
MARTIN, William James, Pfc., USA, WWII, b. 07/26/1914, d. 08/06/1976
MARVEL, Elizabeth F., ssw-James R., b. 1920, d. 1978
MARVEL, James R., ssw-Elizabeth F., b. 1913, d. 1974
MASSEY, Charity P., ssw-William T., b. 1910, d. 1985
MASSEY, Charles H., ssw-Ola E., b. 1888, d. 1963
MASSEY, Elmer T., ssw-Josephine S., b. 1934, d. N/D
MASSEY, Josephine S., ssw-Elmer T., b. 1939, d. N/D
MASSEY, Ola E., ssw-Charles H., b. 1888, d. 1971
MASSEY, William T., ssw-Charity P., b. 1908, d. 1992
MATTHEWS, Christina, ssw-James P., b. 1911, d. N/D
MATTHEWS, James P., ssw-Christina, b. 1911, d. 1990
MATTHEWS, Mary F., b. 1923, d. N/D
MAULL, Alton H., ssw-Margaret W., b. 1922, d. N/D
MAULL, Elva M., b. 1910, d. 1984
MAULL, John T., Sr., b. 1906, d. 1961
MAULL, Margaret W., ssw-Alton H., b. 1925, d. N/D
MAULL, Thomas E., b. 1949, d. 1965
MAWYER, Muriel H., b. 10/31//1926, d. N/D
MAYBEN, Joan Marie, b. 1935, d. N/D

MAYFIELD, Catherine E., ssw-Dennis Lea & Dewey E., Jr., b. 1924, d. N/D
MAYFIELD, Dennis Lea, ssw-Catherine E. & Dewey E., Jr., b. 1947, d. 1969
MAYFIELD, Dewey E., Jr. ssw-Catherine E. & Dennis Lea, b. 1922, d. 1978
MAYFIELD, William Joseph, "Billy Joe," b. 09/08/1965, d. 08/18/1982
MCALLISTER, Clarence W., "Mack," ssw-Helen M., b. 03/15/1930, d. 03/10/1994
MCALLISTER, Clarence W., ssw-Lillian J., b. 1892, d. 1976
MCALLISTER, Helen M., ssw-Clarence W., b. 02/06/1928, d. N/D
MCALLISTER, Lillian J., ssw-Clarence W., b. 1911, d. N/D
MCCANN, Edith M., ssw-John F., b. 1923, d. N/D
MCCANN, John F., ssw-Edith M., Pfc., USA, WWII, b. 06/01/1924, d. 05/07/1990
MCCLELLAND, Carolyn S., b. 03/11/1943, d. N/D
MCCOLLEY, Irene L., ssw-R. Harlan, b. 1914, d. N/D
MCCOLLEY, R. Harlan, ssw-Irene L., b. 1913, d. 1983
MCCONAGHY, Constance M., b. 1947, d. 1963
MCCONNELL, Mildred M., b. 1940, d. N/D
MCDONALD, John V., ssw-Mary A., b. 1888, d. 1966
MCDONALD, Mary A., ssw-John V., b. 1888, d. 1968
MCGEE, Lewis J., ssw-Maude E., b. 1900, d. 1973
MCGEE, Maude E., ssw-Lewis J., b. 1899, d. 1976
MCGINNIS, William H., Jr., RCT, USA, b. 09/08/1929, d. 04/22/1956
MCHARGUE, Joseph C., ssw-Mary C., b. 1929, d. N/D
MCHARGUE, Mary C., ssw-Joseph C., b. 1928, d. N/D
MCHARGUE, Sharon L., ssw-Phillip H. Mulvaney, b. 1956, d. N/D
MCILVAIN, Patricia A., ssw-Robert A., b. 1932, d. N/D
MCILVAIN, Robert A., ssw-Patricia A., b. 1925, d. N/D
MCKENNA, Iris A., ssw-Joseph, b. 1930, d. 1996
MCKENNA, Joseph, ssw-Iris A., b. 1926, d. 1992
MCLAUGHLIN, Edith M., b. 08/11/1921, d. N/D
MCQUAY, John H., ssw-Stella K., b. 02/22/1942, d. N/D
MCQUAY, Stella K., ssw-John H., b. 05/09/1946, d. 03/05/1975
MCSWEENEY, Edna G., ssw-Francis M., b. 1910, d. 1992
MCSWEENEY, Francis M., ssw-Edna G., DE, CM2, USN, WWII, b. 11/08/1910, d. 12/22/1973
MCSWEENEY, Helen M., ssw-Joseph S., b. 1896, d. 1988
MCSWEENEY, Joseph S., ssw-Helen M., b. 1893, d. 1981
MCWILLIAMS, Anna C., ssw-Cyril E., b. 1911, d. 1994
MCWILLIAMS, Cyril E., ssw-Anna C., b. 1907, d. 1973
MEHOLIC, John W., Tec4, USA, WWII, b. 04/08/1914, d. 08/31/1982
MILES, Sonja L., ssw-William B., Jr., b. 1939, d. N/D
MILES, Virginia D., ssw-William B., Sr., b. 1917, d. N/D
MILES, William B., Jr., ssw-Sonja L., SP4, USA, Vietnam, b. 09/23/1943, d. 11/25/1993
MILES, William B., Sr., ssw-Virginia D., b. 1909, d. 1988
MILLER, Elbert F., 2nd Leu., USA, b. 08/14/1905, d. 11/08/1974
MILLER, Gilbert F., ssw-Mary Louise, b. 08/14/1905, d. 11/08/1974
MILLER, Glen N., ssw-V. Wahnita, b. 1949, d. N/D
MILLER, Mary Louise, ssw-Gilbert F., b. 08/19/1918, d. N/D
MILLER, V. Wahnita, ssw-Glen N., b. 1926, d. 1995
MILLMAN, Arithea L., ssw-Henry B., b. 1929, d. N/D
MILLMAN, Henry B., ssw-Arithea L., Sgt., USA, Korea, b. 03/03/1928, d. 02/07/1987

MILLMAN, Lee A., Father of Andrew L., b. 05/22/1956, d. 05/12/1989
MILLS, Ruth Ann, b. 1930, d. N/D
MILTENBERGER, Karl J., Sr., b. 1902, d. 1976
MINTZ, Arthur R., ssw-Betty S., b. 1923, d. 1990
MINTZ, Betty S., ssw-Arthur R., b. 1918, d. N/D
MITCHELL, Agnes L., ssw-Lewin W., b. 1920, d. N/D
MITCHELL, Alexander, ssw-Esther M., b. 1925, d. N/D
MITCHELL, Alfred J., Sr., ssw-Marlyn E., b. 1931, d. N/D
MITCHELL, Charles W., ssw-Mattie L., b. 1904, d. 1993
MITCHELL, Cleo R., ssw-Howard E., b. 1917, d. N/D
MITCHELL, Esther M., ssw-Alexander, b. 1923, d. N/D
MITCHELL, Florence S., ssw-J. Frank, b. 1914, d. N/D
MITCHELL, Howard E., ssw-Cleo R., b. 1918, d. 1986
MITCHELL, Ida M., ssw-Thomas O., b. 09/24/1891, d. 11/11/1967
MITCHELL, J. Frank, ssw-Florence S., b. 1912, d. 1979
MITCHELL, Josephine, b. 04/15/1922, d. 03/09/1988
MITCHELL, Lewin W., ssw-Agnes L., b. 1920, d. N/D
MITCHELL, Lida L., ssw-Theodore W., b. 08/31/1903, d. 03/20/1964
MITCHELL, Lynn West, b. 1955, d. 1959
MITCHELL, Margaret R., ssw-Roscoe W., b. 1910, d. 1987
MITCHELL, Marie E., ssw-William J., b. 04/16/1927, d. N/D
MITCHELL, Marion E., b. 02/12/1915, d. 07/29/1992
MITCHELL, Marlyn E., ssw-Alfred J., Sr., b. 1936, d. N/D
MITCHELL, Mattie L., ssw-Charles W., b. 1916, d. N/D
MITCHELL, Roscoe W., ssw-Margaret R., b. 1911, d. 1976
MITCHELL, Sallie M., ssw-Walter R., b. 1921, d. N/D
MITCHELL, Theodore W., ssw-Lida L., b. 12/06/1896, d. 02/12/1966
MITCHELL, Thomas O., ssw-Ida M., b. 05/03/1887, d. 10/15/1964
MITCHELL, Walter B., b. 06/10/1923, d. 07/20/1980
MITCHELL, Walter R., ssw-Sallie M., b. 1917, d. 1989
MITCHELL, William J., ssw-Marie E., Pvt., USA, b. 01/15/1916, d. 01/10/1993
MOLLOY, Edmund T., b. 1918, d. 1970
MOLLOY, Evelyn E., b. 1916, d. 1991
MONIHAN, E. James, ssw-Mary Jeanette, b. 1937, d. N/D
MONIHAN, Mary Jeanette, ssw-E. James, b. 1935, d. N/D
MONMILLER, Charles L., sswCleora M., Pfc., USA, WWII, b. 04/20/1919, d. 07/18/1989
MONMILLER, Cleora M., ssw-Charles L., b. 08/26/1921, d. N/D
MOORE, A. Douglas, ssw-Marguerite D., b. 1917, d. 1985
MOORE, Anthony C., ssw-Mabel B., b. 1909, d. 1979
MOORE, Charles E., Sr., ssw-Donna F., b. 12/28/1938, d. N/D
MOORE, David, ssw-Mabel E., SN, USN, Korea, b. 12/12/1931, d. 01/16/1994
MOORE, Donna F., ssw-Charles E., Sr., b. 09/12/1959, d. N/D
MOORE, Edwin, "Cap," ssw-Stella, b. 04/18/1904, d. 01/01/1965
MOORE, Eleanor M., ssw-J. T., b. 1925, d. 1974
MOORE, Eli R., b. 1888, d. 1967
MOORE, George G., Sr., FN, USN, Vietnam, b. 01/04/1945, d. 04/07/1994
MOORE, J. T., ssw-Eleanor M., b. 1920, d. N/D
MOORE, Jacob M., Sgt., USA, b. 04/04/1911, d. 06/16/1979

MOORE, Jeanette F., b. 1950, d. N/D
MOORE, John Harry, Pfc., USA, b. 12/08/1938, d. 06/04/1993
MOORE, Louise, b. 1921, d. N/D
MOORE, Mabel B., ssw-Anthony C., b. 1903, d. 1986
MOORE, Mabel E., ssw-David, b. 01/05/1933, d. N/D
MOORE, Marquerite D., ssw-A. Douglas, b. 1920, d. 1989
MOORE, Pearl, b. 1913, d. 1988
MOORE, Stella, "Lib," ssw-Edwin, b. 02/12/1920, d. N/D
MORAN, Betty J., ssw-George M., b. 1926, d. N/D
MORAN, George M., ssw-Betty J., S1, USN, b. 04/04/1925, d. 10/03/1992
MORAN, John A., b. 1903, d. 1970
MORENGO, Anna M., ssw-Lorraine L. Layton, b. 1931, d. N/D
MORGAN, David A., ssw-Jean W., b. 1957, d. N/D
MORGAN, Elwood O., ssw-Violet M., b. 1927, d. N/D
MORGAN, Ethel, ssw-Evans, b. 1899, d. N/D
MORGAN, Evans, ssw-Ethel, b. 1897, d. 1971
MORGAN, Jean W., ssw-David A., b. 1957, d. N/D
MORGAN, Sharon Ann, b. 1953, d. N/D
MORGAN, Violet M., ssw-Elwood O., b. 1926, d. N/D
MORRIS, Jennie E., ssw-Paynter, b. 1908, d. N/D
MORRIS, Paynter, ssw-Jennie E., b. 1902, d. 1985
MORTON, Jack Lloyd, Cpt., USA, WWII, b. 11/28/1918, d. 12/19/1993
MOSS, Charlotte N., ssw-Raymond R., b. 1910, d. 1989
MOSS, Raymond R., ssw-Charlotte N., b. 1913, d. 1993
MUIR, Barnard C., ssw-Katharine E., b. 1910, d. 1980
MUIR, Katharine E., ssw-Barnard C., b. 1921, d. N/D
MULLAHY, Dorothy, b. 1936, d. N/D
MULLANEY, James L., ssw-Mary Lou, b. 1912, d. 1996
MULLANEY, Mary Lou, ssw-James L., b. 1931, d. N/D
MULLEN, John T., ssw-Mary K., b. 1919, d. N/D
MULLEN, Mary K., ssw-John T., b. 1924, d. N/D
MULVANEY, Phillip H., ssw-Sharon L. McHargue, b. 1933, d. 1991
MURK, Leslie J., ssw-Minnie Deitz, b. 1905, d. 1979
MURK, Minnie Deitz, ssw-Leslie J., b. 1912, d. 1993
MURPHY, Norris H., ssw-Sarah A., b. 1910, d. 1980
MURPHY, Sarah A., ssw-Norris H., b. 1918, d. 1989
NAGENGAST, Vivan P., b.1917, d. N/D
NAUMAN, Leona M., b. 1922, d. 1960
NEIL, Mary Jane, b. 1927, d. N/D
NEIL, Thomas Eugene, b. 1929, d. N/D
NEUHAUS, Majorie S., b. 1928
NEVILLE, Catherine J., b. 06/28/1916, d. 04/07/1990
NEWCOMB, Harold W., USA, b. 07/19/1922, d. 12/24/1990
NEWCOMB, Margaret D., b. 01/06/1919, d. N/D
NEWSHAM, Harry Robert, QM2, USN, WWII, b. 01/23/1925, d. 11/27/1993
NIBLET, Margaret B., b. 10/10/1915, d. 01/25/1993
NICHOLS, Elsie L., b. 11/24/1919, d. N/D
NORMAN, Sandra L., b. 1967, d. 1996

NORRMAN, Clifford A. E., ssw-Thelma F., BKR1, USN, WWII, b. 01/20/1918, d. 04/18/1995
NORRMAN, Thelma F., ssw-Clifford A. E., b. 1920, d. N/D
NOTINGHAM, Andrew J., ssw-Frances R., b. 1914, d. 1974
NOTINGHAM, Frances R., ssw-Andrew J., b. 1914, d. N/D
NOVOTNY, Angela, ssw-James A., b. 1924, d. N/D
NOVOTNY, Greg A., b. 1963, d. 1995
NOVOTNY, James A., ssw-Angela, b. 1919, d. N/D
NOVOTNY, James H., b. 1876, d. 1967
NUTTER, Lewis C., ssw-Myrtle E., b. 1885, d. 1970
NUTTER, Myrtle E., ssw-Lewis C., b. 1886, d. 1985
O'CONNOR, Charles J., NY, Sgt., 888 Med. Co., WWII, Korea, b. 07/11/1911, d. 08/22/1972
O'CONNOR, Mary F., b. 1878, d. 1961
O'HAZZA, Francis, "Guy," b. 1925, d. N/D
O'HAZZA, Susie Bell, b. 1925, d. N/D
OAKES, Gerald C., ssw-Stella Mae, b. 1925, d. 1992
OAKES, Stella Mae, ssw-Gerald C., b. 1931, d. N/D
OBZUT, Blanche N., ssw-Jacob, b. 1891, d. 1980
OBZUT, Jacob, ssw-Blanche N., b. 1885, d. 1967
OLP, Maurice L., ssw-Verna S., b. 1912, d. 1987
OLP, Verna S., ssw-Maurice L., b. 1917, d. 1990
OLSEN, Rose Emma, b. 01/14/1962, d. 03/23/1962
OPLINGER, Brenda A., b. 1943, d. 1985
OSADA, Charles R., Sgt., USA, WWII, b. 12/23/1912, d. 04/29/1981
OSTROSKI, Reba, b. 1918, d. N/D
OWEN, Barbara Shon, b. 11/07/1921, d. N/D
PACK, Anna Obzut, ssw-Harry, b. 06/09/1909, d. 04/27/1995
PACK, David, ssw-Rene B., b. 1905, d. 1993
PACK, Harry, ssw-Anna Obzut, b. 03/13/1903, d. 03/19/1994
PACK, Rene B., ssw-David, b. 1906, d. 1981
PALMER, Gaye M., ssw-Lemuel R., b. 1940, d. N/D
PALMER, Lemuel R., ssw-Gaye M., b. 1937, d. N/D
PANUSKA, Evelyn K., b. 02/08/1924, d. N/D
PANUSKA, James B., Pfc., USA, WWII, b. 1920, d. 1980
PAQUETTE, Catharine M., ssw-Wilfred C., b. 1913, d. 1969
PAQUETTE, Wilfred C., ssw-Catharine M., b. 1905, d. 1976
PARKER, Gerald R., USN, b. 03/19/1928, d. 12/16/1994
PARKER, Maurice A., SSgt., USA, b. 05/23/1909, d. 01/21/1984
PARKER, Virginia M., b. 01/22/1887, d. 08/07/1980
PARKER, W. Arthur, b. 02/26/1880, d. 02/22/1960
PARMENTIER, Blanche J., ssw-Joseph A., b. 1921, d. 1992
PARMENTIER, Joseph A., ssw-Blanche J., b. 1924, d. N/D
PARRIS, Margaret V., b. 09/30/1899, d. 12/15/1962
PARRIS, Norman W., Jr., b. 06/26/1922, d. 10/05/1969
PARROTT, Don Allen, ssw-Linda M., b. 1960, d. 1994
PARROTT, Linda M., ssw-Don Allen, b. 1961, d. N/D
PARSONS, Patricia G., b. 09/30/1926, d. 07/14/1987
PASE, Ephatha J., ssw-William J., b. 1898, d. 1988
PASE, Helen A., ssw-John Edgar, b. 1902, d. 1992

PASE, John Edgar, ssw-Helen A., b. 1901, d. 1983
PASE, William J., ssw-Ephatha J., b. 1895, d. 1964
PASSWATERS, Ida B., ssw-Richard A., b. 01/15/1946, d. N/D
PASSWATERS, Raymond W., ssw-Ruby B., b. 07/14/1906, d. 07/23/1964
PASSWATERS, Richard A., ssw-Ida B., b. 07/14/1946, d. 07/10/1995
PASSWATERS, Ruby B., ssw-Raymond W., b. 12/16/1918, d. N/D
PASSWATERS, Victoria E., b. 1930, d. 1996
PAVER, Harvey J., b. 06/27/1920, d. 11/07/1958
PEPPER, Ada L., ssw-C. Arlington, b. 1885, d. 1967
PEPPER, C. Arlington, ssw-Ada L., b. 1882, d. 1956
PEPPER, James, b. 1933, d. 1986
PEPPER, Janice V., b. 1939, d. N/D
PEPPER, Pauline C., ssw-Thomas A., b. 1914, d. N/D
PEPPER, R. Bryan, ssw-Ruth S., b. 1926, d. N/D
PEPPER, Ruth S., ssw-R. Bryan, b. 1928, d. N/D
PEPPER, Thomas A., ssw-Pauline C., b. 1904, d. 1980
PERROTT, Nettie V., ssw-William M., b. 1898, d. 1981
PERROTT, William M., ssw-Nettie V., b. 1896, d. 1969
PETERSON, Judith Ann, b. 07/05/1942, d. 10/07/1981
PHILLIPS, Diane R., ssw-J. Richard A., b. 02/10/1955, d. 06/25/1988
PHILLIPS, J. Richard A., ssw-Diane R., b. 03/18/1956, d. N/D
PHILLIPS, Marilyn Jane, b. 06/13/1927, d. 08/13/1987
PIERSON, Henrietta, ssw-James L., Jr., b. 12/11/1925, d. N/D
PIERSON, James L., Jr., ssw-Henrietta, Pvt., USA, WWII, b. 1922, d.1988
PILKINGTON, Anna T., ssw-Thomas B., b. 1927, d. N/D
PILKINGTON, Thomas B., ssw-Anna T., b. 1920, d. N/D
PIZZUTO, Anthony L., ssw-Mary Anne, b. 01/31/1911, d. 09/25/1981
PIZZUTO, Mary Anne, ssw-Anthony L., b. 04/19/1921, d. 02/22/1971
PLACK, Dorothy M., ssw-William F., Jr., b. 1922, d. 1993
PLACK, William F., Jr., ssw-Dorothy M., b. 1924, d. ND
PLANGGER, August, ssw-Lillie B., b. 1901, d 1985
PLANGGER, Lillie B., ssw-August, b. 1903, d. 1985
PLATT, Anna C., ssw-Thomas M., b. 09/04/1916, d. 06/22/1994
PLATT, Thomas M., ssw-Anna C., MM2, USN, WWII, b. 01/31/1912, d. 05/04/1993
PLOSKON, Thelma G., b. 11/06/1928, d. N/D
PLUMMER, George W., Jr., ssw-Helen V., b. 1914, d. N/D
PLUMMER, Helen V., ssw-George W., Jr., b. 1918, d. N/D
POLITE, Joan Ellen, b. 07/28/1942, d. 11/15/1962
POLITE, Theodore, Jr., USA, WWII, b. 1925, d. 1985
PORST, Carolyn M., b. 10/17/1928, d. N/D
PORTER, Alan Carl, Lt., b. 11/02/1918, d. 05/08/1944
PORTER, Edgar L., ssw-Martha B., b. 11/24/1919, d. 05/23/1992
PORTER, Elizabeth W., ssw-F. Carl, b. 1895, d. 1962
PORTER, F. Carl, ssw-Elizabeth W., b. 1896, d. 1962
PORTER, Martha B., ssw-Edgar L., b. 04/27/1926, d. N/D
POWELL, Elva V., ssw-George S., b. 1910, d. N/D
POWELL, George S., ssw-Elva V., b. 1906, d. 1993
PRICE, Delphos E., Sr., ssw-Michaeline A., b. 1931, d. N/D

PRICE, Michaeline A., ssw-Delphos E., Sr., b. 1936, d. N/D
PRINGLE, Pearl M., b. 02/21/1919, d. N/D
PRITCHETT, Bonnie L., ssw-Wm. Merrill, m. 6-1-1946, b. 1927, d. N/D
PRITCHETT, Wm. Merrill, ssw-Bonnie L., USA, m. 6-1-1946, b. 1913, d. 1996
PROKO, Samuel John, b. 06/08/1911, d. 08/23/1986
PRUITT, L. S., "Pete," b. 1925, d. 1992
PURNELL, Kathleen E., ssw-Leticia Y., b. 1941, d. N/D
PURNELL, Leticia Y., ssw-Kathleen E., b. 1964, d. N/D
PUSEY, Helen Jane, b. 11/04/1925, d. N/D
QUIGLEY, Clyde, Sr., BMC, USCG, WWII, b. 01/01/1907, d. 08/22/1995
QUIGLEY, Helen E., b. 08/27/1905, d. N/D
RANDER, Joseph G., ssw-Mabel, b. 1908, d. 1994
RANDER, Mabel, ssw-Joseph G., b. 1919, d. N/D
REARDON, Sally Ann, b. 1924, d. 1993
RECORDS, Imogene H., b. 1931, d. N/D
REED, Clarence Robert, Pfc., USA, WWII, b. 1919, d. 1976
REED, Frank J., ssw-Helen G., AS, USN, WWII, b. 04/24/1919, d. 05/03/1992
REED, Frank L., Sr., ssw-Margerite K., b. 1915, d. N/D
REED, Frederick E., GM2, USN, WWII, b. 07/17/1921, d. 01/05/1996
REED, Helen G., ssw-Frank J., b. 04/08/1930, d. N/D
REED, Iva Marie, b. 1914, d. 1978
REED, Margerite K., ssw-Frank L., Sr., b. 1916, d. N/D
REED, Mildred H., ssw-Weldon W., b. 1921, d. 1990
REED, Weldon W., ssw-Mildred H., b. 1918, d. 1993
REEDER, George Elwood, Sp2, USN, WWII, b. 1912, d. 1988
REMINGTON, Betty A., b. 1936, d. N/D
RENTZ, Roberta R., b. 1926, d. 1975
REYNOLDS, Doris D., b. 04/03/1917, d. 01/30/1962
REYNOLDS, Esther D., b. 07/05/1935, d. N/D
REYNOLDS, Helen S., ssw-Robert A., b. 1932, d. N/D
REYNOLDS, Katherine R., ssw-William S., b. 1918, d. N/D
REYNOLDS, Lillian M., b. 1944, d. N/D
REYNOLDS, Robert A., ssw-Helen S., b. 1915, d. N/D
REYNOLDS, Walter H., Jr., b. 1906, d. 1967
REYNOLDS, William S., ssw-Katherine R., b. 1906, d. 1976
RICE, Floris P., ssw-Wayland H., b. 10/25/06, d. 09/09/95
RICE, Wayland H., ssw-Floris P., b. 09/03/06, d. N/D
RICHARDS, Charles Harold, ssw-Elizabeth Lee, b. 1905, d. 1969
RICHARDS, Elizabeth Lee, ssw-Charles Harold, b. 1905, d. 1980
RICHARDSON, John H., III, ssw-Lydia Jean, b. 1938, d. N/D
RICHARDSON, Lydia Jean, ssw-John H., III, b. 1937, d. N/D
RICKS, Lucille M., ssw-Thomas E., b. 1919, d. N/D
RICKS, Thomas E., ssw-Lucille M., b. 1919, d. 1993
RITTER, Belinda A., ssw-Bert F., b. 1941, d. 1979
RITTER, Bert F., ssw-Belinda A., b. 1934, d. N/D
ROACH, Gladys M., ssw-William C., b. 1915, d. 1978
ROACH, William C., ssw-Gladys M., b. 1915, d. 1968
ROBERTS, Bobby L., ssw-Shirley L., b. 03/26/1929, d. N/D

ROBERTS, Harvey E., Sr., ssw-Pearl H., b. 1889, d. 1967

ROBERTS, L. June, ssw-Stephen W., b. 1917, d. 1991

ROBERTS, Pearl H., ssw-Harvey E., Sr., b. 1895, d. 1975

ROBERTS, Phoebe K., b. 1931, d. 1990

ROBERTS, Shirley L., ssw-Bobby L., b. 12/06/1929, d. N/D

ROBERTS, Stephen W., ssw-L. June, S1, USN, WWII, b. 06/17/1919, d. 05/01/1983

ROBERTS, Violette B., ssw-Raymond F. Seibert, b. 06/08/1922, d. N/D

ROCKWELL, Judy, ssw-Dennis V. Dangerfield, b. 08/03/1939, d. N/D

RODGERS, Patricia R., b. 1914, d. N/D

RODRIGUEZ, Agatha Vassalo, b. 1970, d. 1993

ROGERS, Etta Mae, ssw-Nelson A., b. 1904, d. 1993

ROGERS, Helen P., ssw-Lloyd T., b. 1906, d. N/D

ROGERS, James E., ssw-Randall C., b. 1919, d. 1984

ROGERS, John A., "Jack," b. 1934, d. N/D

ROGERS, Lloyd T., ssw-Helen P., b. 1908, d. 1979

ROGERS, Margaret M., b. 05/27/1917, d. N/D

ROGERS, Marie Warrington, b. 1935, d. N/D

ROGERS, Merrill L., b. 07/16/1913, d. 11/15/1957

ROGERS, Nelson A., ssw-Etta Mae, b. 1899, d. 1972

ROGERS, Randall C., ssw-James E., b. 1915, d. N/D

ROMIGH, Mary E., b. 1939, d. N/D

ROMIGH, Mike, b. 1938, d. N/D

ROONEY, Della M., ssw-William J., b. 1903, d. 1984

ROONEY, William J., ssw-Della M., b. 1899, d. 1973

ROSCH, Juanita M., b. 1932, d. 1989

ROSS, Donald L., Jr., b. 09/21/1974, d. 04/10/1975

RUBLE, Lloyd C., ssw-Wanda E., Pfc., USA, WWII, b. 1920, d. 1990

RUBLE, Wanda E., ssw-Lloyd C., b. 11/20/1921, d. N/D

RUDDY, Ruth K., ssw-Thomas L., b. 1919, d. N/D

RUDDY, Thomas L., ssw-Ruth K., b. 1914, d. 1991

RUDOLPH, Justine M., b. 1916, d. 1990

RUGER, Helen V., b. 1918, d. N/D

RUMER, Mabel K., b. 1916, d. 1985

RUSKY, Caroline Y., b. 1868, d. 1959

RUSKY, Katherine M., b. 1900, d. 1981

RUSKY, Mary L., b. 1902, d. 1978

RUST, Fred E., ssw-Katherine M., b. 1916, d. 1989

RUST, Katherine M., ssw-Fred E., b. 1919, d. N/D

RUTT, Margaret J., ssw-Reuben J., b. 1918, d. N/D

RUTT, Reuben J., ssw-Margaret J., b. 1908, d. 1983

RYALL, Roger C., b. 1926, d. N/D

RYNKOWSKI, Barbara L., ssw-Richard J., b. 1955, d. N/D

RYNKOWSKI, Richard J., ssw-Barbara L., b. 1954, d. N/D

SABATHNE, Henry A., Jr., ssw-Nancy E., 1st Lt., USA, WWII, b. 1917, d. N/D

SABATHNE, Nancy E., ssw-Henry A., Jr., b. 1932, d. 1988

SACKAWICZ, Emily M., b. 1929, d. N/D

SACKAWICZ, Michael P., b. 1927, d. N/D

SACKETT, Floyd W., PA, Pvt., 33 Co, 163L Depot Brig, WWI, b. 08/08/1897, d. 03/05/1968

SACKETT, Mary F., b. 02/25/1902, d. 01/14/1988
SAMMONS, Andrew J., b. 1904, d. 1954
SAMMONS, Anna M., b. 1913, d. N/D
SAMMONS, Dana Lynn, b. 02/12/1976, d. 04/26/1976
SAMMONS, Daniel R., ssw-Vicki A., b. 1945, d. N/D
SAMMONS, Vicki A., ssw-Daniel R., b. 1946, d. N/D
SAPP, Dewey E., ssw-Ruth P., b. 03/07/1926, d. 01/21/1982
SAPP, Ruth P., ssw-Dewey E., b. 09/25/1926, d. 03/03/1977
SAPP, Timothy Allan, b. 06/16/1950, d. 03/06/1957
SARD, Judith F., ssw-Leroy, b. 1943, d. N/D
SARD, Leroy, ssw-Judith F., b. 1940, d. N/D
SAVAGE, Myrtle, b. 10/08/1918, d. 01/04/1987
SAVAGE, Robert B., FM1, USN, WWII, b. 01/03/1907, d. 09/20/1984
SCHAEFER, Katheryn I., ssw-Richard B., b. 1911, d. 1991
SCHAEFER, Richard B., ssw-Katheryn I., b. 1915, d. 1977
SCHAEFFER, William H., b. 1928, d. N/D
SCHAFFER, Stella V., b. 02/04/1925, d. 08/06/1980
SCHEETZ, Agnes B., ssw-Leo W., b. 12/02/1910, d. N/D
SCHEETZ, Leo W., ssw-Agnes B., Cpl., USA, WWII, b. 06/28/1913, d. 02/24/1994
SCHEIRER, Gerald C., ssw-Sarah L., b. 1922, d. N/D
SCHEIRER, Sarah L., ssw-Gerald C., b. 1928, d. 1984
SCHIERER, Ruth M., b. 1927, d. 1962
SCHIRMER, Charles F., DE, TSgt., USA, WWII, b. 04/19/1919, d. 04/28/1961
SCHLEH, Lester C., ssw-Mildred V., b. 02/20/1912, d. 06/16/1991
SCHLEH, Mildred V., ssw-Lester C., b. 05/16/1916, d. N/D
SCHLITTER, Loretta R., b. 1933, d. N/D
SCHULER, Elizabeth E., ssw-William F., Sr., b. 1911, d. N/D
SCHULER, William F., Sr., ssw-Elizabeth E., b. 1904, d. 1978
SCHULZE, Selma G., ssw-Harold R. & Patricia J. Schulze Smith, b. 1914, d. 1996
SCHUMAN, Joyce H., b. 04/10/1931, d. N/D
SCHUYLER, Richard D., b. 1954, d. 1971
SCHWEBEL, Helen, b. 1921, d. N/D
SCOTT, Edward R., SMSgt., USAF, WWII, Korea, Vietnam, b. 05/07/1923, d. 05/02/1994
SCOTT, Nelda C., b. 1929, d. N/D
SEAMONE, Teresa M., w/o Woody, Age 65y, b. N/D, d. 06/03/1996
SEESMAN, Jacqueline S., ssw-Urban F., b. 1932, d. 1996
SEESMAN, Urban F., ssw-Jacqueline S., b. 1927, d. N/D
SEIBERT, Margaret P., ssw-Violette B. Roberts, b. 1914, d. 1980
SEIBERT, Raymond F., ssw-Violette B. Roberts, b. 1915, d. 1982
SEMPLE, Virginia, ssw-William T., b. 1921, d. N/D
SEMPLE, William T., ssw-Virginia, USCG, b. 09/2/1917, d. 01/03/1994
SHAFER, Allan M., ssw-Jessie E., b. 1919, d. N/D
SHAFER, Jessie E., ssw-Allan M., b. 1917, d. N/D
SHAFFER, Anna E., ssw-Victor L., b. 1922, d. N/D
SHAFFER, Victor L., ssw-Anna E., b. 1918, d. N/D
SHARP, Thelma L., ssw-W. Paynter, b. 10/08/1919, d. N/D
SHARP, W. Paynter, ssw-Thelma L., b. 12/12/1915, d. 12/17/1991
SHARY, Cecilia Rose, b. 02/19/1937, d. N/D

SHAUD, Harry A., ssw-Virginia M., b. 1910, d. N/D
SHAUD, Virginia M., ssw-Harry A., b. 1908, d. 1993
SHAY, Michael J., b. 1948, d. 1967
SHERMAN, Baby Girl, b. 02/02/1965, d. 02/02/1965
SHERMAN, Catherine L., ssw-Edwin L., b. 1933, d. N/D
SHERMAN, Doris A., w/o William, b. 06/13/1926, d. N/D
SHERMAN, Edwin L., ssw-Catherine L., b. 1931, d. N/D
SHERMAN, Howard B., ssw-Thelma L., b. 1935, d. N/D
SHERMAN, Thelma L., ssw-Howard B., b. 1942, d. N/D
SHOCKLEY, Elinor V., b. 1928, d. N/D
SHOCKLEY, Grace M., b. 10/22/1918, d. N/D
SHOOP, George R., ssw-Jeanne G., b. 1915, d. N/D
SHOOP, Jeanne G., ssw-George R., b. 1910, d. N/D
SHORT, Harold L., Pfc., USA, WWII, b. 1923, d. 1977
SHORT, Manford Fisher, Cpl., USA, WWII, b. 10/26/1915, d. 04/01/1978
SHOWELL, Anna M. B., b. 1923, d. N/D
SHUTE, Richard S., PA, Pfc., Btry F., 311 Fld. Arty, WWI, b. 11/21/1892, d. 06/7/1972
SHUTT, Herbert A., Jr., ssw-Rose Marie, b. 1926, d. N/D
SHUTT, Rose Marie, ssw-Herbert A., Jr., b. 1931, d. 1990
SIMMONS, Patsy A., b. 1940, d. N/D
SIMMS, Beatrice L., b. 1926, d. N/D
SIMMS, Richard S., b. 1921, d. N/D
SIMONS, D. Jean, b. 02/16/1929, d. N/D
SIMPERS, Cameron, ssw-Mary E., b. 1914, d. N/D
SIMPERS, Mary E., ssw-Cameron, b. 1919, d. N/D
SIPPLE, Alvetta N., b. 05/20/1931, d. 12/18/1987
SMITH, George V., Sr., PA, BM2, USNRF, WWI, b. 08/30/1897, d. 03/14/1964
SMITH, Cora I., ssw-James C., b. 1906, d. 1976
SMITH, Erma J., b. 11/23/1899, d. 10/12/1981
SMITH, Eugene D., b. 1928, d. 1993
SMITH, Eva M., ssw-James A., b. 1908, d. N/D
SMITH, F. Virginia, ssw-Noah B., b. 12/07/1921, d. 10/03/1995
SMITH, Florence C., b. 1930, d. N/D
SMITH, Gertrude R., ssw-Herman L., b. 08/03/1934, d. N/D
SMITH, Harold R., ssw-Patricia J. Schulze Smith and Selma G. Schulze, b. 1934, d. 1994
SMITH, Harry J., ssw-Marguerite D., b. 1895, d. 1995
SMITH, Henry F., ssw-Katherine M., b. 1900, d. 1975
SMITH, Herman L., ssw-Gertrude R., Tec5, USA, WWII, b. 04/17/1925, d. 06/15/1995
SMITH, Howard L., ssw-Lillian E., b. 08/06/1904, d. 04/25/1989
SMITH, James A., ssw-Eva M., b. 1920, d. N/D
SMITH, James C., ssw-Cora I., b. 1897, d. 1978
SMITH, James C., Jr., m. 6-20-1952, b. 1934, d. 1988
SMITH, Katherine M., ssw-Henry F., b. 1913, d. N/D
SMITH, Lillian E., ssw-Howard L., b. 06/15/1900, d. 11/28/1978
SMITH, Maggie J., b. 01/21/1898, d. 03/28/1993
SMITH, Margaret G., b. 1920, d. N/D
SMITH, Marguerite D., ssw-Harry J., b. 1900, d. 1982
SMITH, Matthew David, b. 07/30/1984, d. 01/28/1985

SMITH, Merritt F., b. 06/27/1893, d. 11/08/1954

SMITH, Noah B., ssw-F. Virginia, b. 08/19/1916, d. N/D

SMITH, Patricia J. Schulze, ssw-Harold R. Smith and Selma G. Schulze, b. 1935, d. N/D

SMITH, William S., Sr., b. 1913, d. 1963

SMYK, C. Sandi Sianni, ssw-Steven H., b. 1943, d. N/D

SMYK, Steven H., ssw-C. Sandi Sianni, b. 1945, d. N/D

SNAVELY, Craig Lee, b. 1964, d. 1989

SNELL, Christopher M., b. 10/24/1966, d. 10/29/1979

SNYDER, Betty A., b. 05/16/1926, d. N/D

SOCKOLOSKY, Jean E., ssw-William J., b. 1920, d. N/D

SOCKOLOSKY, William J., ssw-Jean E., b. 1913, d. 1989

SOOKIASIAN, Edith, b. 1915, d. N/D

SOUDER, Wilmer Emanuel, DE, SC3, USNR, WWII, b. 04/19/1913, d. 12/24/1962

SPICER, Elizabeth D., ssw-Howard N., b. 1917, d. 1977

SPICER, Howard N., ssw-Elizabeth D., b. 1916, d. 1979

SPICER, John S., ssw-Lydia A., b. 1887, d. 1974

SPICER, Lydia A., ssw-John S., b. 1885, d. 1972

SPOSATO, Frederick A., ssw-Jeanne D., DE, Pvt., Btry. B, 81 AAA, Bn. CAC, WWII, b. 11/04/1922, d. 03/19/1971

SPOSATO, Jeanne M., ssw-Frederick A., b. 10/21/1922, d. N/D

STAIB, Clare M., b. 09/14/1938, d. N/D

STANLEY, Florence J., b. 1932, d. N/D

STANSBURY, Phyllis J., b. 08/10/1922, d. N/D

STANSBURY, William F., b. 04/13/1916, d. 02/12/1996

STAUFFER, Daniel W., b. 05/21/1880, d. 05/02/1955

STAUFFER, Doris, A., b. 09/13/1924, d. N/D

STAUFFER, Florence M., b. 1896, d. 1992

STEAD, Edmund P., ssw-Ella Mae T., b. 1915, d. N/D

STEAD, Ella Mae T., ssw-Edmund P., b. 1918, d. N/D

STEELE, Alice M., ssw-George W., b. 1906, d. N/D

STEELE, Ellen L., ssw-Thomas E., b. 01/18/1895, d. 12/22/1957

STEELE, Francis P., ssw-Margaret J., Pfc., USA, WWII, b. 08/06/1923, d. 05/04/1993

STEELE, George W., ssw-Alice M., b. 1905, d. 1967

STEELE, Hazel J., ssw-Ralph T., b. 11/20/1926, d. N/D

STEELE, Joseph F., SSgt., USA, WWII, b. 12/11/1916, d. 08/12/1993

STEELE, Margaret J., ssw-Francis P., b. 05/09/1927, d. N/D

STEELE, Ralph T., ssw-Hazel J., Tec5, USA, WWII, b. 05/15/1914, d. 11/11/1995

STEELE, Suenell G., ssw-W. Darrell, b. 1950, d. N/D

STEELE, Thomas E., ssw-Ellen L., b. 09/30/1899, d. 12/04/1970

STEELE, W. Darrell, ssw-Suenell G., b. 1945, d. N/D

STEELMAN, Elodea C. M., ssw-Howard L., b. 1924, d. 1981

STEELMAN, Howard L., ssw-Elodea C. M., b. 1920, d. 1981

STEVENSON, Mabel E., ssw-Percy D., b. 1898, d. 1990

STEVENSON, Percy D., ssw-Mabel E., b. 1894, d. 1968

STEVENSON Vaughn H., b. 1904, d. 1971

STEVERSON, Yvonne A., b. 1935, d. N/D

STEWART, George W., ssw-Mary C., b. 1897, d. 1994

STEWART, Mary C., ssw-George W., b. 1904, d. N/D

STOTT, Hilda B., ssw-Robert B., b. 1926, d. N/D
STOTT, Robert B., ssw-Hilda B., b. 1916, d. N/D
SULLIVAN, Charles H., ssw-Shirley L., b. 1927, d. 1995
SULLIVAN, Edward, ssw-Elizabeth, b. 1896, d. 1979
SULLIVAN, Elizabeth, ssw-Edward, b. 1897, d. 1994
SULLIVAN, Shirley L., ssw-Charles H., b. 1932, d. N/D
SWINZOW, George, ssw-Wilhelmine, b. 03/11/1906, d. 10/02/1973
SWINZOW, Wilhelmine, ssw-George, b. 06/24/1923, d. N/D
SZEG, Edith, ssw-Louis F., b. 1928, d. N/D
SZEG, Louis F., ssw-Edith, b. 1924, d. N/D
TABOR, James E., ssw-Ruth M., b. 1916, d. 1991
TABOR, Ruth M., ssw-James E., b. N/D, d. N/D
TAYLOR, Donald J., ssw-Martha L., b. 1939, d. N/D
TAYLOR, Mabel E., "Dottie," b. 05/20/1911, d. 05/21/1989
TAYLOR, Martha L., ssw-Donald J., b. 1941, d. N/D
TAYLOR, Mary M., b. 1945, d. N/D
THOMAS, Doris L., ssw-Nelson A., b. 1933, d. N/D
THOMAS, Nelson A., ssw-Doris L., b. 1920, d. 1986
THOMPSON, Alice I., ssw-John B., b. 1919, d. 1990
THOMPSON, Allanora E., ssw-Harry R., b. 1957, d. N/D
THOMPSON, Ethel M., ssw-Joseph J., Sr., b. 1899, d. 1980
THOMPSON, Glenwood E., b. 1922, d. 1979
THOMPSON, Harry R., ssw-Allanora E., b. 1949, d. N/D
THOMPSON, John B., ssw-Alice I., b. 1915, d. 1991
THOMPSON, Joseph J., Sr., ssw-Ethel M., b. 1897, d. 1970
THOMPSON, Kathleen K., b. 1924, d. 1991
THOMPSON, Linda F., b. 1955, d. N/D
THOMPSON, Minnie N., ssw-William H., b. 1909, d. 1993
THOMPSON, William C., ssw-William F. Dickerson, b. 1965, d. N/D
THOMPSON, William H., ssw-Minnie N., b. 1911, d. N/D
TINGLE, Arley Lester, ssw-Rose Jeanette, b. 1910, d. 1989
TINGLE, Charles A., DE, SSgt., USAF, b. 01/31/1926, d. 07/05/1967
TINGLE, Marguerite, ssw-Melvin E., b. 04/21/1914, d. 02/07/1986
TINGLE, Melvin E., ssw-Marguerite, USA, WWII, b. 11/02/1916, d. 10/15/1991
TINGLE, Rose Jeanette, ssw-Arley Lester, b. 1916, d. 1989
TOLBERT, Deborah B., b. 1927, d. N/D
TOLMIE, John Joseph, S1, USN, WWII, b. 01/13/1919, d. 05/18/1994
TORBERT, Herber R., b. 1895, d. 1990
TORBERT, Mary L., b. 1892, d. 1960
TORRACK, Frank A., Jr., ssw-Phyllis K., b. 1921, d. 1993
TORRACK, Phyllis K., ssw-Frank A., Jr., b. 1926, d. N/D
TOWERY, Olen Thomas, b. 06/22/1915, d. 02/17/1995
TRENCH, William R., b. 1940, d. 1981
TRIBBITT, Arthur M., ssw-Hazel, b. 1925, d. 1980
TRIBBITT, Hazel, ssw-Arthur M., b. 1930, d. 1980
TRUITT, Alice B., ssw-William E., b. 1917, d. N/D
TRUITT, Emma W., ssw-Frank W., b. 1922, d. N/D
TRUITT, Frances Wilson, b. 12/21/1923, d. N/D

TRUITT, Frank W., ssw-Emma W., USN, WWII, b. 10/05/1919, d. 06/17/1995

TRUITT, Helen M., b. 08/22/1908, d. 07/26/1985

TRUITT, James Linford, Jr., b. 02/17/1923, d. N/D

TRUITT, Joseph Martin, Sr., ssw-Norma Lee, b. 1926, d. 1979

TRUITT, Kelly Dale, b. 1954, d. 1976

TRUITT, Larry Lee, b. 1952, d. 1970

TRUITT, Norma Lee, ssw-Joseph Martin, Sr., b. 1925, d. N/D

TRUITT, Rowland P., DE, 1st Lt., USMCR, b. 03/01/1920, d. 03/25/1965

TRUITT, Stacy Lynn, b. 04/02/1979, d. 04/02/1979

TRUITT, William E., ssw-Alice B., b. 1917, d. 1964

TRUMBALL, Grace S., b. 1923, d. N/D

TUCKER, Carolyn A., ssw-Ralph L., b. 1939, d. N/D

TUCKER, E. Marie, ssw-R. Elwood, b. 1922, d. N/D

TUCKER, Fannie W., ssw-Raymond A., b. 10/15/1893, d. 03/20/1967

TUCKER, Hazel L., ssw-Ralph, b. 1933, d. N/D

TUCKER, Leon R., b. 1950, d. N/D

TUCKER, R. Elwood, ssw-E. Marie, b. 1922, d. 1986

TUCKER, Ralph, ssw-Hazel L., b. 1930, d. N/D

TUCKER, Ralph L., ssw-Carolyn A., b. 1933, d. N/D

TUCKER, Raymond A., ssw-Fannie W., b. 03/12/1894, d. 11/21/1968

TULL, Randy A., b. 07/06/1960, d. 08/04/1983

TURNER, Emmor F., ssw-Etta M., b. 1900, d. 1974

TURNER, Etta M., ssw-Emmor F., b. 1901, d. 1994

TURNER, Homer M., ssw-Nellie M., b. 1893, d. 1966

TURNER, Linda E., b. 1950, d. 1958

TURNER, Lucille R., b. 1928, d. N/D

TURNER, Nellie M., ssw-Homer M., b. 1894, d. 1983

TURNER, Roy William, Sgt., USA, Korea, b. 1929, d. 1976

TWILLEY, Florence T., b. 1913, d. 1957

TYNDALL, Bernice L., Granville A., b. 1907, d. 1983

TYNDALL, Granville A., ssw-Bernice L., b. 1906, d. 1971

URIE, Elsie M., ssw-Kenneth H., b. 1920, d. N/D

URIE, Kenneth H., ssw-Elsie M., b. 1929, d. N/D

VAN AUKEN, Hazel R., ssw-James W., b. 1906, d. 1989

VAN AUKEN, James W., ssw-Hazel R., b. 1900, d. 1988

VANNESS, Iona M., ssw-Joan M. Dotterer, b. 1926, d. N/D

VARI, Angela M., "Angie," ssw-Francis J., Jr., b. 1938, d. N/D

VARI, Francis J., Jr., ssw-Angela M., b. 1932, d. 1995

VASSALLO, John T., ssw-Marie G., USN, b. 1934, d. N/D

VASSALLO, Marie G., ssw-John T., b. 1934, d. N/D

VEASEY, I. Dallas, Sp4, USA, b. 11/01/1937, d. 02/06/1995

VIENOT, Edna J., ssw-Irving, b. 11/25/1909, d. 12/14/1972

VIENOT, Irving, ssw-Edna J., b. 07/13/1896, d. 04/29/1964

VOGL, Dorothy M., ssw-Frederick Otto, b. 05/12/1916, d. N/D

VOGL, Frederick Otto, ssw-Dorothy M., b. 12/10/1899, d. 01/20/1985

VOLBERDING, Catherine F., ssw-LeRoy G., b. 10/10/1926, d. 09/06/1986

VOLBERDING, LeRoy G., ssw-Catherine F., USN, b. 03/17/1926, d. 08/20/1989

VREELAND, Howard S., 1st Lt., USA, WWII, b. 06/09/1908, d. 03/28/1982

VREELAND, John H., ssw-Luella T., b. 1879, d. 1961
VREELAND, Luella T., ssw-John H., b. 1876, d. 1962
WALKER, Elizabeth J., ssw-J. Dudley, b. 12/30/1893, d. 06/10/1985
WALKER, Gerald James, SSgt., USA, WWII, b. 09/30/1922, d. 08/14/1976
WALKER, J. Dudley, ssw-Elizabeth J., b. 12/06/1894, d. 03/15/1970
WALKER, John N., CPO, USN, b. 02/14/1928, d. 06/05/1993
WALKER, Martha E., ssw-Paul E., Sr., b. 01/31/1933, d. N/D
WALKER, Paul E., Sr., ssw-Martha E., b. 07/16/1930, d. 04/19/1988
WALLS, Cora M., ssw-George T., b. 1905, d. 1981
WALLS, Earl E., Pvt., USA, WWII, b. 11/03/1906, d. 07/21/1977
WALLS, Elizabeth A., ssw-Raymond L., b. 02/12/1912, d. 10/03/1983
WALLS, Elva, ssw-Frank J., b.1909, d. 1987
WALLS, Elwood B., DE, BM1, USCG, WWII, b. 09/23/1907, d. 06/02/1968
WALLS, Frank J., ssw-Elva, b. 1902, d. 1989
WALLS, George T., ssw-Cora M., b. 1897, d. 1968
WALLS, Joseph B., b. 1908, d. 1981
WALLS, Raymond L., ssw-Elizabeth A., b. 07/21/1910, d. 10/05/1975
WALSH, Jerome P., ssw-Madeline A., b. 1894, d. 1967
WALSH, John E., b. 1925, d. N/D
WALSH, Madeline A., ssw-Jerome P., b. 1899, d. 1963
WALSH, Patrick Stanford, b. 10/19/1963, d. 03/04/1964
WALSH, Timothy Gerad, b. 09/18/1961, d. 09/18/1961
WARD, Edith O., ssw-Ridgley W., b. 1916, d. 1990
WARD, John L., b. 1943, d. 1982
WARD, Madison G., ssw-Marian C., b. 09/20/1917, d. 04/08/1965
WARD, Marian C., ssw-Madison G., b.03/17/1928, d. N/D
WARD, Ridgley W., ssw-Edith O., b. 1911, d. 1968
WARNEKE, Thelma M., b. 1915, d. N/D
WARRINGTON, Anna H., ssw-David C., b. 08/21/1927, d. 04/19/1993
WARRINGTON, Daniel Eugene, b. 11/09/1975, d. 02/20/1976
WARRINGTON, David C., ssw-Anna H., SSgt., USAF, WWII, Kora, b. 05/15/1926, d. 09/27/1985
WARRINGTON, Fred C., ssw-Patricia A., b. 1931, d. N/D
WARRINGTON, Howard L., ssw-Virginia Lee, b. 10/18/1923, d. 10/08/1982
WARRINGTON, James H., ssw-Mamie P., b. 1901, d. 1987
WARRINGTON, Mamie P., ssw-James H., b. 1903, d. 1985
WARRINGTON, Patricia A., ssw-Fred C., b. 1933, d. 1993
WARRINGTON, Virginia Lee, ssw-Howard L., b. 07/03/1926, d. 02/02/1996
WATKINS, Georgia A., ssw-Nelson W., b. 03/22/1916, d. N/D
WATKINS, Nelson W., ssw-Georgia A., b. 05/10/1917, d. 03/19/1980
WATSON, Elmer B., DE, Pvt., Med. Dept., WWI, b. 05/25/1896, d. 02/22/1970
WEAVER, Bertha L., ssw-Miles H., b. 1910, d. 1991
WEAVER, Miles H., ssw-Bertha L., b. 1909, d. 1994
WEBB, Cyril D., ssw-Sylvia G., b. 1927, d. 1987
WEBB, J. Willis, ssw-Myrl McN., m. 6-9-1934, b. 12/23/1907, d. 03/27/1987
WEBB, Jesse Colin, DE, Eoh3, USN, b. 06/13/1936, d. 01/10/1972
WEBB, Myrl McN., ssw- J. Willis, m. 6-9-1934, b. 06/12/1909, d. N/D
WEBB, Sylvia G., ssw-Cyril D., b. 1936, d. N/D
WEEMSTEIN, Isaac M., Pvt., USA, WWII, b. 12/25/1912, d. 02/20/1993

WELCH, Glenn F., b. 1902, d. 1984
WELLER, Ruby L., b. 1925, d. N/D
WELLER, Sharon E., b. 1948, d. N/D
WELLS, Baby, b. 06/22/1963, d. 06/22/1963
WELLS, Evelyn M., b. 01/06/1934, d. 04/09/1960
WELLS, James T., b. 1957, d. 1989
WEST, B. Agnes, ssw-M. L., b. 1924, d. N/D
WEST, Charlotte W., ssw-Emory R., Sr., b. 1931, d. N/D
WEST, Doris W., ssw-Lewis W., b. 09/04/1934, d. N/D
WEST, Emory R., Sr., ssw-Charlotte W., b. 1932, d. 1984
WEST, Howard T., ssw-Mary V., b. 1916, d. 1995
WEST, Lewis W., ssw-Doris W., b. 09/24/1933, d. N/D
WEST, M. L., "Sam," ssw-B. Agnes, b. 1923, d. 1995
WEST, Mary V., ssw-Howard T., b. 1912, d. N/D
WESTMAN, Bertel R., ssw-Lora E., b. 1920, d. 1981
WESTMAN, Lora E., ssw-Bertel R., b. 1919, d. 1981
WHALEN, James M., b. 1918, d. 1982
WHEELER, Hugh D., b. 1940, d. 1973
WHITBACK, John A., ssw-Susan E., USN, b. 1929, d. N/D
WHITBACK, Susan E., ssw-John A., b. 1942, d. N/D
WHITE, Anna M., ssw-Hiram T., b. 1908, d. 1982
WHITE, Dorothy, b. 1931, d. N/D
WHITE, Geneva A., b. 1927, d. N/D
WHITE, Hiram T., ssw-Anna M., b. 1894, d. 1983
WHITE, Jack P., Lt., USN, WWII, b. 1911, d. 1981
WHITE, Joan, b. 12/22/1937, d. 11/24/1964
WHITE, Margaret L., b. 1943, d. N/D
WHITE, Virginia M., ssw-Willard H., b. 12/29/1903, d. 04/20/1982
WHITE, Willard H., ssw-Virginia M., b. 01/08/1898, d. 08/14/1928
WHITMAN, E. Jackson, ssw-Margaret R., b. 1900, d. 1985
WHITMAN, Margaret R., ssw-E. Jackson, b. 1901, d. 1978
WIECKOWSKI, Elizabeth M., ssw-Stefan, b. 1894, d. 1979
WIECKOWSKI, Stefan, ssw-Elizabeth M., b. 1893, d. 1969
WIEDEL, Patricia L., b. 03/11/1934, d. N/D
WILKERSON, Edward J., b. 1924, d. 1987
WILKERSON, Everett M., ssw-Margaret Wilkerson James, DE, GM2, USNR, b. 08/12/1917, d. 12/05/1965
WILKERSON, Lillian J., ssw-Walter, b. 1928, d. N/D
WILKERSON, Lovela M., b. 07/05/1914, d. 11/12/1995
WILKERSON, Walter, ssw-Lillian J., b.1926, d. N/D
WILKIE, Donald R., ssw-Doris W., b. 1895, d. 1970
WILKIE, Doris W., ssw-Donald R., b. 1902, d. N/D
WILKIE, Elizabeth L., b. 04/24/1937, d. N/D
WILKIE, Rea W., A1C, USAF, Korea, b. 07/12/1930, d. 06/08/1992
WILKINS, Floyd T., ssw-Mary E., b. 1892, d. 1975
WILKINS, Margaret E., ssw-Roland M., b. 1919, d. N/D
WILKINS, Mary E., ssw-Floyd T., b. 1897, d. 1987
WILKINS, Nora L., ssw-Robert S., b. 1926, d. N/D
WILKINS, Robert S., ssw-Nora L., b. 1918, d. N/D

WILKINS, Roland M., ssw-Margaret E., b. 1915, d. N/D
WILKINSON, Lillian M., ssw-Ralph D., Jr., b. 12/14/1916, d. 10/02/1993
WILKINSON, Ralph D., Jr., ssw-Lillian M., b. 10/17/1906, d. 11/22/1972
WILLEY, Carolyn, b. 1935, d. 1984
WILLEY, Deborah T., b. 1953, d. 1972
WILLEY, Doris L. J., ssw-Paul S., b. 1936, d. 1979
WILLEY, Dorothy E., b. 1923, d. N/D
WILLEY, John L., b. 1884, d. 1957
WILLEY, Paul S., ssw-Doris L. J., b. 1903, d. N/D
WILSON, Albert L., ssw-Gladys I., b. 1906, d. 1996
WILSON, Bertha M., ssw-Harry B., b. 1902, d. 1995
WILSON, Elmer J., ssw-Norma L., b. 1933, d. N/D
WILSON, Frank J., b. 1903, d. 1970
WILSON, Gladys I., ssw-Albert L., b. 1908, d. 1994
WILSON, Harry B., ssw-Bertha M., b. 1900, d. 1983
WILSON, Madeline L., ssw-Wm. Clifford, b. 1910, d. N/D
WILSON, Margaret J., b. 1899, d. 1975
WILSON, Norma L., ssw-Elmer J., b. 1934, d. 1988
WILSON, Vernon D., Cpl., USA, WWII, b. 08/16/1919, d. 02/13/1982
WILSON, Wm. Clifford, ssw-Madeline L., b. 1906, d. 1969
WINGATE, Harold L., Sr., ssw-Joyce A., b. 1940, d. N/D
WINGATE, Joyce A., ssw-Harold L., Sr., b. 1938, d. N/D
WINTERBOTTOM, Edith D., ssw-Thomas L., b. 1922, d. N/D
WINTERBOTTOM, Thomas L., ssw-Edith D., 1st Sgt., USA, WWII, b. 08/11/1917, d. 06/03/1994
WITTENBERG, Claire R., ssw-Leonard C., b. 1919, d. N/D
WITTENBERG, Leonard C., ssw-Claire R., b. 1918, d. N/D
WOLSTENHOLME, Edward V., ssw-Lee O., b. 1913, d. N/D
WOLSTENHOLME, Lee O., ssw-Edward V., b. 1919, d. 1990
WOOD, Anna L., b. 10/16/1907, d. 02/12/1989
WOOD, Florence E., b. 1904, d. 1993
WOODING, Henry C., ssw-Kimberly A., b. 1960, d. N/D
WOODING, Kimberly A., ssw-Henry C., b. 1960, d. N/D
WOODRUM, Marion L., b. 1942, d. N/D
WOODS, Anita J., b. 1925, d. N/D
WOOTERS, Rhoda A., ssw-William T., Sr., b. 1896, d. 1991
WOOTERS, Sara R., ssw-William T., Jr., b. 1918, d. N/D
WOOTERS, William T., Jr., ssw-Sara R., b. 1917, d. 1987
WOOTERS, William T., Sr., ssw-Rhoda A., b. 1892, d. 1988
WORKMAN, Helen E., b. 10/21/1915, d. 05/25/1984
WORKMAN, Louise E., ssw-Willard H., b. 09/07/1916, d. N/D
WORKMAN, Robert, Pfc., USA, b. 01/03/1909, d. 08/16/1974
WORKMAN, Willard H., ssw-Louise E., b. 02/18/1916, d. N/D
WORRELL, Robert N., Cpl., USA, WWII, b. 1906, d. 1987
WRIGHT, Daniel Frederick, Sr., b. 01/14/1936, d. N/D
WRIGHT, Gladys L., ssw-Samuel A., b. 1912, d. 1969
WRIGHT, Samuel A., ssw-Gladys L., b. 1896, d. 1980
WYATT, James H., ssw-Martha E., b. 1918, d. 1983
WYATT, Martha E., ssw-James H., b. 1918, d. 1974

WYATT, Russell C., Sr., b. 1919, d. 1991
WYLAND, Dean R., ssw-Virginia B., b. 1917, d. 1996
WYLAND, Virginia B., ssw-Dean R., b. 1923, d. N/D
YEP, Lilly L., b. 1913, d. 1985
YOURGAL, F. Irene, b. 1928, d. N/D
YOURGAL, John A., TSgt., USA, WWII, b. 04/14/1919, d. 01/27/1985
ZELENSKY, Thomas, Cpl., USA, WWII, b. 12/14/1910, d. 06/29/1983
ZEWSKI, Frances B., b. 07/1920, d. 01/1994
ZIEBER, Lydia K., b. 1922, d. N/D
ZOOK, Ada E., ssw-Clyde, b. 1896, d. 1977
ZOOK, Clyde, ssw-Ada E., b. 1893, d. 1962

(BK-006 & HU-NR) ZION U. M. CHURCH CEMETERY

Located East of Milton on the Northwest side of Broadkill Rd. (Rt. 16) 0.2 miles Southwest of Coastal Highway (Rt. 1).
Recorded: October 14, 1996

AIKINS, Susannah H., w/o John S., Age 27y 10m 24d. b. N/D, d. 10/24/1858
AIKINS, William H., s/o John S. & Susannah H., Age 2y 9m 13d, b. N/D, d. 08/01/1853
ATKIN, Elizabeth, w/o Samuel R., b. 12/26/1830, d. 06/09/1897
ATKIN, John B., b. N/D, d. 02/01/1918
ATKIN, Samuel R., b. 11/14/1829, d. 04/10/1906
ATKIN, Walter F., Age 23y 23d, b. N/D, d. 01/23/1890
BAIRD, Margarete, (Aunt), b. N/D, d. 06/21/1921
BENNETT, Hester A., ssw-Stephen R., b. 05/20/1827, d. 03/02/1891
BENNETT, Stephen R., ssw-Hester A., b. 02/16/1827, d. 01/18/1906
BLACK, Amanda M., ssw-J. Leon, b. 1888, d. 1968
BLACK, J. Leon, ssw-Amanda M., b. 1888, d. 1958
BRITTINGHAM, Elva D., b. 1929, d. 1936
BRITTINGHAM, Granville H., b. 02/10/1933, d. 09/24/1986
BRITTINGHAM, Ralph H., b. 1897, d. 1960
BRITTINGHAM, Richard L., b. 09/13/1939, d. 02/17/1974
BRYAN, Andrew T., ssw-Ella N., b. 01/28/1862, d. 11/04/1915
BRYAN, Annie L., d/o William & Clara, Age 11m 20d, b. N/D, d. 08/08/1883
BRYAN, Arzelia M., d/o William & Clara, Age 11y 1m 28d, b. N/D, d. 03/07/1893
BRYAN, Clara B., w/o William, b. 11/22/1860, d. 12/09/1896
BRYAN, Ella N., ssw-Andrew T., b. 10/28/1873, d. 03/19/1953
BRYAN, George E., b. 02/05/1859, d. 03/19/1906
BRYAN, Mary E., d/o William & Clara, Age 14y 4m 16d, b. N/D, d. 01/01/1892
BRYAN, Mary J., w/o Robt. B., ssw-Robt. B., b. 1833, d. 1908
BRYAN, Robt. B., ssw-Mary J., b. 1828, d. 1892
BRYAN, Sallie S., d/o William & Clara, Age 1y 17d, b. N/D, d. 08/22/1886
BRYAN, Walter J., s/o William & Clara, Age 8m 8d, b. N/D, d. 04/26/1892
BRYAN, Weldon A., s/o Andrew & Ella N., Age 1y 6m, b. 09/07/1894, d. 03/07/1896
BUNTING, Betty M., "Shelly," ssw-Charles S., b. 07/16/1954, d. 05/01/1974
BUNTING, Charles S., ssw-Betty M., b. 07/02/1950, d. N/D
CAHALL, Ethel M., b. 1917, d. 1993
CAMPER, Howard, s/o Thomas & Lena, b. 01/18/1876, d. 01/04/1907

CAREY, Alice S., w/o Wm. E., ssw-Samuel Lofland, b. 04/14/1858, d. 08/05/1889
CAREY, Bertha L., ssw-Ruth R. C. Wagamon, b. 06/23/1898, d. 09/09/1981
CAREY, Henrietta, d/o Henry & Maria, b. 04/09/1860, d. 11/22/1905
CAREY, Leroy E., ssw-Bertha L., b. 11/21/1897, d. 01/30/1986
CLENDANIEL, James F., DE, Pvt., USA, WWI, b. 01/19/1896, d. 03/20/1973
CLIFTON, Elva D., ssw-Otis H., b. 07/07/1913, d. N/D
CLIFTON, Otis H., ssw-Elva D., b. 08/30/1909, d. 01/19/1972
CONWELL, Asa T., ssw-Nancy, b. 1860, d. 1889
CONWELL, Elizabeth A., ssw-Robert R., b. 01/03/1838, d. 08/04/1911
CONWELL, Esther D., w/o Joseph, b. 02/01/1804, d. 09/30/1886
CONWELL, Joseph, s/o Joseph & Esther, b. 06/01/1839, d. 07/01/1839
CONWELL, Joseph, s/o Joseph & Esther, b. 12/18/1830, d. 11/05/1832
CONWELL, Joseph, ssw-Esther D., b. 02/14/1803, d. 10/26/1858
CONWELL, Josephine, d/o Joseph & Esther, b. 01/23/1846, d. 07/30/1846
CONWELL, Lydia Ellen, b. 06/26/1840, d. 11/16/1917
CONWELL, Mary P., w/o Nehemiah J., b. 09/14/1850, d. 03/22/1911
CONWELL, Miers C., ssw-Joseph, died in South America, b. 11/27/1827, d. 11/07/1885
CONWELL, Nancy, ssw-Asa T., b. 1815, d. 1890
CONWELL, Nehemiah J., b. 05/05/1844, d. 03/31/1897
CONWELL, Robert R., ssw-Elizabeth A., b. 05/14/1837, d. 06/15/1902
CONWELL, Sarah A., ssw-Asa T., b. 1830, d. 1895
CONWELL, Sarah A., ssw-Robert R., b. 10/09/1864, d. 09/24/1887
CONWELL, William A., Age 61y 1m 25d, b. N/D, d. 05/04/1877
CONWELL, William E., s/o Joseph & Esther, Captain, b. 03/31/1826, d. 11/27/1883
CONWELL, William J., ssw-Asa T., b. 1858, d. 1908
CONWELL, William O. P., b. 09/25/1876, d. 03/10/1903
CRAIG, Mary A., ssw-Martha A. Jones, b. 04/13/1830, d. 04/01/1911
DAVIDSON, C. Harry, b. 11/16/1882, d. 01/28/1951
DAVIDSON, Cornelius A., b. 10/26/1859, d. 02/19/1945
DAVIDSON, Eddie Walsh, s/o C. A. & Mary S., b. 09/18/1886, d. 09/22/1892
DAVIDSON, Fannie G., ssw-Hyson B., b. 1874, d. 1965
DAVIDSON, George Emily, d/o C. A. & Mary S., b. 09/13/1880, d. 01/31/1898
DAVIDSON, Hyson B., ssw-Fannie G., b. 1870, d. 1934
DAVIDSON, Jane M., ssw-Philip R., b. 1850, d. 1936
DAVIDSON, John R., ssw-James F. Roach, b. 1840, d. 1908
DAVIDSON, Mary S. Johnson, b. 01/30/1864, d. 03/09/1951
DAVIDSON, Philip R., ssw-Jane M., b. 1850, d. 1936
DAVIS, Leroy Vernon, b. 08/17/1878, d. 07/19/1954
DEAN, John E., b. 10/19/1856, d. 04/28/1941
DONOVAN, Gladys E., ssw-Russell E., b. 06/16/1924, d. N/D
DONOVAN, Russell E., ssw-Gladys E., 15th AF, WWII, b. 02/27/1925, d. N/D
DORN, Harry E., ssw-John T. & Emma J.Williams, b. 1870, d. 1952
DORN, Mary E., w/o Harry, ssw-John T. & Emma J. Williams, b. 1866, d. 1960
ELLINGSWORTH, Gary L., b. 05/18/1949, d. 01/20/1996
ELLINGSWORTH, H. Franklin, b. 07/26/1922, d. 07/02/1958
ELLINGSWORTH, Jean E., b. 01/11/1929, d. N/D
GIFFORD, David, b. 03/22/1859, d. 08/08/1925
GIFFORD, Jennie A., b.11/09/1858, d. 03/27/1928

HAZZARD, Coard, ssw-Sarah Wiltbank, Capt. 1st DE. Reg. Milita, Rev. War, b. 04/28/1750, d. 03/13/1831

HEATHER, Hester J., w/o Horatio N., Age 76y 1m 14d, b. N/D, d. 03/07/1898

HEATHER, Horatio N., Age 76y 6m 8d, b. N/D, d. 07/28/1888

HEAVELO, Jonathan, Age 59y 7m 19d, b. N/D, d. 01/09/1825

HILL, Edwin C., b. 09/12/1930, d. 03/16/1969

HUDSON, Clifford L., DE, Pfc., 216 AAA, Gun Bn. CAC, WWII, b. 10/15/1923, d. 05/18/1972

JACKSON, Julias A., Age about 65y, b. N/D, d. 01/03/1864

JEFFERSON, Baby, b. 1930, d. 1930

JEFFERSON, Billy, b. 1931, d. 1933

JEFFERSON, Elnora J., b. 1927, d. 1927

JEFFERSON, Emma Wyatt, ssw-Layton P., b. 05/19/1916, d. N/D

JEFFERSON, Helen J., ssw-Joseph R., b. 1912, d. 1978

JEFFERSON, Joseph R., b. 1917, d. 1918

JEFFERSON, Joseph R., ssw-Helen J., b. 1912, d. 1981

JEFFERSON, Layton P., ssw-Emma Wyatt, b. 03/25/1915, d. 02/06/1984

JEFFERSON, Robert S., b. 1925, d. 1983

JEFFERSON, Samuel B., b. 1899, d. 1945

JEFFERSON, Sarah P., b. 1902, d. 1994

JEFFERSON, William P., b. 1888, d. 1917

JOHNSON, Clara S., b. 09/07/1849, d. 12/31/1931

JOHNSON, Elwood W. L., ssw-Sarah R. Weber, b. 11/27/1921, d. N/D

JOHNSON, Frank W., b. 07/27/1858, d. 03/26/1920

JOHNSON, Geo. A., Capt., b. 1861, d. 1921

JOHNSON, George H., s/o Lydia A. & Harry P., b. N/D, d. N/D

JOHNSON, Harry P., ssw-Lydia A., b. 1887, d. 1928

JOHNSON, Lydia A., ssw-Harry P., b. 1886, d. 1918

JOHNSON, Sarah R. Weber, ssw-Elwood W. L., b. 09/30/1922, d. N/D

JONES, Arthur C., s/o Kensey & Matilda, b. 12/12/1870, d. 02/03/1875

JONES, Arthur R., ssw-Matilda A., b. 07/09/1876, d. 07/12/1969

JONES, Clara M., ssw-Matilda A., b. 06/25/1884, d. 02/23/1977

JONES, Edna F., ssw-Matilda A., b. 1910, d. 1910

JONES, Kensey J., s/o James W. & Elizabeth D., b. 09/04/1831, d. 05/04/1901

JONES, Martha A., ssw-Mary A. Craig, b. 10/02/1856, d. 08/24/1906

JONES, Matilda A., w/o Kensey J., b. 01/25/1836, d. 06/09/1914

KING, Margaret Emily, w/o James King & d/o David & Sarah Wiltbank, b. 08/02/1833, d. 11/09/1921.
    [Note: Also has a stone with Margaret Wiltbank King, b. 1833, d. 1921.]

LEVERAGE, Fannie E., ssw-Nathaniel R., b. 03/28/1880, d. 10/06/1959

LEVERAGE, Nathaniel R., ssw-Fannie E., b. 08/28/1874, d. 01/31/1960

LILLY, Horace W., Age 29y, b. N/D, d. 05/19/1893

LOFLAND, Joseph L., ssw-Samuel, b. 12/22/1866, d. 08/31/1872

LOFLAND, Mary H. Cade, ssw-Samuel, b. 02/08/1839, d. 12/29/1898

LOFLAND, Samuel, ssw-Mary H. Cade, b. 01/29/1835, d. 03/21/1906

LOFLAND, Samuel C., ssw-Samuel, b. 01/06/1864, d. 09/23/1889

LOOCKERMAN, Mae, b. 12/27/1906, d. 11/09/1978

LOOCKERMAN, Samuel G., b. 09/22/1901, d. 05/19/1952

LOOCKERMAN, Sarah A., b. 07/14/1873, d. 07/22/1942

LOOCKERMAN, Sarah E., b. 09/28/1900, d. 12/22/1966

LYNCH, Sarah B., b. 01/09/1801, d. 09/25/1891

MILLIKEN, Sarah, Aunt, b. N/D, d. 07/25/1918
MOORE, Charles M., b. 1880, d. 1936
MOORE, Edna A., b. 1884, d. 1961(
MOORE, John F., ssw-Laura C., b. 1886, d. 1946
MOORE, Joseph K., Capt., b. 10/18/1844, d. 11/271915
MOORE, Laura C., ssw-John F., b. 1890, d. 1974
MOORE, Mary K., b. 11/17/1845, d. 12/27/1921
MORGAN, Charles N., ssw-Sallie W., b. 1877, d. 1962
MORGAN, Sallie W., ssw-Charles N., b. 1883, d. 1988
MORRIS, Ann, w/o Heavelo & d/o Milby & Hester Simpler, Age 80y 10m 10d, b. N/D, d. 05/16/1897
MORRIS, Heavelo, Age 71y 5m 2d, b. N/D, d. 04/18/1887
MORRIS, Susanah, Age 65y 11d, b. N/D, d. 09/26/1845
MORRIS, William R., Age 20y 11m 27d, b. N/D, d. 02/10/1825
NAILOR, Alfred L., b. 09/22/1896, d. 09/04/1961
NAILOR, David B., ssw-Mary E., b. 06/02/1858, d. 07/20/1913
NAILOR, David H., ssw-Isaac W., b. 02/05/1833, d. 11/12/1899
NAILOR, Donald Wayne, b. 06/14/1953, d. 06/14/1953
NAILOR, E. Jane, ssw-Isaac W., b. 04/15/1834, d. 04/06/1914
NAILOR, Frank, s/o David B. & Mary E., b. 06/15/1886, d. 09/13/1886
NAILOR, Harry R., s/o David B. & Mary E., b. 06/15/1886, d. 02/13/1888
NAILOR, Isaac W., ssw-Nora, b. 09/07/1860, d. 04/22/1915
NAILOR, Mary E., ssw-David B., b. 1851, d. 1937
NAILOR, Nora, ssw-Isaac W., b. 1875, d. 1926
NAILOR, Robert B., ssw-Isaac W., b. 1874, d. 1953
PETTYJOHN, Ura J., b. 07/17/1897, d. 10/24/1897
REED, Abraham, ssw-Elizabeth A. Roach, b. 12/31/1826, d. 01/10/1909
REED, Alice H., d/o David H. & Sallie E., b. 11/07/1893, d. 05/24/1894
REED, Anna C., b. 10/03/1878, d. 02/12/1949
REED, Annie V., d/o James E. & Minta, b. 03/14/1880, d. 10/21/1888
REED, Araminta, b. 09/15/1851, d. 07/01/1919
REED, Benjamin D., ssw-Mary E., b. 07/17/1904, d. 03/03/1983
REED, C. Evelyn, ssw-Phillip R., b. 08/17/1908, d. 087/31/1990
REED, Charlotte B., ssw-Philip R., b. 1838, d. 1921
REED, Charlotte R., d/o David H. & Sallie E., ssw-Leah C., b. 04/25/1892, d. 09/17/1892
REED, Clara M., b. 02/13/1906, d. 10/02/1961
REED, Clarence H., b. 08/25/1919, d. N/D
REED, David H., ssw-Sallie E., b. 1863, d. 1935
REED, Delmar D., b. 09/24/1876, d. 06/15/1951
REED, Dorothy E., d/o John P. & Laura A., ssw-Gladys A., b. 01/06/1906, d. 01/10/1906
REED, E. Stockton, b. 1910, d. 1925
REED, Elizabeth A. Roach, w/o Abraham, b. 04/17/1828, d. 07/30/1903
REED, Garrison W., ssw-Lena Camper, b. 1862, d. 1947
REED, George M., b. 07/10/1910, d. 09/24/1910
REED, Gladys A., d/o John P. & Laura A., ssw-Dorothy E., b. 06/10/1908, d. 07/27/1908
REED, Grace Elizabeth, b. 11/17/1940, d. 06/15/1941
REED, Hall D., Sr., b. 01/18/1905, d. 10/15/1987
REED, Inf. d/o David H. & Sallie E., b. N/D, d. 03/19/1891
REED, James C., ssw-Vergie M., b. 01/21/1895, d. 03/14/1972

REED, James Carey, ssw-Sallie A., b. 09/03/1845, d. 06/08/1921
REED, James E., b. 02/07/1849, d. 02/14/1891
REED, John P., ssw-Laura A., b. 07/20/1883, d. 07/19/1973
REED, Joseph R., ssw-Louise, DE, Pvt., 59 Pioneer, Inf., WWI, b. 01/03/1897, d. 12/14/1958
REED, Lana A., b. 09/19/1947, d. 09/24/1970
REED, Laura A., ssw-John P., b. 11/06/1885, d. 10/15/1948
REED, Layton Delmar, b. 12/03/1931, d. 03/10/1932
REED, Leah C., d/o David H. & Sallie E., ssw-Charlotte R., b. 04/25/1892, d.09/17/1892
REED, Lena Camper, ssw-Garrison W., b. 1858, d. 1934
REED, Lilly M., d/o James E. & Minta, b. 02/05/1878, d. 10/23/1892
REED, Louise, ssw-Joseph R., b. 11/08/1919, d. 04/18/1989
REED, Mary E., d/o Jas. E. & Araminta, b. 09/10/1872, d. 02/28/1892
REED, Mary E., ssw-Benjamin D., b. 01/18/1899, d. 06/03/1992
REED, Naomi E., b. 12/01/1924, d. N/D
REED, Philip R., ssw-Charlotte B., b. 1835, d. 1898
REED, Phillip R., ssw-C. Evelyn, b. 09/04/1898, d. 03/05/1986
REED, Sallie A., ssw-James Carey, b. 05/04/1851, d. 01/08/1938
REED, Sallie E., ssw-David H., b.1868, d. 1951
REED, Vergie M., ssw-James C., b. 02/04/1900, d. 11/03/1976
REED, William A., s/o James A. & Armieda, Age 1y 5m 7d, b. N/D, d. 03/27/1877
REYNOLDS, Floyd J., b.12/12/1897, d. 10/26/1968
REYNOLDS, Fonzy B., b. 1872, d. 1946
REYNOLDS, James A., b. 05/20/1833, d. 02/22/1894
REYNOLDS, Nancy, b. 1815, d. 1881
REYNOLDS, Rebecca, b. 02/22/1823, d. 02/18/1907
REYNOLDS, Sallie Sheer, d/o Samuel M. & Fonzy, b. 12/27/1891, d. 04/15/1900
REYNOLDS, Samuel M., b. 1868, d. 1935
ROACH, Bertha, Age 7y, b. N/D, d. 11/15/1889
ROACH, Elizabeth D., ssw-James F., b. 1836, d. 1885
ROACH, James F., ssw-Elizabeth D., b. 1833, d. 1908
ROACH, John Thomas, b. N/D, d. 10/22/1910
ROACH, Sarah Frances, b. 1851, d. 1905
ROBBINS, James G., Age 76y 6m 11d, b. N/D, d. 11/02/1884
ROBBINS, Jane B., Age 79y 7m 12d, b. N/D, d. 05/03/1892
ROBBINS, William C., b. 10/31/1854, d. 08/25/1894
ROBINSON, Charlotte, w/o T. E., ssw-Thomas E., b. 11/06/1851, d. 02/17/1894
ROBINSON, John S., ssw-Sarah H., b. 01/28/1865, d. 12/30/1925
ROBINSON, Sarah H., ssw-John S., b.12/05/1839, d. 10/31/1909
ROBINSON, Thomas E., ssw-Charlotte, b. 08/06/1845, d. 12/23/1914
RUSSELL, Alfred, Capt., ssw-Alfred, Jr., b. 04/01/1826, d. 07/26/1892
RUSSELL, Alfred, Jr., ssw-William, b. 05/12/1875, d. 10/17/1875
RUSSELL, Emanuel, ssw-Esther, Rev., War Vet, Age 69y 16d, b. N/D, d. 09/18/1812
RUSSELL, Esther, ssw-Emanuel, Age 77y 6m 12d, b. N/D, d. 08/31/1824
RUSSELL, Fannie, b. 1864, d. 1941
RUSSELL, Mary E., w/o Alfred, ssw-Alfred, Jr., b. 08/04/1833, d. 01/24/1908
RUSSELL, Robert, Age 77y 9m, b. N/D, d. 03/28/1859
RUSSELL, Samuel, ssw-Sarah, Age 71y 6m 28d, b. N/D, d. 02/19/1885
RUSSELL, Sarah, w/o Robert, ssw-Samuel, Age 73y 29d, b. N/D, d. 08/28/1836

RUSSELL, William, ssw-Alfred, Jr., b. 05/12/1875, d. 10/28/1915
RUST, Sylvester H., Age 66y 3m 6d, b. N/D, d. 01/05/1878
SHORT, Anna Jefferson, b. 1887, d. 1976
SHORT, Lida C., ssw-Joseph Conwell, b. 09/03/1877, d. 12/03/1966
SIMPLER, Andrew M., ssw-Emmeline D. Vaughan, b. 01/15/1807, d. 05/06/1850
SIMPLER, Annie W., d/o J. C. & E. A., Age 1y 5m 19d, b. N/D, d. 09/14/1871
SIMPLER, Emma C., b. 06/08/1845, d. 12/15/1931
SIMPLER, Homer, s/o Geo. W. & Lydia C., Age 1y 9m 11d, b. 12/05/1873, d. 09/16/1875
SIMPLER, William C., s/o J. C. & E. A., Age 4y 2m 16d, b. N/D, d. 01/06/1872
THOMAS, Adeline B., b. 08/07/1914, d. 06/21/1961
THOMAS, Anna K., ssw-Leonard F., b. 1879, d. 1950
THOMAS, James Edwin, b. 1908, d. 1933
THOMAS, Lafe Onal, b. 12/200/1899, d. 04/21/1967
THOMAS, Leonard F., ssw-Anna K., b. 1871, d. 1953
VAUGHAN, Emmeline D., ssw-Andrew M. Simpler, b. 02/20/1815, d. 06/20/1904
WAGAMON, Ruth R. C., ssw-Bertha L. Carey, b. 07/22/1903, d. 12/04/1976
WEST, Dellie H., w/o Philip B., b. 11/30/1878, d. 03/22/1898
WILLIAMS, Emma J., ssw-John T. Williams and Harry E. & Mary E. Dorn, b. 05/28/1845, d. 05/11/1899
WILLIAMS, John T., ssw-Emma J. Williams and Harry E. & Mary E. Dorn, b. 12/22/1840, d. 04/22/1882
WILLIAMS, Sallie L., d/o J. T. & E. J., b. 10/24/1868, d. 08/10/1882
WILSON, Charlie H., s/o Mark D. & Mary C., ssw-Joseph Conwell, b. 06/06/1873, d. 04/13/1889
WILSON, Edna R., ssw-Joseph Conwell, b. 04/11/1894, d. 05/23/1894
WILSON, James A., ssw-Lydia S., b. 09/13/1838, d. 04/03/1905
WILSON, Jennie S., ssw-Joseph C., b. 1872, d. 1926
WILSON, Jos. C., ssw-Joseph Conwell, b. 06/18/1867, d. 07/10/1915
WILSON, Joseph C., ssw-Jennie S., b. 1867, d. 1915
WILSON, Lydia S., ssw-James A., b. 05/12/1842, d. 06/11/1925
WILSON, Margaret, ssw-Zachariah P., Age 77y, b. N/D, d. 03/22/1883
WILSON, Mark D., ssw-Joseph Conwell, b. 04/07/1840, d. 04/28/1874
WILSON, Mary C., ssw-Joseph Conwell, b. 02/04/1843, d. 04/02/1916
WILSON, Sallie D., d/o Mark D. & Mary C., Age 2y 3m 3d, b. N/d, d. 11/02/1868
WILSON, Sallie D., d/o Mark D. & Mary C., ssw-Joseph Conwell, b. 02/21/1862, d. 11/24/1864
WILSON, William J., b. 1863, d. 1929
WILSON, Zachariah P., ssw-Margaret, Age 55y, b. N/D, d. 02/07/1858
WILTBANK, Alice L., ssw-John C., Jr., b. 1866, d. 1956
WILTBANK, David, s/o Cornelius, s/o Isaac, s/o Cornelius, son Helmanius Frederic Wiltbank. He served
        in defense of Lewes in the War of 1812 – 1815, b. 01/28/1789, d. 05/16/1865
WILTBANK, David A., ssw-Hannah F., b. 1842, d. 1924
WILTBANK, Halmanius F., ssw-John C., Jr., b. 1899, d. 1953
WILTBANK, Hannah F., ssw-David A., b. 1843, d. 1926
WILTBANK, Helmanius Frederic, "Emmingrated from Sweden in a Dutch ship, which was wrecked in
        the mouth of The Delaware Bay, saved by swimming and landing on Cape Henlopen about 1650,
        leaving three sons, John, Cornelius and Abraham.
WILTBANK, John C., Jr., ssw-Alice L., b. 1866, d. 1940
WILTBANK, Mollie, d/o David A. & Hannah F., Age 14y 2m 2d, b. N/D, d. 02/09/1891
WILTBANK, Sarah, w/o David & d/o Bevins & Sarah Graves Morris, b. 05/24/1798, d. 02/25/1880
WILTBANK, Willie, s/o David A. & Hannah F., Age 5y 21d, b. N/D, d. 01/29/1875
WORKMAN, Comfort J. Rust, b. 1876, d. 1951

WORKMAN, Frank E., b. 1877, d. N/D
ZOTT, Doris L., b. 03/31/1919, d. 06/06/1991

(BK-007 & HU-NR) WHITES CHAPEL CEMETERY

Located Southeast of Milton on the Northeast side of Coastal Highway (Rt. 1) 0.5 miles north of Cave Neck Rd. (Rd. 88). Recorded: October 9, 1996

ARGOE, Fannie Lank, ssw-Robert Holland, b. 12/25/1881, d. 03/14/1969
ARGOE, Robert Holland, ssw-Fannie Lank, b. 10/30/1869, d. 05/18/1948
BAIRD, Judith Kay, ssw-Ralph Frederick, b. 10/31/1943, d. 03/03/1995
BAIRD, Ralph Frederick, ssw-Judith Kay, b. 06/16/1943, d. N/D
BERNSTEIN, Eleanor Pettyjohn, b. 01/05/1926, d. 08/15/1968
BLANKENSHIP, H. Evelyn, ssw-Newell K., b. 05/26/1921, d. 01/08/1992
BLANKENSHIP, Newell K., ssw-H. Evelyn, b. 06/24/1938, d. N/D
BLIZZARD, Lillian May, b. 10/21/1937, d. Underground
BOHN, Morton D., b. 08/18/1918, d. 10/25/1985
BONE, Malcom W., ssw-Nellie D., b. 08/17/1904, d. N/D
BONE, Nellie D., ssw-Malcom W., b. 07/29/1906, d. 10/03/1991
BRITTINGHAM, Ella, w/o George E., b. 01/06/1870, d. 06/11/1896
BRITTINGHAM, George E. D. W., b. 1870, d. 1949
BRITTINGHAM, Greensbury, ssw-Sadie, b. 1882, d. 1967
BRITTINGHAM, Sadie, ssw-Greensbury, b. 1883, d. 1961
BRITTINGHAM, Sallie N., b. 1874, d. 1952
BRYAN, George T., ssw-Julia A., b. 1849, d. 1926
BRYAN, Gilbert Burton, DE, Pfc., 317 Inf., 80 Div., WWII, Killed in Germany, b. 02/25/1925, d. 03/28/1945
BRYAN, Jacob E., ssw-Margaret J., Brother, b. 1851, d. 1926
BRYAN, Julia A., ssw-George T., b. 1851, d. 1919
BRYAN, Lillian M., ssw-William H., b. 01/25/1891, d. 05/13/1968
BRYAN, Margaret J., ssw-Jacob E., Sister, b. 1845, d. 1920
BRYAN, Mariah Ann, ssw-Weightman, b. 11/11/1814, d. 01/17/1901
BRYAN, Marjorie M., ssw-Robert T., b. 05/06/1921, d. N/D
BRYAN, Robert T., ssw-Marjorie M., b. 07/13/1916, d. 07/14/1980
BRYAN, Weightman, ssw-Mariah Ann, b. 01/10/1814, d. 05/20/1902
BRYAN, William H., ssw-Lillian M., b. 04/09/1893, d. 12/13/1960
CAMPBELL, Arthur B., ssw-Virginia R., b. 12/06/1881, d. 05/05/1971
CAMPBELL, Edward W., ssw-Jennie W., DE, Capt., USA, WWII, b. 02/19/1900, d. 10/31/1972
CAMPBELL, Elizabeth, b. 1860, d. 1939
CAMPBELL, Everett P., b. 05/31/1908, d. 09/22/1947
CAMPBELL, George B., b. 09/23/1863, d. 09/28/1936
CAMPBELL, Jennie W., ssw-Edward W., b. 07/25/1901, d. 02/07/1982
CAMPBELL, Joseph H., b. 1862, d. 1938
CAMPBELL, Maggie L., b. 09/21/1868, d. 01/03/1941
CAMPBELL, Roberta, d/o Arthur B. & Virginia, b. 01/13/1908, d. 03/19/1910
CAMPBELL, Vardie Z., b. 1887, d. 1916
CAMPBELL, Virginia R., ssw-Arthur B., b. 11/15/1886, d. 02/23/1970
CARD, Alfred Rodell, b. 08/15/1895, d. 11/29/1941
CARD, J. Clarence, b. 11/22/1897, d. 05/25/1957

CAREY, Charles V., ssw-Hazel I., b. 09/18/1916, d. 07/03/1968

CAREY, Hazel I., ssw-Charles V., b. 05/08/1917, d. N/D

CARPENTER, Andrew Lee, ssw-Mary Emily, b. 06/15/1879, d. 08/03/1961

CARPENTER, Benjamin E., b. 04/30/1876, d. 05/11/1945

CARPENTER, Clara, b. 02/03/1894, d. 01/31/1895

CARPENTER, Cora D., b. 02/03/1876, d. 02/24/1917

CARPENTER, Emma Walker, ssw-Lemuel J., b. 10/12/1892, d. 01/11/1983

CARPENTER, George W., b. 10/09/1884, d. 06/03/1926

CARPENTER, Gladys M., b. 02/01/1922, d. 02/01/1922

CARPENTER, Hettie A., d/o John H. & Lettie, b. N/D, d. 07/08/1887

CARPENTER, John H., b. 09/07/1852, d. 03/18/1927

CARPENTER, John T., b. 08/11/1900, d. 01/09/1943

CARPENTER, Lemuel J., ssw-Emma Walker, b. 10/25/1882, d. 01/09/1953

CARPENTER, Lettie C., b. 12/07/1856, d. 11/25/1920

CARPENTER, Mary Emily, ssw-Andrew Lee, b. 06/17/1886, d. 12/29/1961

CARPENTER, Robert J., b. 08/13/1925, d. 12/15/1934

CHAPPEL, Charity, b. 1875, d. 1931

CHORMAN, David H., ssw-Eldora C., Pfc., USA, WWII, b. 12/17/1915, d. 09/23/1986

CHORMAN, Earl B., ssw-Mae E., b. 06/05/1913, d. 01/06/1915

CHORMAN, Eldora C., ssw-David H., b. 03/27/1923, d. N/D

CHORMAN, Harold H., ssw-Earl B., b. 01/18/1890, d. 01/31/1980

CHORMAN, Jamie H., b. 05/11/1980, d. 09/27/1980

CHORMAN, Mae E., ssw-Earl B., b. 12/26/1890, d. 03/12/1977

CHORMANN, Alfred Joseph, b. 08/30/1836, d. 02/18/1914

CHORMANN, Mary E., w/o Alfred J., b. 08/24/1842, d. 09/15/1911

CLIFFORD, George Lawson, III, b. 10/31/1964, d. 08/06/1989

CLIFTON, Anna Marie, ssw-Calvin Isaac, b. 12/03/1929, d. 01/30/1962

CLIFTON, Calvin Isaac, ssw-Anna Marie, S1, USN, WWII, b. 04/08/1925, d. 08/03/1981

CLIFTON, F. Neal, Sr., ssw-Kathleen A., RD3, USN, WWII, b. 09/18/1927, d. 09/14/1990

CLIFTON, Kathleen A., Age 73y, b. N/D, d. 11/04/1996

CLIFTON, Kathleen A., ssw-F. Neal, Sr., b. 06/14/1923, d. N/D

COLLINS, Dorothy L., ssw-Daniel J. Givan, b. 1902, d. 1968

COLLINS, Norma Lee, b. 10/21/1954, d. 10/18/1984

CONAWAY, Anna M., ssw-Minos T., b. 04/09/1897, d. 06/01/1982

CONAWAY, Minos T., DE, Pvt., Co. K., 7th Inf., 3 Inf. Div., WWII, Killed in France, b. 04/11/1922, d. 08/15/1944

CONAWAY, Minos T., ssw-Anna M., b. 03/08/1895, d. 12/19/1961

CONNARD, Edward W., h/o Annie E. Connard, b. 04/08/1877, d. 12/21/1918

COOPER, John, Sr., b. 05/10/1910, d. 10/13/1983

CRAIG, James L., b. 01/08/1825, d. 11/13/1909

CRAIG, Mamie M., d/o J. L., b. 03/24/1870, d. 10/12/1884

CRAIG, Mary H., ssw-Wm. S., b. 1885, d. 1967

CRAIG, Wm. S., ssw-Mary H., b. 1873, d. 1943

DAVIDSON, Carl R., ssw-Catherine M., b. 06/23/1913, d. 08/12/1984

DAVIDSON, Catherine M., ssw-Carl R., b. 12/13/1912, d. N/D

DAVIDSON, Helen M., ssw-William V., b. 07/25/1926, d. N/D

DAVIDSON, Uhland T., ssw-Willa A., b. 02/20/1894, d. 12/16/1974

DAVIDSON, Willa A., ssw-Uhland T., b. 03/14/1896, d. 06/10/1973

DAVIDSON, William V., ssw-Helen M., b. 05/11/1929, d. 01/24/1986

DAVIS, James, b. 08/06/1847, d. 06/20/1928

DAYTON, Mildred R., b. 01/17/1900, d. 05/03/1981

DENNIS, Bertha E., ssw-Virgil L., b. 1889, d. 1952

DENNIS, Virgil L., ssw-Bertha E., b. 1895, d. 1972

DICKERSON, Bobby Lee, b. 1944, d. 1945

DICKERSON, Florence M., ssw-Granville L., b. 08/27/1909, d. 12/29/1976

DICKERSON, Granville L., ssw-Florence M., b. 12/29/1902, d. 03/03/1968

DOBLEMAN, Marion W., b. 06/21/1883 d. 08/31/1968

DOCKETY, Sarah H. Green, w/o J. A., ssw-Lucile D. Kerns, b. 08/20/1871, d. 12/26/1911

DODD, Anna Fredonia, ssw-William E., b. 05/13/1916, d. N/D

DODD, Anna May, ssw-William H., b. 1887, d. 1968

DODD, Elva M., ssw-William H., b. 1908, d. 1910

DODD, Helen Constance, b. 01/19/1939, d. 03/21/1939

DODD, Raymond, ssw-William H., b. 1905, d. 1905

DODD, William E., ssw-Anna Fredonia, b. 11/21/1910, d. 09/19/1951

DODD, William H., ssw-Anna May, b. 1880, d. 1939

DONOVAN, Laura B., b. 04/22/1902, d. 01/21/1980

DONOVAN, Marie, Age 39, b. 05/18/1827, d. N/D

DORMAN, Albert E., ssw-Mae E., b. 1906, d. 1993

DORMAN, Mae E., ssw-Albert E., b. 1908, d. N/D

DOTY, De Verne V., ssw-Katherine, Sgt., USA, WWI, b. 04/19/1896, d. 10/25/1978

DOTY, Katherine, ssw-De Verne V., b. 1900, d. 1980

DOUGLASS, Charles M., b. 12/16/1843, d. 02/09/1885

DOUGLASS, Sallie P., b. 10/28/1921, d. 10/28/1921

DUTTON, Charles R., Rev., ssw-Hettie C. Rash, b. 11/03/1874, d. 05/22/1951

DUTTON, Elizabeth J., b. 08/23/1822, d. 11/23/1911

DUTTON, George A., b. 02/14/1821, d. 02/10/1896

DUTTON, Hettie C. Rash, ssw-Rev. Charles R., b. 08/19/1880, d. 09/09/1966

DUTTON, Jesse, ssw-Nellie, b. 08/21/1818, d. 11/27/1896

DUTTON, Jesse C., b. 02/14/1909, d. 06/07/1975

DUTTON, Lillie May, ssw-Jesse, b. 07/11/1875, d. 02/29/1895

DUTTON, Luther, ssw-William A., Son, b. 1884, d. 1901

DUTTON, Mary E., ssw-Peter W., b. 1857, d. 1933

DUTTON, Nellie, ssw-Jesse, b. 05/11/1820, d. 05/04/1907

DUTTON, Peter W., ssw-Mary E., b. 1848, d. 1933

DUTTON, R. Frank, ssw-William A., Son, b. 1900, d. 1925

DUTTON, Sallie, d/o Peter & Mary E., Age 2m 6d, b. N/D, d. 02/14/1882

DUTTON, Samuel J., s/o Peter W. & Mary E., Age 4m 13d, b. N/D, d. 05/06/1884

DUTTON, Sarah V., ssw-William A., b. 1859, d. 1901

DUTTON, William A., ssw-Sarah V., b. 1845, d. 1925

EDWARD, James, s/o Zachariah & Molly, b. 03/17/1870, d. 04/11/1877

EDWARD, Molly, w/o Zachariah, Age abt. 47y, b. N/D, d. 04/04/1878

ELLINGSWORTH, Emma G., ssw-Roy W., b. 06/09/1902, d. 07/21/1973

ELLINGSWORTH, Roy W., ssw-Emma G., b. 08/20/1899, d. 06/03/1982

EMORY, Charles Wm., ssw-Mildred Ann, b. 12/30/1921, d. 01/28/1990

EMORY, Mildred Ann, ssw-Charles Wm., b. 11/03/1925, d. 06/16/1987

EVANS, Maggie S., w/o James C., b. 02/29/1868, d. 11/08/1920

FARLEY, May Howard, b. 02/21/1870, d. 07/17/1922
FISHER, Amanda F. Hopkins, b. 1867, d. 1952
FISHER, Amy H., b. 04/03/1859, d. 06/05/1927
FISHER, Annie E. White, w/o Theodore, b. 08/31/1855, d. 12/17/1949
FISHER, Charles, ssw-Eliza, b. 08/11/1791, d. 08/09/1819
FISHER, Charles W., s/o Myers, b. 1864, d. 1933
FISHER, Charles W., s/o Charles & Eliza, b. 04/17/1838, d. 12/07/1862
FISHER, Clara V., ssw-Maggie P., b. 1870, d. 1893
FISHER, Eliza, d/o John H. & Elizabeth P. Lank, b. 07/03/1889, d. 05/19/1900
FISHER, Eliza, w/o Charles, b. 07/09/1800, d. 02/09/1846
FISHER, Eliza A., ssw-Myers R., b. 10/18/1838, d. 12/23/1910
FISHER, Eliza A. W., b. 02/18/1832, d. 10/28/1920
FISHER, George A., ssw-Maggie P., b. 1869, d. 1947
FISHER, Henry White, s/o Theodore & Annie White, b. 1882, d. 1904
FISHER, Inf. s/o Myers R. & Eliza A., Age 8wks, b. N/D, d/ 06/11/1880
FISHER, James, b. 05/10/1830, d. 11/19/1891
FISHER, James, s/o Maggie, b. Unreadable, d. Unreadable
FISHER, Maggie P., ssw-George A., b. 1868, d. 1949
FISHER, Margaret Landon, w/o William Wright, b. 02/20/1875, d. 11/18/1961
FISHER, Mary E., d/o Myers R. & Eliza A., Age 11y 10m 3d, b. N/D, d. 07/04/1888
FISHER, Myers R., ssw-Eliza A., b. 06/15/1833, d. 01/15/1907
FISHER, Theodore H., s/o John & Lydia, b. 01/10/1855, d. 01/19/1898
FISHER, William Wright, b. 11/24/1866, d. 03/09/1957
FLUHARTY, Harry A., ssw-Leah Truitt, b. 02/07/1901, d. 06/10//1969
FLUHARTY, Leah Truitt, ssw-Harry A., b. 01/23/1923, d. 08/07/1970
FOSKEY, Lydia A., ssw-Robert B., b. 02/18/1866, d. 07/26/1922
FOSKEY, Robert B., ssw-Lydia, b. 06/12/1861, d. 09/17/1940
FRANKLIN, Thomas Ferguson, ssw-John Dorman Robinson, b. 03/20/1870, d. 04/13/1944
FUTCHER, Hannah Jane, w/o Erasmus M. & d/o Mitchell & Hannah Lank, Age 18, b. N/D, d. 11/10/1852
FUTCHER, Inf. d/o E. M. & M., b. N/D, d. N/D
GANRUDE, Dorothy M., ssw-Charles R. Ritter, b. 01/03/1928, d. 08/18/1995
GILLILAND, Alva B., b. 09/03/1901, d. 12/12/1959
GIVAN, Daniel J., ssw-Dorothy J. Collins, b. 05/01/1865, d. 09/02/1943
GIVAN, Martie B., ssw-Daniel J., b. 10/04/1872, d. 10/04/1934
GRAICE, William B., s/o David & Annie, b. 07/21/1829, d. 09/10/1895
GREEN, Charles E., b. 10/11/1878, d. 11/27/1958
GREEN, Emma S., b. 1845, d. 1901
GREEN, James Albert, s/o Wm. T. & Susie, b. 11/25/1903, d. 08/10/1904
GREEN, Mamie A., ssw-William A., b. 09/22/1875, d. 08/01/1947
GREEN, Susie, b. 03/28/1872, d. 04/05/1957
GREEN, William A., ssw-Mamie A., b. 10/02/1873, d. 09/11/1949
GREEN, Wm. T., b. 05/03/1846, d. 09/04/1917
GREENE, Effie M., b. 09/23/1880, d. 03/09/1958
HADDER, George W., ssw-Sallie T., b. 10/26/1906, d. 08/31/1971
HADDER, Sallie T., ssw-George W., b. 03/11/1907, d. 05/03/1976
HALL, Edward, Age 25y 1m 4d, b. N/D, d. 03/23/1847
HALL, Naomi, w/o John M., Age 20y 1m 5d, b. N/D, d. 08/31/1855
HARPER, Jeffery Lamont, b. 12/29/1950, d. 06/26/1976

HARPER, Robert Brian, b. 04/22/1955, d. 04/22/1976

HASTING, Phillip H., b. 1872, d. 1938

HASTINGS, Laura, b. 02/14/1869, d. 02/22/1903

HITCH, Dorothy L., b. 01/21/1911, d. 04/14/1978

HOLLAND, Albert B., Age 31y 9m 14d, b. N/D, d. 10/18/1877

HOLLAND, Alice A., w/o Joseph, b. 08/10/1835, d. 06/25/1926

HOLLAND, Arthur L., s/o Joseph & Alice, b. 03/09/1872, d. 05/30/1896

HOLLAND, Ebenezar, b. 09/04/1801, d. 03/15/1879

HOLLAND, Elisha, ssw-Robert C., b. 03/12/1805, d. 03/16/1888

HOLLAND, Eliza Ebenezar, b. 09/17/1799, d. 08/13/1865

HOLLAND, Frank F., b. 10/14/1870, d. 07/25/1893

HOLLAND, John P., ssw-Sarah H., b. 08/06/1841, d. 12/21/1915

HOLLAND, Joseph, ssw-Joseph L., b. 09/12/1835, d. 08/05/1905

HOLLAND, Joseph L., ssw-Joseph, b. 09/19/1874, d. 11/06/1900

HOLLAND, Louisa A., ssw-Robert C., b. 04/03/1812, d. 02/25/1866

HOLLAND, Maggie W., d/o Joseph & Alice, b. 09/26/1866, d. 05/12/1867

HOLLAND, Robert C., ssw-Elisha, b. 05/22/1846, d. 09/16/1865

HOLLAND, Sarah H., ssw-John P., b. 05/29/1851, d. 06/02/1934

HOLLAND, William D., b. 1839, d. 1884

HORSEY, Virginia D., ssw-William K., b. 09/22/1927, d. N/D

HORSEY, William K., ssw-Virginia D., b. 05/28/1926, d. 08/18/1995

HOWARD, Mazie, d/o William & May, b. 02/14/1898, d. 05/03/1900

HOWARD, William J., b. 1865, d. 1913

HOWETH, H. Wayne, b. 04/01/1963, d. 06/28/1982

HUDSON, John M., ssw-S. Fannie, b. 07/15/1852, d. 02/06/1912

HUDSON, Levin L., Age 49, b. 03/17/1861, d. N/D

HUDSON, Lillie M., b. 03/09/1876, d. 03/29/1913

HUDSON, Margret A., w/o L. L., b. 10/20/1889, d. Unreadable

HUDSON, S. Fannie, ssw-John M., b. 1856, d. 1931

HUDSON, Samuel P., Age 20y 11m, b. N/D, d. 06/22/1861

HUGHEY, Leah A., b. 1955, d. 1995

HULTAPPLE, Earl Michael, ssw-Merle Thornhill, WWI 1917-1918, b. 04/10/1897, d. 01/25/1990

HULTAPPLE, Merle Thornhill, ssw-Earl Michael, b. 11/17/1922, d. N/D

HUNT, Bessie Jane, ssw-William O., b. 08/04/1890, d. 06/23/1979

HUNT, Verdis O., b. 1911, d. 1961

HUNT, William O., ssw-Bessie Jane, b. 04/22/1887, d. 05/18/1953

JACKSON, Beatrice M., b. 1900, d. 1982

JACKSON, Elaine BusBee, b. 06/24/1934, d. N/D

JACKSON, Leo H., Sgt., USA, WWI, b. 08/22/1901, d. 05/18/1977

JAMES, Everett E., ssw-Laura S., b. 1899, d. 1981

JAMES, Laura S., ssw-Everett E., b. 1904, d. 1969

JEFFERSON, Sarah E., ssw-Weightman Bryan, b. 11/11/1847, d. 12/15/1887

JOHANSEN, Alfred, Capt., ssw-Rowland P. Warrington, b. 1871, d. 1940

JOHANSEN, Estella W., Carleton E. Vincent, b. 1877, d. 1963

JOHNSON, Alberta R., b. 11/07/1921, d. 04/02/1989

JOHNSON, Annie E. Connard, ssw-William R., b. 10/30/1881, d. 10/11/1964

JOHNSON, Baby, ssw-William R., b. 01/20/1926, d. 01/20/1926

JOHNSON, Nathaniel W., ssw-Sallie A., b. 1857, d. 1933

JOHNSON, Sallie A., ssw-Nathaniel W., b. 1859, d. 1927

JOHNSON, Theodore C., b. 03/09/1890, d. 12/12/1967

JOHNSON, William R., ssw-Annie E. Connard, b. 04/06/1879, d. 02/17/1950

JORDAN, Bertha J., b. 11/21/1893, d. 02/06/1986

KERNS, James A., ssw-Sarah H. Green Dockety, b. 02/12/1870, d. 06/21/1932

KERNS, Lucile D., ssw-Sarah H. Green Dockety, b. 10/11/1895, d. 09/15/1947

KING, Ada W., d/o C. H. & M. E., b. 03/27/1880, d. 01/25/1881

KING, Alfred H., ssw-L. Annie, b. 12/09/1853, d. 10/03/1916

KING, Archa J., s/o A. H. & L. A., b. 01/14/1801, d. 02/19/1801

KING, Cornelius H., b. N/D, d. 02/29/1859. [Note: Hard to read.]

KING, Cornelius H., Age 56y 11m 21d, b. N/D, d. 06/24/1887

KING, David H., Age 63y 1m, b. N/D, d. 08/08/1881

KING, James H., s/o Cornelius H. & Emma, b. 08/06/1870, d. 04/04/1903

KING, L. Annie, ssw-Alfred H., b. 10/28/1864, d. 03/04/1940

KING, Letty C., d/o C. H. & M. E., Age 4m 19d, b. N/D, d. 09/23/1874

KING, Maggie E., w/o Cornelius, Age 20y 5m, b. N/D, d. 08/10/1870

KING, Mary E., w/o Cornelius & d/o Wilkins, Age 52y 3d, b. N/D, d. 08/23/1887

KING, Mary J., w/o Charles H., b. 08/05/1825, d. 07/12/1898

KING, Willis N., s/o A. H. & L. A., b. 06/01/1889, d. 09/06/1889

LANK, Adelia, ssw-Samuel J., b. 1869, d. 1946

LANK, Albert H., ssw-Ella N., b. 05/11/1862, d. 06/02/1922

LANK, Albert M., ssw-Letitia B., b. 1878, d. 1931

LANK, Alzo James Wm., s/o Wm. J., b. N/D, d. N/D

LANK, Annie P., ssw-James T., b. 01/15/1874, d. 01/08/1930

LANK, Baby, b. N/D, d. N/D

LANK, Callie, b. 05/1872, d. 04/19/1904

LANK, Catharine, w/o John C. & d/o Samuel & Mary Reynolds, Age 31y 1m 16d, b. N/D, d. 02/16/1855

LANK, Catharion W., d/o Cathar., b. Unreadable, d. Unreadable

LANK, Elizabeth Parker, d/o John H. & Elizabeth P. Lank, b. 05/12/1893, d 06/05/1893

LANK, Ella (Little), d/o James & Maria, b. 05/26/1851, d. N/D

LANK, Ella, w/o Robert W. & d/o James & Betty Wilkers, Age 22y 10m 8d, b. N/D, d. 03/15/1884

LANK, Ella D., ssw-Mary L., b. 09/30/1900, d. 12/24/1900

LANK, Ella N., ssw-Albert H., b. 03/03/1868, d. 07/08/1950

LANK, Esther B., ssw-Mary L., b. 02/09/1905, d. 07/01/1906

LANK, George Ella, w/o Henry E., b. 02/22/1859, d. 03/07/1936

LANK, Hannah, w/o John, Age 27y, b. N/D, d. 12/04/1879

LANK, Hannah, w/o John H. & d/o Myers R. & Eliza A. Fisher, b. 02/03/1861, d. 07/10/1932

LANK, Hannah, w/o Mitchell, Age 40y 2m 17d, b. N/D, d. 05/12/1839

LANK, Hannah C., d/o James & Maria, Age 2y 8m 21d, b. 03/10/1871, d. N/D

LANK, Henry C., 2nd, Lt., AAC, WWII, b. 1896, d. 1946

LANK, Henry E., ssw-George Ella, b. 03/15/1855, d. 09/27/1929

LANK, Henry W., s/o J. C. & Hester W., Age 4y 2m 3d, b. N/D, d. 01/22/1875

LANK, Hester W., Age 62y 4m 8d, b. N/D, d. 05/18/1897

LANK, James, ssw-Maria, b. 04/12/1825, d. 02/18/1902

LANK, James T., ssw-Annie P., b. 01/25/1874, d. 11/05/1952

LANK, John C., Age 59y 3m 9d, b. N/D, d. 03/27/1878

LANK, John C., b. 10/1868, d. 02/19/1902

LANK, John D., s/o Albert M., b. 03/05/1908, d. 03/05/1908

LANK, John H., b. 02/11/1856, d. 08/28/1946
LANK, Joseph, b. 10/25/1859, d. 12/21/1909
LANK, Letitia B., w/o Albert, b. 1882, d. 1941
LANK, Maria, d/o Henry E. & Ella, Age 4y 9m 17d, b. N/D, d. 03/19/1899
LANK, Maria, ssw-James, b. 06/18/1827, d. 10/09/1905
LANK, Mary, d/o James, b. N/D, d. N/D
LANK, Mary, w/o Wm. J. & d/o C. & Mary Reynolds, Age 42y 5m 17d, b. N/D, d. 10/08/1853
LANK, Mary Ann R., d/o Peter C. & Mary S., Age 11y 1m 15d, b. N/D, d. 12/21/1854
LANK, Mary L., ssw-Ella D., b. 01/02/1898, d. 10/02/1898
LANK, Mary S., b. 02/12/1822, d. 04/02/1900
LANK, Mary S., c/o Wm. & Anne E., ssw-Robert J. & William B., b. N/D, d. N/D
LANK, Mitchell, Age 60y 9m 11d, b. N/D, d. 04/23/1854
LANK, Nemiah, s/o John C. & Harriet, Age 2y, b. N/D, d. 1860
LANK, Peter C., Age 71y 6m 20d, b. N/D, d. 07/02/1891
LANK, Robert J., c/o Wm. & Anne E., ssw-Mary S. & William B., b. N/D, d. N/D
LANK, Samuel J., ssw-Adelia, b. 1842, d. 1927
LANK, Sarah H., w/o Samuel J., b. 06/14/1842, d. 08/26/1909
LANK, Sophia, 2nd w/o Mitchell, Age 73y 4m 18d, b. N/D, d. 01/04/1874
LANK, William B., c/o Wm. & Anne E., ssw-Mary S. & Robert J., b. N/D, d. N/D
LANK, William T., s/o John C. & Catherine, Age 38y 1m 27d, b. N/D, d. 07/07/1887
LAWSON, Doris Journey, b. 10/03/1923, d. N/D
LEE, Bertha N., ssw-James E., Jr., b. 04/09/1907, d. N/D
LEE, James E., 3rd, b. 02/21/1932, d. 02/18/1933
LEE, James E., Jr., ssw-Bertha N., b. 06/09/1909, d. 02/12/1988
LEE, Richard A., b. 01/05/1931, d. N/D
LEGATES, William N., Jr., b. 01/07/1941, d. 02/29/1972
LINGO, Anna W., ssw-Capt. John H., b. 10/28/1870, d. 01/10/1964
LINGO, John H., Capt., ssw-Anna W., b. 04/22/1865, d. 09/07/1921
LITTLE, Floyd T., b. 05/18/1910, d. 07/19/1965
LITTLE, Lewis T., b. 06/14/1950, d. 11/18/1965
LOGUE, James Park, ssw-Mary S. Lank, b. 08/30/1873, d. 01/15/1952
LOGUE, Mary S. Lank, ssw-James Park, b. 02/25/1882, d. 06/16/1948
LOWE, Ethel H., b. 1898, d. 1984
LOWE, James R., DE, Pvt., 303 Eng. 78 Div., WWI, b. 08/18/1894, d. 07/27/1950
LOWE, Mary E., b. 11/06/1917, d. 01/18/1979
LYNCH, Beatrice A., ssw-Felix W., b. 09/01/1923, d. 12/13/1974
LYNCH, Elizabeth A., ssw-Roy E., b. 06/25/1912, d. 01/01/1983
LYNCH, Felix W., ssw-Beatrice A., b. 11/23/1917, d. N/D
LYNCH, Lillie A., ssw-Doris E. Smack, b. 1907, d. 1995
LYNCH, Roy E., ssw-Elizabeth A., b. 03/15/1913, d. N/D
MAGEE, Clara A. Douglass, b. 10/23/1871, d. 05/08/1957
MARSH, William L., b. 01/13/1951, d. 04/21/1976
MARTIN, Elsie E., ssw-Ralph A., Sr., b. 01/31/1909, d. 04/02/1979
MARTIN, Lena C., ssw-William E., b. 11/06/1872, d. 03/10/1958
MARTIN, Ralph A., Jr., ssw-Ralph A., Sr., b. 08/14/1939, d. 03/17/1941
MARTIN, Ralph A., Sr., ssw-Elsie E., b. 07/23/1910, d. N/D
MARTIN, William E., ssw-Lena C., b. 06/06/1870, d. 05/02/1951
MARVEL, Elizabeth S., ssw-William L., b. 04/14/1916, d. N/D

MARVEL, Jency, ssw-Joseph C., b. 06/19/1890, d. 06/23/1972
MARVEL, Joseph C., ssw-Jency, b. 05/20/1889, d. 11/23/1952
MARVEL, William L., ssw-Elizabeth S., b. 01/14/1917, d. N/D
MCCALAISTER, John A., c/o Cyrus & Eliza A., b. 06/25/1883, d. 03/04/1884
MCCALAISTER, Sarah F., s/o Cyrus & Eliza A., b. 08/02/1880, d. 03/04/1884
MCCALISTER, Annie France, d/o Wm. & Levina, b. 09/08/1887, d. 07/07/1889
MCGEE, Jane E., b. 11/18/1925, d. 09/11/1926
MELOTT, Gladys M., ssw-Raymond G., b. 11/20/1906, d. 02/26/1985
MELOTT, Raymond G., ssw-Gladys M., b. 12/21/1907, d. N/D
MESSICK, Anna M., ssw-Bayard W., b. 05/13/1901, d. 05/26/1992
MESSICK, Bayard W., ssw-Anna M., b. 08/21/1898, d. 03/25/1974
MESSICK, Charles R., b. 1844, d. 1922
MESSICK, Joseph Oscar, s/o C. R. & Sarah, b. 06/30/1870, d. 02/27/1880
MESSICK, Laura V., b. 05/22/1851, d. 09/01/1929
MESSICK, Sarah, b. 1851, d. 1931
METZNER, Anna L., ssw-Harry G., b. 1905, d. 1966
METZNER, Denise L., ssw-Gary H., b. 11/18/1952, d. N/D
METZNER, Frank A., b. 1903, d. 1930
METZNER, Gary H., ssw-Denise L., Sgt, USMC, Vietnam, b. 12/24/1951, d. 09/13/1985
METZNER, Harry G., ssw-Anna L., b. 1901, d. N/D
METZNER, Mary Ann, ssw-Roland H., b. 12/04/1929, d. N/D
METZNER, Roland H., ssw-Mary Ann, b. 04/07/1925, d. N/D
MILBY, Hettie J., ssw-John T., b. 06/04/1853, d. 10/27/1937
MILBY, John T., ssw-Hettie J., b. 06/17/1856, d. 03/11/1934
MILLMAN, Bessie M., ssw-Edward, b. 12/08/1888, d. 10/22/1971
MILLMAN, Edward, ssw-Bessie M., b. 02/27/1884, d. 08/12/1972
MILLMAN, Edward Michael, s/o Edward P. & Nellie T., b. 01/29/1935, d. 01/31/1935
MILLMAN, Edward P., b. 11/17/1910, d. 12/08/1984
MILLMAN, Enoch Preston, b. 08/14/1937, d. 09/12/1991
MILLMAN, Fred A., ssw-Maxine C., b. 01/08/1921, d. 01/05/1982
MILLMAN, G. June, ssw-Roland P., Jr., b. 12/17/1951, d. N/D
MILLMAN, Harold C., ssw-Vietta R., b. 05/27/1914, d. 03/01/1989
MILLMAN, Helen T., b. 10/14/1908, d. 05/04/1956
MILLMAN, Howard E., ssw-Una C. Rust, b. 03/04/1909, d. 02/22/1995
MILLMAN, Inf. Son, ssw-M. Frances, b. 06/19/1939, d. 06/19/1939
MILLMAN, M. Frances, ssw-Roland P., b. 03/11/1920, d. N/D
MILLMAN, Maxine C., ssw-Fred A., b. 03/05/1924, d. N/D
MILLMAN, Roland P., ssw-M. Frances, b. 08/20/1916, d. 06/20/1996
MILLMAN, Roland P., Jr., "Sonny," ssw-G. June, b. 05/11/1950, d. 11/22/1993
MILLMAN, Una C. Rust, ssw-Howard E., b. 10/01/1912, d. 07/24/1978
MILLMAN, Vietta R., ssw-Harold C., b. 01/08/1918, d. N/D
MINCY, Fay N., ssw-William R., Sr., b. 09/11/1916, d. N/D
MINCY, William R., Sr., ssw-Fay N., b. 08/08/1914, d. 05/21/1987
MITCHELL, Charles H., DE, Pvt., 59 Pioneer Inf., b. 04/05/1896, d. 02/24/1935
MITCHELL, Cordelia Ann, ssw-Jacob, b. 1881, d. 1945
MITCHELL, Eliza Jane, ssw-Rufus Thomas, b. 05/06/1865, d. 05/07/1937
MITCHELL, Elizabeth W., ssw-George R., b. 02/25/1882, d. 05/21/1957
MITCHELL, Emma J., ssw-John C., b. 06/28/1893, d. 01/26/1963

MITCHELL, Enoch L., b. 10/28/1883, d. 02/12/1954

MITCHELL, George R., ssw-Elizabeth W., b. 09/20/1879, d. 11/24/1972

MITCHELL, Henry W., ssw-Levenia C., b. 06/01/1867, d. 12/23/1947

MITCHELL, Ida G., ssw-Rufus W., b. 1894, d. 1954

MITCHELL, Isaac A., ssw-Mollie A., b. 07/26/1866, d. 04/09/1943

MITCHELL, Jacob, ssw-Cordelia Ann, b. 1871, d. 1951

MITCHELL, James L., b. 05/17/1854, d. 10/08/1942

MITCHELL, John C., ssw-Emma J., b. 11/30/1895, d. 02/12/1960

MITCHELL, John H., ssw-Minnie E., b. 09/05/1889, d. 05/01/1952

MITCHELL, Julia E., w/o James L., b. 05/28/1861, d. 03/21/1915

MITCHELL, Lenora B. Hudson, w/o Leonard B., ssw-Leonard B., b. 1861, d. 1918

MITCHELL, Leonard B., ssw-Lenora B. Hudson, b. 1850, d. 1936

MITCHELL, Levenia C., ssw-Henry W., b. 02/07/1870, d. 01/14/1944

MITCHELL, Mary J., b. 1860, d. 1937

MITCHELL, Minnie E., ssw-John H., b. 11/23/1891, d. 1969

MITCHELL, Mollie A., ssw-Isaac A., b. 06/08/1867, d. 05/29/1929

MITCHELL, Preston A., BTC, USN, WWII, Korea, b. 01/19/1919, d. 10/09/1980

MITCHELL, Rufus Thomas, ssw-Eliza Jane, b. 01/06/1865, d. 04/29/1953

MITCHELL, Rufus W., b. 1835, d. 1915

MITCHELL, Rufus W., ssw-Ida G., b. 1893, d. 1981

MOORE, Alice V., b. 1882, d. 1947

MOORE, Annie, w/o Wm. T., Age 62y, b. N/D, d. 05/08/1917

MOORE, Edward, ssw-Parris T., Brothers, b. 1878, d. 1943

MOORE, Harry J., ssw-Mabel L., b. 08/20/1896, d. 06/05/1986

MOORE, James E., b. 1849, d. 1932

MOORE, Mabel L., ssw-Harry J., b. 09/07/1900, d. 03/29/1989

MOORE, Parris T., ssw-Edward, Brothers, b. 1876, d. 1954

MOORE, William E., b. 1884, d. 1963

MOSS, Warren H., St. Sgt., USA, WWII, b. 04/28/1921, d. 07/05/1983

MUMFORD, Ella H., ssw-Neal & William H., b. 1882, d. 1928

MUMFORD, Frances S., ssw-Harry E., Frank E. & James N., b. 1925, d. N/D

MUMFORD, Frank E., ssw-Harry E., Frances S., & James N., b. 1954, d. N/D

MUMFORD, Harry E., ssw-Frances S., Frank E. & James N., b. 1917, d. 1971

MUMFORD, James N., ssw-Harry E., Frances S. & Frank E., b. 1947, d. 1984

MUMFORD, Neal, ssw-Ella H. & William H., b. 1882, d. 1961

MUMFORD, William H., ssw-Ella H. & Neal, b. 1916, d. 1940

NEFF, Maud H., ssw-Norman C., b. 1897, d. 1981

NEFF, Norman C., ssw-Maud H., b. 1892, d. 1969

OTT, Emma B., ssw-Robert & Millie C., b. 09/07/1902, d. 08/06/1955

OTT, Millie C., ssw-Emma B. & Robert, b. 1909, d. 1975

OTT, Robert, ssw-Emma B. & Millie C., b. 10/12/1905, d. 08/05/1970

PALMER, Elmer E., b. 03/05/1879, d. 02/08/1965

PALMER, Gertrude, w/o Robert E. & d/o John L. & Mary C. Prittchett, b. N/D, d. 07/17/1907

PALMER, John J., s/o J. Samuel & Lizzie P., b. 11/03/1882, d. 10/03/1903

PALMER, John S., b. 01/27/1845, d. 10/11/1928

PALMER, Lizzie P., b. 03/04/1854, d. 03/29/1943

PALMER, Mary L., b. 12/08/1882, d. 03/19/1966

PALMER, Robert E., s/o Samuel & Elizabeth, b. 07/09/1880, d. 04/22/1915

PALMORE, Mezzey, b. 11/09/1817, d. 08/26/1882

PALMORE, Silvester, b. 0/08/1818, d. 10/09/1889

PANUSKA, Chad Linden, Age 19y, b. 08/03/1976, d. 07/02/1996

PARKER, Elizabeth, ssw-Joseph L. Holland, b. N/D, d. 1858

PARKER, Elizabeth, w/o John H. & d/o James & Eliza A. W. Fisher, b. 03/07/1858, d. 05/17/1893

PARSONS, Adolphus, ssw-Julia B., b. 1879, d. 1952

PARSONS, Arpie J., d/o T. H. & L. H., b. 10/14/1899, d. 03/03/1909

PARSONS, Catherine L., ssw-G. R. Cleave, b. 1896, d. N/D

PARSONS, Effie M., d/o Mathew & Berlinda Roach, b. 06/26/1890, d. 11/07/1956

PARSONS, G. R. Cleave, ssw-Catherine L., b. 1894, d. 1960

PARSONS, John C., b. 12/23/1889, d. 07/0/1962

PARSONS, Julia B., ssw-Adolphus, b. 1884, d. 1954

PARSONS, Lavinnia H., w/o Thomas H., b. 04/08/1859, d. 12/19/1947

PARSONS, Thomas H., b. 06/01/1842, d. 01/06/1915

PARSONS, Thomas V., b. 09/01/1883, d. 06/02/1949

PEPPER, Grace Vincent, ssw-Marshall H. Vincent, b. 03/29/1918, d. 03/30/1940

PETTYJOHN, Emma T., ssw-John P. Thomlinson, b. 1862, d. 1942

PETTYJOHN, Frances V., b. 03/20/1904, d. 02/04/1975

PETTYJOHN, Linford R., b. 11/08/1902, d. 04/10/1970

PETTYJOHN, Willard S., b. 06/08/1869, d. 05/24/1894

PETTYJOHN, Zachariah, b. 11/20/1828, d. 04/08/1898

PRETTYMAN, Charles P., b. 08/04/1887, d. 09/07/1965

PRETTYMAN, Gideon W., Age 52y 10m 2d, b. N/D, d. 02/20/1873

PRETTYMAN, Hettie E., b. 06/21/1831, d. 09/13/1913

PRETTYMAN, John A., b. 1865, d. 1952

PRETTYMAN, Shepards, Age 28y 10m 26d, b. N/D, d. 09/25/1889

PURCELL, Hayden D., b. 09/01/1927, d. 11/20/1994

PURCELL, Marian H., b. 10/20/1921, d. N/D

RAEA, Catherine, ssw-William, b. 1902, d. 1964

RAEA, William, ssw-Catherine, b. 1881, d. 1948

REGISTER, George M., b. 11/24/1862, d. 10/30/1864

REGISTER, Wilbur F., b. 02/01/1865, d. 02/04/1865

REYNOLDS, Bessie W., d/o N. D. & Lizzie C., b. 12/14/1887, d. 04/28/1905

REYNOLDS, Burton E., ssw-Hannah D., b. 08/02/1846, d. 02/23/1930

REYNOLDS, Dorothy M., ssw-Paynter I., b. 04/30/1913, d. N/D

REYNOLDS, Eleanor, ssw-Linford, b. 06/04/1908, d. N/D

REYNOLDS, Elhanan B., Age 63y, b. N/D, d. 07/23/1880

REYNOLDS, Frederick T., ssw-Orna C., b. 01/18/1882, d. 01/29/1918

REYNOLDS, Hannah D., ssw-Burton E., b. 11/05/1846, d. 01/29/1918

REYNOLDS, Hazel Wright, d/o Homer & Bessie, b. 01/12/22, d. N/D

REYNOLDS, Helen P., b. 12/25/1935, d. 03/19/1938

REYNOLDS, Herbert T., DE, Capt., Inf., Korea, BSM, b. 04/02/1927, d. 11/26/1970

REYNOLDS, Jacob R., ssw-Marie H., b. 10/28/1925, d. 05/16/1979

REYNOLDS, James F., s/o Burton & Hannah, b. 08/23/1875, d. 07/17/1896

REYNOLDS, Jeanette G., b. 1931, d. N/D

REYNOLDS, John H., ssw-Lillie M., b. 1883, d. 1949

REYNOLDS, Leon J., ssw-Mabel C., Pfc, USA, WWII, b. 02/19/1921, d. 11/07/1995

REYNOLDS, Lillie M., ssw-John H., b. 1882, d. 1957

REYNOLDS, Linford, ssw-Eleanor, b. 12/31/1900, d. 02/16/1986
REYNOLDS, Lizzie C., ssw-Nehemiah D., b. 11/30/1864, d. 09/20/1952
REYNOLDS, Mabel C., m. 07-06-1943, b. 10/11/1925, d. 09/29/1993
REYNOLDS, Marie H., ssw-Jacob R., b. 05/16/1935, d. 08/04/1988
REYNOLDS, Nehemiah D., ssw-Lizzie C., b. 01/20/1862, d. 05/20/1918
REYNOLDS, Orna C., ssw-Frederick T., b. 03/31/1887, d. 06/02/1941
REYNOLDS, Paynter I., ssw-Dorothy M., b. 01/11/1911, d. 10/31/1987
REYNOLDS, Robert H., s/o E. B. & Margaret, Age 26, b. N/D, d. 06/02/1885
REYNOLDS, Robert R., s/o Fred & Orna, b. 01/17/18, d. 07/01/80
REYNOLDS, Sallie W., w/o Richard, b. 12/14/1844, d. 11/29/1925
REYNOLDS, Thomas, s/o Ellen D., b. N/D, d. 05/26/1881
RICE, Rosalie C., ssw-W. Andrew, b. 09/14/1932, d. N/D
RICE, W. Andrew, ssw-Rosalie C., b. 12/27/1930, d. 04/07/1986
RICHARDS, Ann R., w/o Barak, b. 01/07/1829, d. 03/10/1880
RICHARDS, Barak, b. 04/09/1826, d. 09/03/1896
RICHARDS, Beatrice H., ssw-Jacob H., b. 01/22/1909, d. 03/25/1990
RICHARDS, Elizabeth H., d/o Ann & Barak, b. 03/05/1854, d. 10/18/1879
RICHARDS, Jacob H., ssw-Beatrice H., b. 10/30/1900, d. 07/23/1993
RICHARDS, Jacob H., ssw-Theodore W., b. 10/27/1836, d. 06/16/1866
RICHARDS, Rachel C., ssw-Theodore W., b. 02/13/1840, d. 02/27/1917
RICHARDS, Theodore W., ssw-Jacob H., b. 11/17/1864, d. N/D
RITTER, Carl H., DE, WT3, USNR, WWII, b. 09/30/1924, d. 04/02/1965
RITTER, Charles R., ssw-Dorothy M. Ganrude, b. 10/31/1932, d. N/D
RITTER, Doris R. Noel, b. 03/14/1926, d. 08/22/1979
RITTER, Frances M., ssw-Charles R., b. 06/23/1938, d. 04/18/1989
ROACH, Berlinda C., ssw-Mathew M., b. 1864, d. 1931
ROACH, Mathew M., ssw-Berlinda C., b. 1857, d. 1911
ROBINSON, Alfred B., ssw-Lydia E. White, b. 08/29/1847, d. 02/14/1915
ROBINSON, John Dorman, ssw-Margaret Franklin, Pvt., USA, b. 02/16/1891, d. 07/19/1973
ROBINSON, Lydia E. White, w/o Alfred B., ssw-Alfred B., b. 07/16/1858, d. 06/06/1935
ROBINSON, Margaret Franklin, ssw-John Dorman, b. 01/16/1895, d. 07/28/1964
RUST, Absalom, ssw-William T., b. 12/07/1808, d. 01/07/1891
RUST, Anna H., b. 1903, d. D/N
RUST, Annie E., ssw-William T., b. 1850, d. 1928
RUST, Exa A., b. 1875, d. 1974
RUST, Maria, ssw-William T., b. 10/24/1801, d. 05/31/1851
RUST, Maria E., ssw-William T., b. 03/30/1843, d. 05/23/1917
RUST, Victor A., b. 1902, d. 1953
RUST, William E., b. 1870, d. 1931
RUST, William T., ssw-Annie E., b. 01/16/1841, d. 10/14/1917
SCHEDER, Mary V., b. 07/11/1939, d. 01/07/1994
SEUTTER, Miriam V., ssw-Walter H., Jr., b. 07/13/1926, d. N/D
SEUTTER, Walter H., Jr., ssw-Miriam V., b. 11/14/1924, d. 10/27/1986
SHARP, Clara E., ssw-George R., b. 1876, d. 1946
SHARP, Elizabeth J., ssw-Nathaniel & Sarah E., b. 1837, d. 1925
SHARP, Ella A., ssw-Wm. W., Geo. W. & John H. Sharp and Albert H. Smith and William Van Wright,
    b. 05/17/1862, d. 08/08/1951

SHARP, Geo. W., ssw-Wm. W., Ella A. & John H. Sharp and Albert H. Smith and William Van Wright, b. 11/28/1880, d. 02/03/1881

SHARP, George R., ssw-Clara E., b. 1869, d. 1941

SHARP, John H., ssw-Wm. W., Ella A. & John H. Sharp and Albert H. Smith and William Van Wright, b. 04/29/1863, d. 08/15/1885

SHARP, Nathaniel, ssw-Elizabeth J. & Sarah E., b. 1835, d. 1919

SHARP, Sarah E., ssw-Nathaniel & Elizabeth J., b. 1858, d. 1920

SHARP, Wm. W., ssw-Ella A., Geo. W., & John H. Sharp and Albert H. Smith and William Van Wright, b. 04/19/1856, d. 03/31/1954

SHOCKLEY, Bessie C., ssw-Viral E., b. 03/27/1908, d. N/D

SHOCKLEY, James W., b. 12/09/1844, d. 08/28/1911

SHOCKLEY, Ruth A., b. 10/03/1842, d. 04/07/1922

SHOCKLEY, Viral E., ssw-Bessie C., b. 11/20/1902, d. 02/26/1951

SHORT, Albert W., s/o W. B. & Anna D., b. 09/03/1916, d. 09/12/1917

SHORT, Anna D., ssw-W. Bruce & E. Marguerite, b. 1883, d. 1959

SHORT, E. Marguerite, ssw-W. Bruce & Anna D., b. 1910, d. 1996

SHORT, W. Bruce, ssw-Anna D. & E. Marguerite, b. 1883, d. 1974

SIMPLER, Alfred, b. 01/20/1856, d. 07/05/1915

SIMPLER, Matilda, Age 60y 4m 1d, b. N/D, d. 12/12/1874

SIMPLER, William H., Age 62y 6m 1d, b. N/D, d. 03/19/1872

SMACK, Doris E., ssw-Lillie A. Lynch, b. 08/21/1918, d. 12/01/1975

SMITH, Albert H., ssw-Wm. W., Ella A., John H. & Geo. W. Sharp and William Van Wright, Grandson, b. 02/06/1911, d. 07/15/1911

SMITH, Joseph, b. 1879, d. 1938

SMITH, Martha E., ssw-William G., b. 1867, d. 1937

SMITH, William G., ssw-Martha E., b. 1864, d. 1950

STEELE, George, ssw-John & Minnie, b. 1907, d. 1961

STEELE, John, ssw-Minnie & George, b. 1890, d. 1963

STEELE, Minnie, ssw-John & George, b. 1886, d. 1948

STEPHENS, Mary Jane, d/o Clara H. & Wm. H. Stephens, b. 11/06/1881, d. 04/05/1883

STEWART, Elizabeth Marie, b. 06/22/1975, d. 01/02/1983

SWISHER, Robert S., ssw-Thomas W. Turner, b. 1903, d. 980

TAYLOR, Howard W., Pop, b. 10/01/1901, d. 02/19/1976

TEAS, Eliza Holland, d/o Joseph & Alice Holland, b. 1860, d. 1950

TEES, Delma M., ssw-Victor A., b. 08/08/1902, d. 03/17/1991

TEES, Victor A., ssw-Delma M., b. 12/22/1897, d. 01/01/1971

THOMLINSON, John P., Capt., ssw-Emma T. Pettyjohn, b. 11/21/1855, d. 12/06/1912

TITTERMARY, Howard C., b. 1908, d. 1911

TITTERMARY, Jennie C., b. 1885, d. 1918

TITTERMARY, Raymond J., b. 1905, d. 1955

TITTERMARY, Robert C., b. 1876, d. 1949

TRUITT, Benjamin Franklin, ssw-Elenor, b. 07/10/1858, d. 03/03/1945

TRUITT, Cora M., b. 1894, d. 1958

TRUITT, Joseph B., b. 1890, d. 1937

TRUITT, L. Delema, ssw-W. Harry, b. 01/15/1890, d. 06/16/1951

TRUITT, Louisa A., w/o Wm. A., b. 08/16/1839, d. 06/16/1899

TRUITT, Mary Elenor, ssw-Benjamin Franklin, b. 03/16/1865, d. 12/05/1948

TRUITT, W. Harry, ssw-L. Delema, b. 11/16/1884, d. 08/06/1949

TRUITT, William A., b. 04/22/1822, d. 03/27/1894

TURNER, M. Elizabeth, ssw-Thomas W., b. 1877, d. 1952

TURNER, Thomas W., ssw-M. Elizabeth, b. 1871, d. 1926

UNKNOWN, Baby, b. N/D, d. N/D

UNKNOWN, Mary C., b. N/D, d. 09/1886

UNKNOWN, Willard H., Age 27d, b. N/D, d. 07/17/1887

VAN WRIGHT, William, ssw-Wm. W., Ella A., Geo. W. & John H. Sharp and Albert H. Smith, Grandson, b. 04/28/1901, d. 07/15/1901

VESSELS, Ollie T., ssw-Rowland P. Warrington, b. 1873, d. 1895

VINCENT, Bertha E., b. 12/02/1876, d. 10/23/1931

VINCENT, Burton R., b. 11/30/1906, d. 05/29/1926

VINCENT, C. P. Warrington, ssw-Lillian H., b. 12/10/1914, d. 04/27/1987

VINCENT, C. Paul, ssw-Lena R., b. 10/23/1902, d. 03/31/1994

VINCENT, Carleton E., ssw-Rowland P. Warrington, b. 1882, d. 1914

VINCENT, Charles H., ssw-Medora J., b. 02/12/1873, d. 12/25/1926

VINCENT, Dora W., w/o Myers W., b. 02/02/1848, d. 01/09/1914

VINCENT, Durand M., b. 1885, d. 1955

VINCENT, Ella N., b. 05/16/1879, d. 04/08/1905

VINCENT, Elsie May, d/o Henry D. P. & Ida, Age 4d, b. N/D, d. 01/11/1900

VINCENT, Ethel P., b. 1883, d. 1960

VINCENT, Fannie E., ssw-Herbert J., b. 04/01/1882, d. 05/15/1964

VINCENT, Henry D. P., ssw-Iowa D., b. 08/08/1874, d. 01/16/1922

VINCENT, Herbert J., ssw-Fannie E., b. 01/06/1878, d. 06/01/1948

VINCENT, Iowa D., ssw-Henry D. P., b. 04/10/1879, d. 05/19/1961

VINCENT, Lena R., w/o C. Paul, ssw-C. Paul, b. 01/26/1902, d. 12/28/1965

VINCENT, Lillian H., ssw-C. P. Warrington, b. 11/23/1917, d. N/D

VINCENT, Marshall H., ssw-Grace Vincent Pepper, b. 05/17/1901, d. 05/02/1923

VINCENT, Mary E., d/o Medora J. & Chas. H., b. 09/04/1889, d. 01/06/1900

VINCENT, Medora J., ssw-Charles H., b. 07/26/1876, d. 11/21/1913

VINCENT, Minnie Warrington, w/o Carleton E., ssw-Carleton E., b. 1882, d. 1963

WALSH, Ella E., w/o James, ssw-James, b. 11/26/1850, d. 02/28/1926

WALSH, James, h/o Ella E., ssw-Ella E., b. 11/09/1846, d. 04/03/1918

WARRINGTON, Ida M., ssw-Rowland P., Nora C. & Mary R., b. 1878, d. 1878

WARRINGTON, Mary R., ssw-Rowland P., Ida M. & Nora C., b. 1853, d. 1940

WARRINGTON, Nora C., ssw-Rowland P., Ida M. & Mary R., b. 1875, d. 1895

WARRINGTON, Rowland P., ssw-Mary R., Ida M. & Nora C., b. 1848, d. 1932

WEBB, Anna, ssw-George, b. 05/09/1853, d. 08/27/1930

WEBB, Charles, ssw-George, b. 08/09/1843, d. 01/25/1923

WEBB, George, ssw-Anna, b. 06/18/1883, d. 09/07/1967

WELLS, Ada E., ssw-Martin A., b. 06/11/1912, d. N/D

WELLS, Betsy M., ssw-J. Carlton, b. 04/16/1926, d. N/D

WELLS, D. Alfred, ssw-Ollie W., b. 1888, d. 1954

WELLS, David T., b. 09/17/1856, d. 04/14/1928

WELLS, Eliza J., b. 01/08/1865, d. 01/29/1935

WELLS, Florence M., ssw-Irvin D., b. 1902, d. 1990

WELLS, Harvey H., ssw-Lovie M., b. 1893, d. 1970

WELLS, I. Stanley, b. 03/14/1924, d. 12/23/1964

WELLS, Irvin D., ssw-Florence M., b. 1898, d. 1979

WELLS, J. Carlton, ssw-Betsy M., b. 09/17/1926, d. N/D
WELLS, Kelly Sue, b. 08/21/1969, d. 08/21/1969
WELLS, Lovie M., ssw-Harvey H., b. 1897, d. 1995
WELLS, Martin A., ssw-Ada E., b. 08/09/1916, d. N/D
WELLS, Ollie W., ssw-D. Alfred, b. 1896, d. 1950
WELLS, Richard D., II, "Dickie," Age 32y, b. N/D, d. 11/05/1996
WHITE, Alfred R., ssw-Margaret E., b. 11/13/1840, d. 06/13/1915
WHITE, Ann D., consort o/Robert, Age 71y, b. 01/08/1807, d. 10/22/1877
WHITE, Bessie Sterling, d/o Maggie E. & Alfred, b. 10/24/1891, d. 01/01/1895
WHITE, Elizabeth P., d/o A. R. & Maggie, b. 11/21/1893, d. 09/06/1896
WHITE, Henry H., ssw-Ruth C., b. 1829, d. 1911
WHITE, James J., b. 12/28/1827, d. 11/20/1861
WHITE, James J., ssw-Margaret P., b. 09/08/1867, d. 09/08/1927
WHITE, Lew F., ssw-Mary A., b. 08/27/1890, d. 05/26/1957
WHITE, Lizzie M., d/o Wallace & Tabitha, Age 19y 22d, b. N/D, d. 10/14/1889
WHITE, Margaret E., ssw-Alfred R., b. 12/10/1855, d. 03/03/1951
WHITE, Margaret P., ssw-James J., b. 11/15/1879, d. 07/25/1957
WHITE, Marguerite T., b. 04/14/1906, d. 03/12/1988
WHITE, Mary A., ssw-Lew F., b. 07/06/1893, d. 02/08/1981
WHITE, Mary A., ssw-Ruth C., b. 1834, d. 1912
WHITE, Mary E., ssw-Ruth C., b. 1870, d. 1894
WHITE, Mary L., w/o W. Harry H., b. 1883, d. 1927
WHITE, Robert H., b. 05/18/1902, d. 07/05/1965
WHITE, Ruth C., ssw-Henry H., b. 1879, d. 1912
WHITE, Tabitha, w/o Wallace W., Age 37y 10m 18d, b. N/D, d. 12/29/1874
WHITE, Wallace W., Age 36y 7m 14d, b. N/D, d. 07/17/1875
WILLEY, Arzie Anna, b. 10/14/1904, d. 06/17/1936
WILLEY, Margaret L., ssw-Russell C., b. 10/13/1926, d. N/D
WILLEY, Marion Anna, b. 1929, d. 1929
WILLEY, Neal C., b. 12/26/1952, d. 10/17/1982
WILLEY, Patricia Ann, b. 04/19/1948, d. 12/05/1954
WILLEY, Russell C., ssw-Margaret L., b. 07/18/1918, d. 08/19/1976
WILLEY, Theodore N., Pvt., USA, b. 03/02/1933, d. 02/10/1954
WILLIAMS, Evelyn T., ssw-Raymond J., b. 05/27/1901, d. 05/23/1988
WILLIAMS, Raymond J., ssw-Evelyn T., b. 04/23/1904, d. 06/16/1983
WILSON, Bertha M., c/o T. P. & M. E., ssw-Sarah E., Age 1m 29d, b. N/D, d. N/D
WILSON, Clarric V., Age 8y 4m 23d, b. N/D, d. 01/29/1879
WILSON, Eldridge J., ssw-Pearl, b. 04/05/1894, d. 02/27/1963
WILSON, Margaret Robinson, w/o Wells Warren Wilson, D.D.S., b. 01/29/1895, d. 01/31/1989
WILSON, Mary E., ssw-Theodore P., b. 03/15/1855, d. 04/29/1924
WILSON, Pearl, ssw-Eldridge J., b. 07/24/1884, d. 0/14/1968
WILSON, Raymond Emery, s/o T. P. & M. E., b. 05/24/1897, d. 10/01/1897
WILSON, Sarah E., c/o T. P., ssw-Bertha M., Age 5m 10d, b. N/D, d. N/D
WILSON, Theodore P., ssw-Mary E., b. 03/10/1851, d. 12/25/1940
WORKMAN, Myrtis G., b. 12/08/1904, d. 08/20/1951
WORKMAN, Norman J., b. 01/13/1904, d. 11/03/1964
WRIGHT, Eliza Ann, 1st consort o/Elisha Holland, b. 01/17/1800, d. 03/08/1832

WYLIE, Emile, Taken from the southern home of Phila. 9/4/1900 by A. R. White, age 17, b. N/D, d. 06/07/1907

(BK-008 & HU-NR) WEIGAN CEMETERY

Located S. E. of Milton on the Northeast Side of Cave Neck Rd. (Rt. 88) 0.2 miles S. E. of Round Pole Bridge Rd. (Rd. 257).
Recorded: November 7, 1996

ANDRIE, Baby, ssw-Gertie & Wallace E., b. N/D, d. 1912
ANDRIE, Gertie, ssw-Baby & Wallace E., b. N/D, d. 1909
ANDRIE, Wallace E., ssw-Gertie & Baby, b. N/D, d. 1920
DONOVAN, Martha J., d/o Charles M. & Laura F., b. 03/10/1904, d. 11/08/1910
DONOVAN, Nancy J., b. 07/03/1849, d. 01/04/1919
DONOVAN, Peter S., b. 10/19/1848, d. 01/17/1919
JOHNSON, Abram, b. Stone Broken, d. 12/28/1913
JOHNSON, Martha Jane, w/o Abram, Age 81y 6m 20d, b. N/D, d. 10/01/1913
JOHNSON, Wm. E., b. 08/02/1903, d. 09/10/1909
MAULL, Annie, w/o James E., ssw-James E., b. 07/21/1850, d. 05/30/1919
MAULL, Frances A., w/o Purnell J., Age 79y 3m 22d, b. N/D, d. 02/12/1899
MAULL, Gladys M., d/o W. A. & E. M., b. 02/28/1909, d. 02/28/1909
MAULL, James E., ssw-Annie, b. 05/01/1843, d. 07/07/1921
MAULL, Purnell J., Age 73y 7m 12d, b. N/D, d. 03/26/1892
PEPPER, Comfort A., w/o Thomas B., b. 12/12/1845, d. 09/18/1912
PEPPER, Raymond, s/o Thos. T. & Mary E., b. 03/23/1896, d. 03/28/1896
PEPPER, Thomas B., Co. H., 3rd Rec., Del. Vol. Inf., b. 02/18/1840, d. 02/07/1916

(BK-009 & HU-301) HARBESON CEMETERY, aka BEAVER DAM CEMETERY

Located in Harbeson on the S. W. corner of Harbeson Rd., (Rt. 5) and Seashore Highway (Rt. 9)
Recorded: October 23, 1996

ABBOTT, Angeline, b. N/D, d. N/D
ABBOTT, George H., b. 01/22/1909, d. 11/08/1983
ABBOTT, Lydia L., b. 1863, d. 1935
ABBOTT, Lehemiah J., b. 1859, d. 1924
ADAMS, Elizabeth M., ssw-William L., b. 08/03/1917, d. 05/19/1991
ADAMS, William L., ssw-Elizabeth M., b. 06/17/1912, d. 03/04/1978
ALLEN, Carmen Mae, b. 03/03/1926, d. 03/19/1993
ARMSTRONG, Mary Verena, b. 03/02/1891, d. 09/08/1991
ATKINS, Annie L. Rolden, d/o Allen H. & Sarah L., Age 2y 18d, b. N/D, d. 08/09/1877
ATKINS, James P., ssw-Mary C., b. 1852, d. 1919
ATKINS, Lettie C., d/o Loday W. & Sarah Ann, b. 09/11/1849, d. 04/25/1918
ATKINS, Loda W., s/o James & Aletta, Age 44y 2m 15d, b. 11/16/1817, d. 01/01/1862
ATKINS, Mary C., w/o James P., ssw-James P., b. 1861, d. 1929
ATKINS, Sarah A. Wilson, w/o Loda W., Age 80y 10m 27d, b. 06/09/1823, d. 04/06/1904
ATKINS, Sarah Jane, d/o Loda & Sarah, b. 07/11/1848, d. 01/22/1931
AUERBACH, Lora May, b. 01/02/1883, d. 08/07/1962

BARKER, Edith H., b. 1892, d. 1988

BARKER, Harry, b. 1882, d. 1931

BAUM, Charles, ssw-Clara E., b. 06/09/1888, d. 01/16/1970

BAUM, Clara F., ssw-Charles, b. 02/29/1892, d. 12/07/1978

BAYNUM, Harry T., ssw-Lela L., b. 06/23/1924, d. 11/05/1986

BAYNUM, Lela L., ssw-Harry T., b. 12/24/1927, d. N/D

BELL, Charles William, ssw-Pauline Moore, b. 11/30/1905, d. 09/12/1973

BELL, Pauline Moore, ssw-Charles William, b. 02/24/1912, d. 05/31/1996

BENNETT, Hilda M., ssw-Howard W., b. 1918, d. 1990

BENNETT, Howard W., ssw-Hilda M., b. 1914, d. 1972

BETTS, James B., b. 1867, d. 1955

BETTS, Leonard James, DE, Cpl, Ordance Corps., b. 05/22/1931, d. 08/18/1961

BLAKE, Robert Lee, DE, Sgt, 5th Cav., b. N/D, d. 03/11/1920

BLIZZARD, Rachel A. Atkins, w/o John E., b. 04/15/1856, d. 12/16/1878

BOWDEN, Harry H., b. 196, d. 1981

BRICKNER, Helen L., ssw-John W., b. 04/03/1899, d. 09/18/1963

BRICKNER, John W., ssw-Helen L., b. 05/02/1896, d. 07/24/1980

BRITTIAN, D. Scott, b. 01/26/1960, d. 01/29/1996

BRITTINGHAM, Annie A., ssw-William T. & Fred W. Brittingham and Bessie M. Patterson, b. 1878, d. 1954

BRITTINGHAM, Fred W., ssw-William T. & Annie A. Brittingham and Bessie M. Patterson, b. 1905, d. 1970

BRITTINGHAM, William T., ssw-Annie A. & Fred W. Brittingham and Bessie M. Patterson, b. 1873, d. 1940

CAREY, A. Russell, ssw-Kathryn P., b. 12/09/1914, d. N/D

CAREY, Alletta J., d/o Louis J. & Estella M., b. 11/10/1899, d. 02/21/1903

CAREY, Alton J., ssw-Delema M., b. 09/19/1904, d. 11/11/1958

CAREY, Annie S. Roach, w/o Henry H., b. 01/09/1872, d. 04/03/1925

CAREY, Angeline W., ssw-John P., b. 1828, d. 1902

CAREY, Charles E., b. 10/31/1869, d. 05/07/1948

CAREY, Delema M., ssw-Alton J., b. 02/09/1910, d. 02/15/1980

CAREY, Della E., d/o Joseph H. & Virgie, b. 12/13/1902, d. 01/23/1903

CAREY, Estella M., ssw-Louis J., b. 1880, d. 1963

CAREY, Frederic W., s/o J. T. & Harriet J., b. 07/23/1873, d. 09/15/1908

CAREY, Harriet J., w/o J. Tull, b. 05/03/1845, d. 07/02/1915

CAREY, James H., b. 02/05/1813, d. 05/02/1887

CAREY, James T., b. 09/15/1838, d. 02/19/1928

CAREY, James Tull, ssw-Marion Pollitt, b. 08/18/1912, d. N/D

CAREY, John P., ssw-Angeline W., b. 1860, d. 1925

CAREY, Joseph, ssw-John P., b. 1823, d. 1904

CAREY, Joseph H., b. 07/17/1878, d. 05/15/1921

CAREY, Kathryn P., ssw-A. Russell, b. 07/28/1916, d. 10/30/1992

CAREY, Louis J., ssw-Estella M., b 1868, d. 1943

CAREY, Loura L., b. 03/13/1869, d. 10/11/1949

CAREY, Lucy, d/o W. M. & Mary L. M., Age 21d, b. N/D, d. 07/20/1902

CAREY, Marion Pollitt, ssw-James Tull, b. 07/13/1910, d. N/D

CAREY, Martha E., ssw-Willard M., b. 12/29/1886, d. 04/16/1965

CAREY, Mary A., b. 09/04/1811, d. 02/22/1865

CAREY, Mary L. M., w/o Willard M., b. 05/18/1871, d. 06/29/1902
CAREY, Paynter F., b. 1852, d. 1928
CAREY, Ralph D., b. 1897, d. 1920
CAREY, Sue T., b. 04/17/1855, d. 10/10/1932
CAREY, Willard C., s/o W. M. & Mary L. M., Age 2m 18d, b. N/D, d. 06/15/1900
CAREY, Willard M., ssw-Martha E., b. 10/16/1866, d. 10/21/1959
CAREY, William B., b. 01/15/1852, d. 01/14/1899
CARMEAN, David H., b. 1895, d. 1985
CARPENTER, Benton H., b. 05/03/1813, d. 04/24/1895
CARPENTER, George T., ssw-Mary H. Carpenter and William S. Martin, Jr., b. 02/17/1858, d. 11/22/1922
CARPENTER, Lida Jane, ssw-Oscar, b. 1864, d. 1952
CARPENTER, Louvenia, ssw-William S. Martin, Jr., b. 04/18/1839, d. 10/11/1874
CARPENTER, Mary H., ssw-George T. Carpenter and William S. Martin, Jr., b. 04/08/1861, d. 08/07/1921
CARPENTER, Mary H., w/o Benton H., b. 12/24/1829, d. 08/17/1895
CARPENTER, Oscar, ssw-Lida Jane, b. 1865, d. 1954
CARPENTER, Virgie M., ssw-Oscar, b. 1899, d. 1945
CARPENTER, William S., ssw-William S. Martin, Jr., b. 02/17/1838, d. 05/18/1919
CARTER, Mary B., b. 1915, d. 1982
CATCHELL, George W., b. 1864, d. 1915
CHAMBERLAIN, Tenie, b. 1884, d. 1946
CLAVETTE, Unknown, b. N/D, d. N/D
CLENDANIEL, Arabella, w/o Jos. G., b. 07/29/1858, d. 09/23/1914
CONLEY, Harriet H., b. 1882, d. 1951
CONNOR, Dorothy V., ssw-Dorothy F. Rogers, b. 09/15/1925, d. 03/14/1993
CONNOR, Thaddeus, b. 1988, d. 1988
COULSTON, Fannie T., b. 1907, d. 1986
COULSTON, William R., EM2, USN, WWII, b. 10/24/1903, d. 01/20/1986
COULTER, Benjamin B., s/o James & Rhoda F., Age 19y 10m 16d, b. 12/17/1850, d. 11/03/1870
COULTER, Harry M., b. 06/08/1878, d. 01/23/1934
COULTER, James, b. 07/04/1820, d. 08/23/1889
COULTER, James Andrew, ssw-Susan Elizabeth, b. 07/08/1853, d. 03/23/1922
COULTER, Rhoda F., w/o James, b. 07/27/1829, d. 06/29/1898
COULTER, Susan Elizabeth, ssw-James Andrew, b. 10/20/1855, d. 07/27/1938
COULTER, Susie C., d/o James A. & Susan E., b. 10/08/1889, d. 07/27/1892
COULTER, Zena P., c/o William E. & Mary C., b. 02/18/1886, d. 10/06/1890
DAVIDSON, Albert C., b. 12/27/1907, d. 07/24/1978
DAVIDSON, Charles A., b. 09/22/1875, d. 01/31/1947
DAVIDSON, Charles R., ssw-Eugenia C., b. 1864, d. 1948
DAVIDSON, Donna A., b. 08/08/1924, d. N/D
DAVIDSON, Edna L., b. 01/25/1905, d. 09/14/1992
DAVIDSON, Effie M., b. 06/29/1911, d. 01/01/1995
DAVIDSON, Eugenia C., ssw-Charles R., b. 1867, d. 1949
DAVIDSON, Frank, b. 08/28/1904, d. 07/21/1984
DAVIDSON, John W., ssw-Leah R., b. 1832, d. 1926
DAVIDSON, Leah R., ssw-John W., b. 1833, d. 1907
DAVIDSON, Lizzie, b. 12/13/1878, d. 04/19/1941
DAVIDSON, Martin L., NC, Tec4, USA, WWII, b. 07/28/1899, d. 01/12/1971
DAVIDSON, Olga M., b. 11/25/1908, d. 11/28/1987

DAVIDSON, Robert M., b. 04/01/1924, d. 10/06/1963
DIRKS, Lilley, ssw-Thomas, Sr., b. 1912, d. 1986
DIRKS, Thomas, Sr., ssw-Lilley, b. 1900, d. 1960
DODD, Elsie L. K. (Kopple), b. 10/29/1902, d. 01/24/1995
DODD, Frank A., Sfc, USA, WWI, b. 01/08/1893, d. 0/11/1977
DODD, John Ed., b. 06/02/1858, d. 10/26/1882
DODD, Pearl L., b. 03/31/1908, d. N/D
DODD, Shirley Ann, b. 07/16/1939, d. 03/25/1940
DODD, W. Conwell, b. 08/21/1910, d. 05/29/1951
DONOVAN, Avery K., b. 09/01/1898, d. 07/04/1967
DONOVAN, Carrie E., d/o J. H. & Ida E. F., b. 09/05/1888, d. 02/12/1907
DONOVAN, Edison W., b. 12/07/1896, d. 05/25/1950
DONOVAN, Ida E. F., ssw-James H., b. 05/21/1858, d. 02/06/1946
DONOVAN, James H., ssw-Ida E. F., b. 02/26/1858, d. 11/17/1906
DONOVAN, Mildred V., b. 06/04/1905, d. 01/25/1973
DONOVAN, NFN, b. 0/18/1885, d. 07/21/1887
DONOVAN, NFN, b. 07/21/1887, d. 08/20/1887
DONOVAN, Sallie R., d/o J. H. & Ida E., b. 08/09/1881, d. 11/14/1901
DONOVAN, William W., Pfc, USA, b. 05/22/1930, d. 11/08/1994
DUTTON, Annie M., b. 1862, d. 1939
DUTTON, James I., b. 04/11/1848, d. 08/19/1919
ECKSTEIN, Edward F., ssw-Emma T., b. 03/18/1906, d. 05/29/1964
ECKSTEIN, Emma T., ssw-Edward F. b. 04/14/1911, d. N/D
ELLINGSWORTH, Mary D., ssw-Willard S., b. 1857, d. 1887
ELLINGSWORTH, Willard S., ssw-Mary D., b. 1854, d. 1933
ENNIS, Alice Salenia, w/o David Roland, ssw-David Roland, b. 06/161851, d. 11/28/1911
ENNIS, Charles S., b. 11/03/1872, d. 11/17/1923
ENNIS, David Roland, ssw-Alice Salenia, b. 02/12/1838, d. 03/01/1915
ENNIS, Jesse J., Age 73y 9m 17d, b. N/D, d. 12/15/1878
ENNIS, John Roland, s/o Chas. & Nora V., b. 07/23/1904, d. 02/03/1906
ENNIS, Margaret H., Age abt. 92y, b. N/D, d. 10/18/1867
ENNIS, Marie D., d/o Chas. & Nora V., b. 03/20/1908, d. 09/25/1908
ENNIS, Nora V., b. 12/12/1875, d. 11/30/1971
ENNIS, Sallie E., w/o J. J., Age 40y 8m 23d, b. N/D, d. 07/02/1855
FISHER, Charles T., b. 02/13/1847, d. 12/29/1912
FORST, Joseph F., b. 1879, d. 1960
FORST, Matilda, b. 1881, d. 1933
GOETZ, Clara, Sophia, Sisters, b. 02/01/1909, d. 02/01/1909
GOETZ, Isabella, d/o Max & Lottie, b. 1901, d. 1902
GOETZ, Sophia, ssw-Clara, Sisters, b. 02/10/1907, d. 02/10/1907
GOFF, Ervin A., ssw-Margie D., b. 04/08/1914, d. 04/26/1985
GOFF, Margie D., ssw-Ervin A., b. 04/21/1922, d. N/D
GRAHAM, Minnie M., ssw-S. Alson, b. 1886, d. 1951
GRAHAM, S. Alson, ssw-Minnie M., b. 1885, d. 1968
GREEN, Clifford O., ssw-Marie L., b. 05/10/1897, d. 11/29/1961
GREEN, Margaret V., ssw-William G., b. 1890, d. 1946
GREEN, Marie L., ssw-Clifford O., b. 04/14/1899, d. 12/15/1976
GREEN, William G., ssw-Margaret V., b 1887, d. 1972

GRIERSON, Grace B., ssw-Roy, b. 1913, d. N/D
GRIERSON, Roy, ssw-Grace B., b. 1904, d. 1993
HACKETT, John B., ssw-Ruth V., b. 1912, d. 1941
HACKETT, Ruth V., ssw-John B., b. 1887, d. 1963
HAND, Eugene M., "Marty," b. 12/03/1970, d. 03/22/1978
HAND, Theresa M., b. 06/01/1933, d. 06/16/1987
HASTINGS, David H., ssw-Phillip D., DE, Tec5, USA, WWII, b. 01/01/1920, d. 09/16/1972
HASTINGS, Ethel W., ssw-David H., b. 10/18/1922, d. 02/05/1996
HASTINGS, James Carr, ssw-Joshua C. & Jennie Pride, b. 1916, d. 1917
HASTINGS, Jennie Pride, ssw-Joshua C. & James Carr, b. 1893, d. 1949
HASTINGS, Joshua C., ssw-Jennie Pride & James Carr, b. 1896, d. 1976
HASTINGS, Phillip D., ssw-David H., b. 07/01/1947, d. 06/30/1967
HASTINGS, Phyllis H., ssw-Theodore A., b. 12/24/1927, d. N/D
HASTINGS, Theodore A., ssw-Phyllis H., b. 11/29/1924, d. N/D
HAZEL, Kensey S., b. 05/18/1886, d. 10/07/1917
HAZEL, Kensey S., ssw-Sarah M., b. 06/29/1899, d. 06/10/1925
HAZEL, Sarah M., w/o Kensey S., ssw-Kensey S., b. 01/31/1851, d. 11/28/1913
HAZEL, Thomas Martin, b. 03/23/1884, d. 04/14/1968
HICKMAN, Annias W., b. 12/14/1877, d. 06/18/1956
HICKMAN, Cora, ssw-William H., b. 1909, d. N/D
HICKMAN, Harry G., ssw-William H., b. 1929, d. 1959
HICKMAN, Harry W., ssw-Martha J., b. 07/20/1955, d. 02/23/1992
HICKMAN, Josephine M., d/o Wm. & Cora, b. 1931, d. 1933
HICKMAN, Martha J., ssw-Harry W., b. 10/05/1958, d. N/D
HICKMAN, Viola T., b. 10/29/1885, d. 07/02/1950
HICKMAN, William H., ssw-Harry G., b. 1907, d. 1979
HITCHENS, Carrie S., b. 1898, d. 1976
HITCHENS, Daniel H., b. 1893, d. 1990
HODGDON, Fannie E., ssw-William R., b. 1883, d. 1978
HODGDON, William R., ssw-Fannie E., b. 1877, d. 1947
HOLLAND, Andrew J., Age 79y 25d, b. 01/09/1820, d. 01/03/1899
HOLLAND, Andrew S., ssw-Arabella B., b. 1849, d. 1925
HOLLAND, Arabella B., w/o Andrew S., ssw-Andrew S., b. 1853, d. 1937
HOLLAND, Elizabeth M., w/o Andrew J., Age 69y 10m, b. 03/13/1822, d. 01/13/1892
HOLLAND, Margaret M., d/o Andrew J. & Mary, b. 02/23/1864, d. 05/14/1865
HOLLOWAY, Grace E., b. 06/02/1922, d. N/D
HOLLOWAY, Grace R., b. 08/22/1970, d. 08/24/1970
HOLLOWAY, James A., Sr., ssw-Myrtle, b. 09/06/1882, d. 05/14/1961
HOLLOWAY, James W., ssw-John, Jr., b. 03/11/1943, d. N/D
HOLLOWAY, Jesse E., DE, T5, Hq. Btry, 561 AAA AW BN CAC, WWII, b. 07/28/1915, d. 06/02/1970
HOLLOWAY, John, Jr., ssw-James W., b. 09/1945, d. N/D
HOLLOWAY, John W., Sr., Pfc., USA, WWII, b. 11/19/1920, d. 06/26/1992
HOLLOWAY, Myrtle, ssw-James A., Sr., b. 1882, d. 1913
HOUCK, Lavina E., b. 05/01/1888, d. 04/25/1971
HOWARD, Ebe W., ssw-Nora M. & Leroy J., b. 1873, d. 1939
HOWARD, Leroy J., ssw-Ebe W. & Nora M., b. 1901, d. 1915
HOWARD, Nora M., ssw-Ebe W. & Leroy J., b. 1869, d. 1958
HUDSON, Alletta M., b. 1883, d. 1933

HUDSON, Dian Ellen, b. 03/01/1952, d. 10/12/1990

HUDSON, Douglas C., ssw-Olivia Draper, MM1, USN, Seabees, WWII, b. 07/09/1920, d. 03/19/1986

HUDSON, Elizabeth I., b. 06/30/1905, d. 03/22/1982

HUDSON, Ella R., b. 09/14/1889, d. 08/23/1981

HUDSON, Francis, b. 1928, d. 1947

HUDSON, Frederick W., b. 1921, d. 1937

HUDSON, Harry H., b. 1877, d. 1942

HUDSON, Harry H., DE, MM11, USN, WWII, b. 06/29/1913, d. 08/25/1968

HUDSON, Louis C., b. 02/18/1879, d. 08/06/1955

HUDSON, Myrtle E., b. 1903, d. 1980

HUDSON, Nettie E., b. 01/30/1870, d. 12/23/1960

HUDSON, Olivia Draper, "Candy," ssw-Douglas C., b. 04/16/1930, d. N/D

HUDSON, Richard T., Sr., b. 1898, d. 1985

HUDSON, S. Eward, b. 1929, d. 1948

HUDSON, Stephen P., b. 10/07/1878, d. 08/16/1965

HUDSON, William H., b. 1920, d. 1955

HUDSON, Winifred N., b 03/18/1918, d. N/D

HUGHES, Delema Stooms, b. 08/24/1894, d. 10/28/1962

HUNTER, Edgar S., b. 1905, d. 1960

HUNTER, Lillian P., b. 1909, d. N/D

HUNTER, Robert O., b. 1911, d. N/D

JARVIS, Elizabeth B., b. 07/10/1888, d. 12/21/1980

JARVIS, James Tarr, b. 08/28/1916, d. 10/30/1965

JARVIS, Sidney A., b. 03/22/1909, d. 05/11/1939

JARVIS, Theodore M., b. 05/21/1888, d. 07/23/1955

JEFFERSON, Gertie M., d/o James H. S. & Laura E., ssw-John W. Wilson, b. 02/04/1898, d. 08/05/1898

JEFFERSON, James H., b. 01/09/1855, d. 03/26/1934

JEFFERSON, Laura E., w/o James H., b. 12/14/1862, d. 12/14/1918

JEFFERSON, Sallie G. Sherman, w/o James H., b. 11/29/1864, d. 02/28/1883

JEFFERSON, Sarah E., b. 06/18/1897, d. 09/26/1925

JEFFERSON, Walter B., b. 08/03/1893, d. 02/28/1980

JENSEN, Clifford, s/o Fred & Ella Z., b. 07/24/1906, d. 09/09/1906

JOHNSON, C. Ronald, b. 10/03/1936, d. N/D

JOHNSON, Clara M., ssw-Clarence R., b. 09/20/1913, d. 06/02/1994

JOHNSON, Clarence R., ssw-Clara M., b. 10/15/1913, d. 05/19/1987

JOSEPH, Carlton W., ssw-Juanita P., b. 04/02/1916, d. 08/28/1973

JOSEPH, Charles H., ssw-Lydia, b. 04/13/1847, d. 07/21/1921

JOSEPH, Charles W., s/o C. H. & Lydia, b. 10/24/1896, d. 05/27/1915

JOSEPH, Effie M., ssw-Mildred E., b. 1885, d. 1967

JOSEPH, Guernie D., ssw-Ida M., b. 08/28/1892, d. 10/27/1971

JOSEPH, Guernie D., Jr., b. 12/01/1927, d. 04/15/1929

JOSEPH, Helen M., ssw-Howard M., b. 1914, d. N/D

JOSEPH, Howard M., ssw-Helen M., b. 1909, d. 1966

JOSEPH, Ida M., ssw-Guernie D., b. 08/17/1899, d. 10/27/1992

JOSEPH, Juanita P., ssw-Carlton W., b. 06/21/1911, d. 11/18/1986

JOSEPH, Leroy, ssw-Maggie, b. 09/20/1896, d. 05/13/1956

JOSEPH, Lydia, ssw-Charles H., b. 05/23/1855, d. 01/05/1924

JOSEPH, Maggie, ssw-Leroy, b. 08/14/1900, d. 01/29/1992

JOSEPH, Mildred E., ssw-Effie M., b. 1899, d. 1989
KEANE, J. Leslie, b. 05/29/1900, d. 01/08/1923
KING, James W., ssw-Margaret J., b. 01/18/1937, d. N/D
KING, James W., Jr., b. 03/01/1959, d. 03/05/1964
KING, Margaret J., ssw-James W., b. 02/24/1938, d. 04/07/1984
KOEPPEL, Addie V., b. 1914, d. 1994
KOEPPEL, Albert E., ssw-Theresa, b. 1904, d. 1987
KOEPPEL, Alma Virginia, b. 1937, d. N/D
KOEPPEL, Frank Charles, s/o Joseph & Louise, b. 08/12/1875, d. 01/12/1898
KOEPPEL, Gustav H., b. 1878, d. 1936
KOEPPEL, Henrietta V., b. 1882, d. 1979
KOEPPEL, James B., b. 1917, d. 1959
KOEPPEL, Joseph A., ssw-Louise B., b. 1842, d. 1924
KOEPPEL, Louise B., ssw-Joseph A., b. 1839, d. 1931
KOEPPEL, Priscilla E., b. 1878, d. 1937
KOEPPEL, Rudolph W., b. 1909, d. 1984
KOEPPEL, Theresa, ssw-Albert E., b. 1914, d. N/D
KOPPLE, Charles F., b. 11/03/1914, d. N/D
KOPPLE, Clara S., b. 1883, d. 1973
KOPPLE, Gary Lee, b. 05/19/1956, d. N/D
KOPPLE, Hugo E., b. 1873, d. 1944
KOPPLE, Margaret E., b. 05/03/1924, d. 10/13/1962
LINE, Mary Ann, b. 10/10/1898, d. 10/08/1993
LINGO, Ella J., b. 06/15/1870, d. 07/25/1915
LINGO, J. Floyd, ssw-Nancy B., b. 07/05/1931, d. N/D
LINGO, Nancy B., ssw-J. Floyd, b. 03/18/1931, d. N/D
LINN, Lowvina Carpenter, ssw-William S. Martin, Jr., b. 01/23/1865, d. 04/05/1942
LOGAN, Phillip, Age 9y, b. N/D, d. 08/05/1896
LOVENGUTH, Clara G., b. 1870, d. 1958
LOVENGUTH, Edward, ssw-Laura, b. 05/04/1904, d. 05/29/1970
LOVENGUTH, Laura, ssw-Edward, b. 07/02/1914, d. 09/13/1983
MANSHIP, Alena A., d/o Charles R. & Sarah J., b. 03/22/1885, d. 02/26/1912
MANSHIP, J. Martin, Sr., b. 04/11/1911, d. 07/28/1984
MARINER, Leona P., b. 1884, d. 1941
MARTIN, Annie E., ssw-John A., b. 11/03/1862, d. 04/13/1936
MARTIN, Annie M., b. 1873, d. 1958
MARTIN, Edward, b. 1867, d. 1930
MARTIN, George S., ssw-Mary M., b. 10/14/1890, d. 02/19/1957
MARTIN, John A., ssw-Annie E., b. 03/20/1855, d. 03/21/1921
MARTIN, John D., ssw-Mary M., b. 04/10/1823, d. 04/10/1899
MARTIN, Lulu, b. 03/31/1894, d. 09/22/1964
MARTIN, Mary M., ssw-George S., b. 08/04/1893, d. 03/03/1920
MARTIN, Mary M., w/o J. D., b. 03/21/1833, d. 10/28/1902
MARTIN, William S., Jr., ssw-Lowvina Carpenter Linn, b. 10/11/1865, d. 10/21/1930
MARVEL, Ava R., ssw-Edgar T., b. 09/07/1874, d. 09/24/1949
MARVEL, Edgar T., ssw-Ava R., b. 06/20/1875, d. 12/13/1938
MASON, Lawrence F., ssw-Meta M., b. 1889, d. 1979
MASON, Meta M., ssw-Lawrence F., b. 1893, d. 1983

MCCHESNEY, Samuel C., b. 1901, d. 1975
MCGEE, Alfred H., ssw-Elva N., b. 1865, d. 1933
MCGEE, Elva N., ssw-Alfred H., b. 1868, d. 1956
MCGEE, Emory R., s/o A. H. & Elva N., b. 04/03/1906, d. 04/09/1906
MCGEE, Ernest E., b. 05/18/1891, d. 04/03/1980
MCGEE, Ressie I., b. 02/22/1888, d. 12/28/1968
MCILVAIN, Joan Amelia, ssw-William R., Sr., b. 12/12/1958, d. 02/01/1962
MCILVAIN, William R., Sr., ssw-Joan Amelia, Sgt, USA, WWII, b. 06/09/1910, d. 08/05/1991
MEGEE, Alfred, ssw-Maymie, b. 04/19/1900, d. 10/18/1973
MEGEE, Maymie, ssw-Alfred, b. 07/15/1900, d. 11/15/1987
MESSICK, Edgar W., ssw-Mae V., b. 10/29/1889, d. 04/06/1978
MESSICK, James E., Sr., b. 03/08/1904, d. 03/25/1973
MESSICK, Mae V., ssw-Edgar W., b. 01/10/1897, d. 03/11/1980
MIDEL, Emma M., ssw-Frederick B., b. 1890, d. 1972
MIDEL, Frederick B., ssw-Emma M., b. 1892, d. 1977
MIRCH, Hallie B., ssw-Hiram W., b. 1873, d. 1950
MIRCH, Hiram W., ssw-Hallie B., b. 1870, d 1955
MITCHELL, Elwood H., ssw-Marion P., b. 02/01/1930, d. 10/21/1991
MITCHELL, Granville T., ssw-Mary Ann, Pvt., USA, WWII, b. 06/02/1914, d. 02/08/1989
MITCHELL, Harley W., ssw-Manuella, b. 10/03/1893, d. 08/25/1970
MITCHELL, Ida Mae, ssw-Peter Ott, b. 08/03/1890, d. 07/25/1975
MITCHELL, Manuella, ssw-Harley W., b. 01/18/1898, d. 04/05/1967
MITCHELL, Marion P., ssw-Elwood H., b. 11/20/1925, d. N/D
MITCHELL, Mary Ann, ssw-Granville T., b. 09/01/1913, d. 11/13/1991
MITCHELL, Nellie M., b. 09/13/1911, d. 09/05/1977
MITCHELL, Peter Ott, ssw-Ida Mae, b. 01/08/1889, d. 05/27/1944
MONTGOMERY, Daren Rodger, b. N/D, d. 01/14/69
MOORE, Goldie H., ssw-Wilson E., b. 08/12/1927, d. 04/23/1972
MOORE, James W., DE, Pfc., Co. H., 290 Inf. Reg., WWII, b. 12/09/1919, d. 02/20/1957
MOORE, Norma W. P., b. 03/09/1923, d. 06/22/1961
MOORE, Samuel, ssw-Viva D., b. 08/10/1866, d. 05/08/1964
MOORE, Viva D., ssw-Samuel, b. 11/05/1886, d. 08/30/1966
MOORE, Wilson E., ssw-Goldie H., b. 03/07/1929, d. 07/10/1993
MORRIS, George A., b. 03/15/1898, d. 06/04/1928
MORRIS, James A., b. 02/17/1877, d. 10/17/1894
MORRIS, Jennie, b. 1866, d. 1933
MORRIS, John P., b. 04/30/1855, d. 10/30/1944
NICHOLS, Marion L., Co. A, 7 MI, Calvary, b. N/D, d. N/D
NICKLE, Elva Elizabeth McGee, w/o J. Harry, b. 01/12/1917, d. N/D
NICKLE, John Harry, Pfc., USA, WWII, b. 03/12/1912, d. 11/30/1993
PATTERSON, Bessie M., ssw-Annie A., Fred W. & William T. Brittingham, b. 1897, d. 1959
PAYNTER, Joseph M., ssw-Leeora M., b. 08/01/1895, d. 01/30/1982
PAYNTER, Leeora M., ssw-Joseph M., b. 09/24/1897, d. 10/11/1991
PEPPER, Althea G., ssw-Edwin, b. 1920, d. N/D
PEPPER, Annie S., w/o Joshua M., b. 07/16/1853, d. 07/07/1909
PEPPER, Bessie, b. 1875, d. 1936
PEPPER, Edwin, ssw-Althea G., b. 1916, d. 1991
PEPPER, Laura W., b. 10/16/1907, d. 04/25/1982

PEPPER, T. Ralston, b. 10/08/1902, d. 04/10/1991

PEPPER, Thomas G., b. 12/14/1872, d. 09/01/1900

PEPPER, Truitt, b. 1871, d. 1959

PETTYJOHN, Anna M., b. 01/11/1878, d. 11/06/1963

PETTYJOHN, Arthur, b. 09/09/1858, d. 11/12/1937

PETTYJOHN, Bertha G., w/o Charles E., b. 11/24/1879, d. 01/31/1917

PETTYJOHN, Charles E., b. 10/05/1877, d. 12/29/1954

PETTYJOHN, Charles E., Jr., b. 03/31/1923, d. 06/05/1953

PETTYJOHN, Fannie, w/o Arthur, b. 01/12/1864, d. 11/01/1908

PETTYJOHN, Hilda M., ssw-William H., b. 02/10/1920, d. 05/13/1994

PETTYJOHN, Howard T., b. 02/21/1894, d. 04/20/1975

PETTYJOHN, Inf. s/o Linford & Frances, b. N/D, d. 05/28/1922

PETTYJOHN, Julia E., b. 04/11/1895, d. 12/07/1989

PETTYJOHN, Mary M., b. 04/03/1916, d. 08/05/1917

PETTYJOHN, Sallie A., ssw-Truitt, b. 02/08/1852, d. 05/15/1927

PETTYJOHN, Theodore A., s/o Arthur & Fannie, b. 02/12/1898, d. 10/23/1919

PETTYJOHN, Truitt, ssw-Sallie A., b. 03/10/1859, d. 04/10/1921

PETTYJOHN, William H., ssw-Hilda M., b. 10/11/1917, d. 12/26/1986

PETTYJOHN, Willie T., s/o Truitt & Sallie A., b. 06/12/1890, d. 06/15/1890

PHILLIPS, Margaret R., b. 09/15/1918, d. 01/13/1988

POWERS, Charles H., ssw-Mary Ida, b. 1870, d. 1941

POWERS, Mary Ida, ssw-Charles H., b. 1868, d. 1947

PRETTYMAN, Carl B., ssw-Eugenia H., b. 01/10/1899, d. 07/09/1974

PRETTYMAN, Cora Etta, b. 1879, d. 1963

PRETTYMAN, Esther West, b. 09/14/1903, d. 08/20/1986

PRETTYMAN, Eugenia H., ssw-Carl B., b 05/10/1901, d. 01/01/1967

PRETTYMAN, Irma McCullough, b. 01/23/1932, d. N/D

PRETTYMAN, James West, b. 04/14/1944, d. N/D

PRETTYMAN, Koretta Adelia, b. 09/24/1933, d. N/D

PRETTYMAN, Melvin F., b. 10/08/1903, d. 0/20/1965

PRETTYMAN, Mollie E., b. 11/23/1911, d. 10/04/1991

PRETTYMAN, Naama Murre, w/o Wm. b. 09/27/1827, d. 01/26/1867

PRETTYMAN, William, ssw-Naama Murre, b. 11/06/1821, d. 03/03/1899

PRETTYMAN, William, IV, b. 04/06/1930, d. N/D

PRETTYMAN, William Henry, b. 1850, d. 1922

PRETTYMAN, William Henry, III, b. 06/17/1902, d. 03/08/1989

PRIDE, Guss B., ssw-Una E., b. 1872, d. 1958

PRIDE, Una E., ssw-Guss B., b. 1892, d. 1975

PUSEY, Walter Thompson, b. 07/06/1912, d. 0/22/1996

REDHEFFER, Augustus T., ssw-Emma J., b. 1858, d. 1946

REDHEFFER, Emma J., ssw-Augustus T., b. 1882, d. 1970

REED, Anna E., b. 07/13/1860, d. 04/22/1926

REED, Carlton L., Md., Pvt., USA, Korea, b. 03/02/1929, d. 03/31/1974

REED, James Tull, b. 08/21/1896, d. 10/04/1918

REED, John M., b. 09/16/1891, d. 12/29/1945

REED, John W., ssw-Mary E., b. 09/22/1850, d. 03/07/1901

REED, Joseph A., b. 03/30/1889, d. 06/14/1904

REED, Lester James, b. 01/13/1919, d. 09/08/1932

REED, Lloyd, ssw-Susie, b. 09/26/1893, d. 05/09/1966
REED, Loreta B., d/o J. W. & M. E., b. 06/15/1892, d. 06/22/1891
REED, Mary E., ssw-John W., b. 01/16/1861, d. 03/01/1919
REED, Rathell W., b. 02/09/1895, d. 10/02/1967
REED, Robert James, USN, b. 07/23, 1937, d. 12/05/1988
REED, Sallie M., b. 04/29/1892, d. 11/17/1977
REED, Somerset, b. 06/26/1853, d. 08/15/1929
REED, Susie, ssw-Lloyd, b. 09/17/1900, d. 01/30/1974
REED, Wilburk, b. 06/22/1890, d. 12/29/1943
REYNOLDS, Elsie D., ssw-John S., b. 09/25/1896, d. 12/15/1993
REYNOLDS, John S., ssw-Elsie D., b. 03/26/1901, d. 04/23/1994
ROACH, Angeline, b. 0/18/1833, d. 12/15/1911
ROACH, Clara B., ssw-George E., Linie & Sallie J., b. 1870, d. 1880
ROACH, George E., ssw-Linie, Clara B. & Sallie J., b. 1863, d. 1871
ROACH, Linie, ssw-Clara B., George E. & Sallie J., b. 1875, d. 1876
ROACH, Sallie J., ssw-George E., Linie & Clara B., b. 1863, d. 1881
ROACH, Thomas L., b. 1832, d. 1885
ROGERS, Daisy C., ssw-Mattford, b. 10/08/1895, d. 06/19/1987
ROGERS, Dorothy F., ssw-Dorothy V. Connor, b. 07/17/1900, d. 02/27/1991
ROGERS, John W., b. 1892, d. 1946
ROGERS, Julia K., b. 1895, d. 1936
ROGERS, Madolin Ellen, b. 1928, d. 1929
ROGERS, Mattford, ssw-Daisy C., b. 09/02/1883, d. 08/01/1973
ROGERS, Norman B., b. 1900, d. 1942
ROGERS, Riley B., b. 1878, d. 1931
ROGERS, Sarah J., b. 1884, d. 1927
ROGERS, Sarah K., b. 1928, d. 1936
RUPE, Grover J., b. 11/21/1893, d. 07/04/1965
RUPE, Rose Kuhn, b. 07/31/1912, d. 08/05/1987
RUSSELL, Edith W., ssw-T. Stuart, b. 03/11/1910, d. N/D
RUSSELL, Judith, b. 10/03/1943, d. 10/05/1943
RUSSELL, S. S., ssw-Sarah P., b. 1865, d. 1939
RUSSELL, Sarah P., ssw-S. S., b. 1862, d. 1927
RUSSELL, T. Stuart, ssw-Edith W., b. 07/19/1910, d. N/D
RUST, Absalom, ssw-Mary A., b. 11/10/1842, d. 02/12/1935
RUST, Amanda J., b. 05/01/1893, d. 08/23/1979
RUST, Clara B., b. 1856, d. 1933
RUST, Clara E., b. 01/27/1867, d. 02/16/1939
RUST, George A., b. 12/14/1865, d. 06/01/1955
RUST, Harry D., b. 02/11/1885, d. 10/06/1969
RUST, Inf. d/o Lloyd & V. A., b. 1938, d. 1938
RUST, John R., b. 11/13/1892, d. 05/03/1984
RUST, Lila E., b. 01/01/1899, d. 01/23/1899
RUST, Lillie May, d/o Luther & Mary, b. N/D, d. 08/05/1893
RUST, Lloyd, ssw-Virginia M., b. 1898, d. 1979
RUST, Luther Edgar, h/o Mary S., b. 04/28/1871, d. 02/19/1909
RUST, Marguerite E., b. 05/23/1920, d. N/D
RUST, Mary A., w/o Absalom, ssw-Absalom, b. 11/15/1846, d. 10/01/1916

RUST, Nellie A., b. 04/02/1898, d. 12/29/1984

RUST, Robert M., b. 04/04/1917, d. N/D

RUST, Robert R., b. 1852, d. 1921

RUST, S. Edna Veasey, w/o Edward Rust & d/o R. B. & B. D. Veasey, b. 1901, d. 1920

RUST, Virginia M., ssw-Lloyd, b. 1915, d. N/D

SAVAGE, Fannie, w/o Reuben L., b. 05/15/1870, d. 11/08/1898

SAVAGE, Thomas H., s/o Reuben L. & Fannie, b. 10/20/1896, d. 09/21/1897

SCHUYLER, Clara W., b. 02/11/1934, d. 03/10/1996

SHAFFER, Helena C., ssw-Raymond O., Jr., b. 12/20/1926, d. 08/05/1974

SHAFFER, Raymond O., Jr., ssw-Helena C., b. 06/01/1924, d. 09/04/1975

SHERMAN, Arthur W., ssw-Dorothy E., b. 10/26/1912, d. 04/19/195

SHERMAN, Dorothy E., ssw-Arthur W., b. 01/03/1916, d. 11/04/1969

SHERMAN, E. Elizabeth, ssw-W. Walter, b. 1899, d. 1982

SHERMAN, Ellen, ssw-John, b. 06/20/1829, d. 10/10/1899

SHERMAN, Fannie D., ssw-G. Roy, b. 11/16/1895, d. 05/21/1970

SHERMAN, G. Roy, ssw-Fannie D., b. 09/25/1889, d. 12/28/1973

SHERMAN, George P., ssw-Lea D., b. 03/12/1920, d. 11/27/1994

SHERMAN, George W., ssw-Mary M., b. 1846, d. 1912

SHERMAN, John, ssw-Ellen, b. 01/31/1824, d. 03/03/1904

SHERMAN, John William, ssw-Peggy L., SP4, USA, Vietnam, b. 08/13/1948, d. 12/22/1978

SHERMAN, Lea D., ssw-George P., b. 07/06/1918, d. 08/09/1995

SHERMAN, Marie, b. 1928, d. 1944

SHERMAN, Mary M., w/o George W., ssw-George W., b. 1854, d. 1891

SHERMAN, Peggy L, ssw-John William, b. 08/03/1947, d. N/D

SHERMAN, Raymond, b. 1933, d. 1936

SHERMAN, W. Walter, ssw-E. Elizabeth, b. 1887, d. 1976

SHOCKLEY, Estella R., ssw-Luther, b. 06/15/1899, d. 08/29/1965

SHOCKLEY, Luther, ssw-Estella R., b. 09/20/1898, d. 07/20/1959

SHORT, Estella A., ssw-Ira D., b. 01/02/1888, d. 03/02/1986

SHORT, Ira D., ssw-Estella A., b. 09/01/1882, d. 04/08/1973

SIMPLER, Annie, ssw-George W., b. 04/12/1864, d. 05/03/1920

SIMPLER, Elizabeth W., wid/o James, b. 06/18/1808, d. 04/21/1892

SIMPLER, George W., ssw-Annie, b. 06/05/1867, d. 03/28/1949

SIMPLER, James, Corp'l., b. 1784, d. 1862

SIMPLER, Vergie H., b. 11/15/1881, d. 05/10/1961

SMITH, Emma, b. 01/17/1914, d. 04/25/1996

SMITH, Gary Wayne, Age 44, b. 06/02/1952, d. 05/29/1994

SMITH, John A., ssw-Sylvia M., b. 12/28/1912, d. N/D

SMITH, Sylvia M., ssw-John A., b. 04/10/1920, d. 05/16/1970

SOCKRITER, Amanda M., (Nee Waples), b. 11/04/1892, d. 11/10/1965

SOCKRITER, Billie Jean, (Baker), b. 01/28/1934, d. 01/12/1982

SPARKS, E. Jennie Keane, (Nee Waples), b. 03/05/1876, d. 03/15/1953

STEELE, Harry T., ssw-Lemuel, b. 1888, d. 1909

STEELE, James A., ssw-Rosa B. & James B., b. 1908, d. 1921

STEELE, James B., ssw-Rosa B. & James A., b. 1868, d. 1941

STEELE, Lemuel, ssw-Susan E., b. 1866, d. 1946

STEELE, Susan E., ssw-Lemuel, b. 1860, d. 1910

STEELE, Theo., b. 1870, d. 1946

STEELE, Rosa B., ssw-James A. & James B., b. 1870, d. 1953

STEINER, Elise, b. 1860, d. 1936

STEINER, Frederick, b. 1849, d. 1934

STEVENSON, Edna Martin, w/o W. W. Stevenson, ssw-William S. Martin, Jr., b. 04/12/1886, d. 03/09/1925

STEWART, Annie B., ssw-Ebe T., b. 1858, d. 1938

STEWART, Delema D., ssw-Juanita P., b. 1885, d. 1967

STEWART, E. Gilbert, b. 1903, d. 1940

STEWART, Ebe T., ssw-Annie B., b. 1847, d. 1913

STEWART, Frederick T., DE, Pvt., Co. M., 312 Inf., WWI, b. 07/05/1888, d. 05/29/1960

STEWART, Juanita P., ssw-Delema D., b. 1911, d. 1986

STEWART, William S., ssw-Juanita P., b. 1880, d. 1959

STOOMS, Annie M., w/o Fred, ssw-Maggie, b. 09/14/1877, d. 05/06/1900

STOOMS, Maggie, ssw-Annie M., b. 10/07/1897, d. 08/19/1901

STUCHLIK, Glen, b. 08/19/1962, d. 08/21/1962

TARR, James E., b. 09/10/1863, d. 01/22/1941

TAYLOR, Harry T., b. 11/17/1863, d. 11/12/1929

TAYLOR, Lloyd H., ssw-Sarah B., b. 01/31/1895, d. 10/05/1987

TAYLOR, Margaret M., b. 10/30/1867, d. 01/08/1950

TAYLOR, Sarah B., ssw-Lloyd H., b. 08/23/1895, d. 03/12/1993

THOMAS, Herman A., ssw-Nora R., b. 11/25/1911, d. 11/11/1991

THOMAS, Nora R., ssw-Herman A., b. 03/30/1917, d. N/D

THOMPSON, Albert Wiltbank, b. 04/11/1906, d. 05/25/1946

THOMPSON, John C., ssw-Mary S., b. 11/08/1839, d. 04/29/1919

THOMPSON, Mary S., b. 08/08/1869, d. 02/03/1907

THOMPSON, Mary Walton, b. 06/30/1907, d. 02/09/1937

THOMPSON, Sallie W., b. 12/16/1872, d. 03/18/1961

THOMPSON, Walton, b. 02/10/1869, d. 01/03/1921

TINGLE, Ella E., w/o William H., Age 26y, b. N/D, d. 11/16/1885

TUCKER, Avery I., Sr., b. 05/16/1912, d. 06/05/1990

TULL, Robert T., b. 06/15/1843, d. 01/22/1910

TULLEY, John, b. 1858, d. 1931

VAUGHN, Benjamin O., b. 07/28/1862, d. 03/01/1913

VAUGHN, Charles F., b. 02/06/1884, d. 11/22/1912

VAUGHN, Margaret M., b. 09/12/1869, d. 08/25/1919

VEASEY, Addie M., b. 04/02/1868, d. 02/14/1951

VEASEY, Alfred P., ssw-Sallie V., b. 11/09/1881, d. 04/07/1914

VEASEY, Annie H., b. 1862, d. 1946

VEASEY, Annie R., ssw-Charles S., b. 06/13/1869, d. 12/08/1937

VEASEY, Bessie M., ssw-John C., b. 1899, d. 1975

VEASEY, Bessie M., ssw-Robert B., Miriam T., Ruth T., Karle W. & William R., b. 1882, d. 1904

VEASEY, Charles S., ssw-Annie R., b. 11/19/1868, d. 12/10/1939

VEASEY, Edna K., d/o C. E. & Virginia, b. 06/13/1915, d. 02/12/1916

VEASEY, Edward L., b. 1946, d. 1947

VEASEY, Ethel Betts, ssw-N. Courtland, b. 10/08/1908, d. 11/07/1992

VEASEY, Ethel C., d/o Charles S. & Annie R., b. 05/22/1894, d. 12/18/1896

VEASEY, Evelyn M., ssw-Harry, b. 01/22/1932, d. N/D

VEASEY, G. E., b. 1880, d. 1940

VEASEY, G. Edward, Jr., b. 12/23/1916, d. 04/24/1983

VEASEY, Grace Marie, d/o Alfred P. & Sallie V., b. 12/26/1907, d. 06/10/1908

VEASEY, Harriet V., b. 12/18/1919, d. 09/20/1936

VEASEY, Harry, ssw-Evelyn M., Sgt., USA, WWII, b. 01/03/1923, d. 07/14/1986

VEASEY, Harry, ssw-Jennie Dodd, b. 10/23/1879, d. 06/20/1922

VEASEY, James P., b. 11/02/1862, d. 11/01/1892

VEASEY, Jennie Dodd, ssw-Harry, b. 09/13/1880, d. 09/19/1942

VEASEY, John A., b. 1942, d. 1950

VEASEY, John C., ssw-Bessie M., b. 1901, d. 1960

VEASEY, John H., b. 1914, d. 1955

VEASEY, John S., b. 04/05/1888, d. 02/07/1947

VEASEY, John S., ssw-Sarah J., b. 1854, d. 1926

VEASEY, Joseph W., b. 05/05/1860, d. 10/03/1920

VEASEY, Karle W., ssw-Robert B., Bessie M., Miriam T., Ruth T. & William R., b. 1900, d. 1900

VEASEY, Lillian Ruth, d/o C. E. & Virginia, b. 06/27/1912, d. 03/19/1913

VEASEY, Lloyd T., s/o C. E. & Virginia, b. 01/27/1902, d. 07/21/1902

VEASEY, Lottie B., b. 1890, d. 1949

VEASEY, Luther B., b. 1879, d. 1955

VEASEY, Mabel (Baby), b. 1909, d. 1910

VEASEY, Margaret A., d/o Harry & Jennie, b. 04/20/1909, d. 12/23/1909

VEASEY, Miriam T., ssw-Robert B., Bessie M., Karle W., Ruth T. & William R., b. 1908, d. 1909

VEASEY, N. Courtland, ssw-Ethel Betts, b. 03/18/1906, d. 09/23/1985

VEASEY, N. T., b. 1849, d. 1931

VEASEY, Nellie L., ssw-Thomas P., b. 1909, d. 1947

VEASEY, Preston L., b. 1940, d. 1940

VEASEY, Robert B., ssw-Bessie M., Karle W., Miriam T., Ruth T. & William R., b. 1874, d. 1965

VEASEY, Russell T., b. 05/26/1921, d. 05/08/1962

VEASEY, Ruth T., ssw-Robert B., Bessie M., Karle W., Miriam T. & William R., b. 1884, d. 1954

VEASEY, Sallie V., ssw-Alfred P., b. 10/29/1882, d. 06/09/1913

VEASEY, Sarah J., ssw-John S., b. 1867, d. 1957

VEASEY, Thomas P., ssw-Nellie L., b. 1906, d. 1962

VEASEY, Vergie, b. 1882, d. 1965

VEASEY, William R., ssw-Robert B., Bessie M., Karle W., Miriam T. & Ruth T., b. 1904, d. 1904

VICK, Marguerite E., ssw-Thomas B., b. 1916, d. 1990

VICK, Thomas B., ssw-Marguerite E., b. 1926, d. 1990

VIRNSTEIN, Minnie M., b. 07/18/1886, d. 06/10/1969

WALKER, Elender, d/o Thomas & Elettie, his wife, b. 1803, d. 1884

WALKER, Lydia H., w/o Thomas W., b. 03/02/1844, d. 01/10/1921

WALKER, Thomas, s/o Thomas & Elettie, b. 1806, d. 1885

WALKER, Thomas W., s/o Purnell & Elettie, his wife, b. 05/15/1833, d. 05/14/1909

WALKER, William P., s/o Thomas W. & Lydia H., his wife, b. 05/27/1872, d. 06/10/1890

WALLS, Alena P., d/o Ollie D. & Elzay M., b. 05/29/1900, d. 02/14/1904

WALLS, Annie E., ssw-Frederic A., b. 02/18/1886, d. 04/22/1968

WALLS, Annie V., w/o Edgar L., b. 02/21/1889, d. 06/16/1916

WALLS, Charlie M., ssw-Georgia A., b. 1866, d. 1939

WALLS, Edgar L., b. 03/22/1881, d. 04/30/1954

WALLS, Elsie, ssw-Ethel, b. N/D, d. 06/08/1915

WALLS, Elzay M., ssw-Ollie D., b. 11/25/1877, d. 03/21/1959

WALLS, Essie L., d/o E. L. & Annie V., b. 02/17/1910, d. 06/21/1911

WALLS, Ethel, ssw-Elsie, b. N/D, d. 10/22/1915
WALLS, Florence A., b. 12/31/1918, d. 07/09/1975
WALLS, Frederic A., ssw-Annie E., b. 04/10/1884, d. 03/12/1967
WALLS, George A., b. 08/31/1864, d. 04/24/1944
WALLS, Georgia A., ssw-Charlie M., b. 1873, d. 1972
WALLS, Georgia A., ssw-Ira T., b. 1875, d. 1952
WALLS, Greenbury, ssw-Lavinia L., Co. D, 3 DE. Inf., b. N/D, d. N/D
WALLS, Harry B., ssw-James Lufland, b. 03/25/1919, d. 10/04/1988
WALLS, Harvey H., b. 1870, d. 1953
WALLS, Ira T., ssw-Georgie A., b. 1878, d. 1958
WALLS, James Lufland, ssw-Harry B., DE, Pvt., USA, WWII, b. 07/13/1914, d. 06/21/1967
WALLS, John H., Co. D., 3 DE Inf., b. N/D, d. N/D
WALLS, L. Hester, b. 11/10/1883, d. 06/11/1959
WALLS, Lavinia L., ssw-Greenbury, b. 1857, d. 1928
WALLS, Lawrence A., b. 1909, d. 1956
WALLS, Leah J., w/o Luther S., b. 07/04/1876, d. 07/10/1912
WALLS, Luther S., b. 09/30/1875, d. 02/01/1938
WALLS, Lydia Burton, b. 12/27/1912, d. 09/26/1915
WALLS, Mabel G., b. 12/28/1893, d. 11/17/1986
WALLS, Mildred G., ssw-James Lufland, b. 04/20/1922, d. 04/04/1990
WALLS, Ollie D., ssw-Elzay M., b. 10/15/1881, d. 02/19/1934
WALLS, Samuel J., ssw-Carrie M., b. 05/28/1894, d. 09/01/1969
WAPLES, Alma B., b. 03/04/1906, d. 11/12/1973
WAPLES, Benjamin S., b. 08/12/1898, d. 01/24/1983
WAPLES, Bertha M., ssw-Harry C., b. 04/27/1895, d. 06/20/1968
WAPLES, Emma C., w/o Wm. Edgar, b. 03/23/1872, d. 05/12/1907
WAPLES, George R., DE, H. Co., 59 Pioneer Inf., WWI, b. 09/09/1896, d. 09/13/1923
WAPLES, Harry C., ssw-Bertha M., b. 03/04/1891, d. 11/18/1963
WAPLES, Lida M., ssw-William D., b. 04/24/1892, d. 03/13/1983
WAPLES, Margaret, d/o W. E. & Emma C., b. 02/10/1906, d. 03/19/1911
WAPLES, W. Edgar, b. 02/25/1865, d. 12/18/1931
WAPLES, William D., ssw-Lida M., b. 11/20/1894, d. 03/17/1959
WARRINGTON, Ada M., b. 1936, d. 1936
WARRINGTON, Anna K., ssw-Emma, b. 03/13/1895, d. 12/21/1987
WARRINGTON, Carrie F., ssw-John W., b. 1902, d. 1951
WARRINGTON, Charles E., ssw-Kathleen P., Tec5, USA, WWII, b. 10/10/1923, d. 03/26/1994
WARRINGTON, David P., ssw-Emma, b. N/D, d. 12/13/1900
WARRINGTON, Emma, d/o David & Sarah, ssw-David P., b. 05/12/1890, d. 01/08/1908
WARRINGTON, Frank W., b. 12/25/1867, d. 12/19/1945
WARRINGTON, Harry R., b. 1917, d. N/D
WARRINGTON, Helena M., b. 1918, d. N/D
WARRINGTON, Ida E., b. 1884, d. 1931
WARRINGTON, John S., ssw-Emma, b. 02/13/1888, d. 06/18/1963
WARRINGTON, John W., ssw-Carrie F., b. 1899, d. 1995
WARRINGTON, Kathleen P., ssw-Charles E., b. 12/17/1923, d. N/D
WARRINGTON, Kendal O., b. 1896, d 1939
WARRINGTON, Leander R., b. 1871, d. 1941
WARRINGTON, Leta E., ssw-Sheridan W., b. 1886, d. 1989

WARRINGTON, Margaret E., ssw-Silas M., b. 1848, d. 1930

WARRINGTON, Mettie A., b. 1897, d. 1975

WARRINGTON, Sheridan J., AMM2, USN, WWII, b. 09/16/1920, d. 03/06/1991

WARRINGTON, Sheridan W., ssw-Leta E., b. 1884, d. 1923

WARRINGTON, Silas M., ssw-Margaret E., b. 1838, d. 1896

WATSON, Edw. S., ssw-John T., Mary A. & Wm. R., b. 05/31/1869, d. 07/04/1926

WATSON, John T., ssw-Mary A., Edw. S. & Wm. R., b. 04/10/1843, d. 04/22/1885

WATSON, Mary A., ssw-John T., Edw. S. & Wm. R., b. 12/29/1840, d. 07/21/1899

WATSON, Wm. R., ssw-John T., Edw. S. & Mary A., b. 01/10/1873, d. 11/22/1900

WELLS, Florence M., ssw-Willard S., b. 1901, d. 1966

WELLS, Willard S., ssw-Florence M., b. 1906, d. 1981

WHITE, Doris B., ssw-Levin M., b. 06/09/1918, d. 03/02/1994

WHITE, Levin M., ssw-Doris B., b. 04/07/1915, d. 04/29/1978

WILKERSON, Claude S., Pfc., USA, WWII, b. 01/09/1912, d. 01/26/1986

WILKERSON, Emma J., b. 1917, d. N/D

WILSON, Annie E., d/o Barkley & Louise A., Age 1y 5m 15d, b. 07/02/1864, d. 12/17/1865

WILSON, Annie R., d/o Hiram & Nancy, b. 09/26/1866, d. 03/05/1875

WILSON, Barkley, Age 64y 3m 29d, b. N/D, d. 07/08/1864

WILSON, Barkley, b. 1860, d. 1937

WILSON, Barkley E., b. 09/08/1935, d. N/D

WILSON, Bessie, ssw-Kendal D., b. 03/04/1906, d. 01/12/1981

WILSON, Bonnie P., b. 03/01/1944, d. 11/28/1984

WILSON, Carl E., ssw-Dora L., b. 10/21/1917, d. 01/17/1969

WILSON, Clara J., ssw-William T., b. 03/20/1867, d. 03/27/1935

WILSON, Clara W., w/o Ebe T., b. 05/06/1871, d. 03/24/1923

WILSON, Cora M., b. 11/04/1890, d. 12/26/1956

WILSON, Della M., b. 1873, d. 1933

WILSON, Dora L., ssw-Carl E., b. 11/03/1914, d. N/D

WILSON, Ebe T., ssw-Clara W., b. 1866, d. 1935

WILSON, Elizabeth A., ssw-William H., b. 02/22/1863, d. 03/13/1901

WILSON, Elizabeth D., b. 1884, d. 1928

WILSON, Elizabeth J., w/o John, b. 02/14/1839, d. 03/06/1875

WILSON, Elzey, b. 1870, d. 1935

WILSON, Ernest B., b. 11/22/1908, d. 11/04/1986

WILSON, Gladys C., ssw-Miller, b. 1899, d. 1984

WILSON, Grace E., b. 12/19/1908, d. 12/29/1978

WILSON, Harold T., b. 1900, d. 1962

WILSON, Hiram A., s/o Barkley & Tabitha, Age 69y 2m 1d, b. 12/30/1830, d. 04/01/1900

WILSON, Jacob M., s/o Thomas S. & Julia J., Age 1y 9m 10d, b. N/D, d. 10/31/1883

WILSON, John W., ssw-Gertie M. Jefferson, Father, b. 01/09/1829, d. 03/04/1887

WILSON, Julia J., w/o Thomas S., b. 01/12/1855, d. 02/25/1900

WILSON, Kendal D., ssw-Bessie, DE, Pvt., USA, WWII, b. 02/17/1904, d. 01/12/1968

WILSON, Lillie M., b. 1875, d. 1931

WILSON, Louisa A., Age 39y 3m 27d, b. 03/18/1830, d. 07/15/1869

WILSON, Maggie M., b. 1902, d. 1919

WILSON, Mary E., b. 11/26/1931, d. 10/21/1979

WILSON, Mildred M., b. 1910, d. 1948

WILSON, Miller, ssw-Gladys C., b. 1929, d. 1984

WILSON, Nancy, w/o Hiram A., Age 88y 1m 9d, b. 09/30/1826, d. 11/19/1914
WILSON, Neoma, w/o William P., b. 05/27/1802, d. 01/23/1877
WILSON, Rachel J., d/o William P. & Neonia, b. 05/17/1839, d. 06/02/1851
WILSON, Sarah A., d/o Thomas S. & Julia J., Age 11y 5m 28d, b. 06/17/1877, d. 12/02/1891
WILSON, Thomas H., b. 1886, d. 1929
WILSON, Thomas P., s/o William P. & Neoma, b. 07/04/1825, d. 06/01/1897
WILSON, Thomas S., ssw-Julia J., b. 07/02/1835, d. 09/18/1925
WILSON, William H., s/o John & Elizabeth J., b. 02/05/1857, d. 07/22/1876
WILSON, William H., ssw-Elizabeth A., b. 10/05/1854, d. 12/02/1928
WILSON, William P., s/o Joshua, b. 07/03/1800, d. 01/28/1862
WILSON, William T., ssw-Clara J., b. 07/12/1863, d. 04/01/1935
WILSON, Wm. B., b. 08/11/1903, d. 11/08/1963
WOLSTENHOLME, Gertrude, ssw-Walter G., b. 06/22/1884, d. 05/15/1960
WOLSTENHOLME, Walter G., ssw-Gertrude, b. 05/28/1881, d. 06/18/1962
WORKMAN, Ella Ada, b. 11/06/1885, d. 12/22/1940
WORKMAN, James Alfred, b. 05/26/1883, d. 10/08/1969
WYATT, Alton J., ssw-Edith E., m. 09/01/1934, d. 03/16/1913, d. 04/11/1982
WYATT, Alton L., ssw-Phyllis A., m. 08/03/1973, b. 03/19/1937, d. N/D
WYATT, Annie Belle, ssw-John B., b. 1886, d. 1957
WYATT, Edith E., ssw-Alton J., m. 09/01/1934, b. 02/10/1917, d. 08/16/1991
WYATT, John B., ssw-Annie Belle, b. 1875, d. 1950
WYATT, Phyllis A., ssw-Alton L., m. 08/03/1973, b. 01/07/1934, d. N/D
WYATT, Virgil Lee, b. 02/09/1927, d. 06/16/1975

The following stone was recorded by the Hudson Survey but is now missing or unreadable:
MORRIS, James A., s/o John P. & Elizabeth R., Age 19y 7m 21d, b. N/D, d. 12/04/1894

(BK-010 & HU-302) JOSIAH VEASEY CEMETERY
Located South of Harbeson, approximately 300 yds. S.W. side of a point on Harbeson Rd. (Rt. 5) said
point being 0.4 miles south of Doddtown Rd. (Rd. 293).
Recorded: November 11, 1996

VEASEY, George H. s/o Josiah & Julia, Age 7y 3m 17d, b. N/D, d. 01/11/1873
VEASEY, Josiah M., b. 01/29/1817, d. 10/13/1888
VEASEY, Julia A., w/o Josiah, Age 62y, b. N/D, d. 03/04/1883
VEASEY, Laura A., d/o Josiah & Julia, Age 5y 1m 17d, b. N/D, d. 12/21/1862
VEASEY, Lydia A., d/o Josiah & Julia, Age 19y 11m 21d, b. N/D, d. 12/21/1862
VEASEY, Susan B., d/o Josiah & Julia, Age 2y 3m 10d, b. N/D, d. 10/19/1963

(BK-011 & HU-NR) ELI G. COLLINS CEMETERY
Located North of Milton, approximately 500 yards west of Union St., Ext. (Rt. 5) and approximately 100
yards north of Williams Farm Rd. (Rd. 135A)
Recorded: November 12, 1996

COLLINS, Eli G., ssw-Patience, Age 89y 21d, b. N/D, d. 10/17/1882
COLLINS, George, Age 25y 26d, b. N/D, d. 02/17/1849
COLLINS, George, s/o Thomas & Mary, Age 61y 1m 11d, b. N/D, d. 02/20/1855
COLLINS, Harry W., s/o John A. & Cassie, Age 1y 4m 22d, b. N/D, d. 12/03/1874

COLLINS, Patience, w/o Eli G., Age 87y 6m, b. N/D, d. 09/29/1890
COLLINS, Sallie G., d/o John A. & Cassie, Age 3m 2d, b. N/D, d. 05/02/1871

(BK-012 & HU-NR) HOLLAND CEMETERY
Located S. E. of Milton on the Southside of Eagles Crest Rd. (Rd. 264) 0.4 miles west of Coastal Highway (Rt. 1)
Recorded: March 7, 1997

BURTON, Henry, Age 67y, b. N/D, d. 03/15/1905 [Note: stone is broken.]
CUMMINGS, Sophie, b. 03/15/1881, d. 10/16/1960
HOLLAND, J. M., Rev., ssw-Mary A., b. 06/24/1861, d. 10/13/1939
HOLLAND, Jeremiah, Sr., ssw-Ruth E., b. 10/28/1834, d. 05/05/1913
HOLLAND, Lillie T., ssw-T. Winchester, b. 01/09/1898, d. 10/01/1973
HOLLAND, Mary A., ssw- J. M., b. 10/26/1868, d. 12/25/1972
HOLLAND, Ruth E., w/o Jeremiah, Sr., ssw-Jeremiah, Sr., b. 05/18/43, d. N/D
HOLLAND, Solomon, b. 12/27/1899, d. 04/05/1955
HOLLAND, T. Winchester, ssw-Lillie T., b. 10/11/1890, d. 04/15/1974
NLN, NFN, b. 1906, d. 1978
POOLE, Iris, b. 1920, d. 1977
STURGIS, Handy L., ssw-Laura E., b. N/D, d. 12/25/1898
STURGIS, Laura E., ssw-Handy L., b. 05/28/1897, d. 07/21/1971
TURNER, Frederick S., Co. F., 30 Inf., b. 1829, d. 1907
TURNER, Minnie, b. 1893, d. 1970
WOOLSEYS, Allen, Pvt., USAA, WWII, b. 01/31/1902, d. 03/10/1967

(BK-013 & HU-527) OLD PRESBYTERIAN CHURCH CEMETERY
Located in Milton on the S. W. side of Church St., between Chestnut & Federal Streets.
Recorded: September 19, 1992 [Note: No further burials as of October 13, 1997.]

BAILEY, Isaac, b. 05/19/1887, d. 06/15/1919
BAILEY, Joshua W., Age 72y 11m 1d, b. N/D, d. 02/27/1910
BAILEY, Sarah L., b. 02/14/1841, d. 02/22/1928
BARKER, Henry L., b. 10/05/1822, d. 10/22/1856
CARPENTER, Eliza B., w/o Benton, Age 35y 7m 26d, b. N/D, d. 10/29/1853
COOPER, Jennett, w/o Capt. James Cooper, Age 38y 5d, b. N/D, d. 10/01/1844
JOHNSON, Rosa, d/o Abraham W. & Martha J., b. 08/13/1870, d. 07/12/1884
LEWIS, Ellen E., w/o John, ssw-John, b. 09/13/1843, d. 06/21/1917
LEWIS, John, ssw-Ellen E., b. 02/05/1842, d. N/D
LEWIS, Joshua, b. 12/13/1844, d. N/D
NLN, Harrison W., ssw-Margarette V., b. 1907, d. 1909
NLN, Margarette V., ssw-Harrison W., b. 1895, d. 1897
SCOTT, Joseph H., s/o Wm. A. & Lizzie H., Age 1m 4d, b. N/D, d. 03/29/1862
SCOTT, Mary A., d/o Wm. A. & M. B., Age 6m, b. N/D, d. 01/06/1858
SCOTT, Mary L., d/o Lizzie H., Age 1y 4m 1d, b. N/D, d. 01/15/1862
SPENCER, Mary E., ssw-Thomas B., b. 1869, d. 1953
SPENCER, Thomas B., ssw-Mary E., b. 1861, d. 1945
TATTERSAIL, Thomas, Pfc., DE, 59 Pioneer Inf., WWI, b. 02/22/1895, d. 08/26/1947
WILSON, Hannah, b. 1844, d. 1876

The following stones were recorded by the Hudson Survey but are now missing or unreadable:
SCOTT, Clara G., d/o Wm. A. & M. B., Age 1y, b. N/D, d. 01/1854
SCOTT, Mary, w/o William A., Age 26y 4m, b. N/D, d. 02/16/1856

(BK-014 & HU-525) GOSHEN M. E. CHURCH CEMETERY
Located in Milton, between Chestnut, Mill, Coulter and Walnut Streets.
Recorded: Between November 7, 1996 and July 30, 1997

ATKINS, Anna Francis, ssw-David T., b. 1845, d. 1932. Children: Fannie, Mary, Nannie, Joseph & Raymond
ATKINS, Annie S., ssw-Clara E., Joseph R., Nannie C. Shermer & Shermer T., b. 1850, d. 1932
ATKINS, Bertha May, d/o Wm. H. & Fannie, b. 09/19/1886, d. 07/25/1887
ATKINS, Charles Henry Copes, s/o Joseph & Sallie Maull, b. 10/07/1851, d. 11/26/1913
ATKINS, Clara E., ssw-Annie S., Joseph R., Nannie C. Shermer & Shermer T., b. 1847, d. 1926
ATKINS, David T., ssw-Anna Francis, b. 1842, d. 1933
ATKINS, Fannie Darby, b. 02/20/1870, d. 06/27/1943
ATKINS, Fannie H., ssw-Wm. Henry, b. 1865, d. 1957
ATKINS, George W., ssw-Lucy A., b 11/30/1852, d. 12/03/1915
ATKINS, John S., b. 07/15/1867, d. 02/01/1949
ATKINS, Joseph C., ssw-Sallie Maull, b. 07/20/1813, d. 12/16/1906
ATKINS, Joseph C., s/o David H. & Almira, b. 03/16/1870, d. 07/21/1870
ATKINS, Joseph R., ssw-Annie S., Clara E.., Nannie C. Shermer & Shermer T., b. 12/04/1852, d. 09/14/1931
ATKINS, Joseph T., b. 03/14/1878, d. 03/24/1888
ATKINS, Louisa, d/o Joseph C. & Sally, Age 4y 4m 16d, b. N/D, d. 12/01/1853
ATKINS, Lucy A., ssw-George W., b. 11/17/1855, d. 03/09/1930
ATKINS, Maggie Ethel, d/o Wm. H. & Fannie, b. 04/04/1889, d. 02/04/1890
ATKINS, Mary Ann, consort o/Capt. Jos. C., Age 24y 3m, b. N/D, d. 09/07/1846
ATKINS, Mary C., d/o T. J. & S. A., b. 1855, d. 1882
ATKINS, Mary E. M., b. 08/29/1885, d. 02/09/1905
ATKINS, Nannie C. Shermer, w/o J. R., ssw-Joseph R., Annie S., Clara E. & Shermer T., b. 10/19/1859, d. 07/02/1940
ATKINS, Peter E. P., ssw-Sallie A. Burton, b. 07/12/1822, d. 12/23/1907
ATKINS, Sallie A. Burton, ssw-Peter E. P., b. 05/05/1831, d. 10/17/1915
ATKINS, Sallie maul, ssw-Joseph C., b. 08/27/1828, d. 08/12/1897
ATKINS, Sara A. Wiltbank, w/o Thomas J., b. 1818, d. 1872
ATKINS, Sarah L., b. 01/06/1894, d. 12/21/1976
ATKINS, Shermer T., ssw-Nannie C. Shermer, Annie S., Clara E., & Joseph R., b. 1889, d. 1891
ATKINS, Thomas J., ssw-Sara A. Wiltbank, b. 1818, d. 1907
ATKINS, Virginia Tomlinson, w/o Charles Henry & d/o William Burton Tomlinson & Lydia Ann Burton, b. 08/27/1855, d. 03/27/1927
ATKINS, Wm. Henry, ssw-Fannie H., b. 1854, d. 1911
BARKER, Eliza, w/o Joseph R., Age 74y 10m 25d, b. 06/17/1796, d. 05/12/1871
BARKER, Harriett E., ssw-John B., b. 1863, d. 1948
BARKER, John B., ssw-Harriet E., b. 1850, d. 1927
BARKER, John L., b. 1828, d. 1897
BARKER, Joseph R., Age 76y 5m 9d, b. N/D, d. 07/01/1865
BARKER, Sarah E., b. 1830, d. 1892

BARKER, Thomas R., Age 48y 1m 23d, b. N/D, d. 02/20/1879

BARNES, Frances L., b. 02/29/1880, d. 09/06/1947

BAYNUM, Ann E., b. 02/28/1827, d. 06/19/1907

BAYNUM, Delphenia G., d/o Jas. M. & Ann E., Age 5y, b. N/D, d. 03/07/1856

BAYNUM, James M., Capt., b. 11/08/1822, d. 09/04/1901

BAYNUM, John C., s/o Seth H. & Catherine G., b. 02/10/1863, d. 11/10/1876

BAYNUM, Seth, Age 54y 3m 11d, b. N/D, d. 12/31/1835

BAYNUM, Seth H., Age 30y 8m 16d, b. N/D, d. 10/17/1868

BENNETT, Virginia C. Lynch, w/o John W., ssw-Zadoc P. Lynch, b. 10/16/1852, d. 06/16/1919

BENNUM, George W., s/o Henry O. & Isabella, Age 66y 11m 3d, b. N/D, d. 11/13/1874

BLACK, Charlotte E., ssw-Samuel L., b. 10/27/1862, d. 11/05/1949

BLACK, Eliza G., ssw-Thomas L., b. 10/29/1830, d. 10/05/1914

BLACK, Jane Lingo, ssw-Martin L., b. 03/12/1912, d. N/D

BLACK, John R., b. 1853, d. 1914

BLACK, Joseph L., b. 05/19/1947, d. 11/16/1994

BLACK, Joseph L., ssw-Maggie P., b. 03/13/1858, d. 06/24/1920

BLACK, Letitia L., b. 1884, d. 1952

BLACK, Maggie P., ssw-Joseph L., b. 12/15/1860, d. 10/04/1933

BLACK, Margaret A., b. 11/25/1890, d. 05/17/1986

BLACK, Marianna, b. 1853, d. 1929

BLACK, Martin L., ssw-Jane Lingo, b. 06/03/1913, d. 09/01/1989

BLACK, Robert B., b. 03/17/1889, d. 05/13/1977

BLACK, Samuel L., ssw-Charlotte E., b. 02/10/1860, d. 03/18/1923

BLACK, Samuel Martin, s/o Joseph L. & Maggie P., b. 03/24/1890, d. 03/27/1891

BLACK, Thomas L., b. 1891, d. 1955

BLACK, Thomas L., ssw-Eliza G., b. 11/19/1828, d. 06/24/1891

BLACK, W. Morris, ssw-Charlotte E., b. 11/12/1891, d. 07/18/1982

BLACK, William L., b. 1882, d. 1883

BLEW, Mary, w/o Joel, Age 24y, b. N/D, d. 09/24/1826

BLOCKSOM, Anna L., w/o David, Age 24y, b. N/D, d. 02/23/1856

BLOCKSOM, David, Brother of Capt. John L., b. 09/13/1826, d. 08/19/1869

BLOCKSOM, Elizabeth, ssw-Richard, b. 12/14/1810, d. 07/08/1884

BLOCKSOM, Hetty, w/o Jesse, ssw-Jesse, b. 01/19/1810, d. 03/04/1859

BLOCKSOM, Jesse, ssw-Hetty, b. 11/29/1797, d. 12/24/1851

BLOCKSOM, John L., Capt., Brother of David, b. 11/25/1844, d. 03/14/1877

BLOCKSOM, Richard, ssw-Elizabeth, b. 09/24/1801, d. 04/06/1881

BOLLES, Anna R., ssw-Sarah V. Lofland, b. 1868, d. 1948

BOSMAN, Sarah J. Prettyman, w/o Wm. J., b. 03/01/1844, d. 01/11/1914

BRADLEY, John H., s/o Joseph & Catherine M., Age 2y 11m 20d, b. N/D, d. 12/02/1874

BROCKINGTON, Mary L., ssw-Virginia A., b. 10/29/1865, d. 03/22/1942

BROCKINGTON, Virginia A., ssw-Mary L., b. 11/07/1886, d. 07/17/1971

BROWN, Joseph R., ssw-Patricia P., b. 04/20/1934, d. 04/28/1989

BROWN, Patricia P., b. 09/01/1935, d. N/D

BROWN, Ruth J., b. 10/14/1913, d. 10/24/1978

BRYAN, Frank O., b. 1885, d. 1951

BRYAN, George A., ssw-Sallie A. & Susan M., b. 08/09/1849, d. 02/27/1928

BRYAN, Mary C., b. 04/13/1815, d. 07/06/1891

BRYAN, Sallie A., w/o Geo. A., ssw-George A. & Susan M., b. 09/05/1857, d. 07/19/1909

BRYAN, Susan M., ssw-Sallie A. & George A., b. 07/13/1891, d. 06/15/1892

BURNS, Henry M., ssw-Mary Anna, b. 08/13/1878, d. 06/21/1967

BURNS, Mary Anna, ssw-Henry M., b. 02/12/1882, d. 08/21/1977

BURRIS, Daniel C., ssw-George P., Infant, Lydia I, Manan S., Mary E. & Thomas C., b. 1870, d. 1871

BURRIS, George P., ssw-Daniel C., Infant, Lydia I., Manan S., Mary E. & Thomas C., b. 1840, d. 1925

BURRIS, Infant, ssw-ssw-Daniel C., George P., Lydia I., Manan S., Mary E. & Thomas C., b. 1882 , d. 1882

BURRIS, Lydia I., ssw-Daniel C., George P., Infant, Manan S., Mary E. & Thomas C., b. 1873, d. 1891

BURRIS, Manan S., ssw-Daniel C., George P., Infant, Lydia I., Mary E. & Thomas C., b. 1877, d. 1887

BURRIS, Mary E., w/o George P., ssw-George P., Daniel C., Infant, Lydia I, Manan S. & Thomas C.,
    b. 1845, d. 1891

BURRIS, Thomas C., ssw-Daniel C., George P., Infant, Lydia I., Manan S. & Mary E., b. 1872, d. 1873

BURROUS, Amos A., ssw-Mildred J., b. 1896, d. 1964

BURROUS, Carrie M., d/o Capt. James W. & Eliza J. Oliver, ssw-Charles A., b. 1870, d. 1929

BURROUS, Charles A., Capt., s/o Capt. Eli N. & Mahaley W., ssw-Carrie M., b. 1863, d. 1931

BURROUS, Charles A., Sr., USN, WWI, b. 1894, d. 1957

BURROUS, Eli W., ssw-Mahala W., b. 09/30/1824, d. 09/24/1914

BURROUS, Florence, ssw-Maggie S., b. 01/12/1871, d. 02/15/1871

BURROUS, James A. H., b. 01/18/1900, d. 05/19/1948

BURROUS, Maggie S., d/o Eli W. & Mahala W., ssw-Florence, b. 05/11/1860, d. 02/05/1870

BURROUS, Mahala W., ssw-Eli W., b. 03/08/1826, d. 02/28/1911

BURROUS, Mary L., b. 01/27/1921, d. 12/12/1981

BURROUS, Maude N., b. 03/11/1892, d. 05/16/1978

BURROUS, Mildred J., ssw-Amos A., b. 1898, d. 1992

BURROUS, Samuel G., s/o Capt. Eli W. & Mahala W., b. 09/26/1851, d. 05/31/1934

BURTON, Daniel R., ssw-Emma W., b. 03/15/1835, d. 04/29/1891

BURTON, Emma W., ssw-Daniel R., b. 11/28/1845, d. 06/25/1930

BURTON, Eunice Prettyman, ssw-Henry Purnell, b. 10/06/1846, d. 10/26/1926

BURTON, Henry Purnell, ssw-Eunice Prettyman, b. 03/31/1841, d. 11/24/1926

CADE, Emory Wolfe, ssw-Samuel, b. 09/25/1874, d. 11/15/1884

CADE, John H., Capt., Co. H, 3rd DE. Inf., ssw-Mary C., b. 11/04/1833, d. 09/06/1885

CADE, Lillian, b. 05/23/1855, d. 03/19/1953

CADE, Mary C., ssw-John H., b. 05/24/1835, d. 08/21/1922

CADE, Raymond A., b. 09/20/1871, d. 06/28/1937

CADE, Samuel, ssw-Emory Wolfe, b. 05/18/1859, d. 05/24/1859

CADE, Samuel Henry, s/o John & Eliza, Age 1y 7m 11d, b. N/D, d. 08/26/1834

CALHOON, G. Edward, b. 1858, d. 1930

CALHOON, Laura, b. 1869, d. 1945

CAMP, Mabel S. Pettyjohn, w/o George H., b. 04/19/1881, d. 08/06/1913

CANNON, Lydia Ann B., b. 1888, d. 1973

CAREY, Anna S., ssw-James A., b. 12/02/1843, d. 10/12/1924

CAREY, Annie E., Age 68y 5m 16d, b. 04/9/1851, d. 10/15/1919

CAREY, Arthur C., ssw-Hannah Carey Lank, b. 1845, d. 1878

CAREY, Charles Stockley, b. 07/10/1859, d. 08/14/1939

CAREY, Clara Waples, w/o Theodore C., b. 09/05/1857, d. 06/07/1894

CAREY, Edward J., Age 8m 26d, b. N/D, d. N/D

CAREY, Eli, Age 51y 5d, b. N/D, d. 01/18/1827

CAREY, Elizabeth H., b. 02/01/1818, d. 04/16/1888

CAREY, Ella Collins, b. 10/25/1860, d. 08/22/1942

CAREY, Frank B., ssw-Margaret Wilson, b. 06/24/1875, d. 02/18/1941
CAREY, Gertrude Voshage, w/o Joseph, b. 04/24/1895, d. 09/16/1948
CAREY, Harold H., ssw-John F., b. 02/05/1891, d. 04/20/1891
CAREY, Harry, Eldest s/o James & Eliza A., Age 2y 11m 15d, b. N/D, d. 02/27/1875
CAREY, James A., ssw-Anna S., b. 02/06/1843, d. 01/26/1895
CAREY, Jas. M., Capt., b. 04/30/1817, d. 07/26/1881
CAREY, John F., M. D., Born in Milton, DE, Died in Cheyenne, Wyo., b. 07/04/1842, d. 07/27/1911
CAREY, John P., Age 62y 7m 10d, b. 10/12/1842, d. 05/22/1905
CAREY, Joseph M., Interred at Cheyenne, WY., b. 1845, d. 1924
CAREY, Joseph Maull, II, b 09/07/1892, d. 06/10/1965
CAREY, Margaret Wilson, ssw-Frank B., b. 02/17/1877, d. 08/07/1941
CAREY, Martin B., ssw-Rilla P., b. 05/28/1885, d. 01/10/1896
CAREY, Mary C., w/o John F., b. 06/14/1841, d. 08/02/1881
CAREY, Rilla P., ssw-Martin B., b. 10/10/1890, d. 01/13/1896
CAREY, Robert Davis, b. 05/06/1839, d. 06/08/1907
CAREY, Robert H., ssw-Susan P., b. 07/12/1811, d. 09/02/1891
CAREY, Sallie M., d/o Robert H. & Susan P., b. 05/21/1851, d. 08/09/1925
CAREY, Sarah J., m/o John P., b. 03/24/1826, d. 03/24/1907
CAREY, Susan D., d/o Robert H. & Susan P., b. 12/02/1855, d. 08/04/1935
CAREY, Susan P., w/o Robert H., b. 11/28/1813, d. 08/08/1881
CAREY, Susan Waples, b. 09/02/1886, d. 04/23/1888
CAREY, Theodore C., s/o Theodore Campbell & Clara Waples, b. 11/02/1888, d. 09/10/1916
CAREY, Theodore C., ssw-Clara Waples, b. 10/26/1847, d. 12/24/1895
CARPENTER, Benjamin E., ssw-John B., b. 04/22/1843, d. 04/29/1925
CARPENTER, Georgetta, ssw-Henrietta, Age 7m, b. N/D, d. 09/30/1892
CARPENTER, Henrietta, w/o George T., Age 34y, b. N/D, d. 03/11/1893
CARPENTER, Jensie, Age 57y, b. N/D, d. 04/05/1882
CARPENTER, John B., ssw-Benjamin E., Age 82y 2m 10d, b. N/D, d. 02/21/1896
CHANDLER, Clarence J., ssw-Mary Elliott, b. 10/01/1875, d. 07/18/1876
CHANDLER, Lewis Bernard, ssw-Mary Elizabeth, b. 09/19/1840, d. 04/13/1908
CHANDLER, Mary Elizabeth, ssw-Lewis Bernard, b. 06/21/1843, d. 10/20/1921
CHANDLER, Mary Elliott, ssw-Clarence J., b. 08/01/1868, d. 10/21/1881
CHANDLER, Sara Russell, ssw-William Hazzard, b. 03/11/1868, d. 02/20/1940
CHANDLER, William H., Jr., b. 06/16/1890, d. 07/09/1929
CHANDLER, William Hazzard, ssw-Sara Russell, b. 12/01/1866, d. 01/03/1949
CLEMENTS, Lillie D., d/o Wm. C. & Mary E., Age 7y 2m 11d, b. N/D, d. 01/25/1886
CLEMENTS, Mary E., ssw-William C., b. 08/24/1858, d. 10/17/1950
CLEMENTS, William C., s/o William C. & Mary E., b. 10/04/1889, d. 05/24/1894
CLEMENTS, William C., ssw-Mary E., b. 07/04/1851, d. 04/22/1914
CLIFTON, Betsy, ssw-Nathan, b. 12/27/1785, d. 10/10/1866
CLIFTON, Clarence E., b. 10/22/1880, d. 05/25/1955
CLIFTON, Nathan, ssw-Betsy, b. 03/23/1782, d. 05/03/1866
COLLINS, Aletta J., ssw-James L., b. 03/16/1837, d. 06/26/1920
COLLINS, Austin I., ssw-Virginia, b. 1887, d. 1887
COLLINS, Cassie, ssw-John A., b. 10/24/1851, d. 08/30/1931
COLLINS, George, s/o George & Elizabeth, b. 09/05/1849, d. 06/01/1876
COLLINS, Harry W., ssw-Sallie C., b. 1873, d. 1874
COLLINS, James L., ssw-Aletta J., b. 02/09/1836, d. 03/12/1907

COLLINS, John A., ssw-Cassie, b. 09/27/1845, d. 01/13/1907
COLLINS, Sallie C., ssw-Walter E., b. 1871, d. 1871
COLLINS, Sarah, Age 86y, b. N/D, d. 12/17/1844
COLLINS, Virginia, ssw-Cassie, b. 1876, d. 1885
COLLINS, Walter E., ssw-Austin L., b. 1889, d. 1889
CONAWAY, Ida M., c/o John H. & Mary M., b. 03/13/1872, d. 03/29/1877
CONAWAY, John H., b. 03/07/1852, d. 10/11/1916
CONAWAY, Mary M., w/o John H., b. 12/14/1854, d. 07/30/1922
CONAWAY, Matilda, w/o Rev. W. N. Conaway, b. 01/22/1833, d. 07/29/1906
CONAWAY, Minie J., c/o John H. & Mary M., b. 03/30/1875, d. 10/31/1893
CONAWAY, Samuel M., c/o John H. & Mary M., b. 08/20/1882, d. 07/03/1886
CONNER, David A., b. 12/27/1841, d. 09/25/1919
CONNER, Mary E., b. 12/14/1845, d. 11/30/1901
CONWELL, Annie M., d/o Asa F. & Mary, Age 1y 5m 16d, b. N/D, d. 09/13/1865
CONWELL, Asa F., ssw-Mary Adaline, b. 11/07/1827, d. 01/21/1911
CONWELL, Clara R., b. 12/08/1864, d. 04/20/1950
CONWELL, David M., ssw-Lydia J., b. 1852, d. 1933
CONWELL, Edith C., b. 1891, d. 1993
CONWELL, Eliza A., w/o Capt. W. E., Age 38y, b. N/D, d. 01/27/1868
CONWELL, Elizabeth T., b. 01/04/1852, d. 11/07/1900
CONWELL, Elsie, d/o James C. & Clara, b. 08/12/1891, d. 01/04/1892
CONWELL, H. Ernest, b. 1887, d. 1964
CONWELL, James C., Capt. b. 03/02/1861, d. 08/25/1931
CONWELL, John L., Rev., Age 54y, b. N/D, d. 09/05/1838
CONWELL, John M., s/o John T. & Susan, b. 08/26/1848, d. 04/08/1874
CONWELL, John T., s/o Asa F. & Mary A., Age 1y 5m 6d, b. N/D, d. 01/18/1875
CONWELL, John T., ssw-Susan Morris, b. 10/15/1814, d. 04/29/1903
CONWELL, Lydia J., ssw-David M., b. 1855, d. 1945
CONWELL, Mary Adaline, w/o Asa F., ssw-Asa F., b. 05/09/1832, d. 02/02/1866
CONWELL, Susan, w/o John L., Age 40y 6m 28d, b. N/D, d. 04/15/1836
CONWELL, Susan B., Age 61y 1m 28d, b. N/D, d. 06/23/1892
CONWELL, Susan Morris, w/o John T., b. 03/23/1823, d. 12/02/1892
CONWELL, William E., b. 03/31/1828, d. 11/27/1883
COOPER, Samuel Castner, s/o James, Jr. & Piercy J., Age 5m 6d, b. N/D, d. 10/16/1857
COPANS, Infant, b. 04/02/1985, d. 04/02/1985
COPANS, Janet Lee, b. 1951, d. 1951
COPANS, Paula Veronica, b. 06/06/1931, d. 12/10/1986
COULTER, Cornelius, Age 75y, b. N/D, d. 11/15/1856
COULTER, Eliza, Age 80y, b. N/D, d. 04/29/1867
COULTER, John M., Capt., Age 34y, b. N/D, d. 04/04/1844
COULTER, Sally, w/o Cornelius, Age 63y 8m 5d, b. N/D, d. 10/28/1848
COULTER, Sarah A. Martin, wid/o Cornelius, b. 07/01/1810, d. 03/09/1890
COVERDALE, L. J., ssw-Sallie J. McKeag, Age 60y, b. N/D, d. 02/01/1909
COVERDALE, Mary L., b. 1845, d. 1910
COVERDALE, Minnie, d/o L. J. & S. J., Age 1y 8m 18d, b. N/D, d. 05/04/1880
COVERDALE, Sallie J. McKeag, w/o L. J., ssw-L. J., b. 12/24/1849, d. 06/18/1888
COVERDALE, Wesley, b. 09/15/1832, d. 10/29/1924

COX, Willard Patterson, s/o Washington & Catharine, born in Wilmington, died in Milton, b. N/D, d. 03/27/1902

CREAMER, Maude Browne, ssw-Sarah Virginia Andrews, b. 08/03/1875, d. 01/16/1922

CREAMER, Sarah Virginia Andrews, w/o Rev. Thomas Robinson, b. 04/07/1851, d. 11/27/1923

CREAMER, Simpson Andrew, s/o Rev. T. K. & S. J., b. 06/24/1890, d. 05/20/1891

CREAMER, T. R., Rev., Pastor of the Church of Milton 3 years 9 months, b. 08/01/1846, d. 01/10/1892

DARBY, Amelia, ssw-Myers C., Age 85y 7m 9d, b. N/D, d. 07/24/1891

DARBY, Ephraim, Capt., Age 57y 9m 17d, b. N/D, d. 05/04/1857

DARBY, Ephraim J., s/o Ephraim & Mary M., Age 31y 5d, b. 09/09/1836, d. 10/14/1867

DARBY, Estella A., b. 10/06/1876, d. 04/12/1911

DARBY, James M., Capt., ssw-Sarah J., b. 07/24/1836, d. 05/09/1908

DARBY, Julia C., ssw-Willie C., b. 03/21/1873, d. 06/21/1873

DARBY, Lettia L., d/o Miers J. & Susan, Age 1y 8m 20d, b. N/D, d. 07/20/1864

DARBY, Mary M., w/o Capt. E. Darby, ssw-Harriet E. Vaughan, Age 64y 5m 3d, b. N/D, d. 03/20/1870

DARBY, Miers J., Capt., ssw-Susan T., b. 12/06/1825, d. 01/15/1910

DARBY, Myers C., ssw-Amelia, Age 73y 10m 21d, b. N/D, d. 08/08/1875

DARBY, Sarah J., ssw-Capt. James M., b. 07/28/1846, d. 01/10/1902

DARBY, Susan T., ssw-Capt. Miers J., b. 08/09/1829, d. 12/09/1913

DARBY, Willie C., ssw-Julia C., b. 02/25/1868, d. 07/11/1869

DAVIDSON, Andrew J., ssw-Mary Eliza, John T. & Emma M., Age 47y 4m 5d, b. N/D, d. 05/07/1880

DAVIDSON, Annie M., d/o Chas. & Mary, b. 06/09/1888, d. 06/30/1889

DAVIDSON, C. C., b. 12/24/1827, d. 03/09/1917

DAVIDSON, Chas. H., b. 11/13/1861, d. 06/25/1914

DAVIDSON, Edward T., ssw-Emma M., b. 07/25/1880, d. 01/13/1959

DAVIDSON, Emma C., ssw-Hannah J., b. 07/26/1870, d. 02/17/1960

DAVIDSON, Emma M., w/o Andrew J., ssw-Andrew J., Mary Eliza & John T., b. 1844, d. 1936

DAVIDSON, Emma M., ssw-Edward T., b. 02/17/1887, d. 12/12/1976

DAVIDSON, Emma M., w/o C. C., Age 38y 11m 5d, b. N/D, d. 06/11/1879

DAVIDSON, Geo. R., ssw-Lillie G., b. 1864, d. 1951

DAVIDSON, Hannah J., ssw-John H., b. 10/10/1839, d. 05/09/1916

DAVIDSON, Inf. w/o C. C. & Emma, b. N/D, d. N/D

DAVIDSON, James P., ssw-Sarah E., b. 12/01/1844, d. 10/14/1915

DAVIDSON, John H., ssw-Hannah J., b. 01/29/1837, d. 06/22/1916

DAVIDSON, John T., s/o Andrew J. & Emma M., ssw-Andrew J., Mary Eliza & Emma M., Age 3m 18d, b. N/D, d. 07/11/1865

DAVIDSON, Joseph Alfred, c/o John & Hannah, b. 06/10/1860, d. 06/28/1860

DAVIDSON, Josiah H., Age 57y 11m, b. 01/01/1835, d. 12/01/1892

DAVIDSON, Lillie G., ssw-Geo. R., b. 1868, d. 1953

DAVIDSON, Mahala, b. 04/07/1851, d. 09/24/1935

DAVIDSON, Marie, b. 03/15/1912, d. 10/27/1912

DAVIDSON, Mary E., b. 09/10/1865, d. 12/21/1919

DAVIDSON, Mary E., ssw-Joseph A., Age 9m 17d, b. 09/27/1866, d. 07/14/1867

DAVIDSON, Mary Eliza, c/o John & Hannah, ssw-Andrew J., Emma M. & John T., b. 01/16/1872, d. 06/23/1873

DAVIDSON, Sallie G., b. 06/29/1880, d. 05/07/1908

DAVIDSON, Sarah E., ssw-James P., b. 06/30/1841, d. 04/24/1922

DAVIDSON, Susie B., w/o William H., ssw-William H., b. 1872, d. 1945

DAVIDSON, William H., ssw-Susie B., b. 1873, d. 1962

DAVIDSON, William J., ssw-Mary E., Age 9m 5d, b. 10/28/1868, d. 07/31/1869
DAVIS, Carol, b. 11/04/1926, d. 03/21/1990
DAVIS, Elizabeth A., b. 03/04/1833, d. 01/29/1891
DAVIS, Fannie C., ssw-James A., b. 1872, d. 1953
DAVIS, George S., b. 06/04/1826, d. 09/21/1866
DAVIS, George W., s/o George & Elizabeth, b. 07/28/1865, d. 09/14/1866
DAVIS, James A., ssw-Fannie C., b. 1864, d. 1934
DAVIS, James H., s/o William & Ann, Age 16y 2m, b. N/D, d. 06/06/1852
DAVIS, William, Age 67y, b. N/D, d. 09/26/1852
DEAN, Elizabeth, ssw-John W., b. 05/15/1823, d. 01/26/1910
DEAN, John W., ssw-Elizabeth, b. 06/02/1820, d. 02/02/1892
DICKERSON, Abbie B., b. 10/15/1879, d. 03/12/1970
DICKERSON, Annie M., b. 08/01/1856, d. 03/19/1931
DICKERSON, Catharine H., w/o Richard, b. 07/04/1830, d. 07/30/1886
DICKERSON, Charles M., b. 07/06/1862, d. 10/25/1899
DICKERSON, Elmer, b. 04/27/1876, d. 02/12/1962
DICKERSON, Richard, Capt., ssw-Catharine H., b. 12/28/1828, d. 05/18/1894
DODGE, George E., Capt., ssw-Jessie A., b. 1858, d. 1933
DODGE, Jessie A., ssw-George E., b. 1864, d. 1942
DONOVAN, Hatty A., w/o Peter, ssw-Peter, b. 1824, d. 1874
DONOVAN, Peter, ssw-Hatty A., b. 1817, d. 1889
DORMAN, Ann E., d/o David & Elenor, Age 13y 25d, b. N/D, d. 03/19/1854
DORMAN, David, Age 52y 3m 24d, b. N/D, d. 12/21/1853
DORMAN, Eleanor, d/o Jas. H. & Sarah H., b. 1855, d. 1915
DORMAN, Elenor, w/o David, Age 50y 6m 7d, b. N/D, d. 08/11/1843
DORMAN, Eliza, d/o David & Elenor, Age 19d, b. N/D, d. 09/14/1828
DORMAN, Hetty J. Coverdale, w/o Capt. N. E., b. 08/08/1827, d. 02/11/1899
DORMAN, Hetty J., ssw-John B., b. 06/03/1858, d. 07/18/1928
DORMAN, James H., Capt., ssw-Sarah H., b. 1830, d. 1869
DORMAN, John B., ssw-Hetty J., b. 08/19/1843, d. 02/18/1901
DORMAN, Mary E., Age 1y 6m, b. N/D, d. 08/30/1829
DORMAN, Nehemiah E., Capt., ssw-Hetty J. Coverdale, Buried at sea. b. 05/10/1826, d. 06/21/1869
DORMAN, Samuel D., s/o David & Elenor, Age 20y 2m 26d, b. 05/21/1847, d. 08/17/1867
DORMAN, Sarah E., d/o David & Elenor, Age 7y, b. N/D, d. 10/06/1842
DORMAN, Sarah H., w/o Jas. H., b. 1834, d. 1912
DRAPER, James W., Age 79y, b. N/D, d. 01/29/1879
DUTTON, Addie May, Age 1y 2m 26d, b. N/D, d. N/D
DUTTON, George W., b. 1863, d. 1939
DUTTON, Lovenia H., w/o George, Age 38y 3m 9d, b. 12/08/1861, d. 03/07/1900
DUTTON, Peter F., b. 09/16/1850, d. 04/22/1926
ELLINGSWORTH, Annie M., b. 1863, d. 1940
ELLINGSWORTH, Elizabeth B., b. 12/11/1811, d. 09/03/1892
ELLINGSWORTH, John C., b. 1862, d. 1937
ELLINGSWORTH, Robert B., b. 1890, d. 1891
ELLINGSWORTH, William W., b. 03/25/1842, d. 08/29/1891
ELLINGSWORTH, Lydia E., (William W. & Lydia W.), b. 12/11/1842, d. 04/10/1913
ELLINGSWORTH, Noble, b. 10/10/1865, d. 01/02/1928
ELLINGSWORTH, Noble C., Capt., b. 06/12/1806, d. 11/01/1881

EVANS, Jiney, w/o Robert M., Age 68y 6d, b. N/D, d. 04/18/1874

EVANS, John R., Age 36y, b. N/D, d. 12/31/1840

EVANS, John R., s/o John R. & Nancy, Age 7y, b. N/D, d. 10/05/1844

EVANS, Rilla Lekites, ssw-Harry & Phoebe Lekites, b. 1886, d. N/D

EWING, Mary E., d/o Wm. & Sarah A., Age 14y 6m, b. N/D, d. 11/12/1856

FAUCETT, Nancy J. Parker, w/o Jacob & d/o Peter, Esq., b. 1802, d. 1843

FEARING, Lydia M., ssw-William B., b. 04/02/1843, d. 05/27/1922

FEARING, Vivia G., ssw-Willie E., b. 03/25/1870, d. 01/31/1875

FEARING, William G., ssw-Lydia M., b. 11/29/1837, d. 02/12/1928

FEARING, Willie E., s/o William G. & Lydia M., b. 09/19/1867, d. 01/17/1875

FERL, James Everett, ssw-Janet Guerrin & Samuel Robert, b. 02/10/1956, d. N/D

FERL, Janet Guerrin, ssw-James Everett & Samuel Robert, b. 10/03/1961, d. N/D

FERL, Samuel Robert, s/o James Everett & Janet Guerrin, ssw-James Everett & Janet Guerrin,
     b. 08/22/1991, d. 02/23/1996

FIELDS, Frank F., b. 1889, d. 1922

FIELDS, Joseph H., Age 62y 9m 16d, b. N/D, d. 10/23/1905

FIELDS, Mary E. Johnson, w/o Joseph H., b. 03/05/1849, d. 07/06/1918

FISHER, Eliza A., w/o John H., b. 09/08/1823, d. 07/15/1883

FISHER, Eliza A., ssw-Thomas G., b. 03/25/1887, d. 07/12/1887

FISHER, George T., b. 03/13/1883, d. 07/23/1883

FISHER, John F., Capt., b. 03/14/1849, d. 08/14/1924

FISHER, John H., Capt., ssw-Thomas C., b. 08/18/1818, d. 10/03/1851

FISHER, Mary Hazzard, ssw-William H., b. 09/12/1842, d. 10/25/1929

FISHER, Thomas C., Capt., s/o Capt. J. H. & Eliza A., b. 10/01/1846, d. 06/16/1884

FISHER, Thomas G., ssw-Eliza A., b. 03/26/1887, d. 06/27/1887

FISHER, William H., s/o Capt. J. H. & Eliza A., b. 08/18/1844, d. 11/20/1871

FOWLER, Eliza E., wid/o William, Age 77y, b. N/D, d. 07/01/1903

FOWLER, Elizabeth, b. 04/17/1837, d. 04/20/1922

FOWLER, Robert H., Age 50, b. N/D, d. 03/21/1883

FOWLER, William, Age 76y, b. N/D, d. 12/02/1885

FOX, Ida J. Wilson, b. 11/15/1873, d. 05/08/1953

FOX, Lydia H., b. 06/20/1831, d. 12/19/1910

FOX, Samuel J. Wilson, s/o Wm. H. & Ida J., b. 02/10/1895, d. 02/18/1897

FOX, William H., b. 08/27/1868, d. 10/29/1919

FOX, William H., Jr., b. 08/10/1891, d. 09/07/1919

FRANTZ, Louise H., b. 1903, d. 1924

GILMER, Frederick, ssw-Hester Ann, Age 70y, b. N/D, d. 05/31/1879

GILMER, Hester Ann, ssw-Frederick, Age 73y, b. N/D, d. 04/01/1880

GOODEN, Darvilia, d/o T. R. & Helen, Age 1m 3d, b. N/D, d. 07/14/1856

GOODEN, Helen G., w/o Thomas, Age 79y 2m 5d, b. N/D, d. 12/25/1915

GORDEN, Sallie B., Age 63y 6m 17d, b. N/D, d. 10/06/1861

GOSLEE, Hetty Ann, d/o Mary Davis & Samuel L., Age 10y 2m 20d, b. N/D, d. 09/23/1864

GOSLEE, Mary Davis, w/o Samuel L., b. 02/24/1844, d. 01/21/1908

GOSLEE, Samuel L., b. 04/13/1816, d. 04/06/1891

GOTHARD, Elisha, Age 39y 6m 7d, b. N/D, d. 05/20/1857

GOTHARD, Lydia C., wid/o Elisha, ssw-Mary E., b. 03/17/1817, d. 01/31/1900

GOTHARD, Mary E., d/o Lydia C. & Elisha, ssw-Lydia C., Age 22y, b. N/D, d. 08/30/1879

HALL, Annie E. R., d/o John M. & Elizabeth, b. 11/24/1862, d. 03/10/1887

HALL, Eli, Age 72y 2m 6d, b. N/D, d. 05/13/1846

HALL, Eliza W., b. 03/16/1824, d. 01/21/1891

HALL, Elizabeth, w/o John M., b. 08/29/1829, d. 12/10/1894

HALL, Emma Adelaid, d/o Robert M. & Nancy, Age 2y b. N/D, d. 07/13/1847

HALL, George, Age 74y, b. N/D, d. 05/25/1864

HALL, Houston, b. 12/07/1815, d. 04/15/1888

HALL, Jane, b. N/D, d. 01/29/1855

HALL, Jincy, w/o Robert M., Age 68y 6d, b. N/D, d. 04/18/1874

HALL, John M., b. 07/08/1829, d. 07/06/1890

HALL, Laura Catharine, d/o Houston & Eliza W., Age 19y 3m 11d, b. N/D, d. 10/23/1864

HALL, Mariah C., Age 17y, b. N/D, d. 02/14/1846

HALL, Nancy, w/o Eli, Age 62y 6m 20d, b. N/D, d. 04/24/1849

HALL, Nancy, w/o Robert M., Age 40y, b. N/D, d. 03/25/1849

HALL, Sarah, w/o George, Age 59y, b. N/D, d. 02/22/1859

HAMMOND, May, b. 08/10/1900, d. 04/08/1990

HARRINGTON, Lydia J., b. 07/05/1878, d. 04/24/1903

HATFIELD, Charles H., s/o Wm. H. & Sarah E., b. 04/19/1884, d. 07/02/1884

HATFIELD, Eliza E., w/o Wm. H., b. 05/20/1849, d. 04/22/1875

HATFIELD, Sarah E., w/o Wm. H., b. 06/18/1853, d. 06/04/1884

HATFIELD, Wm. H., Capt., b. 11/14/1846, d. 12/18/1893

HAZZARD, Agnes Lacey, b. 12/29/1890, d. 12/06/1970

HAZZARD, David, Hon., Governor of State of DE, Associate Judge of Superior Court, Age 84y, b. N/D, d. 07/08/1864

HAZZARD, David E., s/o William A. & Mary P., b. N/D, d. 10/16/1841

HAZZARD, David T., b. 09/13/1840, d. 11/14/1879

HAZZARD, David W., s/o Hon. David Hazzard, Age 57y 8m 11d, b. N/D, d. 12/26/1872

HAZZARD, Elizabeth, ssw-John H., Age 55y 11m 8d, b. N/D, d. 01/06/1831

HAZZARD, Elizabeth, w/o Hon. David, Age 71y, b. N/D, d. 02/25/1854

HAZZARD, Erasmus, Age 28y 10d, b. N/D, d. 04/13/1849

HAZZARD, Franklin William, b. 07/31/1921, d. 10/17/1952

HAZZARD, Hannah, w/o John, Age 60y, b. N/D, d. 02/02/1813

HAZZARD, John Benjamin, b. 11/20/1885, d. 02/27/1946

HAZZARD, John H., DE, 2nd Lt., Capt. Wm. Perry's Co., Revoluntary War, b. 04/28/1754, d. 12/26/1825

HAZZARD, Margaret Anna, d/o William A. & Mary P., Age 10y 1m 16d, b. N/D, d. 04/19/1866

HAZZARD, Mary P., w/o William A., b. 08/0/1822, d. 0/08/1902

HAZZARD, Mary W., d/o Stephen & Eliz., Age 18m, b. N/D, d. 03/22/1862

HAZZARD, Sarah E., d/o Stephen & Eliza, Age 4y 6m, b. N/D, d. 06/12/1862

HAZZARD, Sarah J., Age 25y 10m 24d, b. N/D, d. 05/15/1849

HAZZARD, William A., b. 04/29/1813, d. 05/19/1895

HOLLAND, Albert, Age 30y 10m 21d, b. N/D, d. 05/19/1845

HOLLAND, John C., s/o Albert B. & Susan, Age 11y 6m 28d, b. N/D, d. 07/29/1852

HOLLAND, John S., b. 02/05/1823, d. 01/21/1885

HOLLAND, Mary Arabella, w/o Charles F. & d/o N. D. & Mary P. Welch, b. N/D, d. 11/25/1883

HOLLAND, Sarah G., w/o John S., b. 1829, d. 893

HOLLAND, Virginia, d/o Andrew S. & Anna R., b. 05/27/1878, d. 08/14/1879

HOPKINS, Anna R., ssw-Lena, b. 06/16/1837, d. 07/01/1919

HOPKINS, Josiah, Capt., b. 02/10/1826, d. 09/29/1891

HOPKINS, Lena, Infant daughter, ssw-Anna R., b. 07/24/1868, d. 08/09/1868

HOUSTON, Mary C., w/o Robert, Age 21y 9m 12d, b. N/D, d. 12/22/1829

HUDSON, David A., s/o David & Mary J., Age 1m 3d, b. N/D, d. 10/02/1858

HUDSON, Henry C., Capt., ssw-Mary A., b. 10/25/1817, d. 10/23/1912

HUDSON, M. Margaret, Age 77y, b. N/D, d. 05/23/1860

HUDSON, Mary A., w/o Capt. Henry, Age 63y 8m 8d. b. N/D, d. 09/16/1889

HUDSON, Miers C., s/o David & Mary J., Age 12d, b. N/D, d. 01/30/1863

HUNTER, Alice G., w/o George B., ssw-George B., b. 01/20/1855, d. 03/06/1900

HUNTER, Emma F., d/o Thomas L. & Eliza Black, b. 07/21/1856, d. 07/11/1937

HUNTER, George B., Capt., ssw-Alice G., b. 08/06/1857, d. 10/16/1926

INGRAM, Lavina Dutton, b. 05/17/1879, d. 06/21/1954

IRWIN, A. Wallace, ssw-Sara M., b. 1871, d. 1925

IRWIN, Annie Hall Megee, ssw-Edward Gwin, Edward Gwin W., Jr., Elizabeth Blain, Frances Houston,
Henry Hardcastle & William Noah, b. 11/06/1844, d. 05/26/1919

IRWIN, Carolyn Fisher, b. 04/21/1878, d. 01/15/1965

IRWIN, Charles McGee, b. 07/19/1873, d. 12/03/1930

IRWIN, Dorothy, b. 05/17/1907, d. 04/26/1985

IRWIN, Edward Gwin W., Jr., ssw-Edward Gwin, Annie Hall Megee, Elizabeth Blain, Frances Houston,
    Henry Hardcastle & William Noah, b. 02/22/1875, d. 12/29/1881

IRWIN, Edward Gwin (Reverend), ssw-Annie Hall Megee, Edward Gwin W., Jr., Elizabeth Blain, Frances
    Houston, Henry Hardcastle & William Noah, b. 08/23/1829, d. 03/12/1879

IRWIN, Elizabeth Blain, ssw-Edward Gwin, Annie Hall Megee, Edward Gwin W., Jr., Frances Houston,
    Henry Hardcastle & William Noah, b. 04/10/1863, d. 02/07/1912

IRWIN, Frances Houston, ssw-Edward Gwin, Annie Hall Megee, Edward Gwin W., Jr., Elizabeth Blain,
    Henry Hardcastle & William Noah, b. 08/23/1867, d. 03/25/1950

IRWIN, Henry Hardcastle, ssw-Edward Gwin, Annie Hall Megee, Edward Gwin W., Jr., Elizabeth Blain,
    Frances Houston & William Noah, b. 10/13/1876, d. 03/19/1877

IRWIN, Sara M., ssw-A. Wallace, b. 1882, d. 1940

IRWIN, William Noah, ssw-Edward Gwin, Annie Hall Megee, Edward Gwin W., Jr., Elizabeth Blain,
    Frances Houston & Henry Hardcastle, b. 05/12/1866, d. 05/25/1866

JACKSON, Ann, ssw-Dr. Peter R., Elizabeth H. Wiltbank & Peter B., b. 01/15/1783, d. 05/14/1852

JACKSON, Elizabeth H. Wiltbank, w/o Peter B., ssw-Peter R., Peter B. & Ann, b. 07/23/1827, d. 12/11/1908

JACKSON, Peter B., ssw-Elizabeth H. Wiltbank, Ann & Peter R., b. 06/22/1822, d. 08/03/1892

JACKSON, Peter R., Dr., ssw-Elizabeth H., Wiltbank, Ann & Peter B., b. 02/21/1793, d. 12/03/1863

JARVIS, Margaret A., w/o Sidney A., b. 05/01/1856, d. 11/12/1902

JARVIS, Sidney A., b. 12/04/1837, d. 03/17/1928

JARVIS, Sidney A., s/o Sidney & Maggie, b. 08/13/1884, d. 09/07/1884

JEFFRIES, Peter W., Age 44y 11m 25d, b. N/D, d/ 03/11/1862

JEFFRUS, Mary V., d/o Peter W. & Mary, Age 4y 1m 10d, b. N/D, d. 08/02/1866

JENKINS, Millard L., ssw-Nellie J., b. 08/21/1931, d. N/D

JENKINS, Nellie J., ssw-Millard L., b. 09/10/1935, d. 10/10/1995

JOHNSON, Alena A., ssw-William A., b. 07/27/1879, d. 12/30/1969

JOHNSON, Charlotta, w/o Thomas, ssw-Edward T., b. 1844, d. 1883

JOHNSON, Edward T., s/o Thomas & Charlotta, b. 1869, d. 1876

JOHNSON, Edwin P., Age 55y, b. 1867, d. 02/12/1912

JOHNSON, Florence E., b. 1853, d. 1931

JOHNSON, G. William, b. 08/12/1875, d. 04/12/1904

JOHNSON, Georgia M. Maull, b. 1885, d. 1964

JOHNSON, Harry J., s/o Thomas & Charlotta, b. 1877, d. 1888

JOHNSON, Ida V., b. 1886, d. 1922

JOHNSON, James A., ssw-Maggie E., b. 11/11/1861, d. 02/24/1922

JOHNSON, Leroy H., b. 10/10/1899, d. 09/30/1958

JOHNSON, Maggie E., ssw-James A., b. 10/30/1847, d. 01/29/1933

JOHNSON, Maggie M., b. 07/01/1877, d. 01/19/1903

JOHNSON, Purnel K., b. 1834, d. 1913

JOHNSON, Sarah E., b. 09/03/1866, d. 02/22/1956

JOHNSON, Thomas, b. 1841, d. 1924

JOHNSON, Thomas W., Jr., b. 11/13/1871, d. 12/10/1924

JOHNSON, William A., ssw-Alena A., b. 03/29/1876, d. 10/29/1957

JOHNSON, Winnie A., b. 1834, d. 1914

JONES, Burton Stewart, s/o Charles Gerald & Virginia Burton, b. 09/23/1905, d. 04/16/1906

JONES, C. Richard, b. 12/18/1887, d. 10/17/1918

JONES, Charles Burton, s/o Charles Gerald & Virginia Burton, b. 11/20/1906, d. 08/10/1907

JONES, Charles Gerald, s/o John T. & Emeleene, b. 09/01/1877, d. 10/02/1944

JONES, Emma H., b. 1912, d. 1933

JONES, Grace W., b. 03/24/1888, d. 11/27/1967

JONES, Virginia B., w/o Charles Gerald, b. 03/13/1883, d. 03/06/1976

KIMMEY, Abbie, ssw-Mary, b. 1846, d. 1907

KIMMEY, Abraham, Capt., ssw-Carrie Seixas, b. 11/16/1804, d. 01/09/1848

KIMMEY, Carrie Seixas, ssw-Fannie A., b. 01/17/1869, d. 05/18/1897

KIMMEY, Fannie A., ssw-George, b. 1845, d. 1907

KIMMEY, George, ssw-Abbie, b. 1876, d. 1918

KIMMEY, George E., Capt., ssw-James P., b. 1839, d. 1917

KIMMEY, Ida, ssw-Sarah, b. 09/29/1867, d. 02/27/1868

KIMMEY, James P., ssw-George E., b. 1843, d. 1907

KIMMEY, Mary, ssw-Ida, b. 10/12/1865, d. 03/27/1885

LACEY, Charles F., Capt., s/o Priscilla S. & Robert L., b. 09/21/1852, d. 01/23/1924

LACEY, De Lafayette Fletcher, Dr., b. 09/07/1794, d. 03/19/1866

LACEY, Elizabeth, w/o Fletcher, Age 62y 11m, b. N/D, d. 02/23/1863

LACEY, George, s/o Robert L. & Hester A. P., Age 9y 3m 28d, b. N/D, d. 10/14/1865

LACEY, Hannah Black, ssw-Charles F., b. 03/26/1859, d. 12/14/1940

LACEY, James E., s/o Robert L. & Priscilla, Age 8m 14d, b. N/D, d. 05/09/1852

LACEY, Mary A., d/o Fletcher De Lafayette & Elizabeth, Age 67y, b. 05/04/18__

LACEY, Priscilla S., w/o Robert L., Age 35y, b. N/D, d. 02/05/1855

LACEY, Robert L., Age 53y 8m 29d, b. 05/28/1815, d. 01/27/1869

LACEY, William H., Eldest s/o Robert L. & Priscilla S., b. 10/28/1849, d. 09/30/1914

LAMBDIN, Daniel L., s/o Daniel & Elisa, Age 5m 26d, b. N/D, d. 06/24/1834

LANK, Alena Davidson, ssw-John Clarence, b. 08/16/1878, d. 09/29/1963

LANK, Carolyn C., ssw-Edgar W., b. 1875, d. 1950

LANK, David E., ssw-William P., Lost at sea, b. 12/01/1858, d. abt. 01/08/1884

LANK, Edgar W., ssw-Carolyn C., b. 1874, d. 1937

LANK, Elizabeth Emma, ssw-Joseph Milton, b. 1883, d. 1972

LANK, Hannah Carey, ssw-Arthur C. Carey, b. 1851, d. 1922

LANK, Harry W., s/o James T. & Amanda A., b. 04/09/1866, d. 06/12/1866

LANK, James A., Capt., b. 07/14/1850, d. 01/18/1916

LANK, John Clarence, ssw-Alena Davidson, b. 12/13/1877, d. 05/16/1963

LANK, John H., Capt., b. 06/14/1819, d. 07/26/1885

LANK, John R., Capt., b. 1879, d. 1944

LANK, Joseph E., b. 01/01/1909, d. 11/13/1933

LANK, Joseph E., ssw-Mary S., b. 02/01/1848, d. 01/07/1898

LANK, Joseph Milton, ssw-Elizabeth Emma, b. 1876, d. 1964

LANK, Letitia, b. 09/15/1827, d. 03/29/1903

LANK, Mary S., ssw-Joseph E., b. 01/10/1851, d. 12/05/1930

LANK, Sarah A., ssw-William D., b. 12/16/1832, d. 01/09/1919

LANK, William D., ssw-William P., b. 10/22/1828, d. 05/29/1897

LANK, William P., ssw-David E., Lost at sea, b. 10/16/1863, d. abt. 01/08/1884

LANK, William Smithers, Dr., Died in Silver City, New Mexico, b. 10/28/1883, d. 10/31/1915

LEAVY, Maurice J., Tec5, USA, WWII, b. 1909, d. 1985

LEAVY, Robert R., b. 06/14/1937, d. 02/28/1985

LEAVY, Roberta W., b. 1915, d. 1995

LEKITES, Eliza J., ssw-George, b. 1857, d. 1922

LEKITES, George, Capt., ssw-Eliza J., b. 1850, d. 1898

LEKITES, Harry, ssw-Phoebe Lekites and Rilla Lekites Evans, b. 1881, d. 1950

LEKITES, Ollie, Age 9y 6m 23d, b. N/D, d. 10/08/1889

LEKITES, Phoebe, ssw-Harry Lekites and Rilla Lekites Evans, b. 1819, d. 1903

LEONARD, Eliza A. Clifton, ssw-James P., b. 1847, d. 1936

LEONARD, James P., ssw-Eliza A. Clifton, Co. H., 3 DE Inf., b. 1845, d. 1934

LINDLE, Nancy J., ssw-William, b. 1822, d. 1909

LINDLE, William, ssw-Nancy J., b. 1806, d. 1887

LINGO, Albert B., b. 05/12/1919, d. 09/09/1920

LINGO, Charles A., b. 12/25/1912, d. 02/16/1971

LINGO, Elizabeth B., ssw-Robert D., b. 1885, d. 1949

LINGO, Joseph L., ssw-Marguerite E., b. 01/05/1911, d. 09/19/1981

LINGO, Marguerite E., ssw-Joseph L., b. 11/06/1906, d. 11/08/1991

LINGO, R. Davis, b. 1892, d. 1972

LINGO, Robert D., ssw-Elizabeth B., b. 1878, d. 1944

LINGO, Sara W., b. 1894, d. 1988

LINGO, Willard E., b. 1915, d. 1920

LINGO, Willard S., b. 1858, d. 1894

LOFLAND, Caroline Carey, b. 08/11/1848, d. 01/21/1887

LOFLAND, David, b. 01/14/1839, d. 06/09/1882

LOFLAND, Eleanora Alphonza, d/o Jonathan F. & Eleanora, b. 05/24/1897, d. 01/19/1898

LOFLAND, Elias, ssw-Eliza F., b. 1846, d. 1904

LOFLAND, Eliza F., ssw-Elias, b. 1854, d. 1935

LOFLAND, Erasmus, ssw-Mary M., b. 02/19/1834, d. 08/14/1908

LOFLAND, Mary M., ssw-Erasmus, b. 04/12/1836, d. 01/23/1924

LOFLAND, Sallie A., d/o Elias & Eliza, Age 12y 1m 7d, b. N/D, d. 07/16/1887

LOFLAND, Sarah V., ssw-Anna R. Bolles, b. 1864, d. 1952

LYNCH, Zadoc P., ssw-Virginia C. Bennett, b. 04/17/1848, d. 01/14/1886

MAGEE, George L., Jr., s/o George L. & Josephine, b. 09/25/1891, d. 06/21/1892

MAGEE, Josephine, b. 1861, d. 1949

MANSHIP, Agnes Lacey, c/o A. H. & M. V., b. 01/26/1899, d. 07/06/1899

MANSHIP, Alfred Franklin, c/o A. H. & M. V., b. 08/14/1906, d. 01/24/1907

MANSHIP, Alfred H., b. 1864, d. 1927

MANSHIP, Alfred H., ssw-Eliza J., b. 04/08/1837, d. 09/22/1904

MANSHIP, Annie, w/o Alfred, Age 31y 3m 11d, b. 12/14/1841, d. 03/25/1873

MANSHIP, Annie Cornelia, c/o A. H. & M. V., b. 03/03/1902, d. 10/06/1902

MANSHIP, Araminta, w/o Charles, b. 09/12/1812, d. 11/28/1882

MANSHIP, Caleb Rodney, c/o A. H. & M. V., b. 07/19/1889, d. 08/23/1891

MANSHIP, Carrie, d/o Alfred H. & Annie E., b. 07/01/1870, d. 07/08/1870

MANSHIP, Charles, ssw-Araminta, b. 01/01/1810, d. 12/24/1882

MANSHIP, Charles R., ssw-Sarah J., b. 1859, d. 1896

MANSHIP, Clyde, s/o Alfred H. & Annie, Age 1y 1m, b. N/D, d. 10/16/1862

MANSHIP, Eliza J., w/o Alfred H., b. 11/28/1847, d. 08/22/1898

MANSHIP, Elsie, c/o A. H. & M. V., b. 02/28/1894, d. 03/15/1895

MANSHIP, Henry Burton, c/o A. H. & M. V., b. 04/09/1891, d. 11/08/1892

MANSHIP, John F., Dr., s/o William E. & Margaret Emma, b. 05/26/1867, d. 12/04/1892

MANSHIP, Joseph H., ssw-Annie, b. 06/10/1872, d. 07/27/1872

MANSHIP, Maggie V., b. 1864, d. 1943

MANSHIP, Margaret Emma, w/o William E. & d/o Peter C. Parker, ssw-Sheridan P. & William E.,
        b. 03/08/1838, d. 12/27/1873

MANSHIP, Martha J. T., d/o Charles & Araminta, Age 18y, b. 07/16/1845, d. 07/21/1863

MANSHIP, Sarah J., ssw-Charles R., b. 1866, d. 1894

MANSHIP, Sheridan P., M. D., ssw-Margaret Emma & William E., b. N/D, d. 12/14/1933

MANSHIP, William E., ssw-Margaret Emma & Sheridan P., b. 05/08/1835, d. 11/01/1912

MANSHIP, Wm. L., b. 1874, d. 1890

MARKER, Anna A. West, w/o Isaac M., b. 10/20/1872, d. 06/20/1924

MARTIN, Elizabeth, w/o Samuel, Age 57y 5m 6d, b. N/D, d. 09/30/1862

MARTIN, Emma B., d/o Samuel & Elizabeth, Age 1y 10m, b. N/D, d. 07/10/1850

MARTIN, Samuel, Age 73y 9m 27d, b. N/D, d. 02/20/1879

MARTIN, Samuel J., ssw-Sarah E. Parker, b. 1840, d. 1918

MARTIN, Samuel P., s/o Samuel & Sarah E., Age 3w 3d, b. N/D, d. 12/03/1863

MARTIN, Sarah E. Parker, ssw-Samuel J., b. 1839, d. 1896

MASON, Alice V., ssw-William S., Charles H., James T., Mary C. & Mary H., b. 1866, d. 1887

MASON, Charles H., Capt., ssw-William S., Alice V., James T., Mary C. & Mary H., b. 1849, d. 1927

MASON, James L., ssw-Virginia L., b. 05/24/1861, d. 09/15/1938

MASON, James T., ssw-William S., Alice V., Charles H., Mary C. & Mary H., b. 1851, d. 1857

MASON, Mary C., ssw-William S., Alice V., Charles H., James T. & Mary H., b. 1846, d. 1857

MASON, Mary H., w/o William S., ssw-William S., Alice V., Charles H., Mary C. & James T., b. 1824,
        d. 1908

MASON, Virginia L., ssw-James L., b. 11/23/1864, d. 05/27/1912

MASON, William S., Capt., ssw-Mary H., Alice V., Charles H., James T. & Mary C., b. 1819, d. 1876

MAULL, Arthur C., b. 1880, d. 1952

MAULL, Frank G., s/o Wm. W. & Annie A., Age 1y 8m 11d, b. N/D, d. 06/18/1873

MAULL, Henry G., ssw-Margaret E., Age 37y, b. 1845, d. 1882

MAULL, Margaret E., ssw-Henry G., Age 24y 7m 19d, b. 1846, d. 1870

MCFEE, Charlotte Wolfe, w/o John R., b. 10/05/1831, d. 09/01/1911

MCFEE, John R., b. 07/26/1816, d. 08/20/1889

MCFEE, Mary M., only c/o Charlotte W. & Jno R., Age 2y 2m 9d, b. N/D, d. 08/01/1856

MCFERRAN, Joseph A., Dr., ssw-Nancy E., b. 11/23/1826, d. 01/03/1910

MCFERRAN, Margaret, w/o Robert, Age 71y, b. N/D, d. 04/01/1859

MCFERRAN, Nancy E., ssw-Joseph A., b. 11/14/1835, d. 01/14/1912

MCFERRAN, Robert, Age 45y, b. N/D, d. 09/11/1843

MCFERREN, Alice Dashiell, d/o J. A. & Ellen, b. 11/30/1854, d. 09/24/1861

MCGEE, Thomas P., Age _7y 8m, b. N/D, d. 01/24/1897

MEGEE, Anna A., w/o Capt. John R., b. 11/03/1856, d. 08/03/1928

MEGEE, Carrie, d/o Capt. W. H. & Luella, Age 9m 20d, b. N/D, d. 01/25/1877

MEGEE, Charles E., ssw-Lucinda E. Wilson, b. 1867, d. 1896

MEGEE, Frances P., ssw-Herman F., b. 10/13/1918, d. 03/22/1974

MEGEE, Frank L., Pvt., USA, b. 12/17/1900, d. 02/15/1974

MEGEE, George E., s/o Theodore B. & Lizzie M., b. 11/04/1883, d. 10/09/1889

MEGEE, Herman F., ssw-Frances P., b. 08/30/1924, d. N/D

MEGEE, John H., b. 09/03/1899, d. 07/02/1900

MEGEE, John R., Capt., ssw-Anna A., b. 01/17/1842, d. 05/28/1920

MEGEE, Johny Burton, s/o Noah W. & Lydia H., b. Unreadable, d. 08/01/1866

MEGEE, Lizzie M., w/o Theodore B., ssw-George E., b. 04/04/1860, d. 07/20/1888

MEGEE, Lucinda E. Wilson, w/o Charles E., ssw-Charles E., b. 1872, d. 1967

MEGEE, Luella, ssw-William H., b. 04/23/1854, d. 04/18/1932

MEGEE, Lydia G., w/o Capt. J. R., b. 04/10/1855, d. 07/07/1888

MEGEE, Lydia H. Burton, w/o Noah W., b. 03/19/1833, d. 03/11/1916

MEGEE, Lydia J., ssw-Theodore B., b. 05/31/1871, d. 04/01/1950

MEGEE, Mary C., b. 06/27/1831, d. 03/13/1891

MEGEE, Mary L., b. 12/11/1862, d. 02/23/1937

MEGEE, Mary L., d/o Emily J. & John L., b. 10/21/1890, d. 03/17/1894

MEGEE, Moses, b. 02/21/1819, d. 07/09/1888

MEGEE, Noah W., ssw-Patience W., Age 69y, Died in Milton, DE, b. N/D, d. 09/11/1883

MEGEE, Patience W., w/o Noah W., ssw-Noah W., Age 47y, Died in Milton, DE, b. N/D, d. 11/18/1859

MEGEE, Robert Lincoln, b. 1896, d. 1963

MEGEE, Theodore B., Capt., ssw-Lydia J., b. 11/19/1854, d. 02/02/1905

MEGEE, W. Burton, Capt., b. 1883, d. 1935

MEGEE, William H., Capt., ssw-Luella, b. 07/26/1848, d. 11/21/1909

MESSICK, Anna, ssw-Theodore W., b. 1890, d. N/D

MESSICK, Hannah L., d/o D. T. & S. J. Hazzard, ssw-Sara J., b. 11/18/1876, d. 10/05/1890

MESSICK, Jos. H., b. 1845, d. 1919

MESSICK, Sarah J., ssw-Hannah L., b. 11/19/1860, d. 02/12/1901

MESSICK, Theodore W., ssw-Anna, b. 1882, d. 1951

MIELDS, Hugh, Jr., ssw-Irene H., T Sgt., USAAC, WWII, b. 03/03/1923, d. 07/07/1995

MIELDS, Irene H., ssw-Hugh, Jr., b. 2/27/1924, d. N/D

MILLER, Catherine Herman, b. 03/16/1874, d. 12/05/1936

MIRCH, Matthew J., Age 76y 4m 18d, b. 10/07/1815, d. 02/25/1892

MIRCH, Sarah A., w/o M. J., b. 03/02/1841, d. 10/26/1930

MOORE, Anna Pinkston, d/o Rev. Thomas & Louisa, Age 3m, b. N/D, d. 12/05/1857

MORRIS, Annie M., w/o Joseph B., b. 07/18/1846, d. 07/09/1897

MORRIS, Caleb L., ssw-Emma J., b. 11/17/1827, d. 03/01/1882

MORRIS, Emma J., ssw-Caleb L., b. 11/12/1832, d. 07/06/1919

MORRIS, Emmaline, ssw-James D., b. 02/04/1841, d. 02/26/1903

MORRIS, James D., ssw-Emmaline, b. 06/12/1829, d. 10/04/1916

MORRIS, John C., c/o Emmaline & James D., b. 1875, d. 1876

MORRIS, John J., b. 08/18/1842, d. 06/14/1910

MORRIS, Joseph B., b. 0/06/1848, d. 01/18/1923

MORRIS, Katie C., c/o Emmaline & James D., b. 1882, d. 1882

MORRIS, Lula V., b. 1886, d. 1951

MORRIS, Margaret H., ssw-William H., b. 1862, d. 1932

MORRIS, Mary E., ssw-Robert R., b. 05/01/1852, d. 05/24/1943

MORRIS, Mary W., b. 03/23/1840, d. 02/23/1922

MORRIS, Minnie M., c/o Emmaline & James D., b. 1873, d. 1874

MORRIS, Robert R., ssw-Mary E., b. 05/10/1839, d. 08/26/1899

MORRIS, William H., ssw-Margaret H., b. 1858, d. 1913

MUSTARD, J. Millard, c/o John B. & Martha J., b. 07/18/1881, d. 07/21/1885

MUSTARD, John H. B., ssw-Martha H., b. 1835, d. 1898

MUSTARD, Letitia B., Age 55y 2m 24d, b. N/D, d. 03/31/1890

MUSTARD, Lora H., c/o John B. & Martha J., b. 08/11/1878, d. 09/12/1879

MUSTARD, Martha H., w/o John H. B., b. 1840, d. 1925

MUSTARD, Martha J., w/o John B., b. 10/22/1859, d. 06/16/1889

NAILOR, Lemetta, d/o Wm. B. & Emma, b. 05/07/1891, d. 09/28/1891

NAILOR, Sarah E., b. 1868, d. 1953

NAILOR, William B., b. 1862, d. 1925

NEAL, George M., b. 01/15/1893, d. 07/10/1893

NEAL, Hester A., b. 03/04/1830, d. 07/23/1916

NEAL, John W., s/o Wm. H. & Hester, b. 05/24/1873, d. 02/05/1875

NEAL, William H., ssw-John W., b. 11/20/1829, d. 08/19/1874

NELSON, Elizabeth, d/o William C. & Lydia, Age 1m 14d, b. N/D, d. N/D

NELSON, Lydia A., w/o William C., Age 29y 6m 18d, b. N/D, d. 04/24/1864

NORMAN, Sallie A., d/o R. H. & Anna E., Age 7y 3m 21d, b. N/D, d. 12/16/1874

OLIVER, Eliza J., ssw-James W., Elvira, Jennie W. & John E., b. 1848, d. 1899

OLIVER, Elvira, ssw-James W., Eliza J., Jennie W. & John E., b. 1878, d. 1901

OLIVER, James W., ssw-Eliza J., Elvira, Jennie W. & John E., b. 1849, d. 1895

OLIVER, Jennie W., ssw-Eliza J., Elvira, James W. & John E., b. 1881, d. 1883

OLIVER, John E., ssw-Eliza J., Elvira, James W. & Jennie W., b. 1874, d. 1895

OUTTEN, J. Franklin, ssw-Mary E., Husband, b. 1850, d. 1933

OUTTEN, Mary E., w/o J. Franklin, ssw-J. Franklin, b. 1853, d. 1935

PALMER, Comfort N., w/o Capt. John C., ssw-Herald A. & John C., b. 03/11/1843, d. 03/31/1911

PALMER, Herald A., Capt., ssw-John C. & Comfort N., b. 11/25/1887, d. 01/31/1909

PALMER, John C., Capt., ssw-Herald A. & Comfort N., b. 09/14/1833, d. 03/22/1909

PARKER, Amanda M., d/o Peter S. & Hetty B., b. 04/05/1831, d. 09/24/1837

PARKER, Clara, d/o Deborah & Theodore W., b. 09/10/1849, d. 06/03/1856

PARKER, Deborah Maull, w/o Theodore W. & d/o Henry F. & Mary B. W., Born in Lewes, DE,
        b. 10/10/1825, d. 06/17/1903

PARKER, Eliza B., w/o John E., d/o W. M. & W., b. 12/06/1826, d. 04/09/1852

PARKER, Frederic J., s/o Peter & Hetty, Age 2y 18d, b. N/D, d. 07/01/1829

PARKER, Hetty B., w/o Peter S., ssw-Peter S., Age 75y, b. N/D, d. 05/07/1870

PARKER, John E., b. 02/11/1852, d. 07/02/1879

PARKER, John E., b. 11/19/1822, d. 08/12/1851

PARKER, Joseph B., ssw-Joseph C., Age 6m, b. N/D, d. 03/20/1845

PARKER, Joseph C., s/o Peter C. & Eliza, ssw-Joseph B., Age 2y 11m 16d, b. N/D, d. 11/13/1845

PARKER, Peter, Esqr., Age 80y, b. N/D, d. 01/13/1853

PARKER, Peter S., ssw-Hetty B., b. 02/03/1794, d. 12/23/1849

PARKER, Peter S., s/o Deborah & Theodore W., b. 09/14/1852, d. 10/02/1852

PARKER, Priscilla A., w/o Samuel P., Age 73y 7m 6d, b. N/D, d. 04/13/1892

PARKER, Rebecca, Consort o/Peter Parker, Sr., Age 55y 9m 24d, b. N/D, d. 12/02/1835

PARKER, Samuel P., Age 52y 18d, b. N/D, d. 09/11/1862

PARKER, Theodore W., s/o Peter S. & Hetty B., b. 10/15/1825, d. 07/07/1902

PARKER, Theodore W., s/o Theodore W. & Deborah M., Age 18y 11m 14d, b. N/D, d. 09/14/1874

PAYNTER, Alice, d/o John & Elizabeth Parker, Age 44y 7m 21d, b. N/D, d. 08/01/1834

PENTA, Gertrude B., b. 01/13/1898, d. 03/21/1981

PENTA, Michael J., M. D., b. 04/13/1897, d. 10/28/1975

PETTYJOHN, Jacob S., b. 05/12/1843, d. 06/24/1910

PETTYJOHN, Leona, d/o Jacob & Sarah, b. 03/15/1867, d. 08/22/1884

PETTYJOHN, Sarah A., b. 10/07/1848, d. 03/04/1894

POLK, Annie E., b. 01/08/1845, d. 06/14/1904

POLK, Elizabeth B., b. 1840, d. 1924

POLK, John C., b. 04/16/1834, d. 01/15/1899

POLK, Samuel M., s/o J. C. & A. E., Age 3m, b. N/D, d. 06/15/1882

POLK, Sarah, ssw-William Age 77y, b. N/D, d. 09/19/1875

POLK, William, ssw-Sarah, Age 47y, b. N/D, d. 04/07/1847

PONDER, Ida, b. 04/12/1852, d. 07/04/1934

PONDER, James, s/o James & Sallie W., Age 6y 9m 10d, b. 01/13/1859, d. 10/23/1865

PONDER, James, ssw-Sallie W., Governor of Delaware 1870-1874, b. 08/31/1819, d. 11/05/1897

PONDER, James Waples, b. 09/20/1868, d. 02/08/1942

PONDER, John, b. 04/25/1855, d. 01/10/1934

PONDER, Mary R., d/o Thomas L. & Eliza Black, b. 03/24/1862, d. 11/28/1925

PONDER, Sallie W., ssw-James, b. 03/20/1835, d. 10/02/1907

PONDER, Sara E., b. 05/12/1838, d. 02/26/1921

POOL, Mary E., w/o John F., b. 10/24/1852, d. 03/21/1914

PRETTYMAN, Anna V., d/o J. N. & Annie S. b. 03/21/1887, d. 10/31/1888

PRETTYMAN, Florence, d/o W. N. C. & Margaret, b. 06/15/1853, d. 08/27/1854

PRETTYMAN, G. W., ssw-Wm. C., b. 05/12/1849, d. 12/27/1890

PRETTYMAN, George, ssw-Hannah E., b. 01/24/1840, d. 09/12/1904

PRETTYMAN, Hannah E., ssw-George, b. 12/24/1843, d. 12/14/1921

PRETTYMAN, Jennie, c/o J. N. & Annie S., b. 11/13/1895, d. 11/23/1895

PRETTYMAN, Joseph, Age 34y 10m 6d, b. 05/14/1861, d. 03/20/1896

PRETTYMAN, Joseph V., c/o J. N. & Annie S., b. 08/22/1889, d. 08/23/1889

PRETTYMAN, Joshua S., ssw-Mary J., b. 05/26/1849, d. 11/28/1923

PRETTYMAN, Margaret J., ssw-Wm. C., b. 03/17/1828, d. 02/23/1907

PRETTYMAN, Mary J., w/o Isaac, ssw-Joshua S., b. 01/28/1817, d. 04/04/1891

PRETTYMAN, Wm. C., ssw-Margaret J., b. 11/04/1815, d. 02/09/1901

PRIMROSE, Ann, ssw-George M., Elizabeth L., Margaret & Theodore E., b. 04/22/1860, d. 02/06/1867

PRIMROSE, Elizabeth L., ssw-George M., Ann, Margaret & Theodore E., b. 06/13/1824, d. 02/10/1906

PRIMROSE, George M., ssw-Ann, Elizabeth L., Margaret & Theodore E., b. 04/15/1851, d. 11/29/1872

PRIMROSE, John W., Capt., Age 46y 11m 23d, b. N/D, d. 01/31/1860

PRIMROSE, Margaret, ssw-Ann, George M., Elizabeth L. & Theodore E., b. 10/31/1863, d. 02/07/1920

PRIMROSE, Theodore E., ssw-Ann, George M., Elizabeth L. & Margaret, b. 05/26/1825, d. 04/20/1907

RADKE, Cordelia H., b. 11/28/1898, d. 02/12/1987

RADKE, Lester A., ND, CWO, USN, WWII, b. 10/02/1900, d. 04/13/1967

REED, Katie L., d/o John & Martha C., b. 12/11/1856, d. 09/01/1857

REED, Mary E., b. 1856, d. 1936

REED, Viva F., b. 12/13/1876, d. 08/05/1946

REYNOLDS, William E. & Family, b. 1803, d. 1885

ROBBINS, James Coard, ssw-S. Amanda Dorman, b. 1847, d. 1926

ROBBINS, S. Amanda Dorman, w/o James Coard, ssw-James Coard, b. 1844, d. 1924

ROBINSON, Burton M., ssw-Mary, John, Nehemiah D. & Samuel J., b. 1836, d. 1916

ROBINSON, John, ssw-Burton M., Mary, Nehemiah D. & Samuel J., b. 1790, d. 1872

ROBINSON, Mary, ssw-Burton M., John, Nehemiah D. & Samuel J., b. 08/27/1838, d. 04/07/1907

ROBINSON, Nehemiah D., ssw-Burton M., John, Mary & Samuel J., b. 08/02/1868, d. 07/18/1869

ROBINSON, Samuel J., ssw-Burton M., John, Mary & Nehemiah D., b. 01/08/1865, d. 02/16/1865

RUSSELL, Elizabeth Conwell, w/o Wm. b. 10/14/1841, d. 07/09/1866

RUSSELL, George W., Age 29y 3m, b. N/D, d. 06/25/1892

RUSSELL, Lester, ssw-May Burrous, b. 1878, d. 1963

RUSSELL, May Burrous, ssw-Lester, b. 1875, d. 1959

RUSSELL, Mollie, w/o Capt. Wm. B., b. 04/08/1847, d. 05/30/1933

RUSSELL, William, Capt., Lost at sea, Age 44y 9m, b. N/D, d. 03/1872

RUSSELL, Willie, s/o Wm. & Eliz., b. 09/09/1865, d. 10/28/1866

SCOTT, Delphenia, ssw-Virginia B., b. 12/21/1862, d. 06/18/1867

SCOTT, Emily B., ssw-James C., Age 32y 8m 17d, b. 07/02/1834, d. 03/19/1867

SCOTT, Emma, ssw-James C., Age 2m 10d, b. 01/09/1869, d. 03/19/1869

SCOTT, Frances B., b. 06/04/1901, d. 10/19/1993

SCOTT, James C., ssw-Emily B., Age 1y 2m 9d, b. 05/02/1852, d. 08/16/1853

SCOTT, Ralph Lee, b. 08/30/1898, d. 01/17/1954

SCOTT, Virginia B., ssw-Delphenia, b. 03/18/1854, d. 03/12/1858

SHARP, Charles H., ssw-Mollie A., b. 1863, d. 1947

SHARP, Mollie A., ssw-Charles H., b. 1867, d. 1940

SHIVELHOOD, David Kalbach, Dr., ssw-Elizabeth Lank, b. 1907, d. 1944

SHIVELHOOD, Elizabeth Lank, ssw-David Kalback, b. 1907, d. 1984

SHORT, Charles, ssw-Mary F., Age 72y, b. N/D, d. 07/26/1884

SHORT, Mary F., ssw-Charles, Age 68y, b. N/D, d. 07/25/1895

SHORT, William H. C., s/o John & Eliza D., Age 1y 10m 20d, b. N/D, d. 09/23/1853

SKIDMORE, Sarah, nee Kimmey, ssw-James P. Kimmey, b. 04/22/1816, d. 06/04/1868

SMITHERS, Cornelia L., d/o Wm. H. & Virginia L., b. 02/28/1891, d. 08/04/1891

SMITHERS, Lizzie, d/o Wm. H. & Mary J., Age 8y, b. N/D, d 03/23/1857

SMITHERS, Mary J., b. 06/12/1830, d. 06/04/1907

SMITHERS, W. H., Capt., Age 39y 4m, Died in Phila., b. N/D, d. 05/19/1865

STARKEY, Clara P., b. 1862, d. 1953

STARKEY, Wm. T., b. 1856, d. 1931

STEELMAN, Sallie C. West, b. 1869, d. 1944

STEPHENSON, Sally Cornelius Coulter, Adopted d/o C. & S. Coulter, Age 9y 2m 11d, b. N/D,
     d. 06/18/1838

TAYLOR, Herbert H., b. 01/17/1882, d. 07/19/1905

THAYER, Oliver P., b. 05/27/1932, d. N/D

THOMPSON, Mary C. Lingo, b. 1861, d. 1935

TILNEY, Ann E., d/o John & Lydia, Age 5y 8m 12d, b. N/D, d. N/D

TILNEY, Hannah C., w/o John, b. 09/10/1794, d. 10/01/1865

TILNEY, John, Age 50y 11m 26d, b. N/D, d. 07/28/1855

TILNEY, John, Age 56y 4m 25d, b. N/D, d. 01/14/1821

TILNEY, Lydia, Consort o/Jno, Age 39y, b. N/D, d. 10/18/1844

TILNEY, Mary A., Consort o/Robert W., Age 30y 15d, b. N/D, d. 12/03/1848

TILNEY, Mary S., w/o Robert W., Age 68y 10m 1d, b. N/D, d. 03/19/1888

TILNEY, Robert H., Age 26y 6m 26d, b. N/D, d. 08/23/1864

TILNEY, Robert W., Age 59y 3m 4d, b. 04/01/1813, d. 07/05/1872

TILNEY, Stringer, Age 55y 11m 19d, b. N/D, d. 05/01/1826

TILNEY, Susan S., d/o John & Lydia, Age 11m 23d, b. N/D, d. N/D

TOMLINSON, Bathsheba, w/o Thomas & d/o Daniel Reynolds & Susan Robinson, b. 05/10/1803,
        d. 03/18/1886

TOMLINSON, Lydia Ann, w/o William Burton & d/o Mary Manlove Davis & Benjamin Franklin Burton,
        b. 01/25/1832, d. 08/28/1902

TOMLINSON, Thomas, s/o James & Anna Cullen, ssw-Bathsheba, b. 09/14/1806, d. 10/30/1854

TOMLINSON, William Burton, s/o Thomas & Bathsheba Reynolds, b. 05/17/1829, d. 12/10/1913

TOMLINSON, William Thomas, s/o William & Lydia Ann Burton, b. 03/21/1863, d. 03/11/1921

TULL, James, Age 63y, b. N/D, d. 03/19/1864

TULL, Martha Hall, w/o James, Age 72y 27d, b. 11/08/1792, d. 12/05/1864

TUNISON, George H., USA, b. 01/01/1912, d. 02/17/1985

VAUGHAN, Charles, Capt., b. 12/19/1802, d. 07/14/1883

VAUGHAN, Clara, b. 1858, d. 1924

VAUGHAN, Edward M., Age 45y 3m 7d, b. N/D, d. 01/17/1873

VAUGHAN, Eliza Ann Evans, w/o Edward M., b. 1834, d. 1917

VAUGHAN, Harriet E., ssw-Robert H., b. 02/17/1844, d. 01/04/1929

VAUGHAN, Joseph M., b. 02/07/1818, d. 04/09/1862

VAUGHAN, Mary W., Age 12y 5m 16d, b. N/D, d. 04/21/1828

VAUGHAN, Robert H., ssw-Harriet E., b. 09/16/1840, d. 03/15/1923

VAUGHAN, Sarah, b. 09/13/1807, d. 04/21/1849

VEASEY, N. T., Capt., Age 39y 8m, b. N/D, d. 04/26/1866

VENT, Abel, ssw-Nancy, Age 84y 6m 9d, b. N/D, d. 01/61/1868

VENT, Charles T., b. 1882, d. 1955

VENT, Elenor, w/o Capt. Joseph, Age 84y 8m, b. N/D, d. 08/31/1883

VENT, Elizabeth J., Age 36y 1m 27d, b. N/D, d. 10/28/1874

VENT, Ellender, wid/o Wm., Age 84y 3m 19d, b. 09/30/1799, d. 01/19/1884

VENT, Emma, ssw-Nancy Emily, b. 05/21/1890, d. 07/29/1890

VENT, Ferris L., ssw-Emma, b. 02/28/1895, d. 07/14/1895

VENT, Gove S., b. 1866, d. 1937

VENT, John S., Capt., s/o Capt. Joseph, Age 41y 3m 5d, b. N/d, d. 02/15/1864

VENT, Joseph, b. 04/12/1786, d. 11/22/1853

VENT, M. Louisa, b. 10/09/1835, d. 12/16/1895

VENT, Mable P., b. 1890, d. 1938

VENT, Mary, w/o Wm., Age 28y, b. N/D, d. 02/07/1818

VENT, Mary E., b. 1880, d. 1920

VENT, Nancy, w/o Abel, Age 68y 7m 3d, b. N/D, d. 06/18/1863

VENT, Nancy Emily, w/o Wm. J., b. 03/13/1862, d. 01/05/1915

VENT, Sarah E., b. 1831, d. 1898

VENT, Sarah Jane, d/o Abel & Nancy, Age 17y 1m 1d, b. N/D, d. 08/27/1838

VENT, William, Age abt. 55y, b. N/D, d. 02/02/1836

VENT, William J., ssw-Ellender, b. 04/30/1829, d. 01/29/1904

VENT, William J., ssw-Nancy Emily, b. 1854, d. 1918

VIRDEN, Eddie W., ssw-Fannie E. & Ethel L. Virden and Henry E. & Eliza A. Willey, b. 1881, d. 1883

VIRDEN, Ethel L., ssw-Eddie W. & Fannie E. Virden and Henry E. & Eliza A. Willey, b. 1890, d. 1892

VIRDEN, Fannie E., ssw-Eddie W. & Ethel L. Virden and Henry E. & Eliza A. Willey, b. 1860, d. 1892

WACHSMAN, Maggie Mae, nee Dutton, b. 01/31/1896, d. 07/26/1947

WAGAMON, Hamilton K., b. 1859, d. 1935

WAGAMON, Hettie J., b. N/D, d. 07/13/1966

WAGNER, John, b. 06/01/1892, d. 03/15/1941

WALLS, Charles E., b. 10/24/1840, d. 10/26/1882

WALLS, Elizabeth D., w/o John E., b. 09/12/1835, d. 12/05/1914

WALLS, John E., b. 03/10/1832, d. 04/16/1902

WALLS, S. Winsmer, s/o John E. & Elizabeth D., Age 13y 5m 24, d. N/D, d. 11/24/1880

WALLS, Sallie, b. 04/09/1893, d. 07/05/1894

WALLS, Sarah, Age 75y, b. N/D, d. 02/12/1901

WAPLES, Benjamin F., ssw-Sarah, b. 11/15/1819, d. 06/29/1862

WAPLES, Charles G., b. 1860, d. 1862

WAPLES, Conwell, b. 1892, d. 1892

WAPLES, Cornelius M., ssw-Sara Ellen Conwell, b. 12/26/1845, d. 07/16/1917

WAPLES, Estella E., b. 1887, d. 1929

WAPLES, Gideon, ssw-Sarah, Age 37y 1m 22d, b. N/D, d. 08/18/1837

WAPLES, John Conwell, b. 10/18/1857, d. 10/02/1943

WAPLES, Margaret P., b. 1864, d. 1949

WAPLES, Mary, ssw-Sarah W., Age 74y 2m 21d, b. N/D, d. 01/31/1843

WAPLES, Mary A., d/o Gideon & Sarah, Age 1d, b. N/D, d. 10/13/1831

WAPLES, Miers B., s/o Gideon S. & Priscilla, Age 1y 8m, b. N/D, d. 09/09/1831

WAPLES, Priscilla L, w/o Gideon, Age 20y 1m 25d, b. N/D, d. 05/20/1828

WAPLES, Sara Ellen Conwell, ssw-Cornelius M., b. 04/18/1846, d. 03/27/1934

WAPLES, Sarah, w/o Gideon, Age 59y 5m 2d, b. N/D, d. 02/11/1860

WAPLES, Sarah, ssw-Benjamin F., b. 03/09/1862, d. 09/07/1862

WAPLES, Sarah W., ssw-Mary, Age 91y 5m 21d, b. 02/22/1798, d. 08/19/1889

WAPLES, Susan R. Draper, b. 02/06/1822, d. 08/16/1907

WAPLES, William P., b. 1896, d. 1950

WARREN, Annie W., d/o Wm. W. & Sarah J., ssw-Fannie & Mary, Age 16y 11m 13d, b. 01/21/1871, d. 01/04/1888

WARREN, E. Wise, ssw-Ida P., b. 05/17/1856, d. 12/29/1910

WARREN, Fannie, d/o Wm. W. & Sarah J., ssw-Mary & Annie W., b. 04/04/1866, d. 03/29/1868

WARREN, Frances L., d/o W. & M. R., Age 2y, b. N/D, d. 11/25/1842

WARREN, George H., Age 84y, b. N/D, d. 09/08/1913

WARREN, Henry C., s/o Willen & Mary R., Age 3d, b. N/D, d. 03/23/1839

WARREN, Ida P., ssw-E. Wise, b. 06/26/1859, d. 09/28/1911

WARREN, Mary, d/o Wm. W. & Sarah J., ssw-Fannie & Annie W., b. 04/12/1864, d. 04/13/1864

WARREN, Mary R., w/o Willen, Age 47y 8m 10d, b. N/D, d. 08/21/1851

WARREN, Sarah A. Blockson, w/o Geo. H., b. 03/06/1831, d. 09/23/1886

WARREN, William W., Age 55y 6m 14d, b. N/D, d. 01/08/1886

WARRINGTON, Horace W., s/o Horace & Willie, b. 02/05/1891, d. 08/10/1891

WARRINGTON, James H., ssw-Susan E., b. 04/23/1850, d. 12/17/1904

WARRINGTON, Susan E., ssw-James H., b. 05/24/1854, d. 01/10/1936

WARRINGTON, Willie M., b. 05/28/1857, d. 08/07/1937

WATSON, Alice, wid/o Isaac, Age 67y 10d, b. N/D, d. 12/03/1828

WELCH, Amanda A., d/o N. D. & Mary R., b. 09/15/1838, d. 08/27/1839

WELCH, Annie E. Cox, w/o Peter P., ssw-Peter P., b. 1850, d. 1927

WELCH, Eddie B., s/o J. B. & Eliza, b. 12/11/1876, d. 08/30/1889

WELCH, Eliza N., w/o John B., 11 children, b. 11/27/1852, d. 06/07/1915

WELCH, Fannie F., d/o Nehemiah D. & Mary Parker, b. 1864, d. 1945

WELCH, Florence J., d/o N. D. & Mary P., b. 11/23/1852, d. 04/20/1870

WELCH, John B., Druggist, Age 54y, b. 04/03/1848, d. 01/18/1926

WELCH, Lizzie C., d/o N. D. & Mary P., b. 06/07/1861, d. 10/12/1880

WELCH, Mary W. Parker, w/o N. D., b. 03/04/1818, d. 02/28/1912

WELCH, N. D., Esq., Senior Warden of St. John Baptist Church, Milton, b. 1808, d. 1892

WELCH, Peter P., ssw-Annie C. Cox, b. 1850, d. 1940

WELCH, Walter Ray, s/o J. B. & Eliza, b. 08/20/1890, d. 06/18/1891

WEST, James B., b. 1844, d. 1911

WHARTON, Benjamin B., b. 11/30/1816, d. 02/16/1889

WHARTON, Matilda C., b. 04/14/1820, d. 05/17/1903

WHARTON, Matthew B., ssw-Robert K., Drowned at Tacony, Pa., b. 03/10/1858, d. 06/15/1875

WHARTON, Robert K., ssw-Matthew B., Died in Andersonville, Ga. Prison, b. 04/01/1847, d. 06/13/1864

WHITE, Annie A., d/o N. Wallace & Sallie C., Age 1y 3m 27d, b. N/D, d. 09/19/1872

WHITE, Arnsy K., Cpl, USA, WWI, b. 07/02/1891, d. 06/17/1978

WHITE, Charles H., s/o Robert C. & Elizabeth A., Age 15m, b. N/D, d. 09/30/1853

WHITE, Delmar S., b. 11/03/1878, d. 10/19/1939

WHITE, Elizabeth A., wife & companion o/Robert C., b. 12/22/1822, d. 06/12/1867

WHITE, Ethel C., b. 07/22/1903, d. 10/26/1938

WHITE, Isaac, ssw-Katie E., b. 1808, d. 1884

WHITE, Jacob M., ssw-Sarah R., b. 1812, d. 1866

WHITE, Katie E., ssw-William J., b. 1855, d. 1922

WHITE, Laura C., b. 02/19/1857, d. 09/10/1928

WHITE, Mary, w/o Isaac, ssw-Isaac, b. N/D, d. N/D

WHITE, Mary H. W., ssw-Isaac, b. N/D, d. N/D

WHITE, Maud T., d/o Jacob & Sarah, b. 1858, d. 1881

WHITE, N. Wallace, ssw-Sarah C., b. 09/23/1850, d. 12/16/1923

WHITE, Robert C., b. 07/16/1858, d. 06/28/1919

WHITE, Robert C., Age 41y 10m 22d, b. 08/11/1827, d. 07/03/1869

WHITE, Sarah C., ssw-N. Wallace, b. 05/15/1858, d. 01/17/1926

WHITE, Sarah R., w/o Jacob M., b. 1815, d. 1874

WHITE, Viva R., d/o Wm. J. & Kate E., b. 1876, d. 1879

WHITE, William J., ssw-Katie E., b. 07/28/1840, d. 05/16/1910

WILLEY, Eliza A., ssw-Henry E. Willey and Eddie W, Ethel L. & Fannie E. Virden, b. 1821, d. 1900

WILLEY, Henry E., ssw-Eliza A. Willey and Eddie W., Ethel L. & Fannie E. Virden, b. 1824, d. 1898

WILSON, Aletta Ann, ssw-Theodore S., b. 1836, d. 1917

WILSON, Aletta M. C., b. 02/22/1832, d. 09/29/1916

WILSON, Elizabeth, b. 1869, d. 1959

WILSON, Elizabeth Katherine, ssw-John Peter, b. 11/11/1883, d. 02/20/1972

WILSON, Emma H., ssw-Robert H. T., b. 1864, d. 1931

WILSON, Fannie H., d/o Samuel j. & Martha J., Age 2y 5m 6d, b. N/D, d. 02/05/1875

WILSON, Gertrude, ssw-James W., b. 11/13/1824, d. 12/05/1884

WILSON, Inf. s/o John C. & Mary L., b. N/D, d. 03/01/1863

WILSON, James W., ssw-Gertrude, b. 09/23/1820, d. 12/28/1897

WILSON, Jemmie White, s/o Theodore S. & Aletta, Age 1y 4m 17d, b. N/D, d. 04/25/1863

WILSON, John A. B., Rev., ssw-Mary E. Jefferson, b. 09/14/1848, d. 04/30/1906

WILSON, John C., b. 02/02/1824, d. 03/09/1899
WILSON, John P., Capt. Age 59y 9m 8d, b. N/D, d. 05/05/1884
WILSON, John Peter, ssw-Elizabeth Katherine, b. 11/19/1879, d. 01/31/1950
WILSON, Martha Jane, b. 11/30/1853, d. 03/15/1936
WILSON, Mary C., b. 06/07/1807, d. 05/09/1881
WILSON, Mary E. Jefferson, ssw-John A. B., b. 07/30/1850, d. 09/26/1930
WILSON, Mary L., b. 11/07/1845, d. 01/28/1921
WILSON, Mary Mallelieu, d/o John A. B. & Mary, b. 03/30/1886, d. 09/03/1886
WILSON, Olevia Della, b. 07/27/1898, d. 11/09/1986
WILSON, Robert H. T., Dr., ssw-Emma H., b. 1865, d. 1935
WILSON, Samuel James, ssw-Velma Anderson, b. 02/08/1919, d. 08/21/1953
WILSON, Samuel James, Col., b. 08/15/1850, d. 02/07/1937
WILSON, Sarah A., w/o John P., Age 65y 9m 3d, b. N/D, d. 12/01/1887
WILSON, s/o Wm. B. & A. M. C., b. N/D, d. 03/01/1863
WILSON, Theodore S., ssw-Aletta Ann, Age 57y 10m 26d, b. 02/10/1832, d. 01/06/1890
WILSON, Velma Anderson, ssw-Samuel James, b. 07/19/1913, d. 11/14/1989
WILSON, William R., b. 01/16/1828, d. 03/14/1900
WILTBANK, John C., Doctor, ssw-Lizzie P., b. 1868, d. 1934
WILTBANK, John H., ssw-Martha A. Hudson, b. 06/09/1823, d. 03/29/1897
WILTBANK, Lizzie P., ssw-John C., b. 1868, d. 1942
WILTBANK, Martha A. Hudson, w/o John H., b. 01/21/1832, d. 08/19/1900
WINE, Esther J., d/o Joseph H. & Leah, b. 08/27/1850, d. 06/26/1866
WOLFE, Ann, w/o William W. & d/o Hon. David Hazzard, Age 63y, b. N/D, d. 07/19/1866
WOLFE, David E., Dr., b. 12/29/1833, d. 04/02/1906
WOLFE, Maria H., d/o William W. & Ann, b. 08/30/1829, d. 08/31/1830
WOLFE, Sarah Jane, b. 10/02/1839, d. 07/24/1895
WOLFE, William W., Dr., ssw-Ann, Age 65y, b. N/D, d. 03/17/1866
YOUNG, David Hazzard, b. 04/06/1838, d. 11/18/1872
YOUNG, Mary Ann, ssw-Rouse F., Age 76y, b. N/D, d. 06/02/1892
YOUNG, Rouse F., ssw-Mary Ann, Age 46y, b. N/D, d. 05/13/1857

The following stones were recorded by the Hudson Survey but are now missing or unreadable:
BARKER, Darvilia, d/o Thomas R., Age 1m 6d, b. N/D, d. 07/04/1856
BAYNUM, Celia Messick, w/o Capt. John M., b. 12/06/1812, d. 06/12/1889
BAYNUM, John M., Capt. b. 1810, d. 1891
CAREY, Edward, s/o James M., Jr. & Elizabeth, Age 3m 14d, b. N/D, d. 12/15/1849
CAREY, Joseph, s/o J. M. & Elizabeth, Age 1d, b. N/D, d. 08/04/1841
CAREY, Lena, d/o Arthur C. & Hannah J., Age 1m 28d, b. N/D, d. 07/06/1872
CAREY, Lizzie Arthur, d/o Arthur C. & Hannah, Age 1y 1m, b. N/D, d. 07/16/1879
DAVIDSON, Mary J., w/o Josiah H. & d/o James & Mary Lank, b. 09/05/1833, d. 07/28/1873
DORMAN, David, s/o David & Eleanor, b. N/D, d. 08/26/1887
FISHER, Eliza A., w/o John F., b. 11/05/1852, d. 04/06/1887
FOWLER, Joseph H., Age 62y 9m 16d, b. N/D, d. 10/23/1905
FOWLER, Mary E., w/o Joseph H., b. 03/05/1849, d. 07/06/1918
HAZZARD, Sarah J., w/o David T., b. 11/19/1860, d. 02/02/1901
HAZZARD, Unknown, d/o David T. & Sarah J., Age 18m, b. N/D, d. N/D
LOFLAND, Carrie, b. 06/30/1872, d. 08/30/1872
LOFLAND, James H., b. 06/01/1868, d. 08/01/1868

LOFLAND, Joseph B., b. 06/30/1872, d. 07/09/1872
PARKER, Joseph R., Age 76y 7m, b. N/D, d. 07/01/1865
PARKER, Unknown, w/o Joseph R., b. 1796, d. 1871
REED, Adell, d/o Rev. John T. & Martha, b. 12/11/1856, d. 09/01/1857
WARREN, James H., b. 04/23/1850, d. 12/17/1904
WARREN, Mary A., d/o Willen & Mary R., Age 5y, b. 07/13/1840, d. N/D
WILTBANK, Sarah A., w/o Thomas J., b. 1818, d. 1872
WILTBANK, Thomas J., b. 1818, d. 1907

(BK-015 & HU-167) REYNOLDS M. E. CHURCH CEMETERY
Located N. W. of Milton on the S. E. corner of Isaacs Rd. (Rd. 30) and Reynolds Pond Rd. (Rd. 231)
Recorded January 21, 1998

ABBOTT, George A., ssw-Mary E., b. 02/05/1867, d. 01/25/1907
ABBOTT, James F., s/o Henry H. & Sarah F., b. 11/17/1876, d. 08/13/1877
ABBOTT, Mary E., ssw-George A., b. 06/23/1870, d. 01/02/1908
BAILEY, Edward J., b. 1859, d. 1935
BAILEY, Ella, b. 1871, d. 1937
BAKER, Nancy G., b. 1795, d. 1887
BANNING, Leona Mabel, ssw-Orveal H., b. 07/01/1901, d. 07/28/1970
BANNING, Orveal H., ssw-Leona Mabel, b. 01/06/1895, d. 09/11/1983
BARDSLEY, Ida C., ssw-James C., b. 06/20/1907, d. ND
BARDSLEY, James C., ssw-Ida C., b. 11/04/1916, d. 06/29/1977
BEIDEMAN, Catherine E., b. 05/27/1858, d. 05/24/1925
BEIDEMAN, Charles, b. 05/25/1850, d. 06/29/1929
BEIDEMAN, Franklin, b. 12/06/1890, d. 01/15/1963
BEIDEMAN, Ida Eveline, d/o Catharine & Willoughbey, b. 03/22/1881, d. 01/20/1893
BEIDEMAN, James W., b. 03/14/1886, d. 05/27/1956
BEIDEMAN, Julia A., Mot6her, b. 02/28/1829, d. 10/02/1894
BEIDEMAN, Louisa Anna, ssw-Wilmina S., b. 891, d. 1901
BEIDEMAN, Louisa Isabella, ssw-Oliver, b. N/D, d. N/D
BEIDEMAN, Mabel G., ssw-Louisa Anna, b. 1886, d 1886
BEIDEMAN, Oliver, ssw-Louisa Isabella, b. 1854, d. 1936
BEIDEMAN, Rachel, b. 03/20/1852, d. 02/07/1933
BEIDEMAN, Walter, b. 02/27/1888, d. 05/03/1966
BEIDEMAN, William, b. 07/17/1884, d. 06/29/1951
BEIDEMAN, William, Father, b. 03/28/1819, d. 04/11/1882
BEIDEMAN, Willoughbey, b. 10/24/1856, d. 06/11/1938
BEIDEMAN, Wilmina S., ssw-Oliver, b. 1868, d. 1939
BETTS, Mary E., b. 09/09/1858, d. 03/02/1950
BETTS, Robert H., b. 1879, d. 1934
BETTS, Willie M., b. 1879, d. 1954
BLIZZARD, Angieline E., ssw-Eugene H., b. 10/22/1893, d. 10/21/1975
BLIZZARD, Eugene H., ssw-Angieline E., b. 02/25/1893, d. 02/27/1984
BLOCKSOM, Nancy D. Vaughan, w/o Richard, ssw-Richard, b. 10/19/1772, d. 09/24/1843
BLOCKSOM, Richard, ssw-Nancy D. Vaughan, b. 1762, d. 04/01/1822
BOWLES, Keturah Beideman, ssw-Dawsie Biedman Fouche, b. 12/10/1861, d. 07/14/1942
BURTELLE, Ida K., ssw-Joseph F., b. 10/23/1891, d. 05/04/1955

BURTELLE, Joseph F., ssw-Ida K., b. 11/20/1897, d. 05/28/1945
CAREY, Ada, b. 02/22/1843, d. 09/27/1891
CAREY, Cornelius J., b. 02/25/1824, d. 02/02/1911
CAREY, Eli B., b. 03/13/1831, d. 04/21/1909
CAREY, Henry H., h/o Annie S., b. 09/04/1874, d. 12/30/1941
CAREY, Sarah Ellen Reynolds, w/o Eli B., b. 04/13/1846, d. 09/08/1889
CARPENTER, Burton D., b. 12/29/1855, d. 01/27/1943
CARPENTER, Emma E., b. 07/13/1848, d. 12/02/1925
CARPENTER, Inf. o/Burton D. & Emma E., b. 07/16/1886, d. 07/17/1886
CECIL, Lewis M., b. 03/31/1895, d. 06/16/1970
CHADWICK, Geneva, ssw-Harry G., b. 1888, d. 1990
CHADWICK, Harry G., ssw-Geneva, b. 1880, d. 1941
CLENDANIEL, Frederick E., s/o J. C. & M. A., b. 01/12/1891, d. 08/11/1891
CLENDANIEL, John B., s/o J. C. & M. A., b. 10/02/1881, d. 01/02/1885
CLENDANIEL, Mary A., w/o J. C., b. 08/06/1849, d. 01/22/1894
CLIFTON, Caddie E., d/o John G. & Miranda E., b. 10/17/1866, d. 12/29/1886
CLIFTON, Clara V., b. 05/06/1878, d. 02/19/1881
CLIFTON, George A., b. 09/26/1844, d. 07/25/1921
CLIFTON, George W., s/o John G. & Sallie A., b. 06/10/1871, d. 09/03/1892
CLIFTON, Grover C., b. 06/21/1890, d. 03/16/1963
CLIFTON, Helen Catherine, Inf. d/o Wm. Carlton & Beatrice Hudson, b. N/D, d. 05/25/1936
CLIFTON, Hester, b. 1890, d. 1969
CLIFTON, Hester, ssw-William E., b. 03/25/1868, d. 04/29/1939'
CLIFTON, Jehu G., ssw-Miranda E., b. 1856, d. 1930
CLIFTON, John O., ssw-Sarah G., b. 11/23/1839, d. 08/21/1905
CLIFTON, Mary M. Jones, w/o Willard, b. 04/25/1859, d. 02/27/1913
CLIFTON, Miranda E., ssw-Jehu G., b. 1860, d. 1912
CLIFTON, Philip V., b. 1863, d. 1916
CLIFTON, R. Davis, ssw-R. Dawson & Robert T., b. 1900, d. 1901
CLIFTON, R. Dawson, ssw-R. Davis & Robert T., b. 1907, d. 1926
CLIFTON, Robert T., ssw-R. Davis & R. Dawson, b. 1863, d. 1916
CLIFTON, Sallie H., d/o John G. & Sallie G., b. 11/10/1880, d. 04/29/1884
CLIFTON, Sarah A., ssw-William D., b. 1820, d. 1882
CLIFTON, Sarah E., b. 01/13/1857, d. 01/25/1941
CLIFTON, Sarah E., w/o George A., b. 03/07/1848, d. 04/06/1914
CLIFTON, Sarah G., ssw-John O., b. 07/06/1842, d. 12/13/1920
CLIFTON, Willard S., ssw-Mary M. Jones, b. 11/25/1858, d. 09/13/1945
CLIFTON, William D., ssw-Sarah A., b. 1816, d. 1892
CLIFTON, William E., ssw-Hester, b. 01/15/1869, d. 05/23/1943
CLIFTON, William W., b. 07/03/1850, d. 11/20/1898
COFFIN, Emma E., b. 10/27/1853, d. 11/22/1930
COLLINS, E. Lizzie, ssw-Esther E., b. 12/21/1866, d. 04/19/1884
COLLINS, Esther E., ssw-William T., b. 08/06/845, d. 03/03/1923
COLLINS, William T., ssw-Esther E., b. 10/22/1842, d. 10/12/1931
DAVIS, Allie P., ssw-Laura Collins, b. 12/22/1885, d. 05/19/1889
DAVIS, Laura Collins, ssw-Virginia G. Walls, b. 05/27/1865, d. 01/16/1887
DEPUTY, Emma, b. 04/02/1900, d. 08/24/1900
DEPUTY, Jeremiah, ssw-Eliza Deputy Messick, b. 1855, d 1908

DODD, Irma P., ssw-Myers, b. 09/09/1887, d. 08/15/1907
DODD, James, Co. C., 9th DE Inf., Civil War, b. N/D, d. N/D
DODD, Jesse, Age 58y 13d, b. 07/04/1837, d. 03/17/1888
DODD, Myers, ssw-Irma P., b. 1862, d. 1940
DODD, Priscilla A., Age 76y 11m 28d, b. 08/08/1835, d. 08/06/1912
DODD, Sallie, ssw-Irma P., b. 1863, d. 1954
DODD, William B., b. 1868, d. 1926
DONOVAN, Charles M., b. 06/16/1876, d. 10/31/1936
DONOVAN, Elsie W., b. 1908, d. 1959
DONOVAN, Laura D., w/o J. W., ssw-William J., b. 07/02/1881, d. 05/20/1904
DONOVAN, Laura F., b. 06/01/1877, d. 06/17/1951
DONOVAN, William J., ssw-Laura D., b. 04/13/1901, d. 04/03/1908
DUKES, Mildred L., b. 01/03/1917, d. 08/10/1994
ELLINGSWORTH, Amanda C., b. 1869, d. 1941
ELLINGSWORTH, Annie W. Veasey, w/o Rufus N., b. 02/11/1849, d. 06/30/1887
ELLINGSWORTH, Jonah, b. 07/07/1900, d. 10/16/1911
ELLINGSWORTH, Rufus, Jr., s/o R. N. & Annie, Age 7m, b. N/D, d. 11/27/1890
ELLINGSWORTH, Sallie, w/o John A., b. 09/03/1873, d. 11/25/1900
ELLINGSWORTH, John A., b. 05/07/1860, d. 03/17/1927
ELLINGSWORTH, Rufus N., ssw-Annie W. Veasey, b. 06/28/1848, d. 05/22/1921
FOUCHE, Dawsie Beideman, ssw-Keturah Beideman Bowles, b. 1882, d. 1957
FOWLER, James B., ssw-Lydia Nancy, b. 08/25/1847, d. 06/15/1922
FOWLER, Lydia Nancy, ssw-James B., b. 09/10/1850, d. 06/28/1942
HANBY, Delema P., b. 02/24/1898, d. 10/26/1982
HARRINGTON, Joseph Howard, s/o Wm. A. C. & Laura, b. 03/26/1894, d. 09/10/1894
JACKSON, Amanda B., w/o Jas. B., b. 04/17/1843, d. 05/30/1917
JACKSON, Charles Lowber, ssw-Leona Bertha, b. 1875, d. 1966
JACKSON, Clara L., ssw-J. Harold, b. 05/29/1872, d. 05/12/1911
JACKSON, J. Harold, ssw-Clara L., b. 05/01/1908, d. 05/10/1911
JACKSON, James B., ssw-Amanda B., b. 07/09/1841, d. 02/20/1923
JACKSON, Leona Bertha, ssw-Charles Lowber, b. 1881, d. 1982
JEFFERS, Hannah R. Warren, w/o George H., b. 03/17/1826, d. 11/29/1902
JEFFERSON, Alletta C., ssw-C. Frank, b. 02/17/1864, d. 04/06/1952
JEFFERSON, Annie J., d/o Nathaniel T. & Emma, b. 10/16/1876, d. 10/24/1907
JEFFERSON, C. Frank, ssw-Alletta C., b. 05/06/1859, d. 11/30/1932
JEFFERSON, Clarence F., s/o C. F. & A. C., Age 1y 4m 1d, b. N/D, d. 08/07/1883
JEFFERSON, Eliza A., ssw-Thomas W., b. 09/13/1844, d. 03/02/1927
JEFFERSON, Elizabeth M., b. 10/24/1862, d. 08/03/1953
JEFFERSON, Emma, w/o Nathaniel T., b. 07/11/1856, d. 04/11/1898
JEFFERSON, James K. P., b. 02/07/1847, d. 05/02/1911
JEFFERSON, Jennie, w/o James K. P., Age 35y 8m 17d, b. N/D, d. 06/03/1885
JEFFERSON, Leah J., d/o C. F. & A. C., b. 11/16/1901, d. 01/12/1912
JEFFERSON, Lydia A., ssw-Thomas P., Age 73y 3m 10d, b. N/D, d. 10/02/1882
JEFFERSON, Thomas P., ssw-Lydia A., Age 47y 8m 26d, b. N/D, d. 06/05/1852
JEFFERSON, Thomas W., ssw-Eliza A., b. 12/05/1841, d. 06/12/1906
JESTER, James H., ssw-Lydia W., b. 1860, d. 1930
JESTER, Lydia A., ssw-Thomas R., b. 1830, d. 1902
JESTER, Lydia W., ssw-James H., b. 1864, d. 1928

JESTER, Ralph V., b. 01/28/1883, d. 06/22/1883

JESTER, Samuel Roland, Age 29y 5m 11d, b. 07/22/1873, d. 01/03/1903

JESTER, Thomas R., ssw-Lydia A., b. 1820, d. 1892

JOHNSON, Benton H., ssw-Lydia A., b. 01/15/1821, d. 05/03/1894

JOHNSON, C. Raymond, ssw-Lulu C., b. 1914, d. 1960

JOHNSON, Charles B., b. 03/31/1869, d. 02/20/1942

JOHNSON, Charlotte E., b. 06/08/1936, d. 06/08/1936

JOHNSON, Clarence B., ssw-Lulu C., b. 1882, d. 1965

JOHNSON, Eva H. Bennett, w/o James S., b. 10/28/1872, d. 03/28/1897

JOHNSON, Greensbury P., ssw-Miranda A., Age 80y 8m 10d, b. 01/10/1823, d. 09/20/1903

JOHNSON, James S., b. 05/05/1857, d. 04/21/1947

JOHNSON, John W., ssw-Lucy M., b. N/D, d. 09/19/1889

JOHNSON, Lucy M., ssw-John W., b. N/D, d. 12/14/1898

JOHNSON, Lulu C., ssw-C. Raymond, b. 1884, d. 1971

JOHNSON, Lydia A., w/o Benton H., ssw-Benton H., b. 04/03/1821, d. 12/03/1910

JOHNSON, M. Hessie, b. 1889, d. 1890

JOHNSON, M. Hessie, w/o James S., b. 03/15/1856, d. 06/07/1888

JOHNSON, Marietta Havelka, d/o Clarence B. & Lulu C., b. 01/17/1910, d. 11/09/1927

JOHNSON, Martha E., b 07/19/1880, d. 12/04/1946

JOHNSON, Mary E., ssw-Oscar P., b. 05/30/1883, d. 03/11/1962

JOHNSON, Millard R., s/o C. R. & Lulu, b. 05/01/1907, d. 06/02/1907

JOHNSON, Miranda A., w/o Greensbury P., Age 70y 8m, b. N/D, d. 02/01/1901

JOHNSON, Oscar P., ssw-Mary E., b. 01/07/1883, d. 03/29/1958

JOHNSON, Theodore B., b. 1847, d. 1924

JOLINE, Almira C., b. 03/14/1870, d. 10/21/1917

JONES, Addie, ssw-Benjamin B., (Interred Conley Chapel), b. 1874, d. 1927

JONES, Benjamin B., ssw-Addie, b. 1855, d. 1941

JONES, Benjamin F., b. 10/19/1846, d. 08/19/1853

JONES, Elizabeth D., ssw-James W., b. 01/05/1811, d. 08/25/1898

JONES, Elizabeth T., ssw-Erasmus, b. 03/09/1831, d. 11/08/1914

JONES, Erasmus, ssw-Elizabeth T., b. 09/12/1829, d. 12/24/1912

JONES, George W., b. 02/22/1853, d. 01/03/1930

JONES, Henry C., b. 03/17/1838, d. 11/14/1914

JONES, James B., b. 03/18/1836, d. 09/26/1844

JONES, James W., ssw-Frances A. Short Rust, b. 03/19/1801, d. 07/25/1865

JONES, John B., ssw-Sarah Prettyman, b. 08/25/1769, d. 06/27/1852

JONES, John B., b. 12/05/1833, d. 10/12/1909

JONES, Kensey J., b. 09/04/1831, d. 05/04/1901

JONES, Robert B., b. 02/14/1842, d. 07/24/1893

JONES, Sara E., b. 1910, d. 1911

JONES, Sarah Prettyman, w/o John B., ssw-John B., b. 12/09/1772, d. 01/10/1848

LONG, Matilda May, b. 03/06/1896, d. 10/06/1971

LYNCH, Annie P., w/o Willard, b. 06/19/1870, d. 07/24/1900

MARSH, Fannie V., b. 10/09/1898, d. 04/13/1975

MESSICK, Eliz Deputy, ssw-Jeremiah Deputy, b. 1858, d. 1938

MOORE, Pearl Clifton, b. 09/08/1914, d. N/D

MORRIS, Annie, b. 09/07/1856, d. 10/18/1922

MORRIS, Sarah A., ssw-William A., b. 1833, d. 1910

MORRIS, William A., ssw-Sarah A., b. 1832, d. 1892

PARSONS, Preston T., b. 07/14/1912, d. 10/14/1912

PETTYJOHN, Annie M., ssw-G. William, b. 1862, d. 1946

PETTYJOHN, G. William, ssw-Annie M., b. 1860, d. 1944

PETTYJOHN, Myrtle, b. 02/28/1900, d. 03/15/1989

PURNELL, Inf. s/o John S. & Laura, b. 09/22/1901, d. 09/22/1901

REED, Curtis C., ssw-Sarah E., b. 1873, d. 1950

REED, Curtis G., b. 04/09/1824, d. 11/29/1910

REED, Elizabeth, b. 01/26/1835, d. 09/09/1905

REED, Hettie J., w/o Curtis G., b. 03/26/1834, d. 08/31/1905

REED, Lizabeth, w/o Levin, Age abt. 82y, b. N/D, d. 04/05/1882

REED, Mary E., d/o Curtis G. & Sarah E., b. 07/04/1911, d. 08/09/1917

REED, Peter, b. 11/17/1832, d. 06/22/1881

REED, Priscilla, w/o Benjamin, b. 12/31/1805, d. 08/30/1879

REED, Sarah E., w/o Curtis C., ssw-Curtis C., b. 1873, d. N/D

REYNOLDS, Annie E., b. 1864, d. 1946

REYNOLDS, Gove S., b. 1860, d. 1893

REYNOLDS, Myers H., b. 08/17/1886, d. 11/05/1960

REYNOLDS, Pansie Mildred, ssw-William W., Sr., b. 02/07/1904, d. 07/26/1985

REYNOLDS, Roderick S., b. 1861, d. 1928

REYNOLDS, William W., Sr., ssw-Pansie Mildred, b. 06/09/1902, d. 09/04/1974

ROBINSON, Beatrice, Inf. c/o Mary Etta, ssw-Mary Etta & Preston, b. N/D, d. N/D

ROBINSON, John P., ssw-Julia, b. N/D, d. N/D

ROBINSON, Julia, w/o John P., ssw-John P., b. N/D, d. N/D

ROBINSON, Mary Etta, ssw-Beatrice & Preston, b. 07/29/1888, d. 11/15/1915

ROBINSON, Preston, Inf. c/o Mary Etta, ssw-Mary Etta & Beatrice, b. N/D, d. N/D

ROBINSON, Sarah, w/o William E., ssw-William E., b. N/D, d. N/D

ROBINSON, Shawn Michael, b. 10/18/1996, d. 10/18/1996

ROBINSON, William E., ssw-Sarah, b. N/D, d. N/D

RUST, Amy Dodd, ssw-Sylvester H., Grandmother, b. 04/22/1814, d. 10/07/1868

RUST, Frances A. Short, ssw-Frederick A., b. 11/06/1876, d. N/D

RUST, Frederick A., b. 02/04/1919, d. 01/23/1996

RUST, Frederick A., ssw-Hester H., b. 11/06/1876, d. 10/30/1967

RUST, George A., ssw-Sallie E., Father, b. 01/25/1846, d. 06/11/1908

RUST, George J., b. 11/06/1912, d. 06/14/1935

RUST, Hester H., ssw-Frederick A., b. 04/15/1884, d. 07/29/1967

RUST, Sallie, ssw-George A., Mother, b. 05/01/1849, d. 06/06/1923

RUST, Sylvester H., ssw-Sallie E., Grandfather, b. 09/29/1811, d. 01/05/1878

SHOCKLEY, Arthur E., ssw-Georgia Clifton, b. 1877, d. 1949

SHOCKLEY, Charlotte Emily, wid/o David V., last w/o George H. Warrington, b. 03/22/1853, d. 03/04/1935

SHOCKLEY, David V., b. 09/13/1851, d. 03/25/1904

SHOCKLEY, Edgar M., b. 10/24/1890, d. 09/17/1976

SHOCKLEY, Fannie Verlinda, d/o David & Charlotte E., b. 07/30/1879, d. 11/18/1893

SHOCKLEY, Georgia Clifton, ssw-Arthur E., b. 1878, d. 1958

SHOCKLEY, John W., b. 1864, d. 1894

SHOCKLEY, Lester G., s/o A. E. & G. C., b. 02/27/1906, d. 02/17/1914

SHORT, Elmer B., ssw-Fannie A. & Sara E., b. 1863, d. 1936

SHORT, Fannie A., ssw-Elmer B. & Sara E., b. 1876, d. 1957
SHORT, Sara E., ssw-Fannie A. & Elmer B., b. 1915, d. 1969
STEELMAN, Ary B., ssw-Daniel M., b. 10/22/1875, d. 04/18/1909
STEELMAN, Cora W., ssw-John S., b. 1878, d. 1906
STEELMAN, Daniel M., ssw-Ary B., b. 06/06/1871, d. 07/07/1955
STEELMAN, Emma T., ssw-Robert R., b. 10/21/1870, d. N/D
STEELMAN, John, ssw-Matilda, b. 1826, d. 1906
STEELMAN, John S., ssw-Cora W., b. 1859, d. 1939
STEELMAN, Matilda, ssw-John, b. 1838, d. 1913
STEELMAN, Raymond E., s/o R. R. & Emma, b. 07/21/1901, d. 04/25/1904
STEELMAN, Robert R., ssw-Emma T., b. 03/23/1868, d. 08/06/1925
STEELMAN, Samuel, b. N/D, d. N/D
STEEN, Elizabeth, w/o James b. 02/06/1836, d. 08/20/1883
STEEN, Otus, b. 07/05/1891, d. 10/23/1898
STEVENSON, Peter R., ssw-Susan, b. 09/09/1827, d. 04/26/1912
STEVENSON, Susan, w/o Peter R., ssw-Peter R., b. 01/02/1828, d. 03/05/1912
STOUT, Charles, ssw-Mary E., m. 12/24/1916, b. 1892, d. 1975
STOUT, Frances S., b. 09/25/1921, d. 01/13/1928
STOUT, Lucinda, b. 06/03/1926, d. 10/27/1928
STOUT, Margaret P., ssw-William F., b. 06/21/1931, d. N/D
STOUT, Mary E., ssw-Charles, m. 12/24/1916, b. 1899, d. 1984
STOUT, William F., ssw-Margaret P., b. 03/22/1932, d. 02/19/1987
UNKNOWN, Bethany Ann, Inf. d/o Henry & Christy, b. 10/10/1989, d. 12/07/1989
WALLS, Carlton Lindberg, ssw-J. Robert, Gertrude S., Gordon, Irene G., John H., Matilda W., May
    McBride, William T., Jr. & William T., Sr., b. 1927, d. 1928
WALLS, Catherine, b. 11/22/1851, d. 09/19/1934
WALLS, Della A., ssw-Lydia A. & Wallace B., b. 1884, d. 1886
WALLS, Gertrude S., ssw-William T., Jr., Carlton Lindberg, Gordon, Irene G., J. Robert, John H., Matilda
    W., May McBride & William T., Sr., b. 1907, d. 1931
WALLS, Gordon, ssw-Gertrude S., Carlton Lindberg, Irene G., J. Robert, John H., Matilda W., May
    McBride, William T., Jr. & William T., Sr., b. 1938, d. 1946
WALLS, Irene G., ssw-Carlton Lindbert, Gertrude S., Gordon, J. Robert, John H., Matilda W., May
    McBride,William T., Jr. & William T., Sr., b. 1900, d. 1967
WALLS, J. Robert, ssw-Gordon, Carlton Lindberg, Gertrude S., Irene G., John H., Matilda W., May
    McBride,William T., Jr. & William T., Sr., b. 1941, d. N/D
WALLS, Jesse, b. 08/01/1850, d. 09/07/1907
WALLS, Jesse H., ssw-Winnie B., b. 07/22/1893, d. 11/29/1941
WALLS, John H., ssw-Matilda W., Carlton Lindberg, Gertrude S., Gordon, Irene G., J. Robert, May
    McBride, William T., Jr. &William T., Sr., b. 1827, d. 1894
WALLS, Lawrence R., s/o T. F. & L. A., b. 07/18/1887, d. 01/02/1889
WALLS, Lizzie A. Clifton, w/o Al, ssw-T. Frank, b. 04/12/1867, d. 05/30/1947
WALLS, Lydia A., ssw-Wallace B. & Della A., b. 1873, d. 1874
WALLS, Mary A., ssw-William T., b. 05/08/1891, d. 06/02/1971
WALLS, Matilda W., ssw-John H., Carlton Lindberg, Gertrude S., Gordon, Irene G., J. Robert, Matilda W.,
    May McBride, William T., Jr. & William T., Sr., b. 1839, d. 1905
WALLS, May McBride, ssw-William, T., Sr., Carlton Lindberg, Gertrude S., Gordon, Irene G., J. Robert,
    John H., Matilda W., & William T., Jr., b. 1873, d. 1910
WALLS, Nemiah, DE, Cpl., 316 SNTN, 91st Div., WWI, b. 09/22/1884, d. 07/15/1945

WALLS, Robert J., ssw-Sarah E., b. 05/05/1839, d. 05/14/1912

WALLS, Sallie Delemo, d/o T. F. & Lizzie A., b. 05/03/1893, d. 09/25/1894

WALLS, Sarah E., w/o Robert J., ssw-Robert J., b. 07/16/1844, d. 01/23/1926

WALLS, T. Frank, ssw-Lizzie A. Clifton, b. 01/28/1863, b. 01/20/1918

WALLS, Virginia G., ssw-Laura Collins Davis, b. 03/12/1867, d. 04/09/1901

WALLS, Wallace B., ssw-Lydia A. & Della A., b. 1870, d. 1874

WALLS, William T., ssw-Mary A., b. 09/26/1884, d. 09/07/1949

WALLS, William T., Jr., ssw-May McBride, Carlton Lindberg, Gertrude S., Gordon, Irene G., J. Robert, John H.,Matilda W. & William T., Sr., b. 1905, d. 1957

WALLS, William T., Sr., ssw-Matilda W., Carlton Lindberg, Gertrude S., Gordon, Irene G., J. Robert, John H., May McBride & William T., Jr., b. 1875, d 1938

WALLS, Winnie B., ssw-Jesse H., b. 04/14/1899, d. 10/23/1980

WARD, Eliza V., ssw-Robert Curtis & Robert G., b. 1875, d. 1946

WARD, Robert Curtis, ssw-Eliza V. & Robert G., b. 1904, d. 1925

WARD, Robert G., ssw-Eliza V. & Robert Curtis, b. 1879, d. 1951

WARREN, Beatrice A., d/o Dora & Sallie b., 02/10/1905, d. 03/28/1905

WARREN, Della V., b. 1874, d. 1964

WARREN, Dora, ssw-Sallie G., b. 1874, d. 1928

WARREN, Edwin, s/o Noah E. & Della V., b. 11/10/1914, d. 08/28/1915

WARREN, Hettie F., b. 02/25/1840, d. 11/30/1898

WARREN, Nelson Benjamin, s/o Noah E., & Della V., b. 01/03/1916, d. 01/17/1917

WARREN, Noah E., b. 1867, d. 1963

WARREN, Ruth E., b. 1906, d. 1974

WARREN, Sallie G., ssw-Dora, b. 1883, d. 1968

WARREN, William E., s/o Noah E. & Della V., b. 09/12/1908, d. 11/08/1909

WARRINGTON, George H., ssw-Sarah Ida, b. 08/04/1856, d. 07/31/1947

WARRINGTON, Inf. d/o Geo. H. & Sarah Lou, Age 4d, b. N/D, d. 06/23/1890

WARRINGTON, Lambert, b. 1886, d. 1938

WARRINGTON, Mary B., ssw-Stephen H., b. 07/22/1828, d. 11/12/1914

WARRINGTON, Robert L., ssw-Mary Warrington Webb, b. 1886, d. 1938

WARRINGTON, Sarah Ida, w/o Geo. H., b. 02/06/1859, d. 02/22/1907

WARRINGTON, Stephen H., ssw-Mary B., b. 09/25/1824, d. 01/30/1900

WARRINGTON, Stephen W., ssw-Robert L., b. 04/25/1862, d. 07/03/1900

WATSON, Mark L., b. 1868, d. 1956

WATSON, Rachel C., b. 1869, d. 1955

WEBB, Mary Warrington, ssw-Mary B. Warrington, b. 12/26/1865, d. 12/19/1936

WILLEY, Ada Mae, ssw-Wilson P., b. 05/07/1909, d. 08/13/1959

WILLEY, John H., ssw-Maggie G., b. 1873, d. 1944

WILLEY, Linford C., ssw-Mary E., b. 07/14/1902, d. 12/29/1958

WILLEY, Lloyd W., M. D., Pvt., USA, b. 02/17/1928, d. 03/16/1969

WILLEY, Maggie G., ssw-John H., b. 1884, d. 1958

WILLEY, Mary E., ssw-Linford C., b. 07/15/1916, d. N/D

WILLEY, Russell E., b. 06/05/1936, d. 03/26/1982

WILLEY, Wilson P., ssw-Ada Mae, b. 03/28/1906, d. 01/26/1975

WILSON, Emasmus J., ssw-Mazie M., b. 09/07/1889, d. N/D

WILSON, Emma Jones, w/o James H., ssw-James H., b. 09/13/1861, d. 02/23/1934

WILSON, James H., ssw-Emma Jones, b. 04/22/1860, d. 09/24/1919

WILSON, Mazie M., ssw-Emasmus J., b. 10/04/1887, d. 01/02/1963

WINGATE, Isaac C., s/o Matthew C. & Hetty, b. 10/28/1860, d. 05/13/1863
WORKMAN, Elizabeth S., b. 1840, d. 1913
WORKMAN, Jacob R., b. 1842, d. 1922
WORKMAN, Rhoda A., b. 1865, d. N/D
WRIGHT, Floyd, ssw-Mable A., b. 1907, d. 1966
WRIGHT, Ira, b. 1878, d. 1961
WRIGHT, Mable A., ssw-Floyd, b. 1910, d. 1986

The following stones were recorded by the Hudson Survey but are now missing or unreadable:
DODD, Julia, w/o Jesse, b. 08/08/1835, d. 08/06/1912
MORRIS, Nelson Benjamin s/o Noah E. & Della V., b. 01/03/1916, d. 01/17/1917
MORRIS, William E., s/o Noah E. & Della V., b. 09/12/1908, d. 11/08/1909
STEVENSON, Caddie, d/o Joseph B. & Hannah E., b. 11/13/1880, d. 11/23/1900
STEVENSON, Hannah E., w/o Joseph B., b. 08/30/1858, d. 07/16/1918
STEVENSON, Joseph B., b. 08/09/1850, d. 09/05/1918
WORKMAN, Walter J., b. 10/05/1873, d. 07/06/1919

(BK-016 & HU-528) DORMAN – RICHARDS FAMILY CEMETERY
Location: East of Milton approximately 50 yards from the N. W. side of Oyster Rocks Rd. (Rd. 264) 0.7
miles N. E. off Coastal Highway (Rt. 1)
Recorded: April 7, 1998

DORMAN, Eliza P., w/o Nehemiah, Age 28y 6m, b. N/D, d. 02/02/1845
DORMAN, Mary, w/o Capt. Nehemiah, Age 58y 10d, b. N/D, d. 11/27/1831
DORMAN, Nehemiah, Age 56y 4m 8d, b. N/D, d. 04/02/1862
DORMAN, Nehemiah, Captain, Age 48y 8m 10d, b. N/D, d. 04/10/1823
GORDON, Frances R., w/o David, Age 68y 7m 21d. b. N/D, d. 01/12/1867
RICHARDS, Jacob H., Age 30y, b. N/D, d. 06/16/1866
RICHARDS, Sarah, w/o Theodore W., Age 38y 4m 29d, b. N/D, d. 11/07/1848
RICHARDS, Theodore W., Age 53y 5m 9d, b. N/D, d. 11/28/1857

The following stones were recorded by the Hudson Survey but are now missing or unreadable:
HAZZARD, Stephan, b. 03/13/1785, d. 06/23/1831
PEPPER, Mary Hall, wid/o Theodore Richards & w/o Joshua Pepper, Age 68y 7m 27d, b. N/D,
        d. 02/06/1885
RICHARDS, Nathaniel, s/o Theodore, Age 23y 10m 5d, b. N/D, d. 09/22/1852
WRIGHT, Sarah R., w/o Ellis & d/o Stephen & Mary Hazzard, b. 08/02/1812, d. 09/07/1851

(BK-017 & HU-NR) ALEXANDER WARRINGTON CEMETERY
Location: East of Harbeson approximately 100 yards west of Coolspring Rd. (Rd. 290) between Seashore
Highway (Rt. 9) and Log Cabin Hill Rd. (Rd. 247)

WARRINGTON, Alexander, b. 07/09/1786, d. 09/20/1847
WARRINGTON, Eliza Helen, d/o Eliza A. & ___, Age 6m 26d, b. 10/1848, d. 03/05/1849
WARRINGTON, Mary Hall, w/o Alexander, b. 07/07/1793, d. 11/16/1849

CEDAR CREEK HUNDRED

(CC-001 & HU-269) STAYTONVILLE CHURCH CEMETERY

Located N. W. of Greenwood at the N. E. corner of Memory Rd. (Rd. 613) and Staytonville Rd. (Rd. 629) approximately 0.1 mile north of Shawnee Rd. (Rt. 36)
Recorded: April 19, 1995

BAILEY, John S., Co. H, 9th Del. Inf., b. N/D, d. N/D
CLIFTON, Mark, b. 03/07/1872, d. 01/16/1877
HATFIELD, Jonathan H., s/o Jonathan & Ida M., b. 06/27/1889, d. 07/22/1890
HOLSTON, Ann R., w/o William, Age 81y, b. N/D, d. 05/11/1905
JOHNSON, David, b. 07/08/1818, d. 04/29/1888
JOHNSON, Erimina, d/o Wm. & Wilmina, b. 08/04/1881, d. 11/16/1884
PARDEE, Charlie, b. N/D, d. 09/13/1889
PARDEE, Charlotte W., b. N/D, d. 06/04/1897
PARDEE, D. W., Age 27y 4m 5d, b. N/D, d. 06/28/1884
PARDEE, John, b. N/D, d. 07/23/1903
STAYTON, James B., b. 10/30/1775, d. Unreadable [Note: Stone is broken.]
STAYTON, Rachel, Age 25y 8m 6d, b. 10/09/1781, d. 06/15/1807
WEBB, Isaac C., s/o Wm. & Rhoda, b. 11/13/1854, d. 10/28/1892
WEBB, James T., s/o Wm. B. & Rhoda, b. 09/30/1866, d. 07/08/1894
WEBB, Mark H., s/o Wm. B. & Rhoda, b. 12/29/1863, d. 08/06/1886
WEBB, Rhoda W., w/o William B., b. 07/26/1829, d. 08/29/1886
WEBB, William B., Father, b. 12/08/1830, d. 11/17/1920

The following stones were recorded by the Hudson Survey but are now missing or unreadable:
CARLISLE, James, Age 73y, b. N/D, d. 03/16/1926
CLIFTON, Garrett W., b. 08/03/1828, d. 01/25/1909
CLIFTON, John W., Age 82y, b. N/D, d. 08/16/1875
COATES, Franklin G., b. 01/08/1865, d. 02/15/1894
COATES, Mary Clifton, b. 04/05/1841, d. N/D
COATES, Sallie M., b. 12/18/1872, d. 08/22/1884
COATES, Thomas, b. 05/27/1862, d. 09/29/1884
COATES, Thomas D., Capt., Age 67y, b. N/D, d. 08/13/1897
KNOWLES, Mark, s/o Joseph D. & Louisa, b. 09/10/1886, d. 10/26/1887
LASSELLE, Marie S., d/o William F. & Mary E., b. 08/18/1882, d. 07/04/1884
PARDEE, Mary E., b. N/D, d. 05/09/1917
STUART, George, s/o Henry W. & Sarah, Age 17y 11m 3d, b. N/D, d. 04/03/1875
STUART, Sarah Lizzie, d/o James H. & Eliza J., Age 1y 5m, b. N/D, d. 07/16/1875
WARREN, Charles H., b. 09/24/1865, d. 04/17/1902
WEBB, Mary A., Age 80y, b. N/D, d. 11/15/1897
WEBB, Virginia, b. 12/28/1860, d. 12/13/1907

(CC-002 & HU-458) SLAUGHTER NECK UNITED METHODIST CHURCH CEMETERY
Located S. E. of Milford on the East side of Argo's Corner Rd. (Rd. 14E) Approximately 200 yards, NE of
Coastal Highway (Rt. 1)
Recorded: September 6, 1995

ABBOTT, George May, ssw-Ruth Ann, b. 03/13/1903, d. 08/29/1961
ABBOTT, Russell B., s/o William M. & Florence M., b. 01/12/1912, d. 05/10/1913
ABBOTT, Ruth Ann, ssw-George May, b. 01/26/1907, d. 05/13/1989
ADAMS, George F., ssw-Margaret F., b. 03/27/1913, d. 06/17/1991
ADAMS, Margaret F., ssw-George F., b. 12/27/1913, d. 03/08/1994
ALEXANDER, John J., ssw-Thelma B., SSgt, USA, WWII, b. 04/21/1913, d. 04/24/1985
ALEXANDER, Thelma B., ssw-John J., b. 04/20/1917, d. N/D
ARGO, Albert, ssw-Ida, b. 09/15/1839, d. 10/19/1913
ARGO, Annie, d/o A. T. & Sallie E., Age 10m 20d, b. N/D, d. 01/10/1862
ARGO, Annie, ssw-Ida, b. 06/07/1859, d. 02/22/1939
ARGO, Annie M., ssw-John P., b. 05/25/1868, d. 06/05/1946
ARGO, Annie W., ssw-Edward B., b. 06/14/1893, d. 02/10/1975
ARGO, Carlton E., ssw-Esther G., b. 05/22/1905, d. 12/05/1981
ARGO, Clara J., ssw-Harry H., b. 11/29/1891, d. 05/20/1945
ARGO, Clarence, s/o Edward B. & Annie W., b. 05/29/1914, d. 08/17/1914
ARGO, David H., ssw-Margaret E., b. 03/08/1858, d. 09/10/1931
ARGO, Dorothy Marie, d/o Harry H. & Clara J., b. 01/17/1917, d. 02/01/1919
ARGO, E. Hubbard, ssw-Sallie J., b. 11/11/1880, d. 11/27/1963
ARGO, Eddie Grey, ssw-William B., b. 08/21/1878, d. 11/05/1879
ARGO, Edna Gray, ssw-George Earl, George Earl, Jr. & Hubbard Earl, b. 12/23/1904, d. 06/13/1980
ARGO, Edward B., ssw-Annie W., b. 09/21/1891, d. 09/19/1967
ARGO, Ellen N., w/o Ira C., b. 01/08/1870, d. 10/28/1893
ARGO, Esther G., ssw-Carlton E., b. 01/12/1908, d. 01/29/1988
ARGO, Florence E., ssw-John S., b. 09/02/1884, d. 06/02/1972
ARGO, Frankie Credrick, s/o Samuel E. & Lydia R., b. 09/15/1872, d. 05/10/1875
ARGO, George Earl, ssw-Edna Gray, George Earl, Jr. & Hubbard Earl, b. 07/08/1906, d. 05/11/1937
ARGO, George Earl, Jr., ssw-George Earl, Edna Gray & Hubbard Earl, b. 04/25/1936, d. 07/14/1937
ARGO, Harry H., ssw-Clara J., b. 09/28/1889, d. 12/16/1970
ARGO, Hester Ann, ssw-John A., b. 01/01/1837, d. 04/28/1924
ARGO, Hubbard Earl, ssw-George Earl, Edna Gray & George Earl, Jr., b. 06/28/1934, d. 07/08/1934
ARGO, Ida, ssw-Albert, b. 08/19/1899, d. 04/29/1969
ARGO, John A., ssw-Hester Ann, b. 05/16/1836, d. 05/26/1911
ARGO, John E., ssw-Viola C., SSgt., USA, WWII, b. 01/30/1921, d. 09/15/1984
ARGO, John P., ssw-Annie M., b. 12/03/1864, d. 09/15/1939
ARGO, John P., ssw-Mary J., b. 07/05/1934, d. N/D
ARGO, John S., ssw-Florence E., b. 08/29/1882, d. 12/27/1953
ARGO, John Stephen, II, Inf. s/o Richard J. & Doris C., b. N/D, d. 01/27/1971
ARGO, Joseph L., s/o David A. & Clara J., Age 6m 13d, b. N/D, d. 06/30/1889
ARGO, Lena, d/o David A. & Clara J., Age 9y 9m 9d. b. N/D, d. 08/16/1893
ARGO, Lola Exley, b. 1895, d. 1978
ARGO, Lydia R., w/o Samuel E., ssw-Samuel E., b. 01/02/1846, d. 10/28/1914
ARGO, Lydia R., w/o William B., Age 57y 10m 23, d. N/D, d. 04/24/1904
ARGO, Margaret E., ssw-David H., b. 02/05/1861, d. 08/06/1933

ARGO, Mary, b. 1870, d. 1930

ARGO, Mary J., ssw-John P., b. 09/02/1935, d. N/D

ARGO, Sallie E., ssw-Samuel B., b. 04/02/1865, d. 05/15/1954

ARGO, Sallie J., ssw-E. Hubbard, b. 03/07/1884, d. 09/24/1969

ARGO, Samuel B., ssw-Sallie E., b. 06/10/1860, d. 04/12/1946

ARGO, Samuel E., ssw-Lydia R., b. 12/05/1841, d. 01/04/1885

ARGO, Viola C., ssw-John E., b. 05/12/1927, d. N/D

ARGO, William B., ssw-Eddie Grey, b. 02/17/1849, d. 10/29/1896

ARGOE, Hester, ssw-Joseph, b. 08/07/1821, d. 07/17/1890

ARGOE, Joseph, ssw-Hester, b. 05/16/1826, d. 08/02/1904

ARGOE, Mary H., ssw-William A., b. 1868, d. 1930

ARGOE, Wilber C., b. 1870, d. 1928

ARGOE, William A., ssw-Mary H., b. 1862, d. 1947

ATKINS, Henry E., b. 06/02/1918, d. 03/06/1995

ATKINS, Hilda W., b. 12/21/1917, d. 08/13/1990

ATKINS, Virginia J., ssw-Walter C., b. 12/18/1886, d. 07/07/1973

ATKINS, Walter C., ssw-Virginia J., b. 08/09/1884, d. 02/06/1963

BABY CHOICE, Victim of Abortion, b. 05/03/1986, d. N/D

BAER, Alta R., ssw-Russell A., b. 07/13/1883, d. 05/17/1967

BAER, Russell A., ssw-Alta R., b. 10/30/1890, d. 05/21/1941

BARDEN, Sarah J., ssw-Ada L. Roach, b. N/D, d. 01/09/1942

BENNETT, Alice H., ssw-David Burton, b. 12/24/1866, d. 04/30/1946

BENNETT, Alice M., ssw-Walter B., b. 11/30/1896, d. N/D

BENNETT, Amos Gray, ssw-Gertrude S., b. 04/18/1878, d. 03/18/1967

BENNETT, Anna E. Davis, ssw-John Riley, b. 05/08/1852, d. 10/23/1935

BENNETT, Annie P., b. 03/25/1853, d. 04/19/1884

BENNETT, Carrie E., ssw-Mary E., b. 10/11/1866, d. 07/23/1896

BENNETT, Catherine R., w/o James D., b. 08/06/1845, d. 04/09/1926

BENNETT, Clarence W., b. 12/18/1870, d. 09/05/1952

BENNETT, David Burton, ssw-Alice H., b. 05/20/1855, d. 03/29/1921

BENNETT, David W., ssw-Emma D., b. 02/20/1826, d. 07/21/1885

BENNETT, Edgar, ssw-Ira Hazzard, Age 6w, b. N/D, d. 04/05/1876

BENNETT, Edgar H., ssw-Ella M., b. 05/11/1887, d. 03/12/1970

BENNETT, Elias Prettyman, s/o Elias T. & Mary E., b. 11/11/1906, d. 07/26/1907

BENNETT, Elias T., Age 54y 8m 4d, b. 09/06/1814, d. 05/10/1869

BENNETT, Elias T., ssw-Mary V., b. 11/09/1855, d. 08/27/1928

BENNETT, Elizabeth, wid/o Elias T., b. 04/30/1820, d. 12/05/1905

BENNETT, Elizabeth S., w/o Riley W., b. 05/09/1818, d. 09/14/1893

BENNETT, Ella Davis, ssw-Horace E., b. 04/21/1866, d. 08/01/1931

BENNETT, Ella M., ssw-Edgar H., b. 02/07/1894, d. 07/16/1954

BENNETT, Emma D., ssw-David W., b. 08/02/1840, d. 08/27/1890

BENNETT, F. Layton, ssw-Sallie A., b 04/28/1889, d. 04/14/1976

BENNETT, Frederick A., ssw-Carrie E., b. 01/25/1858, d. 05/25/1948

BENNETT, Gertrude S., ssw-Amos Gray, b. 05/19/1886, d. 01/28/1975

BENNETT, Hammond Carey, ssw-Jeannette Isaacs, b. 11/27/1917, d. N/D

BENNETT, Henry C., ssw-Mary S., b. 06/16/1895, d. 11/18/1980

BENNETT, Henry Draper, b. 12/30/1878, d. 08/19/1966

BENNETT, Herschel D., ssw-Margaret E., b. 08/20/1896, d. 07/13/1941

BENNETT, Hester, w/o Nehemiah, Age 83y 1m 11d, b. N/D, d. 02/11/1845
BENNETT, Hester A., b. 06/15/1845, d. 08/15/1904
BENNETT, Hester Ann, w/o Purnel S., b. 02/01/1841, d. 09/25/1915
BENNETT, Horace E., ssw-Ella Davis, b. 08/26/1863, d. 01/20/1948
BENNETT, Ira Hazzard, s/o John W. & Mary E., ssw-Edgar, Age 1y 2m 9d, b. N/D, d. 10/09/1874
BENNETT, James D., ssw-Catherine R., b. 02/04/1842, d. 01/11/1926
BENNETT, Janice M., b. 12/29/1928, d. 08/24/1979
BENNETT, Jeannette Isaacs, ssw-Hammond Carey, b. 01/02/1921, d. N/D
BENNETT, Joanne Isaacs, ssw-Hammond Carey, b. 03/31/1941, d. N/D
BENNETT, John, Age 12y 2, b. N/D, d. 09/22/1862
BENNETT, John Riley, ssw-Anna E. Davis, b. 06/03/1851, d. 05/20/1899
BENNETT, John W., ssw-Mary E., b. 04/27/1840, d. 12/07/1922
BENNETT, Joshua, Age 52y 2m 23d, b. N/D, d. 09/05/1846
BENNETT, Joshua D., b. 05/30/1866, d. 01/10/1882
BENNETT, Lena L., ssw-Riley W., b. 04/04/1895, d. 05/02/1965
BENNETT, Lester F., b. 1898, d. 1961
BENNETT, Lizzie B., ssw-P. Frank, b. 10/18/1874, d. 07/02/1947
BENNETT, Margaret E., ssw-Herschel D., b. 06/21/1898, d. 03/03/1970
BENNETT, Mary, w/o Joshua, Age 54y 4m 12d, b. N/D, d. 03/17/1851
BENNETT, Mary E., ssw-Carrie E., b. 01/15/1863, d. 11/13/1919
BENNETT, Mary E. w/o John W., b. 07/24/1839, d. 10/02/1915
BENNETT, Mary S., ssw-Henry C., b. 06/23/1896, d. 08/01/1973
BENNETT, Mary V., ssw-Elias T., b. 11/15/1866, d. 02/22/1930
BENNETT, Oscar, s/o Purnel & Hester, Age 4y 10m 3d, b. N/D, d. 08/31/1877
BENNETT, P. Frank, ssw-Lizzie B., b. 01/23/1869, d. 08/11/1950
BENNETT, Purnel S., b. 12/29/1834, d. 11/23/1904
BENNETT, Riley W., b. 07/15/1817, d. 08/23/1888
BENNETT, Riley W., ssw-Lena L., b. 04/25/1890, d. 09/03/1973
BENNETT, Sallie A., ssw-F. Layton, b. 12/04/1890, d. 08/08/1963
BENNETT, Sallie E., Draper, w/o John H. & d/o Alexander & Abbie D. Draper, b. 05/19/1834,
        d. 01/08/1858
BENNETT, T. Adolphus, b. 1902, d. 1932
BENNETT, Walter B., ssw-Alice M., b. 03/05/1892, d. 05/15/1956
BENNETT, Walter Elias, s/o John W. & Mary E., Age 10y 8m 14d, b. N/D, d. 03/23/1877
BENNETT, William H., ssw-Mary C. Jones, b. 05/07/1843, d. 11/02/1881
BENSON, Beatrice M., ssw-Davis G., b. 10/12/1919, d. 03/26/1983
BENSON, Davis G., ssw-Beatrice M., b. 07/23/1912, d. 04/19/1991
BETTS, William T., s/o William T. & Helen P., b. 10/14/1908, d. 08/04/1909
BILLINGS, Bruce B., b. 07/24/1956, d. 09/02/1956
BILLINGS, Powell E., MSgt., USA, WWII, b. 05/16/1919, d. 10/20/1989
BILLINGS, Rosella C., b. 06/15/1920, d. N/D
BOSWELL, Benjamin H., b. 05/04/1892, d. 08/31/1957
BOYCE, Arthur F., ssw-Mary E., b. 01/11/1877, d. 06/24/1958
BOYCE, Arthur J., ssw-Mary E., b. 02/16/1909, d. 03/13/1996
BOYCE, Benjamin O., ssw-Mollie E, M. Wilbert & Winona R., b. 05/10/1895, d. 04/16/1911
BOYCE, Bessie G., ssw-Howard C., b. 1881, d. 1924
BOYCE, Edna E., ssw-Samuel W., b. 1907, d. 1918
BOYCE, Herman D., b. 02/12/1894, d. 10/09/1963

BOYCE, Howard C., ssw-Bessie G., b. 1874, d. 1942

BOYCE, Ida, w/o James H., b. 06/11/1874, d. 11/27/1904

BOYCE, James H., b. 02/16/1871, d. 10/16/1904

BOYCE, M. Wilbert, ssw-Benjamin O., Mollie E. & Winona R., b. 01/15/1871, d. 05/03/1953

BOYCE, Mary E., ssw-Arthur F., b. 09/07/1878, d. 10/21/1970

BOYCE, Mary E., ssw-Arthur J., b. 12/20/1900, d. N/D

BOYCE, Mary E., ssw-Minnie W., b. 10/13/1900, d. 04/30/1918

BOYCE, Mary E. Clendaniel, w/o James Henry, ssw-Minnie W., b. 04/1845, d. 03/1922

BOYCE, Minnie W., ssw-Mary E., b. 09/01/1883, d. 12/11/1904

BOYCE, Mollie E., ssw-Benjamin O., M. Wilbert & Winona R., b. 08/09/1871, d. 11/09/1914

BOYCE, Samuel W., ssw-Edna E., b. 1911, d. 1912

BOYCE, Winona R., ssw-Benjamin O., Mollie E. & M. Wilbert, b. 03/22/1875, d. 06/18/1970

BRADLEY, Lavina Mae, ssw-Russell M., Sr., b 07/23/1916, d. 09/29/1993

BRADLEY, Russell M., Sr., ssw-Lavina Mae, b. 06/21/1910, d. N/D

BRANDT, Robert H., b. 1940, d. 1945

BRITTINGHAM, Calvin, b. 08/21/1907, d. 08/25/1988

BRITTINGHAM, Edith K., b. 1886, d. 1964

BRITTINGHAM, Margaret J., b. 10/05/1909, d. 06/26/1986

BRITTINGHAM, Robert K., Del., AA, USN, b. 01/15/1938, d. 10/20/1956

BUCHANAN, Hannah P., Age 34y 25d, b. N/D, d. 08/01/1850

BUCKSON, Charles V., b. 02/28/1894, d. 02/10/1983

BURLINGAME, Thelma M., Age 65y, b. N/D, d. 05/28/95

BYERS, Dorothy Morgan, ssw-Mahlon I., b. 07/08/1914, d. 11/19/1985

BYERS, Mahlon I., ssw-Dorothy Morgan, b. 11/05/1908, d. 1991

CALHOON, Annie V., ssw-Peter R., b. 1874, d. 1966

CALHOON, Eliza A., w/o Joseph A., Age 35y 10m 26d, b. N/D, d. 02/04/1866

CALHOON, Joseph A., b. 12/16/1832, d. 05/23/1896

CALHOON, Peter R., ssw-Annie V., b. 1865, d. 1951

CALHOUN, Elsie, ssw-Joseph L., India J., Rachel B. & Ida R., b. 03/13/1893, d. 08/28/1893

CALHOUN, Ida R., ssw-Joseph L., India J., Rachel B. & Elsie, b. 03/07/1863, d. 03/15/1897

CALHOUN, India J., ssw-Joseph L., Elsie, Ida R., & Rachel B., b. 1870, d. 1957

CALHOUN, Joseph L., ssw-Ida R., Elsie, India J. & Rachel B., b. 1860, d. 1935

CALHOUN, Rachel B., ssw-Joseph L., Elsie, Ida R. & India J., b. 1844, d. 1925

CAMPBELL, Hester Ann, d/o John & Mary, Age 28y 18d, b. N/D, d. 03/22/1847

CAMPBELL, Hester Ann, d/o Robert & Eliza, Age 5m 2d, b. N/D, d. 06/25/1845

CAMPBELL, John, Age 68y 10m 19d, b. N/D, d. 02/25/1853

CAMPBELL, John H., s/o Robert & Eliza, b. N/D, d. N/D

CAMPBELL, John P., s/o Robert & Eliza, Age 1y 6m 12d, b. 12/21/1843, d. N/D

CAMPBELL, Mary, Age 81y 29d, b. 01/23/1789, d. 02/22/1870

CAMPBELL, Robert S., Esq., s/o John & Mary, b. 07/08/1816, d. 11/16/1855

CAMPBELL, Susan J., d/o John & Mary, Age 51y 13d, b. 12/20/1821, d. 01/03/1873

CAREY, Bertha L. M., ssw-George Prettyman, b. 1880, d. 1972

CAREY, George Prettyman, ssw-Bertha L. M., b. 1883, d. 1970

CAREY, Hessie P., ssw-Vinal H., b. 02/13/1893, d. 07/09/1974

CAREY, Josephine, ssw-Willis J., b. 02/21/1867, d. 08/31/1946

CAREY, Vinal H., ssw-Hessie P., b. 11/05/1900, d. 04/02/1976

CAREY, Willis J., ssw-Josephine, b. 03/20/1867, d. 04/25/1938

CARMEAN, Sarah Agnes, d/o Cynthia E., ssw-Van L. G., Age 3m 29d, b. 12/20/1898, d. 04/19/1899

CARMEAN, Van L. G., s/o Fannie A. & J. J., ssw-Sarah Agnes, Age 29y 11m 2d, b. 12/19/1874, d. 11/21/1904

CARPENTER, Benjamin, b. 03/22/1896, d. 04/16/1974

CARPENTER, Blanche R., d/o John B. & Clara H., b. 01/25/1903, d. 03/18/1904

CARPENTER, Comfort J., w/o Robert S., ssw-Robert S., b. 01/11/1861, d. 06/10/1937

CARPENTER, George B., b. 08/20/1849, d. 02/08/1933

CARPENTER, Harry, s/o George & Mary E., b. 12/06/1871, d. 08/11/1900

CARPENTER, Isaac, Age 61y, b. 1790, d. 11/16/1851

CARPENTER, Mary E., w/o George B., b. 10/16/1822, d. 06/19/1903

CARPENTER, Robert S., ssw-Comfort J., b. 11/14/1855, d. 12/12/1926

CARROLL, Evelyn F., ssw-Lester A., b. 09/24/1936, d. N/D

CARROLL, George A., b. 1937, d. 1993

CARROLL, Lester A., ssw-Evelyn F., b. 06/26/1931, d. N/D

CARROLL, Roy Lee, b. 01/18/1858, d. 06/03/1973

CIRWITHEN, Caleb, Age 52y 11m 12d, b. N/D, d. 01/31/1845

CIRWITHEN, Caleb B., s/o Isaac & Catherine, Age 26y 6m 26d, b. 08/07/1848, d. 03/03/1875

CIRWITHEN, Catherine E., w/o Isaac, Age 34y 5m 17d, b. N/D, d. 02/11/1860

CIRWITHEN, Elizabeth C., b. 08/09/1853, d. 05/08/1927

CIRWITHEN, Isaac, Age 69y 11m 8d, b. N/D, d. 02/28/1892

CIRWITHEN, Mary A., w/o Isaac, Age 78y 3m 23d, b. N/D, d. 02/27/1903

CIRWITHEN, Patience, w/o Caleb, Age 68y 4m 17d, b. N/D, d. 07/23/1861

CIRWITHEN, William I., b. 02/25/1864, d. 09/30/1954

CLEAVER, Anna M., ssw-John P., b. 01/11/1906, d. 12/08/1985

CLEAVER, John P., ssw-Anna M., b. 11/27/1899, d. 01/31/1985

CLEMONS, Flora, ssw-Howard, b. 1912, d. 1977

CLEMONS, Howard, ssw-Flora, b. 1919, d. 1989

CLENDANIEL, Alice G., ssw-John H., b. 1867, d. 1952

CLENDANIEL, Dawsie, b. 07/31/1898, d. 04/08/1911

CLENDANIEL, Emma B., ssw-George W., b. 02/13/1881, d. 11/18/1944

CLENDANIEL, Fannie Dawsie, d/o John H. & Alice G., b. 09/06/1889, d. 06/10/1898

CLENDANIEL, George W., ssw-Emma B., b. 02/27/1875, d. 01/13/1955

CLENDANIEL, Harry C., ssw-Minnie M., b. 1873, d. 1936

CLENDANIEL, Harvey B., ssw-M. Elizabeth, b. 01/01/1887, d. 09/07/1941

CLENDANIEL, John H., ssw-Alice G., b. 1862, d. 1937

CLENDANIEL, M. Elizabeth, ssw-Harvey B., b. 07/06/1895, d. 07/20/1990

CLENDANIEL, Marie W., ssw-William J., b. 02/27/1910, d. N/D

CLENDANIEL, Mary S., ssw-William W., b. 09/22/1849, d. 05/07/1918

CLENDANIEL, Minnie M., ssw-Harry C., b. 1879, d. 1921

CLENDANIEL, Purnell, ssw-William W., b. 03/15/1840, d. 06/30/1922

CLENDANIEL, Sarah, Age 76y 10m 6d, b. 08/08/1832, d. 06/14/1909

CLENDANIEL, Thomas E., ssw-William W., b. 04/01/1838, d. 11/01/1908

CLENDANIEL, Thomas H., ssw-Harry C., b. 1909, d. 1909

CLENDANIEL, William H., Age 57y 1m 14d, b. 04/29/1832, d. 06/13/1889

CLENDANIEL, William J., ssw-Marie W., b. 01/01/1905, d. 11/06/1974

CLENDANIEL, William S., s/o William H. & Sarah, Age 1y 8m 19d, b. N/D, d. 10/11/1876

CLENDANIEL, William W., ssw-Thomas E., b. 06/15/1871, d. 03/10/1925

CLENDANIEL, Zechariah T., s/o William H. & Sarah, Age 20y 6m 17d, b. N/D, d. 10/20/1876

CLIFTON, Beatrice Hudson, ssw-William Carlton, b. 1906, d. N/D

CLIFTON, David Brooks, b. 07/14/1961, d. 08/04/1977

CLIFTON, Emma V., ssw-Harold L., b. 1888, d. 1931

CLIFTON, Harold L., ssw-Emma V., b. 1888, d. 1946

CLIFTON, Marshall D., s/o Harold L. & Emma V., b. 10/20/1912, d. 02/01/1920

CLIFTON, William Carlton, ssw-Beatrice Hudson, b. 1903, d. 1980

COATS, Hattie, ssw-Joseph, b. 1872, d. 1949

COATS, Joseph, ssw-Hattie, b. 1870, d. 1949

COFFEN, Annie E., ssw-David B., b. 05/10/1851, d. 02/19/1921

COFFEN, David B., ssw-Annie E., b. 07/29/1842, d. 01/19/1921

COFFEN, David Roy, b. 01/16/1888, d. 03/03/1970

COFFEN, George, b. 04/25/1883, d. 05/22/1945

COFFIN, Charles, ssw-Lulu, b. 1877, d. 1957

COFFIN, John A., b. 07/09/1901, d. 03/24/1936

COFFIN, Lulu, ssw-Charles, b. 1884, d. 1963

COFFIN, S. P., b. N/D, d. N/D

COLLINS, B. Harrison, ssw-Helen May, b. 07/30/1889, d. 03/13/1945

COLLINS, Helen May, ssw-B. Harrison, b. 05/11/1897, d. 08/05/1972

CONAWAY, Jenny Stewart, b. 1890, d. 1957

COOPER, Mildred S., ssw-Walter H., b. 12/28/1916, d. N/D

COOPER, Walter H., ssw-Mildred S., b. 10/08/1894, d. 08/02/1973

COVERDALE, Annie R., ssw-John H., b. 1885, d. 1963

COVERDALE, Bertha S., ssw-Wilbert L., Edgar D., Leighton W. & Otis R., b. 1880, d. 1960

COVERDALE, Claro, d/o Jennie M. & Nathaniel, b. 07/01/1894, d. 06/10/1901

COVERDALE, Earnest, b. N/D, d. 07/27/1921

COVERDALE, Edgar D., ssw-Wilbert L., Bertha S., Leighton W. & Otis R., b. 1915, d. 1988

COVERDALE, Elizabeth, b. N/D, d. 05/06/1918

COVERDALE, Henry, b. N/D, d. 03/13/1920

COVERDALE, Howard G., s/o Nathaniel & Jennie, b. 02/24/1896, d. 02/26/1898

COVERDALE, Jennie M., ssw-Nathaniel, b. 1871, d. 1950

COVERDALE, John H., ssw-Annie R., b. 1876, d. 1973

COVERDALE, John H., ssw-Margaret E., b. 05/15/1836, d. 1899

COVERDALE, Leighton W., ssw-Wilbert L., Bertha S., Edgar D. & Otis R., b. 1913, d. 1956

COVERDALE, Margaret E., w/o John H., b. 01/10/1838, d. 08/13/1913

COVERDALE, Mildred, b. 04/30/1913, d. 02/03/1930

COVERDALE, Naomi, b. N/D, d. 11/18/1928

COVERDALE, Nathaniel, ssw-Jennie M., b. 1868, d. 1947

COVERDALE, Otis R., ssw-Wilbert L., Bertha S., Leighton W. & Edgar D., b. 1910, d. 1981

COVERDALE, Roy M., b. 09/11/1906, d. 05/12/1915

COVERDALE, Ruth, b. N/D, d. 01/21/1928

COVERDALE, Wilbert L., ssw-Bertha S., Edgar D., Leighton W. & Otis R., b. 1870, d. 1941

DALLAS, Elizabeth, ssw-D. Arthur Edwards, b. 1894, d. 1920

DALLAS, Lida J., ssw-D. Arthur Edwards, b. 01/03/1874, d. 09/05/1901

DALLAS, Lydia H., b. 1876, d. 1937

DANIEL, Molton R., Age 75y 9m 17d, b. 10/12/1813, d. 07/29/1889

DANIEL, Nehemiah James, s/o Nehemiah & Priscilla, Age 31y 9m 17d, b. N/D, d. 09/11/1854

DARBY, James W., b. 12/26/1864, d. 09/27/1907

DARBY, Jencie M., b. 1888, d. 1957

DARBY, John H., b. 1861, d. 1940

DARBY, Mary E., ssw-D. Arthur Edwards, b. 1871, d. 1904
DARBY, Mary E., w/o John H., b. 03/22/1869, d. 12/31/1901
DARBY, Nancy, ssw-D. Arthur Edwards, b. 10/15/1808, d. 10/08/1892
DARBY, Wm. J., Co. C., 9 Del. Inf., Civil War, b. N/D, d. N/D
DAVIDSON, Alfred B., ssw-Emma J., b. 1880, d. 1942
DAVIDSON, Ann, w/o John W., Age 44y 7m, b. N/D, d. 10/21/1864
DAVIDSON, Annie C. Robinson, w/o James Cooper, b. 04/10/1844, d. 04/24/1916
DAVIDSON, Davie R., s/o John W. & Ann, Age 13y 3m 27d, b. N/D, d. 11/15/1864
DAVIDSON, Ella V. Gue, ssw-William P., b. 09/01/1881, d. 08/25/1964
DAVIDSON, Emma J., ssw-Alfred B., b. 1882, d. 1959
DAVIDSON, James Cooper, ssw-Annie C. Robinson, b. 08/24/1846, d. 10/19/1927
DAVIDSON, John K., s/o John W. & Ann, Age 19y 9m, b. N/D, d. 10/15/1864
DAVIDSON, John W., Age 71y, b. N/D, d. 08/15/1887
DAVIDSON, Mary H., ssw-Oscar S., b. 12/16/1901, d. 09/21/1974
DAVIDSON, Mildred L., ssw-Nelson H., b. 12/17/1916, d. 08/02/1992
DAVIDSON, Nelson H., ssw-Mildred L., b. 01/15/1913, d. 01/17/1968
DAVIDSON, Oscar S., ssw-Mary H., b. 08/01/1897, d. 01/29/1970
DAVIDSON, Robert F., s/o John W. & Ann, Age 21y 8m 21d, b. N/D, d. 08/27/1864
DAVIDSON, William P., ssw-Ella V. Gue, b. 05/06/1878, d. 12/16/1921
DAVIS, Allie P., ssw-Laura H., b. 1885, d. 1889
DAVIS, Annie L., ssw-Carlton M., b. 1858, d. 1945
DAVIS, Carlton M., ssw-Edwin P., b. 02/28/1893, d. 01/13/1919
DAVIS, Charles W., b. 1858, d. 1935
DAVIS, Edwin P., ssw-Carlton M., b. 12/16/1897, d. 11/11/1969
DAVIS, Eliza J., ssw-Robert W., Age 37y 9m 6d, b. N/D, d. N/D
DAVIS, Elizabeth C., ssw-Joseph Gray, b. 03/17/1857, d. 01/28/1942
DAVIS, Emma R., ssw-Joseph H. & Eliza J. Headley, b. 1875, d. 1936
DAVIS, Esther, w/o Nehemiah, Age 69y 8m 1d, b. N/D, d. 01/25/1850
DAVIS, Harry, ssw-Carlton M., b. 1860, d. 1931
DAVIS, Hester A., ssw-Nehemiah H., b. 1846, d. 1928
DAVIS, John S., Age 70y 11m 14d, b. N/D, d. 04/11/1887
DAVIS, John W., b. 09/14/1841, d. 09/13/1914
DAVIS, Joseph Gray, ssw-Elizabeth C., b. 02/21/1857, d. 12/04/1937
DAVIS, Laura H., ssw-Allie P., b. 1865, d. 1887
DAVIS, Lott W., b. 01/11/1823, d. 02/24/1915
DAVIS, Maria, w/o John S., Age 19y 6m 2d, b. N/D, d. 03/20/1862
DAVIS, Maria, w/o Joseph M., Age 49y 2m 4d, b. 10/20/1822, d. 12/24/1871
DAVIS, Mary E., b. 11/22/1852, d. 07/07/1915
DAVIS, Mary R., w/o Lott W., b. 02/19/1826, d. 12/11/1890
DAVIS, Nehemiah, b. 01/10/1770, d. 04/14/1859
DAVIS, Nehemiah H., ssw-Hester A., b. 1846, d. 1928
DAVIS, Otis C., b. 12/19/1858, d. 08/29/1880
DAVIS, Patience S., ssw-Purnel T., b. 07/23/1833, d. 03/27/1914
DAVIS, Purnel T., ssw-Patience S., b. 11/02/1834, d. 12/13/1899
DAVIS, Robert W., ssw-Eliza J., Age 76y 7m 9d, b. N/D, d. N/D
DAVIS, Roberta C., sswWalter B., b. 04/14/1918, d. N/D
DAVIS, Virginia A., ssw-Robert W., Age 4m 25d, b. N/D, d. N/D
DAVIS, Walter B., ssw-Roberta C., b. 08/12/1916, d. 03/28/1983

DEMPSEY, Arleen M., ssw-James I., b. 03/19/1954, d. N/D

DEMPSEY, Grave Y., ssw-William T., b. 07/31/1927, d. 12/22/1994

DEMPSEY, James I., ssw-Arleen M., b. 06/05/1950, d. 07/04/1988

DEMPSEY, William T., ssw-Grace Y., b. 12/29/1924, d. N/D

DODD, Carrie M., ssw-George E., Everett & Pearl, b. 1893, d. 1961

DODD, Everett, ssw-Carrie M., George E., & Pearl, b. 1921, d. 1922

DODD, George E., ssw-Carrie M., Everett & Pearl, b. 1885, d. 1972

DODD, Pearl, ssw-Carrie M., Everett & George E., b. 1928, d. 1931

DONOVAN, Benjamin Franklin, s/o Thomas W. & Deborah, Age 6y 9m 27d, b. N/D, d. 04/02/1860

DONOVAN, Gibson, b. 11/06/1809, d. 01/31/1882

DONOVAN, Hester Hevalow, w/o Gibson, b. 06/04/1808, d. 11/22/1894

DORMAN, Fred, SSgt., USA, WWII, Korea & Vietnam, b. 07/07/1919, d. 01/11/1996

DOUGLAS, Grace E., b. 1908, d. 1958

DRAPER, Alexander S., Age 37y 6m 22d, b. N/D, d. 12/31/1853

DRAPER, Audrey Owens, ssw-Harry Ross, b. 04/21/1910, d. 11/30/1978

DRAPER, Davis C., ssw-Josephine, Ella S., Eva B., Grover C., Grover C., Jr. & Infant., b. 05/20/1894,
        d. 11/22/1983

DRAPER, Edith M., ssw-Horace P., b. 06/30/1893, d. 09/16/1977

DRAPER, Eliza Riley, ssw-Lawrence R., b. 02/28/1819, d. 05/25/1857

DRAPER, Ella S., ssw-Grover C., Davis C., Josephine, Eva B., Infant & Grover C., Jr., b. 02/26/1902,
        d. 08/15/1959

DRAPER, Ethel H., ssw-Joseph F., b. 11/05/1892, d. 05/28/1965

DRAPER, Ernest Armstrong, s/o Harry R. & Mabel A., b. 03/11/1897, d. 12/14/1900

DRAPER, Eva B., ssw-Davis C., Ella S., Grover C., Josephine, Infant & Grover C., Jr., b. 01/26/1895,
        d. 03/13/1977

DRAPER, Everett C., b. 1917, d. 1919

DRAPER, Grover C., ssw-Ella S., Davis C., Eva B., Josephine, Infant & Grover C., Jr., b. 03/02/1892,
        d. 05/12/1967

DRAPER, Grover C., Jr., ssw-Grover C., Ella S., Davis C., Eva B., Josephine & Infant, b. 10/27/1924,
        d. 08/09/1925

DRAPER, Harry Ross, ssw-Audrey Owens, b. 09/03/1911, d. 10/07/1980

DRAPER, Harry Ross, ssw-Mable Armstrong, b. 06/23/1873, d. 06/17/1912

DRAPER, Henry C., b. 09/05/1838, d. 12/01/1890

DRAPER, Henry R., ssw-Mary J., b. 11/16/1817, d. 04/04/1870

DRAPER, Horace P., ssw-Edith M., b. 05/21/1884, d. 08/07/1922

DRAPER, Infant son, ssw-Davis C., Ella S., Eva B., Grover C., Josephine & Grover C., Jr., b. 02/27/1930,
        d. 02/27/1930

DRAPER, Jack Armstrong, s/o Harry R. & Mabel A., b. 09/18/1902, d. 03/27/1906

DRAPER, Jay Layton, b. 1919, d. 1933

DRAPER, Joseph F., ssw-Ethel H., b. 12/29/1890, d. 02/13/1964

DRAPER, Josephine, ssw-Davis C., Ella S., Eva B., Grover C., Grover C., Jr. & Infant, b. 02/16/1894,
        d. 03/12/1932

DRAPER, Lawrence R., ssw-Sallie Davis, b. 10/09/1846, d. 02/25/1918

DRAPER, Mable Armstrong, w/o Harry Ross, ssw-Harry Ross, b. 01/09/1879, d. 12/13/1964

DRAPER, Margaret H., b. 01/21/1837, d. 01/29/1912

DRAPER, Martha J., ssw-Thomas Reed, b. 10/16/1884, d. 10/30/1969

DRAPER, Mary H., w/o Miers C., Age 27y 3m 4d, b. 10/11/1830, d. 01/15/1858

DRAPER, Mary J., w/o Henry R., b. 03/10/1822, d. 08/21/1884

DRAPER, Maud, ssw-Lawrence R., b. 12/09/1814, d. 02/25/1867

DRAPER, Miers C., Age 52y 11m 9d, b. N/D, d. 09/13/1870

DRAPER, Olivia Belle, ssw-Thomas Reed, b. 02/14/1863, d. 03/19/1904

DRAPER, Sallie Davis, ssw-Lawrence R., b. 03/18/1849, d. 09/30/1932

DRAPER, Sarah, b. 12/09/1818, d. 08/20/1904

DRAPER, Sarah, w/o Leonard D., Age 41y 13d, b. N/D, d. 11/26/1816

DRAPER, Sarah E., w/o Miers C., Age 29y 7m 27d, b. N/D, d. 08/27/1852

DRAPER, Sarah Jane, consort o/Thomas Draper, Age 20y 11m 17d, b. N/D, d. 12/29/1844

DRAPER, Thomas Reed, ssw-Olivia Belle, b. 08/30/1859, d. 04/08/1919

DRAPER, Walter, s/o John H. & Abbie R., b. 08/11/1872, d. 12/13/1875

DRAPER, William, s/o Miers & Sarah E., Age 16y 8m, b. N/D, d. 10/08/1866

EDMUNDS, Mary Ella Cirwithen, w/o James V., b. 04/01/1863, d. 05/17/1899

EDWARDS, D. Arthur, ssw-Mollie, b. 1856, d. 1936

EDWARDS, Mollie, ssw-D. Arthur, b. 1866, d. 1951

ENNIS, Elizabeth V., ssw-Stephen M., b. 04/03/1806, d. 02/20/1881

ENNIS, Stephen M., ssw-Elizabeth V., b. 10/01/1816, d. 01/08/1894

EXLEY, Walter Eckert, b. 1921, d. 1979

FARENS, Alvertia M., ssw-J. Davis, b. 05/17/1911, d. 02/04/1990

FARENS, Clara C., ssw-James W., Donald C. & David Olson, b. 1878, d. 1921

FARENS, David Olsen, ssw-James W., Clara C. & Donald C., DE, Sgt, USA, WWI, b. 1900, d. 1935

FARENS, Donald C., ssw-James W., Clara C., & David Olsen, b. 1915, d. 1972

FARENS, J. Davis, ssw-Alvertia M., b. 03/09/1906, d. 12/01/1994

FARENS, James W., ssw-Clara C., David Olsen & Donald C., b. 1868, d. 1935

FARENS, Sallie J., ssw-Thomas Z., b. 07/14/1877, d. 03/21/1949

FARENS, Thomas Z., ssw-Sallie I., b. 02/26/1871, d. 11/14/1951

FASSEL, Lyda M. Darby, b. 01/27/1907, d. 07/21/1984

FINNITY, John H., ssw-Ruth E., b. 08/29/1904, d. 06/01/1979

FINNITY, Ruth E., ssw-John H., b. 04/18/1911, d. N/D

FINNITY, Wendy Dawn, b. 1971, d. 1971

FOUNTAIN, John H., ssw-William H. & Sarah A., Age 54y, b. N/D, d. 08/21/1916

FOUNTAIN, Sarah A., ssw-William H. & John H., Age 75y, b. N/D, d. 12/05/1899

FOUNTAIN, William H., ssw-John H. & Sarah A., Age 68y, b. N/D, d. 02/15/1912

FOWLER, Marian, ssw-William G., b. 1888, d. 1944

FOWLER, William G., ssw-Marian, b. 1888, d. 1969

FRANK, Margaret E., ssw-Samuel H., b. 04/19/1915, d. 07/21/1942

FRANK, Samuel H., ssw-Margaret E., b. N/D, d. N/D

GILLESPIE, Howard Lee, b. 11/04/1964, d. 06/19/1972

GOBAY, Carl, ssw-Rose, b. 06/06/1909, d. 10/17/1983

GOBAY, Rose, ssw-Carl, b. 08/14/1931, d. N/D

GOONER, Edward, ssw-Mary E., b. 03/07/1892, d. 09/20/1976

GOONER, Francis Willis, s/o Willis & Rena M., b. 07/14/1921, d. 04/21/1930

GOONER, Harry Russell, DE, Sgt., Svc Btry, 45 Field Arty, WWII, b. 08/03/1917, d. 01/05/1968

GOONER, Martha C., ssw-Michael, b. 09/01/1872, d. 05/27/1948

GOONER, Mary E., ssw-Edward, b. 11/06/1897, d. 02/23/1955

GOONER, Michael, ssw-Martha C., b. 08/22/1862, d. 11/10/1918

GOONER, Rena M., ssw-Willis, b. 07/21/1902, d. 03/27/1991

GOONER, Thelma, d/o Willis & Rena M., b. 06/27/1922, d. 10/27/1922

GOONER, Viola, d/o Mike & Cada, b. 09/02/1888, d. 09/13/1912

GOONER, William Edward, Pvt., USA, WWII, b. 02/23/1921, d. 04/02/1978

GOONER, Willis, ssw-Rena M., b. 06/22/1895, d. 10/15/1967

HAMMOND, Catherine, w/o Eli F., Age 51y, b. N/D, d. 08/15/1865

HARRISSON, Chas. B., b. 1924, d. N/D

HARRISSON, Evan M., b. 1936, d. N/D

HARRISSON, Joseph W. E., DSC, b. 1896, d. 1973

HARRISSON, Roslyn Cirwithen, b. 1900, d. 1993

HARRISSON, William J., b. 1922, d. 1973

HAZEL, Rob't., Co. E, 1st DE Inf. Civil War, b. N/D, d. N/D

HEADLEY, Eliza J., ssw-Joseph H. Headley and Emma R. Davis, b. 1863, d. 1963

HEADLEY, Joseph H., ssw-Eliza J. Headley and Emma R. Davis, b. 1876, d. 1950

HEATHER, Howard Melvin, s/o Thomas Howard & Mary P., b. 01/02/1898, d. 03/17/1905

HEATHER, Mary P., w/o T. Howard & d/o Samuel E. & Lydia R. Argo, b. 10/21/1876, d. 09/30/1901

HICKMAN, Emma M., ssw-William S., b. 07/14/1882, d. 12/23/1942

HICKMAN, Lloyd J., s/o Wm. J. & Mary, b. 02/28/1885, d. 09/25/1891

HICKMAN, Mary E., w/o William J., b. 05/02/1854, d. 08/28/1892

HICKMAN, Mary W., d/o William & Eliza W., Age 6y 8m 10d, b. N/D, d. 09/09/1828

HICKMAN, Viola M., 2nd w/o W. S., b. 1890, d. 1961

HICKMAN, Vurna M., d/o Wm. J. & Mary, b. 11/26/1892, d. 02/14/1986

HICKMAN, William J., b. 05/06/1851, d. 03/01/1920

HICKMAN, William S., ssw-Emma M., b. 02/17/1881, d. 05/13/1968

HILL, Christopher, b. 10/18/1977, d. 12/12/1977

HILL, Sarah A., w/o George, b. 04/06/1830, d. 04/27/1893

HOLLAND, David Ervin, s/o David H. & Mary E., Age 2y 6m 8d, b. N/D, d. 04/13/1862

HOLLAND, Willie, s/o David H. & Mary E., Age 4y 7m 22d, b. N/D, d. 10/09/1862

HOUSTON, Clement, b. 10/02/1819, d. 12/29/1917

HOUSTON, Henrietta, w/o Clement, Age 70y 6m 10d, b. 08/28/1824, d. 03/08/1895

HOUSTON, Maria Catharine, d/o Clement & Selea, b. 10/28/1848, d. 06/12/1890

HOUSTON, Mary T., d/o Clement & Seleah Y., Age 4y 4m 5d, b. N/D, d. 03/01/1856

HOUSTON, Sarah Jane, b. 10/09/1846 d. 08/01/1936

HOUSTON, Seleah, w/o Clement, Age 36y 5m 19d, b. N/D, d. 03/29/1857

HOUSTON, Susan Simpson, Age 3y 9m 20d, b. 06/11/1866, d. 03/31/1870

INGRAM, Amanda H., ssw-Charles J., b. 1875, d. 1951

INGRAM, Ann Virginia, ssw-Anthony, Sarah Ann, Eliza Jane, Nathaniel T., William R. C., Jacob, Babe,
Ollie May & Mary, b. 1850, d. 1851

INGRAM, Anthony, ssw-Sarah Ann, Eliza Jane, Nathaniel T., William R. C., Jacob, Ann Virginia, Babe,
Ollie May & Mary, b. 1817, d. 1896

INGRAM, Anthony P., s/o N. & Sarah, Age 1y 4m 26d, b. 03/09/1851, d. 08/03/1852

INGRAM, Babe, ssw-Anthony, Sarah Ann, Eliza Jane, Nathaniel T., William R. C., Jacob, Ann Virginia,
Ollie May & Mary, b. 1857, d. 1857

INGRAM, Benjamin F., ssw-Lillian M., b. 1887, d. 1978

INGRAM, Bertha M., ssw-Ralph, b. 01/22/1884, d. 09/05/1906

INGRAM, Charles A., ssw-Elsie M., b. 08/07/1883, d. 02/01/1963

INGRAM, Charles E., ssw-Edward J., b. 09/27/1953, d. N/D

INGRAM, Charles Edward, Pvt., USA, WWII, b. 01/03/1904, d. 04/14/1977

INGRAM, Charles J., ssw-Amanda H., b. 1877, d. 1957

INGRAM, Edward J., ssw-Charles E., b. 04/05/1942, d. 02/09/1989

INGRAM, Eliza Jane, ssw-Anthony, Sarah Ann, Nathaniel T., William R. C., Jacob, Ann Virginia, Babe, Ollie May & Mary, b. 1842, d. 1929

INGRAM, Elsie M., ssw-Charles A., b. 07/12/1896, d. 02/02/1977

INGRAM, Frank R., ssw-Ruth Ann, b. 07/11/1932, d. 05/13/1967

INGRAM, George M., b. 1871, d. 1872

INGRAM, Gladys S., ssw-John A., b. 06/25/1925, d. 12/28/1995

INGRAM, Hester Catherine, b. 09/03/1849, d. 11/26/1922

INGRAM, Hilda Louise, ssw-Wilson S., b. 01/01/1918, d. N/D

INGRAM, Ida E., b. 1876, d. 1881

INGRAM, Isaac W., ssw-Benjamin F., b. 1892, d. 1916

INGRAM, Jacob, ssw-Anthony, Sarah Ann, Eliza Jane, Nathaniel T., William R. C., Ann Virginia, Babe, Ollie May & Mary, b. 1844, d. 1852

INGRAM, John, b. 1815, d. 1877

INGRAM, John A., ssw-Gladys S., Pfc., USA, WWII, b. 02/10/1920, d. 08/21/1982

INGRAM, John Brinkley, b. 05/10/1848, d. 11/11/1937

INGRAM, Joseph Leon, Pfc., USA, WWII, b. 11/16/1918, d. 06/30/1979

INGRAM, Lillian M., ssw-Benjamin F., b. 1887, d. 1962

INGRAM, Mary, sis/o Anthony, ssw-Anthony, Sarah Ann, Eliza Jane, Nathaniel T., William R. C., Jacob, Ann Virginia, Babe & Ollie May, b. N/D, d. N/D

INGRAM, Mary Frances, w/o Nehemiah R., ssw-Nehemiah R., b. 1848, d. 1940

INGRAM, Naomi L., ssw-Paynter C., b. 01/30/1924, d. N/D

INGRAM, Nathaniel T., ssw-Anthony, Sarah Ann, Eliza Jane, William R. C., Jacob, Ann Virginia, Babe, Ollie May & Mary, b. 1847, d. 1863

INGRAM, Nehemiah R., ssw-Mary Frances, b. 1841, d. 1914

INGRAM, Ollie May, ssw-Anthony, Sarah Ann, Eliza Jane, Nathaniel T., William R. C., Jacob, Ann Virginia, Babe & Mary, b. 1871, d. 1874

INGRAM, Paynter C., ssw-Naomi L., b. 08/10/1906, d. 01/31/1961

INGRAM, Ralph, ssw-Bertha M., b. 08/27/1906, d. 10/08/1906

INGRAM, Ruth Ann, ssw-Frank R., b. 01/17/1935, d. N/D

INGRAM, Sarah Ann, ssw-Anthony, Eliza Jane, Nathaniel T., William R. C., Jacob, Ann Virginia, Babe, Ollie May & Mary, b. 1822, d. 1864

INGRAM, Smart R., w/o Nathaniel, Age 44y 1m 21d. b. N/D, d. 03/15/1862

INGRAM, Virginia M., ssw-W. Wood, b. 10/18/1920, d. N/D

INGRAM, W. Wood, ssw-Virginia M., b. 07/27/1917, d. 12/08/1989

INGRAM, William R. C., ssw-Anthony, Sarah Ann, Eliza Jane, Nathaniel T., Jacob, Ann Virginia, Babe, Ollie May & Mary, b. 1861, d. 1862

INGRAM, Wilson S., ssw-Hilda Louise, b. 11/27/1916, d. 05/09/1979

JACKSON, Frank L., b. 11/02/1873, d. 02/11/1933

JACKSON, Levi H., Co. 1, 5 MD Inf., Civil War, b. N/D, d. N/D

JACKSON, Matthew Ryan, b. 04/18/1980, d. 04/18/1980

JACKSON, Wesley, FIFER, 5 MD INF., Civil War, b. N/D, d. N/D

JEFFERSON, Bertha C., ssw-Otis P., b. 1895, d. 1985

JEFFERSON, Davis C., ssw-Estella J., b. 1894, d. 1971

JEFFERSON, Emma C., ssw-H. Lester, b. 08/25/1911, d. N/D

JEFFERSON, Emma Farens, ssw-Harry R., b. 03/23/1865, d. 06/27/1949

JEFFERSON, Estella J., ssw-Davis C., b. 1896, d. 1972

JEFFERSON, H. Lester, ssw-Emma C., b. 08/08/1907, d. 01/19/1989

JEFFERSON, Harry R., ssw-Emma Farens, b. 03/05/1874, d. 10/13/1937

JEFFERSON, Harry R., ssw-Mildred C., b. 07/05/1910, d. 01/13/1974
JEFFERSON, Josephine, ssw-William P., b. 1867, d. 1951
JEFFERSON, Kinmoth N., b. 1894, d. 1924
JEFFERSON, Leah J., ssw-William P., b. 10/17/1833, d. 06/15/1907
JEFFERSON, Marshall, DE, Tec5, Co. M. 60 Inf., 9 Inf. Div., WWII, b. 07/02/1919, d. 09/03/1961
JEFFERSON, Mildred C., ssw-Harry R., b. 08/31/1908, d. 01/21/1971
JEFFERSON, Otis D., b. 1893, d. 1893
JEFFERSON, Otis D., Rev., ssw-Bertha C., b. 1896, d. 1963
JEFFERSON, William P., ssw-Josephine, b. 1857, d. 1931
JEFFERSON, William P., ssw-Leah J., b. 05/11/1828, d. 11/08/1906
JESTER, Jennifer Lyn, "Stillborn," b. 06/02/1979, d. 06/02/1979
JOHNSON, Barbara Marie, b. 05/02/1954, d. 01/10/1974
JOHNSON, Carrie B., ssw-Horace C., b. 02/04/1912, d. N/D
JOHNSON, Carrie R., w/o James S., b. 05/30/1876, d. 12/15/1920
JOHNSON, Florence M., b. 12/21/1892, d. 10/20/1937
JOHNSON, George L., ssw-Lena H., b. 08/06/1898, d. 11/05/1971
JOHNSON, Horace C., ssw-Carrie B., b. 03/30/1911, d. 12/07/1985
JOHNSON, Lena H., ssw-George L., b. 10/01/1900, d. 06/11/1968
JONES, Charles Edward, ssw-Emma, b. 10/08/1857, d. 07/05/1929
JONES, David W., ssw-Charles Edward, b. 10/04/1854, d. 02/14/1929
JONES, Elizabeth E., ssw-Robert C., b. 09/19/1893, d. 10/27/1941
JONES, Emma, w/o Charles Edward, ssw-Charles Edward, b. 01/15/1865, d. 11/23/1951
JONES, Ethel, d/o T. W. & N. W., b. 1898, d. 1898
JONES, George Griffith, s/o Henry B. & Eliza J., ssw-Theodore W., b. 08/08/1855, d. 09/12/1917
JONES, Harry M., b. 06/13/1898, d. 09/07/1971
JONES, Helen M., ssw-John C., b. 1921, d. 1994
JONES, John C., ssw-Helen M., b. 1911, d. N/D
JONES, Marie, b. 04/03/1925, d. 06/23/1980
JONES, Mary C., ssw-William H. Bennett, b. 12/01/1845, d. 06/08/1906
JONES, Mary E., w/o James H., b. 01/04/1853, d. 10/40/1906
JONES, Mary Elizabeth, w/o William W., ssw-William W., b. 11/05/1854, d. 08/05/1916
JONES, Nancy W. Clifton, w/o Theodore W., ssw-Theodore W., b. 09/08/1862, d. 02/06/1955
JONES, Robert C., ssw-Elizabeth E., b. 01/25/1887, d. 09/24/1964
JONES, Robert C., Jr., b. 09/23/1922, d. 04/16/1963
JONES, Theodore W., s/o Henry B. & Eliza J., ssw-Nancy W., b. 02/18/1852, d. 11/30/1924
JONES, Theodore W., Jr., s/o Theo. W. & Nancy W., b. 12/07/1899, d. 09/09/1936
JONES, William W., ssw-Mary Elizabeth, b. 07/20/1852, d. 12/07/1887
KEMP, Clarence E., ssw-Elizabeth R., b. 12/08/1900, d. 12/04/1956
KEMP, Elizabeth R., ssw-Clarence E., b. 01/06/1900, d. 09/07/1972
KENTON, Barbara A., ssw-Lawrence M., b. 09/21/1942, d. N/D
KENTON, Lawrence M., ssw-Barbara A., b. 02/11/1939, d. N/D
KOLODZIEJ, Anna, b. 1917, d. 1987
LANK, Margaret W., ssw-Robert W., b. 12/23/1862, d. 03/24/1927
LANK, Robert W., ssw-Margaret W., b. 09/17/1858, d. 01/05/1916
LARSEN, Gladys T., ssw-Paul M., Sr., b. 04/18/1908, d. 02/27/1982
LARSEN, Harvey William, SSgt., USA, Korea & Vietnam, b. 05/11/1932, d. 03/03/1979
LARSEN, James E., b. 10/10/1943, d. 03/17/1967
LARSEN, Paul M., Sr., ssw-Gladys T., b. 08/13/1908, d. 09/07/1981

LAWSON, Mary A., b. 02/28/1867, d. 09/20/1942

LAWSON, William J., b. 01/13/1861, d. 03/23/1935

LEVERAGE, Mannie, d/o Robert & Mary, b. 05/23/1882, d. 12/03/1900

LEVERAGE, Mary A., ssw-R. Norton, b. 02/28/1914, d. N/D

LEVERAGE, Mary J., w/o Robert, b. 07/15/1846, d. 09/17/1918

LEVERAGE, R. Norton, ssw-Mary A., b. 04/02/1915, d. N/D

LEVERAGE, Robert J., ssw-Mary J., b. 05/01/1841, d. 03/05/1925

MARKER, Bessie V., ssw-Cora R., b. 02/06/1887, d. 05/25/1932

MARKER, Cora R., w/o Jos. F. & d/o John D. & Sallie Messick, b. 08/09/1876, d. 07/18/1904

MARKER, Edith C., ssw-Cora R., b. 06/28/1919, d. 03/17/1943

MARKER, John F., ssw-Cora R., b. 10/11/1874, d. 01/27/1958

MARTIN, John J., PA, SSgt., Co. A., 25 AVMD Engrs., WWII, b. 03/02/1916, d. 01/25/1965

MARTIN, Sarah E. Morgan, s/o John J., b. 03/04/1916, d. 06/20/1992

MCCLUNE, Bessie E., ssw-James, b. 1905, d. 1948

MCCLUNE, James, ssw-Bessie E., b. 1888, d. 1960

MCCLUNE, Richard J., ssw-Bessie E., b. 1936, d. 1936

MCDANIEL, Baby, b. 07/29/1940, d. 07/29/1940

MCDOWEN, Eliz. May Prettyman, b. 09/19/1886, d. 12/17/1955

MELLON, Dorothy Argo, b. 06/19/1926, d. 07/21/1977

MELLON, Thomas P., b. 01/05/1924, d. N/D

MELVIN, No other information

MESSICK, Adelaide, ssw-Nehemiah J., b. N/D, d. 04/03/1876

MESSICK, Arthur R., b. 05/14/1910, d. 08/04/1978

MESSICK, Charles Vennel, ssw-Nehemiah J., Age 9y, b. N/D, d. N/D

MESSICK, Elmer H., ssw-Mildred E., b. 01/18/1901, d. 10/03/1982

MESSICK, Essie Townsend, d/o Joseph & Hettie A., b. 06/21/1880, d. 07/12/1880

MESSICK, Herbert Willis, Age 11m 4d, b. N/D, d. 10/23/1862

MESSICK, Hester A., w/o Josephus, b. 03/11/1834, d. 04/23/1903

MESSICK, Inf. d/o John D. & Sallie P., Age 5wks, b. N/D, d. 07/02/1893

MESSICK, John D., b. 05/02/1844, d. 07/04/1920

MESSICK, Josephus, ssw-Hester A., b. 1830, d. 1904

MESSICK, Lila Hope, b. 10/11/1985, d. 10/11/1985

MESSICK, Lizzie Harden, ssw-Nehemiah J., b. N/D, d. 03/21/1876

MESSICK, Mary Hill, Age 4y 6m 18d, b. N/D, d. 11/23/1870

MESSICK, Mary Jane, w/o Nehemiah J., ssw-Nehemiah J., b. 10/08/1844, d. 01/11/1923

MESSICK, Mildred E., ssw-Elmer H., b. 12/03/1906, d. 06/02/1996

MESSICK, Nehemiah, Age 63y 7m 13d, b. N/D, d. 07/03/1866

MESSICK, Nehemiah J., ssw-Mary Jane, b. 05/29/1835, d. 04/10/1909

MESSICK, Patience K., ssw-Nehemiah J., b. 10/18/1811, d. 05/01/1890

MESSICK, Ruth H., b. 10/02/1917, d. 09/10/1986

MESSICK, Sallie P., w/o John D., b. 05/15/1849, d. 12/08/1919

MILBY, Howard A., ssw-Lois R., b. 01/31/1916, d. 05/24/1968

MILBY, Lois R., ssw-Howard A., b. 12/23/1925, d. N/D

MILLMAN, Annie L., ssw-Samuel S., b. 10/31/1869, d. 09/27/1958

MILLMAN, David S., b. 12/22/1859, d. 02/07/1918

MILLMAN, Gerald B., ssw-R. Carolyn, m. 07/06/1963, b. 1944, d. N/D

MILLMAN, R. Carolyn, ssw-Gerald B., m. 07/06/1963, b. 1945, d. 1971

MILLMAN, Samuel S., ssw-Annie L., b. 12/08/1858, d. 08/04/1932

MILLS, Baby Boy, b. 01/11/1973, d. 01/11/1973

MILLS, Dorothy M., ssw-Gilbert, b. 05/03/1928, d. N/D

MILLS, Gilbert, ssw-Dorothy M., b. 11/05/1923, d. 10/16/1976

MINNER, Baby Boy, b. 01/20/1972, d. 01/20/1972

MINNER, Roger, b. 12/04/1932, d. 10/11/1991

MITCHELL, Alfred R., ssw-Mildred E., b. 04/07/1911, d. 01/30/1981

MITCHELL, Cora May, b. 1886, d. 1939

MITCHELL, Lorenzo, b. 1875, d. 1944

MITCHELL, Mildred E., ssw-Alfred R., b. 02/25/1921, d. N/D

MONET, Benjamin, s/o Benjamin & Sarah b. N/D, d. 01/27/1858

MONET, Purnel T., Age 7y 7m 4d, b. N/D, d. 08/30/1858

MONET, Sarah M., d/o Benjamin & Sarah, Age 11m 14d, b. N/D, d. 08/29/1858

MOORE, Lee W., ssw-T. Marie, b. 12/24/1936, d. N/D

MOORE, T. Marie, ssw-Lee W., b. 03/17/1936, d. 06/30/1993

MORGAN, Agnes R., ssw-Arthur C., b. 06/27/1895, d. 04/28/1982

MORGAN, Arthur C., ssw-Agnes R., b. 11/04/1889, d. 04/03/1972

MORGAN, Lucius C., "Our Son," Pvt., HQ & HQ Btry., 207th FABN, WWII, b. 1918, d. 1950

MORGAN, Lucius C., Jr., b. 09/07/1948, d. 09/07/1948

MORGAN, Sallie F., ssw-D. Arthur Edwards, b. 01/26/1860, d. 08/09/1901

MORGAN, Sallie I., b. 1860, d. 1901

MORRIS, Esther Draper, ssw-William Wesley, Sr., b. 04/02/1921, d. N/D

MORRIS, William Wesley, Sr., ssw-Esther Draper, b. 03/24/1916, d. 07/29/1992

MURPHY, Clara H., b. 09/13/1907, d. 05/06/1982

MURPHY, Herman R., b. 1904, d. 1952

NLN, Deborah C., b. 09/23/1956, d. 11/24/1956

NORTON, Myron H., b. 1858, d. 1925

O'CONNELL, Clara Edna Miller, b. 10/02/1911, d. 09/18/1993

O'CONNOR, Nellie M., b. 05/13/1905, d. 07/21/1984

PEARCE, Vernon B., b. 02/29/1892, d. 01/10/1951

PENUEL, O. Joseph, ssw-Susan C., b. 05/11/1923, d. N/D

PENUEL, Susan C., ssw-O. Joseph b. 03/28/1924, d. 04/30/1981

PITMAN, Albert, b. 1874, d. 1945

PLUMMER, Charles N., Pvt., USA, WWII, b. 09/11/1916, d. 12/27/1981

PLUMMER, Clarence J., Sr., ssw-Florence E., b. 12/31/1889, d. 03/20/1980

PLUMMER, Florence E., ssw-Clarence J., Sr., b. 08/21/1892, d. 04/17/1966

PONDER, James, b. 1883, d. 1955

PONDER, Linda L., b. 1887, d. 1954

PRETTYMAN, Annie S., w/o W. J., Age 28y 8m 22d, b. N/D, d. 10/26/1878

PRETTYMAN, Annie W., b. 1878, d. 1958

PRETTYMAN, Cora E., ssw-Harry L., b. 09/17/1886, d. 03/22/1955

PRETTYMAN, George H., ssw-Maggie H., b. 10/20/1866, d. 08/25/1936

PRETTYMAN, Harry B., Father, b. 1892, d. 1948

PRETTYMAN, Harry L, ssw-Cora E., b. 05/03/1886, d. 04/14/1972

PRETTYMAN, John B., ssw-Sarah C., b. 10/26/1848, d. 04/16/1917

PRETTYMAN, Joseph Pierce, b. 07/13/1891, d. 10/14/1943

PRETTYMAN, Lewis W., ssw-Mary S., b. 11/13/1853, d. 07/23/1922

PRETTYMAN, Maggie H., ssw-George H., b. 03/27/1872, d. 08/21/1922

PRETTYMAN, Mary Jane, ssw-William J., b. 1851, d. 1918

PRETTYMAN, Mary S., ssw-Lewis W., b. 11/23/1862, d. 05/18/1933

PRETTYMAN, Sarah C., ssw-John B., b. 03/16/1853, d. 06/15/1937

PRETTYMAN, William Burton, s/o Harry B. & Ella, b. 01/10/1915, d. 06/16/1920

PRETTYMAN, William J., ssw-Mary Jane, b. 1851, d. 1910

PURKS, Elizabeth B. Bennett, ssw-William A., b. 1890, d. 1981

PURKS, William A., ssw-Elizabeth B. Bennett, b. 1874, d. 1946

PURNELL, Mary W., d/o Sila & Elizabeth, Age 20y 6m, b. N/D, d. 07/06/1863

RATLEDGE, Abbie R., w/o John H., b. 04/08/1845, d. 08/18/1883

REVELLE, Katherine M., b. 03/27/1930, d. 05/30/1968

REYNOLDS, Annie J., w/o Walter, ssw-David, Eliza R., Herman D. & Walter W., b. 04/07/1882, d. 09/28/1960

REYNOLDS, David, ssw-Eliza R., Annie J., Herman D. & Walter W., Father, b. 09/06/1848, d. 08/10/1899

REYNOLDS, Elie Edwin, b. 02/10/1862, d. 01/01/1937

REYNOLDS, Eliza R., w/o David, ssw-Annie J., David, Herman D. & Walter W., b. 02/10/1859, d. 11/18/1894

REYNOLDS, Emma H., ssw-Ernest L., b. 1893, d. 1977

REYNOLDS, Ernest L, ssw-Richard P., b. 1921, d. 1948

REYNOLDS, Francis W., s/o Myers & Mary J., b. 05/11/1863, d. 10/08/1899

REYNOLDS, Herman D., ssw-David, Annie J., Eliza R. & Walter W., Brother, Supply Co., 20th Inf. Camp Funston, KS, b. 01/17/1890, d. 10/15/1918

REYNOLDS, Mary J., ssw-Myers, b. 01/01/1825, d. 12/24/1899

REYNOLDS, Myers, ssw-Mary J., b. 01/08/1822, d. 11/21/1884

REYNOLDS, Richard J., b. 07/30/1919, d. 07/11/1988

REYNOLDS, Richard P., ssw-Ernest L., b. 1884, d. 1970

REYNOLDS, Roderick, b. 03/08/1850, d. 04/04/1895

REYNOLDS, Walter W., ssw-David, Annie J., Eliza R. & Herman D., b. 05/10/1882, d. 09/12/1945

ROACH, Ada L., ssw-Sarah J. Barden, b. N/D, d. 05/29/1945

ROACH, Alfred K., b. 1855, d. 1924

ROACH, Alice Willis, d/o William & Rosalee, b. 02/17/1867, d. 08/11/1882

ROACH, Catherine, ssw-Thomas, b. 03/16/1812, d. 02/25/1897

ROACH, Charles N., ssw-Josephine, b. 08/26/1858, d. 03/05/1925

ROACH, David S., ssw-Martha J., b. 1846, d. 03/15/1927

ROACH, Edward, b. 09/04/1821, d. 06/20/1896

ROACH, Ethel R., b. 11/29/1903, d. 12/16/1984

ROACH, Fannie T., b. 1856, d. 1893

ROACH, George B., ssw-Thomas, Age 52y, b. N/D, d. 12/01/1890

ROACH, George B., Age 4y 7m 24d, b. N/D, d. N/D

ROACH, Hannah Emma, w/o Theodore, b. 05/25/1853, d. 04/01/1942

ROACH, Harry B., b. 06/30/1872, d. 09/07/1951

ROACH, Harvey W., s/o Chas. N. & Josephine, b. 09/11/1888, d. 02/14/1914

ROACH, Hettie M., b. 03/06/1878, d. 07/24/1856

ROACH, Horace B., s/o William & Rosalee, b. 05/30/1868, d. 09/18/1895

ROACH, Infant Daughter, Age 4 m, b. N/D, d. N/D

ROACH, James, DE, Co. C., 9th Inf., b. N/D, d. N/D

ROACH, James H., b. 05/03/1835, d. 11/04/1885

ROACH, Josephine, ssw-Charles N.., b. 10/24/1867, d. 01/11/1930

ROACH, Marshall T., b. 03/25/1899, d. 06/20/1941

ROACH, Martha J., ssw-David S., b. 07/09/1847, d. 03/17/1920

ROACH, Mary Ann Hargis, w/o Robert, b. 02/26/1834, d. 01/24/1892

ROACH, Oscar B., b. 05/08/1884, d. 08/27/1903

ROACH, Rachel N., Former w/o Josiah H. Smith, b. 03/08/1822, d. 07/07/1893

ROACH, Ralton C., s/o Chas. N. & Josephine, Age 5m, b. N/D, d. 09/22/1904

ROACH, Robert, b. 08/02/1829, d. 01/04/1905

ROACH, Robert D., b. 03/08/1902, d. 09/01/1923

ROACH, Sarah J., ssw-Thomas J., b. 12/22/1856, d. 11/10/1925

ROACH, Theodore H., ssw-Thomas, b. 01/26/1849, d. 12/16/1930

ROACH, Thomas, ssw-Catherine, b. 01/13/1799, d. 11/06/1875

ROACH, Thomas J., ssw-Sarah J., b. 05/30/1849, d. 11/12/1904

ROBINSON, Bessie E., b. 1880, d. 1941

ROBINSON, Clara Draper, ssw-Roy W., b. 10/01/1918, d. N/D

ROBINSON, Roy W., ssw-Clara Draper, b. 08/26/1920, d. 05/11/1996

ROGERS, Grace Darby, b. 11/30/1920, d. 04/26/1986

RUSSELL, Jennie L., ssw-Willis T., b. 10/01/1876, d. 07/14/1949

RUSSELL, Mary G., w/o William Russell, b. 02/29/1846, d. 06/28/1918

RUSSELL, William, ssw-Mary G., Age 62y 5d, b. N/D, d. 05/20/1904

RUSSELL, Willis T., ssw-Jennie L., b. 08/09/1868, d. 02/16/1944

RUTT, Frank K., ssw-Mary J., b. 1864, d. 1943

RUTT, Mary J., ssw-Frank K., b. 1867, d. 1950

SALMONS, Elizabeth D., w/o James, b. 01/23/1803, d. 07/23/1870

SALMONS, James, Age 45y 4m 20d, b. 03/11/1804, d. 08/12/1850

SALMONS, Rhoda R., w/o Thomas J., Age 35y 9m 20d, b. N/D, d. 05/01/1869

SANDERSON, James F., ssw-Lucy H., b. 10/25/1918, d. N/D

SANDERSON, Lucy H., ssw-James F., b. 01/31/1920, d. 01/06/1983

SCHURMAN, Raymond, SSgt., USAAC, WWII, b. 08/12/1920, d. 08/14/1992

SCHURMAN, Robert, b. 1921, d. 1987

SHEPARD, Alexander D., ssw-Alice N., b. 12/18/1871, d. 11/19/1946

SHEPARD, Alice N., ssw-Alexander D., b. 05/31/1870, d. 03/12/1958

SHEPARD, Joseph W., s/o Joseph & Maggie, Age 10m 19d, b. N/D, d. 06/10/1860

SHEPARD, Maggie, w/o Joseph K., Age 19y 2m 19d, b. N/D, d. 08/04/1859

SHEPPARD, Joseph B., b. 06/27/1828, d. 12/19/1896

SHEPPARD, Lydia S., b. 09/26/1840, d. 09/28/1916

SHEPPARD, Mabel M. Wilkins, b. 1901, d. 1973

SHERMAN, Charles R., s/o Donald Messick & Millie Sherman, b. 07/09/1967, d. 07/11/1967

SHOCKLEY, Elizabeth, Relict o/William, Age 72y, b. N/D, d. 05/19/1868

SHOCKLEY, Elizabeth B., d/o William & Elizabeth, Age 4y 7m 6d, b. N/D, d. 12/20/1833

SHOCKLEY, William, Age 576 3m 13d, b. N/D, d. 12/30/1863

SHORT, Martha E. Watson Milby, ssw-Lemuel S. Watson, b. 1869, d. 1944

SIMPSON, Elizabeth Nancy, b. 07/31/1895, d. 12/21/1963

SMITH, Celia A., b. 1855, d. 1898

SMITH, Job, ssw-Sarah J., b. 06/02/1837, d. 04/27/1919

SMITH, Mae R., ssw-Ralph R., b. 02/16/1912, d. 12/22/1985

SMITH, Ralph R., ssw-Mae R., b. 06/25/1912, d. N/D

SMITH, Sarah J., ssw-Job, b. 08/15/1844, d. 12/27/1918

SPENCER, Annie, b. 1901, d. 1970

STEEN, Belle D., ssw-Steward H., Betty B. & Donald T., b. 1886, d. 1981

STEEN, Betty B., ssw-Steward H., Belle D. & Donald T., b. 1920, d. 1926

STEEN, Donald T., ssw-Steward H., Belle D. & Betty D., b. 1911, d. 1991
STEEN, Eliza J., ssw-Hiram J., b. 02/01/1856, d. 05/02/1939
STEEN, Hiram J., ssw-Eliza J., b. 05/18/1862, d. 01/25/1922
STEEN, Steward H., ssw-Belle D., Betty B. & Donald T., b. 1889, d. 1973
STEVENSON, Charles R., ssw-Ella F., b. 10/28/1862, d. 07/05/1955
STEVENSON, Charles Reese, b. 12/11/1926, d. 04/16/1975
STEVENSON, Ella F., ssw-Charles R., b. 03/04/1874, d. 03/15/1947
STEVENSON, Joanna B., w/o Samuel E., ssw-Samuel E., b. 10/26/1864, d. 09/17/1913
STEVENSON, Millie Gertrude, d/o Charles R. & Ella F., b. 05/09/1903, d. 03/21/1904
STEVENSON, Robert W., b. 01/18/1867, d. 04/04/1918
STEVENSON, Samuel E., ssw-Joanna B., b. 02/01/1858, d. 11/12/1912
STORMER, Hilda C., b. 05/28/1887, d. 11/28/1976
STORMER, Jacob J., b. 01/05/1886, d. 01/23/1959
STORMER, Joseph A., Jr., ssw-Louisa & Joseph A., Sr., b. 1895, d. 1928
STORMER, Joseph A., Sr., ssw-Louisa & Joseph A., Jr., b. 1860, d. 1928
STORMER, Louisa, ssw-Joseph A., Jr., & Joseph A., Sr., b. 11/14/1859, d. 09/12/1918
SWIFT, Betty, ssw-James, b. 1921, d. N/D
SWIFT, James, ssw-Betty, b. 1913, d. 1992
TAYLOR, Albert E., ssw-Vera M., b. 10/07/1916, d. N/D
TAYLOR, Vera M., ssw-Albert E., b. 01/28/1920, d. 12/13/1983
TEAS, Annie Stockley, b. 11/12/1880, d. 09/19/1916
TEAS, George H., b. 01/16/1851, d. 03/19/1912
TEAS, John, b. 10/21/1814, d. 11/21/1889
TEAS, Mercy B., b. 08/30/1812, d. 01/13/1886
TEAS, Sarah Emily, w/o George H., b. 10/12/1855, d. 07/19/1896
TODD, Jane, w/o Charles, Age 39y, b. N/D, d. 09/02/1843
TOWNSEND, Mary, w/o Purnell, Age 56y 7m 10d, b. N/D, d. 02/07/1865
TOWNSEND, Purnell, Age 61y 6m 1d, b. N/D, d. 11/19/1850
TRUITT, David R., Age 76y 2m 17d, b. 09/15/1811, d. 12/02/1867
TRUITT, Elsie M., ssw-Lloyd F., b. 1898, d. 1973
TRUITT, George W., s/o Benjamin & Nancy, b. 10/22/1806, d. 07/28/1899
TRUITT, John A., ssw-Mabel E., b. 1882, d. 1965
TRUITT, John S., ssw-Rachel C., b. 01/06/1846, d. 03/06/1934
TRUITT, Joseph M., b. 10/23/1889, d. 01/26/1970
TRUITT, Lloyd F., ssw-Elsie M., b. 1903, d. 1958
TRUITT, Mabel E., ssw-John A., b. 1887, d. 1946
TRUITT, Rachel C., ssw-John S., b. 09/10/1844, d. 04/24/1932
TRUITT, Rhoda, w/o Benjamin, Age 86y 8m 12d, b. 05/07/1776, d. 01/29/1862
TRUITT, Sallie, w/o George W., b. 11/21/1807, d. 01/08/1887
TRUITT, William, b. 1869, d. 1937
VINES, Ralph E., Sr., Sgt., USA, WWII, b. 08/02/1914, d. 03/14/1986
VINES, Virginia A., b. 08/27/1915, d. 02/11/1988
WALKER, Carlton V., Sgt., USA, WWII, b. 08/09/1917, d. 02/06/1982
WALKER, Clarence W., ssw-Maria E., b. 09/11/1904, d. 10/06/1984
WALKER, Maria E., ssw-Clarence W., b. N/D, d. N/D
WALKER, Mary Bryan, b. 06/29/1932, d. 05/23/1983
WALLS, Alfred, Jr., b. 06/19/1924, d. 06/10/1969
WALLS, Alfred B., b. 03/04/1871, d. 07/04/1946

WALLS, Annie E., b. 03/12/1873, d. 11/01/1951

WALLS, Chester R., b. 02/09/1912, d. 03/25/1949

WALLS, Edith M., ssw-Howard A., b. 07/22/1918, d. 08/31/1951

WALLS, Elsie Lawson, ssw-Leroy F., b. 1923, d. N/D

WALLS, Frederick A., ssw-Mary Jane, b. 1873, d. 1954

WALLS, George P., s/o Fred A. & Molly J., b. 06/27/1902, d. 12/18/1908

WALLS, Howard A., ssw-Edith M., b. 02/22/1901, d. 08/23/1981

WALLS, John H., b. 09/20/1868, d. 03/25/1916

WALLS, Lawrence H., b. 1892, d. 1949

WALLS, Leroy F., ssw-Elsie Lawson, b. 1915, d. 1968

WALLS, Mary Jane, ssw-Frederick A., b. 1876, d. 1953

WALLS, Ruth Janette, b. 02/06/1935, d. 07/04/1939

WALLS, Sallie E., ssw-William J., b. 01/01/1885, d.07/26/1947

WALLS, William J., ssw-Sallie E., b. 10/15/1864, d. 10/28/1957

WALLS, Willie T., s/o John H. & Annie E., b. 12/12/1899, d. 06/30/1900

WARREN, Amandus B., b. 03/22/1881, d. 10/07/1953

WARREN, Bennett, ssw-C. Emily, b. 10/12/1822, d. 09/24/1899

WARREN, C. Emily, ssw-Bennett, b. 09/16/1842, d. 01/19/1915

WARREN, Clarence B., b. 03/17/1876, d. 05/16/1965

WARREN, Lina Boyce Clifton, b. 10/04/1877, d. 08/29/1942

WARRINGTON, Elizabeth J., ssw-Richard C., b. 07/23/1936, d. N/D

WARRINGTON, James L., ssw-Mary E., b. 04/04/1854, d. 1936

WARRINGTON, Mary E., w/o James L., b. 09/15/1854, d. 11/17/1902

WARRINGTON, Richard C., ssw-Elizabeth J., b. 06/24/1929, d. N/D

WATSON, Bertha M., Wife, b. 04/19/1877, d. 04/11/1968

WATSON, C. Dale, Son, b. 12/19/1910, d. 12/11/1989

WATSON, Clarence Y., Husband, b. 05/03/1875, d. 05/23/1969

WATSON, Elizabeth, ssw-Henry S., b. 1828, d. 1895

WATSON, Frank D., ssw-Mary E., b. 01/08/1857, d. 01/31/1939

WATSON, Hannah, b. 12/17/1794, d. 12/07/1879

WATSON, Henry S., ssw-Elizabeth, b. 1821, d. 1909

WATSON, Lemuel S., ssw-Martha E. Watson Milby Short, b. 04/28/1861, d. 04/22/1920

WATSON, Mary E., ssw-Frank D., b. 09/30/1854, d. 12/10/1942

WATSON, Sarah E., Mother, b. 1853, d. 1937

WEBB, Bertha C., ssw-Charles O., b. 02/13/1884, d. 04/17/1963

WEBB, Charles O., ssw-Bertha C., b. 08/09/1879, d. 12/01/1956

WEBB, Charley Clay, s/o Charles O. & Bertha, b. 12/05/1903, d. 09/26/1918

WEBB, Edward I., ssw-Mayme G., b. 04/25/1895, d. 07/26/1970

WEBB, Mayme G., ssw-Edward I., b. 09/08/1900, d. 03/17/1991

WEBB, Sheldon E., Sr., b. 07/30/1919, d. 10/22/1984

WELLS, Anna J., ssw-Marshall E., b. 08/13/1916, d. 04/23/1992

WELLS, Marshall E., ssw-Anna J., b. 04/01/1918, d. 06/11/1992

WELSH, Elizabeth, b. 10/04/1800, d. 12/15/1855

WHITE, Clara H., ssw-Harry S., b. 02/10/1912, d. 07/06/1948

WHITE, Harry S., ssw-Clara H., b. 12/03/1901, d. N/D

WILKINS, Alex Lester, b. 1904, d. 1934

WILKINS, Alexander, b. 11/24/1861, d. 01/31/1943

WILKINS, Anna Jane, w/o Charles & d/o John D. & Sallie Messick, Age 26y 2m 7d, b. N/D, d. 02/16/1892

WILKINS, Sallie L., w/o Alexander, b. 03/07/1867, d. 11/23/1907
WILSON, Annie B., ssw-Robert R., b. 11/15/1875, d. 01/04/1929
WILSON, Annie S., w/o George H., b. 04/15/1855, d. 12/24/1881
WILSON, Bertha May, d/o Robt. R. & Annie B., b. 03/23/1880, d. 08/09/1881
WILSON, Frances C., b. 1925, d. 1952
WILSON, G. Edward, b. 1910, d. 1975
WILSON, George, ssw-Sarah J., b. 02/04/1820, d. 08/10/1895
WILSON, Harry, ssw-Victor, b. 12/14/1873, d. 06/30/1880
WILSON, Marvin, b. 06/08/1932, d. 06/08/1932
WILSON, Robert R., ssw-Annie B., b. 07/12/1857, d. 06/08/1922
WILSON, S. Richard, b. 10/27/1902, d. 12/30/1964
WILSON, Sarah J., ssw-George, b. 11/27/1824, d. 11/07/1909
WILSON, Stella D., ssw-William T., b. 10/29/1881, d. 09/10/1962
WILSON, Victor, ssw-Harry, b. 05/06/1879, d. 07/14/1881
WILSON, Warrington O., Age 65y 2m 20d, b. 12/10/1799, d. 03/20/1864
WILSON, William T., ssw-Stella D., b. 05/05/1876, d. 11/10/1939
ZOOK, Barbara C., ssw-David M., b. 02/22/1919, d. 09/28/1973
ZOOK, David M., ssw-Barbara C., b. 04/17/1911, d. 03/11/1975

The following stones were recorded by the Hudson Survey but are now missing or unreadable:
BENNETT, Walter, b. 10/13/1883, d. 07/08/1886
DRAPER, Elizabeth, d/o Thomas & Mary C., b. 01/24/1824, d. 02/14/1883
DRAPER, George, s/o George H. & Ella, b. 03/25/1886, d. 05/02/1889
DRAPER, Mary C., w/o Thomas, Age 53y, b. N/D, d. 11/19/1844
DRAPER, Ruth Ann, w/o Thomas, Jr., Age 18y 6m 1d, b. N/D, d. 09/01/1852
DRAPER, Thomas, Age 20y 11m 17d, b. N/D, d. 12/09/1844
DRAPER, Thomas, Age 77y 10m 24d, b. N/D, d. 10/25/1853
RATLEDGE, Walter Draper, s/o John H. & Abbie R., b. 08/11/1872, d. 12/13/1875
REYNOLDS, George, b. 02/21/1845, d. 10/11/1917
REYNOLDS, Martha M., w/o George, b. 02/24/1856, d. 05/28/1876
ROACH, Eliza R., w/o David, b. 02/10/1859, d. 11/18/1894
ROACH, Herman D., b. 01/17/1890, d. 10/15/1918
SALMONS, James, b. 01/03/1803, d. 07/11/1870
SALMONS, Thomas J., Age 35y 9m 20d, b. N/D, d. 05/01/1869
SMITH, Mary W., d/o Silas & Elizabeth, Age 20y 6m, b. N/D, d.07/06/1863

CC-003 & HU-NR) MT. ZION A. M. E. CHURCH CEMETERY
Located in Ellendale on the North side of Milton-Ellendale Highway (Rt. 16) approximately 0.3 miles East
of Du Pont Boulevard (Rt. 113)
Recorded: September 4, 996

ALEXANDER, Stella, b. 1928, d. 1996
ALL, Estella, b. 01/12/1909, d. 02/24/1990
COLEMAN, Ellsworth, Jr., Rev., b. 1944, d. 1994
DOLCE, Seclarie, b. 1956, d. 1993
DRUMMOND, Roland, b. 1924, d. 1995
GIBSON, DaCraig A., b. 02/01/1963, d. 07/15/1994
GIBSON, Dorothy Henry, ssw-Douglas A., b. 04/16/1929, d. N/D

GIBSON, Douglas A., ssw-Dorothy Henry, b. 02/28/1923, d. N/D
GREEN, James T., b. 1936, d. 1995
HARMON, Nelson E., b. 08/22/1938, d. 07/16/1991
HURST, Gregory M., b. 02/01/1960, d. 03/05/1990
REYNOLDS, Susie, b. 1961, d. 1995
STRAND, Blanche, b. 01/05/1920, d. 01/07/1991
VICKERS, Ella, b. 10/24/1902, d. 09/02/1990
WHITE, Missouri, ssw-Morgan, m. 06/02/1935, b. 10/17/1917, d. 06/02/1994
WHITE, Morgan, ssw-Missouri, m. 06/02/1935, b. 09/22/1914, d. 04/16/1990
WILLIAMS, Chester M., ssw-Mildred B., b. 09/18/1922, d. N/D
WILLIAMS, Mildred B., ssw-Chester M., b. 02/06/1925, d. 01/23/1994
WILLIAMS, Ronald D., USA Paratrooper, b. 06/27/1960, d. 02/14/1992

(CC-004 & HU-164) NEW MARKET CEMETERY

Located East of Ellendale on the South side of Reynolds Pont Rd. (Rd. 231) approximately 200 feet west of Holly Tree Rd. (Rd. 226)
Recorded: October 3, 1996

ABBOTT, Alfred, Co. C., 9th DE Inf., b. 04/24/1830, d. 12/19/1888
ABBOTT, David H., b. 12/03/1862, d. 09/10/1881
ABBOTT, Elizabeth, w/o James, ssw-James, b. 1845, d. 1928
ABBOTT, George A., Age 34y 4m 16d, b. N/D, d. 07/21/1872
ABBOTT, George F., Age 73y 2m 3d, b. N/D, d. 10/18/1906
ABBOTT, George R., s/o William & Mary J., b. 03/07/1860, d. 05/04/1896
ABBOTT, James, ssw-Elizabeth, b. 1842, d. 1919
ABBOTT, John H., b. 1857, d. 1931
ABBOTT, John T., b. 09/19/1861, d. 02/05/1887
ABBOTT, Mary E., w/o Geo. A., Age 42y 4m 20d, b. N/D, d. 08/10/1882
ABBOTT, Matilda, w/o Geo. F., Age 53y 11m 20d, b. N/D, d. 06/29/1892
ABBOTT, Minos L., s/o William & Mary J., b. 07/29/1856, d. 01/03/1877
ABBOTT, William, b. 08/23/1831, d. 02/17/1882
BAKER, Elias, Age 57y 10m 25d, b. N/D, d. 01/09/1821
BAKER, Elias B., b. 06/16/1820, d. 12/23/1900
BAKER, Naomi, wid/o Rev. Elias, Age 77y 11m 2d, b. N/D, d. 05/21/1857
BEIDEMAN, Elixena, d/o William & Julia H., b. 07/08/1852, d. 10/26/1863
BENSON, Clara May, b. 12/23/1892, d. 07/15/1893
BENSON, Fannie, d/o W. S. & M. E., b. 09/21/1875, d. 01/09/1876
BENSON, Sallie, d/o W. S. & M. E., b. 11/04/1870, d. 08/11/1875
BRITTINGHAM, Elizabeth, b. 06/19/1805, d. 12/17/1885
BRITTINGHAM, John, b. 09/26/1802, d. 05/18/1855
CLENDANIEL, Ella, d/o John H. & Sarah J., b. 07/21/1884, d. 07/23/1884
CLENDANIEL, J. A., 3rd, DE Inf., Co. C., b. N/D, d. N/D
CLENDANIEL, James L, s/o John H. & Sarah J., b. 10/18/1860, d. 08/11/1866
CLENDANIEL, John H., s/o Benjamin & Catherine, b. 06/16/1839, d. 10/16/1892
CLENDANIEL, Sarah A. Wilkins, w/o John H., b. 04/10/1841, d. 01/20/1912
CLENDANIEL, Sarah C., Sockrider, w/o Willard H., b. 11/21/1865, d. 03/25/1886
COLLINS, James A., b. 05/10/1796, d. 01/29/1876
COLLINS, Katie M., d/o Myres B. & Frances A., b. 07/06/1874, d. 10/12/1901

COLLINS, Kesia, b. 09/19/1803, d. 06/08/1877

DICKERSON, Alanson, Age 40y 6m, b. N/D, d. 12/28/1851

DICKERSON, Jonathan T., Age 22y, b. N/D, d. 04/04/1861

DICKERSON, Wm. J., Age 49y 6m, b. N/D, d. 12/12/1888

DONOVAN, Anna R., w/o Elisha, b. 08/19/1805, d. 02/17/1883

DONOVAN, Annie, w/o Enoch W., b. 04/05/1875, d. 12/29/1899

DONOVAN, Araminta, w/o Wm. H., b. 01/05/1829, d. 05/25/1881

DONOVAN, Bathsheba, d/o Elisha & Anna, b. 06/29/1827, d. 07/23/1870

DONOVAN, Charlie, s/o Wm. H. & Annie, b. 08/01/1868, d. 02/24/1872

DONOVAN, Dorothy, b. 10/01/1924, d. 01/16/1929

DONOVAN, Elisha, s/o Job & Bathsheba, Age 64y 1m 16d, b. N/D, d. 02/23/1863

DONOVAN, Enoch W., ssw-Martha K., b. 12/16/1871, d. 10/17/1957

DONOVAN, Martha K., ssw-Enoch W., b. 12/12/1879, d. 02/17/1969

DONOVAN, Mary E., w/o James H., b. 05/02/1864, d. 03/29/1886

DONOVAN, Mary M., d/o Elisha & Anna, ssw-William H., b. 01/06/1841, d. 02/12/1891

DONOVAN, Rhoda E., b. 08/19/1909, d. 05/25/1921

DONOVAN, William H., s/o Reuben & Sarah, ssw-Mary M., b. 08/15/1829, d. 08/19/1909

ELLINGSWORTH, Salathiel B., s/o James & Annie, Co. E, 9th DE Inf., Age 55y b. N/D. d. 11/03/1892

FISHER, Avis M., ssw-George H., b. 11/30/1843, d. 02/15/1942

FISHER, Comfort, w/o Joseph, Age 91y, b. N/D, d. 02/01/1910

FISHER, George H., ssw-Avis M., b. 12/16/1846, d. 05/22/1913

FISHER, Georgianna, ssw-William S., b. 04/21/1865, d. 09/01/1916

FISHER, Joseph, b. 04/02/1824, d. 09/04/1888

FISHER, William S., ssw-Georgianna, b. 04/19/1865, d. 06/15/1931

FOWLER, Emma J., w/o Geo. M., b. 04/30/1845, d. 10/02/1901

FOWLER, George M., b. 04/18/1845, d. 06/27/1913

FOWLER, Laverna, d/o Geo. M. & Emma J., b. 12/10/1868, d. 01/15/1877

FOWLER, Noah, s/o Noah B. & Phebe, b. 11/13/1847, d. 04/09/1852

FOWLER, Noah B., b. 05/01/1811, d. 03/26/1871

FOWLER, Phebe G., w/o Noah B., Age 76y 10m 10d, b. N/D, d. 07/20/1894

FOWLER, Sallie, d/o Geo. M. & Emma J., b. 02/27/1872, d. 01/08/1877

HEAVELOW, Alfred, b. 10/04/1825, d. 08/23/1877

HEAVELOW, James H., b. 03/25/1837, d. 12/17/1905

HEAVELOW, John, Age 71y 3m 8d, b. N/D, d. 04/23/1870

HEAVELOW, Mary, w/o John, Age 67y 6m 15d, b. N/D, d. 11/01/1870

JEFFERSON, Nancy, w/o Paynter, b. 06/11/1793, d. 06/13/1873

JEFFERSON, Paynter, Age 51y 9m 16d, b. N/D, d. 12/17/1852

JEFFERSON, Samuel B., Age 61y 2m 19d, b. N/D, d. 04/29/1893

JESTER, Sallie C., w/o Samuel, ssw-Samuel, b. 11/13/1840, d. 03/09/1879

JESTER, Samuel, ssw-Sallie C., b. 08/20/1840, d. 02/01/1876

JOHNSON, Wm. A., s/o Purnell & Winnie A., Age 12y 6m 16d, b. N/D, d. 02/03/1875

LOFLAND, Ann, b. 03/13/1812, d. 05/25/1875

LOFLAND, David, b. 07/12/1806, d. 11/29/1973

LOFLAND, John, Age 31y 8m 26d, b. N/D, d. 12/17/1852

LOFLAND, Littleton M., b. 09/23/1820, d. 06/23/1887

LOFLAND, Sarah, b. 02/12/1812, d. 03/20/1873

LOFLAND, Stephen H., s/o John & Martha M., Age 7y 1d, b. N/D, d. 03/25/1845

LYNCH, David L., b. 02/21/1831, d. 08/18/1887

LYNCH, Minos, Rev., Age 60y 7m 6d, b. N/D, d. 08/18/1869

LYNCH, Sarah, w/o Rev. Minos, Age 73y 19d, b. N/D, d. 02/15/1882

MILBY, Nancy, b. 10/11/1814, d. 06/21/1878

MILBY, Peter, Age 72y 4m 20d, b. N/D, d. 06/05/1871

MILBY, William, Age 28y 1m 17d, b. N/D, d. 05/281859

MILLMAN, Ida Ryan, ssw-Joshua L., b. 1869, d. 1925

MILLMAN, Joshua L, ssw-Ida Ryan, b. 1863, d. 1949

MILLMAN, Orpha T., d/o Lazaras & Eunice, b. 06/28/1821, d. 06/29/1906

MILLMAN, Otis, s/o Joshua & Ida C., b. 08/20/1898, d. 05/25/1904

MORRIS, Bivins, ssw-Nellie, Age 85y, b. N/D, d. 06/27/1907

MORRIS, Nellie, w/o Bivins, Age 64y, b. N/D, d. 06/25/1881

PEARCE, Joshua, Age 19y 7m 15d, b. N/D, d. 01/31/1855

PRETTYMAN, Joshua, Age 41y 22d, b. N/D, d. 01/14/1864

REED, Donovan, Age about 82y, b. N/D, d. 08/15/1873

REED, James B., b. 10/05/1816, d. 09/14/1884

REED, Leah, w/o Donovan, Age 69y 4m 15d, b. N/D, d. 07/0/1857

SHOCKLEY, Catharine K., w/o William V., b. 02/02/1819, d. 02/18/1888

SHOCKLEY, Nancy B., w/o Wilson, Age 71y 9m 7d, b. N/D, d. 01/24/1868

SHOCKLEY, William V., Age 65y 6m 8d, b. N/D, d. 08/25/1881

SHOCKLEY, Wilson, Age 68y, b. 11/11/1788, d. 05/05/1856

SHORT, Alfred, b. 11/26/1816, d. 10/20/1905

SHORT, Annie Blanche, d/o John C. & Laura E., b. 07/18/1887, d. 01/23/1899

SHORT, John C., b. 1858, d. 1943

SHORT, Laura E., b. 1861, d. 1932

SHORT, Lydia Estella, b. 11/25/1860, d. 04/12/1911

SHORT, Margaret M., w/o Alfred, b. 04/19/1819, d. 03/26/1896

SHORT, Mary E., b. 08/23/1833, d. 04/17/1928

SHORT, Mary Lovey, d/o Alfred & Margaret M., Age 27y 7m 28d, b. N/D, d. 09/26/1872

SHORT, Willie, s/o Wm. P. & Catherine J., b. 09/18/1878, d. 10/17/1878

VEASEY, Sarah E., w/o Wm. W. & sis/o Alfred & James Heavelow, Age 78y 1m 19d, b. N/D, d. 10/19/1910

WALLS, Burton, Age 68y 6m, b. N/D, d. 09/15/1860

WALLS, Maryam, Consort of Burton, Age 66y, b. N/D, d. 05/29/1858

WARREN, Carrie V., ssw-William H., Emily A. & F. Asbury, b. 1889, d. 1896

WARREN, Eliza A., ssw-William, b. 11/16/1836, d. 12/09/1918

WARREN, Elizabeth, d/o William H. & Ellen, b. 03/25/1889, d. 07/09/1889

WARREN, Emily A., ssw-William H., Carrie V. & F. Asbury, b. 1852, d. 1899

WARREN, F. Asbury, ssw-William H., Carrie V. & Emily A., b. 1850, d. 1925

WARREN, Mary, w/o Wm., b. 07/15/1807, d. 12/20/1886

WARREN, Sarah E., w/o Stephen, b. 03/04/1835, d. 11/01/1909

WARREN, Spicer, Age 66y 3m, b. N/D, d. 11/23/1846

WARREN, William, Age 72y 8m 25d, b. N/D, d. 03/04/1879

WARREN, William, ssw-Eliza A., b. 01/13/1835, d. 12/31/1902

WARREN, William H., ssw-Carrie V., F. Asbury & Emily A., b. 1880, d. 1894

WELCH, Araminta C., w/o Martin, b. 03/16/1860, d. 08/22/1918

WELCH, Carrie G., b. 06/03/1863, d. 10/30/1917

WELCH, George H., ssw-Lydia J., b. 01/23/1833, d. 01/09/1898

WELCH, Inf. d/o Joseph L. & Carrie G., b. 08/06/1897, d. 08/06/1897

WELCH, Joseph L., b. 10/13/1854, d. 10/13/1905

WELCH, Luther M., Age 53y 6m, b. N/D, d. 02/21/1855
WELCH, Lydia J., ssw-George H., b. 03/02/1833, d. 11/07/1904
WELCH, Martin L., ssw-Araminta C., b. 1866, d. 1931
WELSH, Mary, Consort o/Luther M., Age 46y 8m 18d, b. N/D, d. 04/07/1859
WILKINS, Eliza Jane, d/o James & Letty, b. 07/06/1849, d. 04/06/1852
WILKINS, Geo. W., b. 12/07/1876, d. 04/16/1894
WILKINS, James, Age 62y 5m 18d, b. N/D, d. 04/05/1876
WILKINS, Letty, w/o James, b. 01/19/1817, d. 08/19/1869
WILKINS, Rhoda A. Shockley, w/o George W., b. 05/06/1843, d. 03/18/1869
WILSON, Oliver, Age 13y 7m 28d, b. N/D, d. 06/19/1866
WORKMAN, Alonzo M., s/o Phillip & Laura J., b. 01/20/1893, d. 05/26/1894
WORKMAN, Laura J., ssw-Phillip T., b. 11/26/1851, d. 10/24/1938
WORKMAN, Phillip T., ssw-Laura J., b. 06/17/1847, d. 05/02/1921

The following stones were recorded by the Hudson Survey but are now missing or unreadable:
 BENSON, Elizabeth, b. 03/25/1889, d. 07/09/1889
CLENDANIEL, Caroline V., d/o George R., Age 27y 6m 3d, b. N/D, d. 12/09/1884
LOFLAND, David, b. 02/06/1853, d. 04/15/1914
REED, Jane A., w/o James, b. 11/20/1814, d. 08/27/1899
WILKINS, Nancy L., d/o James & Letty, b. 03/27/1848, d. 07/05/1848

(CC-005 & HU-179) UNION CHURCH CEMETERY
Located N. W. of Ellendale on the N. W. side of North Union Church Rd. (Rd. 42) 2.2 miles N. of Ellendale-Greenwood Highway (Rt. 16)

ARNEY, Ella E., b. 07/27/1888, d. 05/28/1956
ARNEY, Harry, DE Pvt., 312 Inf. 78 Div., WWI, b. 08/12/1886, d. 09/03/1948
BARLETT, Joanna, w/o Jonathan, ssw-Jonathan, b. 1863, d. 1948
BARLETT, Jonathan, ssw-Joanna, b. 1864, d. 1951
BETTS, Annie M., ssw-Solomon J., b. 10/12/1846, d. 03/06/1928
BETTS, Annie Virda, d/o Solomon & Annie, b. 06/09/1874, d. 03/12/1877
BETTS, Clara M., d/o Sallie A. & Edward D., b. 01/28/1872, d. 12/18/1891
BETTS, Edward D., ssw-Sallie A., b. 06/15/1837, d. 07/01/1902
BETTS, Elizabeth, w/o Isaac, Age 74y 4m 9d, b. N/D, d. 12/14/1879
BETTS, Emma P., ssw-William H., b. 04/09/1835, d. 11/11/1914
BETTS, Isaac, Age 73y 1m 5d, b. 01/21/1801, d. 02/26/1874
BETTS, James C., Age 37y 8m 23d, b. N/D, d. 05/24/1876
BETTS, John Clark, s/o Sallie A. & Edward D., b. 03/19/1876, d. 09/14/1886
BETTS, Jonathan Torbert, b. 09/10/1830, d. 07/02/1900
BETTS, Joseph Grant, s/o James C. & Eliza A., age 3y 2m 13d, b. N/D, d. 04/21/1876
BETTS, Josephine, b. 09/23/1862, d. 05/20/1934
BETTS, Lida, d/o Sallie A. & Edward D., b. 10/11/1864, d. 04/14/1892
BETTS, Mary Lizzie, d/o Solomon & Annie, b. 10/20/1864, d. 05/31/1890
BETTS, Sallie A., ssw-Edward D., b. 05/09/1844, d. 04/23/1902
BETTS, Solomon J., ssw-Annie M., b. 06/16/1841, d. 01/08/1906
BETTS, William H., ssw-Emma P., b. 11/04/1828, d. 12/02/1879
BETTS, Willie E., s/o Sallie A. & Edward D., b. 12/04/1866, d. 10/28/1891
CAMPBELL, Diana L., b. 02/19/1949, d. 12/05/1951

CAMPBELL, Helen T., b. 07/27/1906, d. 10/09/1964

CAMPBELL, Julian L., b. 04/15/1892, d. 11/24/1950

CAMPBELL, Robert E., b. 01/17/1928, d. 01/14/1965

CAMPBELL, Wayne M., b. 10/15/1950, d. 11/22/1950

CLENDANIEL, Benjamin F., ssw-Samuel H., Mary E., Leroy C. & Vernon M., b. 07/17/1864, d. 05/20/1906

CLENDANIEL, Elizabeth, w/o James M., b. 03/22/1850, d. 04/12/1913

CLENDANIEL, Frank, b. 1858, d. 1884

CLENDANIEL, James M., b. 04/06/1842, d. 01/08/1928

CLENDANIEL, John, b. 1821, d. 1911

CLENDANIEL, Leroy C., ssw-Benjamin F., Samuel H., Mary E. & Vernon M., b. 06/16/1872, d. 04/21/1882

CLENDANIEL, Mary E., ssw-Benjamin F., Samuel H., Leroy C. & Vernon M., b. 03/16/1839, d. 12/05/1905

CLENDANIEL, Samuel H., ssw-Benjamin F., Leroy C., Mary E. & Vernon M., b. 03/20/1830, d. 10/13/1902

CLENDANIEL, Sarah, b. 1835, d. 1922

CLENDANIEL, Vernon M., ssw-Benjamin F., Leroy C., Mary E. & Samuel H., b. 01/12/1874, d. 03/21/1882

DAVIDSON, Rachel B., Age 67y, b. N/D, d. 01/30/1901

DEPUTY, Etta E., b. 1877, d. 1949

DEPUTY, Ida V., ssw-Solomon, b. 11/18/1862, d. 07/07/1938

DEPUTY, James B., ssw-Nancy, b. 03/15/1831, d. 06/16/1906

DEPUTY, Joann, ssw-Marvin Jay, b. 12/09/1944, d. 03/30/1995

DEPUTY, John J., b. 1868, d. 1935

DEPUTY, Lizzie M., d/o Jas. B. & Nancy E., Age 18y 8m 13d, b. N/D, d. 06/01/1890

DEPUTY, Lula Lank, ssw-Thomas Jay B., b. 1912, d. 1994

DEPUTY, Lulu, d/o James & Susan A., b. 03/30/1879, d. 04/18/1881

DEPUTY, Lydia, d/o Chas. T. & Lydia, b. 07/17/1900, d. 08/30/1900

DEPUTY, Marvin Jay, ssw-Joann, b. 06/11/1942, d. N/D

DEPUTY, Nancy, w/o James B., Age 73y, b. N/D, d. 12/19/1905

DEPUTY, Solomon, ssw-Ida V., b. 07/18/1853, d. 09/30/1946

DEPUTY, Thomas Jay B., ssw-Lula Lank, b. 1911, d. 1965

DEPUTY, William W., b. 04/28/1850, d. 02/18/1921

ELLINGSWORTH, Georgia M., ssw-Jona, b. 02/10/1863, d. 05/20/1951

ELLINGSWORTH, Hattie Mae McSorley, d/o Jonathan & Georgianna, b. 07/22/1893, d. 04/22/1895

ELLINGSWORTH, Jona, ssw-Georgia M., b. 04/09/1865, d. 02/21/1942

ELLINGSWORTH, Vardie F., Sgt., USA, b. 06/23/1896, d. 01/23/1974

GRIFFITH, Elizabeth, b. 1816, d. 1902

GRIFFITH, Emma, b. 1852, d. 1882

HERBER, Vernon C., SSgt., USAF, Vietnam, b. 02/22/1943, d. 11/09/1979

JAGGARD, Wilmer Clyde, s/o Wilmer & Annie, b. 02/07/1886, d. 06/20/1886

KASULKE, Lena May, b. 02/19/1880, d. 08/22/1920

LORD, Edwin Luther, b. 1911, d. 1971

MILLER, Charles A., s/o Wm. & Maria, b. 09/16/1859, d. 05/12/1886

MILLER, Maria, b. 05/11/1838, d. 10/24/1905

MILLER, William, b. 01/01/1836, d. 06/18/1890

MORGAN, Bertha, ssw-Hubbard & Nelson, b. 1882, d. 1914

MORGAN, Hubbard, ssw-Bertha & Nelson, b. 1884, d. 1956

MORGAN, Nelson, ssw-Hubbard & Bertha, b. 1912, d. 1918

MORGAN, William, B., b. 08/05/1848, d. 07/08/1906

MURPHY, Ann L., ssw-James, b. 01/06/1847, d. 07/02/1905

MURPHY, James, ssw-Ann L., b. 07/07/1841, d. 07/25/1933

MURPHY, Johanna, b. 12/26/1865, d. 04/03/1939
MURPHY, Mae Mattie, b. 05/03/1892, d. 0/27/1970
MURPHY, Mark J., b. 04/16/1872, d. 12/14/1936
MURPHY, Nancy, b. 11/30/1849, d. 03/15/1930
NUTTER, Elizabeth, Age 81y, b. N/D, d. 05/23/1885
QUIL, W., b. 06/02/____, d. 06/02/____. [Note: Stone broken in small pieces.]
REVELLE, Ethel Lord Raydon, b. 05/24/1914, d. 03/08/1985
RUSSELL, Anna Everla, d/o Clarence & Lema M., Age 14d, b. N/D, d. 05/09/1910
RUSSELL, Clarence L., b. 08/22/1872, d. 06/29/1959
RUSSELL, Lena M., w/o Clarence L., b. 02/06/1878, d. 08/30/1910
RUSSELL, Sarah Marie, d/o Clarence L. & Lena M., Age 7d, b. N/D, d. 05/02/1910
WALLS, Asa B., ssw-Mary E., b. 11/30/1855, d. 05/21/1897
WALLS, Elmer C., s/o Mary L., b. 09/13/1889, d. 11/02/1891
WALLS, Inf. s/o Asa B. & Mary E., b. 08/29/1887, d. 09/05/1887
WALLS, Mary E., ssw-Asa B., b. 09/12/1855, d. 03/21/1939
WALLS, William B., Age 57y 7m 1d, b. N/D, d. 08/17/1878
WEBB, Annie L., w/o Jeremiah, b. 04/26/1863, d. 03/26/1896
WILLIAMS, Whittington, b. 09/1808, d. 07/29/1895

(CC-006 & HU-161) ELLENDALE PUBLIC CEMETERY
Located in Ellendale on the N. W. side of Ponder Avenue, approximately 0.3 miles North of Milton-Ellendale Highway (Rt. 16)
Recorded: September 4, 1996

ABBOTT, Clarence E., ssw-Lillian M., b. 1886, d. 1960
ABBOTT, Clarence E., Jr., Tec5, USA, WWII, b. 12/07/1917, d. 02/24/1993
ABBOTT, Helen L., ssw-James E., Sr., b. 04/07/1935, d. 07/02/1995
ABBOTT, Ida Mae, b. 05/04/1920, d. N/D
ABBOTT, James A., b. 12/09/1924, d. 01/24/1925
ABBOTT, James E., Sr., ssw-Helen L., b. 02/19/1940, d. N/D
ABBOTT, Lillian M., ssw-Clarence E., b. 1886, d. 1964
ALBERT, Henry W., Tec5, USA, WWII, b. 09/02/1916, d. 03/16/1987
ANDERSON, Howard Bateman, b. 08/31/1867, d. 06/10/1914
ANDERSON, Lena Reed, b. 03/16/1880, d. 03/11/1935
ATKINS, Otis J., b. 03/31/1955, d. 07/02/1967
BAKER, Della W., ssw-Isaiah T., b. 1874, d. 1964
BAKER, Frances Betts, ssw-I. Thomas, Jr., b. 06/29/1921, d. N/D
BAKER, I. Thomas, Jr., ssw-Frances Betts, b. 02/03/1909, d. N/D
BAKER, Isaiah T., ssw-Della W., b. 1870, d. 1937
BAKER, Theron T., s/o I. T. & Della W., b. 02/08/1901, d. 06/15/1902
BECK, Billie Dea, ssw-Larry, m. 11/29/1980, b. 03/22/1955, d. 05/31/1994
BECK, Larry, ssw-Billie Dea, m. 11/29/1980, b. 08/08/1945, d. N/D
BEEBE, Ann E., ssw-John David, Jr., b. 11/26/1927, d. N/D
BEEBE, Arthur H., ssw-Hattie A., b. 05/21/1893, d. 10/23/1981
BEEBE, Frank S., b. 04/22/1896, d. 12/12/1918
BEEBE, Gladys F., b. 1938, d. 1938
BEEBE, Hattie A., ssw-Arthur H., b. 05/04/1897, d. 10/27/1918
BEEBE, John B., h/o Minnie C., b. 12/12/1885, d. 07/01/1968

BEEBE, John David, Jr. ssw-Ann E., b. 09/05/1911, d. 06/06/1973

BEEBE, Katie B., w/o John D., b. 04/10/1884, d. 09/05/1945

BEEBE, Kenneth G., b. 1943, d. 1983

BEEBE, Richard Lester, b. 07/04/1938, d. 03/20/1941

BEEBE, Roland W., b. 1908, d. 1944

BEEBE, Vera Golden, b. 02/10/1906, d. N/D

BENSON, Greensbury, ssw-Jane, b. 1859, d. 1937

BENSON, Jane, ssw-Greensbury, b. 1848, d. 1937

CAHN, Elsa C., b. 12/01/1895, d. 07/18/1980

CALDWELL, James M., ssw-Mary A., b. 1869, d. 1947

CALDWELL, Mary A., w/o James M., ssw-James M., b. 1871, d. 1928

CALDWELL, S. A., w/o W. G., b. 10/31/1848, d. 08/13/1943

CALDWELL, W. G., ssw-S. A., Co. C., 11th Inf. Cav., Civil War, b. 07/07/1846, d. 10/17/1928

CAMPBELL, Lydia A., b. 12/16/1877, d. 04/29/1952

CAREY, Alice K., m/o Rhoda C. Workman, b. 05/02/1869, d. 01/17/1965

CARPENTER, Bessie May, d/o Geo. E. & Lizzie M., b. 05/12/1896, d. 08/10/1896

CARPENTER, Charles H., ssw-P. Catharine, b. 09/23/1901, d. 01/23/1991

CARPENTER, Lizzie M., w/o Geo. E., b. 04/13/1865, d. 10/06/1913

CARPENTER, Mary Ethel, d/o Geo. E. & Lizzie M., b. 10/24/1894, d. 05/27/1910

CARPENTER, P. Catharine, ssw-Charles H., b. 12/22/1904, d. 09/07/1990

CLENDANIEL, Alfred, Co. H., 9 DE Inf., b. N/D, d. N/D

CLENDANIEL, Annie V., ssw-Robert J., b. 1875, d. 1946

CLENDANIEL, Annie W., b. 06/17/1858, d. 12/20/1953

CLENDANIEL, Charlie M., s/o John & Sallie M., b. 12/09/1873, d. 05/04/1900

CLENDANIEL, E. Maud, d/o R. J. & Annie V., b. 07/15/1904, d. 04/21/1914

CLENDANIEL, Isaac, b. 07/07/1878, d. 05/28/1951

CLENDANIEL, John of G., ssw-Sallie M., b. 09/30/1841, d. 09/07/1927

CLENDANIEL, Joshua B., ssw-Sallie C. A., b. 02/19/1909, d. 05/21/1968

CLENDANIEL, Linda V., b. 12/21/1883, d. 04/16/1964

CLENDANIEL, Oliver E., Twin s/o Isaac & Linda V., ssw-Otis, b. 10/26/1923, d. 11/18/1928

CLENDANIEL, Otis V., ssw-Oliver E., b. 10/26/1923, d. 06/23/1944

CLENDANIEL, Robert J., ssw-Annie V., b. 1881, d. 1951

CLENDANIEL, Sallie C. A., ssw-Joshua B., b. 01/30/1906, d. 05/30/1986

CLENDANIEL, Sallie M., ssw-John of G., b. 08/30/1845, d. 01/16/1908

CLENDANIEL, Twin d/o R. J. & Annie V., b. 07/13/1905, d. 09/12/1905

CLENDANIEL, Twin d/o R. J. & Annie V., b. 07/13/1905, d. 09/13/1905

CLENDANIEL, William P., b. 05/24/1899, d. 11/29/1950

COLLINS, C. Marshall, b. 04/25/1913, d. 03/24/1986

COLLINS, Charles W., b. 12/24/1886, d. 12/16/1962

COLLINS, Clarence W., b. 05/04/1924, d. 03/02/1974

COLLINS, Jennie W., b. 09/30/1890, d. 06/20/1971

COVERDALE, Albert J., ssw-Fannie W., b. 12/20/1867, d. 10/26/1950

COVERDALE, Della M., ssw-Harvey, b. 1874, d. 1954

COVERDALE, Eliza, ssw-George, b. 1861, d. 1936

COVERDALE, Ella M., b. 02/09/1894, d. 12/20/1963

COVERDALE, Ervin, ssw-Mary W., b. 1870, d. 1954

COVERDALE, Fannie W., ssw-Albert J., b. 03/16/1867, d. 01/16/1955

COVERDALE, George, ssw-Eliza, b. 1862, d. 1952

COVERDALE, George Raymond, b. 1898, d. 1967
COVERDALE, Harvey, ssw-Della M., b. 1870, d. 1940
COVERDALE, Mary W., ssw-Ervin, b. 1871, d. 1944
COVERDALE, Rachel E., b. 01/11/1891, d. 02/23/1941
DANIELS, Elias M., b. 03/03/1882, d. 10/30/1941
DANIELS, Hester A., b. 05/04/1855, d. 05/2/1918
DANIELS, James H., b. 02/08/1848, d. 06/08/1925
DAVIS, Vincent E., b. 05/17/1963, d. 02/18/1979
DAWSON, Catherine, ssw-Waitman, b. 1880, d. 1906
DAWSON, Laura F., ssw-William H., b. 04/05/1874, d. 11/02/1950
DAWSON, Mary E., ssw- W. Webster, b. 06/20/1912, d. N/D
DAWSON, W. Webster, ssw-Mary E., b. 09/20/1915, d. 01/17/1985
DAWSON, Waitman, ssw-Catherine, b. 1875, d. 1928
DAWSON, William H., ssw-Laura F., b. 03/03/1865, d. 08/0/1934
DELONG, Dorothy A. Beebe, b. 02/07/1918, d. 08/11/1995
DICKERSON, Almira, ssw-Henry B. & Ernest L., b. 1872, d. 1944
DICKERSON, Ernest L., ssw-Henry B. & Ernest L., b. 1898, d. 1935
DICKERSON, Harry B., ssw-Lydia C., b. 1909, d. 1968
DICKERSON, Henry B., ssw-Almira & Ernest L., b. 1868, d. 1943
DICKERSON, Lydia C., ssw- Harry B., b. 1911, d. N/D
DICKERSON, Willard S., b. 01/15/1850, d. 07/31/1923
DONOVAN, David M., b. 1857, d. 1926
DONOVAN, Emma H., b. 1862, d. 1939
DONOVAN, Enoch, ssw-Nellie P., b. 02/02/1895, d. 02/03/1958
DONOVAN, Enoch Daniels, b. 11/27/1923, d. N/D
DONOVAN, Josephine S., b. 07/21/1893, d. 03/22/1968
DONOVAN, Mary L, ssw-W. Fred, b. 09/19/1898, d. 05/06/1993
DONOVAN, Nellie P., ssw-Enoch, b. 07/23/1892, d. 01/28/1945
DONOVAN, W. Fred, ssw-Mary L., b. 06/25/1895, d. 04/12/1956
DOWNES, Joseph H., Pvt., USA, WWII, b. 05/25/1919, d. 01/07/1977
DOWNES, Viola L., b. 10/09/1919, d. 03/25/1976
ELLINGSWORTH, Anna May, b. 05/08/1886, d. 12/28/1942
ELLINGSWORTH, Archie M., b. 02/02/1898, d. 12/11/1945
ELLINGSWORTH, Arthur Francis, s/o William D. & Anna M., b. 08/19/1915, d. 08/20/1915
ELLINGSWORTH, Buryl C., b. 1912, d. N/D
ELLINGSWORTH, Carol Lynn, ssw-Phillip J., b. 02/15/1955, d. N/D
ELLINGSWORTH, Charles J., ssw-Myrtle J., Cpl., USA, WWII, b. 07/27/1927, d. 12/13/1992
ELLINGSWORTH, Clara L., ssw-George A., b. 10/28/1888, d. 05/30/1942
ELLINGSWORTH, Ethel K., b. 07/30/1900, d. 06/12/1918
ELLINGSWORTH, George A., ssw-Clara L., b. 10/23/1885, d. 07/30/1983
ELLINGSWORTH, Hazel D., ssw-Isaac W., b. 04/05/1907, d. 05/23/1991
ELLINGSWORTH, Isaac W., ssw-Hazel D., b. 03/26/1906, d. 07/02/1990
ELLINGSWORTH, Jones, b. 1832, d. 1928
ELLINGSWORTH, Jones E., DE, Tec5, 328 Harcft Co. Tc., WWII, b. 04/21/1919, d. 06/02/1968
ELLINGSWORTH, Myrtle J., ssw-Charles J., b. 06/29/1928, d. N/D
ELLINGSWORTH, Phillip J., ssw-Carol Lynn, b. 02/13/1948, d. 02/17/1987
ELLINGSWORTH, Phoebe, b. 1852, d. 1931
ELLINGSWORTH, Rosetta, b. 03/14/1918, d. 07/29/1918

ELLINGSWORTH, William D., Sr., b. 05/17/1878, d. 078/19/1962

ELLIOTT, Crawford D., 3rd, b. 06/12/1995, d. 06/12/1995

ENNIS, Blanche Baker, ssw-Curtis Wesley, Sr., b. 07/30/1906, d. 08/22/1973

ENNIS, Curtis Wesley, Sr., ssw-Blanche Baker, b. 06/03/1904, d. 01/26/1975

ENNIS, Elmer S., ssw-Joyce M., b. 07/30/1924, d. N/D

ENNIS, Jane Marie, b. 09/12/1954, d. 04/28/1955

ENNIS, Joyce M., ssw-Elmer S., b. 07/15/1930, d. N/D

FISHER, Alex, ssw-Elizabeth, b. 1848, d. 1924

FISHER, Elizabeth, ssw-Alex, b. 1861, d. 1928

FISHER, Lina J., ssw-Walter J., b. 10/28/1893, d. 06/04/1984

FISHER, Walter J., ssw-Lina J., b. 03/12/1889, d. 11/23/1967

GIESE, Bessie H., w/o Otto, ssw-Son, b. 12/29/1899, d. 06/09/1922

GIESE, s/o Bessie H. & Otto, ssw-Bessie H., b. N/D, d. N/D

GOLDEN, C. Donald, b. 12/24/1909, d. 10/17/1928

GOLDEN, Charles Henry, ssw-Luella May, b. 12/29/1880, d. 08/27/1974

GOLDEN, Elsie M., ssw-Uby W., b. 04/29/1917, d. 07/28/1994

GOLDEN, Luella May, ssw-Charles Henry, b. 02/19/1885, d. 09/25/1948

GOLDEN, Uby W., ssw-Elsie M., b. 02/26/1903, d. 01/04/1961

GOLDEN, Uby W., Jr., b. 10/20/1947, d. N/D

GOLDSMITH, Cheryl Mae Wooten, ssw-James Edward, 3rd., b. 1962, d. 1985

GOLDSMITH, James Edward, 3rd, ssw-Cheryl Mae Wooten, b. 1983, d. 1985

GUERIN, Joseph H., Tec5, USA, WWII, b. 02/13/1927, d. 03/15/1988

HAFFNER, Florence B., b. 11/25/1892, d. 01/12/1973

HARRISON, Bessie E., ssw-Gordon N., b. 1904, d. N/D

HARRISON, Gordon N., ssw-Bessie E., NY, Cpl., 26 Air Depot GP AAF, WWII, b. 09/15/1912,
    d. 09/15/1959

HARTLEY, Daisy B., b. 12/04/1895, d. 06/13/1968

HARTLEY, Richard, ssw-Rita, b. 05/30/1923, d. N/D

HARTLEY, Rita, ssw-Richard, b. 12/06/1915, d. 12/31/1975

HELLENS, Emma C., ssw-John W., b. 08/29/1880, d. 12/27/1964

HELLENS, John W., ssw-Emma C., b. 09/26/1873, d. 10/04/1944

HITCH, John H., ssw-Lizzie B., b. 12/26/1893, d. 03/20/1955

HITCH, Lizzie B., ssw-John H., b. 05/19/1893, d. 02/14/1936

HOYT, Charles S., b. 08/29/1871, d. 02/12/1954

HOYT, Raylynn C., ssw-Reba B., SSgt., USA, WWII, b. 12/05/1918, d. 08/22/1982

HOYT, Reba B., ssw-Raylynn C., b. 10/20/1921, d. N/D

HOYT, Walter William, b. 04/30/1898, d. 11/05/1967

HUDSON, Edwin Reed, b. 01/02/1913, d. 02/18/1913

INGRAM, Isabel, b. 1855, d. 1938

INGRAM, Manship, b. 1847, d. 1925

JESTER, Benjamin E., ssw-Rachel D., b. 07/01/1827, d. 11/13/1907

JESTER, Cora M., ssw-Harry W., b. 1880, d. 1933

JESTER, Eliza A., ssw-James H., b. 1850, d. 1928

JESTER, Elizabeth M., b. 08/09/1909, d. 08/21/1928

JESTER, Harry W., ssw-Cora M., b. 1870, d. 1934

JESTER, Harry W., Jr., b. 1910, d. 1968

JESTER, James H., ssw-Eliza A., b. 1852, d. 1939

JESTER, Lillian G., b. 09/03/1876, d. 09/30/1965

JESTER, Rachel D., ssw-Benjamin E., b. 07/24/1833, d. 05/11/1897
JESTER, S. Otis, b. N/D, d. N/D
JESTER, Samuel Otis, b. 09/18/1874, d. 03/07/1938
JOHNSON, Emeline, b. 02/14/1848, d. 06/29/1907
JONES, Sallie E., b. 06/22/1827, d. 09/25/1905
JOSEPH, Cheryl Christy, b. 05/25/1969, d. 03/05/1970
JOSEPH, Shirley L., ssw-Theodore H., b. 03/16/1933, d. N/D
JOSEPH, Theodore H., ssw-Shirley L., b. 09/12/1938, d. N/D
KNERR, Robert F., b. 04/09/1880, d. 02/25/1915
KNERR, Robert N., b. 02/19/1912, d. 10/26/1940
KROH, Carrie Knerr, b. 08/14/1881, d. 12/17/1953
LAKE, Harry H., b. 08/22/1913, d. 03/04/1995
LANGABEE, Gordon K., b. 11/03/1918, d. N/D
LANGABEE, Velma O. Golden, b. 04/27/1920, d. N/D
LINDLE, Andrew, b. 04/25/1873, d. 03/28/1917
LINDLE, Joshua, b. 06/25/1835, d. 03/03/1906
LINKER, Edna May, ssw-Otto, b. 1883, d. 1982
LINKER, Otto, ssw-Edna May, b. 1889, d. 1963
LOFLAND, Charles, ssw-Rose L., b. 1870, d. 1943
LOFLAND, Charles H., b. 05/15/1906, d. 07/24/1979
LOFLAND, Joseph, ssw-Lillie V., b. 1871, d. 1929
LOFLAND, Lillie V., ssw-Joseph, b. 1881, d. 1957
LOFLAND, Rose L., ssw-Charles, b. 1880, d. 1955
LYNCH, Elizabeth I., b. 1885, d. 1950
LYNCH, Elwood A., ssw-Pauline W., b. 1905, d. 1953
LYNCH, James H., b. 1884, d. 1934
LYNCH, James H., Jr., Artiller, WWII, b. 1923, d. 1955
LYNCH, Pauline W., ssw-Elwood A., b. 1906, d. 1991
MACKLIN, Allie V., ssw-Tolbert, b. 1862, d. 1951
MACKLIN, Edward F., b. 08/10/1875, d. 07/27/1957
MACKLIN, Edward F., ssw-Emma M., b. 08/10/1875, d. 07/27/1957
MACKLIN, Edward F., Jr., b. 1905, d. 1905
MACKLIN, Elias, ssw-Susie C., b. 1856, d. 1934
MACKLIN, Emma M., b. 12/29/1875, d. 08/19/1951
MACKLIN, Emma M., ssw-Edward F., b. 12/29/1875, d. 08/19/1951
MACKLIN, Henry D., b. 12/25/1825, d. 10/24/1904
MACKLIN, Jessefy, w/o Henry D., b. 01/22/1824, d. 02/15/1886
MACKLIN, M. Crozier, b. 1923, d. 1926
MACKLIN, Nila, b. 02/03/1894, d. 04/06/1957
MACKLIN, Susie C., ssw-Elias, b. 1861, d. 1933
MACKLIN, Tolbert, ssw-Allie V., b. 1854, d. 1938
MAHAN, Mamie T., ssw-Seth Irvin, b. 04/05/1855, d. 07/03/1968
MAHAN, Seth Irvin, ssw-Mamie T., b. 10/19/1874, d. 12/22/1944
MANNERING, Mary V., b. 10/06/1899, d. 09/17/1928
MARKER, Albert W., ssw-Ruth E. Wilson, b. 1903, d. 1967
MARKER, Cora M., b. 02/13/1921, d. N/D
MARKER, Frances A., d/o W. H. & Elizabeth, b. 04/23/1907, d. 10/29/1918
MARKER, Gertrude, b. 1899, d. 1931

MARKER, Harry O., SSgt., AAF, b. 07/24/1918, d. 02/03/1974

MARKER, Harvey, b. 1901, d. 1969

MARKER, Horace S., s/o W. H. & Elizabeth, b. 10/29/1899, d. 12/02/1900

MARKER, Irene, ssw-Oscar, b. 1907, d. 1969

MARKER, Isaac M., b. 01/02/1861, d. 12/30/1925

MARKER, Lina G., b. 09/21/1895, d. 04/13/1982

MARKER, Lizzie B., b. 02/04/1876, d. 12/15/1920

MARKER, Oscar, ssw-Irene, b. 1895, d. 1969

MARKER, Ruth E. Wilson, ssw-Albert W., b. 1902, d. 1928

MCQUAID, Elsie M., b. 08/08/1906, d. 07/01/1966

MELVIN, Andora C., b. 01/31/1904, d. 04/06/1972

MELVIN, James M., Pvt., USA, WWII, b. 01/28/1910, d. 08/07/1980

MEREDITH, Elizabeth, b. 04/12/1924, d. 02/18/1967

MESSICK, Anna E., b. 05/08/1922, d. N/D

MESSICK, Charles F., Pfc., USA, WWII, b. 09/06/1922, d. 09/11/1986

MILLMAN, Albert, ssw-Elsie, b. 10/02/1920, d. N/D

MILLMAN, Alexander J., ssw-Gussie G., b. 03/22/1887, d. 08/25/1968

MILLMAN, Annie E., ssw-Michael, b. 12/25/1847, d. 05/03/1934

MILLMAN, Burton J., ssw-Lillie E., b. 1879, d. 1971

MILLMAN, Ella J., ssw-Willard H., b. 1870, d. 1938

MILLMAN, Elsie, ssw-Albert, b. 06/30/1915, d. 06/04/1994

MILLMAN, Emory E., b. 12/18/1869, d. 10/02/1941

MILLMAN, Fred C., DE, Pvt., 110 Inf., 28 Div., WWI, b. 03/20/1895, d. 05/12/1972

MILLMAN, Gussie G., ssw-Alexander J., b. 02/22/1890, d. 10/31/1969

MILLMAN, John W., b. 01/22/1848, d. 02/12/1926

MILLMAN, Kate Mary Lamsback, w/o John W., b. 07/04/1858, d. 06/30/1912

MILLMAN, Leonard M., b. 12/18/1883, d. 12/17/1932

MILLMAN, Lillie E., ssw-Burton J., b. 1883, d. 1963

MILLMAN, Mary A., b. 02/18/1892, d. 11/22/1980

MILLMAN, Michael, Co. G., 9 DE INF., ssw-Annie E., b. 04/15/1833, d. 01/24/1914

MILLMAN, Willard H, ssw-Ella J., b. 1868, d. 1929

MILMAN, Mary E., ssw-William H., b. 02/10/1850, d. 12/11/1932

MILMAN, William H., ssw-Mary E., Co. E, 9 DE Inf., b. 12/28/1843, d. 08/02/1928

MITCHELL, Ethel D., b. 04/19/1898, d. 08/12/1973

MITCHELL, Joan B., ssw-Merriel, b. 08/12/1932, d. N/D

MITCHELL, Merriel R., ssw-Joan B., Cpl., USA Co. C., 866 Eng. Avn. Bn., Korea, b. 03/24/1932, d. 04/09/1990

MOORE, Bonard D., ssw-Hyacinth L., b. 04/27/1913, d. 05/29/1991

MOORE, Hyacinth L., ssw-Bonard D., b. 02/03/1912, d. 09/12/1993

MORGAN, Clarence W., ssw-George U., Laura J. & Millard J., b. 12/08/1899, d. 03/21/1948

MORGAN, Dorsey G., ssw-Estella M., b. 05/22/1889, d. 01/28/1966

MORGAN, Dorsey G., Jr., Pvt., USAR, WWII, b. 10/16/1921, d. 01/14/1992

MORGAN, Elmer G., ssw-Junie E., b. 09/22/1902, d. 08/23/1978

MORGAN, Estella M., ssw-Dorsey G., b. 08/13/1888, d. 07/27/1965

MORGAN, George U., ssw-Laura J., Clarence W. & Millard J., b. 03/25/1869, d. 07/12/1932

MORGAN, Gilbert P., ssw-Mary Hester, b. 01/17/1864, d. 01/04/1933

MORGAN, Howard J., DE, Pfc., 38 Inf. 2nd Ind. Div, Korea, b. 05/29/1931, d. 08/26/1950

MORGAN, Junie E., ssw-Elmer G., b. 06/30/1900, d. 03/24/1985

MORGAN, Laura J., ssw-George U., Clarence W. & Millard J., b. 12/08/1879, d. 08/31/1961
MORGAN, Mary Hester, ssw-Gilbert P., b. 06/09/1861, d. 03/22/1931
MORGAN, Millard J., ssw-George U., Laura J. & Clarence W., b. 12/25/1904, d. 09/15/1949
MORGAN, Ralph E., b. 02/22/1930, d. 08/15/1987
NEIBERT, Anton, ssw-Elizabeth F., Frank & Grace R., b. 1855, d. 1938
NEIBERT, Charles H., ssw-Edna R. M., b. 07/29/1924, d. N/D
NEIBERT, Edna R. M., ssw-Charles H., b. 09/10/1930, d. N/D
NEIBERT, Elizabeth F., ssw-Anton, Frank & Grace R., b. 1869, d. 1943
NEIBERT, Frank, ssw-Anton, Anton, Grace R. & Elizabeth F., b. 1897, d. 1969
NEIBERT, Grace R., ssw-Anton, Elizabeth F. & Frank, b. 1902, d. N/D
NEIBERT, Jack R., ssw-Robert J., b. 06/04/1958, d. 10/13/1980
NEIBERT, Robert J., ssw-Jack R., b. 06/22/1931, d. 04/27/1994
O'NEILL, Charles, ssw-Willard Short, b. 1867, d. 1937
OLSON, Emma C., b. 04/02/1843, d. 08/23/1930
OLSON, John A., b. 07/22/1878, d. 02/10/1961
OWENS, Eleanor M., ssw-James H., b. 09/09/1875, d. 06/16/1946
OWENS, Frank E., ssw-Sallie A., b. 08/15/1900, d. 04/28/1969
OWENS, James H., ssw-Eleanor M., b. 07/04/1867, d. 10/06/1932
OWENS, Joshua, ssw-Robert C., Margaret L. & Myrtle, b. 1851, d. 1937
OWENS, Margaret L., ssw-Robert C., Joshua & Myrtle, b. 1874, d. 1923
OWENS, Myrtle, ssw-Robert C., Margaret L. & Myrtle, b. 1901, d. 1901
OWENS, Robert B., DE, Pvt., 561 AAF Base Unit, WWII, b. 11/03/1908, d. 10/28/1944
OWENS, Robert C., ssw-Margaret L., Joshua & Myrtle, b. 1874, d. 1944
OWENS, Sallie A., ssw-Frank E., b. 01/25/1897, d. 07/22/1975
PARISI, James M., b. 04/25/1953, d. 07/20/1993
PILIERO, Gertrude, b. 04/16/1906, d. 02/27/1964
PLUMMER, Annie E., b. 03/24/1865, d. 08/01/1943
PLUMMER, Henry R., ssw-S. Catherine, b. 02/09/1902, d. 10/23/1980
PLUMMER, S. Catherine, ssw-Henry R., b. 06/17/1908, d. 07/05/1995
PLUMMER, Thomas W., b. 11/20/1862, d. 03/24/1913
POSTLES, Annie H., ssw-Luke, b. 04/02/1859, d. 06/13/1928
POSTLES, Luke, ssw-Annie H., b. 07/02/1853, d. 03/06/1936
PRETTYMAN, Alice, ssw-John & Annie B., b. 05/22/1903, d. 06/01/1923
PRETTYMAN, Annie B., ssw-John & Alice, b. 05/20/1865, d. 11/08/1931
PRETTYMAN, Howard B., b. 05/17/1888, d. 07/18/1917
PRETTYMAN, John, b. 05/20/1865, d. 11/08/1931
PRETTYMAN, John, ssw-Annie B. & Alice, b. 11/18/1859, d. 05/28/1922
RASPE, John A., Sr., Pvt., USA, b. 02/02/1894, d. 07/07/1952
RASPE, Rose Etta, b. 1919, d. 1923
REED, Annie E., b. 1853, d. 1939
REED, Bessie R., d/o Otis B. & Jennie H., b. 06/09/1904, d. 03/29/1905
REED, D. Henry, b. 1840, d. 1929
REED, David H. ssw-Jennie E., b. 12/28/1884, d. 12/30/1884
REED, David H. of E., ssw-Jannie E., b. 08/08/1859, d. 04/11/1941
REED, Elias B., b. 11/25/1824, d. 09/01/1887
REED, Elias B., ssw-Violet E., Tec5, USA, WWII, b. 03/15/1913, d. 10/25/1985
REED, George M., Sr., ssw-Margaret A., b. 1869, d. 1943
REED, Inf. Twins o/David H. & Jannie E., b. 12/28/1881, d. 12/30/1881

REED, Jannie E., w/o David Reed of E., b. 04/09/1860, d. 11/17/1920
REED, Jennie E., ssw-David H., b. 12/28/1884, d. 12/30/1884
REED, Jennie H., ssw-Otis B., b. 1880, d. 1971
REED, John H., b. N/D, d. N/D
REED, Joseph E., ssw-Mary V., b. 1852, d. 1932
REED, Lydia A., ssw-William J., b. 1847, d. 1922
REED, Margaret A., ssw-George M., Sr., b. 1874, d. 1940
REED, Mary Jester, ssw-Samuel Edwin, b. 02/29/1856, d. 04/01/1919
REED, Mary V., ssw-Joseph E., b. 1868, d. 1935
REED, Otis B., ssw-Jennie H., b. 1882, d. 1966
REED, Rachel T., b. 01/13/1826, d. 01/16/1905
REED, Samuel Edwin, ssw-Mary Jester, b. 01/30/1855, d. 07/12/1910
REED, Violet E., ssw-Elias B., b. 09/08/1918, d. N/D
REED, William J., ssw-Lydia A., b. 1842, d. 1921
ROGERS, Alfred D., ssw-Lillian G., b. 1909, d. 1977
ROGERS, Emma J., ssw-Fred W., b. 11/03/1897, d. 10/07/1973
ROGERS, Fred W., ssw-Emma J., b. 10/04/1893, d. 12/20/1981
ROGERS, Gladys A., d/o F. W. & E., b. 10/16/1925, d. 05/07/1934
ROGERS, Lillian G., ssw-Alfred D., b. 1912, d. 1965
RUSSELL, Arthur R., ssw-Florence C., b. 03/19/1877, d. 09/12/1950
RUSSELL, Florence C., ssw-Arthur R., b. 05/21/1876, d. 08/01/1953
SHENKLE, Sarah Jane, b. 06/17/1848, d. 03/31/1927
SHORT, Willard, ssw-Charles O'Neill, b. 1880, d. 1953
SMITH, B. Helen, ssw-Harvey T., b. 02/15/1896, d. 07/09/1922
SMITH, George, b. 1836, d. 1915
SMITH, Grace H., b. 11/02/1901, d. 08/15/1957
SMITH, Harvey T., ssw-B. Helen, b. 12/22/1892, d. 03/14/1978
SMITH, Rachel, b. 1839, d. 1905
SPICER, Catherine E., ssw-Clarence W., b. 02/25/1923, d. 02/26/1975
SPICER, Clarence W., ssw-Catherine W., b. 01/11/1897, d. 05/26/1960
SPICER, Eva E., ssw-Willard S., b. 08/11/1878, d. 03/01/1945
SPICER, George H., b. 1863, d. 1931
SPICER, Sarah E., b. 02/27/1870, d. 10/01/1945
SPICER, Willard S., ssw-Eva E., b. 10/31/1876, d. 08/15/1943
STONEBERGER, K. Jeanette, ssw-Robert J., b. 02/11/1933, d. 02/05/1990
STONEBERGER, Robert J., ssw-K. Jeanette, b. 09/29/1930, d. 04/22/1990
STUART, James D., DE, Cpl., USA, WWII, b. 02/01/1896, d. 02/24/1972
SWAIN, Mary E., ssw-Robert H., b. 10/08/1868, d. 07/31/1943
SWAIN, Robert H., ssw-Mary E., b. 03/28/1863, d. 01/27/1949
TAYLOR, Baby Girl, b. N/D, d. 1967
THAYER, May, b. 08/02/1891, d. 08/02/1971
TUCKER, Eliza J., ssw-Ray W., b. 06/23/1905, d. 06/24/1987
TUCKER, Grace L., ssw-Robert L., b. 06/14/1926, d. N/D
TUCKER, Ray W., ssw-Eliza J., b. 03/04/1887, d. 06/13/1968
TUCKER, Robert L., ssw-Grace L., b. 09/23/1924, d. N/D
WALIUS, Anna M., ssw-Peter O., b. 10/20/1873, d. 05/28/1950
WALIUS, Joseph M., ssw-Losetta E., b. 05/03/1949, d. N/D
WALIUS, Losetta E., ssw-Joseph M., b. 07/02/1914, d. N/D

WALIUS, Peter O., ssw-Anna M., b. 11/22/1859, d. 12/20/1934
WALIUS, Theodore H., b. 11/05/1908, d. 01/08/1961
WALKER, George E., b. 01/22/1877, d. 06/08/1903
WALKER, Hannie A., b. 1914, d. 1991
WALKER, Mary E., w/o W. M., b. 12/18/1836, d. 02/24/1911
WALLS, Leah Jane, ssw-Webster W., b. 1856, d. 1938
WALLS, Raymond, Sp4, USA, Vietnam, b. 08/12/1943, d. 03/11/1991
WALLS, Webster W., ssw-Leah Jane, b. 1855, d. 1943
WALLS, Joan C., b. 04/08/1945, d. N/D
WARREN, Clara B., ssw-Samuel, b. 1862, d. 1932
WARREN, David Bennett, b. 07/21/1852, d. 03/07/1910
WARREN, Inf./o Luther P. & Ida, b. N/D, d. 04/1909
WARREN, Isaac K., ssw-Virginia F., b. 02/13/1844, d. 03/05/1920
WARREN, James H., b. 02/18/1846, d. 04/17/1926
WARREN, Lydia, w/o R. A., b. 01/04/1872, d. 04/21/1902
WARREN, Lydia W., b. 06/26/1860, d. 12/07/1940
WARREN, Robert A., b. 1860, d. 1950
WARREN, Sallie J., b. 1870, d. 1954
WARREN, Samuel, ssw-Clara B., b. 1858, d. 1940
WARREN, Virginia F., w/o Isaac K., ssw-Isaac K., b. 01/12/1845, d. 04/09/1914
WARRINGTON, Aleine, d/o Stephen & Burnace E. Warrington, b. 02/11/1933, d. 02/05/1990
WEBB, Annie M., d/o Marshall H. & Stella E., b. 11/26/1905, d. 06/24/1906
WEBB, Beatrice A., ssw-James L., b. 1921, d. 1996
WEBB, Henry P., s/o M. H. & S. E., b. 01/27/1904, d. 03/02/1904
WEBB, Irvin M., ssw-Mary M., b. 1908, d. 1950
WEBB, James L., ssw-Beatrice A., b. 1914, d. 1978
WEBB, James P., b. 05/26/1843, d. 10/23/1911
WEBB, Joseph H., s/o George E. & Eunice C., b. 05/03/1899, d. 02/04/1916
WEBB, Marshall H., b. 04/11/1872, d. 02/19/1958
WEBB, Mary M., ssw-Irvin M., b. 1910, d. 1980
WEBB, Stella, w/o Marshall, b. 08/12/1879, d. 09/21/1930
WEST, Annie B., ssw-John W., b. 08/31/1887, d. 04/03/1961
WEST, John W., ssw-Annie B., b. 02/12/1885, d. 09/01/1955
WEST, Mary A. Golden, ssw-Norman A., b. 03/23/1916, d. N/D
WEST, Norman A., ssw-Mary A. Golden, b. 07/23/1902, d. N/D
WHITNEY, Erlis F., b. 1858, d. 1937
WHITNEY, Sarah E., b. 1861, d. 1927
WIBLE, Edith Ennis, b. 1899, d. 1983
WILLEY, Jennie M., b. 04/25/1914, d. 12/02/1982
WILLIAMS, Daniel J., b. 03/11/1912, d. 05/21/1976
WILLIAMS, Frances C., b. 06/13/1917, d. 05/30/1921
WILLIAMS, Howard D., b. 1914, d. 1977
WILLIAMS, James E., b. 1885, d. 1967
WILLIAMS, James P., ssw-Lucy, b. 10/23/1880, d. 07/27/1951
WILLIAMS, Lucy, ssw-James P., b. 04/19/1882, d. 04/05/1963
WILLIAMS, Maggie G., b. 1892, d. 1955
WILSON, Charles R., ssw-Mabel F., b. 07/07/1899, d. 03/13/1960
WILSON, Clara V., ssw-James W., b. 1876, d. 1961

WILSON, Harold A., USN, WWII, b. 12/16/1925, d. 12/20/1985
WILSON, J. Stanley, b. 1904, d. 1944
WILSON, James W., ssw-Clara V., b. 1866, d. 1934
WILSON, John H., b. 07/17/1909, d. 08/19/1936
WILSON, Mabel F., ssw-Charles R., b. 10/23/1902, d. 02/16/1972
WILSON, Thomas P., b. 08/21/1869, d. 04/13/1957
WOLF, Christina, ssw-William, b. 07/04/1876, d. 03/18/1963
WOLF, Helen, b. 05/03/1907, d. 05/11/1918
WOLF, William, ssw-Christina, b. 05/30/1872, d. 02/28/1943
WOOD, Mary A., b. 1860, d. 1936
WOOD, Robert A., b. 1861, d. 1931
WORKMAN, Georgana, ssw-William H., b. 1877, d. 1955
WORKMAN, Lawrence O., b. 07/07/1911, d. 08/15/1929
WORKMAN, Lawrence W., b. 07/16/1941, d. 08/01/1995
WORKMAN, Norman E., b. 01/03/1902, d. 02/18/1967
WORKMAN, Rhoda C., d/o Alice K. Carey, b. 06/26/1902, d. 07/31/1981
WORKMAN, William H., ssw-Georgana, b. 1872, d. 1953
YEARWOOD, Cecil Dudley, Sp3, USA, Korea, b. 07/21/1928, d. 07/02/1992

The following stone was recorded by the Hudson Survey but is now missing or unreadable:
MARKER, William H., b. 08/19/1872, d. N/D

(CC-007 & HU-NR) DEPUTY FAMILY CEMETERY
Located S. E. of Milford, approximately 75 yards S. W. of Coastal Highway (Rt. 1) 0.3 miles South of Johnson Rd. (Rd. 207)
Recorded: March 7, 1997

DEPUTY, Ann Mariah, w/o James H., Age 31y, b. N/D, d. 01/03/1870
DEPUTY, Sarah, w/o Zachariah, Age 83y 7m b. N/D, d. 03/09/1878
DEPUTY, Zachariah, Age 68y, b. N/D, b. 12/03/1855

(CC-008 & HU-NR) SARAH A. WILLIAMS CEMETERY
Located West of Lincoln on the East side of Du Pont Blvd. (Rt. 113) and 0.3 miles South of Johnson Rd. (Rd. 207)
Recorded March 7, 1997

DEPUTY, Nancy Jane, b. 04/25/1856, d. 02/09/1927
DUTTON, Annie, ssw-Ella W. Henson, b. 1846, d. 1930
DUTTON, George, ssw-Annie, b. 1848, d. 1914
HENSON, Ella W., ssw-John W., b. 1876, d. 1964
HENSON, John W., ssw-Ella W., b. 1879, d. 1951
PAGE, George T., USA, WWII, b. 08/24/1915, d. 07/06/1988
WATSON, Camilla V., b. 05/18/1885, d. 11/10/1976
WATSON, Vonda R., b. 05/15/1955, d. 12/24/1956
WATSON, Wilbert, b. 1925, d. 1992
WILLIS, Sarah A., w/o Hiram F., b. 08/05/1863, d. 08/27/1904
WRIGHT, William T., b. 02/22/1892, d. 01/05/1908

(CC-009 & HU-278) OAKLEY CHURCH CEMETERY

Located 2.6 miles west of Ellendale at the S. E. corner of Ellendale-Greenwood Highway, (Rt. 16) and Oakley Rd. (Rd. 610)

Recorded: November 9, 1995

ADAMS, David Thomas, ssw-Sarah J. Cornell, b. 1846, d. 1921
ADAMS, Gertrude D., ssw-Willmont L., b. 1891, d. 1963
ADAMS, Sarah J. Cornell, ssw-David Thomas, b. 1847, d. 1937
ADAMS, Willmont L., ssw-Gertrude D., b. 1883, d. 1975
ANDRIE, James R., ssw-June J., b. 04/06/1934, d. N/D
ANDRIE, June J., ssw-James R., b. 02/12/1938, d. 09/25/1981
BANNING, Bessie D., ssw-Charles T., Norman & Walter, b. 1883, d. 1968
BANNING, Charles T., ssw-Bessie D., Norman & Walter, b. 1869, d. 1947
BANNING, Daniel A., Sgt., Co. C., 104 Inf. Regt., WWII, b. 10/06/1916, d. 01/19/1961
BANNING, Daniel G., b. 07/20/1859, d. 08/20/1938
BANNING, Frances Emily, w/o Mark L. Banning, b. 10/11/1856, d. 03/29/1937
BANNING, Harry E., b. 1879, d. 1957
BANNING, John L., ssw-Mira Anna, b. 1875, d. 1946
BANNING, L. Edwin, b. 1922, d. 1923
BANNING, Lizzie M., b. 1883, d. 1972
BANNING, Mark Lofland, b. 03/16/1857, d. 03/29/1953
BANNING, Mira Anna, ssw-John L., b. 1882, d. 1950
BANNING, Norman, ssw-Bessie D., Charles T. & Walter, b. 1909, d. 1910
BANNING, Thomas O., b. 05/16/1840, d. 02/15/1908
BANNING, Walter, ssw-Norman, Bessie D. & Charles T., b. 1914, d. 1914
BANNING, William, b. 11/05/1837, d. 03/06/1904
BEERS, Luther Weber, S1, USN, WWII, b. 1918, d. 07/22/1989
BELL, Dorsey M., ssw-John R. L. Rogers, b. 1921, d. 1963
BUCKLEY, Allen W., ssw-Cora Alice, b. 08/20/1895, d. 12/06/1970
BUCKLEY, Clara D., ssw-Cyrus J., b. 1868, d. 1940
BUCKLEY, Cora Alice, ssw-Allen W., b. 07/30/1904, d. 02/21/1995
BUCKLEY, Cyrus J., ssw-Clara D., b. 1853, d. 1917
BUCKLEY, Edward Nelson, USA, Vietnam, b. 11/06/1945, d. 11/14/1994
CANNON, Martha A., b. 1889, d. 1973
COLLISON, Debbie L., b. 03/23/1970, d. 09/23/1986
COLLISON, Linda Lee, b. 02/26/1949, d. N/D
DAWSON, John O., b. 02/08/1863, d. 10/11/1903
DEPUTY, C. Fred, ssw-Vina C., b. 06/26/1876, d. 12/02/1966
DEPUTY, Maggie G., ssw-William H., b. 07/22/1874, d. 10/16/1957
DEPUTY, Mary E., b. 1849, d. 1929
DEPUTY, Vina C., ssw-C. Fred, b. 11/16/1880, d. 07/16/1965
DEPUTY, William H., b. 1847, d. 1900
DEPUTY, William H., ssw-Maggie G., b. 01/27/1874, d. 02/25/1965
DISHAROON, Losetta, b. 03/29/1924, d. 01/16/1992
DONNELLY, Eva S., b. 1905, d. 1952
DONOVAN, Horace, b. 12/22/1886, d. 12/31/1914
DONOVAN, Wilhelmina, w/o Asbury, b. 01/08/1871, d. 02/06/1910

DONOVAN, Willard C., b. 1891, d. 1965

DOWNIE, Menolla Banning, b. 09/17/1900, d. 04/09/1971

ECKHARDT, Fritz, Co. H., W. V. Inf., Civil War, b. N/D, d. N/D

ENFIELD, Bertha Lee, b. 10/07/1948, d. 07/29/1960

ENFIELD, Lois, b. 1975, d. 1975

ENFIELD, Matthew, b. 1976, d. 1977

ENFIELD, Wilson, b. 1975, d. 1975

HAASS, Clara M., b. 04/15/1925, d. 11/28/1955

HEMMONDS, Ann E., w/o Joshua M., ssw-Joshua M., b. 07/06/1850, d. 12/08/1905

HEMMONDS, Georganna, ssw-John R., b. 09/06/1866, d. 02/14/1938

HEMMONDS, John R., ssw-Georganna, b. 02/12/1864, d. 02/04/1924

HEMMONDS, Joshua M., ssw-Ann E., b. 03/15/1843, d. 01/04/1914

HEMMONDS, Mary E., b. 01/05/1866, d. 06/17/1932

HEMMONS, Mary P., b. 10/13/1841, d. 04/09/1918

HUFFENS, Barbara, ssw-Peter, b. 1867, d. 1953

HUFFENS, Peter, ssw-Barbara, b. 1859, d. 1942

JERMAN, Delema Porter, ssw-William E., Sr., b. 1925, d. 1985

JERMAN, William E., Sr., ssw-Delema Porter, Cpl., USAAF, WWII, b. 01/10/1916, d. 11/10/1972

JOHNSON, Huldah S., ssw-Otis L., b. 03/08/1910, d. 05/07/1982

JOHNSON, John M., b. 1876, d. 1935

JOHNSON, Otis L., ssw-Huldah S., b. 01/21/1897, d. 03/01/1972

LORD, Lottie S., b. 1890, d. 1914

LORD, S. Elizabeth, b. 1863, d. 1936

LORD, Thomas L., b. 1850, d. 1916

MORROW, Ethel V. Adams, w/o Louis W. Morrow, b. 06/26/1923, d. 01/23/1962

PASSWATERS, Alfred H., ssw-Maggie E., Rachel H. & Lelia Brimer, b. 1876, d. 1962

PASSWATERS, Charlie L., b. 1885, d. 1921

PASSWATERS, Clement, b. 1843, d. 1918

PASSWATERS, Clement, Jr., b. 1875, d. 1931

PASSWATERS, Lelia Brimer, ssw-Rachel H., Alfred H. & Maggie E., b. 1894, d. 1960

PASSWATERS, Maggie E., ssw-Alfred H., Rachel H. & Lelia Brimer, b. 1876, d. 1939

PASSWATERS, Rachel H., ssw-Maggie E., Alfred H. & Lelia Brimer, b. 1901, d. 1955

PASSWATERS, Sara M., b. 1853, d. 1918

PORTER, Wilson A., Pfc., USA, Korea, b. 11/26/1928, d. 10/20/1977

ROGERS, John R. L., ssw-Dorsey M. Bell, b. 1906, d. 1964

SCOTT, Bertha M., ssw-Wilmer, b. 1890, d. 1970

SCOTT, Wilmer, ssw-Bertha M., b. 1905, d. 1976

SHORT, Alice B. Clifton, b. 1909, d. 1934

SHORT, Benjamin Harrison, b. 01/19/1889, d. 07/13/1964

SHORT, Bertha E., w/o Joseph D., b. 12/25/1881, d. 08/28/1929

SHORT, Harry A., ssw-Mary E., b. 01/18/1871, d. 12/11/1931

SHORT, Henry C., ssw-Mary A., b. 10/17/1840, d. 01/14/1914

SHORT, Joseph D., b. 07/10/1880, d. 02/14/1956

SHORT, Mary A., ssw-Henry C., b. 11/05/1844, d. 12/25/1919

SHORT, Mary E., w/o Harry A., ssw-Harry A., b. 08/17/1878, d. 04/25/1927

SIZEMORE, Arkie E., ssw-Grace W., b. 12/25/1900, d. 11/01/1962

SIZEMORE, Grace W., ssw-Arkie E., b. 10/29/1911, d. N/D

SMITH, John, b. 09/01/1875, d. 06/30/1957

SMITH, Joseph H., b. 05/31/1923, d. 09/26/1964
SMITH, Joseph J., b. 1850, d. 1928
SMITH, Laura W., b. 01/04/1886, d. 06/02/1957
SMITH, Walter S., Pvt., 534 CML Mortar Bn., WWII, b. 01/11/1918, d. 09/16/1953
TRUITT, Adeline, b. 1849, d. 1921
TUCKER, Eugene H., b. 12/23/1897, d. 03/11/1971
WAGNER, Ora, b. 1872, d. 1950
WEBB, Charles A., b. 03/12/1939, d. 03/12/1939
WEBB, Charles E., b. 01/04/1885, d. 03/08/1962
WEBB, Charles H., ssw-Mary R., b. 05/16/1854, d. 05/13/1906
WEBB, Delbert J., Tec5, USA, WWII, b. 09/04/1908, d. 08/21/1989
WEBB, Eliza P., b. 11/02/1824, d. 10/12/1910
WEBB, Elizabeth W., ssw-Marshall A., b. 03/18/1873, d. 08/02/1947
WEBB, Elma E., b. 10/27/1917, d. 07/11/1918
WEBB, Elmira F., Age 12y 3m, b. 02/20/1861, d. 05/20/1873
WEBB, Elwood H., ssw-Helen W., b. 10/16/1919, d. N/D
WEBB, Helen W., ssw-Elwood H., b. 01/15/1929, d. N/D
WEBB, Ida F., b. 09/09/1909, d. 07/03/1910
WEBB, Isaac C., Age 68y 1m 15d, b. N/D, d. 04/01/1887
WEBB, John Isaac, Jr., b. 07/14/1980, d. 12/28/1980
WEBB, John P., ssw-Mary E., b. 10/11/1848, d. 05/11/1928
WEBB, Joseph H., ssw-Lida S., b. 1857, d. 1935
WEBB, Lida S., ssw-Joseph H., b. 1866, d. 1939
WEBB, Marie B., b. 11/28/1919, d. 08/21/1989
WEBB, Marshall A., ssw-Elizabeth W., b. 11/20/1867, d. 08/19/1928
WEBB, Mary A., b. 05/04/1886, d. 05/14/1939
WEBB, Mary E., ssw-John P., b. 11/03/1849, d. 02/24/1938
WEBB, Mary R., ssw-Charles H., b. 02/26/1857, d. 01/01/1933
WEBB, Oliver W., b. 02/12/1903, d. 12/30/1967
WEBB, Raymond, b. 09/17/1893, d. 08/19/1976
WEBB, Rena E., ssw-Ward I., b. 08/03/1890, d. 10/16/1971
WEBB, Susan Carol, b. 07/27/1962, d. 08/03/1970
WEBB, Ward I., ssw-Rena E., b. 12/09/1887, d. 02/08/1968
WEBB, William H., b. 06/03/1873, d. 04/27/1950
WHARTON, Edward N., ssw-Ida B., b. 1875, d. 1956
WHARTON, Ida B., ssw-Edward N., b. 1866, d. 1952
WHARTON, Lizzie B., ssw-William R., b. 1854, d. 1926
WHARTON, William R., ssw-Lizzie B., b. 1849, d. 1933
WILLEY, Amanda M., b. 07/19/1906, d. 05/16/1970
WILLEY, Herman E., Pvt., USAAF, WWII, b. 02/14/1902, d. 07/05/1975
WRIGHT, Bryan, ssw-Stella, m. 04/25/1924, b. 01/12/1902, d. 04/10/1984
WRIGHT, Stella, ssw-Bryan, m. 04/25/1924, b. 03/04/1904, d. 01/07/1989

(CC-010 & HU-NR) SILOAM A. M. E. CHURCH CEMETERY
Located S. E. of Milford at the S. E. corner of Pine Haven Rd. (Rd. 224) and Herring Branch Rd. (Rd. 627)
0.3 miles west of Coastal Highway (Rt. 1)

ANDERSON, Harlan, b. N/D, d. 1986
ANORFLEET, Francis, b. 1928, d. 1985
ASKINS, Margariette, b. 1908, d. 1979
BEAVERS, Mildred, b. 1913, d. 1994
BECKWITH, Catherine Taylor, b. 12/23/1942, d. 06/20/1990
BELL, Willie Lee, b. 1937, d. 1974
BENTLEY, David E., b. 09/21/1949, d. 09/06/1983
BIVENS, Solan, b. 1911, d. 1934
BLACKWELL, James E., Cpl., USA, WWII, b. 03/25/1919, d. 12/05/1986
BOONE, John W., b. N/D, d. N/D
BOYKIN, Minnie L., b. 04/28/1922, d. 09/23/1985
BRATTEN, Myanna L., b. 11/20/1967, d. 10/04/1968
BRIGGS, Richard, b. 08/30/1969, d. 01/12/1971
BRITTINGHAM, Elenor, b. 1893, d. 1977
BROCKETT, Herman E., b. 1929, d. 1993
BROOKFIELD, Venia, ssw-Laura C. Macklin, b. 1851, d. 1964
BROOKS, Mildred, b. 1919, d. 1975
BROWN, Carrie L., b. 1932, d. 1993
BROWN, Ember, b. 05/04/1904, d. 02/28/1970
BROWN, Harvey L., b. 1925, d. 1987
BROWN, James R., "Tootsie," b. 03/30/1924, d. 03/14/1988
BROWN, Melvin, b. 1980, d. 1980
BROWN, Nancy, b. 1908, d. 1974
BROWN, Patricia Ann, b. 1969, d. 1980
BROWN, Rayford, b. 1926, d. 1982
BROWN, Roy, b. 1952, d. 1995
BROWN, Sylvester, b. 12/06/1908, d. 03/15/1971
BROWN, Louise, b. 1910, d. 1996
BURTON, Charles, b. 1941, d. 1984
BURTON, Clarence H., b. 09/10/1921, d. 09/30/1989
BURTON, Elmer James, USA, WWII, b. 02/02/1951, d. 01/31/1988
BURTON, Harry J., b. 1932, d. 1995
BURTON, Haywood C., b. 1910, d. 1974
BURTON, Haywood L., b. 09/29/1940, d. 09/08/1994
BURTON, William, b. 1926, d. 1994
BUTLER, Howard S. Pfc., HQ. Co. #4 Army, WWII, b. 02/11/1904, d. 01/24/1967
BUTLER, Solomon R., USA, WWII, b. 1906, d. 1980
BYRD, James B., b. 1942, d. 1997
CARTER, Henry A., Jr., b. 02/03/1943, d. 05/12/1985
CEPHAS, Sarah E., b. 1885, d. 1959
CHANDLER, Lorenzi D., Cook, USA, WWI, b. 1894, d. 1976
CHURCH, Charles H., Jr., b. 1937, d. 1995
CIRWITHIAN, Norman, Pfc., USA, WWII, b. 02/26/1922, d. 03/06/1985
COLEMAN, Raymond, Sp4, USA, b. 02/06/1960, d. 07/08/1985

CONNER, Ruth, b. 1934, d. 1993

COSME, Eliza Ann, b. 06/24/1944, d. 11/16/1984

COVERDALE, Spencer, Pvt., USA, WWII, b. 1918, d. 1983

COXEN, Harry O., Rev., ssw-Martha E., b. 1927, d. 1988

COXEN, Martha E., ssw-Rev. Harry O., b. 1933, d. N/D

CRAPPER, Elmer, Pfc., USA, WWII, b. 10/06/1916, d. 01/17/1982

CRISTA, Diaz A., Baby Girl, b. N/D, d. 11/16/73

CRUZ, Luis, b. 07/10/1934, d. 06/26/1992

CUMMINGS, Clarence, Pvt., USA, WWII, b. 1917, d. 1981

CURRY, John W., b. 1981, d. 1995

DANIELS, Bennie, b. 1915, d. 1978

DANIELS, Clarence, b. 12/03/1897, d. 07/18/1972

DANIELS, Lavinna, b. 07/04/1924, d. 03/20/1968

DAVIS, Abraham, b. 02/16/1935, d. 11/27/1985

DAVIS, Clara, ssw-Emory, b. 1897, d. N/D

DAVIS, Emory, ssw-Clara, b. 1892, d. 1975

DAVIS, Gertrude Macklin, ssw-Charles A. Macklin, b. 1886, d. 1974

DAVIS, Gladys, ssw-Randolph, b. 03/09/1915, d. 09/15/1996

DAVIS, Randolph, ssw-Gladys, b. 01/25/1908, d. 03/09/1983

DESHIELDS, Lillie N., b. 1912, d. 1993

DOWDELL, Caroll L., b. 1965, d. 1993

DRAPER, Anna, b. 03/11/1925, d. 03/02/1941

DRUMMOND, Jessie Mae White, b. 09/23/1951, d. 05/05/1984

DRUMMOND, Paula V., b. N/D, d. 1982

DRUMMOND, Stanford, Sgt., USA, Korea, b. 02/05/1934, d. 06/01/1983

DUKER, Charles L., Cpl., Co. H, 164 Inf., b. 04/15/1933, d. 05/30/1966

DUKER, Shirley L., b. 09/02/1934, d. 05/24/1992

DUKES, Ellaree Frazier, b. 07/04/1934, d. 11/06/1984

DUKES, Mack, b. 1918, d. 1987

FARLOW, Clifford William, STM2, USNR, WWII, b. 02/27/1911, d. 06/14/1956

FARLOW, Elton, b. N/D, d. N/D

FISHER, Marshall, Jr., b. 1948, d. 1993

FOREMAN, Fred, b. 1923, d. 1992

FOREMAN, Lillie M., b. 134, d. 1990

FRAIZER, Mattie H., b. 07/04/1913, d. 05/06/1979

FRANCIS, Mary, b. 1910, d. 1992

FULLMAN, Annie Mae, ssw-Mary E., b. 1915, d. 1939

FULLMAN, John W., ssw-Mary E., b. 1886, d. 1944

FULLMAN, John W., Jr., Interred in Belgium, b. 1911, d. 1945

FULLMAN, Mary E., ssw-Annie Mae, b. 1942, d. 1948

FULLMAN, Mary E., ssw-John W., b. 1884, d. N/D

GADSON, Mabel, b. 09/14/1907, d. 04/10/1977

GALLASHAW, Bertha M., b. 1915, d. 1985

GOLDSBOROUGH, Ida M., b. 06/28/1912, d. 10/17/1989

GOOCH, Jerome, b. 04/30/1935, d. 11/21/1992

GRAY, Melvin, b. 10/08/1965, d. 06/24/1991

GREEN, Blanche T., b. 11/11/1928, d. 06/08/1981

GRIFFITH, Clara B., b. 07/10/1925, d. 12/16/1984

GRIFFITH, Elma Mae, b. 03/10/1898, d. 07/05/1986
GRIFFITH, John I., b. 07/04/1922, d. 03/26/1991
GRIFFITH, Mildred E., b. 1931, d. 1996
GRIFFITH, Roxie, b. 05/22/1905, d. 09/30/1972
HACKET, James, b. 09/22/1936, d. 12/29/1976
HADRICK, James, b. 1912, d. 1985
HAIRSTON, Henry, Pa., Pfc., Co. A, 505 Svc. Bn., QMC, WWI, b. 03/29/1888, d. 09/16/1967
HAIRSTON, Leroy, b. 1957, d. 1982
HALL, Charlie, b. 1922, d. 1994
HANZER, Louis, Pvt., USA, WWI, b. 11/02/1895, d. 11/27/1977
HARDY, Eliza, b. 1904, d. 1989
HARMON, Elva H, b. 1907, d. 1973
HARMON, Gilbert, b. 05/16/1906, d. 03/28/1985
HARMON, Mildred M., b. 04/23/1920, d. 12/27/1982
HARMON, Willie F., b. 1923, d. 1991
HAZZARD, Harvey O., Sr., b. 01/24/1909, d. 11/21/1991
HENRY, Robert, b. 1946, d. 1994
HONEYVILLE, Viola, b. 1899, d. 1986
HOPKINS, Georgia A., b. 05/20/1907, d. 09/08/1988
HOUSTON, John H., b. 1877, d. 1940
HOUSTON, Sarah, b. N/D, d. N/D
HOWELL, Essie A., b. 1913, d. 1987
HOWELL, Lucille, b. 1926, d. 1987
HOWIE, Jennie B., b. 02/26/1890, d. 11/28/1981
HOWIE, Walter E., Sr., Pvt., USA, WWII, B. 1927, d. 1989
HUDSON, Mary E., ssw-William J., b. 1902, d. 1986
HUDSON, William J., ssw-Mary E., b. 1900, d. 1981
IRVIN, Mamie, b. 1898, d. 1990
JACKSON, James W., Pfc., USA, Vietnam, b. 1948, d. 1977
JACKSON, Ruby, b. 1920, d. 1995
JEFFERSON, Wilmer, b. 1923, d. 1980
JENNINGS, J. B., b. 10/19/1920, d. 02/05/1971
JOHNSON, Doris H., b. 12/23/1953, d. 01/20/1993
JOHNSON, Mary A., b. 1953, d. 1980
JOHNSON, Ronald, b. N/D, d. N/D
JOHNSON, Ronald H., b. 05/28/1942, d. 09/22/1993
KEELING, Mary E., b. 09/15/1904, d. 01/10/1970
KELLY, Sue P., b. 1941, d. 1980
LEE, Robert, b. N/D, d. N/D
LEGGINS, Joseph, b. 1905, d. 1972
LILES, Daisy, b. 1906, d. 1997
MACKLIN, Charles A., ssw-Gertrude Macklin Davis, b. 1886, d. 1924
MACKLIN, Laura C., ssw-Venia Brookfield, b. 1887, d. 1976
MACKLIN, Ray Ella, ssw-William Lewis, Sr., b. 07/18/1925, d. 06/13/1968
MACKLIN, William Lewis, Sr., ssw-Ray Ella, b. 06/20/1925, d. 11/21/1991
MARSHALL, Frank P., Jr., b. 09/06/1943, d. 01/25/1944
MARSHALL, Lula F., b. 1937, d. 1996
MARSHALL, Untone, b. 1957, d. 1990

MAULL, Jeffery C., b. 1982, d. 1990
MCCREA, Caroline, b. 05/12/1910, d. 12/01/1986
MERRILL, Noah, b. 1911, d. 1937
MERRILL, Noah F., Rev., b. 1954, d. 1987
MILLER, Ethel, b. 12/10/1910, d. 08/22/1977
MILLER, Kathy, b. 1914, d. 1990
MORGAN, Carrie, b. 1899, d. 1977
MURPHY, Ella, ssw-Louis, b. 1918, d. N/D
MURPHY, Louis, ssw-Ella, b. 1912, d. 1972
NASHAY, Raven, b. N/D, d. N/D
NATSON, Rosson, b. 1913, d. 1991
NEAL, Annabelle, ssw-Wilbur J., b. 01/04/1900, d. 04/21/1933
NEAL, Catherine E., ssw-Daniel W., Age 78y, b. N/D, d. 10/16/1945
NEAL, Daniel W., ssw-Catherine E., Age 64y, b. N/D, d. 06/20/1926
NEAL, Juanita, b. 10/02/1910, d. 09/12/1983
NEAL, Wilbert, Jr., b. 1922, d. 1990
NEAL, Wilbur J., ssw-Annabelle, b. 11/04/1888, d. 03/15/1959
NELSON, Angeline, b. 1991, d. 1991
NESMITH, Cleveland, b. 1941, d. 1993
NESMITH, Eugene, b. 1909, d. 1990
NESMITH, Frances, b. 1914, d. 1989
NESMITH, Lulua, b. 02/07/1910, d. 12/10/1973
NESMITH, Stella, b. 1900, d. 1996
NLN, Alfredo, b. 1952, d. 1993
NLN, Domenick, b. 1939, d. 1992
NLN, John H., b. 1937, d. 1992
NLN, NFN, b. 1919, d. 1991
NLN, Sparky, b. 1968, d. 1980
NLN, Tami, b. 02/23/1975, d. 09/16/1990
ONEY, Paul E., DE, 3133 QM, Svc. Co., WWII, b. 04/07/1921, d. 04/13/1964
PALMER, Edward, Sr., b. 1921, d. 1993
PARKER, Charles, Sr., ssw-Mabel J., b. 1893, d. 1959
PARKER, Edgar, b. 1926, d. 1993
PARKER, Frances Clorice Bayward, b. 11/27/1931, d. 12/23/1977
PARKER, George T., Cpl., USA, b. 1933, d. 1989
PARKER, Mabel J., ssw-Charles, Sr., b. 1897, d. 1969
PERRY, Alverila, b. 1924, d. 1991
PERRY, Robert A., Pvt., USA, WWII, b. 04/12/1902, d. 09/23/1985
PERRY, Theodore W., b. 1919, d. 1987
PERRY, Theodore W., b. 1945, d. 1995
PETTYJOHN, Burl, ssw-Mary, b. 1890, d. 1965
PETTYJOHN, Elijah, ssw-Nelia Ellen, b. 1844, d. 1928
PETTYJOHN, Ernest O., ssw-Gertrude E., b. 11/11/1911, d. 03/04/1983
PETTYJOHN, George H., b. 12/18/1908, d. 05/09/1980
PETTYJOHN, Georgia B., ssw-Robert H. & Helen M., b. 1898, d. 1944
PETTYJOHN, Georgia Ida, b. 1906, d. 1991
PETTYJOHN, Gertrude E., ssw-Ernest O., b. 07/12/1913, d. 04/12/1982
PETTYJOHN, Helen M., ssw-Georgia B. & Robert H., b. 1924, d. 1947

PETTYJOHN, Irene, ssw-Thomas H., b. 1879, d. 1966

PETTYJOHN, Mary, ssw-Burl, b. 1894, d. 1988

PETTYJOHN, Medrania, ssw-Walter J., b. 02/28/1897, d. 08/21/1992

PETTYJOHN, Nelia Ellen, Elijah, b. 1859, d. 1938

PETTYJOHN, Radie Anna, b. 1893, d. 1981

PETTYJOHN, Robert H., ssw-Georgia B. & Helen M., b. 1890, d. 1934

PETTYJOHN, Thomas, b. 05/02/1906, d. 03/28/1976

PETTYJOHN, Thomas H., ssw-Irene, b. 1877, d. 1968

PETTYJOHN, Travis T., b. 1950, d. 1994

PETTYJOHN, Walter J., ssw-Medrania, b. 09/15/1893, d. 08/20/1978

PETTYJOHN, Willis S., Pfc., USA, WWI, b. 04/12/1892, d. 11/15/1975

PHELPS, Leslie H., Tec5, USA, WWII, b. 1920, d. 1984

PINKNEY, Mary, b. 1929, d. 1987

PIPER, Georganna, ssw-Howard H., Sr., b. 06/01/1906, d. N/D

PIPER, Howard H., Sr., ssw-Georganna, b. 10/06/1903, d. 05/10/1975

POWELL, Dorothy F., b. 02/02/1933, d. 11/04/1987

POWELL, Lamont G., b. 1959, d. 1993

POWELL, LesHea M., b. 1990, d. 1990

POWELL, Louis, b. 1932, d. 1989

POWELL, Sharonte, b. 07/11/1984, d. 01/21/1986

PRICE, Edwin, b. 1908, d. 1984

PRICE, Eliza J., ssw-Thomas J., b. 1879, d. 1979

PRICE, Leon, b. 1910, d. 1984

PRICE, Thomas J., ssw-Eliza J., b. 1875, d. 1960

RANDOLPH, Walker B., b. 06/17/1861, d. 03/05/1956

REED, Charles, b. 03/03/1918, d. 02/25/1975

REED, Leon M., b. 01/25/1926, d. 05/30/1984

REYNOLDS, Lillie Bell, b. 11/12/1906, d. 11/04/1990

RHODES, Daniel, Pfc., USA, WWII, b. 03/22/1904, d. 04/18/1972

RHODES, Elsie V., b. 1893, d. 1973

RHODES, Virgie M., b. 1891, d. 1968

ROBINSON, Bessie, b. N/D, d. N/D

ROBINSON, Charles, b. N/D, d. N/D

ROBINSON, Cora, ssw-Walter, b. 1902, d, 1988

ROBINSON, Mary, b. 1897, d. 1981

ROBINSON, Sheppard, b. 1889, d. 1946

ROBINSON, Walter, ssw-Cora, b. 1898, d. 1986

SAMPSON, Zerphlee, b. 12/27/1895, d. 06/08/1978

SCOTT, William M., Sr., b. 1924, d. 1996

SEYMORE, Leroy, Pvt., USA, WWII, b. 1925, d. 1980

SHARP, Lambert, b. 1907, d. 1994

SHARP, Louise, b. 1909, d. 1992

SHARPE, Dwayne K., b. 08/26/1958, d. 12/16/1985

SHELTON, Hattie, b. 1908, d. 1993

SHEPPARD, George, b. 1930, d. 1996

SHORTS, Baby Girl, b. 1990, d. 1990

SIMS, Ned, b. 1913, d. 1985

SMITH, David P., b. 1949, d. 1992

SMITH, Freddie, Tec5, USA, WWII, b. 05/06/1915, d. 03/19/1991
SMITH, Joseph C., b. 1940, d. 1992
SMITH, W. M., "Asbury," b. 1919, d. 1974
SPENCE, Everett Eugene, b. 1949, d. 1978
STANLEY, Margaret, b. 1946, d. 1985
STEVENS, Ollie E., b. 07/23/1897, d. 10/01/1970
SUAREZ, Betty Sarah, b. 1934, d. 1982
SUAREZ, James Leroy, b. 1959, d. 1996
TAYLOR, Teany, b. 07/03/1892, d. 12/29/1992
THOMAS, Eugene, b. 1930, d. 1987
THOMAS, Marsha Yvette, b. 09/02/1962, d. 11/24/1990
THOMAS, Marshall Y., b. N/D, d. N/D
TRUITT, Dorothy Y., b. 1919, d. 1996
TRUITT, James E., b. 07/05/1913, d. 01/09/1982
TUCKER, Carrie, b. 1946, d. 1993
VICKERS, James, b. 1927, d. 1985
WALLS, Joseph Styles, DE, Pvt., 22 Depot Svc. Co., WWI, b. 05/10/1894, d. 10/31/1953
WAPLES, Annie Mae, ssw-Olden W. S., Sr., b. 12/27/1922, d. 12/20/1975
WAPLES, Olden W. S., Sr., ssw-Annie Mae, b. 10/30/1913, d. N/D
WARREN, Alfred, CK 3, USN, WWII, b. 06/27/1912, d. 04/07/1980
WARREN, Margaret M., b. 04/20/1928, d. 11/24/1985
WATERS-MITCHELL, Jack'Kia Tyronda, b. 11/19/1994, d. 01/04/1996
WEAVER, Carrie, b. 1940, d. 1995
WEST, Baby, b. N/D, d. 1991
WHALEN, J. W., Rev., b. 10/10/1880, d. 12/08/1963
WHALEN, John W., Sgt., USA, WWII, b. 06/25/1917, d. 03/21/1973
WHALEY, Delbert, b. 1940, d. 1993
WHALEY, George, b. 1910, d. 1982
WHALEY, John O., ssw-Millie L., b. 07/22/1894, d. 06/03/1981
WHALEY, Millie L., ssw-John O., b. 09/27/1898, d. 09/12/1948
WHEELER, Donald Lee, b. 1957, d. 1994
WHITE, Oscar J. R., 3rd, b. 1952, d. 1974
WHITE, Zemble, b. 1928, d. 1996
WILLIAMS, Edwin Booth, NC, Pfc., USA, b. 08/18/1932, d. 10/23/1966
WILLIAMS, Florence Lee, Pvt., USA, b. 06/14/1936, d. 01/24/1991
WINSTEAD, Henrietta, b. 1922, d. 1984
WRIGHT, James, b. 03/09/1909, d. 08/11/1996
WRIGHT, Jessie Lee, b. 11/28/1915, d. 05/26/1978
YOUNG, Ada J., b. 10/14/1910, d. 06/07/1963
YOUNG, Beneto D., DE, Pfc., Co. I, 808 Pioneer Co., WWI, b. 12/04/1887, d. 05/31/1966
YOUNG, Corrine M., b. 03/09/1927, d. 06/03/1987
YOUNG, Georganna, ssw-Hanson L., b. 03/22/1908, d. 11/17/1968
YOUNG, Hanson L., ssw-Georganna, b. 03/08/1906, d. 01/31/1986
YOUNG, Hanson Lewis, Jr., Cpl., USA, Korea, b. 04/11/1930, d. 02/22/1993
YOUNG, James L., b. 09/15/1902, d. 02/02/1978
YOUNG, James Leroy, Jr., DE, Cpl., Co. F, 32 Inf. Regt., Korea, b. 05/27/1931, d. 03/13/1955
YOUNG, Joseph Titus, b. 08/26/1898, d. 05/02/1978
YOUNG, Pearl V. Whalen, b. 1906, d. 1995

(CC-011 & HU-NR) OLD HICKORY CEMETERY
Located S. E. of Milford on the N. E. side of Herring Branch Rd. (Rd. 627), 0.5 miles South of Pine Haven Rd. (Rd. 224)

ALEXANDER, Willie Mercer, Sr., "Bay," b. 07/01/1916, d. 05/18/1994
ALLEN, Alice C., b. 1926, d. 1989
ALLEN, Darl Payne, USN, WWII, b. 08/23/1925, d. 09/25/1988
ALLEN, Emma Jane, ssw-George, Jr., b. 10/08/1922, d. 08/23/1978
ALLEN, George, Jr., ssw-Emma Jane, b. 04/28/1917, d. 07/18/1967
BAGWELL, Danny S., b. 1910, d. 1996
BARRON, Ubaldo, b. 05/16/1960, d. 05/22/1986
BAYNARD, Alexander, ssw-Carrie D. Powell, b. 09/01/1909, d. N/D
BAYNARD, Gertrude D., b. 10/08/1907, d. 02/06/1962
BENSON, Geneva Shockley, b. 06/10/1903, d. 07/25/1987
BLUNT, Mattie Crapper, b. 1929, d. 1942
BOONE, Leonard A., Jr., ssw-Lorraine E., b. 02/02/1937, d. N/D
BOONE, Lorraine E., ssw-Leonard A., Jr., b. 10/28/1932, d. 10/21/1981
BOWE, Olian, b. 1922, d. 1997
BOWE, Rufus, b. 1937, d. 1988
BOWE, Rufus, Sr., b. 08/17/1915, d. 03/07/1993
BRITTINGHAM, Ebony Andriea, b. 04/20/1985, d. 07/09/1985
BROUTON, Annie, b. 1936, d. 1989
BROWN, Carrie P., ssw-William Maynard, m. 08/14/1953, b. 08/18/1918, d. N/D
BROWN, Muriel C., b. 1961, d. 1995
BROWN, William Maynard, ssw-Carrie P., m. 08/14/1953, Tec5, USA, b. 09/09/1921, d. 02/10/1994
BRUNDGE, Ruth, b. 12/20/1928, d. 02/28/1994
BUNCH, Aletha S., ssw-William, b. 03/28/1905, d. 11/03/1983
BUNCH, William, ssw-Aletha S., b. 05/22/1905, d. 11/09/1970
BURRIS, Reginald W., Sp4, 81 QM PIT, USA, Support Comd., Vietnam, b. 01/18/1948, d. 08/19/1969
BURTON, Alfred J., b. 1855, d. 1931
BURTON, Elsie H., b. 12/04/1898, d. 09/04/1986
BURTON, James H., b. 03/12/1844, d. 04/10/1911
BURTON, Mary I., b. 1881, d. 1954
BUTLER, Willie James, b. 1924, d. 1973
BYNES, Girlena, ssw-Willie, Sr., b. 07/06/1927, d. N/D
BYNES, Willie, Sr., ssw-Girlena, b. 02/17/1920, d. 12/05/1989
CAMPBELL, Lillie Mae, b. N/D, d. N/D
CANNON, Ethel Mae Ross, b. 05/11/1920, d. 03/09/1989
CANNON, Frances H., b. 01/19/1919, d. 12/17/1974
CARBIN, Jamie, b. 1977, d. 1983
CARBIN, Michael, b. 1982, d. 1983
CARBIN, Windi, b. 1980, d. 1983
CARMICHAEL, Steiner, Pvt., 53 Co., 157 Depot Brigade, WWI, b. 02/26/1896, d. 02/20/1962
CARROLL, Dalton S., ssw-Grace A., b. 02/18/1891, d. 10/09/1953
CARROLL, Grace A., ssw-Dalton S., b. 10/27/1896, d. 08/28/1986
CARROLL, Lucinda Ann, "Cindy," b. 10/02/1958, d. 11/18/1995
CARTER, Bertha, b. 1891, d. 1978
CAULK, Christia Ann, b. 10/07/1882, d. 07/17/1964

CEPHAS, Bertie, b. 1888, d. 1895

CEPHAS, Catherine, b. 1920, d. 1967

CEPHAS, Elliott D., Lcpl, USMC, Age 21y, b. 09/08/1966, d. 05/11/1987

CEPHAS, Elsie Y., ssw-Fred G., Sr., b. 03/19/1925, d. N/D

CEPHAS, Fred G., Jr., b. 1951, d. 1997

CEPHAS, Fred G., Sr., ssw-Elsie Y., b. 08/19/1919, d. 06/10/1993

CEPHAS, Jon Edwin, Pvt., USA, b. 09/16/1944, d. 02/02/1995

CEPHAS, NFN, b. N/D, d. 1972

CHURCH, Rachel, b. 11/19/1919, d. 11/30/1938

CIRWITHIAN, Edward, ssw-Ola, b. 1881, d. 1963

CIRWITHIAN, Ola, ssw-Edward, b. 1899, d. 1953

CLAPPER, Roscoe, b. 07/15/1910, d. 04/19/1970

COBBS, Michael, b. 1991, d. 1992

COCKRAN, Pearl S., b. 1921, d. 1986

COLLINS, Alice Shockley, ssw-Charles Stanton Harmon, b. 01/20/1888, d. 06/08/1942

CONWELL, David, b. 10/16/1816, d. 10/21/1897

CONWELL, Elizabeth S., b. 1865, d. 1935

CONWELL, Nathan, b. 11/25/1862, d. 10/12/1941

CONWELL, Rhoda Ella, ssw-Samuel Lewis, b. 1869, d. 1952

CONWELL, Samuel Lewis, ssw-Rhoda Ella, b. 1858, d. 1944

CONWELL, Sarah, b. 06/26/1823, d. 01/27/1879

COOPER, Fowler, b. 1900, d. 1986

CORBIN, Rosanna, b. 1919, d. 1995

CRAPPER, Elwood, Sgt., USA, WWII, b. 09/12/1917, d. 01/01/1993

CRAPPER, Helen Y., b. 04/28/1893, d. 09/16/1986

CRAPPER, Inez, b. 1924, d. 1978

CRAPPER, Joseph, b. 1921, d. 1996

CRAPPER, Mary Holden, Born Wattsville, Va., b. 1915, d. 1992

CRAPPER, Robert B., b. 12/25/1890, d. 09/12/1942

CROPPER, Augustus, Pvt., Co. K, 807 Pioneer Inf., WWI, b. 04/12/1887, d. 1/15/1957

DANIELS, Annie M., b. 07/24/1925, d. 04/18/1991

DANIELS, Daisy V., ssw-Garfield W., Sr., b. 08/07/1917, d. N/D

DANIELS, Garfield W., Jr., Pvt., USA, b. 12/08/1938, d. 06/11/1985

DANIELS, Garfield W., Sr., ssw-Daisy V., b. 06/12/1916, d. 01/24/1995

DANIELS, Keith L., b. N/D, d. 1994

DANIELS, Victor L., Jr., b. N/D, d. 08/24/1989

DAVES, Kezia, b. 1989, d. 1997

DAVIS, Absalom James, S1, USNR, WWII, b. 04/01/1924, d. 04/10/1972

DAVIS, Anthony J., b. 03/1957, d. 06/1990

DAVIS, Charles R., b. 1962, d. 1988

DAVIS, Donelda, b. 1964, d. 1994

DAVIS, Edward S., Tec5, USA, WWII, b. 03/23/1919, d. 10/01/1979

DAVIS, Jacob W., ssw-Margaret E., b. 1899, d. 1980

DAVIS, Leola P., b. 1893, d. 1973

DAVIS, Margaret E., ssw-Jacob W., b. 1899, d. 1982

DAVIS, Mary E., b. 10/22/1921, d. 01/26/1978

DAVIS, Nehemiah H., b. 08/1924, d. 05/1975

DAVIS, Parold G., USA, WWI, b. 01/14/1895, d. 11/14/1984

DENNIS, Patrick, Jr., b. N/D, d. 1995

DOUGLAS, James, b. 1909, d. 1990

DOWNING, Daniel A., Rev., Born Accomac Co., Va. & Died in Milford, b. 10/10/1880, d. 04/07/1971

DOWNING, Elton A., Pfc, USA, WWII, b. 02/28/1911, d. 04/19/1974

DOWNING, Lucy L., w/o Rev. D. A., b. 03/08/1908, d. 01/20/1972

DOWNING, Parthenia, b. 1937, d. 1979

DOYLE, Arnold, b. 1961, d. 1985

DOYLE, Isaac, b. 1964, d. 1993

DREDDEN, Mary Emily, b. 1918, d. 1985

DUFFY, Clarine G., b. 1923, d. 1995

ELLIS, Calvin, b. 1917, d. 1992

ELLIS, Mary V., "Say," b. 0/21/1919, d. 06/21/1988

EVANS, Annie B., b. 10/29/1938, d. 06/13/1988

FAIRCLOTH, Mildred Molock, b. 05/14/1912, d. 04/08/1981

FARLOW, Eva M., b. 03/21/1944, d. 12/31/1990

FAWLKES, Mary F., w/o Maudie, Age 39y, b. N/D, d. 01/26/1909

FINCH, Mary R., b. 1898, d. 1920

FOREMAN, Malinda M., b. 1912, d. 1994

FOREMAN, Vincent, b. 1919, d. 1978

FOUNTAIN, Sarah J., Age 68y, b. N/D, d. 03/09/1912

FRAZIER, Elouise, ssw-Julius, b. 04/13/1922, d. 10/13/1996

FRAZIER, John J., Sfc., USN, b. 05/20/1909, d. 03/10/1991

FRAZIER, Julius, ssw-Elouise, b. 06/02/1919, d. N/D

FREEMAN, David, Jr., Tec5, 390 QM Truck Co., WWII, b. 12/15/1918, d. 05/15/1958

FREEMAN, Pauline, b. 1932, d. 1994

FREEMAN, Shynise I., b. 1995, d. 1996

GAMBLE, NFN, b. 1930, d. 1994

GARRISON, Roscoe, b. 10/31/1926, d. 05/07/1993

GAYLE, Wallace, b. 1909, d. 1997

GIBBS, Macon T., b. 1933, d. 1989

GIBBS, Milton, ssw-Sophia, b. 05/15/1916, d. N/D

GIBBS, Sophia, ssw-Milton, b. 01/16/1922, d. 07/09/1995

GILBERT, Alethea Daniels, b. N/D, d. 05/09/1989

GILL, Catherine Robinson, b. 03/29/1922, d. 02/16/1968

GONAZELZ, Juan, "Jonny," b. 12/24/1941, d. 08/05/1991

GRIFFIN, Eddie Lee, b. 1921, d. 1990

GRIFFIN, Lee W., b. 1919, d. 1987

GRIFFIN, Paul, b. 1925, d. 1996

GRIFFITH, Fred C., ssw-Mabel H., b. 1895, d. N/D

GRIFFITH, Mabel H., ssw-Fred C., b. 1905, d. N/D

GROVES, Elzie, s/o Joseph O & Mary, Pvt., Co. C, 808 Inf., AEF, WWI, b. 1896, d. 1925

GROVES, Walter, b. 05/15/1923, d. 02/16/1979

HALLETT, Ronald L., b. 1944, d. 1993

HAMILTON, Prestizia, b. N/D, d. 1996

HAMMOND, Earlene, b. 1918, d. 1996

HANDY, Raven S., b. N/D, d. 1992

HARMAN, Howard, MM2, USN, WWII, b. 1914, d. 1979

HARMON, Alfred, Jr., A2C, USAF, b. 08/09/1934, d. 05/06/1979

HARMON, Anton, b. 09/06/1957, d. 03/02/1978

HARMON, Charles Stanton, ssw-Alice Shockley Collins, b. 03/15/1943, d. 07/25/1943

HARMON, Cora Watson, b. 1902, d. 1994

HARMON, Ethel M., b. 1925, d. 1988

HARMON, Laurence, b. 1942, d. 1996

HARMON, Mary Edith, b. 1896, d. 1971

HARMON, Ralph, Pvt., USA, b. 02/21/1928, d. 11/06/1988

HARMON, Rosetta M., ssw-Torbert B. S., b. 08/27/1938, d. N/D

HARMON, Torbert B. S., ssw-Rosetta M., Pvt., USA, b. 08/15/1927, d. 01/21/1991

HARRIS, Annie M., b. 1878, d. 1956

HARRIS, Arthur L., b. 08/06/1915, d. 11/13/1984

HARRIS, Clifford, ssw-Roxie Mae, b. 03/18/1888, d. 03/02/1958

HARRIS, Delores A., ssw-Carolyn L. Robinson, b. 03/12/1941, d. 06/04/1954

HARRIS, Oscar E., b. 02/04/1928, d. 10/23/1993

HARRIS, Roxie Mae, ssw-Clifford, b. 03/01/1895, d. 03/19/1985

HAZZARD, Amos T., ssw-Tacie E., b. 1893, d. 1948

HAZZARD, Harvey, Jr., b. 08/29/1925, d. 09/05/1985

HAZZARD, Reginald I., "Buggy," b. 10/13/1936, d. 06/10/1985

HAZZARD, Shanna, b. N/D, d. 1994

HAZZARD, Sufrain A., b. 07/24/1936, d. 10/22/1986

HAZZARD, Tacie E., ssw-Amos T., b. 1897, d. 1978

HEAVELOW, Daisey A., b. 1887, d. 1954

HILL, Sarah, b. 1912, d. 1991

HILL, W. George, b. N/D, d. 07/17/1906

HINTON, Alice B., b. 1930, d. 1978

HINTON, Garfield, b. 1911, d. 1993

HOBBS, Enoch Jasper, b. 1906, d. 1961

HOBBS, Georgeanna, b. 1915, d. 1986

HUGGINS, Mildred F., ssw-Clara J. Ingram, b. 09/11/1905, d. 12/01/1995

HURST, Ada B., ssw-Clifford E., b. 06/12/1936, d. 09/09/1996

HURST, Clifford E., ssw-Ada B., b. 12/27/1934, d. N/D

INGRAM, Clara J., ssw-Mildred F. Huggins, b. 03/07/1872, d. 01/14/1966

INGRAM, Mary E., b. 01/28/1904, d. 05/30/1990

JACKSON, Clifford, b. 1956, d. 1994

JACKSON, Grace C., ssw-Rev. Robert A., b. 01/17/1932, d. N/D

JACKSON, Robert A., DD, Rev., ssw-Grace C., WWII VET, b. 05/20/1923, d. 03/16/1993

JEFFERSON, Mattie S., b. 1919, d. 1986

JENKINS, Charles H., ssw-Mary E., b. 06/20/1922, d. N/D

JENKINS, Mary E., ssw-Charles H., b. 08/28/1922, d. 02/18/1983

JOHNSON, Lee Ann, b. 05/02/1952, d. 07/28/1976

JOHNSON, Ricky, b. N/D, d. 1979

JOHNSON, Rodney, b. 1971, d. 1991

JONES, Ella B., b. 1897, d. 1983

JONES, Frank, A3C, USAF, Korea, b. 05/29/1932, d. 04/16/1989

JONES, Girllena, b. 1923, d. 1994

JONES, Mary L., b. 1910, d. 1996

JONES, Sally I., b. 08/16/1947, d. 02/10/1992

JONES, Wallace, b. 1959, d. 1994

KADIRI, Jasiri N., b. 1949, d. 1996
KEE, McCoy W., b. 1933, d. 1995
KING, Walter C., b. 07/18/1917, d. 02/26/1988
KITTRELL, Georgia L., b. 06/27/1922, d. 12/23/1991
LASSITER, Clara Doris, b. N/D, d. N/D
LEGRAND, Gloria, b. 1953, d. 1997
LEWIS, Lucius L., Jr., MM, FR, USN, b. 1959, d. 1982
LOADHOLT, Willie L., b. 12/08/1928, d. 04/26/1989
LOCKMAN, Jaal T., ssw-Rev. James O., b. 1893, d. 1982
LOCKMAN, James O., Rev., ssw-Jaal T., b. 1885, d. 1961
LOCKWOOD, Bertha E., ssw-Joshua, b. 11/23/1893, d. 01/21/1961
LOCKWOOD, Joshua, ssw-Bertha E., b. 10/15/1876, d. 01/19/1957
LOFLAND, Richard Preston, b. 11/23/1946, d. 08/31/1955
LONG, Charity, b. 1929, d. 1980
LOPER, Elias, b. 1922, d. 1995
LOPER, Phyllis L., b. 11/28/1930, d. 05/22/1961
LOPER, Rodney Nixon, b. 1931, d. 1994
MAPP, Gordon, Jr. b. N/D, d. 1992
MARSHALL, Natalie C., b. N/D, d. 1979
MASON, Jessie J., A1C, USAF, Korea, b. 12/31/1928, d. 03/05/1977
MASON, Lillian D., b. 1902, d. 1986
MASON, Melvin, b. 1900, d. 1996
MCCREA, Alfred, b. 11/23/1905, d. 10/23/1996
MCCREA, Louise, b. 1905, d. 1995
MCDONALD, Shakirah N., b. N/D, d. 1997
MCDUFFIE, Eunice, b. 02/03/1924, d. 01/14/1979
MCDUFFIE, Walter, b. 1880, d. 1969
MICKLE, Clyde Woods, b. 1917, d. 1973
MICKLE, Joshua Wesley, b. 1902, d. 1974
MIQUEL, Gabriel H., b. N/D, d. 1997
MONLEY, Clarence, b. 1940, d. 1987
MOORE, William H., b. 07/25/1925, d. 04/17/1961
MORRIS, Alpenia M., ssw-Clifford W., b. 07/29/1916, d. 02/16/1990
MORRIS, Bruce Bentley, b. 04/18/1960, d. 02/04/1993
MORRIS, Clifford W., ssw-Alpenia M., b. 07/25/1910, d. 09/27/1968
MORRIS, Elzie Stanley, b. 02/02/1939, d. 09/15/1994
MORRIS, Grace J., ssw-Granville W., b. 02/14/1940, d. N/D
MORRIS, Granville W., ssw-Grace J., b. 12/17/1937, d. 07/13/1991
MORRIS, Lillie Mae, b. 1913, d. 1986
MORRIS, Rexall D., b. 01/27/1956, d. 08/12/1973
MULLEN, Birdie K. Johnson, b. 06/04/1914, d. 04/02/1994
MURPHY, Johnny, b. 1921, d. 1996
NEAL, Mary E., ssw-Oliver S., b. 10/09/1896, d. N/D
NEAL, Oliver S., ssw-Mary E., b. 05/12/1893, d. 08/24/1965
NELSON, Eric D., b. 1988, d. 1991
NELSON, Rhina, ssw-Eleanor Pettyjohn, b. 1902, d. 1981
NICHOLS, Baby, b. N/D, d. 1991
NICHOLS, Charles D., b. 10/10/1910, d. 05/02/1984

OGLESBY, Estella, b. 1931, d. 1997

OWENS, Darryl L., b. 1957, d. 1994

OWENS, Lee Vince, USA, WWII, b. 11/18/1924, d. 01/14/1994

PARKER, Archibald Henry, Stm1, USNR, WWII, b. 01/10/1925, d. 12/30/1966

PEARSALL, William, b. 1951, d. 1995

PERKINS, Bertha G., b. 1921, d. 1997

PERRY, James, b. 1905, d. 1992

PETERSON, Archie Lee, Jr., b. 1989, d. 1989

PETTYJOHN, Charlotte J., b. 05/06/1927, d. 08/22/1977

PETTYJOHN, Edith R., b. 08/15/1906, d. 12/30/1962

PETTYJOHN, Edward, b. 1913, d. 1944

PETTYJOHN, Eleanor, ssw-Rhina Nelson, b. N/D, d. N/D

PETTYJOHN, Frances Henry, ssw-Herbert, b. 08/27/1927, d. 12/13/1991

PETTYJOHN, Hattie M., w/o Jeremiah, b. 08/08/1875, d. N/D

PETTYJOHN, Herbert, ssw-Frances Henry, b. 11/04/1924, d. N/D

PETTYJOHN, Herbert, Jr., Pvt., USA, Vietnam, b. 12/21/1950, d. 05/07/1988

PETTYJOHN, Orlando J., b. 1962, d. 1982

PETTYJOHN, Oscar H., b. 04/13/1890, d. 09/11/1972

PETTYJOHN, Raymond L., b. 02/11/1894, d. 08/23/1965

PETTYJOHN, Virginia, b. 1887, d. 1945

PIERCE, Harry, b. 02/06/1956, d. 04/23/1985

PIERCE, Margaret J., b. 12/25/1865, d. 06/11/1944

PIERRE, Aretha Y., b. 1963, d. 1995

PITTS, Margaret, b. 1962, d. 1979

POPE, Gertrude, b. 1926, d. 1994

POULSON, Andrew, b. 1921, d. 1978

POWELL, Carrie D., ssw-Alexander Baynard, b. 08/01/1894, d. 12/27/1990

POWELL, Mary M., b. 11/14/1910, d. 01/28/1993

POWELL, Nathaniel, Sr., b. 08/07/1902, d. 05/01/1983

POWELL, Irving B., Pvt., USA, b. 09/25/1895, d. 11/25/1974

PRETTYMAN, James A., ssw-Katherine A., b. 1916, d. N/D

PRETTYMAN, Katherine, ssw-James A., b. 1915, d. 1986

PRETTYMAN, William J., Pfc., USA, b. 04/21/1943, d. 10/07/1992

PRIDEOUX, Sarah Elizabeth, b. 05/09/1916, d. 10/04/1996

PURNELL, Stella, b. 1900, d. 1997

QUINONES, Elder Mary H., b. 1911, d. 1983

QUINONES, Mary, b. 01/07/1911, d. 07/24/1988

RAYFIELD, Eva, b. 09/28/1900, d. 09/10/1980

REID, Delores, b. 11/30/1932, d. 11/04/1978

REYNOLDS, Jacquel Darris, b. 1990, d. 1993

REYNOLDS, Roxanna, b. 1902, d. 1993

RICHARD, NFN, b. 1934, d. 1982

RICHARDSON, Marie H., b. 09/09/1919, d. 03/14/1997

RICHARDSON, Mary Jane, b. 12/12/1906, d. 09/27/1994

RIDDICK, Connie E., b. 1940, d. 1988

ROBINSON, Carolyn L., ssw-Delores A. Harris, b. 06/07/1943, d. 05/30/1970

ROBINSON, Charles I., b. 02/01/1906, d. 05/04/1991

ROBINSON, Joseph W., b. 04/20/1924, d. 08/26/1971

ROMAN, Clara M., b. 02/20/1930, d. 10/14/1968

ROSS, James, ssw-Hettie, b. 1880, d. 1956

ROSS, James H., b. 1917, d. 1966

ROSS, Lurenzo P., ssw-Virginia I., b. 12/17/1927, d. 11/13/1955

ROSS, Nettie, ssw-James, b. 1885, d. 1956

ROSS, Virginia I., ssw-Lurenzo P., b. 05/15/1928, d. 10/20/1974

SAMPLE, Helen Louise A., b. 04/20/1920, d. 12/27/1995

SAVAGE, Addie Mae, b. 05/01/1928, d. 02/11/1994

SAVAGE, John E., b. 06/10/1924, d. 12/24/1996

SAVAGE, Louis, b. 1949, d. 1986

SCOTT, Bertha L., ssw-Charlie, b. 1934, d. 1991

SCOTT, Carrie L., b. 10/02/1922, d. 01/28/1983

SCOTT, Charlie, ssw-Bertha L., b. 1927, d. 1996

SEARS, Willie M., b. 1927, d. 1993

SHANNON, NFN, b. 1917, d. 1982

SHARP, Elnora, b. 1917, d. 1994

SHEPPARD, Jasmine A., b. N/D, d. 1991

SHOCKLEY, Alma D., b. 1889, d. 1976

SHOCKLEY, Alonzo, Sr., b. 08/03/1878, d. 10/02/1952

SHOCKLEY, Anthony R., b. 11/18/1875, d. 11/29/1951

SHOCKLEY, Anthony R., b. 12/10/1846, d. 08/06/1912

SHOCKLEY, Charles, ssw-Sadie Y., b. 10/07/1874, d. 03/22/1941

SHOCKLEY, Charles W., b. 08/09/1815, d. 07/20/1885

SHOCKLEY, David A., Pastor, b. 10/13/1940, d. 06/17/1983

SHOCKLEY, David H., Rev., b. 1913, d. 1964

SHOCKLEY, Della E., Age 50y, b. N/D, d. 08/09/1906

SHOCKLEY, Dianah, Age 76y 9m 1d, b. 09/08/1809, d. 06/12/1880

SHOCKLEY, Elizabeth Hilton, b. 04/15/1888, d. 12/25/1956

SHOCKLEY, Elmore, ssw-Pattie Virginia, b. 1896, d. 1969

SHOCKLEY, George J., Age 21y 3m 11d, b. 06/18/1847, d. 09/29/1871

SHOCKLEY, Ira, b. N/D, d. N/D [Note: Stone broken.]

SHOCKLEY, James M., s/o Nathan & Naomi, b. 12/28/1859, d. 10/03/1907

SHOCKLEY, James M., ssw-Sarah A., b. 05/18/1821, d. 03/18/1906

SHOCKLEY, Jesse, b. 03/11/1810, d. 07/05/1869

SHOCKLEY, John C., b. 11/14/1839, d. 05/26/1892

SHOCKLEY, Joseph H., h/o Carrie Shockley, b. N/D, d. 04/02/1929

SHOCKLEY, Mary, b. 1869, d. 1942

SHOCKLEY, Mary E., b. 1917, d. 1931

SHOCKLEY, Mary Jane, ssw-William M. & Mary Pettyjohn, b. 10/09/1904, d. N/D

SHOCKLEY, Mary Pettyjohn, ssw-Mary Jane & William M., b. N/D, d. N/D

SHOCKLEY, Naomi Y., w/o Lemuel H., Age 58y, b. N/D, d. 02/22/1901

SHOCKLEY, Pattie Virginia, ssw-Elmore, b. 1900, d. 1971

SHOCKLEY, S. Emmeline, w/o A. R., b. 1847, d. 1932

SHOCKLEY, Sadie Y., ssw-Charles, b. 07/07/1880, d. 12/09/1950

SHOCKLEY, Sarah A., ssw-James M., b. 01/29/1838, d. 01/12/1899

SHOCKLEY, William L., Sr., Sgt, USA, WWII, b. 05/19/1923, d. 06/16/1979

SHOCKLEY, William M., ssw-Mary Jane & Mary Pettyjohn, b. 11/01/1894, d. 12/21/1975

SMITH, Earl Levie, b. 09/06/1937, d. 10/07/1979

SMITH, Glen, b. 09/18/1960, d. 01/19/1988

SMITH, Walter, b. 1933, d. 1991

SPELLMAN, Sarah E., b. 07/05/1905, d. 10/21/1991

STEVENSON, Charlie, b. 1914, d. 1996

SUTTON, Frances B., b. 05/05/1904, d. 01/14/1991

SUTTON, Henry Lee, b. 08/07/1911, d. 02/20/1981

TAYLOR, Robert, b. 1919, d. 1996

THOMAS, Lester, b. 1915, d. 1985

THOMAS, Santay, b. 1973, d. 1983

THOMPSON, Cornell P., b. 1915, d. 1988

TILLEY, Earl, Sr., b. 11/16/1938, d. 12/21/1980

TILLMAN, Ella Ree, b. 1941, d. 1979

TINGLE, Clarence H., b. 1907, d. 1996

TINGLE, Emory, b. N/D, d. N/D

TOWNSEND, Floyd Leroy, b. 03/01/1932, d. 12/29/1971

TOWNSEND, Irene, b. 1891, d. 1984

TOWNSEND, Mildred, b. 1931, d. 1986

TRADER, Carroll J., Pvt., Co. A, 371 Inf., WWI, b. 07/18/1889, d. 12/29/1956

TROTTER, Eugene, Pvt., USA, WWII, b. 08/08/1912, d. 11/24/1973

TUCKER, Lorenzo, b. 1969, d. 1995

TUNNELL, Marie, b. 1904, d. 1986

TURNER, Charles J., Jr., "Bud," ssw-Meredis R., Cpl, USA, WWII, b. 01/10/1924, d. 07/21/1996

TURNER, Mazie, b. 1918, d. 1990

TURNER, Meredis R., "Rita," ssw-Charles J., Jr., b. 12/25/1938, d. N/D

VANN, William, Tec5, USA, WWII, b. 08/31/1918, d. 02/04/1985

WALSTON, Gather, b. 1920, d. 1994

WALTON, Effie, b. 1914, d. 1991

WARREN, David S., Tec4, USA, WWII, b. 06/13/1920, d. 03/27/1990

WARREN, Harry J., Cpl., USA, Korea, b. 08/15/1933, d. 04/30/1992

WATERS, Bessie, b. 1925, d. 1993

WATSON, Augusta, Pfc., USA, WWII, b. 12/27/1921, d. 07/12/1983

WATSON, Elize, ssw-Malinda S., b. 06/11/1884, d. 08/24/1947

WATSON, Malinda S., ssw-Elize, b. 03/11/1891, d. 09/19/1932

WEATHERBY, Viola, b. 1925, d. 1977

WHALEY, Elton T., Cpl., USA, Korea, b. 10/21/1927, d. 07/07/1982

WHITE, Baby, b. N/D, d. 1988

WHITE, Charles, b. 1950, d. 1982

WHITE, Kenyota, b. 1980, d. 1997

WHITE, Teiona, b. N/D, d. 1997

WILCOX, Dorothy, b. 1924, d. 1995

WILLIAMS, Alice, b. 12/03/1923, d. 12/17/1966

WILLIAMS, Anna Lee, b. 1921, d. 1995

WILLIAMS, Baby, b. 1991, d. 1991

WILLIAMS, Darrell, b. 12/02/1957, d. 03/16/1986

WILLIAMS, Delema, ssw-Herman B., b. 01/12/1903, d. 01/20/1961

WILLIAMS, Delores, b. 04/28/1938, d. 01/05/1993

WILLIAMS, Eliat B., b. 1959, d. 1995

WILLIAMS, Frank James, b. 03/28/1953, d. 07/16/1980

WILLIAMS, Herman B., ssw-Delema, Cpl., Btry. F349, Fld. Arty., WWI, b. 11/20/1894, d. 12/04/1963
WILLIAMS, Jessie, Jr., b. 1951, d. 1989
WILLIAMS, Jessie J., b. 08/15/1921, d. 06/11/1990
WILLIAMS, John H., b. 1913, d. 1982
WILLIAMS, Tyesha, b. N/D, d. 1993
WILLIAMS, Vernice, b. 12/28/1922, d. 10/02/1981
WILLIAMS, Victor, b. 04/20/1960, d. 05/12/1973
WINSTEAD, Jason, b. 1928, d. 1997
YOUNG, Bernard, ssw-Bethenia V., Pfc., USA, WWI, b. 12/01/1890, d. 06/29/1964
YOUNG, Bethenia V., ssw-Bernard, b. 1890, d. 1958
YOUNG, Chriffina, b. N/D, d. 05/12/1940
YOUNG, Clara, Age 46y, b. N/D, d. 01/07/1927
YOUNG, Edith E., b. 10/18/1866, d. 07/13/1914
YOUNG, Flossie E., ssw-Justus G., b. 12/18/1930, d. 11/19/1989
YOUNG, Garrison H., b. 09/09/1892, d. 06/28/1926
YOUNG, George W., b. 05/10/1897, d. 12/20/1976
YOUNG, Grace A., b. 06/18/1946, d. 05/04/1994
YOUNG, Harvey, b. 02/22/1905, d. 02/10/1976
YOUNG, Haswell C., b. 1907, d. 1970
YOUNG, Haswell G., Rev., b. 04/24/1934, d. 10/27/1996
YOUNG, James H., b. 11/22/1872, d. 06/20/1939
YOUNG, John Garnett, ssw-Sophia Thelma, b. 07/16/1919, d. N/D
YOUNG, Julia A., b. 07/07/1839, d. 04/22/1894
YOUNG, Justus G., ssw-Flossie E., b. 06/11/1927, d. 02/12/1983
YOUNG, Larah A., w/o Robert, b. 1881, d. 1940
YOUNG, Lorenzo, b. 1924, d. 1996
YOUNG, Mary E., b. 1911, d. 1965
YOUNG, Mattie Lee, b. 06/22/1887, d. 06/09/1963
YOUNG, Nelia A., w/o Little Joseph Young, b. 1829, d. 06/12/1888
YOUNG, Norwell M., b. 1936, d. 1954
YOUNG, Rebecca A., b. 03/11/1852, d. 03/09/1923
YOUNG, Robert A., ssw-Thorris R., m. 10/08/1943, b. 08/02/1921, d. 09/27/1992
YOUNG, Robert C., b. 1900, d. 1962
YOUNG, Robert J., b. 12/04/1836, d. 04/26/1898
YOUNG, Roxie A., b. 1906, d. 1990
YOUNG, Sophia Thelma, ssw-John Garnett, b. 09/11/1921, d. 09/17/1994
YOUNG, Thorris R., ssw-Robert A., m. 10/08/1943, b. 01/05/1926, d. N/D
YOUNG, Toni A., b. 12/14/1971, d. 04/30/1994
YOUNG, Vivian A., b. 1924, d. 1996
YOUNG, William H., b. 05/02/1911, d. 06/06/1990
YOUNG, Willis J., b. 08/28/1902, d. 08/18/1980

(CC-012 & HU-NR) UNION CEMETERY

Located in Milford approximately 75 feet N. E. of Rehoboth Boulevard between S. E. Front St. and S. E. Second St.
Recorded: March 7, 1997

ALDRED, Walter Sudler, Inf. s/o Rev. E. P. & J. A., b. 03/07/1869, d. 01/13/1871

ANDREWS, Eliza Ann, w/o Capt. Wm. H., Age 85y 2m, b. 03/22/1814, d. 05/22/1899

ANDREWS, Margaret Jane, w/o L. L. & d/o Gibson & Sarah M. Collins, Age 24y 20d, Died in Philadelphia, b. N/D, d. 01/28/1875

ANDREWS, W., Capt., Age 88y 9m 7d, b. 11/08/1811, d. 08/15/1900

BETTS, James H., b. 12/31/1822, d. 01/25/1879

CARPENTER, Charles H., b. 06/25/1853, d. 02/08/1882

CARPENTER, Martha G., d/o C. H. & N. A., b. 03/22/1882, d. 06/23/1885

CARROLL, William J., s/o Charles & Mary E., Age 23y 8m 2d, b. N/D, d. 09/20/1882

CHANCE, T. C., Co. F., 1st Del. Inf., b. N/D, d. N/D

CLENDANIEL, S. T., Co. F., US Inf., b. N/D, d. N/D

COLLINS, Charles G., b. 09/11/1856, d. 09/28/1885

COLLINS, Gibson A., s/o Charles & Mary M., b. 05/01/1881, d. 10/13/1882

COLLINS, Sarah A., Age 59y 2m 9d, b. 04/16/1823, d. 06/25/1882

CONDIN, Elizabeth C. Potter, w/o John Condin, b. 1821, d. 1891

CONDIN, John, b. 1814, d. 1891

CONDIN, John Potter, s/o John & Elizabeth, b. 09/20/1863, d. 03/24/1885

CUBBAGE, Louisa, w/o Samuel, Age 73y, b. N/D, d. 10/11/1871

CUBBAGE, Samuel, b. 06/02/1819, d. 06/09/1878

DEPUTY, Abraham M., Age 46y 1m 23d, b. 08/18/1828, d. 10/11/1874

DEPUTY, Adella, ssw-Sarah L. & Bertha E., b. N/D, d. N/D

DEPUTY, Anne M., w/o Col. B. B., b. N/D, d. N/D

DEPUTY, Bertha E., ssw-Sarah L. & Adella, b. N/D, d. N/D

DEPUTY, Bertha L., ssw-Lillian R. & Blanche, b. N/D, d. N/D

DEPUTY, Blanche, ssw-Bertha L., & Lillian R., b. N/D, d. N/D

DEPUTY, Ella, d/o Benj. B. & Annie M., b. 03/17/1868, d. 09/18/1869

DEPUTY, Lillian R., ssw-Bertha L. & Blanche, b. N/D, d. N/D

DEPUTY, Mattie B., d/o Thomas H. & Anna E., Age 2y 9m 18d, b. N/D, d. 01/25/1876

DEPUTY, Sarah L., ssw-Adella & Bertha E., b. N/D, d. N/D

DILLAHAY, John, Co. C., 1 Del. Inf., b. N/D, d. N/D

DOWNING, Margaret D., d/o Wm. J. & Hannah, Age 36y 11m 4d, b. N/D, d. 06/27/1876

EDGELL, Amelia, ssw-Mary J., Age 75y, b. N/D, d. N/D

EDGELL, Mary J., ssw-Amelia, Age 73y, b. N/D, d. N/D

HALL, Mary Hester, d/o Henry M. & Annie, Age 4m 4d, b. N/D, d. 08/11/1878

HALLETT, James B., Age 64y 8m, b. 05/09/1804, d. 01/09/1869

HARRIS, Belle, b. N/D, d. 06/16/1900

HARRIS, Maggie, b. N/D, d. 1876

HARRIS, William H., Capt., Co. K, 193 Rgt., NY, Civil War, b. 08/31/1841, d. 02/10/1895

HARRIS, Willie H., b. 1872, d. 1873

HILL, Mary, w/o John, Age 73y, b. N/D, d. 01/20/1894

HOBBS, George L., Co. B, 1 Del. Inf., Spanish Am. War, b. N/D, d. N/D

HOBBS, Nehemiah, Co. I, 1 Del. Inf., b. N/D, d. N/D

HOLSTEIN, James T., Age 75y, b. N/D, d. 06/12/1893

HOLSTON, George N., b. 01/06/1872, d. 09/20/1908

HOLSTON, Sara A., b. 08/04/1839, d. 10/12/1910

HOLSTON, William J., b. 10/17/1894, d. 06/09/1899

HUDSON, William H., Co. C, 8 Del. Inf., b. N/D, d. N/D

HYNSON, Amanda, b. 1846, d. 1898

HYNSON, J. L., Co. B, 1st Del. Inf., b. N/D, d. N/D

JOHNSON, Anna M., ssw-Mary B. & Jonathan, Daughter, b. 1888, d. 1933

JOHNSON, Jonathan, ssw-Anna M. & Mary B., b. 1856, d. N/D

JOHNSON, Mary B., w/o Jonatha, ssw-Jonathan & Anna M., b. 1864, d. 1935

KALER, Bessie, b. 07/27/1893, d. 12/20/1899

KALER, Edward, b. 12/12/1833, d. 05/23/1905

KALER, Nevada, b. 04/09/1875, d. 09/25/1894

KALER, Oscar, b. 11/04/1849, d. 06/23/1900

KALER, Sarah, b. 01/14/1884, d. 07/18/1885

LANE, Thomas H., b. 09/15/1882, d. 08/26/1883

MCCOLLEY, Anna, ssw-Robert, Age 75y, b. N/D, d. 03/01/1885

MCCOLLEY, Robert, ssw-Anna, Age 93y b. N/D, d. 07/19/1879

MILLER, Addie S., d/o Charles & Mary E. Carroll, b. 05/02/1858, d. 09/01/1905

MILLMAN, T. J., Co. B, 8th Del. Inf., b. N/D, d. N/D

MILLS, Charles, b. 12/15/1811, d. 01/03/1882

MILLS, Charles M., s/o G. & M., b. 10/22/1852, d. 12/18/1882

MILLS, Maria, w/o Charles, b. 04/13/1810, d. 09/07/1881

MORGAN, Margaret A., b. 1860, d. 1925

MORGAN, Sallie A., ssw-Willard S., b. 1851, d. 1898

MORGAN, Willard S., ssw-Sallie A., b. 1856, d. 1943

PAISLEY, Elisha H., Co. I, b. N/D, d. N/D

PAISLEY, Henry, Co. C, 8 Del. Inf., b. N/D, d. N/D

PAISLEY, Lola, Age 65y, b. N/D, d. N/D

PAISLEY, Sallie, Age 42y, b. N/D, d. N/D

PAISLEY, Sussie, Age 75y, b. N/D, d. N/D

PAISLEY, Sussie, Age 81y, b. N/D, d. N/D

PARKER, Allen, S. A. War, b. N/D, d. N/D

POTTER, Elizabeth, ssw-3 babies, John, Wm. & Lizzy, b. N/D, d. 1899

POTTER, John, ssw-Elizabeth, Wm. & Lizzy, 3 Babies, b. N/D, d. N/D

POTTER, Lizzy, ssw-Elizabeth, Wm. & John, 3 Babies, b. N/D, d. N/D

POTTER, Wm., ssw-Elizabeth, John & Lizzy, 3 Babies, b. N/D, d. N/D

PREOLE, Mary E., w/o John D., b. 12/01/1838, d. 03/28/1912

QUILLEN, Edward, b. 12/12/1833, d. 05/23/1905

QUILLEN, Elizabeth, w/o Jacob & d/o William J. & Celia Davis, Age 70y 4m 7d, b. N/D, d. 05/22/1893

QUILLEN, Emma, b. 07/28/1869, d. 07/17/1885

QUILLEN, Jacob, b. 07/27/1828, d. 05/11/1908

QUILLEN, John, s/o Jacob & Elizabeth, Age 16y 7d, b. N/D, d. 01/11/1873

QUILLEN, Joseph B., s/o Jacob & Elizabeth, Age 30y 7m, b. N/D, d. 04/20/1878

QUILLEN, Susan B., d/o Jacob & Elizabeth, Age 14y 3m 4d, b. N/D, d. 09/16/1875

REDDEN, Mary E., d/o John W. & Mary, Age 17y 4m 29d, b. N/D, d. 05/16/1878

RICHTER, Joseph, Co. G, 3rd Del. Inf., b. N/D, d. N/D

ROBINSON, Daniel G., Age 26y, b. N/D, d. 10/29/1875

ROBINSON, Shadrach, Age 51y b. N/D, d. 03/23/1867

SAMMONS, Sallie, w/o William, Age 74y 8m 12d, b. N/D, d. 07/19/1877

SAMMONS, William, Age 65y, b. N/D. d. 10/30/1857

SMOOT, Annie M., w/o William H., b. 03/01/1840, d. 08/13/1871

STOREY, Maggie, w/o John W., Age 26y, b. N/D, d. 09/05/1892

SUYDAM, Ruby L., w/o G. L., Age 25y 8m 6d, b. N/D, d. 10/22/1876

TITUS, Clarence W., s/o J. V. & G. M., Age 4y 2m 3d, b. N/D, d. 12/27/1875

TITUS, Hattie, d/o J. V. & C. M., Age 4m 6d, b. N/D, d. 08/09/1875
VOSS, W. H., Co. G, 3 Del. Inf., b. N/D, d. N/D
WARREN, Amelia, w/o Lobawick, Age 81y, b. N/D, d. 03/25/1886
WARREN, Lobawick, b. N/D, d. N/D [Note: Stone broken.]
WARREN, Robert, Age 59y, b. N/D, d. 06/26/1875

The Captain Jonathan Caldwell Chapter, Daughters of the American Revolution, Milford, Delaware, have researched various historical records, including those of the Delaware Public Archives, and have recorded information from the tombstones of this cemetery. Those persons who they identified as having been interred in this cemetery for whom we could not find stones are:

BRIDGHAM, Samuel & Mary Anna, Buried here, stones at Odd Fellows Cemetery, Milford, DE.
FITZGERALD, John T., b. 12/10/1848, d. 11/14/1909
ROE, Janney, age 24y, b. N/D, d. N/D
STEVENS, Mabel, b. N/D, d. 07/26/1937
VREELAND, Cathaliene P., Age 91y 7m 13d, b. N/D, d. 02/26/1876
VREELAND, Margaret, b. 08/11/1807, d. 03/15/1898

(CC-013 & HU-455) CEDAR NECK UNITED METHODIST CHURCH CEMETERY
Located East of Milford at the Northernly corner of the intersection of Cedar Beach Rd. (Rd. 36) and Shockley Rd. (Rd. 202) 1.9 miles East of Coastal Highway (Rt. 1)

BENNETT, Sadie K., b. 03/25/1882, d. 08/02/1975
BOYCE, James Henry, b. 1838, d. 1894
CARPENTER, Burton D., b. 03/04/1820, d. 12/24/1897
CARPENTER, Mary E., b. 10/07/1825, d. 02/14/1898
COLLINS, Margaret S., w/o Samuel P., b. 09/04/1827, d. 04/28/1891
COLLINS, Samuel P., b. 01/02/1825, d. 05/13/1900
COLLINS, William Henry, s/o John H. & Ollie N., b. 08/14/1904, d. 09/03/1905
COLLINS, William P., b. 09/13/1869, d. 08/24/1901
DRAPER, Samuel, b. N/D, d. N/D
EVANS, John Henry, s/o Jas. & Ruth, b. 03/15/1871, d. 12/21/1875
FITZGERALD, Elizabeth, w/o Ezekiel, Age 91y, b. N/D, d. 04/19/1904
FITZGERALD, Emma J., w/o W. David, b. 11/27/1852, d. 10/27/1917
FITZGERALD, Ezekiel, Age 59y 1m 18d, b. N/D, d. 05/17/1878
FITZGERALD, J. Purnell, b. 11/17/1850, d. 07/23/1941
FITZGERALD, Marshall E., s/o Jno. P. & Belle, b. 03/01/1883, d. 07/30/1885
FITZGERALD, Rachel A. B., w/o John P. & d/o Niles T. & Elizabeth Mills, b. 10/26/1858, d. 07/10/1906
FITZGERALD, W. David, b. 04/08/1845, d. 03/20/1910
HIGMAN, Ella V., w/o Wm. & d/o M. T. & Elizabeth H. Mills, b. 12/26/1867, d. 05/16/1893
KING, Charles Henry, ssw-Ricken Olivia, b. 1864, d. 1938
KING, Ricken Olivia, w/o Charles Henry, ssw-Charles Henry, b. 1862, d. 1929
MILLS, David W., b. 09/01/1849, d. 02/17/1914
MILLS, Elizabeth B., w/o Miles T., b. 02/11/1825, d. 07/17/1897
MILLS, Miles T., b. 01/15/1826, d. 09/04/1908
O'NEIL, Patrick, Died in Scotland, b. 1861, d. 1906
O'NEIL, Sophia, b. 1861, d. 1946
PRETTYMAN, Elizabeth, w/o Joshua, b. 02/14/1826, d. 04/07/1882

SHOCKLEY, Elias, Age 76y 8m 22d, b. N/D, d. 12/05/1896
SHOCKLEY, Mary Elizabeth, d/o Theadore & Joda, b. 03/18/1896, d. 07/25/1896
SHOCKLEY, Mary H., w/o Wilson, b. 11/28/1834, d. 11/16/1912
SHOCKLEY, Michael John, b. 03/13/1967, d. 03/14/1967
SHOCKLEY, Sarah A., w/o Elias, Age 58y 3m 18d, b. N/D, d. 02/07/1890
SHOCKLEY, Wilson, b. 07/26/1827, d. 09/15/1884
STAYTON, Emma Webb, b. 09/12/1853, d. 07/13/1922
VICTOR, John W., 8 Del. Inf., b. N/D, d. N/D
WATSON, Elias S., b. 06/11/1848, d. 01/12/1903
WATSON, John Y., s/o William & Ann, Age 22y 2m 20d, b. 01/14/1854, d. 03/21/1876
WATSON, Mamie, d/o Wm. P. & Sallie B., b. 05/13/1878, d. 09/25/1882
WATSON, Our Babe, b. N/D, d. N/D
WATSON, William M., Age 81y 8m 7d, b. 02/15/1804, d. 10/22/1885
WATSON, William P., Age 73y, b. N/D, d. 03/26/1899
WATSON, William P., b. 12/02/1921, d. N/D
WEBB, John S., b. 06/01/1848, d. 11/21/1905

(CC-014 & HU-22) LINCOLN PUBLIC CEMETERY
Located in Lincoln on the South and West sides of Clendaniel Pond Rd. (Rd. 38) 0.2 miles East of
Greentop Rd. (Rd. 225) Recorded: January 3, 1994

ABBOTT, J. M. C., b. 1879, d. 1940
ABBOTT, Mary M., b. 11/16/1885, d. 06/11/1929
ABBOTT, William H., b. 06/03/1854, d. 02/14/1920
ANDREWS, Mary E., w/o John, b. 07/24/1871, d. 02/18/1930
APPEL, Dick, b. 09/08/1974, d. 09/09/1974
APPEL, Frank E., Jr., b. 07/21/1957, d. 06/03/1978
ARGO, Emma C., b. 07/25/1859, d. 10/27/1904
ARGO, John H., b. 05/11/1846, d. 05/08/1920
ARGO, William M., s/o John H. & Sarah E. & Grdson o/Joshua Webb, b. 09/03/1870, d. 12/27/1915
ARNOLD, Belle, b. 1854, d. N/D
ARNOLD, Erastus, b. 1813, d. 1890
ARNOLD, G. A., b. 1848, d. 1906
ARNOLD, Georgia, b. 1849, d. 1906
ATKINS, Charley R., s/o Robert G. & Cora W., b. 06/04/1892, d. 10/09/1918
ATKINS, Cora M., b. 10/03/1863, d. 08/25/1937
ATKINS, Robert G., b. 04/09/1857, d. 08/16/1892
BACHELDER, Ernest G., NJ, Pvt., 88 Co., Trans Corps, WWI, b. 10/05/1893, d. 09/18/1959
BACHELDER, Lola A., b. 1893, d. 1962
BARRETT, Clarence S., Sgt., USA, WWI, b. 1896, d. 1978
BARRETT, Jennie S., b. 1904, d. 1974
BEARDSLEY, Ethel Jean, b. 1884, d. 1957
BEARDSLEY, Mary Catherine, b. 1861, d. 1941
BEARDSLEY, Nell Augusta, b. 1886, d. 1970
BEARDSLEY, Truman A., b. 11/07/1850, d. 11/23/1909
BEIDEMAN, Caddie C., b. 1883, d. 1980
BEIDEMAN, Howard H., b. 1879, d. 1938
BEIDEMAN, Lula Reed, b. 08/08/1940, d. N/D

BEIDEMAN, Roland H., b. 1905, d. 1947
BENNETT, Annie Macklin, b. 11/21/1887, d. 08/23/1918
BENNETT, Carrie E., b. 02/12/1900, d. 04/17/1985
BENNETT, Joshua S., b. 1891, d. 1959
BENNETT, Myrna L., b. 03/26/1937, d. 05/25/1984
BENNETT, Nora M., b. 1894, d. 1972
BENSON, Agnes J., b. 1918, d. 1943
BENSON, Charles H., b. 1922, d. 1925
BENSON, Charles L., b. 06/07/1889, d. 08/07/1956
BENSON, Eliza A., b. 1860, d. 1931
BENSON, Elmer J., b. 05/09/1897, d. 11/18/1972
BENSON, Herman R., b. 1915, d. 1943
BENSON, Lanah E., b. 01/13/1896, d. 04/02/1981
BENSON, Leonard T., b. 1928, d. 1929
BENSON, Minnie R., b. 04/03/1901, d. 08/12/1975
BENSON, Ruth A., b. 1917, d. 1919
BENSON, Wynter, b. 1892, d. 1972
BERKES, Albert F., b. 02/09/1895, d. 07/29/1974
BERKES, Anne I., b. 10/08/1912, d. 06/15/1990
BERWICK, Elizabeth H., b. 05/03/1915, d. N/D
BERWICK, Ferris E., b. 11/06/1905,n d. 01/31/1973
BERWICK, Gladys E., b. 06/20/1910, d. 03/09/1992
BERWICK, James W., b. 12/03/1908, d. 06/30/1971
BERWICK, Walter S., b. 09/20/1865, d. 06/28/1945
BETTS, Francis B., b. 1908, d. 1984
BIDDLE, Lyde Postles, b. 1891, d. 1956
BOWER, Robert C., Sr., TSgt., USA, WWII, b. 06/14/1915, d. 11/29/1992
BOYD, Eleanor E., b. 1876, d. 1972
BOYD, James, b. 1879, d. 1952
BOYER, Keith D., b. 07/11/1942, d. N/D
BOYER, Nancy L., b. 02/12/1945, d. 03/13/1990
BRADY, Mary Matilda, w/o John W., b. 1877, d. 1939
BREWSTER, Frank P., b. 1891, d. 1946
BRITTINGHAM, Mary, b. 1838, d. 1894
BRITTINGHAM, T. S., b. 1828, d. 1889
BROWN, Virginia E., b. 06/09/1904, d. 01/15/1971
BURRIS, Annie E., b. 11/12/1852, d. N/D
BURRIS, Rachel A., b. 11/27/1832, d. 07/05/1891
BURRIS, William M., b. 09/10/1853, d. 12/27/1920
BURRIS, William T., b. 02/02/1826, d. 03/28/1905
CAIN, Bevins M., b. 06/18/1851, d. 09/23/1914
CALHOON, Ellennora, w/o William T., b. 11/25/1846, d. 01/26/1906
CALHOON, Elmer T., b. 01/16/1877, d. 08/20/1898
CALHOON, James B., b. 10/08/1840, d. 11/29/1918
CALHOON, William T., b. 02/14/1846, d. 05/15/1920
CALHOUN, Dora K., b. 05/28/1884, d. 01/29/1967
CALHOUN, Wm. Marshall, b. 05/02/1871, d. 12/12/1956
CALLAWAY, William, b. 02/26/1878, d. 12/29/1958

CAMPBELL, Hannah A., b. 07/25/1827, d. 03/29/1901

CAMPBELL, John F., b. 06/05/1823, d. 09/22/1893

CAREY, Archie J., m. 02/11/1933, b. 08/03/1910, d. 02/28/1988

CAREY, Baby Boy, s/o Archie & Virgie, b. 12/06/1945, d. 12/06/1945

CAREY, Clara P., b. 08/29/1925, d. N/D

CAREY, Curtis H., b. 1880, d. 1926

CAREY, Edith O., b. 1902, d. 1945

CAREY, Eliza A., w/o Robert F., b. 08/16/1850, d. 02/19/1917

CAREY, Estella F., b. 09/24/1879, d. 05/04/1961

CAREY, Etta M., b. 1912, d. 1966

CAREY, Fred, b. 07/25/1893, d. 03/10/1964

CAREY, Lida C., d/o Andrew F. & Millie H., Age 8y 1m 14d, b. N/D, d. 05/02/1904

CAREY, Mary, w/o Curtis H., b. 1880, d. 1920

CAREY, Melson C., b. 1910, d. 1923

CAREY, Millie Hatfield, w/o Andrew F., b. 12/29/1875, d. 11/14/1911

CAREY, NFN, c/o Robert & Estella, Two children, b. N/D, d. N/D

CAREY, Richard, Sr., b. 06/23/1914, d. 10/04/1985

CAREY, Robert F., b. 01/25/1839, d. 11/03/1913

CAREY, Robert J., b. 09/21/1883, d. 06/07/1949

CAREY, Sallie A., b. 04/01/1896, d. 02/16/1991

CAREY, Sylvia, d/o Archie & Virgie, b. 11/25/1933, d. 02/18/1934

CAREY, Virgie E., w/o Archie J., m. 02/11/1933, b. 03/26/1913, d. 04/18/1986

CAREY, W. Howard, b. 1916, d. 1988

CARLISLE, Alice M., b. 10/13/1924, d. 11/20/1991

CARLISLE, James M., b. 1888, d. 1926

CARLISLE, Mae D., b. 1895, d. 1922

CARLISLE, Minnie Reed, b. 1878, d. 1956

CARLISLE, Norman R., Pfc., USA, WWII, b. 08/20/1922, d. 07/26/1980

CARLISLE, Parist T., Dr., b. 1864, d. 1942

CARPENTER, Flossie M., b. 1896, d. 1966

CARPENTER, George W., b. 09/10/1862, d. 12/20/1952

CARPENTER, Laura Mae, d/o George W. & Nellie B., b. 08/28/1888, d. 10/31/1889

CARPENTER, Nellie B., b. 04/12/1864, d. 02/10/1939

CARPENTER, Onis R., b. 1887, d. 1984

CHIPMAN, Wm. T., b. 1865, d. 1934

CLARK, Clyde J., b. 1893, d. 1944

CLARK, Earl, b. 1895, d. 1943

CLARK, Ella C., b. 1874, d. 1937

CLARK, Elwood, b. 05/11/1914, d. 12/25/1986

CLARK, Elwood Marvin, b. 1935, d. 1967

CLARK, Harry C., b. 1859, d. 1903

CLARK, Harry V., b. 06/13/1903, d. 02/12/1959

CLARK, Helen Mae, b. 1928, d. 1929

CLARK, Lillie, b. 05/16/1915, d. N/D

CLARK, Ralph C., b. 11/21/1921, d. 02/20/1924

CLARK, William R., b. 08/01/1943, d. 09/20/1943

CLAYVILLE, J. Edward, b. 1854, d. 1936

CLAYVILLE, Jesse Robert, Cpl., USA, WWII, b. 09/07/1909, d. 09/06/1990

CLAYVILLE, M. Ellen, b. 1860, d. 1923
CLENDANIEL, Avery F., b. 1881, d. 1959
CLENDANIEL, Bessie E., b. 1889, d. 1973
CLENDANIEL, Caroline V., w/o George R., Age 25y, b. N/D, d. 12/07/1884
CLENDANIEL, Eliza A. Warren, w/o Geo. R., b. 1850, d. 1929
CLENDANIEL, Elizabeth M., b. 04/18/1894, d. 01/30/1974
CLENDANIEL, Elwood M., b. 02/03/1902, d. 12/21/1974
CLENDANIEL, Frederick, b. 1870, d. 1936
CLENDANIEL, Gary Lynn, Sgt., USA, Vietnam, b. 11/04/1952, d. 02/01/1992
CLENDANIEL, George R., b. 1857, d. 1942
CLENDANIEL, George W., b. 05/11/1875, d. 09/09/1933
CLENDANIEL, George Wilkins, b. 12/03/1910, d. 12/11/1910
CLENDANIEL, Harry E., b. 1871, d. 1938
CLENDANIEL, Harry E., b. 1883, d. 1957
CLENDANIEL, Ida A., b. 1869, d. 1933
CLENDANIEL, J. Leonard, b. 09/27/1867, d. 01/04/1950
CLENDANIEL, Jacob, b. 05/28/1835, d. 12/20/1922
CLENDANIEL, Jennie M., b. 11/27/1876, d. 02/18/1954
CLENDANIEL, John H., b. 1876, d. 1961
CLENDANIEL, Joshua, b. 10/02/1838, d. 03/07/1916
CLENDANIEL, Kathryn B., b. 1891, d. 1951
CLENDANIEL, L. Sanson, b. 1898, d. 1926
CLENDANIEL, Leroy W., b. 11/27/1887, d. 12/04/1962
CLENDANIEL, Mabel May, b. 03/28/1900, d. 11/15/1911
CLENDANIEL, Mary E., b. 01/04/1892, d. 04/12/1892
CLENDANIEL, Mary E., b. 08/17/1866, d. 06/02/1941
CLENDANIEL, Mary E., b. 1870, d. 1964
CLENDANIEL, Mary E., b. 10/06/1836, d. 04/16/1882
CLENDANIEL, Mary M., b. 1866, d. 1955
CLENDANIEL, Pauline V., b. 08/11/1913, d. 08/19/1980
CLENDANIEL, Sallie J., b. 1864, d. 1952
CLENDANIEL, Sara Linda, b. 10/28/1901, d. 07/01/1903
CLENDANIEL, Sarah A., w/o Frederick, b. 1873, d. 1924
CLENDANIEL, Virginia K., d/o George R. & Eliza A., b. 03/11/1892, d. 07/24/1892
CLENDANIEL, W. C., b. 1859, d. 1938
CLENDANIEL, Walter F., b. 11/23/1870, d. 01/02/1923
CLENDANIEL, Willard H., b. 1862, d. 1936
CLIFTON, Beatrice, b. 02/27/1865, d. 10/28/1887
CLIFTON, Elizabeth Lawes, b. 10/20/1845, d. 02/24/1928
CLIFTON, Glenn, b. 1868, d. 1949
CLIFTON, Hester L., b. 1859, d. 1950
CLIFTON, Ida Cubbage, w/o W. S., b. 12/13/1868, d. 10/24/1930
CLIFTON, James H., Co. 1, 7 Del. Inf., b. N/D, d. N/D
CLOGG, Darlene w/o John L., Sr., m. 06/15/1963, b. 11/28/1944, d. N/D
CLOGG, John L., Sr., m. 06/15/1963, d. 07/05/1942, d. 08/08/1990
COLEGROVE, Jeanne M., b. 07/06/1929, d. 04/10/1930
COOK, Charles W., b. 1903, d. 1965
COOK, Eleanor C., b. 05/04/1835, d. 07/15/1914

COOK, Ella M., b. 1858, d. 1947

COOK, Hamilton O., b. 06/30/1825, d. 07/10/1906

COOK, Orrin J., Co., E, 1st NY Volunteer Infantry, b. 1840, d. 1925

COOK, Thomas W., b. 09/10/1836, d. 12/25/1908

COOPER, Abbie P., b. 07/03/1859, d. 06/21/1939

COOPER, Charles Elmer, b. 01/08/1889, d. 02/11/1961

COOPER, Eliza B., b. 1848, d. 1932

COOPER, George R., b. 09/15/1858, d. 08/10/1925

COOPER, Grace M., b. 10/16/1900, d. 04/04/1990

COOPER, Mamie Lindale, b. 07/29/1896, d. 02/06/1973

COOPER, Raymond F., Cpl., 167 Inf., 42 Div., WWI, b. 04/05/1897, d. 03/16/1948

COOPER, Ronald W., b. 07/30/1935, d. N/D

CORKRAN, Ethelyn, b. 1870, d. 1938

CORKRAN, Lewis P., Rev., b. 1852, d. 1931

CORLEY, Lucille Southard, b. 08/08/1916, d. 11/11/1966

CORLEY, Philip E., b. 05/08/1954, d. 04/14/1985

CORLEY, Walter B., Jr., b. 01/29/1939, d. 03/07/1979

CORLEY, Walter B., Sr., b. 09/16/1907, d. 11/13/1980

COULTER, Clara E. A., b. 1876, d. 1964

COULTER, Eliza, b. 02/14/1851, d. 03/22/1936

COULTER, Robert L., b. 1874, d. 1941

COULTER, Thomas, b. 1919, d. 1992

COULTER, Thomas J., Age 59y, b. N/D, d. 02/16/1896

CUBBAGE, Samuel C., b. 06/14/1859, d. 02/14/1917

CURTIN, John A., b. 1882, d. 1957

CURTIN, Lillian Morrison, b. 1887, d. 1977

CURTIN, Robert E., b. 1884, d. 1960

DAVIDSON, Maude A., b. 1882, d. 1967

DAVIS, Mary, b. 1846, d. 1916

DELORENZO, Harry M., b. 01/21/1912, d. 04/01/1981

DELORENZO, Mildred L., b. 09/08/1914, d. 03/30/1990

DENNEY, Catherine Johnson, b. 1869, d. 1897

DEPUTY, Wilbert B., b. 07/05/1863, d. 06/25/1947

DEPUTY, Willie Ellen, b. 12/24/1871, d. 05/01/1924

DERRICKSON, Charles Otis, s/o Robert H. & Sallie L., b. 09/18/1884, d. 08/08/1886

DERRICKSON, Christina M., b. 07/02/1889, d. 10/12/1955

DERRICKSON, Dollie H., b. 07/12/1875, d. 03/24/1914

DERRICKSON, Florence V., d/o Robert H. & Sallie L., b. 03/03/1880, d. 07/21/1899

DERRICKSON, Robert H., b. 1859, d. 1929

DERRICKSON, Sallie L., b. 1858, d. 1933

DICKERSON, Neva E., b. 1910, d. 1939

DONALDSON, Anna, b. 1860, d. 1936

DONOHOE, Mary E., b. 10/11/1844, d. 12/28/1916

DONOHOE, William P., b. 12/22/1838, d. 12/24/1915

DONOVAN, Albert Wesley, b. 02/16/1891, d. 08/22/1960

DONOVAN, Alfred B., b. 1847, d. 1925

DONOVAN, B. Frank, b. 1878, d. 1921

DONOVAN, Delema P., b. 1901, d. 1988

DONOVAN, Della M., b. 08/06/1891, d. 12/15/1925

DONOVAN, Randall B., DE, Pvt., 13 Casual Co., WWI, b. 02/19/1896, d. 03/16/1961

DONOVAN, Susan A., b. 1860, d. 1946

DONOVAN, Wilbur H., b. 07/09/1941, d. 07/16/1979

DRAGOO, John C., b. 05/27/1828, d. 01/19/1900

DRAGOO, Rebecca A., b. 09/26/1829, d. 04/17/1905

DWYER, NFN, s/o W. H. H. & Mary J., b. 05/31/1861, d. 08/17/1866

EFFINGER, Charles W., b. 1896, d. 1977

EFFINGER, Letitia S., b. 1891, d. 1931

ELLINGSWORTH, Robert T., b. 07/25/1883, d. 09/30/1964

EVANS, Albert B., b. 10/13/1920, d. 05/02/1976

EVANS, Virginia Elizabeth, b. 06/06/1920, d. 01/19/1971

FAILING, Barbara V., b. 06/27/1938, d. N/D

FAILING, Wylie E., b. 02/27/1963, d. 12/31/1987

FENNER, Orren G., b. 10/10/1843, d. 10/30/1907

FITZGERALD, Charles, b. 12/25/1900, d. 01/17/1984

FITZGERALD, Dennis, b. 11/14/1886, d. 05/09/1981

FITZGERALD, Emma L., b. 11/10/1879, d. 10/28/1914

FITZGERALD, Flossie M., b. 09/01/1893, d. 11/08/1980

FITZGERALD, Grace M., b. 05/17/1911, d. 12/31/1990

FITZGERALD, H. Hazel, b. 10/28/1889, d. 04/09/1957

FITZGERALD, Huriah T., b. 02/26/1884, d. 06/04/1947

FITZGERALD, Huriah T., Jr., ssw-Irene M., m. 03/01/1940, b. 07/28/1916, d. N/D

FITZGERALD, Irene M., ssw-Huriah T., Jr., m. 03/01/1940, b. 12/30/1921, d. N/D

FITZGERALD, J. Edward, b. 05/01/1880, d. 12/09/1954

FITZGERALD, John T., b. 07/07/1908, d. 04/26/1950

FITZGERALD, John T., b. 12/10/1848, d. 11/14/1907

FITZGERALD, Lillie G., b. 07/28/1910, d. 05/01/1979

FITZGERALD, Sallie K., b. 11/14/1885, d. 05/31/1953

FITZGERALD, William Geo., b. 08/19/1881, d. 05/01/1964

FITZGERALD, William J., b. 05/30/1907, d. 06/28/1968

FORKUM, Annie S., b. 06/08/1862, d. 01/05/1945

FORKUM, George W., VA, Pvt., AT. Co. 377 Infantry, WWII, b. 05/04/1921, d. 11/22/1972

FOSTER, Nellie Hatfield, b. 05/09/1878, d. 07/23/1954

FRANKLIN, Charles W., b. 1881, d. 1926

GERE, Alvurda, b. 1854, d. 1932

GERE, Annie Belle, b. 11/15/1865, d. 10/07/1945

GERE, Charlie, b. 03/04/1868, d. 03/05/1961

GERE, Clarissa, b. 10/25/1835, d. 04/27/1919

GERE, John R., b. 1859, d. 1901

GLADDING, Charles L., b. 1864, d. 1945

GRAY, Levenia P., Age 73y, b. N/D, d. N/D

HALFEN, Florence K., b. 1893, d. 1975

HALFEN, Paul R., b. 1927, d. 1943

HALFEN, Paul Robert, b. 1956, d. 1982

HALFEN, Peter A., b. 1880, d. 1957

HALL, Eliza E., b. N/D, d. N/D

HARDER, Ezra F., b. 1845, d. 1927

HARDER, Lucy A., w/o Ezra F., b. 11/26/1844, d. 08/03/1913

HARDER, Myron G., b. 1868, d. 1921

HARDING, Emma L., b. 04/19/1917, d. N/D

HARDING, Frank S., b. 10/05/1914, d. 11/27/1984

HARDING, Gladys J., b. 10/18/1924, d. N/D

HARDING, Robert J., Jr., b. 09/24/1925, d. 01/28/1980

HARRISON, Laura C., w/o James H., b. 06/22/1866, d. 05/19/1909

HASTINGS, Merritt P., b. 04/18/1893, d. 02/23/1976

HATFIELD, George W., b. 06/17/1886, d. 12/29/1922

HATFIELD, Henry, b. 03/26/1869, d. 11/28/1921

HATFIELD, James B., b. 01/30/1871, d. 09/13/1903

HATFIELD, Purnell, b. 10/31/1839, d. 11/26/1900

HATFIELD, William L., NY, Sfc., 265 Areo Sq., WWI, b. 11/29/1894, d. 05/01/1961

HAZZARD, Mary E. Wilkins, b. 1861, d. 1937

HEARN, Caleb, b. 1850, d. 1939

HEARN, Edythe T., b. 08/25/1912, d. 06/19/1979

HEARN, Ida K., b. 05/24/1890, d. 08/09/1973

HEARN, J. Edward, b. 07/09/1883, d. 01/25/1968

HEARN, James Edward, s/o Wm. E. & Edythe T., b. 10/13/1938, d. 10/14/1938

HEARN, William Edward, b. 02/27/1912, d. 11/11/1988

HEARN, William J. and Family, b. N/D, d. N/D

HEITMULLER, Thelma Moore, b. 1909, d. 1982

HEITMULLER, William A., b. 1879, d. 1960

HELLENS, Harvey A., b. 08/02/1894, d. 04/05/1928

HELLENS, Sarah C., b. 01/10/1855, d. 09/29/1917

HENDERSON, Ira M., M. D., b. 1887, d. 1968

HENDERSON, Maysie Reed, b. 1887, d. 1978

HENDRICKS, John Burton, b. 1892, d. 1979

HENDRICKS, Mae M., b. 1896, d. 1970

HENDRICKSON, Cassie W., b. 02/25/1890, d. 02/08/1972

HERMAN, Charlotte, b. 1901, d. 1982

HERMAN, Rachel, b. 1903, d. 1908

HERMAN, William b. 1873, d. 1944

HILL, George P., b. 1888, d. 1973

HILL, Liley C., b. 1884, d. 1970

HILL, Marian, b. N/D, d. N/D

HILL, Robert John, b. N/D, d. N/D

HITCH, Almira Daisey, b. 1846, d. 1933

HITCH, Reba P., b. 1891, d. 1976

HITCH, Richard P., s/o Roscoe C. & Reba M., b. 09/10/1912, d. 07/15/1914

HITCH, Roscoe C., b. 1884, d. 1969

HITCH, Thomas Anderson, b. 1850, d. 1929

HOLLIS, Sarah W., b. N/D, d. N/D

HORTON, Lucy E., b. 10/12/1855, d. 10/29/1931

HORTON, Seymour C., b. 03/11/1837, d. 02/29/1912

HOSTEDLER, Harold E., Cpl., USMC, WWII, b. 12/18/1924, d. 08/03/1981

HOUSTON, Curtis S., b. 03/29/1814, d. 07/09/1893

HOUSTON, Hester A., w/o Curtis S., b. 09/11/1827, d. 03/30/1912

HUDSON, Bessie C., d/o Frederick & Florence, b. 06/02/1898, d. 08/14/1899
INGRAM, Carolyne M., b. 10/12/1922, d. 09/12/1987
INGRAM, Robert F., b. 07/28/1916, d. N/D
INGRAM, Robert J., b. 12/22/1943, d. N/D
JACKSON, Lucy H. W., b. 06/22/1817, d. 01/11/1896
JEFFERSON, Elihu, b. 1868, d. 1934
JEFFERSON, Julia C., b. 1874, d. 1915
JEFFERSON, Leslie, b. 1894, d. 1911
JESTER, Dorothy B., b. 06/23/1911, d. 07/16/1986
JESTER, F. Irene, b. 1891, d. 1961
JESTER, George A., b. 1885, d. 1949
JESTER, Sarah E., b. 04/07/1851, d. 02/18/1929
JESTER, William W., b. 06/04/1856, d. 02/05/1937
JEWELL, Catherine L., b. 11/06/1930, d. N/D
JEWELL, Elizabeth L., b. 06/04/1904, d. 03/24/1987
JEWELL, Kathryn F., b. 03/03/1889, d. 12/14/1967
JOHNSON, George B., b. 1871, d. 1933
JOHNSON, George H., b. 1839, d. 1912
JOHNSON, J. Paxson, b. 07/22/1869, d. 05/29/1946
JOHNSON, Joseph A., b. 1860, d. 1922
JOHNSON, Joseph Yardley, s/o Albert T. & Louisa K., Died in London, England, Body moved after
        5 years, b. 02/03/1864, d. 01/22/1904
JOHNSON, Louisa Kohler, w/o A. T., b. 01/06/1837, d. 10/02/1868
JOHNSON, M. Louise, b. 06/15/1912, d. 11/25/1980
JOHNSON, Mary A., b. 1872, d. 1946
JOHNSON, May Young, b. 10/28/1873, d. 01/05/1955
JOHNSON, Paris P., b. 02/25/1909, d. N/D
JOHNSON, Sarah T. Lecompte, w/o George H., b. 1841, d. 1918
JONES, Edith L., b. 1919, d. N/D
JONES, George W., b. 05/07/1911, d. 01/20/1971
JONES, Hattie A., b. 1857, d. 1951
JONES, James H., b. 1865, d. 1947
JONES, Lois G., b. 10/06/1928, d. 01/30/1929
JONES, Mary M., w/o James H., b. 10/31/1869, d. 04/20/1923
JONES, Sabelia P., b. 12/11/1926, d. 01/01/1930
KERSEY, Elsie May, b. 10/07/1898, d. 04/28/1964
KIBLER, Myrtle B., b. 1894, d. 1974
KING, Betty M., b. 06/29/1924, d. 01/17/1988
KING, Edwin Chester, Pfc., USA, WWII, b. 12/25/1919, d. 10/13/1979
KING, Edwin Larry, b. 11/01/1947, d. 01/13/1950
KING, James A., b. 08/21/1923, d. 08/24/1981
KING, Naomi P., b. 06/01/1975, d. 03/31/1978
KING, Oscar, b. 05/20/1895, d. 10/19/1974
KING, Virgil LeRoy, b. 09/29/1932, d. 03/08/1955
KING, William Earl, Pfc., USA, WWII, b. 07/06/1923, d. 09/01/1987
KIRBY, Hobe Gere, b. 1870, d. 1960
KIRBY, William G., b. 02/24/1859, d. 06/13/1915
KLETT, Charles W., b. 02/17/1872, d. 02/09/1953

KLETT, Ellen, w/o Charles W., b. 03/14/1870, d. 08/27/1947

KOMOROWSKI, Janice F., b. 02/25/1958, d. 07/04/1958

KOVAR, Frances, b. 1890, d. 1959

KOVAR, Josephine, b. 1859, d. 1927

KOVAR, Rudolph, b. 1888, d. 1960

KOVAR, William, b. 1857, d. 1925

KRAUS, George P., Jr., Cpl., USA, WWII, b. 09/29/1898, d. 11/25/1992

KRAUS, Jennie P., b. 03/07/1922, d. N/D

LACEY, Mary B., b. 1857, d. 1951

LADD, Leona S., b. 02/25/1916, d. N/D

LADD, Lowell D., b. 03/23/1910, d. 02/02/1978

LADD, Pearl J., b. 06/18/1913, d. 03/28/1976

LECOMPTE, Herman H., s/o John N. & Mary D., b. 05/18/1889, d. 06/18/1905

LECOMPTE, John N., b. 05/10/1844, d. 10/13/1918

LECOMPTE, Mary D., b. 01/20/1855, d. 01/21/1940

LINDALE, James T., b. 02/21/1855, d. 03/13/1927

LINDALE, Mary E., b. 10/17/1857, d. 10/07/1941

LINTHICUM, Evelyn (Pete), b. 01/08/1916, d. 06/14/1967

LOFLAND, Howard, b. 11/06/1907, d. N/D

LOFLAND, Leroy, b. 11/15/1913, d. N/D

LOFLAND, Nelson H., b. 04/02/1919, d. N/D

LOWRY, M. Delema, b. 05/12/1913, d. 06/30/1974

LOWRY, William H., b. 06/01/1908, d. N/D

LULL, Cora, b. 1864, d. 1930

LULL, Fred, b. 1853, d. 1926

LYNCH, Anzey E., b. 12/17/1859, d. 05/13/1937

LYNCH, Charles C., b. 03/23/1850, d. 02/14/1930

LYNCH, W. David, b. 02/12/1881, d. 02/05/1956

MACKLIN, Anna Ellen Short, w/o Wm. B., b. 05/16/1854, d. 12/29/1916

MACKLIN, Bartley T., b. 01/31/1831, d. 06/03/1895

MACKLIN, Curry A., b. 02/14/1862, d. 12/24/1921

MACKLIN, Hall A., Sr., b. 02/10/1898, d. 02/14/1971

MACKLIN, Letha E., b. 10/30/1902, d. N/D

MACKLIN, Letha F., b. 10/12/1923, d. 11/08/1988

MACKLIN, Raymond H., b. 06/21/1891, d. 12/03/1959

MACKLIN, Roy A., s/o Curry A. & Willie S., b. 12/14/1888, d. 08/13/1889

MACKLIN, William Bert, b. 04/10/1855, d. 11/20/1915

MACKLIN, Willie, b. 01/06/1866, d. 03/29/1943

MAREL??, Herbert Oliver, b. Unreadable, d. 10/07/1878

MARKER, Carrie E., d/o Cyrus & Mary E., b. 09/24/1896, d. 11/14/1906

MARKER, Cyrus A., Age 75y 8m, b. 07/14/1848, d. 03/14/1924

MARKER, Mary D., b. 1879, d. 1956

MARKER, Mary E., b. 1854, d. 1930

MARKER, Robert J., b. 1878, d. 1950

MARKER, Robert J., s/o Robt. J. & Mary D., b. 08/05/1916, d. 08/28/1917

MARQUISETTE, James, b. 12/25/1903, d. 12/16/1967

MASTEN, Clement, b. 1833, d. 1915

MASTEN, Sarah A., b. 1837, d. 1924

MAY, Frank J., b. 1876, d. 1950
MAY, Nora L., b. 1894, d. 1971
MCCANN, Etta M., b. 04/25/1894, d. 02/25/1970
MCCANN, Harry F., Pa, MM2, USNRF, WWI, b. 05/05/1896, d. 09/11/1956
MCCLEARY, Priscilla L., b. 07/23/1943, d. 04/02/1987
MCHENRY, Eleanor A., b. 1889, d. 1925
MCHENRY, John J., b. 1857, d. 1928
MCHENRY, Winifred H., b. 1861, d. 1947
MEREDITH, Anna, b. 03/31/1867, d. 11/25/1944
MEREDITH, Bethuel, b. 07/31/1864, d. 06/12/1940
MESSICK, Grace T., b. 10/29/1923, d. N/D
MESSICK, Hannah M., b. 06/10/1913, d. 01/17/1957
MESSICK, Jennie T., b. 1876, d. 1964
MESSICK, Joseph W., b. 1872, d. 1944
MESSICK, Lester, b. 11/24/1918, d. 11/22/1990
MESSICK, Norman L., b. 09/05/1908, d. 07/10/1971
MILES, Minnie Beardsley, b. 02/02/1889, d. 10/26/1982
MILES, Sara N., b. 1831, d. 1917
MILLMAN, Charles, b. 01/23/1918, d. 03/27/1918
MILLMAN, Charlie, b. 05/14/1875, d. 04/24/1925
MILLMAN, Chester A., b. 12/06/1903, d. 12/08/1908
MILLMAN, David D., b. 11/20/1862, d. 05/18/1942
MILLMAN, Elva M., b. 10/18/1902, d. N/D
MILLMAN, Floyd C., b. 08/17/1900, d. 01/11/1978
MILLMAN, Mary H., b. 03/01/1871, d. 04/20/1937
MILLMAN, Samuel J., b. 01/01/1893, d. 03/03/1959
MILLMAN, Virgie, b. 11/22/1879, d. 11/27/1946
MILLS, Catherine Elizabeth, d/o Miles Elwood & Minnie Aline, b. 11/26/1912, d. 09/14/1915
MILLS, Henrieta C., b. 04/07/1903, d. 05/26/1991
MILLS, Lloyd E., b. 10/07/1900, d. N/D
MILLS, Miles Elwood, b. 11/11/1889, d. 10/19/1972
MILLS, Robert J., b. 11/13/1937, d. 01/12/1938
MOORE, Mary F., b. 09/23/1867, d. 08/08/1952
MOORE, Robert E., b. 1897, d. 1952
MORGAN, A. Marshall, b. 11/11/1879, d. 03/09/1949
MORGAN, Anita S., b. 07/23/1912, d. N/D
MORGAN, Bessie N., b. 1882, d. 1951
MORGAN, Bradbury, b. 02/01/1845, d. 06/25/1918
MORGAN, Douglas G., b. 07/30/1917, d. 04/28/1976
MORGAN, Joseph Eugene, Sgt., USA, WWII, b. 11/07/1920, d. 05/23/1975
MORGAN, Joseph H., b. 1875, d. 1946
MORGAN, Kathleen E., b. 01/02/1924, d. N/D
MORGAN, Marceil E., b. 04/28/1917, d. N/D
MORGAN, May, b. 05/10/1883, d. 06/25/1968
MORGAN, Rachel A., w/o Bradbury, b. 05/02/1850, d. 12/21/1933
MORGAN, Rena M., b. 07/27/1919, d. N/D
MORGAN, Sallie E., b. 08/17/1885, d. 06/23/1963
MORGAN, William B., b. 08/23/1881, d. 06/07/1963

MORGAN, William B., Jr., b. 11/25/1917, d. 02/21/1989

MORGAN, Woodrow W., b. 07/03/1912, d. 04/11/1978

MORLEY, John Winfield, Inf. s/o John W. & Rosa, b. N/D, d. N/D

MORRISON, Frank, b. 04/09/1853, d. 12/12/1894

MORRISON, George, Jr., b. 10/25/1845, d. 01/19/1888

MORRISON, George A., b. 10/18/1823, d. 07/13/1890

MORRISON, George A., b. 10/23/1889, d. 01/20/1965

MORRISON, Hobart R., b. 02/10/1897, d. 12/08/1915

MORRISON, Jennie Shew, b. 1860, d. 1940

MORRISON, Julia A., w/o George A., b. 09/15/1824, d. 02/05/1917

MORRISON, Kate, d/o George A. & Julia A., b. 11/30/1864, d. 07/08/1878

MORRISON, Ray, b. 09/13/1880, d. 10/12/1920

MORRISON, Robert M., b. 02/10/1897, d. 12/18/1915

MORRISON, V. Lou, b. 01/05/1888, d. 11/11/1956

MORRISON, William, b. 1850, d. 1929

MURPHY, Gilbert D., b. 01/18/1916, d. 10/05/1989

MURPHY, John, Pvt., USA, WWII, b. 1909, d. 1984

MURPHY, Kathryn Morrison, w/o Gilbert D., b. 10/25/1914, d. N/D

NEIBERT, Charles, Sr., b. 04/22/1895, d. 05/14/1954

NEIBERT, Grace L., b. 1903, d. N/D

PASSWATERS, Bruce M., b. 12/07/1962, d. 04/12/1981

PASSWATERS, Charles M., b. 07/29/1943, d. 07/03/1975

PASSWATERS, Cordelia L., b. 04/20/1943, d. N/D

PASSWATERS, Franklin A., b. 03/01/1922, d. 04/08/1987

PASSWATERS, Harry, b. 1884, d. 1959

PASSWATERS, Martha K., b. 03/06/1903, d. 07/04/1966

PASSWATERS, Mary E., b. 06/28/1922, d. 04/11/1993

PASSWATERS, William B., b. 11/30/1898, d. 06/04/1991

PASSWATERS, William B., Jr., b. 07/06/1935, d. 02/03/1987

PETTYJOHN, Blanche, b. 02/05/1889, d. 06/18/1968

PIERCE, James F., b. 09/19/1865, d. 04/12/1948

PIERCE, Jennie Wilkins, w/o James F., b. 03/01/1862, d. 04/23/1899

PIERCE, Maggie Carey, w/o Foster, b. 01/10/1876, d. 09/24/1949

PIERCE, William, Age 75y, b. N/D, d. 03/09/1904

PLEASANTON, John T., b. 1909, d. 1992

PLEASANTON, Sallie M., b. 1911, d. 1986

POOLE, Joseph, b. 08/25/1881, d. 06/05/1973

POOLE, Mae, b. 01/14/1887, d. 02/17/1977

POORE, Margaret M., b. 1898, d. 1981

POSTLES, Donald H., b. 1916, d. 1974

POSTLES, Edna Peggy, b. 1917, d. 1985

POSTLES, Francis E., b. 1891, d. 1932

POSTLES, Francis W., b. 1924, d. N/D

POSTLES, Virginia O., b. 1862, d. 1934

POSTLES, William T., b. 1860, d. 1947

PRIDE, Annie L., b. 12/25/1871, d. 01/06/1924

PRIDE, Esther E., b. 12/26/1909, d. 01/04/1982

PRIDE, John C., b. 10/12/1840, d. 10/22/1934

PRIDE, Raymond, Jr., b. 06/22/1927, d. 10/02/1990
RATHBUN, John A., b. 07/01/1816, d. 10/01/1897
REED, Belle, c/o E. G. & Elida, b. 01/26/1890, d. 05/26/1890
REED, Charlie C., s/o E. G. & Elida, b. 11/08/1882, d. 01/02/1884
REED, Elias G., b. 1857, d. 1952
REED, Esther J., b. 02/18/1908, d. 11/06/1982
REED, George D., b. 04/08/1852, d. 02/23/1930
REED, George M., Jr., b. 08/14/1908, d. 11/28/1987
REED, Gertrude Chipman, b. 1859, d. 1951
REED, J. Vernon, b. 1902, d. 1953
REED, James Henry, b. 10/18/1870, d. 02/02/1924
REED, James V., Jr., b. 1924, d. 1992
REED, Josephine, b. 1901, d. 1929
REED, Lena, b. 12/01/1891, d. 11/30/1892
REED, Lida V., b. 1860, d. 1935
REED, Mary E. Shockley, w/o Geo. D., b. 11/08/1845, d. 01/21/1911
REED, Vernie Mabel, c/o E. G. & Elida, b. 06/12/1880, d. 05/04/1902
REED, Viola P. Coulter, b. 12/23/1871, d. 06/07/1947
REYNOLDS, John E., b. 1897, d. 1959
REYNOLDS, Rhea C., b. 1916, d. 1984
RICE, Caroline Horton, w/o George L., b. 1835, d. 1910
RICE, George L., b. 1836, d. 1905
RISLER, Eugene S., Jr., b. 1917, d. 1936
RISLER, Eugene S., Sr., b. 1889, d. 1970
RISLER, Mahlon R., s/o William, R. & Sarah, b. 11/04/1894, d. 06/18/1908
RISLER, Sarah I., b. 1871, d. 1941
RISLER, William R., Sr., b. 1860, d. 1932
ROLLE, Henry, b. 1830, d. 1906
ROWELL, Fred N., b. 1870, d. 1947
RUST, Christina Morgan, b. 1941, d. 1973
RUZICKA, No other information
RWYER, Judson, s/o W. H. & Mary J., b. 06/21/1861, d. 08/17/1866
RYAN, Ethel Marie, b. 10/04/1925, d. 10/05/1925
RYDER, David C., b. 04/16/1799, d. 01/28/1868
RYDER, Mary A., b. 09/25/1812, d. 03/11/1899
SACKETT, Allena, d/o Chas. H. & Louisa E., b. 04/09/1882, d. 05/14/1882
SACKETT, Charles H., b. 1848, d. 1928
SACKETT, Charles J., b. 05/08/1901, d. 04/12/1971
SACKETT, George, b. 1820, d. 1901
SACKETT, Gertrude M., b. 02/10/1888, d. 10/31/1907
SACKETT, Louisa E., b. 1853, d. 1925
SACKETT, Orpha C., b. 1823, d. 1891
SANCHEZ, Alicia, b. 04/11/1953, d. 05/03/1988
SANSON, Francis E., M. D., b. 03/15/1861, d. 03/17/1918
SANSON, Nellie S., b. 10/24/1878, d. 04/26/1924
SATTERFIELD, Calvin, b. 1890, d. 1942
SATTERFIELD, Elizabeth H., b. 07/05/1889, d. 09/13/1966
SAVAGE, Beva L., b. 06/15/1912, d. N/D

SAVAGE, Eurie M., b. 1878, d. 1954

SAVAGE, Laura A., w/o Eurie M., b. 1878, d. 1938

SAVAGE, Dawin C., b. 09/12/1910, d. N/D

SAXTON, Beatrice, b. 08/14/1895, d. 12/04/1990

SAXTON, Leroy P., b. 05/21/1888, d. 04/03/1969

SCOTT, David, One of the founders of Houston, Delaware, b. 01/22/1822, d. 11/15/1905

SCOTT, Eliza Jane Johnston, w/o David, b. 02/12/1828, d. 02/06/1908

SELBY, Earl F., Jr., s/o E. F. & Mildred, b. 08/04/1920, d. 09/15/1920

SENNETT, Winnita M., b. 02/09/1945, d. 02/21/1992

SHELDON, Earl P., b. 05/27/1902, d. 03/07/1966

SHELDON, Helena Southard, b. 03/26/1902, d. N/D

SHEW, Anne M., b. 1916, d. 1988

SHEW, Charles C., b. 04/13/1876, d. 04/21/1916

SHEW, Cornelia G., w/o Frank C., b. 01/08/1848, d. 10/19/1936

SHEW, Frank C., b. 09/18/1847, d. 03/27/1925

SHEW, George S., b. 1868, d. 1895

SHEW, Harry S., (Col.), b. 1909, d. 1979

SHEW, Josie Allena, b. 1894, d. 1940

SHEW, Leva L., b. 1892, d. 1971

SHEW, Louis P., b. 1874, d. 1958

SHEW, Maria A., b. 1871, d. 1944

SHEW, Minnie R., b. 1868, d. 1950

SHEW, Putman, b. 1821, d. 186

SHEW, Ruth Allene, d/o Louis P. & Maria A., b. 04/29/1900, d. 08/28/1908

SHIELDS, Bessie M., b. 07/02/1911, d. N/D

SHIELDS, Richard E., b. 01/15/1913, d. 04/04/1981

SHOCKLEY, Anna E., b. 1851, d. 1914

SHOCKLEY, Charles M., b. 1865, d. 1932

SHOCKLEY, Elias, b. 1824, d. 1890

SHOCKLEY, Emma, w/o S. W. b. 05/02/1851, d. 10/25/1879

SHOCKLEY, Emma May, b. 05/28/1897, d. 05/08/1898

SHOCKLEY, Estella Gere, b. 1856, d. 1938

SHOCKLEY, Gardner W., b. 1873, d. 1879

SHOCKLEY, George lacey, b. 1899, d. 1953

SHOCKLEY, George R., b. 1875, d. 1879

SHOCKLEY, Harold S., b. 1897, d. 1954

SHOCKLEY, Harry, b. 11/13/1863, d. 12/01/1927

SHOCKLEY, Ida M., b. 12/20/1896, d. 07/26/1981

SHOCKLEY, James B., b. 1856, d. 1922

SHOCKLEY, John R., b. 09/21/1888, d. 03/17/1965

SHOCKLEY, Joseph H., b. 1869, d. 1926

SHOCKLEY, Joseph H., Jr., Interred Ft. Benning Memorial Cemetery, b. 1912, d. 1965

SHOCKLEY, Laura J., b. 03/15/1871, d. 04/25/1949

SHOCKLEY, Lula A., b. 09/15/1868, d. 11/10/1947

SHOCKLEY, Lydia B., b. 1831, d. 1888

SHOCKLEY, Mabelle E., b. 11/02/1903, d. 02/04/1928

SHOCKLEY, S. W., b. 1848, d. 1895

SHOCKLEY, Sallie B., b. 1870, d. 1969

SHOCKLEY, Sallie J., b. 1863, d. 1950

SHOCKLEY, Samuel Gere, b. 1881, d. 1895

SHOCKLEY, William B., b. 1859, d. 1936

SHOURDS, Catherline W., b. 02/12/1919, d. N/D

SHOURDS, Evan T., Sr., AS, USN, WWII, b. 08/01/1918, d. 10/09/1990

SLAUGHTER, Laura J., b. 1865, d. 1944

SMALL, Abel S., b. 07/19/1823, d. 01/06/1889

SMALL, Alphonsia W., b. 04/26/1845, d. 04/11/1920

SMALL, Emma Egbert, b. 01/02/1850, d. 02/27/1927

SMALL, Mary R., w/o William B., b. 10/09/1878, d. N/D

SMALL, W. B., Co. F, 104th PA Inf., b. N/D, d. N/D

SMITH, Bessie Laws, b. 11/06/1875, d. 03/06/1974

SMITH, George M., b. 07/26/1852, d. 06/29/1917

SMITH, Kenneth Lee, b. 02/26/1953, d. 05/02/1972

SMITH, Laura A., b. 12/14/1835, d. 08/12/1897

SMITH, Thompson R., b. 11/17/1834, d. 03/20/1905

SOCKRIDER, Audie F., b. 1876, d. 1955

SOCKRIDER, Paul, b. 1903, d. 1945

SOCKRIDER, William T., b. 1863, d. 1939

SOCKRIDER, Wilson H., b. 1870, d. 1899

SOUTHARD, Charles A., s/o I. Eugene & Phebe C., b. 06/16/1869, d. 01/13/1873

SOUTHARD, Ella Marie, b. 10/07/1907, d. 02/14/1908

SOUTHARD, Harry C., Jr., b. 07/09/1900, d. 10/07/1907

SOUTHARD, Harry Carter, b. 11/17/1873, d. 12/13/1944

SOUTHARD, I. Eugene, b. 09/12/1845, d. 03/30/1901

SOUTHARD, I., Eugene, III, b. 1909, d. 1965

SOUTHARD, James Paul, b. 04/29/1913, d. 05/10/1920

SOUTHARD, Mary Curtin, b. 03/16/1880, d. 11/12/1943

SOUTHARD, Phebe Carter, w/o I. Eugene, b. 01/30/1849, d. 10/31/1896

SOUTHARD, Philip C., b. 06/19/1918, d. 04/06/1981

SOUTHARD, William Steven, USAF, WWII, b. 02/19/1906, d. 05/02/1977

SPENCER, G. Frank, b. 10/28/1874, d. 06/26/1952

SPENCER, Ida V., b. 11/14/1884, d. 12/06/1970

SPICER, Edward E., b. 1881, d. 1972

SPICER, Katie E., b. 1884, d. 1955

STANTON, Willie, Inf. s/o David & Marvet, b. N/D, d. N/D

STAYTON, A. Jay, b. 12/14/1935, d. 02/10/1992

STAYTON, Amos J., b. 01/10/1909, d. 01/17/1988

STAYTON, Nora M., b. 02/10/1913, d. N/D

STAYTON, Roger Lee, b. N/D, d. 1960

STEEN, Grace W., b. 09/01/1908, d. N/D

STEEN, William A., b. 10/07/1912, d. 01/19/1975

STERRITT, Reuben Washburn, b. 10/19/1885, d. 02/13/1966

STERRITT, V. Mabel, b. 11/06/1903, d. 03/20/1986

STEVENS, Alexander McCulley, Dr., b. 05/26/1885, d. 01/31/1954

STEVENS, Angeline E., b. 02/21/1833, d. 12/10/1909

STEVENS, Annie E., d/o Dr. J. A. & Janie P., b. 12/29/1882, d. 06/28/1884

STEVENS, George L., b. 08/25/1830, d. 01/22/1904

STOUT, Achsah Wilcox, w/o David, Age 54y 16d, b. N/D, d. 12/06/1881
STRAIT, Benjamin F., b. 1832, d. 1890
STRAIT, Fred, s/o Benjamin F. & Melissa A., b. 1867, d. 1887
STRAIT, Melissa A., w/o Benjamin F., b. 1841, d. 1887
SWAIN, Bernice A., b. 02/17/1887, d. 06/14/1942
SWAIN, Charles H., b. 07/31/1887, d. 04/12/1972
SWAIN, Dorothy I., b. 03/18/1932, d. N/D
SWAIN, G. Harvey, b. 08/10/1891, d. 10/04/1975
SWAIN, George Riggs, b. 08/30/1897, d. 07/11/1968
SWAIN, George W., b. 1864, d. 1929
SWAIN, Harry J., Sr., m. 1933, b. 10/27/1910, d. N/D
SWAIN, Hazel B., b. 12/21/1912, d. 02/07/1992
SWAIN, Inf. s/o Charles H. & Bernice, b. N/D, d. 03/20/1918
SWAIN, Iris I., b. 01/01/1900, d. N/D
SWAIN, M. Elizabeth, b. 1869, d. 1959
SWAIN, Palmer E., b. 11/29/1929, d. 10/28/1983
SWAIN, Pearl P., b. 11/20/1901, d. N/D
SYMONDS, James S., b. 1860, d. 1941
TAYLOR, Florine L., b. 01/19/1920, d. 11/24/1981
TAYLOR, Hiram J., Jr., b. 06/10/1917, d. N/D
THOMAS, Dennie E., b. 1877, d. 1955
THOMAS, Iris M., b. 12/06/1925, d. N/D
THOMAS, Robert H., b. 1873, d. 1951
THOMAS, William E., b. 08/22/1921, d. N/D
TINGLE, Emma P., b. 1876, d. 1927
TINGLE, Roland L., USS Memphis, b. 1896, d. 1916
TRACY, Joseph B., b. 12/28/1806, d. 05/07/1884
TRACY, Maria L., b. 02/23/1818, d. 01/25/1901
TRANSEAU, Annie C., b. 1839, d. 1889
TRANSEAU, Edith L., b. 10/28/1894, d. 10/11/1961
TRANSEAU, Elise R., b. 1899, d. 1986
TRANSEAU, Mary Eliz., w/o Wm. Sherman, b. 1868, d. 1952
TRANSEAU, Sherman T., b. 1897, d. 1984
TRANSEAU, William R., b. 09/09/1891, d. 05/20/1975
TRANSEAU, Wm. Sherman, b. 1866, d. 1935
TRAVIS, William J., b. 08/21/1910, d. 03/14/1986
TRAVIS, Naomi G., b. 01/15/1913, d. N/D
TRAYLOR, Ora Hitch, b. 1882, d. 1937
TRIPLETT, Harles H., b. 03/05/1921, d. 09/12/1986
TRIPLETT, Pauline L., b. 10/23/1921, d. N/D
TRUITT, Donald Harry, s/o Harry B. & Edna L., b. 01/30/1914, d. 05/10/1914
TRUITT, Edna L., b. 08/09/1882, d. 07/02/1969
TRUITT, Joshua W., b. 02/22/1836, d. 07/26/1915
TRUITT, Mary E. Kidler, b. 09/27/1881, d. 04/28/1971
TRUITT, Mary R., b. 06/11/1855, d. 03/07/1940
TRUITT, Nancy B., b. 02/07/1845, d. 03/03/1928
TRUITT, Roy C., b. 04/23/1885, d. 05/20/1970
TRUITT, William S., b. 11/13/1851, d. 04/02/1923

TUCKER, Minnie M., b. 1878, d. 1961
TUCKER, William E., b. 1869, d. 1935
UNSINN, John A., b. N/D, d. 01/02/1924
UNSINN, Joseph A., Mus 1, USN, WWI, b. 01/31/1894, d. 06/26/1977
UNSINN, Thelma S., b. 06/13/1898, d. 02/09/1990
VADAKIN, Frank W., b. 11/18/1879, d. 12/18/1965
VADAKIN, Mary V., b. 09/26/1886, d. 12/31/1939
WALLS, Arthur H., b. 1888, d. 1949
WALLS, Arthur H., b. 1915, d. 1979
WALLS, Carrie L., b. 1868, d. 1926
WALLS, Gertrude S., b. 1914, d. N/D
WALLS, Julia S., b. 1887, d. 1957
WALLS, Laura C., b. 06/13/1881, d. 02/14/1967
WARREN, Alice, w/o Joseph E., b. 11/23/1859, d. 07/27/1892
WARREN, Arthur F., b. 03/24/1893, d. 04/23/1927
WARREN, Charles H., b. 11/28/1915, d. N/D
WARREN, Edna Mae, b. 12/29/1919, d. N/D
WARREN, Emily N., b. 07/01/1920, d. N/D
WARREN, Ethel H., b. 05/04/1883, d. 08/30/1971
WARREN, Frank, b. 05/31/1857, d. 02/11/1926
WARREN, Frank N., b. 1887, d. 1934
WARREN, Frederick C., b. 04/25/1886, d. 09/21/1947
WARREN, Gary Charles, b. 07/30/1948, d. 01/09/1965
WARREN, George H., b. 02/16/1880, d. 09/19/1957
WARREN, Harry F., b. 09/12/1879, d. 07/12/1946
WARREN, Joseph E., b. 01/06/1862, d. 04/13/1946
WARREN, Laura V., b. 1885, d. 1966
WARREN, Lillie M., b. 1883, d. 1970
WARREN, Margaret A., w/o Frank, b. 04/15/1855, d. 10/08/1923
WARREN, Mary E., b. 1893, d. 1983
WARREN, Perry, b. 1860, d. 1930
WARREN, Rose M., b. 06/22/1888, d. 06/15/1971
WARREN, Virginia R., b. 10/01/1880, d. 08/24/1937
WARREN, William R., b. 01/27/1918, d. 04/25/1991
WARRINER, Jairus David, b. 01/22/1852, d. 08/12/1922
WARRINER, Matilda, b. 08/29/1858, d. 10/24/1946
WARRINER, Priscilla, w/o Levi Clark, b. 02/01/1850, d. 12/07/1926
WARRINER, Raymond Jairus, b. 05/29/1887, d. 10/27/1945
WARRINGTON, Edith V., b. 03/30/1892, d. 07/09/1952
WARRINGTON, William E., b. 08/04/1874, d. 10/23/1950
WATERS, Grace C., b. 12/26/1899, d. 12/23/1979
WATERS, Mildred Pauline, b. 03/18/1938, d. 10/08/1960
WATERS, Thomas Ashby, Sr., DE, S1, USN, WWII, b. 05/19/1906, d. 08/27/1971
WATSON, Annie E., b. 08/26/1859, d. 09/01/1908
WATSON, Jesse L., b. 1854, d. 1938
WEATHERLY, Charles E., b. 1867, d. 1944
WEATHERLY, Nellie E., b. 1870, d. 1943
WEBB, Addie J., b. 12/07/1866, d. 09/19/1957

WEBB, Bessie, w/o George L., b. 09/09/1888, d. 02/23/1917

WEBB, Elwood Z., b. 01/01/1907, d. 02/04/1973

WEBB, George L., b. 11/13/1886, d. 12/06/1967

WEBB, Lydia Passwaters, b. 1903, d. 1987

WEBB, William F., b. 05/14/1861, d. 07/19/1953

WELCH, Frederick C., b. 05/31/1868, d. 06/11/1900

WELCH, I. Fisher, b. 09/22/1860, d. 04/17/1927

WELCH, Lillie C., b. 01/26/1871, d. 06/21/1953

WELCH, Mark H., b. 08/17/1865, d. 01/18/1948

WELCH, Nathaniel H., Age 74y 8m 2d, b. 02/04/1831, d. 10/06/1905

WELCH, Sallie H., w/o I. Fisher, b. 06/13/1864, d. 12/26/1933

WELCH, Sarah T., w/o Nathaniel H., Age 74y, b. 1835, d. 09/24/1909

WILKINS, Alice M., b. 1889, d. 1959

WILKINS, Donald E, b. 07/30/1923, d. N/D

WILKINS, Elmer T., b. 1887, d .1963

WILKINS, Eva, b. N/D, d. N/D

WILKINS, Florence C., b. 09/13/1930, d. 09/06/1991

WILKINS, Frances E. Campbell, w/o John, b. 12/29/1827, d. 04/20/1911

WILKINS, Grace L., b. 11/11/1916, d. 03/16/1964

WILKINS, Herbert, Adopted s/o John & Frances E., b. 06/07/1877, d. 06/22/1884

WILKINS, Hirschel D., b. 09/14/1921, d. 08/02/19876

WILKINS, Howard E., b. 01/25/1916, d. N/D

WILKINS, James Burton, b. 12/10/1990, d. 07/16/1965

WILKINS, Jane E., b. 10/27/1929, d. N/D

WILKINS, John, b. 02/22/1829, d. 10/12/1900

WILKINS, Joyce D., w/o Kenneth H., m. 01/25/1963, d. 03/03/1944, d. 05/28/1988

WILKINS, Julia E., b. 04/19/1917, d. 03/26/1974

WILKINS, Kenneth H., m. 01/25/1963, b. 05/29/1942, d. N/D

WILKINS, Martha Hatfield, b. 08/22/1871, d. 09/08/1963

WILKINS, Ruth Clendaniel, b. 02/24/1904, d. 04/06/1981

WILKINS, Sherman C., b. 06/02/1864, d. 07/09/1893

WILLEY, Delema, b. 12/08/1920, d. 03/03/1985

WILLEY, Donna O., b. 02/08/1942, d. 04/14/1977

WILLEY, Herman V., DE, SP3, 21015 Vc Comd. Unit, Korea, b. 10/09/1928, d. 09/04/1970

WILLEY, Navada, b. 09/07/1935, d. 09/07/1935

WILLIAMS, Benjamin F., b. 06/30/1827, d. 04/07/1914

WILLIAMS, Clara P., b. 05/18/1889, d. 08/14/1982

WILLIAMS, Margaret J., b. 01/21/1854, d. 08/08/1925

WILLIAMS, William D., b. 10/29/1888, d. 04/24/1974

WILSON, Charlie, b. 11/17/1881, d. 03/08/1917

WILSON, George Thomas, Capt., b. 12/15/1933, d. 01/31/1989

WILSON, James R., Pvt., Died in N. Africa Area, b. 10/01/1913, d. 07/09/1944

WINN, Joy Reed, b. 1923, d. 1948

WIREMAN, Wm. b. 1898, d. 1957

WOODEN, Benjamin, b. 02/14/1824, d. 08/27/1917

WORKMAN, Charles H., b. 03/16/1875, d. 01/15/1964

WORKMAN, Della E., b. 11/02/1876, d. 02/18/1969

WORKMAN, Virginia, d/o Charles H. & Dolly E., b. 12/01/1913, d. 04/06/1914

WYATT, Anna J., b. 09/14/1861, d. 09/15/1943
WYATT, Anna May, b. 08/17/1880, d. 07/07/1976
WYATT, Ira Murray, b. 01/22/1880, d. 05/02/1944
WYATT, William J., b. 02/22/1850, d. 12/26/1915
YAGER, Mary L., b. 03/14/1955, d. 03/14/1955

The following stones were recorded by the Hudson Survey but are now missing or unreadable:
BENSON, Ida, b. 1874, d. N/D
BENSON, John H., b. 1869, d. 1930
COLLINS, W. H., Age 72y, b. N/D, d. N/D
HARRIS, Elsie Mabel, d/o Peter & Minnie, b. 10/07/1878, d. 04/10/1881
HARRIS, Herbert Clair, s/o Peter & Minnie, b. 01/25/1877, d. 04/06/1881
HARRISON, E. James, b. 07/14/1897, d. 07/10/1925
SMALL, A. Eugene, b. 01/08/1866, d. 02/28/1919
SMALL, Elizabeth D., b. 05/25/1827, d. 08/19/1900

(CC-015 & HU-176) WEBB CEMETERY
Located S. W. of Ellendale at the Northerly corner of the intersection of South Union Church Rd. (Rd. 42) and Oakley Rd. (Rd. 610) Recorded: November 9, 1995

PASSWATERS, Jeremiah M., ssw-Laura F., b. 1869, d. 1936
PASSWATERS, John H., Age 34y 9m 11d, b. 11/28/1871, d. 09/09/1906
PASSWATERS, Laura F., ssw-Jeremiah M., b. 1888, d. 1910
PASSWATERS, Sarah, b. 12/25/1844, d. 02/09/1914
WEBB, Eunice C., w/o George F., Age 44y 4m 19d, b. 05/02/1858, d. 09/22/1899
WEBB, Helen N., d/o George F. & Mary V., b. 10/26/1912, d. 08/09/1913
WEBB, Inf. o/Isaac F. & Mollie, b. 05/17/1909, d. 05/19/1909
WHARTON, Laura W., d/o Lizzie, b. 11/28/1878, d. 11/10/1884

The following stones were recorded by the Hudson Survey but are now missing or unreadable:
PASSWATERS, Jennie, w/o Thomas T., b. 01/17/1878, d. 08/02/1910
PASSWATERS, Oscar, s/o T. T. & J., b. 09/17/1909, d. 06/30/1910

(CC-016 & HU-459) BENIAH SHARP FAMILY CEMETERY
Located Southeast of Milford, approximately 500 yards N. W. of Sharps Rd. (Rd. 200) 0.6 miles N. E. of Coastal Highway (Rt. 1) Recorded: January 6, 1998

SHARP, Beniah, Age 25y, b. 1812, d. 02/10/1869
SHARP, R. P., b. 10/13/1878, d. 08/08/1964
SHARP, Rhoda, w/o Beniah, Age 48y 2m, b. N/D, d. 03/26/1858
SHARP, William H., s/o Rhoda K. & Beniah, Age 25y 6m 2d, b. 11/25/1845, d. 06/07/1871

DAGSBORO HUNDRED

(DA-001 & HU-101) THOMPSON FAMILY CEMETERY

Located S. E. of Millsboro approximately 150 feet from the S. E. side of Thorogood Rd. (Rd. 333) 0.4 miles N. E. of Dagsboro Rd. (Rd. 334)
Recorded: April 4, 1992

THOMPSON, Daniel B., s/o Isaac C. & Mary C., Age 65y, b. N/D, d. 09/28/1889
THOMPSON, Emoline, w/o Isaac J., b. 09/20/1824, d. 11/23/1887
THOMPSON, Isaac J., b. 09/10/1826, d. 07/05/1904

(DA-002 & HU-228) LEVIN STEEN FAMILY CEMETERY

Located West of Millsboro at the Western corner of the intersection of Hardscrabble Rd. (Rt. 20) and Homestead Rd. (Rd. 442)
Recorded: March 30, 1992

DAVIS, Ulisus Sharp, Age 55y, b. N/D, d. 04/15/1929
STEEN, Eliza A., wid/o Levin Steen, b. 11/13/1842, d. 03/09/1901
STEEN, Sarah E., b. 07/28/1866, d. 10/02/1915
THOMPSON, Benjamin F., b. 02/03/1886, d. 07/02/1916

The following stones were recorded by the Hudson Survey but are now missing or unreadable:
HITCHENS, Edward S., b. 01/20/1863, d. 01/13/1883
STEEN, Levin, b. 11/28/1847, d. 04/01/1920
STEEN, Otis, b. 12/18/1901, d. 03/16/1903
STEEN, Sallie M., b. 04/11/1884, d. 09/08/1887

(DA-003 & HU-231) FOOKS-SHORT FAMILY CEMETERY

Located S. W. of Georgetown on N. E. side of Whaley's Corner Rd., (Rd. 329), 0.2 miles N. W. of East Trap Pond Rd. (Rd. 62)
Recorded: March 30, 1992

SHORT, Abron D., s/o Daniel & Mary M. E., b. 08/19/1890, d. 06/21/1891
SHORT, Cyrus O., s/o Daniel E. & Mary M. E., Age 1y 7m 15d, b. N/D, d. 03/08/1881
SHORT, Inf. o/Daniel & Mary M. E., b. 12/26/1886, d. 03/07/1887
SHORT, Mary M. E., w/o Daniel, b. 04/28/1854, d. 07/31/1890

The following stone were recorded by the Hudson Survey but are now missing or unreadable:
FOOKS, Cyrus Q., Age 63y, b. N/D, d. 04/28/1880
FOOKS, Priscilla N. C., d/o Cyrus & Mary, Age 9y 4m 29d, b. N/D, d. 03/18/1853

(DA-004 & HU-478) GREEN FAMILY CEMETERY

Located West of Millsboro on the N. E. side of Godwin School Rd. (Rd. 410), 50 yards S. E. of Country Living Rd. (Rd. 433).
Recorded: March 22, 1992

GREEN, Mary K., Age 63y 7m 23d, b. N/D, d. N/D
GREEN, Theresa, Age 1y 1m, b. N/D, d. 12/02/1863

The following stone was recorded by the Hudson Survey but is now missing or unreadable:
GREEN, Jesse, age 55y, b. N/D, d. N/D

GEORGETOWN HUNDRED

(GN-001 & HU-240) HEBRON M. E. CHURCH CEMETERY
Located West of Georgetown on the South side of Seashore Highway (Rt. 404), 1.5 miles west of the Du Pont Boulevard (Rt. 113).
Recorded: October 19, 1993

BOTJER, Mildred J., ssw-Clarence E. Joines, b. 1908, d. 1970
BRITTINGHAM, Beatrice Helen, b. 03/09/1935, d. N/D
BRITTINGHAM, Dalton Vance, b. 11/19/1933, d. 03/18/1989
BRITTINGHAM, Dalton Vance, Jr., b. 04/11/1959, d. 10/22/1959
CONAWAY, Elizabeth, w/o Thomas, Age 95y, b. N/D, d. 04/26/1909
CONAWAY, Thomas, Age 78y, b. N/D, d. 04/01/1900
DAVIS, Helen L., ssw-John H., b. 10/13/1931, d. N/D
DAVIS, John H., ssw-Helen L., b. 11/13/1929, d. N/D
HITCHENS, Elwood James, Jr., b. 05/09/1963, d. 05/14/1963
HITCHENS, Florence D., ssw-Samuel P., b. 05/31/1899, d. 01/27/1992
HITCHENS, Robert A., ssw-Virginia B., Pfc., USA, WWII, b. 06/10/1926, d. 01/17/1987
HITCHENS, Samuel P., ssw-Florence D., b. 08/28/1888, d. 02/05/1950
HITCHENS, Virginia B., ssw-Robert A., b. 06/08/1931, d. N/D
HUDSON, Joseph, s/o George W. & Ida, b. 03/02/1913, d. 11/01/1918
JEFFERSON, Sallie West, b. 01/22/1859, d. 08/11/1933
JESTER, George, ssw-Nellie I., b. 03/08/1927, d. 06/12/1982
JESTER, Nellie I, ssw-George, b. 08/22/1934, d. N/D
JOINES, Clarence E., ssw-Mildred J. Botjer, b. 1900, d. 1965
KING, Addie, ssw-Thomas, b. 06/16.1862, d. 11/26/1932
KING, Addie C., w/o Clarence C., b. 09/19/1884, d. 03/03/1907
KING, Arinthia E., ssw-James F., b. 06/20/1888, d. 12/03/1962
KING, Catherine, w/o Bivens C., b. 01/25/1902, d. 06/13/1961
KING, Catherine M., d/o Lloyd T. & Mary A., b. 07/16/1920, d. 07/19/1920
KING, Charles E., s/o Charles & Carrie J., Baby Boy, b. 1920, d. 1921
KING, Charley H., s/o John & Julia A., Age 2m 17d, b. N/D, d. 03/01/1889
KING, Dorothy M., ssw-Preston L., b. 12/10/1933, d. N/D
KING, Edwin G., ssw-Ida King & Harrington Savage, b. 1895, d. 1930
KING, Elijah, b. 1880, d. 1953
KING, Elwood J., Del., Pvt., QM Corps., WWII, b. 05/17/1917, d. 07/11/1965
KING, Herman W., b. 12/01/1912, d. 05/17/1913
KING, James B., b. 04/27/1831, d. 09/17/1915
KING, James F., ssw-Arinthia E., b. 02/03/1884, d. 06/14/1953
KING, John, b. 1916, d. 1937
KING, John, Sr., b. 10/18/1847, d. 11/19/1929
KING, Julia A., w/o John, b. 04/16/1856, d. 03/18/1915

KING, Lloyd T., ssw-Mary A., b. 10/18/1897, d. 12/17/1969

KING, Mary A., ssw-Lloyd T., b. 06/21/1897, d. 10/23/1987

KING, Mary Ellen, w/o Wingate, b. 07/30/1859, d. 09/03/1902

KING, Preston L., ssw-Dorothy M., b. 01/15/1923, d. N/D

KING, Robert Thurman, s/o Thurman & Jane, b. 1941, d. 1941

KING, Sarah A., w/o James B., b. 05/08/1835, d. 11/08/1911

KING, Thomas, ssw-Addie, b. 07/21/1860, d. 03/08/1930

KING, Wingate, Pvt., Co. B, 6 DE Inf., b. 08/10/1839, d. 03/08/1923

LLOYD, James T., b. 1931, d. 1989

MAGEE, Carlton, b. 04/26/1911, d. 03/05/1948

MAGEE, Edith M., ssw-Silas J., b. 1883, d. 1968

MAGEE, Florence, ssw-Flossie, b. 1915, d. 1916

MAGEE, Flossie, ssw-Florence, b. 1907, d. 1908

MAGEE, Silas J., ssw-Edith M., b. 1881, d. 1933

MCDOWELL, Harrison C., s/o Philip W. & Sara, Age 3y 2m 3d, b. N/D, d. 03/03/1891

MEREDITH, James Allen, Foster s/o Linda & Frank Jewell, b. 03/26/1968, d. 04/08/1991

MURRAY, Frank E., ssw-Mildred M., b. 10/26/1924, d. N/D

MURRAY, Mildred M., ssw-Frank E., b. 04/12/1925, d. 12/07/1991

QUILLEN, Henry O., ssw-Norma L., b. 12/12/1941, d. N/D

QUILLEN, Norma L., ssw-Henry O., b. 01/28/1945, d. 09/03/1988

REYNOLDS, Estella B., ssw-William D., b. 07/12/1903, d. 10/01/1992

REYNOLDS, William D., ssw-Estella B., b. 03/31/1898, d. 06/10/1980

SALMONS, Arthur C., b. 1890, d. 1937

SAMMONS, Charlie, ssw-Ida Bell, b. 06/18/1868, d. 05/04/1909

SAMMONS, Ida Bell, ssw-Charlie, b. 11/19/1868, d. 02/16/1934

SAVAGE, Harrington, ssw-Ida King Savage and Edwin G. King, b. 1905, d. 1975

SAVAGE, Ida King, ssw-Harrington Savage and Edwin G. King, b. 1899, d. 1975

SCOTT, Inf. s/o Glenn & Ethel K., Baby Boy, b. N/D, d. N/D

SHOEMAKER, Agnes A., ssw-Denver J., b. 12/04/1928, d. N/D

SHOEMAKER, Denver J., ssw-Agnes, GM3, USN, WWII, b. 12/18/1924, d. 09/25/1976

SHOEMAKER, Ralph Karl, b. 07/09/1957, d. 08/03/1957

SMITH, Agustus E., s/o H. D. & Mary C., b. 07/18/1884, d. 11/03/1889

SMITH, David R., b. 03/12/1844, d. 12/03/1917

SMITH, Hiram D., ssw-Mary C., b. 04/17/1858, d. 04/16/1939

SMITH, Mary C., ssw-Hiram D., b. 10/01/1857, d. 11/07/1950

SMITH, Willie, d/o H. D. & Mary C., b. 04/25/1896, d. 07/28/1896

TALLENT, Elsie, b. 1918, d. 1940

TALLENT, Frank B., ssw-Reba N., Pvt., USA, WWII, b. 01/29/1910, d. 07/06/1986

TALLENT, Reba N., ssw-Frank B., b. 03/14/1912, d. N/D

THOMAS, H., b. 01/03/1862, d. 03/31/1942

TUNIS, Frank Allen, b. 10/22/1968, d. 11/01/1985

WEST, Avery S., ssw-Julia I., b. 09/06/1896, d. 06/11/1961

WEST, Clara May, ssw-George W., b. 1878, d. 1946

WEST, Edward B., b. 1867, d. 1948

WEST, Effie L., b. 10/20/1879, d. 02/07/1915

WEST, Eliza E., w/o John T., b. 01/14/1863, d. 09/05/1926

WEST, George W., ssw-Clara May, b. 1873, d. 1957

WEST, John T., b. 06/07/1854, d. 01/06/1893

WEST, Julia I., ssw-Avery S., b. 03/15/1898, d. 06/10/1976
WEST, Robert R., ssw-Sarah E., b. 11/07/1863, d. 01/25/1937
WEST, Sarah E., ssw-Robert R., b. 09/23/1868, d. 05/31/1913
WEST, W. A., b. 1856, d. 1942
WHITE, Aline E., ssw-John O., Jr., b. 05/23/1927, d. N/D
WHITE, John O., Jr., ssw-Aline E., b. 09/26/1927, d. 12/09/1980
WHITE, Ronald Lee, b. 10/14/1929, d. 12/17/1952
WILLEY, Grace E., ssw-Samuel W., b. 12/27/1916, d. 06/29/1956
WILLEY, James G., b. 10/21/1940, d. 08/21/1958
WILLEY, Samuel W., ssw-Grace E., b. 07/15/1916, d. N/D
WILSON, William Brent, s/o Gloria Jean & Steven F. Wilson, b. N/D, d. 03/29/1981
WINGATE, John C., b. 05/23/1829, d. 03/02/1899
WINGATE, George R., s/o John C. & Julia A., b. 12/07/1875, d. 11/01/1889
WINGATE, Larenzo C., b. 08/28/1879, d. 07/30/1929

(GN-002 & HU-NR) OLD PATHS CHURCH OF CHRIST CEMETERY
Located N. W. of Georgetown at the N. W. corner of Du Pont Boulevard (Rt. 113) and Redden Rd. (Rt. 40)

ATKINS, S. Lee, ssw-Sarah R., b. 08/01/1938, d. 10/27/1993
ATKINS, Sarah R., ssw-S. Lee, b. 12/06/1936, d. N/D
BENNETT, David L., ssw-Polly S., b. 08/27/1935, d. N/D
BENNETT, Polly S., ssw-David L., b. 05/06/1936, d. N/D
BENNETT, Steven S., b. 02/23/1958, d. 08/19/1983
CHERKOWSKY, Vincent P., b. 1938, d. 1995
GOEHRINGER, Benjamin Arthur, b. N/D, d. 01/11/1994
SHANE, G. Hayes, ssw-Gaile K., b. 12/13/1967, d. 10/18/1968
SHANE, Gaile K., ssw-G. Hayes, b. 03/08/1947, d. 10/18/1968
WILLEY, Atwood R., ssw-Mildred E., b. 05/08/1913, d. 01/28/1992
WILLEY, Mildred E., ssw-Atwood R., b. 02/25/1922, d. N/D

(GN-003 & HU-195) JOSHUA PEPPER MEMORIAL CEMETERY
Located in Georgetown, on the N. W. corner of Kimmey St. & Tracey St.
Recorded: October 31, 1996

CEMETERY MARKER
JOSHUA & ELIZABETH PEPPER
This is the burial place of Joshua & Elizabeth McCauley Pepper who were the ancestors of the Pepper family of Sussex County. Joshua was the great-grandson of Robert Pepper who had emigrated from England to Roxbury, Mass. In 1640. Joshua served in the Snow Hill Battalion during the Revolutionary War. He was the original owner of some of the land which became Georgetown in 1791.

This marker was erected by the Joshua Pepper Memorial Cemetery Inc., in 1991 to commemorate the 350th anniversary of Robert Pepper's arrival in America and the 200th Aniversary of Georgetown.

CHASE, George, s/o James S. & Mary R., b. 08/20/1844, d. 10/19/1883
CHASE, James S., b. 07/13/1817, d. 06/26/1857
CHASE, Mary R., b. 09/06/1820, d. 03/15/1886
KOLLOCK, Alfred R., Age 46y 8m 24d, b. N/D, d. 05/03/1886

KOLLOCK, Mary Exinna, w/o Phillip, Age 73y 1m 29d, b. 06/27/1809, d. 03/26/1882
KOLLOCK, Mary H., b. 02/16/1845, d. 01/15/1920
KOLLOCK, Phillip, Age 40y 8m 12d, b. 09/10/1809, d. 04/22/1850
MAYWOOD, George Frederick, s/o Sam. & Sarah J., Age 2y 16d, b. N/D, d. 06/18/1884
PEPPER, Anna, w/o Thomas B., Age 78y 19d, b. N/D, d. 01/26/1863
PEPPER, Bessie C., d/o Charles C. & Beulah J., Age 8m 15d, b. N/D, d. 06/08/1877
PEPPER, Edward G., Age 66y 5m 28d, b. N/D, d. 03/14/1883
PEPPER, Francis V., w/o Edw. G., Age 20y 3m 26d, b. N/D, d. 12/24/1880
PEPPER, Joshua, SAR, b. 01/18/1720, d. 12/28/1808
PEPPER, Margaret, d/o E. G. & M. T., Age 5y 6m 24d, b. N/D, d. 10/06/1860
PEPPER, Margaret T., w/o Edward G., Age 62y 15d, b. N/D, d. 11/20/1877
PEPPER, Rachel, w/o Thomas B., Age 57y 8m 16d, b. N/D, d. 09/17/1870
PEPPER, Thomas, Age 45y 5m 13d, b. N/D, d. 08/05/1845
PEPPER, Virginia C., d/o E. G. & M. T., Age 6y 1m 10d, b. N/D, d. 03/22/1862
PEPPER, William E., s/o E. G. & M. T., Age 10m 28d, b. N/D, d. 06/29/1842
SHORT, Harlan, s/o Sam & Amanda E., Age 1y 2m, b. N/D, d. 01/23/1897
SHORT, Herb M., Age 22y 2m 1d, b. 09/01/1870, d. 11/02/1892
SHORT, Samuel M., Age 43y 9m 3d, b. N/D, d. 09/02/1886
WILSON, Eliza L., b. N/D, d. N/D

The following stone was recorded by the Hudson Survey but is now missing or unreadable:
PEPPER, Thomas B., b. 01/30/1811, d. 12/14/1891

(GN-004 & HU-208) SAND HILL CHURCH CEMETERY
Located N. E. of Georgetown at the S. E. corner of Sand Hill Rd. (Rd. 319) and Huff Rd. (Rd. 252) 2.3 miles
North of Seashore Highway (Rt. 9).
Recorded: October 3, 1996

ABBOTT, Angeline, ssw-Willard S., b. 02/26/1891, d. 04/21/1914
ABBOTT, Charlotte J., w/o Willard S., b. 08/01/1864, d. 01/01/1908
ABBOTT, Willard S., ssw-Angeline, b. 02/09/1869, d. 10/11/1913
BOKAN, Alfred, b. 08/10/1924, d. 10/07/1957
BRITTINGHAM, Arcadia Leah, w/o Moses M., Age 67y, b. N/D, d. 05/01/1891
BRITTINGHAM, Mary A., ssw-Moses S., b. 1846, d. 1924
BRITTINGHAM, Moses S., ssw-Mary A., b. 1843, d. 1926
BRITTINGHAM, Wallace Edward, s/o Lafayette & Bessie, b. 05/09/1901, d. 08/12/1901
BRITTINGHAM, William H., s/o Moses M. & Arcadia L., Age 21y 7m 26d, b. N/D, d. 06/20/1869
BRYAN, Henry E., Pvt., AAF, b. 04/22/1922, d. 09/21/1974
BRYAN, Letta A., w/o Robert B. & d/o Wm. S. & Mary Pepper, Age 35y 1m 15d, b. N/D, d. 03/27/1870
BRYAN, Mary A., d/o Robert B. & Letty A., Age 18y 10m 14d, b. 09/22/1852, d. 08/06/1871
BURNS, Melvina B., b. 07/21/1901, d. 01/22/1975
BURNS, Samuel Herbert, b. 01/19/1900, d. 06/07/1974
CLIFTON, John W., ssw-Sallie P., b. 1871, d. 1949
CLIFTON, Joseph W., s/o John W. & Sallie, b. 08/05/1900, d. 07/18/1901
CLIFTON, Sallie P., ssw-John W., b. 1872, d. N/D
COOPER, Anna J., w/o Harry J., b. 10/16/1886, d. 05/25/1910
COOPER, Harvey D., s/o Harry J. & Anna J., b. 05/24/1909, d. 08/19/1909
COOPER, Louisa, w/o Wm. J., b. 04/02/1847, d. 03/22/1905

217

COOPER, Nora C., b. 1873, d. 1906

COOPER, Raymond, b. 1906, d. 1906

COOPER, Wilbur T., b. 1870, d. 1951

COOPER, William J., b. 03/23/1838, d. 07/08/1904

COOPER, Willie, b. 11/22/1877, d. 05/08/1877

DANIELS, Elias M., ssw-Margaret E., b. 11/24/1851, d. 02/13/1922

DANIELS, Margaret E., ssw-Elias M., b. 01/15/1872, d. 07/20/1939

DANIELS, Preston, b. 09/11/1909, d. 09/11/1909

DICKERSON, Annie, b. 03/31/1864, d. 11/25/1949

DICKERSON, George M., b. 12/18/1852, d. 07/27/1936

DICKERSON, William E., s/o G. & Annie, b. 12/24/1884, d. 07/10/1889

DODD, Jesse E., b. 02/11/1852, d. 04/13/1900

DODD, Mary J., w/o Jesse, Age 34y 1m 14d, b. N/D, d. 02/15/1891

DONOVAN, Arthur G., b. 02/18/1903, d. 03/22/1961

DONOVAN, Burton, ssw-Luvenia H., b. 11/30/1859, d. 03/12/1922

DONOVAN, Edna M., ssw-Frank W., b. 06/23/1907, d. 06/09/1995

DONOVAN, Emma, Age 10d, b. N/D, d. 08/06/1891

DONOVAN, Frank W., ssw-Edna M., b. 10/27/1903, d. 07/05/1994

DONOVAN, Hannah R., w/o Wm. T., Age 40y 8m, b. N/D, d. 05/17/1888

DONOVAN, James R., Age 57y 8m 15d, b. N/D, d. 09/08/1858

DONOVAN, Janey C., ssw-Robert T., b. 1858, d. 1935

DONOVAN, John O., b. 12/28/1846, d. 06/02/1915

DONOVAN, Lester, s/o W. H. & M. H., b. 07/29/1906, d. 08/17/1907

DONOVAN, Lillie Ward, b. 1882, d. 1974

DONOVAN, Luvenia H., ssw-Burton, b. 04/22/1864, d. 11/30/1936

DONOVAN, Maggie P., d/o Wm. T. & H. R., b. 08/13/1875, d. 01/23/1876

DONOVAN, Mary A., d/o Wm. T. & H. R., b. 08/13/1875, d. 08/18/1875

DONOVAN, Mary H., ssw-Willard H., b. 10/19/1879, d. 04/04/1959

DONOVAN, Mary J., w/o Robert P., Age 82y 5m 15d, b. 01/18/1816, d. 07/03/1898

DONOVAN, Rachel A., ssw-William of P., b. 1870, d. 1967

DONOVAN, Robert T., ssw-Janey C., b. 1856, d. 1939

DONOVAN, Sarah Elizabeth, w/o John O., b. 07/17/1849, d. 11/14/1912

DONOVAN, Willard H., ssw-Mary H., b. 10/25/1874, d. 10/12/1954

DONOVAN, William of P., ssw-Rachel A., b. 1864, d. 1935

DONOVAN, William T., Age 55y 11m 21d, b. N/D, d. 01/06/1892

DRAKE, Mary J., b. 1855, d. 1938

DUKES, Florence E., b. 1899, d. 1960

DUKES, Harry E., DE, Pvt., Co. C, 32 E. Batt., WWII, b. 01/08/1919, d. 02/05/1960

DUKES, Harry L., b. 1896, d. 1956

DUTTON, Edith S., d/o Thomas & Clara, b. 05/22/1882, d. 01/08/1897

DUTTON, Elizabeth, wid/o Truitt, Age 98y 10m 25d, b. 02/06/1792, d. 12/31/1890

DUTTON, James H., b. 08/02/1817, d. 04/11/1884

DUTTON, Levin P., b. 11/24/1824, d. 07/02/1912

DUTTON, Nancy, w/o Levin, b. 02/13/1833, d. 11/02/1913

DUTTON, Robert, Age 62y, b. N/D, d. 01/31/1884

DUTTON, Sarah H., w/o Robert, b. 05/01/1834, d. 02/08/1910

DUTTON, Zed C., Capt., b. 08/31/1861, d. 04/12/1930

FLEETWOOD, Clara B., ssw-Harry A. & Oscar H., b. 1901, d. 1987

FLEETWOOD, Delia M., b. 02/02/1870, d. 11/13/1920

FLEETWOOD, Harry A., ssw-Clara B. & Oscar H., b. 1922, d. 1929

FLEETWOOD, John A., b. 07/08/1854, d. 05/18/1915

FLEETWOOD, Oscar H., ssw-Clara B. & Harry A., b. 1889, d. 1955

GOOD, Amanda M., ssw-John J. & Wilbur, b. 07/06/1867, d. 06/07/1934

GOOD, John J., ssw-Amanda M. & Wilbur, b. N/D, d. N/D

GOOD, Wilbur, ssw-Amanda M. & John J., b. N/D, d. N/D

GREEN, Eliza J., b. 12/29/1841, d. 08/13/1921

GREEN, Helen M., d/o Charles E. & Ruth, Age 7m 14d, b. N/D, d. 07/10/1890

GREEN, Inf. d/o R. T. & Katie E., b. 02/09/1904, d. 02/19/1904

GREEN, Lloyd B., s/o Harvey & Hettie J., b. 12/16/1901, d. 09/17/1903

GREEN, Jessie, b. 10/10/1842, d. 06/01/1895

GREENLY, Betsy, w/o David, b. 11/03/1792, d. 12/26/1873

GREENLY, David, ssw-Eunice A., Age 84y, b. N/D, d. 08/22/1873

GREENLY, Eunice A., ssw-David, b. 1836, d. 1917

GREENLY, Rob't, ssw-Betsy, b. 12/03/1825, d. 08/17/1891

JOSEPH, Flossie E., b. 1901, d. 1951

LINGO, Lydia H., w/o Joseph H., b. 09/08/1857, d. 10/15/1876

LYNCH, Elizabeth, w/o Joshua A., Age 34y, b. N/D, d. 05/30/1859

LYNCH, Jane, d/o Joshua A. & Elizabeth, b. 09/17/1863, d. 09/14/1867

LYNCH, Joshua A., ssw-Elizabeth, b. 09/24/1824, d. 02/27/1910

MARVEL, Carrie M., ssw-Nehemiah P., b. 02/14/1896, d. 04/22/1960

MARVEL, Nehemiah P., ssw-Carrie M., b. 10/08/1886, d. 01/21/1962

MASSEY, Amelia, Age 75y, b. 10/09/1830, d. 11/24/1905

MASSEY, Frank, b. 1813, d. 1890

MASSEY, Hester, w/o Ed. T., Age 21y, b. 1869, d. 1890

MASSEY, John T., b. 09/01/1882, d. 09/20/1887

MASSEY, Moyrus, b. 06/08/840, d. 08/11/1911

MASSEY, Sallie, Age 74y, b. 09/25/1863, d. 01/25/1938

MASSEY, William M., b. __/03/1868, d. __/22/1929

MATSON, Elmina T., b. 07/08/1866, d. 11/27/1927

MCGEE, Florence, d/o Geo. E. & Georgianna, b. 09/13/1890, d. 07/05/1904

MCGEE, George E., ssw-Georgeanna, b. N/D, d. 01/29/1939

MCGEE, Georgeanna, ssw-George E., b. N/D, d. 03/24/1943

MCGEE, Stella M., Age 11m, b. N/D, d. 05/05/1887

MEGEE, Fannie L., w/o Clarence A., b. 11/05/1875, d. 10/17/1910

MEGEE, Martha L., b. 10/25/1844, d. 03/12/1895

MEGEE, Theodore M., b. 02/13/1844, d. 02/17/1908

OLIVER, John W., Capt., ssw-Mary, b. 1822, d. 1902

OLIVER, Mary, ssw-Capt. John W., b. 1831, d. 1888

PALMER, Charley G., ssw-Lavenia P., b. 06/02/1870, d. 11/06/1956

PALMER, Dolphus L., ssw-Ethel M., b. 1906, d. 1962

PALMER, Ethel M., ssw-Dolphus L., b. 1904, d. 1987

PALMER, George E., ssw-George W. & Mary A., b. 1889, d. 1935

PALMER, George W., ssw-George E. & Mary A., b. 1864, d. 1954

PALMER, Greensbury W., ssw-Mary E., b. 02/26/1839, d. 06/08/1918

PALMER, Lavenia P., ssw-Charley G., b. 09/26/1870, d. 12/08/1956

PALMER, Mary A., ssw-George W. & George E., b. 1866, d. 1947

PALMER, Mary E., w/o Greensbury W., ssw-Greensbury W., b. 07/21/1839, d. 06/24/1935
PEPPER, Elizabeth E., w/o Greensbury H., b. 03/24/1831, d. 03/20/1895
PEPPER, Eunice, w/o Henry, Age 65y, b. N/D, d. 11/18/1881
PEPPER, Greensbury H., b. 03/05/1814, d. 04/03/1897
PEPPER, Greensbury Harrison, ssw-Priscilla Caroline, b. 07/01/1855, d. 05/02/1918
PEPPER, Henry H., b. 12/26/1816, d. 01/08/1891
PEPPER, Inf. s/o Greensbury H. & Priscilla Caroline, b. 03/24/1883, d. 03/24/1883
PEPPER, James H., s/o Henry N. & Eunice, Age 15y 5m 9d, b. N/D, d. 02/09/1869
PEPPER, Lillian Ethel, d/o Greensbury H. & Priscilla Caroline, Age 5y 7m 16d, b. N/D, d. 11/09/1885
PEPPER, Priscilla Caroline, ssw-Greensbury Harrison, b. 12/06/1860, d. 10/29/1941
PEPPER, Viola, d/o Greensbury H. & Priscilla C., Age 10y 8m 23d, b. N/D, d. 02/24/1905
PETTYJOHN, Alva L., d/o H. B. & Lina, b. 1927, d. 1933
PETTYJOHN, Andrew J., b. 10/15/1818, d. 09/12/1906
PETTYJOHN, Annie, Age 64y 8m 14d, b. 04/28/1800, d. 01/12/1865
PETTYJOHN, B. Thos., ssw-Maggie P., b. 03/16/1846, d. 02/06/1917
PETTYJOHN, Everett J., b. 03/29/1908, d. 01/15/1951
PETTYJOHN, Frederick R., ssw-Minnie S., b. 1867, d. 1946
PETTYJOHN, Geo. W., ssw-Mary H., b. 09/15/1827, d. 07/27/1907
PETTYJOHN, Horace B., b. 1904, d. 1955
PETTYJOHN, Horace B., s/o B. T. & Maggie P., Age 17y 10m 2d, b. N/D, d. 05/28/1898
PETTYJOHN, John H., ssw-Nora E., b. 12/19/1872, d. 04/09/1953
PETTYJOHN, Lina, ssw-Mary H., b. 1869, d. 1926
PETTYJOHN, Maggie P., ssw-B. Thos., b. 03/26/1848, d. 08/12/1922
PETTYJOHN, Mary H., w/o Geo. W., b. 09/23/1835, d. 09/04/1905
PETTYJOHN, Minnie S., ssw-Frederick R., b. 1874, d. 1938
PETTYJOHN, Nora E., ssw-John H., b. 09/29/1877, d. 03/05/1930
PETTYJOHN, Raymond S., ssw-Frederick R., b. 1902, d. 1906
PETTYJOHN, Virginia S., ssw-Frederick R., b. 1911, d. 1911
PETTYJOHN, Willie J., s/o Benjamin J., Age 2y 8m 10d, b. N/D, d. 1871
PRIDE, James, ssw-Josephine, b. 1863, d. 1949
PRIDE, James M., ssw-Mary E., b. 10/22/1829, d. 02/23/1884
PRIDE, Josephine, ssw-James, b. 1869, d. 1927
PRIDE, Margaret L., b. 01/31/1904, d. 11/12/1986
PRIDE, Mary E., ssw-James M., b. 02/14/1838, d. 08/20/1904
PRIDE, Samuel, b. 04/10/1899, d. 11/16/1987
RAYNE, Elenah A., b. 02/25/1833, d. 01/20/1929
RAYNE, John A., b. 07/04/1833, d. 08/21/1908
REED, Fannie T., d/o Philip R. & Charlotte B., Age 10m 20d, b. N/D, d. 09/03/1869
REED, George B., s/o James T. & Priscilla, Age 1y 3m 7d, b. N/D, d. 12/15/1862
REED, Hannah V., d/o James T. & Priscilla, Age 13y 8m 1d, b. N/D, d. 01/28/1870
REED, James Ponder, s/o Jas. & Priscilla, Age 1y 9m 3d, b. N/D, d. 01/01/1870
REED, Mary Jane, d/o James T. & Priscilla, b. 11/11/1859, d. 03/16/1867
REED, Priscilla, w/o James T., Age 44y 9m 15d, b. N/D, d. 10/15/1885
RENDFREY, Lenora M., b. 1883, d. 1946
RITTINGHOUSE, Robert C., DE, Cpl., Co. B, 752 Tank Bn., WWII, b. 04/27/1927, d. 03/02/1964
ROACH, Eli J., ssw-Nancy Chase, b. 03/24/1831, d. 11/05/1904
ROACH, Nancy Chase, w/o Eli J., b. 1827, d. 1884
ROGERS, Delia E., w/o E. L., b. 09/17/1867, d. 04/06/1919

ROGERS, Edward L., b. 1864, d. 1944

ROGERS, Elmer, ssw-Mary L., b. 1894, d. 1953

ROGERS, Effie L., b. 04/05/1889, d. 08/28/1937

ROGERS, Elizabeth, b. 04/10/1912, d. 07/01/1930

ROGERS, Emma, b. 1876, d. 1945

ROGERS, Greensbury H., b. 05/22/1892, d. 01/10/1893

ROGERS, Inf. s/o Roland & Blanche, b. 04/21/1935, d. 04/21/1935

ROGERS, Ira, b. 1901, d. 1967

ROGERS, Mary L., ssw-Elmer, b. 1900, d. 1981

ROGERS, Ottis, DE, CMM, USCG, WWII, b. 11/23/1884, d. 07/23/1962

SHARP, A., Age 69y 10m 21d, b. N/D, d. 12/30/1874 [Note: Footstone only]

SHARP, Asa J., Age 83y 11m 12d, b. 12/31/1842, d. 12/12/1926

SHARP, Bertha May, d/o Asa J. & Addie B., b. 12/29/1910, d. 04/18/1913

SHARP, Edda, s/o Asa J. & Mary H., b. 05/24/1885, d. 01/26/1888

SHARP, Elenah May, d/o Asa J. & Mary H., b. 05/26/1882, d. 06/22/1888

SHARP, Ethel, d/o Asa J. & Addie B., b. 09/10/1912, d. 09/17/1912

SHARP, Henry, b. 09/27/1992, d. 09/27/1992

SHARP, Inf. s/o Isaac W. & Milly A., b. 11/1898, d. 11/1898

SHARP, Isaac M., b. 12/09/1836, d. 04/01/1898

SHARP, Jacob T., s/o Kensey & Mollie, Age 22y 12d, b. N/D, d. 10/20/1862

SHARP, Josiah G., b. 12/17/1834, d. 12/17/1902

SHARP, Kensey, Age abt. 76y, b. N/D. d. 08/02/1882

SHARP, Kensey J., Age 36y 6m 2d, b. N/D, d. 07/02/1884

SHARP, Louisa Elizabeth, w/o Josiah G., b. 02/05/1835, d. 03/08/1912

SHARP, Mary H., w/o Asa J, b. 11/14/1849, d. 11/10/1922

SHARP, Mollie, w/o Kensey, Age 69y, b. N/D, d. 11/06/1880

SHARP, Norman J., b. 04/17/1920, d. 09/07/1920

SHARP, Walter A., ssw-Annie M., b. 1900, d. 1954

SHARP, William E., b. 09/05/1839, d. 05/27/1901

SHARP, William H., ssw-Annie M., b. 1873, d. 1938

SHORT, Caleb A., b. 1864, d. 1942

SHORT, Gardner W., s/o Isaac W. & Elema A., b. 09/08/1853, d. 11/07/1885

SHORT, Hannah L., w/o John W., Age 41y 7m 4d, b. N/D, d. 03/09/1901

SHORT, Isaac W., Age 62y 10m 22d, b. N/D, d. 07/27/1881

SHORT, John W., b. 02/28/1853, d. 02/27/1923

SHORT, Noah J., ssw-Sarah A., b. 1862, d. 1951

SHORT, Sarah A., ssw-Noah J., b. 1861, d. 1950

SIMPSON, Walter B., b. 09/18/1865, d. 02/18/1918

SPICER, George W., s/o Wm. J. & Mary A., Age 4y 2m 19d, b. N/D, d. 04/18/1864

SPICER, Granville W., s/o John C. & Jennie, b. 1896, d. 1896

SPICER, James, Age 84, b. N/D, d. N/D

SPICER, James T., b. 1860, d. 1909

SPICER, John, b. 1872, d. 1887

SPICER, John C., ssw-Mary J., b. 05/20/1856, d. 03/02/1940

SPICER, Levenia E., w/o Wm. J., Jr., b. 03/27/1857, d. 05/17/1922

SPICER, Lizzie H., w/o James, b. 09/12/1829, d. 10/30/1892

SPICER, Mary A., w/o Wm. J., Age 87y, b. N/D, d. 09/02/1915

SPICER, Mary J., ssw-John C., b. 08/12/1858, d. 01/28/1931

SPICER, Theodore A., b. 02/05/1850, d. 03/19/1895
SPICER, Wm. J., ssw-Mary A., Age 63y, b. 03/24/1827, d. 08/17/1890
SPICER, Wm. J., Jr., ssw-Levenia E., b. 05/13/1854, d. 05/29/1936
STANTON, Charlotte E. Lynch, w/o Geo. W., b. 06/12/1855, d. 04/18/1910
STANTON, Geo. W., ssw-Charlotte E. Lynch, b. 02/01/1846, d. N/D
STERBUTZL, Gertrude, b. 02/22/1865, d. 10/19/1943
SWAIN, Elizabeth P., w/o Spencer P., b. 11/14/1840, d. 02/21/1912
SWAIN, Kingsberry S., ssw-Mary Jane, b. 1861, d. 1933
SWAIN, Mary Jane, ssw-Kingsberry S., b. 1867, d. 1941
SWAIN, Ralph W., s/o Kingsberry S. & Mary J., b. 08/26/1888, d. 06/05/1902
SWAIN, Spencer P., ssw-Elizabeth P., b. 02/16/1833, d. 02/11/1926
T., E. H., b. N/D, d. N/D [Note: Footstone only.]
TAYLOR, Doris M., w/o E. S., b. 1926, d. 1950
THORTON, Fanny P., nee Dutton, ssw-O'Ferall, b. 09/28/1895, d. 04/18/1936
THORTON, O'Ferall, ssw-Fanny P., WWI, b. 06/10/1896, d. 05/12/1966
UNKNOWN, Eliah, Dates underground
UNKNOWN, Infant, Dates underground [Found between Charley P. & George F. Workman]
UTTS, Nancy A., w/o Charles W., b. N/D, d. 10/22/1915
WARD, Bessie M., b. 1906, d. 1908
WARD, Frank B., b. 1879, d. 1942
WARD, George, b. 1886, d. 1963
WARD, Inf. s/o W. H. & Orpha J., b. 07/30/1886, d. 07/30/1886
WARD, Joseph B., b. 09/20/1873, d. 08/30/1895
WARD, Marshall S., b. 1913, d. 1993
WARD, Orpha J., w/o William H., b. 05/28/1846, d. 01/05/1916
WARD, William H., b. 10/04/1840, d. 08/02/1895
WARREN, Charlie H., s/o Robert & Mary, Age 3y 9m 22d, b. N/D, d. 09/13/1868
WARREN, James H., s/o W. G. & Wilhelmina, ssw-Ratie M., b. 06/20/1900, d. 01/18/1901
WARREN, Ratie M., c/o W. G. & Wilhelmina, ssw-James H., b. 12/01/1891, d. 09/02/1892
WARREN, Sallie E., w/o James H., Age 35y 7m 21d, b. N/D, d. 10/31/1880
WARREN, Wilhelmina, ssw-William G., b. 02/07/1871, d. 02/09/1950
WARREN, William G., ssw-Wilhelmina, b. 11/24/1866, d. 05/28/1949
WEYL, Albert, b. 09/25/1851, d. 02/22/1919
WILKINS, Adaline, w/o John P., Age 80y, b. N/D, d. 01/07/1906
WILKINS, Catherine, b. 1927, d. Unreadable (19__)
WILKINS, Comfort T., w/o John H., b. 03/29/1849, d. 10/15/1928
WILKINS, Eli Wesly, b. 1846, d. 1922
WILKINS, Ida V., b. 1865, d. 1942
WILKINS, John H., ssw-Comfort T., b. 11/19/1845, d. 07/23/1906
WILKINS, John P., b. 12/24/1818, d. 12/20/1903
WILKINS, Lee B., Age 15y 7m 26d, b. N/D, d. 06/04/1903
WILKINS, Mahalia A., d/o James P. & Mary A., b. 04/04/1894, d. 11/20/1898
WILLEY, Clara Mae, ssw-Marvin, b. 10/10/1905, d. 12/10/1989
WILLEY, Marvin, ssw-Clara Mae, b. 06/15/1912, d. 07/11/1973
WILSON, Albert H., b. 1885, d. 1908
WILSON, Annie E., ssw-George T., b. 08/15/1860, d. 04/21/1914
WILSON, Caroline, b. 06/07/1828, d. 05/23/1892
WILSON, Charles H., b. 1855, d. 1934

WILSON, Eli W., b. 02/06/1827, d. 08/07/1905

WILSON, Elizabeth A., w/o Wm. J., b. 10/12/1852, d. 08/29/1915

WILSON, Emma L., d/o Nathanial & Hester A., b. 02/11/1873, d. 11/01/1874

WILSON, George T., ssw-Annie E., b. 09/26/1858, d. 02/23/1926

WILSON, Hester Anna, w/o Nathanial C., Age 69y, b. N/D, d. 03/16/1908

WILSON, John Edward, b. 02/25/1871, d. 02/28/1947

WILSON, Kendle B., s/o William W. & Mary, Age __y 9m 23d, b. N/D, d. 12/09/1859

WILSON, Lovey Ellenia, d/o Rhoades & Sarah, b. 12/19/1856, d. 05/07/1858

WILSON, Martha J., b. 1860, d. 1940

WILSON, Mary, w/o William W., Age 49y 3m 29d, b. N/D, d. 12/20/1867

WILSON, Nathanial C., b. 08/09/1847, d. 03/27/1916

WILSON, Nehemiah J., ssw-Sarah E., b. 09/24/1845, d. 10/04/1936

WILSON, Rhoades S., b. 01/30/1815, d. 01/22/1864

WILSON, Sarah E., b. 02/24/1822, d. 08/10/1896

WILSON, Sarah E., w/o Nehemiah, b. 01/29/1852, d. 01/26/1926

WILSON, William W., Age 84y, b. N/D, d. 06/19/1897

WILSON, Wm. J., ssw-Elizabeth A., b. 03/02/1853, d. 06/30/1925

WORKMAN, Alva L., d/o George R. & Loreta B., b. 07/05/1922, d. 10/11/1922

WORKMAN, Arthur B., b. 04/26/1886, d. 03/18/1976

WORKMAN, Arthur H., s/o John W. & Sallie A., Age 21y 4m 21d, b. N/D, d. 08/31/1835

WORKMAN, C. Rodney, b. 06/19/1920, d. 06/02/1933

WORKMAN, Catherine E., d/o A. B. & Ella M., b. 08/03/1914, d. 11/14/1914

WORKMAN, Charley P., Age 30y 2m 9d, b. N/D, d. 02/15/1890

WORKMAN, Courtland E., b. 03/25/1893, d. 07/01/1941

WORKMAN, Delia M., b. 09/11/1897, d. 02/16/1963

WORKMAN, Ebenezer A., Civil War, b. 1843, d. 1936

WORKMAN, Ella M., b. 07/07/1891, d. 10/03/1918

WORKMAN, George E., b. 04/10/1853, d. 04/23/1906

WORKMAN, George R., ssw-Loreta B., b. 08/14/1884, d. 06/14/1972

WORKMAN, Inf. s/o George & Loreta B., b. 09/16/1918, d. 07/06/1922

WORKMAN, Isaiah, s/o E. A. & Mary E., b. 05/12/1876, d. 01/28/1893

WORKMAN, John W., b. 09/10/1817, d. 11/14/1903

WORKMAN, Loreta B., ssw-George R., b. 04/24/1887, d. 07/10/1985

WORKMAN, Martha G., b. 1860, d. 1954

WORKMAN, Mary E., w/o E. A., Age 25y 22d, b. N/D, d. 06/14/1877

WORKMAN, Sallie A., Age 63y 6m 6d, b. N/D, d. 10/25/1884

WORKMAN, William A., s/o John & Sallie A., Age 21y 10m 8d, b. 10/13/1851, d. 08/23/1873

WURSTER, Lena R., ssw-Sallie P. Fleetwood, b. 1895, d. 1922

YAGAR, Helen, b. 08/18/1905, d. 07/20/1976

YAGAR, Steve, NY, Pvt., Co. B, 12th Ammunition TN, WWI, b. 08/08/1895, d. 07/09/1962

YAGER, Joseph, ssw-Olga, b. 1889, d. 1964

YAGER, Olga, ssw-Joseph, b. 1893, d. 1977

YORK, Mary L., b. 11/11/1927, d. 12/15/1952

YOUNG, Jeanne Joyce, b. 07/13/1942, d. 04/24/1946

YOUNG, William Penn, VA, COX USN, WWI, b. 11/28/1899, d. 01/24/1965

The following stones were recorded by the Hudson Survey but are now missing or unreadable:

ABBOTT, Fannie M., d/o Willard S. & Charlotte J., Age 2m 26d, b. N/D, d. 01/16/1890

DUTTON, L. Perry, b. 11/17/1865, d. 08/09/1907
HURLEY, Delema, d/o N. & Hester, b. 05/11/1886, d. 03/03/1888
MASSEY, Johnny, b. N/D, d. N/D
MCGEE, Emory, s/o W. J. & Ella, b. 10/19/1891, d. 10/19/1891
MCGEE, Willie, s/o W. J. & Ella, b. 09/07/1890, d. 09/07/1890
PETTYJOHN, Mamie, d/o W. T. & Clara, b. 07/12/1898, d. 08/03/1898
PETTYJOHN, Nattie Leroy, s/o Ira E. & Maggie E., Age 6m 17d, b. N/D, d. 07/12/1899
SHARP, Hannah L., w/o John W., Age 41y 7m 4d, b. N/D, d. 03/09/1901
SHARP, Horace K., s/o Kensey J. & Sallie A., b. 08/16/1906, d. 01/30/1907
SHARP, Infants (son & daughter), b. N/D, d. N/D
SHARP, Maggie, w/o Kensey J., b. 10/13/1879, d. 12/25/1903
THOMAS, Ella H., d/o Frank & Emma B., b. 11/22/1887, d. 02/04/1890
WILSON, Inf. d/o Wm. J. & E. A., b. 03/09/1874, d. 03/09/1874

(GN-005 & HU-NR) PROSPECT A. M. E. CHURCH CEMETERY
Located in Georgetown on the S. W. Corner of South Railroad Avenue & East Adams Street
Recorded: January 6, 1998

ANDREW, John H., Age 65y 11m, b. N/D, d. 01/02/1910
BRADLEY, Basha, ssw-George E., Joseph W., Mary E. & Edward, b. N/D, d. 10/18/1892
BRADLEY, Edward, ssw-George E., Joseph W., Mary E. & Basha, Age 84y, b. N/D, d. 12/09/1924
BRADLEY, George E., ssw-Joseph W., Basha, Edward & Mary E., Age 38y 8m 13d, b. N/D, d. 03/08/1918
BRADLEY, Joseph W., ssw-George E., Basha, Mary E. & Edward, b. 10/23/1884, d. 06/01/1929
BRADLEY, Mary E., ssw-George E., Basha, Edward & Joseph W., b. 10/15/1845, d. 02/05/1921
FAUCETT, Major, b. 06/24/1837, d. 08/27/1902
FRAME, Dinah, b. 01/10/1818, d. 03/19/1873
HOPKINS, Frank Wright, Age 58y, b. N/D, d. 03/20/1910
INGRAM, Alfred Martin, ssw-Osceola H., b. 1924, d. 1995
INGRAM, Alfred W., DE, Pvt., 549 Field Arty., 92 Div., b. N/D, d. 01/14/1941
INGRAM, Eva C., b. 08/07/1894, d. 12/27/1947
INGRAM, Josephine, ssw-Martin F., b. 1859, d. 1939
INGRAM, Martin F., ssw-Josephine, b. 1880, d. 1938
INGRAM, Osceola H., ssw-Alfred Martin, b. 1920, d. 1981
MITCHELL, Cynthia, b. N/D, d. 09/25/1886
MITCHELL, Geo. H., Age 45y 5m 1d, b. 01/02/1857, d. 06/02/1902
PETTYJOHN, John W., Age 47y, b. N/D, d. 08/15/1914
ROBINSON, Rachael, w/o Moses, Age abt. 65y, b. N/D, d. 11/18/1864
SHORT, Fred A., b. 1884, d. 1935
STURGIS, Denise M., b. 1955, d. 1995
STURGIS, Toyia, b. 08/03/1970, d. 06/27/1978
WARRINGTON, William E., b. 03/14/1872, d. Unreadable
WILLEY, Henry, Age 67y, b. N/D, d. N/D
WILLIN, Maurice, Age 47y, b. N/D, d. 02/10/1914
WOOLFORD, Ann, d/o Robert & Margaret, b. 11/21/1868, d. 06/09/1879
WOOLFORD, Robert, b. 02/18/1826, d. 02/18/1891

GUMBORO HUNDRED

(GU-001 & HU-NR) SHARP MITCHELL CEMETERY

Located South of Gumboro on the East side of Cooper Rd. (Rd. 415A) 0.2 miles south of Millsboro
Highway (Rts. 26 & 30).
Recorded: June 20, 1994

AKE, Mary Alice, b. 1860, d. 1942
AKE, Thomas J., b. 1855, d. 1947
BAKER, Joseph D., Age 51y 2m 4d, b. N/D, d. 05/24/1889
BETTS, Edgar, ssw-M. Catherine, b. 1870, d. 1951
BETTS, M. Catherine, ssw-Edgar, b. 1868, d. 1944
BURTON, Earl T., b. 12/28/1872, d. 04/11/1915
BURTON, Eliza J., b. 05/01/1833, d. 05/28/1920
BURTON, Thomas J., b. 07/18/1835, d. 03/03/1927
DONOWAY, Charlie, b/o George, b. N/D, d. N/D
DONOWAY, George B., b/o Charlie, Private, Co. G., 77 Inf., MD, WWI, b. 02/16/1890, d. 03/23/1965
DUKES, Inf. s/o William & L. Jane, b. N/D, d. N/D
DUKES, L. Janie, d/o Sharp Mitchell, b. 03/12/1861, d. 07/16/1940
DUKES, William F., b. 06/27/1861, d. 06/22/1938
EVANS, Martha E., b. 1865, d. 1915
FOSKEY, Annie, d/o Benj. & Eliza, b. 07/05/1868, d. 07/12/1882
GOSWELLEN, Starrie, b. 1895, d. 1932
HOLLAND, Lambert, Civil War – Salisbury, Age abt. 95y, b. N/D, d. 1935
HOLLAND, Mary, Age abt. 90y, b. N/D, d. 1953
MITCHELL, Gertrude, b. 10/05/1904, d. 03/04/1963
MITCHELL, John S., b. 05/14/1856, d. 12/04/1927
MITCHELL, Mariah, ssw-Sharp, Age 30y, b. 1841, d. 1871
MITCHELL, Sewell H., ssw-Stella M., b. 1891, d. 1950
MITCHELL, Sharp, ssw-Mariah, Age 95y, b. 1839, d. 1935
MITCHELL, Stella M., ssw-Sewell H., b. 1897, d. 1969
PHILLIPS, Charlotte C., w/o John H., b. 06/15/1845, d. 02/16/1901
WELLS, Nancy P., w/o William T., Age 27y 4m 12d, b. 07/06/1864, d. 11/20/1891
WORKMAN, Charles E., s/o Charles T. & Sallie, b. 12/05/1888, d. 03/07/1902
WORKMAN, Chales I, s/o Charles T. & Sallie J., b. 09/16/1886, d. 08/11/1892

(GU-002 & HU-293) GUMBORO CEMETERY

Located in Gumboro within a triangle formed by Millsboro Highway (Rt. 26 & 30), Pear Tree Rd. (Rd 424)
& Shell Station Rd. (Rd. 427).
Recorded: June 11, 1994

ARTERS, Susanna, w/o Rev. Joseph A., Age, 33y 3m, b. N/D, d. 09/02/1870
BRIMER, Sarah I., w/o Joshua H., Age 20y 10m 9d, b. N/D, d. 10/11/1868
GRAY, Elizabeth, ssw-Isaac A., b. 1830, d. 1907
GRAY, Henry W., b. 08/26/1860, d. 04/20/1895
GRAY, Horace W., s/o Henry W. & Martha, b. 07/15/1888, d. 07/19/1891
GRAY, Isaac A., ssw-Elizabeth, b. 1831, d. 1895

GRAY, Martha A., w/o Henry W., b. 10/25/1858, d. 11/14/1924
GUNBY, David, Age abt. 70y, b. N/D, d. 07/10/1868
GUNBY, Edward P., s/o Jacob & Nancy, Age 26y, b. N/D, d. 05/26/1863
GUNBY, Henry, Age Abt. 62y, b. N/D, d. 11/30/1903
GUNBY, Jacob, Age 83y 10m 6d, b. 07/31/1800, d. 06/06/1884
GUNBY, Jene E., d/o D. & P., Age 2m 20d, b. N/D, d. 09/22/1871
GUNBY, John B., b. 07/22/1825, d. 01/14/1879
GUNBY, Lucy E., b. 04/15/1832, d. 01/02/1919
GUNBY, Nancy, w/o Jacob, Age 65y, b. N/D, d. 03/31/1872
GUNBY, Parron A., b. 02/22/1876, d. 08/27/1902
GUNBY, Polley, w/o David, Age 52y, b. N/D, d. 06/1810
GUNBY, Steven P., b. 12/14/1827, d. 01/03/1896
KING, Annie L. M., ssw-George W., Age 1y 12d, b. N/D, d. 09/20/1871
KING, Bertha, d/o George & Mary, b. 04/19/1886, d. 07/02/1886
KING, George E., Age 69y 10m 27d, b. 04/26/1836, d. 03/23/1906
KING, George W., ssw-Laurie D., Age 2y 11m 16d, b. N/D, d. 09/15/1871
KING, John T., s/o George E. & Mary A., b. 06/11/1876, d. 07/03/1876
KING, Laurie D., ssw-George W., Age 5y 11m 12d, b. N/D, d. 09/10/1871
KING, Mary A., w/o George E., Age 62y 1m 6d, b. 02/06/1844, d. 03/12/1906
KING, Mary V. W., d/o George & Mary, b. 09/26/1872, d. 07/18/1875
LYNCH, Sarah E., b. 06/27/1868, d. 09/30/1912
MARTIN, Elizabeth Gunby, Consort o/ John H. Martin, Age 41y, b. N/D, d. 06/25/1865
RADIS, No other information
RICHARDS, Joseph H., Age abt. 42y, b. N/D, d. 07/08/1892
RICHARDS, Verdie May, b. 12/09/1889. d. 05/27/1907
RICHARDS, Willie J., s/o Joseph H. & Sarah, b. 12/08/1891, d. 04/13/1892
SHORT, Mary J., wid./o Shadrach, Age 26y 2m 25d, b. N/D, d. 06/05/1855
WELLS, Bertha, d/o W. B. & G. E., b. 03/04/1880, d. 01/22/1886
WELLS, Pernetta, b. 08/04/1825, d. 02/24/1903
WELLS, William H., b. 08/14/1820, d. 12/13/1890
WINSER, Giben, Consort o/John, Age 76y, b. N/D, d. 07/21/1846

The following stone was recorded by the Hudson Survey but is now missing or unreadable:
KING, Lavinia E., d/o Geo. E. & Mary A., b. 07/05/1884, d. 09/22/1884

(GU-003 & HU-296) WEST WOODS CEMETERY
Located North of Gumboro about 200 yards from the west side of Westwoods Rd. (Rd 426) 0.6 miles N. W. of Millsboro Highway (Rts. 26 & 30).
Recorded: June 11, 1994

BAKER, Magnolia Alie, w/o Peter A., b. 08/15/1882, d. 01/29/1916
BARR, Barnie, ssw-Alice West, b. 1874, d. 1914
BRASUR, George W., s/o John W. & Anna B., Age 2y 8m, b. N/D, d. 01/03/1901
DOWNS, Pleta A., w/o William S., Age 85y, b. N/D, d. 02/22/1894
DOWNS, Sarah, w/o Robert J., b. 06/04/1847, d. 02/26/1877
ESHAM, Beatrice F., b. 07/29/1934, d. N/D
ESHAM, Calvin J., Jr., b. 08/06/1927, d. 11/24/1981
ESHAM, Calvin J., Sr., b. 1900, d. 1977

ESHAM, Evelyn P., b. 1905, d. 1981

MITCHELL, Lillie R., baby d/o J. J. & M., b. 12/27/1906, d. 03/09/1909

MITCHELL, Rufus M., b. 06/20/1866, d. 08/16/1908

MITCHELL, Virginia C., s/o Minus & Mary, b. 03/15/1878, d. 11/11/1883

MOORE, Amelia, b. N/D, d. N/D

MOORE, Hettie R., w/o Levin T., b. 06/09/1818, d. 06/01/1895

MOORE, Levin T., b. 06/15/1818, d. 06/11/1901

MOORE, Roxanne, d/o Levin T. & Hettie B., Age 25y, b. N/D, d. 08/11/1886

PARKER, Infant, b. N/D, d. 01/22/1921

PARKER, Infant, b. N/D, d. 04/04/1928

PARKER, Infant, b. N/D, d. 10/10/1926

PARKER, Infant, b. N/D, d. 11/26/1936

REVEL, Eddie, ssw-Ella, b. 1837, d. 1924

REVEL, Ella, ssw-Eddie, b. 1858, d. 1924

REVEL, Ethel M., ssw-Willie E., b. 1898, d. 1967

REVEL, Willie E., ssw-Ethel M., b. 1892, d. 1965

REVELL, Elizabeth A., b. 1898, d. 1898

REVELL, Nettie M., d/o H. R. & G. A., b. 1915, d. 1916

REVELL, Virgie M., d/o H. R. & G. A., b. 1908, d. 1909

ROGERS, Carrie Ellen, b. 12/12/1923, d. 04/23/1973

ROGERS, Charles E., b. 11/24/1912, d. 11/17/1991

SHORT, Flora M., d/o J. H. & M. L., b. 09/29/1910, d. 03/05/1911

SHORT, Fred B., b. 09/15/1916, d. 02/28/1917

SHORT, Harold, b. 05/11/1921, d. 05/07/1974

SHORT, Harvey J., b. 1876, d. 1935

SHORT, Mannie, b. 1885, d. 1966

SHORT, William C., DE, Pfc., USA, WWII, b. 09/26/1918, d. 03/10/1973

SMITH, Felix, Grandfather, b. 1847, d. 1926

SMITH, Kate, b. N/D, d. N/D

SMITH, Mary Hester, Grandmother, b. 1850, d. 1903

STEELE, Mary A., w/o Joshua, Age 75y, b. N/D, d. 02/01/1900

TRUITT, Flora May, d/o James B. & Lavenia H., b. 03/30/1883, b. 09/25/1883

TRUITT, George B., s/o Philip T. & Mary C., b. 10/17/1883, d. 06/09/1899

TRUITT, Ida J., d/o Philip T. & Mary C., b. 10/14/1891, d. 06/09/1899

TRUITT, Mattie G., d/o Philip T. & Mary C., b. 11/08/1885, d. 10/08/1886

TRUITT, Philip T., Age 26y 11m 18d, b. N/D, d. 10/23/1886

TRUITT, William H., s/o Philip T. & Mary C., b. 02/18/1880, d. 05/20/1902

VICKERS, Cathern, w/o William G., b. 06/17/1862, d. 05/11/1903

WEST, Alice, ssw-Barnie Barr, d/o H. B. & L. West, b. 1876, d. 1930

WEST, Andy E., b. 05/12/1866, d. 07/21/1953

WEST, Burton, ssw-Plettie, Parent of Joshua G., b. N/D, d. N/D

WEST, Ebe J., s/o Joseph B. & Mary C., Age 18y 3m 15d, b. N/D, d. 08/13/1896

WEST, John A., s/o Handy B. & Leah A., b. 05/09/1868, d. 02/22/1869

WEST, John P., s/o Handy B. & Leah A., b. 05/12/1882, d. 12/20/1882

WEST, Joseph B., ssw-Mary C., b. 07/06/1853, d. 04/29/1926

WEST, Joshua G., b. 06/23/1832, d. 03/31/1911

WEST, Joshua J., b. 03/24/1884, d. 11/18/1929

WEST, Lee M., s/o Joshua A. & Andy E., b. 03/10/1893, d. 12/14/1909

WEST, Mary C., ssw-Joseph B., b. 09/22/1848, d. 04/24/1926
WEST, Mary H., d/o Joseph B. & Mary C., Age 17y 6d, b. N/D, d. 09/10/1896
WEST, Philip, s/o Bradlie & Eplety, Age 23y 18m 9d, b. N/D, d. 10/24/1859
WEST, Plettie, ssw-Burton, Parent of Joshua G., b. N/D, d. N/D
WEST, Sallie H., d/o Joshua G. & Sallie M., Age 9m 1d, b. N/D, d. 06/17/1870
WEST, Sallie M., w/o Joshua G., Age 37y 2m 17d, b. N/D, d. 07/20/1870
WEST, William H., s/o Joshua G. & Julia, Age 2y 1m 10d, b. N/D, d. 08/04/1875
WILKERSON, Alice M., ssw-William J., b. 01/22/1880, d. 06/05/1952
WILKERSON, Baby Boy, b. 1943, d. 1943
WILKERSON, Elisha E., b. 1914, d. 1915
WILKERSON, Elisha T., b. 1850, d. 1920
WILKERSON, Ethel Mae, b. 1898, d. 1944
WILKERSON, Eva M., b. 1938, d. 1938
WILKERSON, Herman, b. 1916, d. 1918
WILKERSON, John A., b. 1919, d. 1923
WILKERSON, John Lee, b. 1888, d. 1968
WILKERSON, Leon, DE, Pvt., Co. B, Americal Div., WWII, b. 07/22/1920, d. 04/16/1971
WILKERSON, Leon, Jr., b. 1945, d. 1976
WILKERSON, Lettie Ann, b. 1853, d. 1927
WILKERSON, Levin H., b. 02/06/1878, d. 05/18/1922
WILKERSON, Ninna, b. 07/18/1922, d. 09/12/1923
WILKERSON, Sarah T., b. 1922, d. 1973
WILKERSON, William J., ssw-Alice M., b. 09/24/1882, d. 09/28/1977

The following stones were recorded by the Hudson Survey but are now missing or unreadable:
CAREY, Ebey V., s/o Arley & Mary, b. 02/10/1897, d. 10/07/1899
MOORE, Nancy E., w/o H. C., Age 85y, b. N/D, d. 02/01/1909
WEST, Katholeen, d/o Henry J. & Eva L., b. 12/07/1916, d. 07/26/1918

INDIAN RIVER HUNDRED

(IR-001 & HU-NR) CHRIST CHURCH (NON-DENOMINATIONAL) CEMETERY
Located S. E. of Harbeson at the N. E. corner of Hollymount Rd. (Rd. 48) and Beaverdam Rd. (Rd. 285)
Recorded: November 24, 1992

ALLEN, Edward, ssw-Katie E., b. 1923, d. 1992
ALLEN, Katie E., ssw-Edward, b. 03/14/1926, d. 01/06/1986
BAILEY, Daniel W., b. 1898, d. 1979
BURTON, Donelda M., ssw-Harry C., Jr., m. 01/07/1950, b. 1921, d. N/D
BURTON, Harry C., Jr., ssw-Donelda M., m. 01/07/1950, b. 1910, d. 1972
COURSEY, Aaron C., ssw-Anna Louise, m. 11/20/1937, Pvt., USA, WWII, b. 11/02/1916, d. 08/30/1987
COURSEY, Ann Louise, ssw-Aaron C., m. 11/20/1937, b. 02/23/1914, d. N/D
DAY, Melchia B., MSgt., USA, WWII, b. 1920, d. 1981
DRAINE, Daniel G., Pvt., USA, WWI, b. 03/06/1887, d. 12/30/1980
DRAINE, Luther D., ssw-Minnie C., b. 1890, d. 1961
DRAINE, Margaret M., b. 1895, d. 1988
DRAINE, Minnie C., ssw-Luther D., b. 1901, d. 1992

DRUMMOND, John W., ssw-Viola E., b. 1923, d. N/D
DRUMMOND, Viola E., ssw-John W., b. 1922, d. 1991
HARMON, Alberta, b. 02/06/1906, d. 07/11/1986
HARMON, Baby, ssw-Lamont Peny, b. 1982, d. 1982
HARMON, Cecil E., ssw-Clara A., Tec4, USA, WWII, b. 07/21/1913, d. 11/19/1979
HARMON, Clara A., ssw-Cecil E., b. 03/26/1906, d. 07/15/1989
HARMON, Edith M., ssw-John H., b. 11/12/1915, d. 12/22/1990
HARMON, Ella F., ssw-Maggie L., Mother, b. 02/04/1872, d. 05/11/1965
HARMON, Elmer Lee, b. 09/11/1898, d. 10/19/1971
HARMON, Jeffrey S., b. 1972, d. 1992
HARMON, John H., ssw-Edith M., b. 02/10/1910, d. 01/18/1971
HARMON, Maggie L., ssw-Ella F., Daughter, b. 04/07/1892, d. 11/25/1974
HARMON, Nellie, ssw-William T., m. 07/29/1944, b. 05/14/1919, d. 09/05/1988
HARMON, Sharon Melinda, ssw-William Augustus, b. 07/21/1960, d. N/D
HARMON, Thelma Hazel, b. 02/14/1914, d. 12/25/1976
HARMON, William Augustus, "Dickie," ssw-Sharon Melinda, b. 09/09/1955, d. 07/01/1984
HARMON, William T., ssw-Nellie, m. 07/29/1944, USA, WWII, b. 08/11/1917, d. 09/25/1984
HARRIS, William E., Sp4, USA, b. 09/29/1957, d. 09/13/1991
HITCHENS, Bernice, b. 03/13/1903, d. 08/11/1982
HOLLOMAN, Mildred W., ssw-William L., b. 09/01/1904, d. N/D
HOLLOMAN, William H., Sr., Sfc., USA, b. 1939, d. 1991
HOLLOMAN, William L., ssw-Mildred W., b. 10/05/1898, d. 05/10/1984
HOPKINS, Preston J., Cpl., USA, WWII, b. 1925, d. 1976
JOHNSON, Alvin S., ssw-Carlos C., b. 06/26/1903, d. 01/12/1974
JOHNSON, Annie Marie, ssw-Joseph M., Sr., b. 07/04/1918, d. N/D
JOHNSON, Bertha E., ssw-Lester E., b. 03/29/1920, d. 06/19/1967
JOHNSON, Carlos C., ssw-Alvin S., b. 01/14/1911, d. 07/05/1964
JOHNSON, Elva M., ssw-Paris N., Sr., b. N/D, d. N/D
JOHNSON, George B., ssw-Rosa M., b. 08/12/1900, d. 11/24/1982
JOHNSON, Joseph M., Sr., ssw-Annie Marie, b. 07/19/1908, d. 06/21/1971
JOHNSON, Lester E., ssw-Elva M., b. 1914, d. 1988
JOHNSON, Paris N., Sr., ssw-Elva M., b. 1914, d. 1988
JOHNSON, Rosa M., ssw-George B., b. 12/31/1907, d. 04/03/1984
MADDOX, Roberta C., b. 01/25/1916, d. 10/26/1975
MARIANO, Anatalio N., b. 1892, d. 1967
MORRIS, Elmer, ssw-Eva M., b. 1890, d. 1958
MORRIS, Eonar Earl, b. 1938, d. 1984
MORRIS, Eva M., ssw-Elmer, b. 1896, d. 1989
MORRIS, John W., Sr., ssw-Vera C., b. 11/12/1934, d. 04/14/1986
MORRIS, Vera C., ssw-John W., Sr., b. 06/04/1932, d. N/D
MUNTZ, Viola S., b. 1949, d. 1985
NORWOOD, Charles A., b. 1911, d. 1990
PAYNTER, Caleb, ssw-Rose May, b. 08/07/1909, d. N/D
PAYNTER, Herman C., ssw-Caleb, b. 11/28/1954, d. N/D
PAYNTER, Rose May, ssw-Caleb, b. 05/10/1910, d. 10/21/1990
PENY, Lamont, ssw-Baby Harmon, b. 07/19/1965, d. 07/26/1991
SAMMONS, Lorenzo, b. 07/06/1897, d. 02/27/1979
TAYLOR, George W., ssw-Inez Neuble, m. 09/18/1924, b. 07/28/1901, d. N/D

TAYLOR, Inez, Neuble, ssw-George W., m. 09/18/1924, b. 04/13/1904, d. 12/26/1991
THOMPSON, Gertrude E., b. 01/28/1892, d. 08/23/1977
WARD, Emily F., b. 1910, d. 1978
WRIGHT, Clara, ssw-Harry & Elsie, b. 1877, d. 1963
WRIGHT, Elsie, ssw-Harry & Clara, b. 01/08/1899, d. 06/11/1947
WRIGHT, Harry, ssw-Clara & Elsie, b. 1874, d. 1956
WRIGHT, Trevanion Leon, Pfc., USA, WWII, b. 12/26/1915, d. 08/02/1981
YOUNG, Beatrice, b. 1910, d. 1991
YOUNG, Walter Jones, Pfc., USA, WWII, b. 09/12/1912, d. 08/18/1983

(IR-002 & HU-NR) INDIAN MISSION CHURCH CEMETERY
Located S. E. of Harbeson at the Eastern corner of Indian Mission Rd. (Rt. 5) and Hollymount Rd. (Rd. 48)
Recorded: November 24 & 30, 1992

BATTY, Charles A., Tec4, USA, WWII, b. 08/12/1915, d. 07/25/1992
BATTY, Lillian S., Wife, b. 09/02/1908, d. 02/15/1982
BUMBRAY, Ralph, Sr., Age 54y, b. N/D, d. 05/03/1916
CHRISTIAN, Joseph W., ssw-Myrtle V., b. 05/01/1909, d. 09/16/1985
CHRISTIAN, Myrtle V., ssw-Joseph W., b. 09/23/1909, d. N/D
CLARK, Alice, b. 1886, d. 1887
CLARK, Benjamin R., b. 1904, d. 1904
CLARK, Elios Pennrose, b. 11/25/1889, d. 09/23/1919
CLARK, Ephriam, b. 1888, d. 1888
CLARK, Ferdinand, "Chief Sea Gull," b. 1891, d. 1932
CLARK, Florence, b. 1897, d. 1897
CLARK, Florence A., w/o Chief Wyniaco, b. 1859, d. 1939
CLARK, Florence A., b. 1912, d. 1913
CLARK, James F., b. 1885, d. 1945
CLARK, James H., b. 1885, d. 1885
CLARK, James H., ssw-Nancy, b. 1831, d. 1907
CLARK, Laura, b. 1889, d. 1889
CLARK, Nancy, ssw-James H., b. 1830, d. 1907
CLARK, Rhoda A., b. 1896, d. 1912
CLARK, Sarah J., b. 1883, d. 1897
CLARK, William R., "Chief Wyniaco," ssw-Florence A., b. 1855, d. 1928
CLARK, William R., b. 1916, d. 1916
COOPER, Minnie E., d/o Charles & Eva Johnson, b. 07/28/1916, d. 11/16/1961
COURSEY, Alberta M., b. 03/05/1937, d. 02/09/1971
COURSEY, Amelia A., w/o Charles L., b. 10/30/1862, d. 04/29/1931
COURSEY, Amos S., b. 1893, d. 1958
COURSEY, Carrie M., ssw-Charles L., b. 1871, d. 1905
COURSEY, Cecelia E., ssw-Charles M., b. 06/29/1904, d. 03/04/1984
COURSEY, Charles L., ssw-Carrie M., b. 1869, d. 1941
COURSEY, Charles M., ssw-Cecelia E., b. 08/06/1902, d. 10/23/1986
COURSEY, Helen Cecelia, d/o Cecelia & Marshall Coursey, b. 05/28/1927, d. 09/07/1930
COURSEY, William A., s/o Charles L. & Carrie M., b. 04/01/1900, d. 07/05/1901
DAVIS, Lillie M., ssw-Robert H., m. 09/26/1913, b. 1896, d. 1986
DAVIS, Robert H., ssw-Lillie M., m. 09/26/1913, d. 1891, d. 1981

DRAINE, Nora S., b. 11/15/1901, d. 04/22/1988
DRAINE, Richard E., SSgt., USA, WWII, b. 1921, d. 1981
FUSSELL, Viola V., ssw-William, b. 1912, d. 1973
FUSSELL, William, ssw-Viola V., b. 1911, d. N/D
GRAHAM, Joanna W., b. 1860, d. 1931
HARMAN, David S., s/o J. W. & Anna, b. 07/04/1887, d. 07/04/1887
HARMAN, Elizabeth P., b. 05/29/1895, d. N/D
HARMAN, Ellen N., Age 85y, b. N/D, d. 04/22/1909
HARMAN, Ephraim L., Ex. Chief, b. 04/16/1891, d. 05/18/1967
HARMAN, Eunice, d/o Isaac W. & Vina A., b. 11/11/1879, d. 05/22/1914
HARMAN, Eunice E., ssw-Noah, b. 03/17/1872, d. 02/12/1954
HARMAN, Isaac L., s/o J. W. & Anna, Age 6m, b. N/D, d. 03/17/1885
HARMAN, Isaac W., ssw-Vina A., b. 1862, d. 1931
HARMAN, Isaac W., Jr., ssw-Isaac W., Jr., b. 03/05/1927, d. 09/1927
HARMAN, Isaac W., Jr., ssw-Isaac W., Jr., b. 1904, d. 1986
HARMAN, John W., Age 33y 6m 15d, b. N/D, d. 07/13/1890
HARMAN, Levin T. S., s/o Isaac W. & Vina A., b. 06/16/1900, d. 10/31/1900
HARMAN, Lindbergh, ssw-Isaac W., Jr., b. 04/09/1928, d. 01/1929
HARMAN, Noah, ssw-Eunice E., b. 07/14/1870,d. 12/25/1943
HARMAN, Noah G., s/o Isaac W. & Vina A., b. 01/23/1908, d. 10/11/1908
HARMAN, Ralph B., b. 11/02/1885, d. 04/26/1927
HARMAN, Salina A., d/o Noah & Eunice, b. 10/07/1912, d. 04/28/1913
HARMAN, Sarah M., d/o J. W. & Annie, b. N/D, d. 09/20/1890
HARMAN, Vina A., w/o Isaac W., b. 1867, d. 1939
HARMAN, William C., s/o I. W. & V. A., b. 01/11/1895, d. 11/26/1910
HARMON, Albert, ssw-Anna M., b. 1909, d. 1966
HARMON, Alston, ssw-Helen, b. 09/16/1912, d. N/D
HARMON, Anna M., ssw-Albert, b. 1907, d. 1983
HARMON, Anna W., ssw-Theodore, b. 02/01/1888, d. 01/09/1976
HARMON, Annie P., ssw-Theodore P., b. 09/21/1890, d. 01/07/1971
HARMON, Archie, b. 03/30/1886, d. 05/10/1957
HARMON, Charlie L., b. 03/02/1922, d. 07/20/1922
HARMON, Eliza J., w/o Ralph B., b. 06/30/1893, d. 01/07/1918
HARMON, Eunice P., b. 10/22/1915, d. 08/02/1987
HARMON, Fannie G., b. 09/18/1893, d. 09/28/1923
HARMON, Fred, b. 11/20/1883, d. 10/17/1964
HARMON, Gerald Wayne, b. 02/07/1951, d. 05/04/1986
HARMON, Hamrilton W., s/o Noah & Eunice E., b. 04/19/1896, d. 08/10/1896
HARMON, Helen, ssw-Alston, b. 03/03/1916, d. 03/12/1976
HARMON, Helen R., b. 05/16/1911, d. 02/19/1966
HARMON, Herman G., b. 04/18/1923, d. 01/31/1924
HARMON, Inf. s/o Noah & Eunice E., b. 11/26/1892, d. N/D
HARMON, Inf., s/o T. & A. W., b. N/D, d. 03/18/1904
HARMON, Isaac Clinton, b. 10/23/1916, d. 03/25/1992
HARMON, Isaac M., b. 10/25/1885, d. 03/10/1967
HARMON, J. Wesley, b. 1881, d. 1940
HARMON, Joseph M., b. 1926, d. 1939
HARMON, Joseph W., ssw-Sarah I., b. 1897, d. 1958

HARMON, Kenneth Wendell, b. 08/23/1924, d. 06/04/1986
HARMON, Leon E., b. 02/18/1902, d. 06/29/1982
HARMON, Leon E., Jr., b. 11/18/1941, d. 11/29/1957
HARMON, Leonard A., Artist, b. 06/29/1952, d. 04/03/1989
HARMON, Levin T., ssw-Rebecca P., b. 1860, d. 1940
HARMON, Marietta L., b. 10/15/1927, d. 02/21/1981
HARMON, Myrtle E., b. 10/25/1910, d. 05/10/1985
HARMON, Rebecca P., ssw-Levin T., b. 1861, d. 1944
HARMON, Sarah, d/o T. & A. W., b. 07/07/1909, d. 02/17/1911
HARMON, Sarah I., ssw-Joseph W., b. 1897, d. 1983
HARMON, Theodore, ssw-Anna W., b. 01/01/1874, d. 07/30/1965
HARMON, Theodore P., b. 04/14/1840, d. 12/04/1912
HARMON, Theodore P., ssw-Annie P., b. 06/10/1889, d. 04/04/1962
HARMON, Thomas H., ssw-Virginia F., b. 12/03/1902, d. 01/16/1975
HARMON, Viola, Age 2y 1m 8d, b. N/D, d. 04/14/1906
HARMON, Virginia F., ssw-Thomas H., b. 08/26/1907, d. 03/21/1984
HARMON, William A., s/o R. B. & E. J., b. 06/24/1914, d. 09/13/1915
JACKSON, Blaine, "Gray Fox," Assist. Chief 1975-1991, ssw-Gladys M., m. 04/14/1928, b. 05/29/1907,
        d. 06/17/1991
JACKSON, Elizabeth, b. 01/01/1820, d. 01/06/1896
JACKSON, Gladys M., "Bright Dawn," ssw-Blaine, m. 04/14/1928, d. 09/15/1909, d. N/D
JACKSON, Harold B., ssw-Gladys M., b. 12/28/1925, d. 06/12/1988
JACKSON, Helen, w/o William W., b. 01/01/1859, d. 10/14/1913
JACKSON, John A., ssw-Lovenia P., b. 04/02/1869, d. 01/08/1939
JACKSON, John H., Age 47y 2m 18d, b. 01/08/1853, d. 03/26/1906
JACKSON, Lillie May Harmon, w/o John A., Age 18y 2m 15d, b. N/D, d. 04/23/1893
JACKSON, Lovenia P., w/o John A., ssw-John A., b. 02/22/1877, d. 10/17/1928
JACKSON, Lyda A., w/o Robert B., ssw-Robert B., Age 54y 7m 1d, b. N/D, d. 05/03/1901
JACKSON, Raymond S., b. 04/22/1909, d. 10/24/1968
JACKSON, Robert B., ssw-Lyda A., Age, 73y 10m 15d, b. N/D, d. 12/29/1915
JACKSON, William M., Sgt., USA, WWII, b. 10/26/1916, d. 06/15/1989
JAMESON, James L., b. 07/04/1887, d. 08/28/1961
JOHNSON, Aimus S., s/o Wm. H. & Eliza A., Age 1m b. N/D, d. 08/02/1899
JOHNSON, Ann W., b. N/D, d. 10/07/1885
JOHNSON, Anna Delores, b. 04/16/1929, d. 10/10/1934
JOHNSON, Charles R., ssw-Eva M., b. 1887, d. 1946
JOHNSON, Curtis W., b. 11/04/1891, d. 08/28/1976
JOHNSON, Dorothy, b. 1915, d. 1936
JOHNSON, Eliza A., ssw-William Howard, b. 1878, d. 1929
JOHNSON, Elizabeth, ssw-William A., b. 10/25/1850, d. 07/29/1920
JOHNSON, Eva M., w/o Charles R., b. 1889, d. 1981
JOHNSON, Fannie G., w/o R. B., b. 02/07/1864, d. 02/21/1912
JOHNSON, Helen C., ssw-J. Wesley, b. 08/23/1897, d. 03/29/1982
JOHNSON, Helen M., d/o C. R. & E. M., b. 1913, d. 1920
JOHNSON, Helen V., ssw-Lacey, b. 06/24/1910, d. 03/23/1988
JOHNSON, Infant, b. N/D, d. 02/15/1912
JOHNSON, J. Wesley, ssw-Helen C., b. 10/24/1900, d. 12/21/1985
JOHNSON, Lacey, ssw-Helen V., b. 03/14/1907, d. N/D

JOHNSON, Luther C., b. 03/21/1878, d. 01/30/1961

JOHNSON, Mary E., Age 78y, b. N/D, d. 03/02/1914

JOHNSON, Mary Ella, b. 05/31/1875, d. 09/19/1954

JOHNSON, Nelson, DE, Cpl. C of 368 Inf., 92 Div., WWII, b. 07/13/1888, d. 02/09/1915

JOHNSON, Return W., b. 05/12/1897, d. 01/22/1976

JOHNSON, Robert B., b. 07/18/1842, d. 05/23/1926

JOHNSON, Robert P., s/o R. B. & F. G., b. N/D, d. N/D

JOHNSON, Thelma E., "Earth Woman," b. 04/02/1923, d. 12/09/1990

JOHNSON, William A., ssw-Elizabeth, b. 12/29/1848, d. 03/21/1924

JOHNSON, William Howard, ssw-Eliza A., b. 1874, d. 1981

MAULL, Howard N., ssw-Lillian H., USA, WWII, b. 12/04/1920, d. 12/05/1984

MAULL, Lillian H., ssw-Howard N., b. 01/21/1915, d. 05/12/1987

MILLER, Gardner C., ssw-William E., William L. & Sarah A., b. 1943, d. N/D

MILLER, Nelson R., Sr., b. 1934, d. 1989

MILLER, Sarah A., ssw-William E., William L. & Gardner C., b. 1904, d. 1972

MILLER, William E., ssw-Sarah A., Gardner C. & William L., b. 1899, d. 1952

MILLER, William L., ssw-William E., Gardner C. & Sarah A., b. 1927, d. 1941

MORGAN, Alberta H., ssw-Leamond, b. 09/17/1900, d. N/D

MORGAN, Leamond, ssw-Alberta H., b. 01/12/1898, d. 11/14/1976

MORRIS, Charles T., ssw-Sophia Isabelle, b. 1867, d. 1940

MORRIS, Sophia Isabelle, ssw-Charles T., b. 1864, d. 1937

MOSLEY, Bertha E., ssw-Charles, b. 10/26/1902, d. 09/13/1970

MOSLEY, Charles, ssw-Bertha E., b. 09/29/1895, d. 03/17/1984

MOSLEY, Vianna I., "Sweety," b. 10/20/1937, d. 03/27/1983

MYERS, Mildred T., ssw-William A., b. 09/13/1911, d. 08/12/1982

MYERS, William A., ssw-Mildred T., b. 05/24/1907, d. 02/23/1972

NORWOOD, Adaline E., b. 1907, d. 1942

NORWOOD, Frank H., Age 42y 6m 12d, b. 03/22/1862, d. 10/01/1904

NORWOOD, James Tyrone, "Tee," ssw-Jean Johnson, b. 10/23/1941, d. N/D

NORWOOD, Janie B., ssw-Richard L., b. 04/16/1918, d. N/D

NORWOOD, Jean Johnson, ssw-James Tyrone Norwood, b. 12/18/1940, d. N/D

NORWOOD, Luther B., b. 1879, d. 1942

NORWOOD, Richard L., ssw-Janie B., b. 12/25/1911, d. N/D

NORWOOD, Robert W., b. 1857, d. 1942

NORWOOD, Samuel B., Age 78y 9m 22d, b. 02/24/1829, d. 12/16/1907

NORWOOD, Sarah A., Age 66y 3m 25d, b. 12/19/1837, d. 04/14/1904

ORTIZ, Ida Harmon, b. 04/25/1932, d. 07/03/1987

REIDER, Harold C., ssw-Marie C., b. 1900, d. 1973

REIDER, Marie C., ssw-Harold C., b. N/D, d. N/D

SAMMONS, Charles C., ssw-Ida N., b. 04/12/1877, d. 11/06/1931

SAMMONS, Ida N., w/o Charles C., ssw-Charles C., b. 09/19/1887, d. 01/28/1985

SMITH, Carlyle W., ssw-Thelma A., b. 06/15/1917, d. 11/01/1990

SMITH, Thelma A., ssw-Carlyle W., USA, WWII, WAC, b. 06/12/1922, d. 09/20/1984

SOCKUME, Levin J., b. 1841, d. N/D

STERRETT, Mary L., Mother, b. 07/26/1882, d. 08/27/1954

STERRETT, Willis A., Son, b. 11/02/1900, d. 12/08/1974

STREET, Anna J., ssw-Willis L., b. 10/06/1901, d. 03/09/1991

STREET, Clara E., ssw-G. R. & Della H., b. 06/21/1879, d. 10/10/1903

STREET, Claracie M., b. N/D, d. N/D
STREET, Clarence Sylvester, s/o Robert P. & Matilda, Age 3m, b. 02/10/1913, d. N/D
STREET, David P., ssw-Matilda A., b. 03/10/1822, d. 04/05/1911
STREET, Della H., ssw-G. R. & Clara E., b. 1885, d. 1935
STREET, Etta P., ssw-Lawrence S., b. 06/17/1909, d. N/D
STREET, Eunice D., b. 02/11/1930, d. 04/07/1931
STREET, Feba May, d/o Robert P. & Matilda, Age 3m, b. 09/09/1905, d. N/D
STREET, G. R., ssw-Della H. & Clara E., b. 01/07/1877, d. 12/14/1955
STREET, Harry, b. 11/25/1885, d. 04/07/1971
STREET, Helen Cassie, b. 12/18/1918, d. 07/12/1921
STREET, Herman, b. 01/24/1920, d. 03/28/1955
STREET, Isaac, ssw-Parnelpa A., b. 07/23/1848, d. N/D
STREET, Lawrence S., ssw-Etta P., b. 01/23/1911, d. 10/24/1957
STREET, Martin, Pvt., USA, WWII, b. 06/03/1914, d. 05/25/1973
STREET, Mary E., b. 08/20/1890, d. 06/12/1975
STREET, Matilda A., ssw-David P., b. 09/30/1840, d. N/D
STREET, Matilda A., ssw-Robert P., b. 1880, d. 1945
STREET, Mervin Earl, b. 06/01/1921, d. 07/15/1939
STREET, Nelson Warren, s/o Robert P. & Matilda, Age 3 m, b. 06/12/1909, d. N/D
STREET, Parnelpa A., ssw-Isaac, b. 01/01/1840, d. 07/11/1926
STREET, Pocahontas E., Mom, b. 09/24/1898, d. 08/19/1969
STREET, Robert, b. 09/05/1900, d. 05/16/1974
STREET, Robert I., NY, Pfc., 377 Inf., 95 Inf. Div., WWII, b. 12/16/1920, d. 11/19/1944
STREET, Robert P., ssw-Matilda, b. 1868, d. 1937
STREET, Rosetta M., b. 01/08/1896, d. 05/31/1932
STREET, Willis L., ssw-Anna J., b. 08/25/1916, d. N/D
TAYLOR, Catherine Street, b. 09/03/1904, d. 10/26/1975
THOMPSON, Asbury, b. N/D, d. 09/28/1881
THOMPSON, Barthalomew, b. 03/30/1886, d. 01/02/1967
THOMPSON, El??, b. 10/16/1883, d. 06/30/1918
THOMPSON, J. W., b. 12/18/1837, d. 07/25/1921
THOMPSON, Maria L., b. 1858, d. 1921
THOMPSON, Marie L., b. 1865, d. 1943
THOMPSON, Sara, b. 02/18/1841, d. 11/08/1921
THOMPSON, Sarah E., Age 21y, b. 1892, d. 08/30/1913
THOMPSON, Snowden A., b. 1869, d. 1961
WRIGHT, A. Warren, ssw-Adele M., b. 07/18/1912, d. 12/24/1981
WRIGHT, Adele M., ssw-A. Warren, b. 10/15/1920, d. N/D
WRIGHT, Alden, b. 1929, d. 1979
WRIGHT, Anna C., ssw-Walter B., b. 12/17/1889, d. 10/06/1983
WRIGHT, Arthur, ssw-Hersel, b. 1907, d. 1966
WRIGHT, Arthur E., ssw-Hersel, b. 1872, d. 1949
WRIGHT, Augustus, b. 05/13/1879, d. 07/05/1963
WRIGHT, Bertha, ssw-Warren T. & Marie L., b. 10/30/1872, d. 04/01/1950
WRIGHT, Caroline, ssw-Hersel, b. 1877, d. 1961
WRIGHT, David W., ssw-Emily C., b. 05/25/1846, d. 10/30/1913
WRIGHT, Emily C., w/o David W., ssw-David W., b. 11/06/1845, d. 05/12/1921
WRIGHT, Fannie M., w/o O. W., b. 03/13/1893, d. 02/24/1916

WRIGHT, Hersel, ssw-Robert W., b. 04/11/1911, d. 08/16/1990
WRIGHT, Howard J., Sr., ssw-Wilda A., b. 02/09/1919, d. N/D
WRIGHT, Joseph R., Sr., b. 03/19/1904, d. 10/21/1973
WRIGHT, Laura, b. 1888, d. 1953
WRIGHT, Lottie E., ssw-William A., b. 1899, d. 1977
WRIGHT, Malcolm C., Cpl., USMC, Korea, b. 01/02/1936, d. 0/03/1982
WRIGHT, Marie L., ssw-Warren T. & Bertha, b. 04/03/1897, d. 06/11/1925
WRIGHT, Mary Ann, ssw-William E., b. 07/18/1914, d. 12/24/1991
WRIGHT, Oscar W., b. 05/31/1889, d. N/D
WRIGHT, Return, b. 09/12/1898, d. 12/16/1989
WRIGHT, Richard H., b. 04/12/1910, d. 04/09/1947
WRIGHT, Robert, ssw-Ruth A., b. 12/04/1851, d. 03/21/1916
WRIGHT, Robert C., Sr., Past Asst. Chief Nanticoke Indian Assoc., b. 06/12/1912, d. 08/09/1985
      Sons: Charles L., Dallas N. & Robert C., Jr.
      Daughters: Trethia Ann Wright, Carrie Davis, Lillie R. Davis & Conchita Clark
WRIGHT, Robert J., s/o Wm. A. & Sarah H., b. 10/12/1896, d. 09/03/1902
WRIGHT, Robert W., b. 04/16/1931, d. 06/03/1974
WRIGHT, Robert W., ssw-Hersel, b. 1901, d. 1971
WRIGHT, Roy, b. 07/12/1897, d. 08/24/1973
WRIGHT, Ruth A., ssw-Robert, b. 02/25/1855, d. 02/12/1938
WRIGHT, Ruth E., b. 05/02/1908, d. 09/13/1984
WRIGHT, Salena F., d/o Nicholas & Anna, b. 07/17/1898, d. 09/30/1898
WRIGHT, Sarah, w/o Wm. A., b. 1874, d. 1920
WRIGHT, Treathia Ann, b. 04/08/1936, d. 11/11/1937
WRIGHT, Walter B., ssw-Anna C., b. 01/21/1881, d. 03/01/1983
WRIGHT, Walter T., Pvt., USA, WWII, b. 08/24/1911, d. 07/08/1976
WRIGHT, Warren T., ssw-Bertha & Marie L.., b. 02/25/1869, d. 12/19/1965
WRIGHT, Wilda A., ssw-Howard J., Sr., b. 08/23/1920, d. N/D
WRIGHT, William A., ssw-Lottie E., b. 1890, d. 1944
WRIGHT, William A., ssw-Sarah, b. 1867, d. 1946
WRIGHT, William E., ssw-Mary Ann, WWII, b. 06/10/1921, d. 01/24/1992
WRIGHT, William M., ssw-Hersel, b. 1904, d. 1926
WRIGHT, Wilson S., b. 04/06/1926, d. 04/23/1979
WRIGHT, Winona J., b. 10/13/1892, d. 05/15/1978

(IR-003 & HU-NR) HARMONY CEMETERY
Located North East of Millsboro on the South East Corner of Townsend Rd. (Rd. 303) and Inland Bay Rd. (Rd. 306)
Recorded: September 2 – 4, 1996

ALLEN, J. Stanford, b. 09/07/1912, d. 03/18/1990
ALLEN, Mayola W., b. 03/04/1917, d. N/D
ANDERSON, Cleo V., b. 1924, d. 1970
BARNUM, Chanley W., b. 02/18/1912, d. 06/07/1945
BAYLIS, Helen, b. 07/10/1910, d. 04/27/1991
BEST, Helen M., b. 01/02/1909, d. 01/18/1969
BRUMBY, Julia Lee, b. 03/08/1905, d. 05/31/1905
BURTON, Ella, b. 1906, d. 1979

BURTON, Emma B., b. 12/07/1881, d. 01/10/1973
BURTON, Harvey B., b. 03/01/1906, d. 10/04/1970
BURTON, Harvey W., b. 02/16/1875, d. 11/02/1970
BURTON, Sarah J., b. 07/04/1900, d. 09/25/1976
BURTON, William, b. 11/08/1915, d. 03/02/1970
BUSH, Amelia I., b. 05/01/1924, d. 06/11/1990
CLARK, Arzie E., b. 01/14/1914, d. N/D
CLARK, Charles L., b. 11/05/1912, d. 05/23/1990
CLARK, Elsie R., b. 09/06/1896, d. 11/09/1939
CLARK, John W., s/o Nathaniel & Eunice, Age 44y 6m 23d, b. N/D, d. 08/07/1875
CLARK, Joseph T., b. 09/02/1900, d. 04/02/1978
CLARK, Louise, b. 1871, d. 1947
CLARK, Norman W., b. 03/22/1930, d. 12/16/1994
CLARK, Robert, b. 02/14/1814, d. 05/03/1893
CLARK, Robert M., b. 1886, d. 1970
CLARK, Sylvia F., b. 02/27/1921, d. 05/10/1995
CLARK, Thomas H., b. 09/05/1847, d. 09/17/1922
CLARK, Vernear A., b. 08/24/1955, d. 03/17/1979
CLARK, Walter L., b. 12/28/1909, d. 02/25/1979
CLARK, William B., b. 1860, d. 1933
CLARK, William B., b. 1895, d. 1951
COVERDALE, Clara P., b. 02/04/1890, d. 05/15/1955
D., No other information [Located between John Harmond & Clara Johnson Hall]
D., E. A., b. N/D, d. N/D [Located between Jean D. Davis & Armela Jackson]
DAISEY, William S., b. N/D, d. 10/06/1941
DAVIS, Charles M., b. 1898, d. 1948
DAVIS, Clarence D., b. 04/18/1925, d. 06/11/1991
DAVIS, Eliza Ann, w/o Morris, b. 12/19/1869, d. 07/03/1889
DAVIS, George A., b. 1909, d. 1986
DAVIS, Hersel R., b. 06/03/1915, d. N/D
DAVIS, Hester A., b. 09/22/1877, d. 11/09/1944
DAVIS, Jean D., b. 10/24/1932, d. N/D
DAVIS, John M., b. 1863, d. 1936
DAVIS, Lillie R., b. 11/20/1939, d. N/D
DAVIS, Mary E., b. 1868, d. 1897
DAVIS, Minnie M., b. 1903, d. 1952
DAVIS, Myrtle P., b. 09/05/1913, d. N/D
DAVIS, Reginald L., b. 05/19/1930, d. 03/26/1987
DAVIS, William A., b. 10/25/1934, d. N/D
DAVIS, William W., b. 06/14/1906, d. 12/20/1961
DIGGS, Theodore, b. 03/02/1895, d. 03/22/1987
DRAIN, Sylvester, Age 27y 5m 13d, b. N/D, d. 10/19/1926
DRAINE, Baby, b. N/D, d. N/D
DRAINE, Elsie Ann Daise, b. 01/07/1899, d. N/D
DRAINE, Eunice H., b. 07/24/1918, d. 06/28/1992
DRAINE, Robert N., b. 06/20/1914, d. N/D
DUNNING, Rena, b. N/D, d. N/D
EVANS, Harold V., "Poochie," b. 01/12/1959, d. 12/12/1980

FRAZIER, Elton L., b. 05/31/1923, d. 03/16/1969
GANTZ, Mary Ellen, Age 53y, b. N/D, d. 05/24/1932
GRAHAM, Donald C., b. 1926, d. 1934
GRAHAM, Elsie, b. 04/02/1894, d. 11/03/1946
GRAHAM, Howard, b. 10/26/1888, d. 03/02/1975
HALL, Albert L., Reverend, b. 06/18/1892, d. 1 2/13/1956
HALL, Amos H., b. 11/25/1902, d. 03/28/1982
HALL, Betty B., M. 04/01/1952, b. 01/04/1932, d. N/D
HALL, Clara Johnson, b. 08/29/1883, d. 09/15/1930
HALL, Elena V., b. 03/18/1918, d. 10/22/1993
HALL, Elsie A., b. 09/02/1900, d. 02/28/1975
HALL, Elva M., b. 10/21/1916, d. 04/07/1945
HALL, Everett L., b. 10/29/1927, d. 10/13/1974
HALL, Everett Lee, b. 12/02/1921, d. 11/08/1990
HALL, Harvey T., b. 06/28/1894, d. 0/26/1966
HALL, Irvin B., b. 12/09/1880, d. 01/10/1962
HALL, Laura K., b. 09/26/1907, d. N/D
HALL, Lenard Albert, s/o Albert L. & Elsie A., Age 2y 2m 2d, b. N/D, d. 04/23/1925
HALL, Lillie M., m. 04/12/1916, b. 09/21/1893, d. 07/20/1984
HALL, Mary E., b. 1900, d. 1961
HALL, S., b. N/D, d. N/D
HANZER, Alexander, b. 10/16/1878, d. 12/18/1941
HANZER, Annie, b. 1868, d. 1950
HANZER, Eugene, b. 10/09/1888, d. 03/12/1922
HANZER, Georgiana, b. 1903, d. N/D
HANZER, Harriet A., b. 1864, d. 1940
HANZER, John C., Age 73y 7m 28d, b. N/D, d. N/D
HANZER, John W., b. 1881, d. 1960
HANZER, Sufphor J., w/o Charles C., b. 04/20/1842, d. 09/18/1912
HANZER, William, b. N/D, d. 03/1916
HARMAN, Gertrude H., b. 11/21/1909, d. 09/21/1935
HARMON, Alvin L., b. 01/23/1922, d. 01/13/1935
HARMON, Annie R., b. 12/03/1873, d. 04/03/1955
HARMON, Baby Edward, b. N/D, d. N/D
HARMON, Clarence H., b. 12/25/1932, d. 10/22/1980
HARMON, E. Belle, b. 1883, d. 1973
HARMON, E. Hester, b. 1888, d. 1979
HARMON, Eliza, d/o Isaac M. & Sarah J., b. below ground, d. below ground
HARMON, Eliza J., b. 12/03/1880, d. 02/28/1965
HARMON, Ella Mae, b. 06/30/1870, d. 07/28/1908
HARMON, Emanuel, b. 1902, d. 1979
HARMON, Enach, b. 1900, d. 1945
HARMON, Eunice W., d/o Isaac M. & Sarah J., Age 2m 8d, b. N/D, d. 01/23/1859
HARMON, Eunice W., d/o Isaac M. & Sarah J., Age 5m, b. N/D, d. 07/14/1869
HARMON, Freddie, b. N/D, d. N/D
HARMON, George, b. N/D, d. N/D
HARMON, George, b. 03/01/1908, d. N/D
HARMON, George F., b. N/D, d. N/D

HARMON, Gloria V., b. 04/30/1941, d. 12/01/1941
HARMON, Helen M., b. 03/15/1919, d. 07/22/1964
HARMON, Helena J., b. 05/28/1934, d. 10/06/1992
HARMON, Horace J., b. 1883, d. 1957
HARMON, Inf. d/o Isaac M. & Sarah J., Age 12d, b. N/D, d. 07/24/1858
HARMON, Isaac H., b. 1913, d. 1990
HARMON, Isaac T., b. 1878, d. 1958
HARMON, Isaac W., "Bud," b. 02/09/1898, d. 03/07/1982
HARMON, James, b. 02/18/1884, d. 10/28/1971
HARMON, Jan F., b. N/D, d. 1908
HARMON, Jean, b. N/D, d. N/D
HARMON, John D., b. 03/30/1891, d. 02/28/1971
HARMON, John M., b. 1882, d. 1954
HARMON, John W., b. 06/29/1850, d. 12/17/1894
HARMON, John W., b. 08/04/1876, d. 09/12/1962
HARMON, Joseph, b. N/D, d. N/D
HARMON, Joseph, b. N/D, d. N/D
HARMON, Kover W., Age 11m 10d, b. N/D, d. N/D
HARMON, L. Jeanette, b. 12/08/1914, d. 10/03/1977
HARMON, Larry A., b. 08/04/1953, d. 12/15/1993
HARMON, Lena F., b. 09/24/1895, d. 09/29/1968
HARMON, Leon, Sr., b. 11/28/1922, d. 07/28/1982
HARMON, Leston A., "Shorty," b. 02/24/1924, d. 09/12/1995
HARMON, Louise, b. 1901, d. 1945
HARMON, Mabel J., b. 1905, d. 1994
HARMON, Madgie, b. 11/02/1894, d. 06/11/1995
HARMON, Mary, b. N/D, d. N/D
HARMON, Matilda, b. 1867, d. 1953
HARMON, Nancy T., d/o Isaac M. & Sarah J., Age 3y 1m 18d, b. N/D, d. 03/02/1869
HARMON, Neocia M., b. 1889, d. N/D
HARMON, Oscar, Sr., b. 06/04/1918, d. 01/31/1957
HARMON, Otis William S., b. 07/04/1898, d. 12/29/1970
HARMON, Phyllis, b. N/D, d. 09/15/1928
HARMON, Phyllis B., b. 11/02/1931, d. N/D
HARMON, Rachel, b. N/D, d. N/D
HARMON, Raymond S., b. 1903, d. 1976
HARMON, Robert, b. 10/1955, d. N/D
HARMON, Robert F., b. 1928, d. 1992
HARMON, Robert Freeman, b. 10/22/1927, d. 05/31/1992
HARMON, Robert M., s/o Isaac M. & Sarah J., Age 1y 10m 17d, b. N/D, d. 03/03/1821
HARMON, Sarah C., b. 06/05/1923, d. N/D
HARMON, Sarah Catherine, b. 02/04/1902, d. 10/27/1995
HARMON, Sarah E., b. 1882, d. 1944
HARMON, Sylvester, b. 1927, d. 1992
HARMON, Thelma A., b. 1944, d. 1945
HARMON, Theodore, b. N/D, d. N/D
HARMON, Thomas, b. 1861, d. 1934
HARMON, Thomas E., b. 1881, d. 1955

HARMON, Unreadable, Age 1y 9m 15d, b. N/D, d. N/D
HARMON, Wilbur, b. 05/27/1897, d. 12/17/1966
HARMON, Willey, b. N/D, d. N/D
HARMON, William C., b. N/D, d. 10/15/1950
HARMON, William E., b. 02/16/1868, d. 08/1929
HARMON, William Edward, b. 05/23/1910, d. 09/24/1986
HENRY, Clarissa, b. 04/03/1917, d. 05/21/1996
HENRY, Jerome, b. 05/27/1904, d. 11/19/1958
J., C. H., No other information. [Located between George E. & Sarah E. Johnson]
JACKSON, Agnes B., b. 09/14/1913, d. N/D
JACKSON, Arvel A., b. 10/22/1911, d. 06/26/1988
JACKSON, Attlee T., b. 1951, d. 1983
JACKSON, Edna L., m. 08/04/1922, b. 1905, d. N/D
JACKSON, Elvanetta, "Babe," b. 11/07/1921, d. 01/30/1996
JACKSON, George B., b. 1937, d. 1992
JACKSON, Helen, b. 1917, d. 1918
JACKSON, Herman S., b. 08/10/1920, d. N/D
JACKSON, Isaac A., b. 1877, d. 1948
JACKSON, Isaac E., b. 1898, d. 1962
JACKSON, James M., b. 11/30/1845, d. 05/26/1926
JACKSON, James Wesley, b. 08/1907, d. 04/1909
JACKSON, Laura E. Street, b. 08/12/1900, d. 03/19/1922
JACKSON, Layton, b. 05/17/1909, d. 06/21/1995
JACKSON, Linia, b. 1905, d. 1981
JACKSON, Mary, b. 1936, d. 1995
JACKSON, Mary E., m. 03/30/1910, b. 08/09/1891, d. 04/19/1979
JACKSON, Minerva E., b. 1878, d. 1918
JACKSON, Preston Coolidge, b. 01/18/1924, d. 12/18/1993
JACKSON, Sallie, b. 1903, d. 1922
JACKSON, Samuel B., b. 01/12/1909, d. 08/10/1989
JACKSON, Samuel H., b. 10/16/1889, d. 09/16/1972
JACKSON, Sarah J., w/o James M., b. 10/24/1856, d. 02/07/1920
JACKSON, Sarah Jane, b. 05/15/1886, d. 11/16/1986
JACKSON, Trudy E., b. 1952, d. N/D
JACKSON, William Earl, b. 03/28/1915, d. 12/19/1990
JACKSON, William W., b. 1885, d. 1970
JOHNSON, Albert Leon, "WAS-QUA," b. 11/21/1907, d. 09/22/1981
JOHNSON, Alma, b. 10/11/1911, d. 06/07/1961
JOHNSON, Annie E., b. 01/26/1893, d. 04/14/1965
JOHNSON, Burton, Age 68y 6m, b. N/D, d. 12/14/1852
JOHNSON, Burton, Age abt. 81y, b. N/D, d. 09/1868
JOHNSON, Calvin H., b. 10/14/1909, d. 12/09/1988
JOHNSON, Charles, b. 10/10/1902, d. 04/20/1978
JOHNSON, Charles H., Age 42y 5m 5d, b. N/D, d. 11/07/1895
JOHNSON, Charles J., b. 04/11/1896, d. 07/05/1973
JOHNSON, Creenie E., d/o George E. & Sarah J., Age 23d, b. N/D, d. 11/24/1872
JOHNSON, David W., s/o M., Age 1y 4m 18d, b. N/D, d. 09/30/1887
JOHNSON, Doris B., b. 06/03/1933, d. 08/28/1973

JOHNSON, Dorsey E., b. 06/25/1892, d. 09/07/1969

JOHNSON, Drewlo J., b. 07/19/1892, d. 02/02/1976

JOHNSON, Edsel C., b. 1926, d. 1982

JOHNSON, Eldridge R., b. 04/20/1929, d. N/D

JOHNSON, Eliza G., Age 60y 4m 7d, b. N/D, d. 08/17/1889

JOHNSON, Ellen, Age 60y, b. N/D, d. 04/10/1848

JOHNSON, George E., Age 82y, b. N/D, d. 03/14/1912

JOHNSON, Harley E., b. 1897, d. 1961

JOHNSON, Herbert R., b. 12/05/1921, d. 10/26/1983

JOHNSON, Inf. o/Annie & Dorsey, b. N/D, d. N/D

JOHNSON, James E., b. 1894, d. 1955

JOHNSON, John, b, 01/20/1891, d. 05/14/1964

JOHNSON, John B., b. 05/25/1843, d. 05/17/1926

JOHNSON, John L., b. N/D, d. 03/20/1956

JOHNSON, Larry L., b. 1894, d. 1959

JOHNSON, Lawrence E., s/o Sarah & H. E., Age 6m 7d, b. 02/08/1917, d. 08/19/1917

JOHNSON, Lillie B., b. 09/14/1898, d. 12/03/1966

JOHNSON, Lucy E., b. 1890, d. 1978

JOHNSON, Madge M., b. N/D, d. 05/17/1892 [Note: stone in ground]

JOHNSON, Marcella M., b. 1907, d. 1972

JOHNSON, Mary A., b. 05/31/1850, d. 04/10/1920

JOHNSON, Mary E., b. 01/22/1849, d. 11//05/1930

JOHNSON, Maymie R., b. 09/06/1902, d. 12/27/1968

JOHNSON, Purnel, Age 76y 8m 5d, b. N/D, d. 07/01/1862

JOHNSON, Sallie M., b. 09/25/1906, d. 06/25/1988

JOHNSON, Samuel L., b. 07/05/1900, d. 03/13/1963

JOHNSON, Sarah E., Age 43y 3m 15d, b. 12/17/1873, d. 04/02/1917

JOHNSON, Sophia E., d/o Return & Ann, Age 25y 4m 11d, b. N/D, d. 03/04/1860

JOHNSON, Unicy A., w/o William, Age 61y 9m 10d, b. N/D, d. 08/05/1877

JOHNSON, Walter D., b. 1898, d. 1929

JOHNSON, William A., b. 08/27/1825, d. 05/20/1965

JOHNSON, William B., b. 06/11/1902, d. 06/01/1983

JOHNSON, William P., b. 10/03/1869, d. 01/05/1870

JOHNSON, William T., Age abt. 36y, b. N/D, d. 04/08/1877

KIRBY, James Wilmont, b. 11/15/1886, d. 03/27/1983

KIRBY, Sarah Jane, b. 05/30/1894, d. 01/10/1970

LEVERETT, Ruth A., b. 1928, d. 1986

M., E., b. N/D, d. 1935 [Located between H. M. & Mary E. Thompson]

M., H., b. 1931, d. 1933 [Located next to Mary Ellen Gantz & E. M.]

MARINELLI, Constantino V., b. 02/21/1906, d. 01/06/1985

MARINELLI, Hilda J., b. 09/24/1912, d. 09/25/1984

MCCALL, Blonnie V., b. 1925, d. N/D

MCCALL, John F., b. 07/04/1927, d. 11/02/1980

MILLER, Charles J., b. 10/29/1898, d. 07/04/1983

MILLER, Chester D., b. 1921, d. 1944

MILLER, Christina, b. 09/20/1901, d. 04/21/1978

MILLER, Nememiah, Age 87y, b. N/D, d. 11/09/1901

MILLER, Rosie E., b. 10/22/1885, d. 01/10/1982

MILLER, William T., b. 06/04/1884, d. 12/02/1952

MORRIS, Annie Mae, d/o John & Adeline, b. 09/09/1882, d. 10/01/1887

MORRIS, Arlenard, b. 1874, d. 1966

MORRIS, Baby, b. N/D, d. N/D

MORRIS, Bertha, Age 21y, b. N/D, d. 03/02/1908

MORRIS, Billy, b. 12/24/1928, d. 01/09/1994

MORRIS, Charley E., s/o John M. & Sarah, Age 25y 9m 22d, b. 09/19/1888, d. 06/05/1914

MORRIS, Clarence, b. 1887, d. 1964

MORRIS, David W., b. 1898, d. 1960

MORRIS, Edgar C., b. 1890, d. 1960

MORRIS, Elena V., b. 1936, d. 1962

MORRIS, Eliza J., b. 1904, d. 1972

MORRIS, Ellen G., b. 10/04/1920, d. 02/20/1968

MORRIS, Elmer L., b. 12/09/1902, d. 04/07/1980

MORRIS, Frances F., w/o Edward F., b. 12/27/1853, d. 12/06/1893

MORRIS, Harvey S., b. 04/03/1913, d. 04/18/1988

MORRIS, Ietia, b. N/D, d. N/D

MORRIS, Inf. o/Maggie & Wolsey, b. 03/12/1902, d. 03/13/1902

MORRIS, John W., b. 06/02/1847, d. 10/31/1930

MORRIS, Joseph L., b. 07/21/1924, d. N/D

MORRIS, Leonard E., s/o Arlenard & L. C., b. 03/27/1911, d. 09/21/1911

MORRIS, Leroy, b. 04/08/1895, d. 12/07/1971

MORRIS, Lydia, b. 1884, d. 1938

MORRIS, Mary L., b. 11/25/1914, d. 02/22/1995

MORRIS, Millie P., b. 02/19/1921, d. N/D

MORRIS, Noah O., b. 10/13/1916, d. 09/10/1991

MORRIS, Oscar S., b. 1914, d. 1965

MORRIS, Radia V., b. 02/27/1925, d. 12/11/1970

MORRIS, Sadie, b. 1894, d. 1968

MORRIS, Sallie, b. 1878, d. 1940

MORRIS, Sarah J., b. 1895, d. 1972

MORRIS, Thurston M., b. 07/04/1898, d. 04/12/1968

MORRIS, William T., b. 1897, d. 1936

MORRIS, Winston F., b. 1934, d. 1990

MOSLEY, Ardith, b. 07/27/1934, d. N/D

MOSLEY, Burton, b. 01/14/1879, d. 06/11/1960

MOSLEY, Carlton, b. 08/29/1909, d. 01/18/1942

MOSLEY, Edith R., b. 09/02/1912, d. 08/28/1970

MOSLEY, Eliza J., b. N/D, d. 11/16/1909

MOSLEY, Elmira, b. 04/24/1893, d. 06/10/1960

MOSLEY, Elnora, b. 08/02/1933, d. 08/07/1933

MOSLEY, George E., b. 03/13/1914, d. 04/27/1983

MOSLEY, George E., b. 1879, d. 1962

MOSLEY, Harry, b. 04/20/1873, d. 03/20/1951

MOSLEY, Maggie, b. 03/06/1883, d. 01/24/1961

MOSLEY, Maurice A., "Snooty," b. 08/15/1934, d. N/D

MOSLEY, Robert B., b. 01/05/1910, d. 09/17/1918

MOSLEY, Sarah A., b. 07/30/1888, d. 07/16/1965

MOSLEY, William, b. 10/13/1882, d. N/D
MOSLEY, William D., b. 10/11/1911, d. 06/10/1946
NORWOOD, Irene Hall, b. 09/07/1882, d. 10/29/1962
NORWOOD, Nancy, Age 55y, b. N/D, d. N/D
NORWOOD, Walter E., Son, b. 1871, d. 1930
PEEKINS, T. Roosevelt, b. 01/03/1897, d. 08/06/1992
POLK, Deliah, b. 08/28/1934, d. 01/09/1964
PRETTYMAN, James, b. N/D, d. 11/13/1928
PRETTYMAN, James E., b. 10/25/1884, d. 09/22/1900
PRETTYMAN, Nancy R., w/o James H., Age 68y, b. N/D, d. 08/29/1927
PRETTYMAN, William, b. N/D, d. 10/15/1937
R. C., Footstone, no other information (Located between Robert D. Street & Helen M. Best.)
REED, James H., b. 1922, d. 1978
S., H. I., No other information. [Located next to John W. Street]
S., M. C., Footstone only [Located between Catharine & John W. Street]
S., M. E., No other information
SAMMONS, George C., b. 12/01/1908, d. 07/17/1991
SHARPER, Joseph M., b. 11/17/1921, d. 02/03/1976
SHARPER, Margaret E., b. 11/10/1911, d. 02/14/1986
SHARPER, Martha E., b. 11/21/1886, d. 08/27/1949
SHELTON, Edith Mae, b. 07/27/1917, d. 04/10/1993
SHELTON, Idelia Hall, b. 11/22/1876, d. 05/30/1952
SHELTON, Isaac W., b. 10/14/1901, d. 11/13/1903
SHELTON, John, Sr., b. 1910, d. 1978
SHELTON, John P., b. 03/01/1878, d. 04/02/1962
SHELTON, Joseph, b. 1905, d. 1972
SHELTON, Roy J., b. 09/05/1900, d. 08/02/1971
SHELTON, Walter Simon, b. 04/09/1915, d. 10/22/1995
SMITH, D., b. 1908, d. 09/17/1958
SOCKUM, S. W., b. N/D, d. N/D
STEVENSON, Alphonso R., Sr., "Steve," b. 09/15/1917, d. 07/18/1987
STEVENSON, Daisy C., b. 09/04/1916, d. N/D
STEVENSON, Norman A., b. 11/26/1949, d. 10/16/1970
STEVENSON, William H. Book, b. 09/27/1952, d. 10/11/1988
STOCKLEY, Pearl S., b. 10/18/1912, d. 01/05/1992
STREET, Anna, w/o David, Age 41y 13d, b. N/D, d. 07/26/1850
STREET, Annie E., b. 1865, d. 1906
STREET, Baby, b. N/D, d. N/D
STREET, Benjamin A., b. 01/07/1925, d. 11/24/1989
STREET, Benton C., b. 1862, d. 1920
STREET, Catharine, b. 03/30/1801, d. 04/13/1868
STREET, Clarence A., b. 04/02/1897, d. 06/07/1980
STREET, Delema, b. 06/03/1924, d. 07/28/1995
STREET, Hattie, b. 09/07/1894, d. 11/30/1974
STREET, Hester I., d/o Theophilus & Sarah, Age 18y 3m 14d, b. N/D, d. 03/10/1884
STREET, John W., s/o Unicy M., Age 3m, b. N/D, d. 10/26/1829
STREET, Martha A., b. 10/07/1895, d. 03/25/1977
STREET, Melvin M., b. 06/29/1918, d. 01/01/1994

STREET, Minerva E., b. 01/09/1928, d. N/D
STREET, Richard, b. 11/20/1918, d. N/D
STREET, Robert D., b. 03/14/1893, d. 07/28/1894
STREET, William B., b. 10/25/1906, d. 11/21/1996
STREET, Wingate, b. 10/22/1890, d. 02/11/1979
STREET, Wingate S., Age 85y 10m 5d, b. N/D, d. N/D
THOMPSON, Annie Z., b. 11/29/1875, d. 12/27/1890
THOMPSON, Charles, b. 10/10/1902, d. 04/20/1978
THOMPSON, Frederick, b. 02/17/1889, d. 09/03/1913
THOMPSON, George C., Age 64y, b. N/D, d. 03/03/1920
THOMPSON, Hiram James, b. 10/30/1856, d. 10/06/1922
THOMPSON, Jeremiah, b. 02/10/1847, d. 08/04/1923
THOMPSON, John, b. 1877, d. 1945
THOMPSON, Josephine, w/o George C., Age 56y 6m 18d, b. 06/01/1856, d. 12/12/1912
THOMPSON, Leeyon, s/o William G. & Ella, b. 06/06/1902, d. 07/08/1905
THOMPSON, Mary E., b. 07/05/1883, d. 08/03/1965
THOMPSON, Mary E., w/o Jerry M., Age 61y, b. N/D, d. 08/28/1918
THOMPSON, Milsey, Age 93y, b. N/D, d. 09/18/1882
TINGLE, Josephine, b. 07/12/1846, d. 06/29/1914
UNKNOWN, Baby, b. N/D, d. 1917
UNKNOWN, NFN, b. N/D, d. 1891
WEEKS, Minty, b. 10/16/1837, d. 02/17/1922
WRIGHT, Ada W., b. 07/07/1914, d. 07/17/1979
WRIGHT, Arrie B., b. 1894, d. 1976
WRIGHT, Ayrie M., b. 03/12/1905, d. N/D
WRIGHT, Fannie Harmon, b. 05/28/1908, d. 11/12/1954
WRIGHT, Frederick, b. 07/12/1880, d. 10/04/1963
WRIGHT, Horace E., b. 1892, d. 1994
WRIGHT, Lawrence H., b. 07/05/1910, d. 08/15/1977
WRIGHT, Luvenia W., b. 05/15/1880, d. 07/23/1964
WRIGHT, Wilda G., b. 10/10/1928, d. 07/02/1946

(IR-004 & HU-NR) HARMAN FAMILY CEMETERY

Located East of Millsboro about 300 yards East of Layton Davis Rd. (Rd. 312A) 0.8 miles SE of John J. Williams Highway (Rt. 24).
Recorded: May 4, 1996

HARMAN, Ceathew, Age 1y 3m 20d, b. N/D, d. 01/27/1882
HARMAN, Daniel, Age 11m 15d, b. N/D, d. 09/22/1877
HARMAN, David, Age 9m 27d, b. N/D, d. 08/04/1877
HARMAN, Ephram L., Age 25y 6m 18d, b. N/D, d. 03/17/1890
HARMAN, Isaac, b. 10/27/1829, d. 04/23/1900
HARMAN, Sarah J., w/o Isaac, b. 08/27/1837, d. 02/19/1908

(IR-005 & HU-494) THOROUGHGOOD FAMILY CEMETERY
Located N. E. of Millsboro 250 yards N. W. of the intersection of Cordrey Rd. (Rd. 308) and William Street Rd. (Rd. 309).
Recorded: May 4, 1996 Revised February 21, 2013

THOROUGHGOOD, Annie E., d/o Simon W. & Sallie H., Age 8y 5m 3d, b. N/D, d. 12/14/1863
THOROUGHGOOD, Burton W., s/o Wm. N. & Sarah T., Age 38y 10m 23d, b. N/D, d. 10/21/1890
THOROUGHGOOD, Infant, b. N/D, d. N/D [Note: Stone broken – unreadable.]
THOROUGHGOOD, Laura B., d/o Simon W. & Sallie H., Age 18y 6m 16d, b. N/D, d. 06/30/1876
THOROUGHGOOD, Sallie H., w/o Simon W., Age 34y 7m 25d, b. N/D, d. 05/01/1867
THOROUGHGOOD, Sarah T., w/o William N., Age 73y, b. N/D, d. 12/03/1892
THOROUGHGOOD, Simon, Age 67y 6m 27d, b. 03/28/1831, d. 10/19/1898
THOROUGHGOOD, Wm. N., Age 61y 9m, b. N/D, d. 07/01/1876

The following stone was recorded by the Hudson Survey but is now missing or unreadable:
THOROUGHGOOD, Elihu, b. 05/17/1768, d. 04/11/1841

(IR-006 & HU-485) CRAIG-PRETTYMAN FAMILY CEMETERY
Located East of Millsboro, down a field road approximately, 0.5 mile from the south east side of Hollyville Rd. (Rd. 305) and 0.2 miles from Harmons Hill Rd. (Rd. 302).
Recorded: May 4, 1996

CRAIG, Betsey M., b. N/D, d. N/D
CRAIG, Eliza B., b. N/D, d. N/D
CRAIG, John L., b. N/D, d. N/D
CRAIG, Lydia B., his wife, b. N/D, d. N/D
CRAIG, Robert, b. N/D, d. N/D
CRAIG, William H., b. N/D, d. N/D
LINGO, William H., s/o Daniel & Catherine, Age 2m, b. N/D, d. 05/31/1816
PRETTYMAN, David M., Age in 60th y, b. N/D, d. 04/27/1875
PRETTYMAN, Lydia Ann, d/o David & Mary, Age 16y 11m 10d, b. N/D, d. 04/18/1865
PRETTYMAN, Mary C., w/o David M., Age 42y 1m 9d, b. N/D, d. 11/11/1859

(IR-007 & HU-NR) ALL SAINTS CEMETERY
Located South East of Harbeson, on the west side of Beaver Dam Rd. (Rd. 285) 1.6 miles north of Indian Mission Rd. (Rd. 5). Recorded: October 30, 1996

ABEL, David H., b. 02/13/1952, d. 06/09/1990
ABEL, Irene M., b. 04/23/1931, d. 08/27/1994
ABEL, John F., b. 06/24/1927, d. 03/10/1982
ADAMS, Alder Ross, ssw-Marguerite Deschamps, b. 02/29/1924, d. N/D
ADAMS, Marguerite "Mimi," Deschamps, ssw-Simone Helen, b. 11/11/1924, d. 12/30/1981
ADAMS, Simone Helen, ssw-Marguerity Deschamps, b. 02/22/1965, d. 02/23/1965
ALLEN, Frederic Burford, USMC, b. 10/22/1924, d. N/D
ALLEN, Jesse Wilson, b. 09/11/1903, d. 03/31/1976
ALLEN, Mildred Burford, b. 08/25/1904, d. 11/12/1980
ALLMAN, Henry H., ssw-Tacy Stokes, b. 06/30/1901, d. 07/18/1977
ALLMAN, Tacy Stokes, ssw-Henry H., b. 07/12/1905, d. 11/27/1975

ASHE, Alice Mildred, ssw-Paul Milton, b. 03/28/1877, d. 09/18/1981
ASHE, Paul Milton, ssw-Alice Mildred, b. 07/16/1897, d. 05/04/1979
BAILEY, Richard Slaght, b. 05/30/1915, d. 03/03/1992
BAKER, Esther Marsh, ssw-Franklin Thomas, b. 09/14/1921, d. N/D
BAKER, Franklin Thomas, ssw-Esther Marsh, TSgt., SAAC, WWII, b. 10/26/1913, d. 05/17/1996
BAKER, Kathaleen Wright, b. N/D, d. N/D
BAKER, Thomas Harding, b. 12/23/1903, d. 12/28/1978
BARTON, Emma Lee, ssw-Lewis Dempsey, b. 04/10/1924, d. 01/26/1984
BARTON, Lewis Dempsey, ssw-Emma Lee, b. 03/01/1911, d. 12/04/1990
BARTON, Lewis Dempsey, Jr., b. 05/12/1948, d. 03/13/1981
BATEMAN, Joseph L., b. 07/03/1926, d. N/D
BATEMAN, Mary Virginia, b. 09/03/1929, d. 10/29/1990
BEAN, Mildred Mitchell, b. 1891, d. 1971
BEAN, William S., Jr., TMC, USN, WWI, WWII, b. 10/23/1884, d. 07/16/1969
BEAN, William Stevens, b. 1861, d. 1942
BENNETT, Mildred E., ssw-Walter L., b. 1895, d. 1982
BENNETT, Walter L., ssw-Mildred E., b. 1891, d. 1970
BISHOP, G. Wayne, ssw-Helen Marie, b. 12/131923, d. N/D
BISHOP, Helen Marie, ssw-G. Wayne, b. 09/19/1921, d. 09/10/1991
BISHOP, Lillian L., ssw-Richard M., Sr., b. 08/27/1913, d. 10/04/1985
BISHOP, Richard M., Sr., ssw-Lillian L., b. 02/25/1907, d. 01/05/1985
BLIGHT, Catherine D., ssw-Edward S., b. 1900, d. 1969
BLIGHT, Edward S., ssw-Catherine D., b. 1906, d. 1977
BLIGHT, Patricia E., ssw-Samuel S., b. 1932, d. 1993
BLIGHT, Samuel S., ssw-Patricia E., b. 1933, d. N/D
BLUGERMAN, Leonid Nicholas, b. 05/25/1899, d. 02/07/1922
BLUGERMAN, Mary Roslee, b. 02/18/1909, d. 07//29/1987
BLUGERMAN, Robert Leonid, Maj., USA, b. 10/19/1937, d. 05/04/1978
BOWMAN, E. Eleanor Davis, ssw-Phillip M., Sr., b. 08/24/1929, d. 12/08/1994
BOWMAN, Phillip M., Sr., ssw-E. Eleanor Davis, b. 01/23/1932, d. 11/16/1994
BRADLEY, Elisabeth G., ssw-John L., b. 08/26/1907, d. 05/31/1984
BRADLEY, John L., ssw-Elisabeth G., b. 05/16/1904, d. 06/10/1994
BRINKLEY, Constance P., ssw-Lemuel W., b. 03/19/1918, d. N/D
BRINKLEY, Lemuel W., ssw-Constance P., b. 08/30/1915, d. 07/04/1986
BROCKWAY, Douglas W., Jr., b. 04/07/1969, d. 10/15/1987
BRYN, Anna Mary, ssw-Sigmund Grilstad, Born in Cynthiana, Kentucky, b. 1904, d. N/D
BRYN, Sigmund Grilstad, ssw-Anna Mary, Born in Oslo, Norway, b. 1899, d. 1982
BUCK, Dorothy S., b. 1896, d. 1974
BUCK, Frank H., b. 1892, d. 1971
BUCKMASTER, Edna P., ssw-Leslie W., b. 1893, d. 1983
BUCKMASTER, Leslie W., ssw-Edna P., b. 1881, d. 1969
BURKE, James R., ssw-Philominia C., b. 01/02/1891, d. 06/30/1967
BURKE, Philominia C., ssw-James R., b. 09/05/1888, d. 08/02/1965
CALDWELL, Marie F., b. 03/22/1907, d. 06/18/1985
CAMPBELL, Evelyn M., ssw-John W., b. 08/04/1907, d. 09/04/1988
CAMPBELL, John W., ssw-Evelyn M., b. 07/07/1902, d. 03/08/1987
CARD, Ruth E. L., b. 10/09/1943, d. 05/08/1991
CARPENTER, Ron, b. 08/23/1935, d. 12/26/1982. Children: Jewell, Sharon, Kenneth & Ronald

CASE, George E., MD, S1, USNR, WWII, b. 09/25/1926, d. 01/14/1968

CHACONAS, John James, Cpl., USN, WWII, b. 06/20/1918, d. 09/27/1993

CHACONAS, Constance, b. 07/06/1954, d. 01/14/1974

CHALLENGER, Dorothy B., ssw-John F., b. 1900, d. 1991

CHALLENGER, John F., ssw-Dorothy B., b. 1897, d. 1984

CLARK, Arthur G., b. 10/06/1928, d. 02/19/1995

COHAN, Sydney A., b. 1912, d. 1956

COLLINS, Lorraine M., ssw-Thomas, b. 05/23/1910, d. 06/26/1974

COLLINS, Thomas, ssw-Lorraine M., b. 10/04/1902, d. 02/20/1974

COMPTON, Lenore C., b. 08/03/1894, d. 08/22/1994

COMPTON, Nancy Devan, b. 12/20/1921, d. 01/31/1978

COMPTON, Robert Sayre, b. 02/18/1922, d. 09/11/1972

COVELESKI, Frank L., b. 1917, d. 1977

COVERDALE, Martha E., ssw-Miles E., b. 05/30/1912, d. 07/27/1995

COVERDALE, Miles E., ssw-Martha E., b. 03/01/1911, d. N/D

COVIELLO, Betty, ssw-Patrick F., b. 1932, d. 1980

COVIELLO, Patrick F., ssw-Betty, Sgt., USMC, Korea, b. 04/22/1932, d. 06/29/1995

CRAEMER, Florence Colclough, ssw-Raymond Charles, b. N/D, d. 03/20/1992

CRAEMER, Raymond Charles, ssw-Florence Colclough, b. N/D, d. 11/06/1980

CRAFT, Dorothy C., ssw-Herbert C., b. 1888, d. 1977

CRAFT, Herbert C., ssw-Dorothy C., b. 1888, d. 1947

CRAFT, Naon J., ssw-Herbert C., b. 1915, d. N/D

CRANE, Harold T., b. 1913, d. 1995

CRISFIELD, Arthur Woodland, ssw-Kathleen Goodloe, b. 11/08/1900, d. 08/21/1986

CRISFIELD, Kathleen Goodloe, ssw-Arthur Woodland, b. 07/18/1902, d. N/D

CROOK, Carolyn Blight, b. 12/02/1902, d. 06/28/1989

CROWLEY, Eleanor Townsend, ssw-Joseph John, b. 04/20/1922, d. 07/19/1978

CROWLEY, Joseph John, ssw-Eleanor Townsend, b. 09/02/1921, d. N/D

CUNNINGHAM, Jo White, b. 12/03/1911, d. 04/30/1980

CUNNINGHAM, William H., LCDR, USN, WWII, b. 06/28/1911, d. 04.23.1983

CURREY, Anna K., b. 07/12/1926, d.10/22/1988

CURTIS, Glenna Esther, ssw-Ralph William, b. 09/09/1922, d. 04/26/1994

CURTIS, Ralph William, ssw-Glenna Esther, b. 10/06/1920, d. N/D

DAVENPORT, Frances A., ssw-Frank J., b. N/D, d. N/D

DAVENPORT, Frank J., ssw-Frances A., b. N/D, d. N/D

DAVIS, Anna K., ssw-Clifford Smith, Sister, b. 07/04/1911, d. 10/28/1994

DAVIS, Clifford Smith, ssw-Anna K., Brother, b. 10/15/1915, d. N/D

DAVIS, Elizabeth A. ssw-Thurston Kenneth, b. 08/04/1910, d. N/D

DAVIS, Thurston Kenneth, ssw-Elizabeth A., b. 08/28/1907, d. 04/20/1988

DAWSON, Ella Jacquot, ssw-Ralph, b. 09/09/1901, d. 01/28/1990

DAWSON, Ralph, ssw-Ella Jacquot, WWI, b. 07/15/1899, d. 02/15/1983

DEPPE, Charles T., Sr., m. 10/25/1944, TSgt., USMC, WWII, b. 03/18/1921, d. 07/28/1993

DEPPE, Ruth M., m. 10/25/1944, b. 09/22/1923, d. N/D

DIAMOND, Mary Elizabeth, ssw-Mary Elizabeth, II, b. N/D, d. N/D

DIAMOND, Mary Elizabeth, II, ssw-Robert Stafford, b. 1962, d. 1984

DIAMOND, Robert Stafford, ssw-Mary Elizabeth, II, b. N/D, d. N/D

DICK, John Redstreake, ssw-Lena Rebecca, b. 01/25/1900, d. 11/09/1974

DICK, Lena Rebecca, ssw-John Redstreake, b. 02/10/1897, d. 11/21/1984

DICKINSON, Eldred Given, ssw-Norfleet Dunlop, b. 1905, d. 1987

DICKINSON, Norfleet Dunlop, ssw-Eldred Given, b. 1908, d. 1973

DIFFENDERFER, J. Bruce, ssw-Mary Elisabeth, b. 11/20/1906, d. 10/20/1989

DIFFENDERFER, Mary Elisabeth, ssw-J. Bruce, b. 07/11/1910, d. N/D

DILCER, Frances M., ssw-Maude S., b. 1900, d. 1980

DILCER, Maude S., ssw-Frances M., b. 1906, d. 1981

DIVVER, Anne O'Toole, ssw-Paul Belton, b. 1929, d. N/D

DIVVER, Paul Belton, ssw-Anne O'Toole, b. 1928, d. 1988

DODGE, Marion Ruckman, b. 06/03/1928, d. 05/24/1966

DOLAN, James J., ssw-Jayne A., b. 01/12/1921, d. 07/21/1990

DOLAN, Jayne A., ssw-James J., b. 07/05/1921, d. 09/18/1985

DOUD, Philip D., b. 01/26/1939, d. 06/12/1992

DOUGALL, James L., Capt., USA, WWII, b. 03/02/1900, d. 05/11/1980

DOUGHERTY, Rachel Townsend, b. 04/13/1970, d. 04/26/1970

DOUGLAS, Dave, b. 01/01/1918, d. 11/16/1978

DOUGLAS, Evelyn E., b. 1970, d. 1996

DRAPER, Dorothy Dickerson, b. 10/07/1917, d. 10/29/1989

DRAPER, George H., III, b. 10/25/1917, d. 09/19/1990

DREW, Evelyn Blight, b. 06/04/1900, d. 07/30/1975

DUNN, Carolyn Wortendyke, b. 09/21/1900, d. 03/25/1981

DUNN, Talbot Wortendyke, b. 12/25/1940, d. 03/08/1959

DUNN, Talbot Bedell, b. 09/04/1843, d. 07/04/1963

EGAN, Roberta C., ssw-William R., b. 1914, d. 1993

EGAN, William R., ssw-Roberta C., b. 1914, d. 1964

EMMERT, David Guy, b. 02/09/1926, d. 10/30/1982

ENNIS, Anne Kelly, b. 02/27/1888, d. 03/27/1962

ENNIS, Howard T., b. 07/17/1889, d. 06/19/1972

ENNIS, John H., USA, WWII, b. 05/06/1921, d. 03/28/1988

FAIVRE, Frances C., ssw-Victor W., b. 10/16/1904, d. 04/13/1983

FAIVRE, Victor W., ssw-Frances C., b. 05/23/1911, d. 06/21/1994

FERRARI, Maria, b. 05/28/1912, d. 09/11/1993

FILLIUS, Helen H., ssw-Mary S. Henning, b. 1882, d. 1963

FISHER, Anna Wilson, ssw-DeWitt, b. N/D, d. N/D

FISHER, DeWitt, ssw-Anna Wilson, CDR, USN, WWI, WWII, b. 01/02/1898, d. 04/21/1990

FLAHERTY, Gerald L., ssw-Rachel E., b. 07/14/1924, d. 05/25/1988

FLAHERTY, Rachel E., ssw-Gerald L., b. 10/17/1925, d. N/D

FLATT, Brian Charles, s/o Karen & John, b. 12/11/1972, d. 12/11/1972

FLATT, Christopher Howell, s/o Karen & John, b. 08/25/1971, d. 10/08/1971

FORMICHELLA, Gene A., S1, USN, WWII, b. 02/01/1925, d. 06/08/1991

FORSYTH, Edwin F., b. 1903, d. 1964

FREAR, Allison Louise, b. 03/05/1961, d. 03/23/1985

FRENCH, Mary E., ssw-Stella W., b. 1915, d. 1979

FRENCH, Stella W., ssw-Mary E., b. 1895, d. 1976

GALE, Enoch R., Jr., ssw-Ruth M., b. 07/24/1903, d. 08/22/1992

GALE, Ruth M., ssw-Enoch R., Jr., b. 08/02/1907, d. 04/20/1981

GALLAGHER, Wallise, ssw-Richard C. Rhoades, b. 04/12/1904, d. 11/24/1983

GELDER, Charlotte Walton, b. 05/02/1914, d. 04/18/1979

GIBSON, Baby, b. 08/28/1971, d. 08/28/1971

GOODRICH, Beulah Lenfest, ssw-Edgar Jennings, b. 07/20/1896, d. 11/11/1986
GOODRICH, Edgar Jennings, ssw-Beulah Lenfest, b. 11/15/1896, d. 04/10/1969
GOODY, John William, b. 1909, d. 1982
GOODY, Phyllis Burton, b. 1911, d. 1977
GRAHAM, James Butler, ssw-Louise N., b. 1922, d. 1996
GRAHAM, Louise N., ssw-James Butler, b. 1925, d. N/D
GRAHAM, Milton E., ssw-Sara B., b. 01/13/1895, d. 07/18/1949
GRAHAM, Sara B., ssw-Milton E., b. 06/27/1894, d. 12/24/1970
GRANTHAM, Dolores M., ssw-Larry, b. 08/26/1929, d. N/D
GRANTHAM, Larry, ssw-Dolores M., b. 08/08/1925, d. 06/07/1987
GRAVIET, Clifford M., USN, HMC, b. 1920, d. 1980
GRAVIET, Kathleen E., b. 1956, d. 1976
GRAVIET, Kathryn E., b. 1924, d. 1987
GRENOBLE, Catherine Blanche, w/oWinfield Scott & d/o Cyrus & Clara Moore, ssw-Winfield Scott,
        b. 11/10/1890, d. 03/08/1978
GRENOBLE, Winfield Scott, h/o Catherine Blanche, ssw-Catherine Blanche, Maj., USQM Corp., Interred
        Gettysburg National Cemetery, b. 11/15/1880, d. 12/02/1961
GRIEVES, Ethel R., ssw-Harry M., b. 03/14/1894, d. 11/10/1972
GRIEVES, Harry M., ssw-Ethel R., b. 10/31/1892, d. 06/11/1974
GUENVEUR, Jane T., b. 01/25/1918, d. 11/30/1969
GUNDRY, Alice P., ssw-Jesse K. H., b. 1903, d. 1980
GUNDRY, Jesse K. H., ssw-Alice P., b. 1902, d. 1979
HABIG, Paul G., ssw-Rosalie, b. 01/14/1923, d. N/D
HABIG, Rosalie, ssw-Paul G., b. 05/16/1923, d. 07/24/1988
HALE, Mary Proctor, ssw-Ernest W. & Mary S. Proctor, b. 1896, d. 1981
HALL, Anna Hartman, ssw-William Gilbert, b. 10/16/1925, d. N/D
HALL, Barbara, ssw-Ralph Emmons, Jr., b. 09/14/1941, d. N/D
HALL, Carolyn Ann, ssw-William Gilbert, b. 02/05/1959, d. 02/27/1959
HALL, Dorothy Murphy, ssw-Ralph Emmons, b. 12/21/1900, d. 10/08/1993
HALL, Helen Santo, ssw-Robert Murphy, b. 05/05/1927, d. N/D
HALL, Ralph Emmons, ssw-Dorothy Murphy, b. 02/28/1885, d. 05/02/1961
HALL, Ralph Emmons, Jr., ssw-Barbara, b. 11/20/1931, d. N/D
HALL, Robert Murphy, ssw-Helen Santo, b. 08/09/1927, d. 11/29/1976
HALL, William Gilbert, ssw-Anna Hartman, b. 01/14/1924, d. 02/21/1996
HAMILTON, Jane P., "Polly," ssw-Russell D., b. 05/14/1932, d. 01/28/1989
HAMILTON, Russell D., ssw-Jane P., b. 05/076/1928, d. 02/13/1994
HAMILTON, Sara Chandler, ssw-Russell D., b. 10/04/1894, d. 11/18/1993
HANBY, Frances Cross, b. 12/28/1917, d. N/D
HANBY, Victor Dure, Jr., b. 01/12/1913, d. 03/14/1981
HANNAGAN, James F., AM1, USN, WWII, b. 03/14/1922, d. 07/28/1987
HEARN, Danielle Christian, b. 04/14/1984, d. 07/21/`1984
HENNING, Carl S., ssw-Marion D., b. 1880, d. 1956
HENNING, Marion D., ssw-Carl S., b. 1897, d. 1989
HENNING, Mary S., ssw-Helen H. Fillius, b. 1860, d. 1943
HENNING, Ruth P., b. 1898, d. 1963
HENNING, William F., b. 1890, d. 1961
HOLMGREN, Curtis E., b. 1920, d. 1959
HOLSON, A. Kathryn, b. 11/06/1923, d. 04/27/1989

HOLSON, Edward Orlando, SSgt, WWII, b. 11/07/1923, d. 06/24/1962

HOLSON, Joann, b. 11/30/1941, d. 11/22/1992

HOOPER, Charles, III, b. 10/20/1949, d. 03/05/1992

HORN, Allassie B., ssw-Charles S., Jr., b. 1899, d. 1985

HORN, Charles S., Jr., ssw-Allassie B., b. 1899, d. 1975

HORST, Louise, b. 04/13/1904, d. 11/05/1995

HUNTLEY, Howard White, b. 1887, d. 1963

HYDE, Lila M., b. 11/29/1890, d. 05/05/1974

IDE, Laurence Edward, ssw-Naomi Weaver Alexander, b. 05/03/1909, d. N/D

IDE, Naomi Weaver Alexander, ssw-Laurence Edward, b. 09/26/1907, d. 01/12/1996

JACK, Robert William, II, ssw-Ruth Wood, b. 10/14/1908, d. N/D

JACK, Ruth Wood, ssw-Robert William, II, b. 09/08/1910, d. 07/07/1986

JACKSON, Charlotte Bramble, b. 08/13/1895, d. 02/22/1980

JACKSON, Irving Lester, b. 12/09/1896, d. 09/24/1980

JAFFREY, Florence Wilson, b. 10/19/1891, d. 01/08/1978

JEGLUM, Jack Boylan, b. 03/31/1917, d. 05/18/1970

JENKINS, Barbara M., ssw-Bruce Ashley, b. 08/15/1923, d. 07/06/1993

JENKINS, Bruce Ashley, ssw-Barbara M., b. 11/09/1922, d. N/D

JOHNCOX, Clifford Francis, ssw-Vera Lacy, b. 09/11/1904, d. 08/21/1985

JOHNCOX, Vera Lacy, ssw-Clifford Francis, b. 10/18/1909, d. 12/07/1984

JOHNSTON, Willard J., b. 03/11/1913, d. 11/25/1980

JONES, Edward G. P., Sea 2, USN, WWI, b. 02/21/1899, d. 02/28/1984

JONES, James Merrill, ssw-Lenore King, b. 07/01/1914, d. N/D

JONES, Lenore King, ssw-James Merrill, b. 07/22/1912, d. 09/22/1977

JONES, Martha Tikob, b. N/D, d. 01/13/1974

KEIPER, Frederick Warren, Capt., USA, WWII, b. 05/31/1917, d. 02/15/1986

KELLETT, Fred, b. 1903, d. 1963

KEMPER, Charles F., ssw-Evadne J., b. 10/06/1891, d. 07/01/1961

KEMPER, Evadne J., ssw-Charles F., b. 09/12/1897, d. 04/05/1987

KENNEDY, John J., b. 11/14/1920, d. 02/18/1991

KER, Henry L., ssw-Mary M., b. 01/17/1914, d. 01/06/1990

KER, Mary M., ssw-Henry L., b. 08/16/1913, d. 07/19/1982

KEWLEY, Mary E., ssw-Thomas H., b. 08/26/1916, d. N/D

KEWLEY, Thomas H., ssw-Mary E., b. 07/04/1911, d. 05/30/1992

KINGMAN, Edward R., ssw-Margaret N., Capt., USN, b. 1917, d. N/D

KINGMAN, Margaret N., ssw-Edward R., Ensign, USNR, b. 1923, d. 1988

KINTER, Susan B., b. 09/25/1911, d. 02/06/1981

KNOTTS, Grace J., b. 03/10/1909, d. N/D

KNOTTS, James T., Jr., b. 09/19/1903, d. 12/29/1993

KRAMEDAS, John, b. 03/18/1933, d. 03/10/1985

KRAMEDAS, Margaret A. Neilen, b. 06/27/1901, d. 06/09/1989

KRAMER, Murray W., 2nd Lt., USA, b. 02/19/1918, d. 01/31/1983

KUSIK, Victor, (Priest), b. 09/18/1926, d. 08/03/1983

LAFFERTY, Emma Eisele, ssw-Rudolph Straube, b. 04/25/1899, d. N/D

LAFFERTY, Helen Morton, b. 10/26/1905, d. 06/28/1974

LAFFERTY, Mervyn Lewis, b. 09/28/1899, d. 03/05/1970

LAFFERTY, Mervyn Lewis, Jr., b. 1934, d. 1984

LAFFERTY, Rudolph Straube, ssw-Emma Eisele, b. 04/29/1899, d. 01/19/1993

LAMERE, Eugene W., ssw-Gertrude B., b. 1920, d. N/D
LAMERE, Gertrude B., ssw-Eugene W., b. 1919, d. 1985
LAMPIE, Marion H. Smith, b. 09/16/1919, d. 01/09/1987
LANK, Florence M., ssw-William D., b. 1904, d. 1992
LANK, William D., ssw-Florence M., b. 1897, d. 1992
LAWVER, Charles Waters, 1st Lt., USA, WWII, b. 11/29/1912, d. 01/05/1978
LAYTON, Caleb Rodney, ssw-Marie Brooke, b. 07/04/1907, d. 05/06/1988
LAYTON, Daniel John, Jr., ssw-June McDermott, b. 07/02/1910, d. 08/04/1963
LAYTON, June McDermott, ssw-Daniel John, Jr., b. 12/06/1923, d. 03/23/1979
LAYTON, Marie Brooke, ssw-Caleb Rodney, b. 06/20/1911, d. 10/05/1991
LEACH, Mary Hall, ssw-Sanford Burdette, b. 11/16/1909, d. 04/27/1996
LEACH, Sanford Burdette, ssw-Mary Hall, b. 03/08/1907, d. 08/22/1995
LECATO, Esther V., ssw-John M., b. 1889, d.1979
LECATO, John M., ssw-Esther V., b. 1889, d. 1969
LEE, Ralph W., Jr., b. 05/08/1899, d. 12/04/1976
LEE, Sarah Elizabeth Chase, b. 07/06/1904, d. 08/27/1983
LEHMAN, Franklin Alexander, b. 11/12/1973, d. 11/17/1973
LEHMAN, Robert Armstrong, b. 04/20/1911, d. 07/01/1974
LEWIS, Betty V., ssw-Howard, b. 1929, d. 1985
LEWIS, Howard, ssw-Betty V., b. 1927, d. 1996
LICHTENSTEIN, Evelyn N., ssw-Victor, b. 09/25/1907, d. N/D
LICHTENSTEIN, Victor, ssw-Evelyn N., b. 10/24/1904, d. 02/20/1995
LIGHTHIPE, Harold Hoagland, ssw-Mary Ansley Short, b. 11/03/1909, d. N/D
LIGHTHIPE, Harold Hoagland, Jr., ssw-Harold Hoagland, b. 01/23/1951, d. 01/05/1988
LIGHTHIPE, Mary Ansley Short, ssw-Harold Hoagland, b. 03/15/1917, d. N/D
LINGO, Amy Elizabeth, d/o John & Carol, b. 11/21/1970, d. 04/14/1974
LINGO, Beatrice, b. 08/12/1904, d. 08/26/1981
LINGO, Clarence N., b. 02/24/1928, d. 01/07/1989
LINGO, Derrick Oliver, ssw-Martha Boyd, b. 07/20/1901, d. 10/10/1977
LINGO, Eleanor W., ssw-William H., b. 01/24/1915, d. N/D
LINGO, June Elizabeth, ssw-Kenneth King, b. 08/26/1927, d. 01/30/1988
LINGO, Kenneth King, ssw-June Elizabeth, b. 06/16/1928, d. 04/08/1976
LINGO, Martha Boyd, ssw-Derrick Oliver, b. 06/18/1902, d. 11/21/1982
LINGO, Norma Lee, b. 08/23/1931, d. N/D
LINGO, William H., ssw-Eleanor W., b. 11/19/1914, d. 08/02/1981
LINK, William J., TSgt., USA, WWII, b. 03/29/1919, d. 11/17/1982
LOFLAND, Joyce Fay, b. 09/09/1966, d. N/D
LOWDEN, Henry M., ssw-Jean B., Capt., USA, WWII, b. 11/01/1903, d. 01/28/1982
LOWDEN, Jean B., ssw-Henry M., b. 10/14/1913, d. 12/02/1991
LUDWIG, Helen Holder, ssw-John N., Jr., b. 02/04/1894, d. 03/25/1976
LUDWIG, John N., Jr., ssw-Helen Holder, b.10/08/1891, d. 04/05/1972
LYNCH, Edda G., ssw-Robert T., b. 11/18/1918, d. 08/08/1986
LYNCH, Robert T., ssw-Edda G., b. 10/05/1910, d. N/D
LYON, Dorothy B., b. 07/25/1909, d. 02/13/1970
MAHONEY, Harriet A., ssw-Joseph R., b. 1915, d. 1987
MAHONEY, Joseph R., ssw-Harriet A., b. 1914, d. 1990
MARKIEWICZ, Leon, ssw-Ruth N., b. 12/21/1923, d. N/D
MARKIEWICZ, Ruth N., ssw-Leon, b. 09/22/1922, d. 06/14/1986

MARTIN, Elizabeth Hall, b. 07/19/1909, d. 02/17/1979

MARVEL, Hugh, ssw-Ruth Lanning, b. 03/02/1914, d. 04/13/1991

MARVEL, Ruth Lanning, ssw-Hugh, b. 04/18/1931, d. N/D

MARVIL, Comfort Ingram, ssw-James Edward, b. 08/26/1910, d. 08/24/1982

MARVIL, James Edward, M.D., ssw-Comfort Ingram, b. 03/02/1904, d. 01/23/1996

MASSEY, Francis A., BMC, USCG, WWII, b. 04/27/1907, d. 05/30/1983

MASSEY, Mildred R., b. 05/18/1908, d. 09/02/1994

MAYNADIER, Helen L., w/o Seton M., b. 08/24/1909, d. 11/09/1981

MAYNADIER, Seton M., b. 03/31/1901, d. 06/16/1973

MCDERMOTT, Marguerite Davis, w/o Matthew James, ssw-Matthew James, b. 06/13/1891, d. 01/02/1976

MCDERMOTT, Matthew James, ssw-Marguerite Davis, b. 09/30/1888, d. 12/04/1974

MCKINNEY, Frances A., ssw-James R., b. 06/17/1941, d. N/D

MCKINNEY, James R., ssw-Frances A., b. 04/27/1940, d. 04/05/1983

MCMANUS, John A., b. 1910, d. 1966

MCNEIL, Clarid Fee, ssw-Francis Catherine, b. 1908, d. 1992

MCNEIL, Francis Catherine, ssw-Clarid Fee, b. 1910, d. 1992

MCNEILLY, Mary Helen McDermott, w/o John Jere McNeilly, b. 08/10/1925, d. 02/23/1980

MCWILLIAMS, Lora F., b. 11/06/1897, d. 09/06/1977

MCWILLIAMS, William A., USA, WWI, WWII, b. 1899, d. 1977

MENNELLA, William A., b. 03/23/1951, d. 02/22/1993

MEYERS, Grace V., ssw-Lester A., b. 12/13/1925, d. N/D

MEYERS, Lester A., ssw-Grace V., b. 01/28/1930, d. N/D

MIFFLIN, Eleanor D., b. 05/10/1922, d. 04/14/1987

MIFFLIN, James Edward, 1st Lt. USA, WWII, b. 06/20/1915, d. 09/18/1985

MILLER, Archie L., ssw-Ocia, b. 04/21/1895, d. 12/17/1975

MILLER, Marybelle Dick, b. 11/29/1898, d. 05/09/1994

MILLER, Ocia, ssw-Archie L., b. 06/01/1902, d. 08/06/1970

MILLER, William, b. 04/26/1887, d. 02/03/1969

MILLS, Charles Wilson, ssw-Mary Esther, b. 1901, d. 1993

MILLS, Mary Esther, ssw-Charles Wilson, b. 1897, d. 1993

MONTE, John David, ssw-Mariko Taeko, b. 03/27/1930, d. 08/11/1996

MONTE, Mariko Taeko, ssw-John David, b. 02/16/1934, d. N/D

MOORE, Florence Darlington, ssw-Leon Greene, b. 06/24/1895, d. 12/22/1988

MOORE, Leon Greene, ssw-Florence Darlington, b. 10/13/1893, d. 01/28/1966

MOOTZ, Eric Andrew, b. 1959, d. 1959

MORGAN, Henry Williams, Jr., ssw-Theodora Polk Pyle, m. 06/13/1928 at VMI, b. 07/14/1903,
        d. 04/15/1967

MORGAN, Theodora Polk Pyle, ssw-Henry Williams, Jr., m. 06/13/1928 at VMI, b. 04/27/1905,
        d. 12/10/1991

MORRIS, Berton Edward, b. 10/24/1914, d. 02/27/1974

MUNCY, Carolyn Elaine, ssw-Thomas Walter, b. 10/06/1930, d. N/D

MUNCY, Thomas Walter, ssw-Carolyn Elaine, b. 11/14/1923, d. 10/23/1988

MURPHY, J. Edward, b. 12/01/1900, d. 03/05/1984

NAYLOR, Jane Hind, b. 10/16/1878, d. 03/26/1964

NELTE, Linda T., w/o Frank M. Nelte, Jr., b. 05/30/1930, d. 07/11/1984

NICHOLS, Lewis Ray, Cpl., USA, Korea, b. 06/08/1928, d. 07/22/1994

O'LEARY, Marguerite M., b. 03/01/1890, d. 10/14/1984

O'NEILL, Paul A., ssw-Dorothy T., Capt., USA, WWII, b. 06/23/1912, d. 03/24/1984

O'NEILL, Dorothy T., ssw-Paul A., b. 12/07/1916, d. N/D

OGONOWSKI, Catherine M., ssw-Joseph A., m. 07/03/1941, b. 08/16/1917, d. 03/23/1996

OGONOWSKI, Joseph A., ssw-Catherine M., m. 07/03/1941, b. 03/19/1917, d. N/D

ORTON, Lewes D., ssw-Madeline S., b. 1906, d. 1984

ORTON, Madeline S., ssw-Lewes D., b. 1906, d. 1982

OWENS, Charles Allen, Jr., b. 01/21/1907, d. 03/03/1987

OWENS, Laura Lee Corley, b. 09/11/1909, d. 12/07/1991

PACHIDES, Theo, ssw-Thomas, b. 05/15/1897, d. 01/12/1999

PACHIDES, Thomas, ssw-Theo, b. 01/18/1891, d. 01/23/1984

PAYNE, Robert H., Lt., USCG, WWII, b. 08/24/1912, d. 01/23/1982

PEARSON, Charles Edgar, ssw-Elizabeth Kirkbride, USNR, WWI, b. 12/11/1872, d. 06/27/1958

PEARSON, Elizabeth Kirkbride, ssw-Charles Edgar, b. 1876, d. 1961

PENNIMAN, Lenore C., b. 04/12/1924, d. 04/28/1980

PENNIMAN, William T., Jr., b. 03/24/1920, d. 01/20/1992

PERRY, Marjorie H., b. 11/14/1913, d. 01/10/1980

PHILLIPS, John Trump, ssw-Mildred, b. 08/28/1912, d. 02/22/1968

PHILLIPS, Mildred, "Smitty," ssw-John Trump, b. 09/04/1918, d. 05/19/1991

PICHILLI, Mary, ssw-Natale, b. 1903, d. 1978

PICHILLI, Natale, ssw-Mary, b. 1895, d. 1981

PONDER, Jane Clark, b. 1917, d. N/D

PONDER, Lula McDowell, ssw-William Hungerford, b. 1884, d. N/D

PONDER, William Hungerford, ssw-Lula McDowell, b. 1884, d. 1959

PONDER, William McDowell, b. 1913, d. 1969

POULTERER, Betty B., ssw-William T., Jr., b. 02/02/1915, d. N/D

POULTERER, William T., Jr., ssw-Betty B., Lt. Col., USA, WWII, b. 01/13/1909, d. 02/26/1993

PRENGER, James P., ssw-Mary Irene, b. 09/27/1919, d. N/D

PRENGER, Mary Irene, ssw-James P., b. 06/23/1920, d. N/D

PROCTOR, Ernest W., ssw Mary S., b. 1874, d. 1963

PROCTOR, Harry Evans, ssw-Margaret W., b. 11/29/1905, d. 04/18/1979

PROCTOR, Margaret W., ssw-Harry Evans, b. 11/26/1907, d. N/D

PROCTOR, Mary S., ssw-Ernest W., b. 1870, d. 1942

QUILLEN, Dorothy C., b. 05/03/1902, d. 03/24/1980

QUIMBY, Ellen Boyd, ssw-Frederick Davis, b. 05/13/1908, d. 04/27/1971

QUIMBY, Frederick Davis, ssw-Ellen Boyd, b. 07/18/1910, d. 11/19/1964

RATLEDGE, Baby Boy, b. 12/19/1960, d. 12/25/1960

RATLEDGE, Donald S., Cpl., USA, Korea, b. 06/07/1931, d.04/27/1982

RHOADES, Richard C., ssw-Wallise Gallagher, b. 05/09/1907, d. 01/14/1995

RICHESON, Hughe, b. 07/02/1907, d. 07/04/1988

RICHESON, Marjorie M., b. 11/25/1913, d. N/D

RIGGIN, George Hall, M. D., b. 04/07/1879, d. 12/22/1962

RIGGIN, Sarah Elizabeth, b. 03/07/1889, d. 01/20/1966

RILEY, Edgar Heisler, ssw-Lila Stevenson, b. 1893, d. 1982

RILEY, Lila Stevenson, ssw-Edgar Heisler, b. 1894, d. 1986

RITCHIE, Carl L., ssw-Helen M., Pfc., USA, WWI, b. 02/13/1897, d. 03/23/1984

RITCHIE, Helen M., ssw-Carl L., b. 05/19/1902, d. 12/26/1991

ROBERTS, William Ashton, M. D., b. 07/31/1900, d. 02/09/1978

ROCHELEAU, Robert F., Capt., USA, WWII, b. 12/28/1920, d. 02/24/1991

ROSEMARY, Urban D., USN, WWII, b. 02/29/1924, d. 08/06/1993

ROSS, Clarence A., Cdr., USN, WWII, b. 08/31/1899, d.04/22/1992
ROWE, Jeffry C., Cpl., USMC, b. 11/12/1951, d. 02/08/1994
RUCKMAN, John Hamilton, ssw-Mary Armstrong, Col., USA, WWI, WWII, b. 08/03/1888, d. 08/10/1966
RUCKMAN, Mary Armstrong, ssw-John Hamilton, b. 10/26/1896, d. 09/04/1966
RUSSELL, Edward J. C., Born in England, b. 09/25/1905, d. 06/08/1978
RUSSELL, Minna G., Born in England, b. 12/06/1908, d. 04/09/1991
RUTHERFORD, Dorothy C., b. 1908, d. 1983
RUTHERFORD, Dorothy Q., ssw-William, Jr., b. 05/09/1916, d. 02/27/1989
RUTHERFORD, William, Jr., ssw-William H., b. 11/08/1941, d. N/D
RUTHERFORD, William H., ssw-William, Jr., b. 07/04/1906, d. 08/22/1983
SAULSBURY, Anne Roe, ssw-James Keene, b. 1900, d. 1987
SAULSBURY, James Keene, ssw-Anne Roe, b. 1899, d. 1972
SAVOY, Jean Dawson, ssw-Ralph Dawson, b. 03/25/1929, d. N/D
SAVOY, Lyla Townsend, b. 08/27/1894, d. 07/29/1983
SAVOY, Prew, II, ssw-Ralph Dawson, b. 11/11/1928, d. N/D
SCHLUMPF, Katherine M., b. 10/04/1930, d. 07/11/1996
SCHREIBER, William, b. 1928, d. 1996
SCHULER, Eric Tristan, ssw-Melitta Eugenie, b. 09/09/1901, d. 01/14/1989
SCHULER, Melitta Eugenie, ssw-Eric Tristan, b. 12/04/1907, d. 02/08/1995
SEIDLE, N. Robert, Lt. Col., USA, WWII, b. 06/20/1910, d. 12/30/1978
SEIDLE, Virginia M., b.1911, d. N/D
SELDEN, Albert A., b. 1888, d. 1973
SHAW, Benjamin Franklin, b. 05/18/1908, d. 07/01/1974
SHAW, Lillian Louise Bell, b. 09/21/1912, d. 10/08/1990
SHORT, Vula Morton, b. 04/09/1906, d. 06/10/1967
SHUPARD, Florence (Betty), ssw-Herb R., b. 1918, d. 1984
SHUPARD, Herb R., ssw-Florence, b. 1914, d. N/D
SIMMONS, Robert H., Pfc., USA, WWII, b. 06/07/1923, d. 12/08/1992
SIPPLE, Henry D., R. Adminiral, USN, b. 1913, d. 1992
SIPPLE, Natalie Hamilton, b. 1912, d. 1989
SIPPLE, Sylvia Axford, b. 1917, d. N/D
SMITH, Barbara Todd, ssw-Norman Earl, b. 04/25/1929, d. N/D
SMITH, Ellen C., ssw-James F., b. 1928, d. N/D
SMITH, Herbert A. C., b. 04/17/1902, d. 06/28/1967
SMITH, James F., ssw-Ellen C., b. 1926, d. N/D
SMITH, Norman Earl, ssw-Barbara Todd, b. 07/30/1925, d. N/D
SMITH, Robert Stevenson, II, b. 1919, d. 1987
SMOCK, Effie D., b. 02/10/1907, d. 09/30/1975
SMOCK, Jack M., b. 11/09/1909, d. 06/11/1974
SMOCK, Lawrence J., b. 06/14/1962, d. 06/15/1962
STANISZEWSKI, Evelyn P., ssw-Stanley A., b. 06/24/1929, d. 06/20/1984
STANISZEWSKI, Stanley A., ssw-Evelyn P., b. 11/03/1929, d. 12/06/1985
STEGEMAN, Doris V., b. 1923, d. 1994
STEIN, Maurice, b. 04/05/1906, d. 07/05/1973
STEIN, Melville M., b. 09/10/1911, d. 08/21/1989
STEWART, Frank H., b. 12/26/1912, d.11/24/1987
STEWART, Gertrude E., b. 10/09/1916, d. 03/01/1987
STEWART, Kate M., b. 05/15/1902, d. 11/01/1990

STONESIFER, Jean Fisher, b. N/D, d. N/D
STONESIFER, Joseph Novak, LCdr., USN, WWII, b. 02/24/1914, d. 03/15/1995
STRICKROTH, George M., ssw-Jean L., b. 1916, d. 1979
STRICKROTH, Jean L., ssw-George M., b. 1920, d. N/D
SUTHERLAND, Walter R., Pfc., USA, WWII, b. 02/23/1921, d. 05/20/1984
THOMAS, Joan B., ssw-Robert H., b. 02/26/1920, d. 06/15/1996
THOMAS, Robert H., ssw-Joan B., b. 06/19/1914, d. 03/07/1976
THOMAS, Shirley L., ssw-William H., b. 07/08/1923, d. 04/29/1988
THOMAS, William H., ssw-Shirley L., b. 10/13/1920, d. N/D
THOMPSON, Blanche B., ssw-Leon L., b. 04/30/1909, d. 12/29/1984
THOMPSON, Charles Roberts, b. 08/22/1904, d. 01/21/1970
THOMPSON, Leon L., ssw-Blanche B., LCDR, USNR, WWI, WWII, b. 06/11/1899, d. 01/14/1957
THOMPSON, Patricia Layton, ssw-Wesley Howard, b. 04/14/1922, d. 04/22/1995
THOMPSON, Wesley Howard, ssw-Patricia Layton, b. 05/03/1917, d. 03/10/1987
THOROUGHGOOD, Evelyn Dick, ssw-George Miller, b. 10/07/1920, d. N/D
THOROUGHGOOD, George Miller, ssw-Evelyn Dick, TSgt., USA, WWII, b. 08/07/1917, d. 11/15/1988
THOROUGHGOOD, Robert D., b. 1948, d. 1948
TIKOB, J. Edward, ssw-Mary Helen, b. 09/06/1889, d. 12/03/1974
TIKOB, Mary Helen, ssw-J. Edward, b. 03/18/1891, d. 06/07/1976
TOBIN, George L., b. 1902, d. 1989
TOBIN, Grace A., b. 1908, d. 1974
TORBERT, Charles R., b. 06/29/1890, d. 03/31/1962
TORBERT, Mary R., b. 08/22/1888, d. 11/16/1954
TORREY, Marie Odell, ssw-Morgan Caywood, b. 03/28/1902, d. 01/01/1987
TORREY, Morgan Caywood, ssw-Marie Odell, b. 11/01/1902, d. 07/30/1982
TOWNSEND, Donna S., ssw-John G., II, b. 1925, d. N/D
TOWNSEND, John G., II, "Jack," ssw-Donna S., b. 1918, d. 1991
TOWNSEND, Preston Coleman, b. 03/14/1910, d. 05/13/1984
TSELIOS, Grace Ann Smith, w/o Chris Tselios, b. 05/25/1950, d. 03/07/1968
TUBBS, Marjorie Chapman, b. 1915, d. 1966
TULL, Edna B., ssw-Foster A., b. 12/26/1924, d. N/D
TULL, Foster A., ssw-Edna B., b. 08/12/1922, d. 06/15/1981
VANSANT, Edna Helms, ssw-Joseph Addison, b. 05/16/1903, d. 04/23/1987
VANSANT, Gordon, b. 04/10/1929, d. 04/14/1970
VANSANT, Joseph Addison, ssw-Edna Helms, b. 03/10/1901, d. 03/15/1980
VIOHL, Mary E., ssw-Walter C., b. 1906, d. 1985
VIOHL, Walter C., ssw-Mary E., b. 1906, d. 1988
VOTH, Elsa Schuler, b. 09/29/1880, d. 07/19/1949
WAKEFIELD, Frances Grier, b. 07/05/1910, d. 02/15/1973
WAKEFIELD, Frank Grier, b. 06/14/1945, d. 02/10/1991
WAKEFIELD, Harold Kenneth, b. 07/06/1902, d. 06/12/1972
WALKER, Edmund D., ssw-Sophia N., b. 02/09/1894, d. 12/18/1977
WALKER, Sophia N., ssw-Edmund D., b. 07/12/1896, d. 01/22/1982
WALSMITH, Evelyn D., ssw-Joseph S., Jr., b. 1907, d. 1991
WALSMITH, Joseph S., Jr., ssw-Evelyn D., b. 1906, d. 1973
WALTON, Hilda Munson, b. 1925, d. N/D
WALTON, Margaret Burbage, b. 1889, d. 1983
WALTON, Robert James, III, b. 1922, d. N/D

WARRINGTON, Alton F., b. 01/18/1914, d. N/D
WARRINGTON, Lillian C., b. 10/04/1919, d. N/D
WATSON, Alice Neill, ssw-John William, b. 04/16/1907, d. 06/01/1984
WATSON, John William, ssw-Alice Neill, Col., USA, WWII, Korea, b. 05/30/1903, d. 03/30/1971
WENYON, Forrest P., ssw-Margaret C., b. 06/20/1896, d. 10/28/1974
WENYON, Margaret C., ssw-Forrest P., b. 09/06/1901, d. N/D
WHITE, Charles L., b. 12/24/1898, d. 03/21/1975
WHITE, Virginia Kelly, b. 11/17/1897, d. 10/22/1964
WHITNEY, Frederick P., ssw-Mary I., b. 12/05/1906, d. 08/28/1993
WHITNEY, Mary I., ssw-Frederick P., b. 04/15/1912, d. 07/22/1987
WIGGINS, Clarence S., b. 02/01/1921, d. 11/05/1992
WILDT, Christy Vincent, Jr., ssw-Emily Rodney, b. 12/24/1908, d. 07/24/1992
WILDT, Emily Rodney, ssw-Christy Vincent, Jr., b. 01/20/1912, d. N/D
WILKINSON, James Richard, III, TSgt., USA, WWII, b. 11/21/1922, d. 01/13/19992
WILLIAMS, Barbara M., b. 1948, d. N/D
WILLIAMS, John C., USA, Korea, b. 11/20/1929, d. 07/24/1988
WILSON, Helen Hines, ssw-Thomas W., b. 06/25/1893, d. 01/24/1957
WILSON, Howard Mifflin, ssw-Virginia McCrea, b. 01/15/1878, d. 01/01/1967
WILSON, J. Lee Davis, bb. 12/11/1907, d. 07/01/1966
WILSON, Robert M., Pfc., USA, WWI, b. 08/13/1900, d. 02/14/1996
WILSON, Thomas W., ssw-Helen Hines, b. 09/05/1884, d. 09/08/1973
WILSON, Virginia McCrea, ssw-Howard Mifflin, b. 01/29/1885, d. 02/23/1975
WIVERT, Joyce J., ssw-Warren A., b. 1918, d. 1994
WIVERT, Warren A., ssw-Joyce L., DE Pvt., WWII, b. 03/15/1915, d. 04/30/1971
WOOD, Alfred Whittlesey, b. 12/21/1908, d. 05/11/1988
YARNALL, Marguerite L., ssw-Willard S., b. 1891, d. 1966
YARNALL, Willard S., ssw-Marguerite L., b. 1878, d. 1960
YATES, Elizabeth Lyons, ssw-Richard Taylor, b. 1911, d. 1995
YATES, Richard Taylor, ssw-Elizabeth Lyons, b. 1908, d. N/D
ZOLLER, Carl A., ssw-Hilda Barbara, Capt., USN, b. 02/18/1891, d. 02/24/1959
ZOLLER, Carl A., b. 1960, d. N/D [Note: Dedication at the entrance]
ZOLLER, Hilda Barbara, ssw-Carl A., b. 11/01/1896, d. 05/30/1978

(IR-008 & HU-NR) RITTER FAMILY CEMETERY

Located S. E. of Harbeson, approximately 50 yards west of Beaver Dam Rd. (Rd. 285) behind St. Georges Chapel, 1.6 miles N. or Indian Mission Rd., (Rt. 5).
Recorded: October 30, 1996

BURNSIDE, William E., b. 06/20/1932, d. 05/12/1983
RITTER, Inf. Son, b. N/D, d. 02/15/1930
RITTER, Janet Louise, Age 10w 4d, b. N/D, d. 07/11/1942
RITTER, Margaret D., b. 10/27/1905, d. 12/04/1992
RITTER, William F., b. 10/13/1901, d. 08/26/1982
        Children of William Frederick and Margaret Dallas: Franklin Martin, B. Marie, Ethel Sarah, Mary
        Lou, Bert Frederick, Irvin William, June Lee, Howard Louis (Bud), Joanne (Jo), Janice Ellen,
        Margaret Patricia

(IR-009 & HU-002) MASSEY CEMETERY

Located S. E. of Harbeson, in the Pinewater Farm Development at the N. E. end of Persimmon Lane. Said development is on the S. W. Side of Pine Water Rd. (Rd. 49) 0.7 Miles S. E. of John J. Williams Highway (Rt. 24)
Recorded: October 23, 1993

MASSEY, Alfred, s/o John S. & Eunice, Age 22y 3m, 16d, b. N/D, d. 01/27/1883
MASSEY, Eunice, w/o John S., Age 69y 11m 23d, b. N/D, d. 01/15/1892
MASSEY, Henry, b. N/D, d. N/D
MASSEY, John S., Age 59y 6m 7d, b. N/D, d. 06/27/1886
MASSEY, John S., s/o John B. & Mier, Age 23d, b. N/D, d. 01/__/____
MASSEY, Tabitha, b. N/D, d. N/D
MASSEY, William H., s/o John S. & Eunice, Age 18y 1m 11d, b. N/D, d. 03/21/1866

(IR-010 & HU-003) BRERETON CEMETERY

Located S. E. of Harbeson in the Pinewater Farm Development on the S. E. side of Virden Lane approximately 100 feet N. W. of Multiflora Dr. Said development is on the S. W. side of Pine Water Rd. (Rd. 49) 0.7 miles S. E. of John J. Williams Highway (Rt. 24).
Recorded: October 23, 1993

BRERETON, James J., b. N/D, d. 02/16/1887
BRERETON, John Prettyman, s/o James A. & Lydia E., Age 9y 7m 20d, b. N/D, d. 07/21/1876
BRERETON, Mary Ann, w/o James A., Age 45y 3m 25d, b. N/D, d. 03/03/1854

(IR-011 & HU-304) JAMES R. WARRINGTON FAMILY CEMETERY

Located South of Harbeson, approximately 200 yards west of Hurdle Ditch Rd. (Rd. 290) between Harbeson Rd. (Rd. 5) and Johnson Rd. (Rd. 47).
Recorded: April 10, 1995

WARRINGTON, Benjamin S., b. 11/17/1813, d. 08/08/1854
WARRINGTON, Clara A., d/o William T. & Rhoda A., Age 3y 8m 3d, b. N/D, d. 07/27/1858
WARRINGTON, James T., Age 35y, b. N/D, d. 03/06/1853
WARRINGTON, Mary, w/o James R., Age 40y 5m 9d, b. N/D, d. 06/06/1831

The following stones were recorded by the Hudson Survey but are now missing or unreadable:
WARRINGTON, James R., Age 65y 4m 6d, b. N/D, d. 03/22/1846
WARRINGTON, Mary Eliza, d/o William T. & Rhoda A., Age 10m 17d, b. N/D, d. 08/01/1868
WARRINGTON, William R., s/o James T. & Elizabeth, Age 1, b. N/D, d. 09/07/1854

(IR-012 & HU-479) FRAME FAMILY CEMETERY

Located North of Millsboro on the east side of Gravel Hill Rd. (Rd. 30), 1.1 miles north of John J. Williams Highway (Rt. 24).
Recorded: April 4, 1992

FRAME, George, Age 48y 5m 10d, b. N/D, d. 09/16/1875
FRAME, M. Paynter, Age 45y b. N/D, d. 07/10/1815
FRAME, M. Robert, Age 34y, b. N/D, d. 06/11/1802
HARRIS, Mary, wid/o Paynter Frame and Stephen Harris, Age 92y 8m 8d, b. 10/26/1771, d. 07/04/1864

JERMAN, Ann Eliza, d/o Nobel & Eliza, b. 11/07/1835, d. 09/28/1856

(IR-013 & HU-NR) MILLSBORO SEVENTH DAY ADVENTIST CHURCH CEMETERY

Located N. E. of Millsboro on the north side of Cordrey Rd. (Rd. 308) 0.1 mile West of Streets Rd.
   (Rd. 310)
Recorded: April 29, 1997

BOYKIN, Charles F., b. 10/02/1913, d. 02/05/1979
COTTMAN, George, ssw-Jensie, b. 06/16/1886, d. 06/01/1972
COTTMAN, Jensie, ssw-George, b. 02/22/1887, d. 03/10/1977
COTTMAN, Mildred, ssw-Virgil W., b. 08/23/1916, d. N/D
COTTMAN, Purlies M., DE, CK3, USNR, WWII, b. 08/27/1906, d. 01/08/1968
COTTMAN, Virgil W., ssw-Mildred, b. 02/27/1907, d. 02/14/1961
ELLISON, James H., ssw-Maude Ellison Price, b. 11/12/1922, d. 04/14/1988
GOODMAN, Grace M., b. 06/05/1918, d. 04/04/1996
HARMON, Keshaun, b. 1989, d. 199_
HARMON, Olive S., b. 04/09/1884, d. 06/08/1954
HOOD, James E., b. 1950, d. 1989
JACKSON, Clara B., ssw-William A., b. 01/03/1892, d. 05/08/1977
JACKSON, William A., ssw-Clara B., b. 09/05/1887, d. 09/20/1956
JACKSON, William Dempster, ssw-Verneace J. Jones, Pvt., USA, WWII, b. 11/01/1926, d. 05/04/1986
JOHNSON, Ethel L., b. 1912, d. 1988
JOHNSON, Lucille V., ssw-Bettie J. Lee, b. 10/26/1910, d. 10/11/1976
JONES, Minnie E., ssw-Willie B., b. 10/06/1920, d. 05/07/1985
JONES, Verneace J., ssw-William Dempster Jackson, b. 1918, d. 1988
JONES, Willie B., ssw-Minnie E., b. 05/22/1900, d. 08/16/1961
LEE, Bettie J., ssw-Lucille V. Johnson, Mother, b. 08/14/1886, d. 01/10/1972
LEE, Shepard, b. 03/09/1933, d. 08/06/1996
MCCALL, Claude H., ssw-Gail B., Pvt., USA, Korea, b. 05/18/1930, d. 11/09/1993
MCCALL, Gail B., ssw-Claude H., b. 07/10/1940, d. N/D
MCCRAY, Cornell C., b. 12/14/1950, d. 01/21/1983
MCCRAY, Norman R., DE, Pfc., 41 Engr. CS Regt. WWII, b. 06/22/1926, d.05/04/1963
MOSLEY, Lydia A., ssw-Raymond B., b. 1901, d. 1990
MOSLEY, Raymond B., ssw-Lydia A., b. 1904, d. 1974
NORWOOD, Beverly A., ssw-Charles F., b. 1947, d. N/D
NORWOOD, Charles F., ssw-Beverly A., b. 1941, d. 1981
NORWOOD, Edith J., Medicine Woman, b. 06/28/1918, d. 04/05/1995
NORWOOD, Emery W., ssw-Sarah C., b. 12/17/1899, d. 05/14/1983
NORWOOD, Robert S., Sr., b. 01/31/1914, d. 09/20//1978
NORWOOD, Samuel B., ssw-Thelma E., m. 01/02/1932, b. 12/25/1907, d. 09/10/1996
NORWOOD, Sarah C., ssw-Emery W., b. 06/05/1898, d. 03/22/1990
NORWOOD, Thelma E., ssw-Samuel B., m. 01/02/1932, b. 03/28/1911, d. 11/29/1991
POLK, Karen L., b. 10/26/1967, d. 05/20/1986
PRICE, Dewey A., b. 05/16/1900, d. 03/11/1974
PRICE, Maude Ellison, ssw-James H. Ellison, b. 09/09/1905, d. 03/16/1989
PRITCHET, David A., Sr., b. 09/05/1939, d. 01/05/1969
SHOWELL, Alfred L., ssw-Almeda M., b. 1907, d. 1956
SHOWELL, Alfred R., ssw-M. Almenia, b. 03/19/1938, d. N/D

SHOWELL, Almeda M., ssw-Alfred L., b. 1914, d. 1993
SHOWELL, Arnez R., b. N/D, d. 1981
SHOWELL, James W., b. 04/15/1912, d. 12/22/1970
SHOWELL, M. Almenia, ssw-Alfred R., b. 07/14/1941, d. 07/27/1984
STAFFEL, Kenneth R., b. 11/02/1926, d. 04/18/1992
STREET, Algetha M., ssw-M. Earl, b. 02/03/1914, d. 11/10/1995
STREET, Arnold S., b. 08/11/1903, d. 04/08/1965
STREET, Bertha M., b. 07/23/1890, d. 01/18/1925
STREET, Beulah M., ssw-Levi W., b. 05/29/1898, d. 06/06/1971
STREET, Burton C., b. 02/02/1885, d. 02/06/1959
STREET, Carlos E., ssw-Myrtle B., m. 09/26/1931, b. 07/22/1910, d. 10/171988
STREET, Children o/Levi & Beulah, b. N/D, d. N/D
STREET, Howard D., ssw-Mary E., b. 1874, d. 1945
STREET, John F., Elder, ssw-Ruth E., b. 01/08/1906, d. N/D
STREET, Levi W., ssw-Beulah M., b. 09/09/1897, d. 09/23/1972
STREET, M. Earl, ssw-Algetha M., b. 01/02/1908, d. N/D
STREET, Mary E., ssw-Howard D., b. 1868, d. 1941
STREET, Myrtle B., ssw-Carlos E., m. 09/26/1931, b. 01/01/1908, d. 07/08/1993
STREET, Ruth E., ssw-John F., b. 03/26/1907, d. 08/21/1982
TULL, Alonzo L., ssw-Mary E., m. 08/24/1929, b. 01/11/1905, d. 11/19/1988
TULL, Mary E., ssw-Alonzo L., m. 08/24/1929, b. 06/25/1910, d. 01/15/1996
UPSHUR, Geneva B., w/o William H., b. 11/16/1900, d. 08/08/1989
WALLACE, M. Ellen, b. 1909, d. N/D
WEBB, Alice M., b. 1882, d. 1961
WOOD, George T., b. 03/29/1909, d. 03/291988
WOOD, Lena Mae, b. 05/10/1913, d. 10/12/1962
WRIGHT, Howard C., ssw-Mary E., Sp4, USA, Vietnam, b. 02/28/1943, d. 09/22/1981
WRIGHT, Mary E., ssw-Howard C., b. 1948, d. N/D

LEWES REHOBOTH HUNDRED

(LR-001 & HU-NR) PEOPLES MEMORIAL PARK CEMETERY
Located North of Rehoboth Beach on the East side of Coastal Highway (Rt. 1) at John J. Williams
Highway (Rt. 24)
Recorded: September 26, 1992

ALLEN, Albert, Sr., ssw-Hannah., b. 1886, d. 1975
ALLEN, Charles H., Jr., b. 11/18/1891, d. 05/18/1964
ALLEN, David, b. 1958, d. 1987
ALLEN, Frank W., ssw-Louise, b. 1884, d. 1963
ALLEN, Hannah M., ssw-Albert, Sr., b. 1888, d. 1989
ALLEN, Katie E., b. 12/26/1916, d. 07/01/1981
ALLEN, Lillie Mae, b. 09/21/1919, d. 08/21/1957
ALLEN, Louise, ssw-Frank W., b. 1886, d. 1951
ALLEN, Mary E., b. 06/06/1896, d. 11/19/1984
ARGO, Charles W., ssw-Lillian, b. N/D, d. N/D
ARGO, Charles William, Jr., BM3, USN, b. 12/19/1929, d. 08/02/1977

ARGO, Fannie M., ssw-Nona V. Darden, b. 02/14/1898, d. N/D

ARGO, Lillian, ssw-Charles W., b. N/D, d. N/D

ARGO, Rebecca S., ssw-Walter S., b. 1876, d. 1960

ARGO, Steven D., b. 05/30/1909, d. 10/09/1978

ARGO, Walter S., ssw-Rebecca S., b. 1875, d. 1963

AYERS, Robert P., Tec5, USA, WWII, b. 03/23/1921, d. 05/28/1988

BAUGH, Horace N., b. 12/14/1914, d. 08/26/1972

BECKETT, William A., USA, WWII, b. 06/18/1926, d. 10/10/1991

BOWDEN, James E., b. 09/12/1972, d. 04/19/1979

BRITTINGHAM, Oliver G., NJ, A26, USAF, Korea, b. 06/22/1922, d. 08//14/1973

BRITTINGHAM, Reba L., b. 12/25/1898, d. 12/31/1983

BROWN, Richard, b. 02/12/1908, d. 12/22/1981

BUNDICK, Hezekiah, Pvt., USA, WWI, b. 01/14/1897, d. 04/26/1956

BURNS, Victoria R., b. 1905, d. 1992

BURTON, Annie M., ssw-Benjamin A., b. 1872, d. 1952

BURTON, Benjamin A., ssw-Annie M., b. 1863, d. 1950

BURTON, Benjamin F., Tec4, USA, WWII, b. 1922, d. 1987

BURTON, Benjamin H., DE Co. D, 368 Infantry, WWI, b. 04/22/1890, d. 04/01/1966

BURTON, Bess White, b. 1886, d. 1964

BURTON, Clarence, NY, Pfc., 367 Inf., 92 Div., WWI, b. 06/13/1893, d. 06/03/1947

BURTON, Clarence E., ssw-Mary J., b. 1890, d. 1954

BURTON, Elizabeth H., b. 03/17/1915, d. 06/16/1983

BURTON, Fred D., DE, Pfc., Btry. F, 349 Field Arty., WWI, b. 07/04/1895, d. 05/26/1968

BURTON, Grace E., b. 02/25/1897, d. 03/26/1983

BURTON, Ida J. M., b. 1895, d. 1957

BURTON, Martin Luther, DE, Pfc., 574 Port Co. TC., WWII, b. 08/11/1911, d. 03/19/1957

BURTON, Mary J., b. 08/03/1903, d. 03/11/1979

BURTON, Mary J., ssw-Clarence E., b. 1888, d. 1982

CACKIER, Harold D., b. 06/13/1914, d. 01/19/1962

CAMPBELL, Bruce Maurice, GMM2, USN, b. 09/12/1957, d. 12/06/1981

CANNON, Clara Mae, b. 02/13/1894, d. 08/21/1960

CANNON, Ralph, b. 01/26/18990, d. 07/17/1966

CARTER, Mary D., ssw-Frank R. White, b. 1886, d. 1952

CARTER, Raymond L., DE, Pvt., 4104 Base Unit, AAF, WWII, b. 10/09/1900, d. 08/12/1961

CLARK, Benny, Sr., b. 03/21/1916, d. 04/10/1977

CLARK, Charles C., ssw-Eliza, b. 03/20/1880, d. 02/03/1961

CLARK, Denny O., ssw-Charles C., b. N/D, d. N/D

CLARK, Eliza, ssw-Charles C., b. 02/27/1884, d. N/D

CLARK, Frederick W., b. 07/11/1909, d. 06/20/1976

CLARK, R. Raphael, b. 1 2/22/1922, d. 04/10/1946

COLLICK, Sarah H., b. 06/27/1923, d. 08/31/1984

COLLICK, Thomas H., Jr., b. 12/06/1921, d. 04/07/1977

CONOWAY, Edward, ssw-Sarah, b. N/D, d. N/D

CONOWAY, Sarah, ssw-Edward, b. N/D, d. N/D

COOK, Phillip A., S1, USN, WWII, b. 1907, d. 1980

COVINGTON, Patricia Ann, b. 02/26/1880, d. 02/06/1954

CUMMINGS, Rebecca Argo, w/o Grover W. Cummings & d/o Walter & Rebecca Argo, b. 05/06/1907, d. 10/03/1992

DARDEN, Nona V., ssw-Fannie M. Argo, b. 02/08/1880, d. 01/01/1978
DEAN, Beulah M., b. 03/09/1922, d. 02/02/1980
DEAN, Dallas M., b. 03/12/1916, d. 02/05/1973
DOWNING, Robert Andrew, b. 08/15/1957, d. 05/06/1978
DUBOIS, Louis B., Pvt., USA, WWII, b. 11/24/1922, d. 09/13/1974
DUFFIE, Wm. R., b. 1962, d. 1978
DUFFY, Braven M., ssw-S. Christine, b. 1910, d. 1982
DUFFY, Fred K., b. 11/25/1914, d. 10/03/1985
DUFFY, Idella, b. 1917, d. 1991
DUFFY, John E., Jr., Cpl., USA, WWII, b. 1912, d. 1991
DUFFY, S. Christine, ssw-Braven M., b. 1917, d. 1981
DUFFY, William O., b. 1906, d. 1987
DUNNING, Albert, III, ssw-Albert, Jr., "Our Son," b. 1934, d. 1975
DUNNING, Albert, Jr., ssw-Albert, III, b. 1907, d. 1976
DUNNING, Amy H., ssw-Albert, III, b. 1907, d. 1987
DUNNING, Dewey S., ssw-Edna V., b. 09/27/1898, d. 08/21/1956
DUNNING, Edna V., ssw-Dewey S., b. 06/17/1898, d. 10/29/1966
DUNNING, Hiram Burton, Pfc., USA, WWII, b. 1927, d. 1978
DUNNING, Lewins Curtis, Sr., Pfc., USA, WWII, b. 05/19/1913, d. 02/20/1981
EVANS, Will, DE Pvt., Co. A, 801 Pioneer Inf., WWI, b. 05/03/1887, d. 08/24/1961
FARRINGTON, Marie C., ssw-Frank R. White, b. 1900, d. 1966
FLETCHER, Elijah, VA, Pvt., 15 HQ TNG Cen., WWI, b. 04/16/1894, d. 06/04/1948
FLETCHER, Geneva M., "Big Mom," b. 09/17/1903, d. 02/15/1989
FLETCHER, John Henry, DE, Bugler, 808 Pioneer Inf., WWI, b. 03/25/1895, d. 12/19/1957
FLETCHER, Oneida B., b. 04/13/1896, d. 02/08/1982
FOREMAN, Spencer T., Sgt., USA, WWII, b. 11/03/1912, d. 03/09/1992
FRAME, Effie, ssw-Monica Tunnell, Age 92, of Rehoboth Beach, b. 1900, d. 01/17/1993
FULLER, Clara A., ssw-Guilford, b. 1892, d. N/D
FULLER, Guilford, ssw-Clara A., b. 1878, d. 1963
FURLOW, Fred, NC, Pvt., USA, WWI, b. 06/30/1896, d. 12/30/1958
GIBBS, James L., b. 10/19/1957, d. 06/30/1970
GIBBS, Temple M., b. 1903, d. 1961
GLOVER, Zell T., Pvt., USA, b. 03/15/1922, d. 01/02/1975
GOOCH, Harriet L. M., b. 02/12/1932, d. 11/16/1985
GOOCH, Martin R., DE, Tec5, 3141 OM Serv. Co., WWII, b. 01/05/1916, d. 04/26/1960
GOOCH, Phylis M., b. 1874, d. 1951
GREEN, Moses, NC, SGT., Com. 371 Inf., WWI, b. 07/04/1896, d. 10/08/1965
HALL, Hannah A., "Mother," b. 03/25/1922, d. 11/28/1990
HALL, Vaughn O., DE, Cpl., 321 Arty. 101 Abn. Div., Vietnam, BSM, b. 01/25/1948, d. 05/23/1969
HASSELL, Marie, b. 01/02/1920, d. 09/07/1989
HITCHENS, Nancy C., b. 1906, d. 1974
HOLLAND, Edith E., ssw-Roy E., b. 1897, d. 1991
HOLLAND, Jacob S., Pfc., USA, WWII, b. 1923, d. 1990
HOLLAND, Roy E., ssw-Edith E., b. 1891, d. 1975
HOLLIS, Alexander, ssw-Rachel, b. 1874, d. 1950
HOLLIS, Rachel, ssw-Alexander, b. 1895, d. 1973
HOLMES, Eugene, Pfc., USA, Korea, b. 1930, d. 1982
HOLMES, Roland, DE, A3C, USAF, b. 04/25/1934, d. 11/05/1969

INGRAM, Joshua VA, Pfc., Co. M, 811 Pioneer Inf., WWI, b. 07/15/1893, d. 12/23/1958
JACKSON, Hildegard A., b. 11/16/1912, d. 02/27/1991
JOHNSON, Daniel James, Jr., b. 09/01/1957 d. 07/23/1972
JOHNSON, Lulu K., b. 1888, d. 1960
JOHNSON, Thomas B., b. 1883, d. 1951
JOHNSON, Thomas Henry, DE, Tec5, 3413 OM TRUCK CO., WWII, b. 08/03/1922, d. 11/16/1958
JONES, Cora Lee, b. 10/08/1898, d. 06/21/1971
JORDAN, H. S. and Family, b. N/D, d. N/D
KELLAM, Mary, b. 1929, d. 1992
KELLEY, Marvin W., b. 1913, d. 1990
KEMP, Guss, Pfc., USA, WWII, b. 1922, d. 1984
KENNEDY, Kevin Bernard, b. 04/11/1956, d. 09/28/1974
KING, Jennie, b. 1865, d. 1945
LACEY, Maran W., b. 08/21/1901, d. 01/23/1978
LEWIS, James M., ssw-Levinia F., b. 1892, d. 1971
LEWIS, Levinia F., ssw-James M., b. 1901, d. 1983
LOCKWOOD, Charles C., Pfc., USA, b. 05/23/1911, d. 05/05/1975
LOGAN, Margaret Jordan, b. 04/09/1908, d. 08/02/1991
LONG, Rudolph R., DE, Pfc., 318 Port Co., TC, WWII, b. 03/23/1925, d. 09/28/1969
LORD, Evelyn E., b. 09/20/1919, d. N/D
MALLOY, Mary, ssw-Robert, b. N/D, d. N/D
MALLOY, Robert, ssw-Mary, b. N/D, d. N/D
MALLOY, Sheila, ssw-Robert, b. N/D, d. N/D
MATTHEWS, Andrew, b. 10/26/1927, d. 09/24/1982
MAULL, Alfred L., Jr., DE, Tec5, 254 Port Co. Tc. WWII, b. 09/15/1918, d. 04/22/1951
MAULL, Carlton, b. 1910, d. 1989
MAULL, Joseph E., Sr., Pfc., USA, WWII, b. 1923, d. 1988
MAULL, Lillian M., b. 01/09/1898, d. 06/19/1982
MAULL, Otelia C., b. 11/05/1903, d. 05/03/1975
MCDANIEL, James, b. 1914, d. 1987
MILLER, David, ssw-Marie, b. 1905, d. 1947
MILLER, Henry Richard, b. 04/20/1913, d. 04/26/1983
MILLER, Isabell Elva, b. 1932, d. 1939
MILLER, Marie, ssw-David, b. 1906, d. 1986
MINOR, Alvester, ssw-Greta & Clara, b. 05/01/1910, d. 02/10/1972
MINOR, Clara, ssw-Alvester & Greta, b. 09/16/1931, d. 02/11//1973
MINOR, Greta, ssw-Alvester & Clara, b. 09/19/1911, d. 03/26/1986
MORRIS, Leon W., Sr., ssw-Thelma O., m. 05/03/1952, b. 1924, d. N/D
MORRIS, Thelma O., ssw-Leon W., Sr., m. 05/03/1952, b. 1921, d. 1988
MOSLEY, George H., DE, Pvt., 39 Co., 154 Depot Grigade, WWI, b. 09/11/1891, d. 10/28/1958
MOSLEY, Southern M., DE, Pfc., 319 Port Co., TC, WWII, b. 01/16/1905, d. 07/27/1972
PALMER, William G., Sr., b. 05/08/1915, d. 11/24/1967
PARKER, Ervin E., ssw-Marion S., b. 1943, d. 1990
PARKER, Marion S., ssw-Ervin E., b. 1947, d. N/D
PARKER, Sarah E., b. 1879, d. 1963
PAYNTER, Bertha, b. 1901, d. 1990
PAYNTER, Samuel T., NJ, Cook, USA, WWI, b. 12/24/1890, d. 09/23/1963
PAYNTER, William V., DE, Pfc., 10 Motor Trans Sq., AAF, WWII, b. 10/31/1926, d. 01/07/1958

PHILLIPS, Emma F., b. 01/1913, d. 02/1957

PHILLIPS, Maude Elizabeth, b. 11/12/1902, d. 11/01/1972

PHILLIPS, Pedro, Rev., b. 09/17/1904, d. 05/03/1971

POE, Harry A., NY, Pfc., SVC Dept., USMA, WWII, b. 09/14/1908, d. 10/01/1957

POE, Nettie F., b. N/D, d. N/D

RANSON, Donald T., b. 1951, d. 1974

REED, A., Cpl., USA, Korea, b. 1932, d. 1980

RILEY, Alden C., Pfc., USA, WWI, b. 1894, d. 1979

RILEY, Raymond Robert, Pfc., USA, WWII, b. 1910, d. 1990

ROBERTS, Alwilda L., ssw-Clarence H., b. 09/28/1911, d. 06/02/1985

ROBERTS, Clarence H., ssw-Alwilda L., b. 12/10/1912, d. 09/14/1991

ROBINSON, Frank W., Sr., Rev., b. 03/16/1938, d. 06/03/1990

SALTERS, Matilda H., b. 07/29/1920, d. 03/03/1974

SAVAGE, Julia C., b. 09/06/1929, d. 04/19/1986

SCOTT, Albert P., Jr., DE, CS3, USCG, b. 06/06/1936, d. 07/13/1960

SEYMOUR, Joseph E., Jr., "Joey," b. 05/18/1964, d. 10/30/1987

SEYMOURE, Annie H., ssw-Joseph C., b. 1877, d. 1947

SEYMOURE, Frank B., DE, Sgt., Quartermaster Corps., WWII, b. 12/06/1915, d. 03/28/1970

SEYMOURE, Joseph C., ssw-Annie H., b. 1887, d. 19__

SHORT, Eben A., Sgt., USA, b. 10/07/1919, d. 06/21/1991

SHORT, Myron H., b. 1954, d. 1962

SHOWELL, George M., Pfc., USA, WWII, b. 1910, d. 1992

SINGLETON, Clara E., b. 02/09/1921, d. 08/06/1976

SPENCE, Everett E., b. 1949, d. 1978

SPENCE, Preston P., b. 08/01/1942, d. 07/01/1991

STANLEY, Mary E. Gooch, b. 04/15/1929, d. 11/24/1982

STANLEY, William C., USCG, WWII, b. 1918, d. 1992

STEWART, Charles F., Pfc., USA, WWII, b. 1922, d. 1991

STEWART, Louis, b. 12/03/1903, d. 04/13/1959

STEWART, Paul James, DE, Pvt., Co. C., 1321 Engr. Gs. Bn., WWII, b. 09/05/1927, d. 04/28/1969

STOCKLEY, Louis B., Sr., ssw-Theodosia M., b. 1912, d. 1977

STOCKLEY, Theodosia M., ssw-Louis B., Sr., b. 1914, d. 1982

SUNKETT, Melvin T., Jr., USA, b. 1949, d. 1989

SUNKETT, Melvin T. W., Sr., Pvt., USA, WWII, b. 1919, d. 1988

THOMAS, Frederick D., Jr., SSgt., USA, WWII, b. 1921, d. 1978

THOMPSON, Desazari A., "Desi," b. 05/12/1968, d. 08/23/1988

THOMPSON, Richard, Pvt., USA, WWI, b. 05/20/1896, d. 04/14/1986

THOMPSON, Saddie, b. 1903, d. 1951

TIMMONS, Joseph R., USN, Vietnam, b. 04/02/1950, d. 03/21/1976

TUNNELL, David L., b. 1927, d. 1989

TUNNELL, Edith C., b. 04/02/1931, d. 06/24/1969

TUNNELL, Floyd W., ssw-Mozella C., b. 1917, d. N/D

TUNNELL, Monica, d/o Clinton McWilliams & Albertina R., Tunnell, ssw-Effie Frame, "Moonie,"
        Roseanne, b. 1988,   d. 04/1993

TUNNELL, Mozella C., ssw-Floyd W., b. 1909, d. 1974

TURNER, Hampton M., Sr., Cpl., USA, Korea, b. 1926, d. 1984

WAGNER, Frederick H., b. 06/11/1905, d. 04/15/1964

WALKER, Ethel, b. 1916, d. 1975

WALTERS, Mary H., Mother, b. 1912, d. 1984
WAPLES, Amanda, ssw-Augustus, b. 1903, d. N/D
WAPLES, Augustus, ssw-Amanda, b. 1902, d. 1979
WAPLES, Linford E., Tec5, USA, WWII, b. 1924, d. 1984
WAPLES, Norman L., DE, Pfc., 320 Port Co., TC., WWII, b. 06/20/1913, d. 11/06/1963
WAPLES, Pearline A., b. 08/31/1921, d. 11/17/1985
WARD, Calonia, b. 08/24/1909, d. 04/08/1976
WARD, Clarence, MD, Pvt., Co. 1, 808 Pioneer Inf., WWI, b. 09/17/1894, d. 01/20/1958
WARD, Harry, DE, Cook, USA, WWI, b. 04/15/1896, d. 02/26/1964
WARD, Herman F., A1C, USAF, WWII, b. 1922, d. 1982
WARD, Louise J., b. 10/20/1923, d. 07/17/1978
WARD, Mrshall S., AAE, b. 04/17/1909, d. 09/25/1985
WARD, Mary L., b. 1922, d. 1992
WARD, Richard William, S2, USN, b. 02/29/1920, d. 09/16/1977
WARD, Rodney B., b. 07/09/1913, d. 06/20/1981
WEATHERSBY, Delilian, b. 1927, d. 1993
WHARTON, Estella E., b. 06/01/1914, d. 05/02/1972
WHARTON, Evelyn, b. 1926, d. 1991
WHITE, Frank R., ssw-Mary D. Carter, b. 1892, d. 1971
WHITE, Harriett D., ssw-Frank R., b. 1893, d. N/D
WHITE, Marguerite, b. 1902, d. 1989
WHITE, Rushton C., b. 05/15/1903, d. 07/30/1981
WHITE, Sarah E., b. 1922, d. 1964
WILLIAMS, Eddie, b. 09/26/1955, d. 12/19/1976
WILLIAMS, Hettie J., ssw-Raphael T., b. 1894, d. N/D
WILLIAMS, Raphael T., ssw-Hettie J., b. 1888, d. 1949
WINSTON, John R., b. 01/05/1900, d. 04/10/1962
WOLFE, Maude L., b. 06/06/1909, d. 02/05/1990
WOLFE, Vincent R., b. 12/03/1913, d. 12/12/1989
WOODS, Elmer James, A1C, USAF, WWII, Korea, b. 12/14/1928, d. 11/12/1975
WRIGHT, James M., b. N/D, d. N/D
WYNNE, Felicia Ann, b. 02/20/198, d. 05/07/1963
ZANE, D. Caesar, b. 1960, d. 1987

(LR-002 & HU-541) EPWORTH CEMETERY
Located in Rehoboth Beach on the North side of Henlopen Avenue between Grove Street & Felton Street.
Recorded between March 24 & 30, 1992

ADEN, Floyd R., ssw-Helen B., b. 1913, d. N/D
ADEN, Helen B., ssw-Floyd R., b. 1917, d. N/D
AHERN, William R., III, Baby, b. 08/08/1979, d. 08/10/1979
ALEXANDER, Mary C., b. 1911, d. 1986
ALEXANDER, G. Norman, b. 1911, d. 1989
ALLEN, J. Burton, b. 03/19/1910, d. 09/09/1959
ANDERSON, Ayn B., b. 1905, d. 1982
ANDERSON, LeRoy, b. N/D, d. 01/01/63
ARNOLD, Benjamin F., ssw-Evelyne B., b. 1900, d. 1949
ARNOLD, Evelyne B., ssw-Benjamin F., b. 1904, d. 1976

ARNOLD, Samuel, Jr., ssw-Sarah L., Pfc., 110th Inf., 28th Div., WWI, b. 08/14/1892, d. 05/12/1960

ARNOLD, Sarah L., ssw-Samuel, Jr., b. 1897, d. 1984

BACKER, Edward W., Jr., SC3, USCG, WWII, b. 06/28/1921, d. 01/17/1963

BACKUS, Beulah G., b. 07/25/1891, d. 08/07/1975

BAILEY, Carlton J., ssw-Virginia Ray, b. 09/23/1933, d. N/D

BAILEY, Virginia Ray, ssw-Carlton J., b. 02/20/1935, d. 03/26/1982

BAKER, Ann W., ssw-William T., b. 09/21/1920, d. 04/23/1990

BAKER, Clara P., ssw-William E., b. 1883, d. 1964

BAKER, Eunice I., ssw-William G., m. 03/22/1941, b. 10/29/1921, d. N/D

BAKER, Robert W., ssw-William T., b. 03/26/1949, d. 11/15/1991

BAKER, William E., ssw-Clara P., b. 1885, d. 1971

BAKER, William G., ssw-Eunice I., m. 03/22/1941, d. 10/08/1921, d. 01/12/1981

BAKER, William T., ssw-Ann W., b. 12/27/1911, d. 03/08/1965

BANDORF, Edna V., ssw-Walter, b. 12/17/1891, d. 12/26/1970

BANDORF, Walter, ssw-Edna V, b. 12/03/1890, d. 08/25/1972

BARNES, Ethel L., ssw-John, b. 02/08/1899, d. 03/07/1978

BARNES, John, ssw-Ethel L., b. 04/08/1896, d. 09/23/1971

BARNETT, Elizabeth A., ssw-Robert P., b. 09/08/1922 d. 05/12/1974

BARNETT, Robert P., ssw-Elizabeth A., b. 11/19/1921, d. N/D

BATROH, Irma, SSgt, USAF, b. 06/11/1922, d. 05/11/1991

BAYLIS, Delema, w/o Benjamin R. Baylis & sis/o Raymond E. Wilson, b. 07/23/1902, d. 11/29/1987

BEACHLEY, Jack Witner, b. 11/16/1926, d. 12/27/1991

BECKER, Olive I., b. 08/24/1885, d. 06/20/1952

BECKER, William J., Jr., b. 02/02/1912, d. 07/15/1964

BEIDEMAN, Clyde Allen, ssw-George L., b. 1910, d. 1922

BEIDEMAN, George L., ssw-Kathryn E., b. 01/01/1890, d. 11/23/1941

BEIDEMAN, Helen Louise, ssw-George L., b. 1916, d. 1918

BEIDEMAN, Kathryn E., ssw-George L., b. 10/02/1892, d. 12/22/1973

BEIDEMAN, Lester J., s/o O. C. & Margaret M., b. 03/23/1911, d. 09/30/1914

BEIDEMAN, Margaret M., ssw-Oliver C., b. 05/29/1892, d. 01/23/1968

BEIDEMAN, Oliver C., ssw-Margaret M., b. 04/05/1887, d. 01/04/1951

BEVIS, William W., b. 07/27/1896, d. 09/27/1973

BINGHAM, Margaret Ann, b. 06/12/1926, d. 02/23/1976

BLANER, Andrew H., ssw-Anna V., b. 1890, d. 1965

BLANER, Anna V., ssw-Andrew H., b. 1895, d. 1987

BLANER, Gladys M., ssw-Richard D., b. 1927, d. N/D

BLANER, Richard D., ssw-Gladys M., b. 1929, d. 1991

BOLAND, William L., b. 07/20/1873, d. 09/09/1930

BORGESE, Patricia Ann, b. 1931, d. 1986

BOYCE, Evalyn, ssw-Fred J., b. 10/10/1898, d. 08/18/1986

BOYCE, Fred J., ssw-Evalyn, b. 10/17/1894, d. 10/23/1967

BRANDT, John O., ssw-Maggie B., b. 12/28/1894, d. 11/07/1975

BRANDT, Maggie B., ssw-John O., b. 10/22/1899, d. N/D

BRANFORD, E. Josephine, b. 1922, d. N/D

BRANFORD, Harry V., b. 1888, d. 1961

BRANFORD, Josephine M., b. 1890, d. 1966

BRANFORD, Walter A., DE, LTCOL., USA, WWII, b. 10/24/1909, d. 08/12/1973

BROWN, John, ssw-Marie T., b. 09/17/1903, d. 07/11/1975

BROWN, Marie T., ssw-John, b. 11/09/1906, d. 12/29/1972

BRYAN, Julia Ann Wall, b. 08/28/1926, d. 05/31/1968

BUCKWALTER, Benjamin S., b. 1879, d. 1960

BURNHAM, Audrey M., b. 05/24/1921, d. 12/20/1981

BURNHAM, Paul S., Dr., b. 04/13/1903, d. 02/04/1987

BURRIS, Lewis C., USMC, b. 04/17/1946, d. 10/23/1964

BURTON, Addie E., ssw-Thomas R., b. 1900, d. 1983

BURTON, Amelia A., ssw-Samuel J., b. 10/06/1909, d. N/D

BURTON, Catherine Attix, ssw-James R., b. 05/02/1919, d. N/D

BURTON, Edna S., b. 1901, d. 1958

BURTON, Ervin J., ssw-Son, b. 07/21/1936, d. 11/07/1936

BURTON, Floyd Aden, Baby, b. 09/01/1942, d. 09/20/1942

BURTON, Jackie Gilbert, b. 11/27/1937, d. 02/15/1938

BURTON, James R., Doc., ssw-Catherine Attix, b. 09/20/1911, d. 01/04/1989

BURTON, Julian T., USA, WWII, b. 03/27/1920, d. 08/13/1990

BURTON, Our Son, ssw-Ervin J., b. 04/07/1930, d. 04/07/1930

BURTON, Samuel J., ssw-Amelia A., b. 07/28/1904, d. 12/04/1983

BURTON, Thomas R., ssw-Addie E., b. 1895, d. 1944

BUTTON, Clemmie, ssw-George B., b. 12/29/1881, d. 12/30/1952

BUTTON, George G., ssw-Clemmie, b. 03/31/1874, d. 09/11/1956

BUTTON, J. Ralph, ssw-George B., b. 12/31/1912, d. 04/21/1915

CAIN, J. Watson, ssw-Nellie R., b. N/D, d. 03/21/1950

CAIN, Nellie R., ssw-J. Watson, b. N/D, d. 10/04/1958

CALDWELL, Maude Larkin, ssw-Samuel Craighead V., b. 1914, d. 1978

CALDWELL, Samuel Craighead V., ssw-Maude Larkin, b. 1911, d. 1972

CALHOUN, Thomas S., b. 1911, d. 1992

CARLISLE, Henry, ssw-Lola Grubb, b. 08/09/1869, d. 05/29/1945

CARLISLE, Lola Grubb, ssw-Henry, b. 01/22/1867, d. 01/07/1943

CARMEAN, William C., DE, Cpl., USMC, b. 09/01/1934, d. 02/09/1968

CARTWRIGHT, Lucy E., b. 04/09/1905, d. 04/28/1987

CHING, Robert K., ssw-Udell, b. 12/11/1911, d. 11/28/1968

CHING, Udell (Judy), ssw-Robert K., b. 09/07/1922, d. 01/31/1967

CLENDANIEL, Harry F., ssw-Laura E., b. 12/04/1886, d. 02/21/1976

CLENDANIEL, Laura E., ssw-Harry F., b. 05/28/1899, d. 12/14/1990

CLIFTON, Brooksie T., ssw-Charles E., b. 1884, d. 1945

CLIFTON, Charles E., ssw-Brooksie T., b. 1880, d. 1955

CLIFTON, Edward S., DE, Sgt., USA, WWII, Korea & Vietnam, b. 02/17/1915, d. 02/15/1970

CLIFTON, Lloyd N., AB, USAF, b. 10/31/1938, d. 02/07/1975

CLULEY, Herbert D., ssw-Olia A., b. 08/15/1889, d. 05/29/1963

CLULEY, Olia A., ssw-Herbert D., b. 11/22/1891, d. 04/06/1972

COLE, Alice M., ssw-Edgar B., b. 1914, d. 1972

COLE, Bruce Floyd, b. 04/15/1902, d. 07/05/1974

COLE, Charles W., ssw-Kitty T., b. 08/05/1917, d. 03/18/1986
    Parents of Charles W., George G. & Neil O.
    Grandparents of George B., Jr., Joseph B., Priscilla T., Charles W., II, Neil O., Jr., Dorsey L. & Brock H.

COLE, Edgar B., ssw-Alice M., b. 1884, d. 1970

COLE, Kitty T., ssw-Charles W., b. 07/07/1923, d. N/D
    Parents of Charles W., George G. & Neil O.
    Grandparents of George B., Jr., Joseph B., Priscilla T., Charles W., II, Neil O., Jr., Dorsey L. &
    Brock H.
COLE, Ruth Edna, b. 09/25/1903, d. N/D
COLLIER, Albert F., Jr. ssw-Ruth & Ruth Louise, b. 1917, d. 1982
COLLIER, Ruth, ssw-Albert F., Jr. & Ruth Louise, b. 1914, d. 1979
COLLIER, Ruth Louise, ssw-Albert F., Jr. & Ruth, b. 1943, d. 1952
COLLINS, Mildred N., b. 04/24/1896, d. 07/05/1966
CONANT, Daniel G., ssw-Vera B., b. 10/09/1893, d. 08/07/1969
CONANT, Vera B., ssw-Daniel G., b. 09/27/1893, d. 01/26/1964
CONANT, William H., ssw-Daniel G., b. 12/25/1925, d. 12/05/1932
CONWAY, Ann, b. 1920, d. 1992
CONWAY, William H., Jr., b. 06/16/1914, d. 04/30/1978
COOPER, Samuel J., b. 10/25/1909, d. 02/01/1955
CORNING, Florence R., ssw-Hobart Munson, b. 1889, d. 1987
CORNING, Hobart Munson, ssw-Florence R., b. 1888, d. 1970
CORRIGAN, Bernice H., ssw-John N., b. 1915, d. 1991
CORRIGAN, John N., ssw-Bernice H., b. 1914, d. 1974
COSTELLO, Beatrice, ssw-Francis, b. 1915, d. 1983
COSTELLO, Francis, ssw-Beatrice, b. 1925, d. N/D
COWAN, Rebecca W., b. 07/19/1918, d. 08/27/1990
COWGILL, Anne Irwin, b. 1909, d. 1992
COX, Elzada, ssw-Walter, b. 1850, d. 1920
COX, Walter, ssw-Elzada, b. 1847, d. 1926
CROSBY, Lois H., ssw-William, b. 12/05/1921, d. N/D
CROSBY, William, ssw-Lois H., b. 11/21/1917, d. N/D
CROSS, Amanda May Welker, b. 1895, d. 1983
DAVIES, Elena, b. 09/18/1879, d. 06/19/1945
DAVIS, Effie, ssw-George, b. 1875, d. 1971
DAVIS, George, ssw-Effie, b. 1888, d. 1968
DEAKYNE, Grace A., ssw-James E., b. 1915, d. 1988
DEAKYNE, James E., ssw-Grace A., b. 1916, d. N/D
DEAKYNE, John, ssw-Mabel M., b. 1893, d. 1964
DEAKYNE, Mabel M., ssw-John, b. 1896, d. 1982
DEGRANDIS, Raymond, b. 1946, d. 1985
DELOY, Douglas P., ssw-Ralph A., b. 11/30/1944, d. 09/17/1985
DELOY, Geraldine S., ssw-Ralph A., b. 09/21/1924, d. N/D
DELOY, Mary Ann, ssw-Ralph A., b. 08/03/1958, d. 05/16/1966
DELOY, Ralph A., ssw-Geraldine S., b. 01/13/1922, d. N/D
DEMING, Richard C., b. 10/07/1914, d. 05/15/1967
DENNY, Nadejda, b. 1904, d. 1976
DERRICKSON, Earline, ssw-Harry E., b. 10/20/1925, d. N/D
DERRICKSON, Ethel M., ssw-William B., b. 12/04/1912, d. N/D
DERRICKSON, Harry E., ssw-Earline, b. 03/22/1924, d. 08/10/1990
DERRICKSON, J. Kenneth, b. 05/18/1977, d. 04/09/1987
DERRICKSON, William B., ssw-Ethel M., b. 08/23/1913, d. 08/20/1981
DESCHAMPS, Marie, ssw-Maurice, b. 03/31/1895, d. 12/26/1983

DESCHAMPS, Maurice, ssw-Marie, b. 11/02/1886, d. 02/20/1958

DESMET, Edmund R., ssw-Hester M., Husband, b. 08/04/1920, d. 09/27/1991

DESMET, Hester M., ssw-Edmund R., Wife, b. 10/16/1918, d. 10/16/1988

DONOVAN, Richard Edward, DE, A2C, 2134 Comm. Sq., AF, b. 04/02/1939, d. 03/17/1965

DOUGHERTY, Joseph F., ssw-Kathleen R., b. 1908, d. 1981

DOUGHERTY, Kathleen R., ssw-Joseph F., b. 1915, d. 1986

DOWNING, Elizabeth E., ssw-William S., b. 1874, d. 1965

DOWNING, Floris E., b. 1907, d. 1990

DOWNING, J. Arthur, DE, Surf, USCG, WWI, b. 12/13/1885, d. 08/04/1966

DOWNING, James A., b. 1860, d. 1912

DOWNING, Sarah E., b. 1885, d. 1945

DOWNING, William S., ssw-Elizabeth E., b. 1870, d. 1937

DUTTON, Anna B., ssw-Wm. Elmer, b. 12/23/1885, d. 03/03/1962

DUTTON, Ethel, ssw-Joe, b. 1904, d. 1983

DUTTON, J. T., ssw-S. E., b. 1850, d. 1924

DUTTON, Joe, ssw-Ethel, b. 1899, d. 1978

DUTTON, S. E., ssw-J. T., b. 1856, d. 1926

DUTTON, Wilton E., T/5 Hq. Btry. 27th Armored FA. Bn., Killed in action Italy, b. 04/01/1917,
        d. 04/28/1945

DUTTON, Wm. Elmer, ssw-Anna B., b. 01/14/1877, d. 01/04/1954

DYER, Courtland G., ssw-Elizabeth M., b. 08/14/1906, d. 12/25/1969

DYER, Elizabeth M., ssw-Courtland G., b. 12/01/1905, d. N/D

EATON, Gregory J., ssw-Irma D., b. 1909, d. 1984

EATON, Irma D., ssw-Gregory J., b. 1922, d. 1991

EDER, Edward J., b. 1907, d. 1969

EDGERTON, Anna Hayden, b. 07/27/1935, d. 02/10/1985

EDWARDS, Annie C., ssw-George W., b. 1873, d. 1960

EDWARDS, George W., ssw-Annie C., b. 1871, d. 1947

EICHNER, Walter Gardner, b. 12/05/1907, d. 10/22/1946

ELIAS, Annie, Born Ratzebur-Pommern, Germany, b. 09/21/1896, d. 08/05/1974

ELIAS, John, b. 06/10/1880, d. 02/27/1953

ELLINGSWORTH, George W., DE, Tec3, HQ Co., 1st Army, WWII, b. 07/01/1913, d. 03/17/1968

ELLIS, Edith M., ssw-William J., b. 11/15/1888, d. 11/12/1975

ELLIS, Rebecca B., ssw-William J., b. 08/05/1918, d. N/D

ELLIS, William J., ssw-Edith M., b. 11/17/1888, d. 11/25/1943

ELLIS, William J., ssw-Rebecca B., b. 04/17/1916, d. N/D

ELSASSER, Ernest, ssw-Jenny, b. N/D, d. N/D

ELSASSER, Jenny, ssw-Ernest, b. N/D, d. N/D

ELSASSER, Mabel, ssw-Ernest, b. N/D, d. N/D

EVANS, Ella L., b. 01/19/1890, d. 01/03/1923

EVANS, Lucy C., b. 08/11/1896, d. 02/17/1960

EVANS, Samuel R., Pfc., Co. F, 2nd BA. 8th Inf., Killed in action in Germany, b. 06/16/1916, d. 02/11/1945

EVANS, Scott Samuel, b. 10/26/1894, d. 01/24/1950

EWING, Barbara, ssw-Charles Holland, b. 08/24/1933, d. N/D

EWING, Charles Holland, ssw-Barbara, A2C, USAF, Korea, b. 05/22/1929, d. 06/08/1978

EWING, Clarence A., ssw-Eugenia H., b. 1895, d. 1974

EWING, Eugenia H., ssw-Clarence A., b. 1896, d. 1981

EWING, Mildred H., ssw-Thomas W., Jr., b. 1904, d. N/D

EWING, Thomas W., Jr., ssw-Mildred H., DE, Pvt., Co. M, 167 Inf., WWI, b. 08/17/1896, d. 12/21/1968

FARIES, Charles K., ssw-Helen M., b. 05/23/1911, d. N/D

FARIES, Helen M., ssw-Charles K., b. 02/05/1909, d. 04/10/1991

FICHTER, Lawrence J., Jr., b. 1946, d. 1989

FISHER, Charles, ssw-Mary C., b. 1878, d. 1951

FISHER, Mary C., ssw-Charles, b. 1885, d. 1954

FISHER, Walter N., DE, Sgt., 2521 Svc. Comd. Unit, WWII, b. 03/06/1910, d. 11/06/1962

FRAME, George, b. 04/22/1905, d. 03/25/1974

FRAZER, Alice Virginia, ssw-Henry Sylvester, b. 05/05/1860, d. 08/22/1930

FRAZER, Henry Sylvester, ssw-Alice Virginia, b. 04/09/1853, d. 12/08/1928

FRAZER, Mary Pearle, b. 12/23/1901, d. 07/09/1980

FRESE, Adolf, ssw-Katharina Scholze and Anne & August Stolting, b. 03/29/1901, d. 12/18/1989

FRESE, Martha, ssw-Katharina Scholze and Anne & August Stolting, b. 05/02/1907, d. 12/23/1986

FRITCHMAN, J. Curtis, ssw-Sara L., b. 03/15/1905, d. N/D

FRITCHMAN, Sara L., ssw-J. Curtis, b. 05/27/1911, d. N/D

FRYE, Lucille Reed, Mother, b. 11/14/1916, d. 03/30/1977

FRYLING, Ida P., b. 01/29/1866, d. 06/21/1925

GADOW, Bernhard A., b. 05/28/1911, d. 02/09/1984

GAGNON, Virginia Keen, b. 1902, d. 1965

GANTT, Albert, ssw-Edna S., MD, 1st Sgt., Co. E, 5th Inf., MDNG, WWI, b. 06/06/1887, d. 04/12/1960

GANTT, Edna S., ssw-Albert, b. 11/03/1892, d. 11/17/1971

GILMARTIN, Ida Palmer, ssw-Thomas J., b. 09/01/1915, d. 05/08/1973

GILMARTIN, Thomas J., ssw-Ida Palmer, b. 10/13/1906, d. 08/25/1971

GILTENBOTH, George H., ssw-Marie V., b. 08/20/1908, d. N/D

GILTENBOTH, Marie V., ssw-George H., b. 06/02/1908, d. 10/28/1989

GOBAS, Eudokia Zoides, b. 08/12/1903, d. 02/13/1990

GOBAS, George, Born Galatine, Greece, b. 1893, d. 1967

GOEPEL, Harry C., b. 1900, d. 1963

GOLDEN, Irene C., b. 08/10/1926, d. 11/10/1990

GOODWIN, Hilda S., ssw-Paul Eugene, b. 09/19/1921, d. 05/22/1991

GOODWIN, Paul Eugene, ssw-Hilda S., Cpl, USA, WWII, b. 11/03/1916, d. 01/25/1991

GOVATOS, John G., Jr., b. 07/28/1916, d. 10/15/1985

GOWER, Frances Morgan, b. 1927, d. 1989

GRAHAM, Ella M., ssw-John P., b. 1886, d. 1959

GRAHAM, John P., ssw-Ella M., b. 1884, d. 1969

GREEN, Harvey H., ssw-Hettie J., b. 10/11/1878, d. 02/11/1948

GREEN, Hettie J., ssw-Harvey H., b. 12/09/1876, d. 02/21/1962

GREENE, Charles E., ssw-Ruth E., b. 11/24/1863, d. 03/13/1929

GREENE, Fannie Burton, b. 04/17/1878, d. 06/06/1950

GREENE, Ruth E., ssw-Charles E., b. 12/30/1867, d. 03/22/1926

GRIFFIN, Delma Ewing, ssw-Edwin B., b. 1904, d. 1983

GRIFFIN, Edwin B., ssw-Delma Ewing, DE, SSgt., GHQ, US Forces PAC, WWII, b. 11/05/1906, d. 05/04/1962

GRUBBS, Della E., b. 01/24/1874, d. 04/29/1945

GUTHERIE, Mable Eagleston, ssw-Raymond Stewart, b. 04/09/1901, d. 07/12/1965

GUTHERIE, Raymond Stewart, ssw-Mable Easleston, b. 08/26/1900, d. 04/29/1950

HABIB, Mohamed, b. 1925, d. 1986

HADDER, George F., ssw-Marion H., b. 1933, d. 1978

HADDER, Marion H., ssw-George F., b. 1921, d. 1978

HAFF, Eliza M., ssw-John H., b. 1907, d. N/D

HAFF, John H., ssw-Eliza M., b. 1903, d. 1978

HALEY, Lorraine, ssw-Thomas J., Jr., b. 1914, d. 1972

HALEY, Thomas J., Jr., ssw-Lorraine, b. 1912, d. 1990

HALL, Dorothy Wingate, b. 04/28/1905, d. 01/15/1973

HAMMOND, Dorothy F., ssw-William A., b. 07/05/1921, d. N/D

HAMMOND, William A., ssw-Dorothy F., b. 09/14/1909, d. 03/07/1977

HANNA, George Thomas, b. 1853, d. 1942

HARMON, Florence Quillen, b. 11/13/1922, d. N/D

HARMON, Robert Lee, Major, USA, WWII, Korea, b. 11/18/1920, d. N/D

HARMSTEAD, James L., ssw-Lillian M., b. 1877, d. 1940

HARMSTEAD, Lillian M., ssw-James L., b. 1878, d. 1955

HARPER, Meta M., ssw-Thomas Bayard, b. 02/24/1927, d. N/D

HARPER, Thomas Bayard, ssw-Meta M., DE, LCpl., USMC, Korea, b. 01/10/1930, d. 09/21/1964

HARRIS, Martha B., b. 03/31/1895, d. 12/10/1966

HAYDEN, Edward L., ssw-Emma L., b. 03/31/1901, d. 05/23/1986

HAYDEN, Emma L., ssw-Edward L., b. 10/17/1904, d. 06/30/1944

HAYDEN, Eugene T., Sr., ssw-Mabel Lucas, b. 1894, d. 1948

HAYDEN, Mabel Lucas, ssw-Eugene T., Sr., b. 1900, d. 1984

HAYS, Harry E., ssw-Mary M., b. 05/17/1887, d. 03/18/1959

HAYS, Mary M., ssw-Harry E., b. 06/18/1892, d. 05/27/1978

HAZZARD, Bessie E., ssw-John C., b. 03/18/1906, d. 04/13/1979

HAZZARD, J. Earl, ssw-Lillian E., b. 1903, d. 1979

HAZZARD, James E., Jr., ssw-John C., b. 1905, d. 1990

HAZZARD, John C., ssw-Bessie E., b. 03/18/1930, d. 02/15/1964

HAZZARD, Lillian E., ssw-J. Earl, b. 1908, d. 1991

HAZZARD, Robert Earl, b. 1929, d. 1974

HILL, Amanda Boone, b. 04/24/1863, d. 12/11/1949

HILL, Charles P., b. 1915, d. 1915

HILL, Charles Plummer, b. 01/08/1920, d. 05/14/1956

HILL, Elizabeth S., b. 07/26/1922, d. 11/17/1990

HILL, Emily Amanda, b. 1914, d. 1914

HILL, Frank Smith, b. 1915, d. 1916

HILL, Fred C., b. 03/15/1892, d. 01/14/1950

HILL, George W., b. 08/27/1894, d. 05/16/1931

HILL, Harvey E., ssw-S. Blanche, b. 02/15/1896, d. 05/08/1958

HILL, Helena Quillen, ssw-John W., b. 03/20/1907, d. 11/24/1963

HILL, Joanne, ssw-John W., Jr., b. 04/29/1936, d. N/D

HILL, John E., s/o William P. & Bertha B. Hill, b. 03/20/1946, d. 02/19/1987

HILL, John W., ssw-Helena Quillen, b. 05/30/1899, d. 10/06/1987

HILL, John W., Jr., ssw-Joanne, b. 05/26/1928, d. 07/22/1985

HILL, Phyllis Bennett, ssw-Robert Clarke, III & Robert Clarke, IV, b. 12/14/1919, d. 10/10/1982

HILL, Robert Clarke, III, ssw-Phyllis Bennett & Robert Clarke, IV, b. 11/12/1918, d. 10/19/1989

HILL, Robert Clarke, IV, ssw-Robert Clarke, III & Phyllis Bennett, b. 09/22/1945, d. 12/28/1973

HILL, Ruth, b. 04/04/1897, d. 08/05/1969

HILL, S. Blanche, ssw-Harvey E., b. 07/29/1893, d. 10/05/1990

HILL, Sara A., ssw-William L., b. 11/27/1909, d. 01/03/1991

HILL, William L., ssw-Sara A., b. 10/01/1906, d. 06/22/1966

HILL, William P., Jr., s/o William P. & Bertha B. Hill, b. 02/25/1942, d. 02/01/1947

HINCKLEY, Robert, b. 04/03/1853, d. 06/01/1941

HITCH, Cathy A., b. 12/02/1960, d. 06/05/1962

HITCH, Dorothy J., ssw-John L., b. 03/16/1922, d. N/D

HITCH, John L., ssw-Dorothy J., b. 07/31/1923, d. N/D

HITCHENS, Warren E., TSgt, USA, WWII, b. 08/03/1915, d. 11/12/1975

HOEBEE, Mary, ssw-Ralph, b. 08/24/1916, d. N/D

HOEBEE, Ralph, ssw-Mary, b. 06/10/1913, d. 05/21/1984

HOLLAND, Angie V., ssw-William J., b. 1898, d. 1989

HOLLAND, George, ssw-Mary R., b. 1883, d. 1951

HOLLAND, Gladys, ssw-Mary R., b. 1914, d. 1980

HOLLAND, Harold, ssw-Mary R., b. 1908, d. 1976

HOLLAND, Mary R., ssw-George, b. 1887, d. 1980

HOLLAND, Steven Carl, b. 08/03/1964, d. 04/28/1990

HOLLAND, William J., ssw-Angie V., b. 1893, d. 1949

HUDSON, Alma K. P., ssw-Harland J. Paynter, b. N/D, d. 12/23/1978

HUDSON, Edward S., ssw-Walsie K., b. 12/29/1884, d. 03/27/1970

HUDSON, Ethel Pittman Sadler, ssw-John Norman, Born Whitaker, NC, b. N/D, d. 05/14/1963

HUDSON, Ethelind Sadler, ssw-John Norman, b. 08/11/1902, d. 02/11/1966

HUDSON, J. Fred, b. 1877, d. 1957

HUDSON, James F., Jr., ssw-John Norman, b. 12/11/1965, d. 12/12/1965

HUDSON, Jean Marie, ssw-John Norman, b. 03/10/1936, d. 07/14/1936

HUDSON, John Norman, ssw-Ethelind Sadler, b. 12/31/1899, d. 10/06/1986

HUDSON, John Norman, Jr., ssw-John Norman, b. N/D, d. 11/19/1938

HUDSON, Mae H., b. 1879, d. 1963

HUDSON, Walsie K., ssw-Edward S., b. 08/27/1887, d. 02/17/1987

JAMES, Grace Brown, b. 10/19/1891, d. 01/17/1972

JAMES, William Linden, b. 02/17/1889, d. 05/09/1970

JOHNSON, Arthur H., ssw-Lydia E., Father, b. 1852, d. 1925

JOHNSON, Della A., ssw-Horace P., b. 1853, d. 1930

JOHNSON, Ella F., ssw-Lester F., b. 03/08/1898, d. 01/22/1985

JOHNSON, Horace P., ssw-Della A., b. 1888, d. 1931

JOHNSON, J. Dorman, ssw-Ruth S., b. 07/23/1907, d. 04/16/1971

JOHNSON, John B., ssw-Lucy W., b. 1870, d. 1947

JOHNSON, Lester F., ssw-Ella F., b. 07/17/1897, d. 05/27/1990

JOHNSON, Lucy W., ssw-John B., b. 1873, d. 1947

JOHNSON, Lydia E., ssw-Arthur H., Mother, b. 1856, d. 1930

JOHNSON, Norma Mae, ssw-Arthur H., Sister, b. 1878, d. 1940

JOHNSON, Ruth S., ssw-J. Dorman, b. 08/26/1908, d. N/D

JOHNSON, Samuel R., ssw-Horace P., b. 1849, d. 1927

JOHNSTON, Cleburn Coy, Sr., ssw-Lena Ruth, b. 10/11/1894, d. 12/21/1987

JOHNSTON, Lena Ruth, ssw-Cleburn Coy, Sr., b. 06/11/1898, d. 09/09/1955

JONES, Abram I., b. 1890, d. 1972

JONES, Arminta, b. 1899, d. 1989

JONES, John Gaddis, b. 1906, d. 1989

JOSEPH, A. Frank, ssw-Amelia W., b. 09/14/1861, d. 04/29/1942

JOSEPH, Alfred M., ssw-Sarah E., Herbert B. & Sallie A. Joseph and Kate N. McHenry, b. 1848, d. 1925

JOSEPH, Amelia W., ssw-A. Frank, b. 09/11/1868, d. 10/30/1944

JOSEPH, Carl T., ssw-Edith T., b. 06/13/1894, d. 03/08/1968

JOSEPH, Catherine E., ssw-Harold R., b. 09/13/1909, d. 11/16/1971

JOSEPH, Charles F., ssw-Flossie H., b. 04/06/1892, d. 02/13/1986

JOSEPH, Edith T., ssw-Carl T., b. 05/17/1895, d. 01/12/1959

JOSEPH, Ethel Megee, ssw-John E., b. 11/13/1895, d. 08/20/1961

JOSEPH, Flossie H., ssw-Charles F., b. 02/10/1893, d. 02/23/1949

JOSEPH, Harold R., ssw-Catherine E., b. 08/02/1910, d. 10/05/1987

JOSEPH, Herbert B., ssw-Alfred M., Sarah E. & Sallie A. Joseph and Kate N. McHenry, b. 1881, d. 1950

JOSEPH, John E., ssw-Ethel Megee, b. 06/08/1886, d. 07/05/1965

JOSEPH, Kenneth Megee, DE, Sgt., AAF, WWII, b. 03/03/1922, d. 05/04/1973

JOSEPH, Leona E., b. 1885, d. 1970

JOSEPH, Marjorie M., ssw-Norman B., b. 1916, d. N/D

JOSEPH, Norman B., ssw-Marjorie M., b. 1898, d. 1980

JOSEPH, Sallie A., ssw-Alfred M., Sarah E. & Herbert B. Joseph and Kate N. McHenry, b. 1828, d. 1918

JOSEPH, Sarah E., ssw-Alfred M., Sallie A. & Herbert B. Joseph and Kate N. McHenry, b. 1849, d. 1920

JOYCE, Betty D., ssw-James I., b. 1900, d. 1988

JOYCE, James i., ssw-Betty D., PA, CPL, USMC, WWII, b. 02/07/1903, d. 09/20/1969

KEENE, Cassie Hanna, ssw-Earle Linwood, b. 1891, d. 1984

KEENE, Earle Linwood, ssw-Cassie Hanna, b. 1892, d. 1941

KELSO, Hugh S., Sonny, DE, A1C, 568 Opr. Sq., AF, Korea, b. 02/05/1929, d. 05/14/1970

KENNEY, Winnetta E., b. 07/23/1899, d. 04/27/1975

KENTON, Elsie M., ssw-William H., b. 09/25/1923, d. N/D

KENTON, Fred Charles, b. 03/01/1953, d. 10/01/1954

KENTON, William H., ssw-Elsie M., b. 12/16/1906, d. 04/22/1984

KEY, Eugene Winfield, ssw-Helen Byrd, b. 1908, d. 1965

KEY, Helen Byrd, ssw-Eugene Winfield, b. 1916, d. N/D

KING, Blanche A., ssw-Charles S. & Florence K. Salin, b. 1855, d. 1944

KIRBY, James W., b. 1908, d. 1965

KIRKER, Dimmie S., ssw-Joseph E., b. 04/18/1887, d. 08/08/1966

KIRKER, Joseph E., ssw-Dimmie S., b. 02/07/1883, d. 09/18/1973

KUNSMAN, Electa A., ssw-Granville F., b. 08/07/1918, d. N/D

KUNSMAN, Eliza Jane, ssw-Fred, b. 1863, d. 1934

KUNSMAN, Elsie W., ssw-Joseph S., b. 1883, d. 1957

KUNSMAN, Fred, ssw-Eliza Jane, b. 1862, d. 1940

KUNSMAN, Granville F., ssw-Electa A., b. 02/12/1916, d. N/D

KUNSMAN, Joseph S., ssw-Elsie W., b. 1878, d. 1960

LAFFERTY, John E., USA, WWII, b. 1916, d. 1981

LANGE, Karl F., Born Ratzebuhr-Pommern, Germany, b. 11/15/1892, d. 12/30/1953

LARSEN, Ejner C., ssw-Nan D., b. 04/24/1895, d. 01/07/1969

LARSEN, Nan D., ssw-Ejner C., b. 07/23/1899, d. N/D

LATHROP, Lucy Y., b. 03/19/1890, d. 08/03/1981

LAVACHIA, Joseph, b. N/D, d. 1992

LAVENETS, Steve Henry, b. 08/30/1965, d. 11/19/1965

LAVENETS, Dorothy, b. 02/24/1957, d. 10/20/1979

LAVIN, William F., USA, WWII, b. 07/13/1909, d. 01/16/1989

LEBEGERN, Charles H., Sr., ssw-Helen G., b. 07/04/1899, d. 10/17/1984

LEBEGERN, Helen G., ssw-Charles H., Sr., b. 06/24/1902, d. 03/02/1979

LEWICKI, Apollonia, b. 12/23/1984, d. 01/01/1985
LEWIS, Margaret F., ssw-William E., b. 1915, d. 1973
LEWIS, William E., ssw-Margaret F., b. 1912, d. 1980
LINDALE, Mary P., ssw-William L., b. 1894, d. 1984
LINDALE, William L., ssw-Mary P., DE, Pvt., USA, WWII, b. 10/11/1896, d. 10/03/1973
LINGENFELTER, Helen G., ssw-John S., b. 06/22/1916, d. 08/14/1977
LINGENFELTER, John S., ssw-Helen G., b. 05/03/1946, d. 04/13/1966
LOCASCIO, Alma L., ssw-Michael, b. 1908, d. 1960
LOCASCIO, Michael, ssw-Alma L., NY, Pvt., 1252 Svc. Com. Unit, WWII, b. 04/25/1900, d. 04/03/1969
LOPRESTI, Ignazio, ssw-Mary P., b. 03/24/1897, d. 02/13/1990
LOPRESTI, Mary P., ssw-Ignazio, b. 05/17/1903, d. 03/06/1966
LORAH, Jack J., b. 05/25/1944, d. 09/11/1975
LORAH, Jean M., b. 02/20/1916, d. 09/10/1982
LUTHER, Margaret S., b. 07/31/1913, d. 03/12/1969
LUTKAVAGE, Frank W., ssw-Mary E., b. 1899, d. 1982
LUTKAVAGE, Mary E., ssw-Frank W., b. 1906, d. 1974
LUTZ, Myrtle W., w/o Norman A., b. 09/10/1892, d. 12/29/1980
LUTZ, Norman A., b. 02/05/1893, d. 09/29/1965
LYELL, Eva S., b. 1900, d. 1976
LYNCH, Anna E., ssw-James T., b. 1907, d. N/D
LYNCH, Dorothy R., ssw-George B., b. 05/11/1911, d. N/D
LYNCH, George B., ssw-Dorothy R., b. 09/11/1909, d. 02/21/1987
LYNCH, James T., ssw-Anna E., b. 1902, d. 1965
LYTE, Jamk, b. N/D, d. 07/17/1990
MACABEE, Mamie J., ssw-Thomas M., b. 09/18/1900, d. 03/21/1980
MACABEE, Thomas M., ssw-Mamie J., b. 11/01/1903, d. 01/19/1975
MACDONALD, Elsie M., d/o Edward S. & Amanda Boone Hill, b. 01/28/1901, d. 07/29/1991
MACK, Christian E., ssw-Mary Louise, b. 01/12/1929, d. 04/06/1988
MACK, Mary Louise, ssw-Christian E., b. 04/03/1925, d. N/D
MACLAUGHLIN, Cecil Gordon, Mac, WT3, USN, WWII, b. 11/06/1905, d. 10/11/1976
MAGDALENO, Aureliano G., ssw-Lydia E., b. 06/16/1905, d. 05/24/1983
MAGDALENO, Lydia E., ssw-Aureliano G., b. 02/15/1913, d. 02/27/1982
MAJOR, Elizabeth S., ssw-Harry W., b. 1908, d. N/D
MAJOR, Harry W., ssw-Elizabeth S., b. 1908, d. 1947
MANN, B. Judith, ssw-William Henry, b. 11/03/1929, d. 12/19/1991
MANN, William Henry, ssw-B. Judith, b. 03/13/1917, d. 04/25/1990
MARSH, Emma C., ssw-Nathaniel P., b. 02/29/1896, d. 02/11/1988
MARSH, John J., ssw-Kathryn E., b. 10/28/1913, d. N/D
MARSH, Kathryn E., ssw-John J., b. 10/13/1913, d. N/D
MARSH, Nathaniel p., ssw-Emma C., b. 10/27/1895, d. 04/06/1969
MARTIN, Janet P., ssw-John H., b. 1919, d. 1983
MARTIN, John H., ssw-Janet P., b. 1916, d. 1985
MARVEL, Beatrice E., ssw-Kenly C., b. 10/23/1914, d. 05/27/1984
MARVEL, Kenly C., ssw-Beatrice E., b. 11/05/1913, d. N/D
MARVEL, William H., Jr., Cpl., USA, WWII, b. 10/10/1917, d. 03/17/1979
MASON, Delemo Greene, b. 05/31/1892, d. 07/21/1956
MASSEY, Edward S., DE, CBM, USCG, WWI, b. 09/04/1875, d. 04/09/1947
MASSEY, Florence H., b. 01/21/1913, d. 06/29/1968

MASSEY, G. Dewey, b. 08/14/1898, d. 04/29/1951

MASSEY, John Edmund, s/o John & Florence, b. 07/28/1936, d. 09/25/1939

MASSEY, John W., b. 01/08/1911, d. 05/03/1981

MASSEY, Joshua W., b. 08/21/1837, d. 05/19/1914

MASSEY, Margaret M., b. 11/27/1880, d. 05/06/1957

MASTEN, Fannie C., b. 02/06/1885, d. 03/20/1939

MATTHEWS, John Cecil, ssw-Rita Virginia D., b. 02/24/1902, d. 10/24/1982

MATTHEWS, Rita Virginia D., ssw-John Cecil, b. 10/19/1908, d. N/D

MAULL, Helen Hastings, ssw-Robert Arnell, Sr., b. 05/08/1913, d. N/D

MAULL, Robert Arnell, Sr., ssw-Helen Hastings, b. 11/16/1911, d. 11/28/1969

MCCAULLEY, Estella R., ssw-Henry B., b. 1893, d. 1976

MCCAULLEY, Henry B., ssw-Estella R., b. 1887, d. 1974

MCCULLOCH, Edith E., ssw-Samuel A., b. 02/04/1894, d. 04/04/1981

MCCULLOCH, Samuel A., ssw-Edith E., b. 08/31/1898, d. 02/28/1990

MCDANIEL, NFN, Fire Station 86, b. N/D, d. N/D

MCDOWELL, Alvin Franklin, ssw-Mary Miller, b. 1903, d. 1987

MCDOWELL, Mary Miller, ssw-Alvin Franklin, b. 1904, d. N/D

MCGOVERN, Rebecca J. Toomey, b. 11/01/1891, d. 04/28/1975

MCHENRY, Kate N., ssw-Alfred M., Sarah E., Herbert B. & Sallie A. Joseph, b. 1882, d. 1953

MCNATT, Ronald W., b. 02/17/1938, d. 10/22/1983

MCQUAY, Alice L., ssw-William S., b. 1910, d. 1951

MCQUAY, Mae H., b. 1915, d. 1956

MCQUAY, William S., ssw-Alice L., b. 1908, d. N/D

MELSON, Claudia B., ssw-Joseph B., b. 11/19/1921, d. N/D

MELSON, Gail Ann, b. N/D, d. 08/18/1968

MELSON, Joseph B., ssw-Claudia B., b. 10/15/1919, d. N/D

MELVIN, David G., ssw-Mollie C., b. 11/20/1884, d. 01/25/1940

MELVIN, Mollie C., ssw-David G., b. 07/28/1889, d. 08/06/1978

MELVIN, Victor K., b. 10/05/1905, d. 04/21/1975

MERRITT, Bessie M., b. 12/01/1889, d. 07/31/1968

MERRITT, Harry V., ssw-Mattie H., DE, CBM, USCG, WWI, WWII, b. 08/02/1890, d. 03/17/1962

MERRITT, Jesse M., b. 04/01/1887, d. 08/15/1967

MERRITT, Mattie H., ssw-Harry V., b. 11/26/1899, d. 10/09/1973

MESSICK, Charles G., DE, Pvt., 21 Inf., 24 Inf. Div., Korea, b. 03/20/1931, d. 08/11/1950

MESSICK, Estella H., b. 1889, d. 1966

MESSICK, John S., b. 1887, d. 1972

MESSICK, Margaret M., ssw-Ralph R., b. 05/15/1914, d. 02/10/1986

MESSICK, Nancy Lee, b. 06/28/1959, d. 10/14/1971

MESSICK, Ralph R., ssw-Margaret M., b. 02/09/1909, d. 12/15/1986

MILLANE, Kathryn H., ssw-Richard Daniel, Mother, b. 10/101908, d. N/D

MILLANE, Richard Daniel, s/o Kathryn H., CT, Cpl, USMC, b. 04/20/1947, d. 04/14/1967

MINNER, NFN, b. N/D, d. N/D

MISENER, Mildred Ann, b. 04/16/1905, d. 11/11/1981

MITCHELL, Clara Edna, ssw-William T., b. 1899, d. 1973

MITCHELL, Cole Lawton, b. N/D, d. 10/25/1991

MITCHELL, Delia E., ssw-Larry S., b. 1894, d. 1941

MITCHELL, Eva W., ssw-Oliver H., b. 1884, d. 1962

MITCHELL, Larry S., ssw-Delia E., b. 1886, d. 1970

MITCHELL, Oliver H., ssw-Eva W., b. 1883, d. 1963

MITCHELL, William T., ssw-Clara Edna, b. 1897, d. 1953

MOORE, Clara May, b. 1932, d. 1936

MOORE, Doris H., ssw-R. Carlton, b. 09/11/1909, d. N/D

MOORE, Florence M., ssw-Herbert F., b. 12/07/1909, d. N/D

MOORE, Herbert F., ssw-Florence M., b. 03/02/1907, d. 11/25/1967

MOORE, Ida Mae, b. 1913, d. 1972

MOORE, Jeddie M., b. 05/07/1930, d. 09/21/1953

MOORE, John R., b. 08/22/1939, d. 08/24/1947

MOORE, R. Carlton, ssw-Doris H., b. 09/06/1909, d. 06/01/1979

MOORE, Ralph E., b. N/D, d. 05/07/1951

MORGAN, Marguerite, ssw-Ralph D., b. 1895, d. 1989

MORGAN, Ralph D., ssw-Marguerite, b. 1892, d. 1950

MORRIS, Branche C., ssw-Jeanne L., b. 1902, d. 1984

MORRIS, Jeanne L., ssw-Branche C., b. 1906, d. 1991

MOY, Ni Ton, ssw-Fook Lew Wong, b. 1894, d. 1968

MURCH, Elizabeth, b. 1894, d. 1947

MURCH, J. Harold, b. 1897, d. 1951

MURRAY, Clarence E., b. 11/16/1896, d. 01/21/1961

MUTTI, Johanna Tiede, b. 02/05/1903, d. 10/18/1981

NEELY, Buz, b. 1947, d. 1988

NIBLETT, Jessie D., ssw-Joseph H., b. 10/26/1913, d. N/D

NIBLETT, Joseph H., ssw-Jessie D., b. 04/22/1909, d. 04/17/1988

NIBLETTE, G. Wm., ssw-Marion M., b. 1899, d. N/D

NIBLETTE, Marion M., ssw-G. Wm., b. 1902, d. 1988

NICKERSON, Fae Elaine, b. 09/22/1947, d. 11/07/1947

NOWAKOWSKI, James Brian, ssw-Jo Ann, b. 10/24/1954, d. 03/08/1974

NOWAKOWSKI, Jo Ann, ssw-James Brian, b. 04/08/1950, d. 02/02/1974

O'KEEFE, Hilda F., ssw-Joseph J., b 01/06/1908, d. N/D

O'KEEFE, Joseph J., ssw-Hilda F., b. 03/23/1899, d. 07/18/1977

OLSON, Blanche King, ssw-John Garnett, b. 09/04/1914, d. 01/17/1991

OLSON, John Garnett, ssw-Blanche King, CSC, USCG, WWII, b. 04/19/1912, d. 04/10/1982

OSBORNE, Alice Palmer, ssw-Carroll A., b. 04/24/1905, d. N/D

OSBORNE, Carroll A., ssw-Alice Palmer, b. 09/29/1890, d. 06/01/1968

OSOBA, Edward J., ssw-Nettie K., b. 02/16/1910, d. 02/21/1988

OSOBA, Nettie K., ssw-Edward J., b. 11/02/1906, d. 03/06/1986

OSTERHOLM, Albert V., b. 1907, d. 1986

PALEY, Edna M., b. 03/16/1911, d. 09/05/1991

PALEY, George E., b. 03/15/1906, d. 09/08/1967

PALMER, Alfred, ssw-Vallie, b. 1864, d. 1929

PALMER, Anna B., b. 03/27/1887, d. 03/16/1983

PALMER, Clara E., ssw-Roy W., b. 1897, d. 1970

PALMER, Cora Shockley, ssw-Ralph, b. 02/27/1895, d. 06/14/1983

PALMER, Della May, ssw-Theodore W., b. 1877, d. 1939

PALMER, Elizabeth C., ssw-Elmer T., b. 02/23/1909, d. 07/20/1979

PALMER, Elmer T., ssw-Elizabeth C., b. 06/11/1905, d. 08/24/1979

PALMER, G. Oscar, b. 06/28/1882, d. 03/05/1964

PALMER, Goldia M., ssw-Theodore R., b. 09/10/1909, d. N/D

PALMER, Harry W., b. 02/09/1877, d. 03/08/1965

PALMER, Kate, b. 1882, d. 1976

PALMER, Ralph, ssw-Cora Shockley, b. 11/25/1897, d. 03/11/1967

PALMER, Rebecca H., b. 1911, d. 1991

PALMER, Robert W., Sr., b. 10/12/1910, d. 08/15/1960

PALMER, Robert West, b. 01/21/1934, d. 03/13/1991

PALMER, Roy W., ssw-Clara E., b. 1894, d. 1957

PALMER, Theodore R., ssw-Theodore W., Jr., DE, LCpl., USMC, b. 11/24/1944, d. 12/25/1964

PALMER, Theodore W., ssw-Della May, b. 1869, d. 1943

PALMER, Theodore W., Jr., ssw-Theodore W., b. 10/08/1907, d. 03/18/1977

PALMER, Vallie, ssw-Alfred, b. 1875, d. 1968

PAPANTINAS, Theodore S., Kastoria, Greece, b. 1922, d. 1983

PARISH, C. Joseph, b. 06/08/1929, d. 07/01/1980

PARRY, Archibald Sidney, ssw-Beatrice M., b. 1901, d. 1955

PARRY, Beatrice M., ssw-Archibald Sidney, b. 1905, d. 1968

PAYNTER, Alma K., ssw-Harland J., b. 09/01/1910, d. N/D

PAYNTER, C. Marshall, b. 06/15/1896, d. 10/25/1951

PAYNTER, Calvin H., ssw-Clara V., b. 1901, d. 1971

PAYNTER, Clara V., ssw-Calvin H., b. 1904, d. 1975

PAYNTER, Guelian T., s/o James H. & Hattie A., b. 05/11/1912, d. 08/21/1912

PAYNTER, Harland J., ssw-Alma K., b. 09/15/1903, d. 01/25/1968

PAYNTER, Hettie A., ssw-James H., b. 08/21/1874, d. 09/01/1943

PAYNTER, James D., ssw-James H., b. 1907, d. 1950

PAYNTER, James H., ssw-Hettie A., b. 10/14/1867, d. 08/11/1924

PAYNTER, Lloyd B., ssw-Rachel A. & Lloyd B., Jr., DE, Pfc., USA, WWI, b. 05/13/1898, d. 05/07/1973

PAYNTER, Lloyd B., Jr., ssw-Lloyd B. & Rachel A., b. 1948, d. 1948

PAYNTER, Rachel A., ssw-Lloyd B. & Lloyd B., Jr., b. 1914, d. 1988

PELETIS, George N., b. 1894, d. 1984

PELZER, Agnes, ssw-William A., b. 1883, d. 1968

PELZER, William A., ssw-Agnes, b. 1880, d. 1956

PEPITONE, Nicholas Joseph, ssw-Thelma R., Tec4, USA, WWII, b. 1912, d. 1975

PEPITONE, Thelma R., ssw-Nicholas Joseph, b. 1912, d. 1976

PFISTER, Joseph, ssw-Thelma, b. 1904, d. N/D

PFISTER, Thelma, ssw-Joseph, b. 1910, d. 1976

PHILLIPS, Anna E., ssw-Hance C., Sr., b. 06/30/1908, d. N/D

PHILLIPS, Charles H., ssw-Marie M., b. 1894, d. 1988

PHILLIPS, Clifford F., ssw-H. Mildred, b. 03/29/1902, d. 06/14/1964

PHILLIPS, Edward C., ssw-Florence M., b. 1886, d. 1952

PHILLIPS, Emily E., ssw-Frederick B., b. 04/07/1908, d. N/D

PHILLIPS, Florence M., ssw-Edward C., b. 1891, d. 1976

PHILLIPS, Frederick B., ssw-Emily E., b. 05/30/1905, d. 10/13/1985

PHILLIPS, H. Mildred, ssw-Clifford F., b. 12/24/1909, d. N/D

PHILLIPS, Hance C., Sr., ssw-Anna E., b. 12/23/1900, d. 08/19/1976

PHILLIPS, Jewell P. McQuay, ssw-Maude C., b. 05/18/1922, d. N/D

PHILLIPS, Marie M., ssw-Charles H., b. 1903, d. 1990

PHILLIPS, Maude C., ssw-Jewell P. McQuay, b. 09/04/1884, d. 09/05/1971

PHILLIPS, Patrick R., b. 1982, d. 1982

PIERSON, Cecilia M., ssw-Ralph B., b. 07/14/1908, d. N/D

PIERSON, Ralph B., ssw-Cecilia M., USA, WWI, b. 05/18/1895, d. 02/28/1990
POUPARD, Helen, ssw-Theodore, b. 09/06/1911, d. 09/22/1991
POUPARD, Theodore, ssw-Helen, b. 04/04/1912, d. 10/21/1981
POWELL, Edwin R., ssw-Evelyn E., b. 08/04/1905, d. 06/20/1978
POWELL, Evelyn E., ssw-Edwin R., b. 05/31/1917, d. 08/23/1973
PRICE, Julian C., b. 10/02/1904, d. 09/25/1987
PRICE, Marion Yarnall, b. 1894, d. 1927
PURDY, Dorothy M., ssw-Forrest E., b. 07/06/1909, d. N/D
PURDY, Forrest E., ssw-Dorothy M., b. 03/03/1894, d. 03/14/1981
QUACKENBOSS, M. J., b. 1854, d. 1934
QUILLEN, Ada L., ssw-D. Franklin, Sr., b. 1905, d. 1951
QUILLEN, D. Franklin, Sr., ssw-Ada L., b. 1898, d. 1958
QUILLEN, Harry K., ssw-Sara E., b. 12/22/1912, d. 11/08/1980
QUILLEN, Sara E., ssw-Harry K., b. 11/04/1911, d. N/D
QUINN, Helen T., b. 01/15/1903, d. 11/07/1971
REED, Alva R., ssw-Russell M., b. N/D, d. N/D
REED, B. Mildred, ssw-H. Frank, b. 06/21/1899, d. 12/16/1979
REED, H. Frank, ssw-B. Mildred, b. 01/18/1896, d. 10/29/1978
REED, Russell M., ssw-Alva R., b. 12/10/1908, d. 02/04/1975
REICHHOLD, Laura M. Scheller, ssw-Minnie Scheller & Ralph George, b. 1896, d. 1956
REICHHOLD, Minnie Scheller, ssw-Laura M. Scheller & Ralph George, b. 1894, d. 1988
REICHHOLD, Ralph George, ssw-Laura M. Scheller & Minnie Scheller, b. 1894, d. 1989
REYNOLDS, Elbert R., ssw-Tenie K., b. 01/23/1904, d. 02/12/1972
REYNOLDS, Tenie K., ssw-Elbert R., b. 02/04/1905, d. 09/08/1986
RICKARDS, Irene E., b. N/D, d. 09/07/1951
ROACH, Anna L., ssw-Thomas H., b. 08/12/1866, d. 04/17/1956
ROACH, Ayers W., ssw-Mollie J., b. 02/26/1894, d. 02/03/1925
ROACH, George A., ssw-Rida B., b. 01/18/1884, d. 05/25/1951
ROACH, Louis W., ssw-William T., b. 07/04/1905, d. 10/21/1990
ROACH, Mollie J., ssw-Ayers W., b. 07/21/1893, d. 05/07/1968
ROACH, Rida B., ssw-George A., b. 01/07/1876, d. 07/31/1960
ROACH, Thomas H., ssw-Anna L., b. 11/13/1856, d. 04/13/1913
ROACH, Walter J., ssw-Ayers W., b. 11/20/1922, d. 06/18/1927
ROACH, William T., ssw-Louis W., b. 12/13/1887, d. 07/29/1978
ROBERTS, Charles G., DC, Lcdr., USN, WWII, b. 03/04/1912, d. 02/04/1974
ROBERTS, Elsie Eagleston, ssw-John William, b. 03/18/1920, d. N/D
ROBERTS, John William, ssw-Elsie Eagleston, TSgt, USA, WWII, b. 11/16/1913, d. 04/04/1982
ROBINSON, Helen E., b. 1890, d. 1916
RODGERS, Edward S., ssw-Evelyn M., b. 1912, d. 1973
RODGERS, Evelyn M., ssw-Edward S., b. 1916, d. N/D
ROOPE, Helen L., ssw-John R., Jr., b. 03/17/1936, d. 04/23/1983
ROOPE, John R., Jr., ssw-Helen L., b. 01/08/1934, d. N/D
ROYCE, Essie L., ssw-George E., b. 1893, d. 1973
ROYCE, George E., ssw-Essie L., b. 1888, d. 1960
RUBLE, Vivian C., DE, Pfc., 24 Transport Sq., AAF, WWII, b. 02/18/1901, d. 07/22/1960
RUDDELL, Austin G., b. 08/29/1911, d. 08/08/1971
RUDDELL, Edward C., b. 05/08/1917, d. 05/15/1919
RUDDELL, Frederick B., b. 09/14/1913, d. 02/23/1915

RUDDELL, Maude A., b. 12/22/1885, d. 12/17/1984
RUGE, Tewes C., b. 05/13/1878, d. 04/19/1961
RUGE, William J., b. 01/19/1883, d. 02/04/1964
RUMBOLD, Lila Maitland, ssw-Robert Thomas, b. 09/10/18__, d. N/D
RUMBOLD, Robert Thomas, ssw-Lila Maitland, b. 08/31/18__, d. N/D
RUSSELL, Daisy J., b. 1911, d. 1983
RUSSELL, Robert K., b. 1909, d. 1956
SALIN, Charles S., ssw-Florence K. Salin and Blanche A. King, b. 1880, d. 1936
SALIN, Florence K., ssw-Charles S. Salin and Blanche A. King, b. 1883, d. 1968
SANDERS, Stanley H., Jr., b. 09/20/1961, d. 02/15/1962
SANTANGELD, Anthony, b. 09/08/1903, d. 11/24/1987
SAUNDERS, Charles E., ssw-Hilda M., b. 06/13/1917, d. N/D
SAUNDERS, Hilda M., ssw-Charles E., b. 03/14/1918, d. 11/26/1991
SAVAGE, Dorman F., b. 03/26/1919, d. 03/10/1991
SAVAGE, Dorothy E., ssw-Floyd B., b. 03/25/1900, d. N/D
SAVAGE, Floyd B., ssw-Dorothy E., b. 12/02/1898, d. 05/14/1987
SAVIN, Sannie Mary Adkins, b. 1873, d. 1946
SAVIN, John Edgar, b. 1861, d. 1929
SCHOLZE, Katharina, ssw-Anne & August Stolting and Adolf & Martha Frese, b. 05/08/1880,
        d. 02/23/1974
SCHWARTZ, Carolyn Toomey, b. 03/25/1912, d. 07/15/1988
SCHWARTZ, Mike, DE, Tec5, 1252 Sta. Com. Unit, WWII, b. 05/05/1914, d. 07/27/1954
SEBRING, Mary Ann, b. 1947, d. 1987
SEELEY, Gladys S., b. 03/24/1890, d. 12/26/1966
SHELDON, Eliza, w/o Geo. T. Sheldon, b. 1846, d. 1922
SHOCKLEY, Belle W., ssw-Carol Sue, b. 12/22/1889, d. 12/05/1953
SHOCKLEY, Carol Sue, ssw-George W., b. 05/20/1943, d. 02/06/1944
SHOCKLEY, George E., ssw-Carol Sue, b. 08/07/1887, d. 08/27/1962
SHOCKLEY, George W., ssw-Carol Sue, b. 12/13/1914, d. 03/04/1946
SHORT, C. Travis, b. 07/17/1937, d. 12/25/1940
SHORT, Carl A., b. 1910, d. 1990
SHORT, Francis R., ssw-Madeline C., b. 07/22/1907, d. 06/22/1990
SHORT, Madeline C., b. N/D, d. N/D
SHORT, Ruth, b. 02/26/1925, d. 08/22/1979
SIMPLER, Alvin E., ssw-Helen S., MOMM1, USCG, b. 12/19/1912, d. 10/12/1974
SIMPLER, Amanda W., ssw-Joseph R., b. 1894, d. 1988
SIMPLER, Caleb L., ssw-Miriam N., b. 1895, d. 1975
SIMPLER, Daniel T., DE, Pvt., Pfc., 59th Pioneer Inf., WWI, b. 11/03/1893, d. 11/04/1955
SIMPLER, Helen S., ssw-Alvin E., b. 04/11/1917, d. 06/28/1990
SIMPLER, John C., ssw-Laura M., b. 1892, d. 1969
SIMPLER, John E., ssw-Lettie M., b. 1891, d. 1968
SIMPLER, Joseph R., ssw-Amanda W., b. 1888, d. 1959
SIMPLER, Laura M., ssw-John C., b. 1898, d. 1974
SIMPLER, Lettie M., ssw-John E., b. 1897, d. 1963
SIMPLER, Miriam N., ssw-Caleb L., b. 1898, d. 1982
SIMPSON, Alice C., ssw-Earl, b. 1903, d. 1980
SIMPSON, Earl, ssw-Alice C., b. 1906, d. 1959
SIMPSON, Harry Paul, ssw-Earl, b. 12/17/1960, d. 08/02/1970

SLATER, Blanche M., ssw-Frederick D. & Thomas F., b. 11/27/1930, d. N/D

SLATER, Frederick D., ssw-Blanche M. & Thomas F., b. 12/07/1929, d. 10/18/1977

SLATER, Patrick Scott, USN, Vietnam, b. 03/18/1945, d. 08/30/1987

SLATER, Thomas F., ssw-Frederick D. & Blanche M., b. 01/27/1955, d. 04/16/1970

SLENCZKA, Nora Caon Young, ssw-Ronald Sterline Young, m/o Ronald Sterling Young, b. 10/19/1920, d. 11/10/1984

SMALL, Esther Tuuri, ssw-Frank B., b. 05/04/1899, d. 09/27/1987

SMALL, Frank B., ssw-Esther Turri, DE, BM2, USCG, WWI, b. 04/01/1889, d. 07/29/1953

SNYDER, Forest H., ssw-Jennie R., Born in Piqua, OH, b. N/D, d. 07/19/1953

SNYDER, Jennie R., ssw-Forest H., Born in Berea, KY, b. N/D, d. 11/26/1968

SNYDER, Lois N., ssw-William E., b. 07/18/1918, d. 07/28/1973

SNYDER, William E., ssw-Lois N., b. 07/06/1921, d. N/D

SOUCEK, Frank James, III, b. 01/30/1923, d. 05/20/1982

SPIEGEL, Frank D., b. 1934, d. 1992

STACY, Dorothy W., ssw-William G., b. 1912, d. 1979

STACY, William G., ssw-Dorothy W., b. 1916, d. 1991

STALLINGS, Belle W., b. 1884, d. 1974

STALLINGS, John W., b. 05/09/1912, d. 01/01/1981

STANNART, Hazel Evans, b. 01/27/1919, d. 08/28/1948

STEEDLE, Morris J., NJ, Pvt., USA, WWII, b. 08/14/1903, d. 09/02/1973

STEELE, Barbara Ann, ssw-George A., Jr., Baby, b. 1943, d. 1943

STEELE, Clara Emily, ssw-Thomas Carl, b. 1875, d. 1950

STEELE, Darrell R., DE, Pfc., Co. C, 9th Inf. Regt., Korea, b. 10/01/1930, d. 09/01/1950

STEELE, Dorothy Mae, b. 05/05/1904, d. 12/20/1973

STEELE, George A., ssw-Irene C., b. 09/08/1888, d. 09/21/1957

STEELE, George A., Jr., ssw-Barbara Ann, b 1919, d. 1987

STEELE, Harold Davidson, b. 03/10/1898, d. 08/14/1972

STEELE, Harry Wilmer, ssw-Helen C., b. 1886, d. 1953

STEELE, Helen C., ssw-Harry Wilmer, b. 1892, d. 1989

STEELE, Irene C., ssw-George A., b. 12/10/1914, d. N/D

STEELE, Thomas Carl, ssw-Clara Emily, b. 1883, d. 1931

STEELMAN, Grover C., ssw-Mae W., b. 07/07/1892, d. 12/03/1979

STEELMAN, Joseph, b. 1856, d. 1926

STEELMAN, Mae W., ssw-Grover C., b. 05/07/1902, d. 02/17/1980

STEPHENS, Edward M., ssw-Florence A., b. 1900, d. 1966

STEPHENS, Florence A., ssw-Edward M., b. 1901, d. 1984

STEVENSON, Fred W., b. 10/24/1929, d. 11/03/1981

STEVENSON, Mary E., ssw-Robert D., b. 1893, d. 1954

STEVENSON, Robert D., ssw-Mary E., b. 1879, d. 1964

STOCKLEY, Hattie S., b. 12/02/1896, d. 02/14/1952

STODDART, Naomi, ssw-William, b. 1923, d. N/D

STODDART, William, ssw-Naomi, b. 1918, d. 1975

STOLTING, Anne, ssw-August Stolting and Katharina Scholze and Adolf & Martha Frese, b. 01/29/1906, d. N/D

STOLTING, August, ssw-Anne Stolting and Katharina Scholze and Adolf & Martha Frese, b. 02/22/1902, d. 04/22/1987

STRICKLAND, Bessie F., ssw-Clarence W., b. 1871, d. 1945

STRICKLAND, Clarence W., Rev., ssw-Bessie F., b. 1868, d. 1967

STRICKLAND, Fannie D., ssw-Walter C., b. 1895, d. 1959

STRICKLAND, Walter C., ssw-Fannie D., PA, CE, USN, WWI, b. 08/23/1888, d. 03/25/1956

STURMFELZ, Carl W., Jr., MD, Tec4, HQ Btry, 106 Div. Arty., WWII, b. 02/22/1923, d. 09/13/1957

SULLIVAN, Eugene F., Tec4, USA, WWII, b. 04/08/1917, d. 04/22/1984

SULLIVAN, Howard P., ssw-Mary Ann, b. 1889, d. 1965

SULLIVAN, Mary Ann, ssw-Howard P., b. 1889, d. 1958

SUTER, Elizabeth M., ssw-Kenneth H., b. 02/06/1940, d. N/D

SUTER, Kenneth H., ssw-Elizabeth M., b. 09/22/1936, d. 05/12/1985

SWANN, Florence M., ssw-Robert S., b. 02/17/1920, d. N/D

SWANN, Robert S., ssw-Florence M., b. 08/17/1918, d. 05/03/1977

TAPPAN, Effie J., ssw-W. B., b. 1890, d. 1921

TAPPAN, Florence E., ssw-W. B., b. 1895, d. 1954

TAPPAN, Minnie N., ssw-W. T., b. 1873, d. 1944

TAPPAN, W. B., h/o E. J. & F. E. and f/o F. L., F. E. & Wm., III, b. N/D, d. N/D

TAPPAN, W. T., ssw-Minnie N., b. 1868, d. 1940

TEWELOW, Bessie S., b. 1904, d. 1991

THAWLEY, Addison T., ssw-Fannie H., b. 1891, d. 1972

THAWLEY, Fannie H., ssw-Addison T., b. 1888, d. 1943

THAWLEY, Orath, ssw-Addison T., b. 1893, d. N/D

THOMAS, Everett, ssw-Thelma, b. 1907, d. 1977

THOMAS, Thelma, ssw-Everett, b. 1907, d. 1981

THOMPSON, Clara Dow, ssw-Harry Owen & Harry, Jr., b. 1873, d. 1967

THOMPSON, Harry, Jr., ssw-Harry Owen & Clara Dow, b. 1899, d. 1947

THOMPSON, Harry Owen, ssw-Clara Dow & Harry, Jr., b. 1870, d. 1956

TOOMEY, Alberteen P., ssw-John S. & Alfred L., b. 1853, d. 1923

TOOMEY, Alfred L., ssw-John S. & Alberteen P., b. 1884, d. 1919

TOOMEY, Carolyn G., b. 12/25/1920, d. 04/26/1967

TOOMEY, Daniel O., ssw-John S., b. 1877, d. 1937

TOOMEY, Elmer, ssw-Katharine C., b. 1882, d. 1954

TOOMEY, John S., ssw-Alberteen P. & Alfred L., b. 1851, d. 1933

TOOMEY, John W., ssw-John S., b. 05/25/1975, d. 05/13/1937

TOOMEY, Katharine C., ssw-Elmer, b. 1882, d. 1940

TOOMEY, Robert H., De, Pfc., Med. Dept., WWII, b. 05/09/1921, d. 02/05/1945

TOPPIN, Charles Eliz, ssw-George W., b. 11/20/1900, d. N/D

TOPPIN, George W., ssw- Charles Eliz, b. 07/29/1894, d. 10/19/1985

TOWLSON, Mary Major, Mother, b. 09/06/1882, d. 02/05/1968

TOYER, Huntley M., b. 05/19/1896, d. 11/13/1964

TOYER, Lambert W., b. 1896, d. 1969

TRAVIS, Baby, b. N/D, d. 02/14/1930

TRAVIS, Cathryn, Baby, b. N/D, d. 09/08/1940

TRIFILLIS, Helen M., ssw-William E., b. 08/07/1924, d. 06/13/1972

TRIFILLIS, William E., ssw-Helen M., b. 02/02/1917, d. 10/21/1975

TRUITT, Baby, ssw-James H., b. 1938, d. 1938

TRUITT, Bessie S., ssw-James H., b. 1884, d. 1974

TRUITT, Dorothy S., ssw-James H., b. 1919, d. N/D

TRUITT, Effie May, ssw-Willard S., b. 1890, d. 1944

TRUITT, Elizabeth Ellen, ssw-Willard S., b. 1886, d. 1939

TRUITT, James H., ssw-Bessie S., b. 1875, d. 1955

TRUITT, James S., Sr., ssw-James H., b. 1914, d. 1981

TRUITT, Willard S., ssw-Elizabeth Ellen, b. 1861, d. 1935

TULUS, Eugene, b. 1898, d. 1980

TULUS, Olga J., b. 1896, d. 1982

TYLECKI, Francis J., DE, Tec3, 537 Ord. Hv. Maint. Co. FA, WWII, b. 09/29/1906, d. 01/24/1959

TYNDALL, Anna E., ssw-Doris T., Charles W., Kathryn T. & Oliver H., b. 1889, d. 1963

TYNDALL, Charles W., ssw-Doris T., Anna E., Kathryn T. & Oliver H., b. 1884, d. 1956

TYNDALL, Dora G., ssw-John R., b. 11/08/1881, d. 06/09/1963

TYNDALL, Doris T., ssw-Anna E., Charles W., Kathryn T. & Oliver H., b. 1908, d. 1921

TYNDALL, Fernanda K., Nan, ssw-William Patrick H., b. 07/28/1909, d. N/D

TYNDALL, John R., ssw-Dora G., b. 03/23/1881, d. 12/26/1941

TYNDALL, Kathryn T., ssw-Doris T., Anna E., Charles W. & Oliver H., b. 1879, d. 1943

TYNDALL, Oliver H., ssw-Doris T., Anna E., Charles W. & Kathryn T., b. 1880, d. 1926

TYNDALL, William Patrick H., ssw-Fernanda K., b. 09/04/1905, d. 07/27/1973

TYSON, Frank I., ssw-Rebecca A., DE, Cpl., Co. L, 59th Inf. Regt., WWII, BSM, b. 10/30/1915, d. 04/04/1960

TYSON, Rebecca A., ssw-Frank I., b. 01/11/1919, d. 05/30/1977

VIGNOLA, Anthony R., ssw-Eva Marie, b. 11/17/1913, d. 04/06/1988

VIGNOLA, Eva Marie, ssw-Anthony R., b. 03/05/1915, d. 02/23/1969

VIGNOLA, Stephen Anthony, ssw-Anthony R., b. 01/19/1964, d. 08/19/1991

WALDRON, Marian A., b. 09/04/1917, d. 04/28/1985

WALGUARNEY, Doming A., ssw-Gertrude H., b. 12/05/1914, d. 03/18/1982

WALGUARNEY, Gertrude H., ssw-Doming A., b. 10/17/1916, d. N/D

WALKER, Madeline E., b. 03/08/1919, d. 05/17/1984

WALL, Beulah R., ssw-George Barton, b. 1893, d. 1960

WALL, George Barton, ssw-Beulah R., b. 1890, d. 1978

WALRAVEN, John Paul, ssw-Viola C., b. 1889, d. 1958

WALRAVEN, Viola C., ssw-John Paul, b. 1888, d. 1980

WAPLES, Ina L., w/o John T., ssw-John T., b. 1858, d. 1926

WAPLES, John T., ssw-Ina L., Co. C, 1st Indiana, HA, b. 1843, d. 1915

WAPLES, John T, Jr., ssw-John T., b. 1885, d. N/D

WARDENCKI, Mary, b. 09/09/1902, d. 05/26/1987

WARRINGTON, Annie Downing, b. 1864, d. 1926

WATSON, Charles C., ssw-Lola C., b. 03/10/1877, d. 08/15/1962

WATSON, Edith M., ssw-John A., b. 09/05/1893, d. 04/11/1981

WATSON, John A., ssw-Edith M., b. 04/26/1889, d. 03/22/1982

WATSON, Lola C., ssw-Charles C., b. 02/02/1909, d. 09/13/1958

WATSON, Wheatley W., b. 07/26/1894, d. 01/28/1953

WEART, Charles Reynolds, SM2. USN, WWII, b. 1926, d. 1981

WEBSTER, Charlotte M., b. 1889, d. 1977

WEBSTER, Eden S., b. 1907, d. 1946

WELKER, Frank Melvin, b. 1899, d. 1990

WHITE, Howard L., ssw-Sara E., b. 05/20/1919, d. 10/12/1963

WHITE, Sara E., ssw-Howard L., b. 03/17/1915, d. 10/05/1991

WIEDERSPAHN, Henry J., b. 03/17/1903, d. 09/20/1972

WIEDERSPAHN, Mildred L., b. 06/25/1907, d. 10/21/1973

WILHELM, Raymond W., b. 04/30/1901, d. 10/24/1966

WILLIAMS, John H., Capt., USMC Res., b. 10/03/1944, d. 04/02/1974

WILSON, Albert J., ssw-Lucinda, b. 1885, d. 1951

WILSON, Catherine W., ssw-Josiah H., b. 09/04/1906, d. 02/28/1983

WILSON, Delbert J., ssw-Kathryn K., b. 1912, d. 1975

WILSON, Josiah H., ssw-Catherine W., b. 10/19/1904, d. 05/06/1975

WILSON, Kathryn K., ssw-Delbert J., b. 1908, d. 1989

WILSON, Kendall W., ssw-Josiah H., b. 10/23/1942, d. 12/17/1985

WILSON, Lucinda, ssw-Albert J., b. 1886, d. 1964

WILSON, Marion B., ssw-Ronald Walden, b. 10/01/1898, d. 12/17/1980

WILSON, Raymond E., ssw-Ronald Walden, b. 11/27/1895, d. 06/05/1959

WILSON, Ronald Walden, ssw-Marion B., DE, Sp 5, Signal Corps., b. 12/19/1937, d. 10/26/1958

WILSON, William M., SSgt., USA, WWII, b. 08/25/1915, d. 01/09/1988

WILT, Emilie A., b. 1888, d. 1957

WILT, G. R., ssw-Renee, b. 1906, d. 1976

WILT, Renee, ssw-G. R., b. 1901, d. 1977

WINGATE, Carl D., ssw-Eva A., b. 1876, d. 1941

WINGATE, Clifton S., b. 02/28/1913, d. 09/21/1988

WINGATE, Eva A., ssw-Carl D., b. 1885, d. 1957

WINGATE, Myrtle B., b. 1890, d. 1976

WINGATE, Ralph D., ssw-Carl D., b. 1921, d. 1939

WINGATE, Ralph M., b. 1890, d. 1929

WINGATE, Ralph M., Jr., b. N/D, d. N/D

WITSIL, Gladys Hudson, b. 9/29/1912, d. 04/01/1968

WOLFE, Edward S., b. 06/13/1922, d. 11/30/1990

WOLFE, Edward S., ssw-Lucinda J., b. 1893, d. 1963

WOLFE, Hazel, b. 1893, d. 1973

WOLFE, John W., b. 09/17/1923, d. 03/18/1973

WOLFE, Lucinda J., ssw-Edward S., b. 1895, d. 1984

WOLFE, Russel P., b. 11/06/1925, d. 11/02/1991

WONG, Fook Lew, ssw-Ni Ton Moy, b. 1893, d. 1965

WRIGHT, Harry E., ssw-Margaret B., 1st Lt., USA, WWII, b. 09/19/1916, d. 07/18/1983

WRIGHT, Margaret B., ssw-Harry E., b. 1916, d. N/D

WUNDER, Edna V., ssw-George A., b. 04/22/1900, d. N/D

WUNDER, George A., ssw-Edna V., b. 01/12/1898, d. 10/02/1968

YARNALL, Dorothea Marie, ssw-William Bush, b. 1897, d. N/D

YARNALL, Helen Donoho, ssw-Robert William, b. 1864, d. 1937

YARNALL, Helen H., ssw-Robert W., b. 1920, d. 1962

YARNALL, Joseph Leo, ssw-Mildred Wilson, b. 1891, d. 1943

YARNALL, Mildred Wilson, ssw-Joseph Leo, b. 1901, d. 1924

YARNALL, Robert Keith, b. 05/28/1970, d. 09/01/1973

YARNALL, Robert W., ssw-Helen H., DE, Pvt., HQ. Det. SAC, WWI, b. 05/30/1896, d. 08/31/1959

YARNALL, Robert William, ssw-Helen Donoho, b. 1862, d. 1939

YARNALL, William Bushy, ssw-Dorothea Marie, b. 1897, d. 1944

YARNALL, William Hart, b. 1921, d. 1921

YOCUM, Curtis E., ssw-Idella, b. 1880, d. 1951

YOCUM, Idella, ssw-Curtis E., b. 1878, d. 1970

YOUNG, Robert, b. N/D, d. 12/06/1950

YOUNG, Ronald Sterling, ssw-Nora Caon Young Slenczka, b. 07/04/1941, d. N/D

TAPPAN, Frances L., d/o W. B. & E. J., b. 12/25/1910, d. 10/10/1917

(LR-003 & HU-181) PAYNTER FAMILY CEMETERY

Located South West of Lewes on the North end of Tulip Street, approximately 150 yards north east of Coastal Highway (Rt. 1) and adjacent to St. Judes Catholic Church
Recorded: February 7, 1997

PAYNTER, John, Captain, b. 12/21/1786, d. 01/02/1812
PAYNTER, Mary, w/o Capt. Samuel, Age 51y b. N/D, d. 03/17/1850
PAYNTER, Ruth, w/o Cornelius, b. 09/27/1766, d. 12/07/1799
PAYNTER, Samuel, Captain, s/o Cornelius, Age 58y, b. N/D, d. 11/12/1852

LITTLE CREEK HUNDRED

(LC-001 & HU-540) MT. PLEASANT UNITED METHODIST CHURCH CEMETERY

Located S. W. of Laurel on the West side of Mt. Pleasant Rd. (Rd. 493) 0.1 mile North of Sharptown Rd. (Rt. 24)
Recorded: April 26, 1995

BRADLEY, Alpha Beatrice, ssw-George, b. 02/27/1871, d. 04/05/1942
BRADLEY, Annie E., b. 05/31/1865, d. 05/12/1950
BRADLEY, George, ssw-Alpha Beatrice, b. 02/04/1869, d. 03/30/1945
BRADLEY, Lucretia A., w/o S. J., b. 06/29/1842, d. 06/14/1909
BRADLEY, Samuel J., b. 05/18/1836, d. 04/29/1914
CALLAWAY, Annie G., ssw-Joseph F., b. 02/15/1879, d. 02/13/1957
CALLAWAY, Helen M., ssw-J. Carolton, b. 1909, d. 1962
CALLAWAY, Helen P., b. 10/07/1904, d. 11/20/1905
CALLAWAY, J. Carolton, ssw-Helen M., b. 1900, d. 1986
CALLAWAY, John R., b. 11/18/1962, d. 06/16/1990
CALLAWAY, Joseph F., ssw-Annie G., b. 12/04/1868, d. 09/22/1945
CALLAWAY, Joseph K., ssw-Mary E., Father, b. 01/05/1839, d. 03/10/1926
CALLAWAY, M. LaFayette, ssw-Starrie L., b. 1872, d. 1940
CALLAWAY, Mary E., ssw-Joseph K., Mother, b. 08/15/1844, d. 04/30/1927
CALLAWAY, Paul C., s/o Starrie L. & M. LaFayette, b. 12/23/1898, d. 02/26/1899
CALLAWAY, Starrie L., ssw-M. LaFayette, b. 1878, d. 1954
CAMPBELL, Nelson C., Cpl., USA, WWI, b. 05/12/1899, d. 01/11/1988
COLLINS, Emaline P., w/o Noah W., b. 09/25/1832, d. 03/13/1905
COLLINS, Harriett E., w/o Jacob A., Age 68y 8m 16d, b. 03/28/1853, d. 12/14/1921
COLLINS, Herbert Elwood, s/o Jacob & Hattie, Age 13y 9m 29d, b. N/D, d. 08/05/1901
COLLINS, Hiriam H., b. 05/12/1859, d. 08/05/1897
COLLINS, Ida D., w/o Elmer J., Age 28y 9m 15d, b. N/D, d. 04/12/1902
COLLINS, Isaac E., b. 02/17/1833, d. 01/24/1913
COLLINS, Jacob A., Age 75y 3m 8d, b. 08/06/1837, d. 11/14/1912
COLLINS, Julia J., w/o Jacob A., Age 39y 7m 2d, b. N/D, d. 07/18/1877
COLLINS, Lola J., d/o O. F. & Molano I., b. 04/19/1897, d. 09/22/1911
COLLINS, Lurana E., w/o Joseph J., b. 09/25/1846, d. 11/19/1890

COLLINS, Mary A. B., w/o Levin, Age 52y 3m 26d, b. N/D, d. 07/12/1883
COLLINS, Mary E., w/o Hiram H., b. 05/21/1861, d. 08/23/1892
COLLINS, Miranda A., w/o Joseph J., b. 04/08/1844, d. 01/14/1911
COLLINS, Noah W., b. 09/10//1830, d. 03/29/1906
COLLINS, Olive O., d/o E. J. & E. P., Age 11m 8d, b. N/D, d. 09/29/1899
COLLINS, Sallie E., w/o Henry J., b. 01/03/1828, d. 10/27/1893
COLLINS, Sarah E., w/o Isaac E., b. 05/06/1841, d. 12/08/1917
COLLISON, Helen M., Daughter, b. 11/11/1908, d. 03/03/1966
COLLISON, John W., Father, b. 12/23/1883, d. 04/22/1950
COLLISON, Minnie M., Mother, b. 05/29/1886, d. 07/19/1957
COLLISON, Wm. E., b. 07/08/1833, d. 06/10/1893
COOPER, Anna Mae, ssw-Paul W., Sr., b. 11/28/1940, d. N/D
COOPER, Paul W., Sr., ssw-Anna Mae, b. 11/23/1934, d. 01/20/1985
CORDREY, Elijah A., b. 1838, d. 1917
CORDREY, Isaac E., ssw-Maude E., b. 10/13/1908, d. 02/02/1965
CORDREY, Joseph F., ssw-Mary J., b. 12/03/1873, d. 01/05/1933
CORDREY, Katherine, Baby, b. 07/31/1932, d. 11/26/1932
CORDREY, Mary J., ssw-Joseph F., b. 03/12/1875, d. 09/08/1929
CORDREY, Maude E., ssw-Isaac E., b. 08/24/1909, d. 08/171990
CORDREY, Sarah C., b. 1836, d. 1913
CULVER, Alton R., ssw-Leona M., b. 11/24/1930, d. N/D
CULVER, Baby, s/o F. C. & Mamie E., b. N/D, d. N/D
CULVER, Eva G., ssw-O. Ray, b. 09/07/1900, d. 11/18/1969
CULVER, Harry Straughn, s/o Elias T. & Lauranna E., Age 1y 2m 27d, b. N/D, d. 03/21/188
CULVER, Laura A., b. 06/11/1856, d. 03/09/1933
CULVER, Leona M., ssw-Alton R., b. 06/23/1919, d. 10/12/1985
CULVER, Mamie E., w/o Fred C., b. 04/10/1877, d. 06/18/1899
CULVER, Minos W., Age 62y 2m 6d, b. 06/26/1855, d. 09/01/1917
CULVER, O. Ray, ssw-Eva G., b. 11/19/1891, d. 08/27/1948
CULVER, Sarah E., Age 78y 7m 2d, b. 01/22/1837, d. 08/24/1915
DICKERSON, Bessie E., ssw-John E., b. 02/10/1899, d. 01/08/1981
DICKERSON, Cassie May, b. 02/07/1872, d. 10/29/1957
DICKERSON, Catherine O., b. 1919, d. N/D
DICKERSON, Charles F., b. 1875, d. 1932
DICKERSON, Clarence H., ssw-Myrtle E., b. 1903, d. 1967
DICKERSON, Delila E., b. 08/20/1858, d. 01/23/1955
DICKERSON, Edna L., Mom, b. 08/19/1894, d 03/09/1965
DICKERSON, Edwin F., b. N/D, d. N/D
DICKERSON, Elizabeth E., b. 1877, d. 1951
DICKERSON, Elizabeth J., d/o Frasier A. & O. V., Age 20d, b. N/D, d. 05/08/1892
DICKERSON, Elwood F., "Pop," b. 01/10/1891, d. 03/09/1964
DICKERSON, Frazier A., b. 06/11/1859, d. 03/20/1916
DICKERSON, Geo. S., b. 03/15/1857, d. 04/13/1921
DICKERSON, Gilbert F., b. 1922, d. N/D
DICKERSON, John E., ssw-Bessie E., b. 12/20/1898, d. 06/04/1974
DICKERSON, Larry E., b. N/D, d. N/D
DICKERSON, Lelah E., b. 1894, d. 1958
DICKERSON, Martha E., b. 11/10/1896, d. 09/16/1968

DICKERSON, Martha E., w/o F. A., b. 06/13/1857, d. 10/12/1880
DICKERSON, Mary E., b. 05/20/1908, d. 03/03/1964
DICKERSON, Mollie Jane, b. 10/18/1896, d. 10/26/1896
DICKERSON, Myrtle E., ssw-Clarence H., b. 1906, d. 1977
DICKERSON, Opecheo V., w/o F. A., b. 06/02/1861, d. 10/27/1925
DICKERSON, R. George, b. 03/28/1941, d. 02/08/1975
DICKERSON, Richard, b. 06/29/1919, d. 02/01/1980
DICKERSON, Sophia J., b. 10/17/1880, d. 08/02/1930
DICKERSON, Walter W., b. 1914, d. N/D
DICKERSON, William F., b. 1893, d. 1924
DICKERSON, William G., b. 07/27/1901, d. 11/20/1970
DICKERSON, William W., b. N/D, d. N/D
DUNN, Bealah B., b. 1912, d. 1913
DUNN, Charles Franklin, b. 1948, d. 1949
DUNN, Clifford H., b. 1903, d. 1950
DUNN, Columbus F., b. 1857, d. 1931
DUNN, Doris Anne, b. 01/15/1945, d. 02/07/1950
DUNN, Eliza E., b. 1877, d. 1918
DUNN, George Robert., b. 1947, d. 1949
DUNN, Lottie G., b. 1900, d. 1901
DUNN, William R., b. 1930, d. 1931
ELLIOTT, Debra L., b. 04/17/1953, d. 12/06/1992
ELLIOTT, Dora A., b. 09/06/1865, d. 12/18/1952
ELLIOTT, Mary G., d/o Rufus G. & Dora A., b. 12/22/1893, d. 02/17/1903
ELLIOTT, Rufus G., b. 12/03/1867, d. 10/09/1950
ELLIS, Hanson D., b. 06/04/1870, d. 09/18/1945
ELLIS, Maud Blanch, d/o E. P. & S. A., b. 05/18/1889, d. 07/05/1889
EVANS, A. Margaret, b. 01/21/1913, d. 10/31/1955
GOOTEE, Griffith M., b. 02/06/1831, d. 17/27/1913
GOOTEE, Ida A., ssw-Theo C., b. 12/20/1864, d. 09/27/1922
GOOTEE, Olevia Ann, w/o Griffith M., Mother, b. 01/10/1839, d. 12/15/1909
GOOTEE, Raleigh S., b. 09/05/1892, d. 08/02/1961
GOOTEE, Theo C., ssw-Ida A. b. N/D, d. 01/24/1863
GOOTEE, William T., b. 12/17/1894, d. 03/26/1983
HASTINGS, Euthel C., d/o Elihu T. & Ladonia L., b. 05/05/1888, d. 09/06/1888
HASTINGS, Orion Cleo, s/o E. Thomas & Ladonia L., b. 09/02/1891, d. 12/16/1905
HASTINGS, Robert W., SP4, USA, b. 04/25/1944, d. 11/07/1992
HENDERSON, Adella, b. 1861, d. 1941
HENDERSON, Alda Cora, d/o Wm. J. & Eliza, b. 05/06/1889, d. 02/19/1907
HENDERSON, Baby, b. N/D, d. N/D [Note: stone broken]
HENDERSON, Elizzie, w/o Wm. J., b. 06/20/1862d, 05/13/1893
HENDERSON, Ethel A., b. 03/28/1909, d. 07/25/1979
HENDERSON, George I., b. 09/26/1900, d. 11/02/1983
HENDERSON, Hester Ann, w/o Wm. J., Age 33y 11m 1d, b. N/D, d. 10/11/1886
HENDERSON, Sallie E., w/o Wm. J., b. 10/15/1848, d. 07/12/1924
HENDERSON, William J., b. 06/22/1854, d. 05/27/1929
HENRY, Addie J., w/o John H., b. 07/24/1817, d. 09/05/1894
HENRY, Albert G., ssw-Rachel J., b. 10/29/1874, d. 03/01/1965

HENRY, Annie E., ssw-William W., b. 07/30/1884, d. 04/05/1939
HENRY, Arthur E., b. 10/15/1905, d. 08/24/1966
HENRY, Beaulah C., b. 09/15/1905, d. 10/28.1991
HENRY, Berta M., b. 01/02/1905, d. 11/27/1989
HENRY, Charlie K., ssw-Julia A., b. 06/07/1900, d. 03/08/1971
HENRY, George W., b. 03/30/1850, d. 06/02/1938
HENRY, Inf. Sons/o Stella H. & Walter R., b. 1908, d. 1909
HENRY, Irving S., b. 01/09/1870, d. 07/23/1925
HENRY, John Horsey, b. 09/08/1826, d. 01/19/1907
HENRY, Julia A., ssw-Charlie K., b. 06/05/1901, d. 01/03/1969
HENRY, Julia E., w/o George W., b. 07/31/1857, d. 02/23/1895
HENRY, Lillie M., b. 01/16/1873, d. 04/05/1939
HENRY, Lizzie E., w/o George W., b. 01/22/1861, d. 06/05/1929
HENRY, Mahaley E. C., w/o W. B., Age 70y, b. N/D, d. 06/25/1918
HENRY, Nellie L., d/o A. G. & Rachel J., b. 09/01/1907, d. 07/19/1908
HENRY, Paul F., b. 04/24/1903, d. 11/25/1990
HENRY, Rachel J., ssw-Albert G., b. 01/01/1874, d. 08/10/1968
HENRY, William B., b. 01/03/1842, d. 01/02/1914
HENRY, William W., ssw-Annie E., b. 09/17/1881, d. 12/17/1947
HILL, Madeline A., b. 04/06/1923, d. N/D
HITCH, Kernie D., ssw-William J., b. 1879, d. 1951
HITCH, William J., ssw-Kernie D., b. 1873, d. 1914
HITCHEN, Elsie M., b. 1905, d. 1975
HITCHEN, Lee G., b. 1905, d. 1956
HITCHENS, Claude L., ssw-Mary E., b. 09/10/1903, d. 06/30/1972
HITCHENS, Howard A., ssw-Katherine A., b. 06/12/1926, d. 11/17/1981
HITCHENS, Joseph E., b. 08/04/1878, d. 02/27/1949
HITCHENS, Katherine A., b. 06/30/1925, d. N/D
HITCHENS, Mary E., ssw-Claude L., b. 01/22/1906, d. 03/301991
HORSEY, Martin M., ssw-Myrtle E., b. 1907, d. 1979
HORSEY, Myrtle E., ssw-Martin M., b. 1910, d. 1989
HOWARD, Nellie J., d/o Wm. J. & Alvirdie, b. 10/23/1897, d. 06/11/1898
HOWARD, Nellie J., d/o Wm. J. & Alvirdie, b. 11/19/1888, d. 11/19/1893
KLINE, Linwood L., ssw-Mary L., S1, USN, WWII, b. 02/19/1921, d. 05/21/1982
KLINE, Mary L., ssw-Linwood L., b. 06/01/1931, d. 03/18/1991
KOSTER, Kitty Elizabeth, b. 1958, d. 1995
MANLOVE, George, b. 06/02/1916, d. 09/22/1980
MARLETTE, Madeline Ida, Age 71y, b. 1918, d. 1990
MASSEY, Lillie E., ssw-William M., b. 09/14/1907, d. 09/03/1967
MASSEY, William M., ssw-Lillie E., b. 08/16/1902, d. 06/23/1976
MORRIS, George E., s/o James H. & Ellen, b. 02/09/1887, d. 01/06/1890
MORRIS, Harry C., s/o James H. & Ellen, b. 10/20/1888, d. 12/27/1889
MORRIS, James H., Age 59y 8m 24d, b. 05/09/1846, d. 02/02/1906
MORRIS, Margaret Ellen, w/o James H., b. 06/07/1853, d. 10/28/1908
MORRIS, Thomas C., s/o James H. & Ellen, Age 1y 25d, b. N/D, d. 01/25/1885
MORRIS, Ula Mexa, d/o James H. & Ellen, b. 05/02/1893, d. 11/25/1894
NLN, Luben C., b. N/D, d. N/D [Next to Sarah J. Rhodes]
OLIPHANT, Betty M, ssw-Phyllis A. Pusey, b. 03/19/1939, d. N/D

PARSONS, Gary Lee, b. 10/31/1978, d. 02/12/1985

PARSONS, Sue Ellen, b. 08/12/1963, d. 12/08/1972

PHILLIPS, Earl B., s/o George S. & Guzie E., Age 5m 28d, b. N/D, d. 03/19/1888

PHILLIPS, Katherine, ssw-Layton L., b. 08/14/1918, d. N/D

PHILLIPS, Layton L., ssw-Katherine, b. 03/22/1919, d. N/D

PHILLIPS, Victor W., b. 04/21/1898, d. 08/25/1899

PUSEY, Delema Jane, ssw-Franklin McKinley, b. 1902, d. 1973

PUSEY, Franklin McKinley, ssw-Delema Jane, b. 1901, d. 1961

PUSEY, LeRoy H., b. 10/31/1924, d. 08/05/1964

PUSEY, Melvin Edward, Sr., b. 09/04/1938, d. 07/07/1994

PUSEY, Phyllis A., ssw-Betty M. Oliphant, b. 05/04/1959, d. 02/28/1993

RALPH, Anna L., b. 12/16/1895, d. 09/28/1994

RALPH, D. Guy, b. 05/31/1893, d. 09/14/1973

RALPH, David W., b. 1845, d. 1925

RALPH, Grover W., s/o David W. & Mary P., b. 02/08/1885, d. 02/13/1887

RALPH, James English, b. 02/18/1805, d. 07/30/1849

RALPH, Kate E., b. 1897, d. 1959

RALPH, Lottie H., b. 1897, d. 1981

RALPH, Mary P., b. 1856, d. 1928

RALPH, Sallie B., b. 1888, d. 1987

RALPH, Sarah S., w/o James E., b. 12/25/1812, d. 01/10/1891

RASH, Maggie E., b. 01/11/1836, d. 05/25/1934

RHODES, Fred P. W., s/o Wm. H. & Sarah J., Age 18y 5m 3d, b. N/D, d. 11/28/1892

RHODES, Granville, Age 27y 10m 19d, b.02/08/1861, d. 12/27/1888

RHODES, Sarah J., w/o Wm. J., Age abt. 65y, b. N/D, d. 05/04/1903

RHODES, Susan E., Age 3m 30d, b. 09/13/1888, d. 01/11/1889

SHANER, Berton A., ssw-Kathryn C., b. 1925, d. N/D

SHANER, Kathryn C., ssw-Berton A., b. 1927, d. N/D

SHOCKLEY, Carlton, ssw-Flossie M., b. 07/04/1902, d. 01/06/1983

SHOCKLEY, Flossie M., ssw-Carlton, b. 05/01/1912, d. N/D

TAYLOR, Ernest E., s/o William & Maranda, Age 10y 3m 15d, b. N/D, d. 12/09/1891

TAYLOR, William, Age 80y 6m 10d, b. N/D, d. 11/30/1891

TULL, Beatrice G., b. 02/03/1932, d. 04/30/1980

TWILLEY, Alvah, s/o Robert O. & Annie E., b. 05/07/1878, d. 12/26/1898

TWILLEY, Annie E., w/o Robert O., b. 03/08/1844, d. 04/04/1911

TWILLEY, Clifford F., s/o George S. & Edith T., Age 10m 3d, b. 07/06/1899, d. 05/09/1900

TWILLEY, Edith E., d/o William B. & Mary E., b. 09/06/1922, d. 09/09/1922

TWILLEY, Edith T., b. 11/10/1864, d. 04/08/1935

TWILLEY, George S., b. 11/02/1858, d. 02/19/1941

TWILLEY, Glenn B., s/o George S. & Edith T., Age 2m 6d, b. N/D, d. 08/23/1892

TWILLEY, Jennie C., d/o Robert O. & Annie E., b. 08/12/1874, d. 02/21/1919

TWILLEY, Mary E., b. 11/21/1893, d. 03/24/1965

TWILLEY, May, d/o George S. & Edith T., Age 27d, b. N/D, d. 06/12/1891

TWILLEY, Robert O., b. 12/24/1834, d. 03/23/1899

TWILLEY, William B., b. 07/16/1893, d.10/16/1958

WALLER, Ebenezer, Age 79y, b. N/D, d. 03/02/1896

WALLER, Mary Ann, w/o Ebenezer, Age 61y, b. N/D, d. 06/04/1897

WALSON, Charles M., b. 08/08/1831, d. 06/07/1904

WALSON, Mary Jane, b. 12/27/1847, d. 01/08/1929
WALSON, Sallie A., w/o Chas. M., b. 01/27/1828, d. 07/05/1911
WALSON, Sarah A. C., Age 8m 23d, b. 11/17/1859, d. 08/10/1860
WORKMAN, Mahala H., w/o William, Age 88y 3m 19d, b. N/D, d. 02/06/1904

The following stones were recorded by the Hudson Survey but are now missing or unreadable:
COLLINS, William H., s/o Henry J. & Sallie E., Age 24y 7m 23d, b. N/D, d. 01/21/1887
DUNN, Luther B., b. 09/15/1814, d. 110/18/1904
HASTINGS, Luben G., s/o Virda A., Age 1y 3m 29d, b. N/D, d. 04/06/1887 [Note: Possibly NLN Luben]
HENDERSON, Maggie M., granddaughter o/Phillis, b. 10/15/1875, d. 11/22/1892
HENDERSON, Phillis, b. N/D, d. 01/20/1902
HENDERSON, Olan Ray, s/o William J. & Hester Ann, b. 06/23/1885, d. 06/25/1888
WORKMAN, Ernest C., s/o William & Mahala H., Age 10y 3m 15d, b. N/D, d. 12/091891
WORKMAN, William, Age 80y 6m 10d, b. N/D, d. 11/30/1891

NANTICOKE HUNDRED

(NA-001 & HU-NR) TRESSLER MENNONITE CHURCH CEMETERY
Located East of Greenwood on the East side of B. & R. Road (Rd. 603), approximately 100 yards south east of Ellendale-Greenwood Highway (Rt. 16).
Recorded: April 19, 1995

CONDON, Bretton Ryan, b. 04/17/1995, d. 04/17/1995
GAUMER, Albert R., ssw-Olive T., m. 12/05/1942, b. 04/26/1912, d. 09/09/1994
GAUMER, Olive T., ssw-Albert R., m. 12/05/1942, b. 02/03/1907, d. N/D
MASSEY, Dorothy S., ssw-Ronald J., b. 04/11/1943, d. 05/16/1994
MASSEY, Ronald J., ssw-Dorothy S., b. 01/21/1943, d. N/D
YODER, Ina M., ssw-Ronald G., b. 02/04/1943, d. 07/29/1994
YODER, Ronald G., ssw-Ina M., b. 05/28/1941, d. N/D

(NA-002 & HU-238) ASBURY UNITED METHODIST CHURCH CEMETERY
Located South West of Georgetown on both sides of Asbury Road (Rd. 446) at the intersection with County Seat Highway (Rt. 9)
Recorded May 15, 1996

ADAMS, Annie M., b. 01/08/1877, d. 02/26/1948
ADAMS, Baby, b. 1949, d. 1949
ADAMS, Bertha M., b. 1903, d. 1935
ADAMS, George T., b. 07/25/1873, d. 11/09/1940
ADAMS, Hilda W., ssw-Norvil I., b. 12/17/1910, d. N/D
ADAMS, John L. Briggs, b. 07/01/1969, d. 07/25/1994
ADAMS, Landeth C., b. 1900, d. 1971'
ADAMS, Norvil I., ssw-Hilda W., b. 01/04/1911, d. 06/30/1979
ATKINS, Donald J., b. 11/11/1954, d. 08/07/1974
ATKINS, Joseph E., ssw-Thelma G., b. 06/01/1928, d. 04/07/1989
ATKINS, Thelma G., ssw-Joseph E., b. 11/11/1932, d. N/D
BAILEY, Cleveland H., ssw-Elva M., MD, Y2, USN, WWI, b. 04/22/1892, d. 08/10/1970

BAILEY, Elva M., ssw-Cleveland H., b. 1900, d. 1995
BAILEY, Estella E., ssw-Francis A., Mother, b. 03/22/1911, d. 10/14/1933
BAILEY, Francis A., ssw-Estella E., Father, b. 05/02/1905, d. 01/05/1952
BAILEY, Thomas Lee, Son, b. 06/27/1939, d. 07/08/1941
BAKER, Albert S., s/o Alfred F. & Helen, b. 1942, d. 1942
BAKER, Flora A., d/o T. P). & M. E., b. 03/03/1877, d. 10/16/1878
BAKER, Lizzie T., ssw-Wilbert S., b. 1859, d. 1932
BAKER, Wilbert S., ssw-Lizzie T., b. 1887, d. 1929
BANKS, Dorothy W., ssw-John Walter, b. 01/16/1917, d. N/D
BANKS, John Walter, ssw-Dorothy W., b. 10/24/1909, d. 04/26/1966
BARR, Charles Emory, b. 07/23/1910, d. 01/12/1961
BARR, David W., b. 11/27/1890, d. 12/25/1931
BARR, Everett M., ssw-Herbert E., b. 1867, d. 1950
BARR, Herbert E., ssw-Everett M., b. 1909, d. 1993
BARR, Ida F., b. 04/23/1866, d. 04/07/1942
BARR, Robert, ssw-Sarah E., b. 1857, d. 1933
BARR, Sarah E., ssw-Robert, b. 1865, d. 1942
BARR, William, b. 06/02/1861, d. 09/25/1926
BLACKSON, Lillian O., ssw-Norris L., b. 10/23/1906, d. 07/27/1973
BLACKSON, Norris L., ssw-Lillian O., b. 02/15/1898, d. 10/17/1963
BLACKSON, Richard C., ssw-Ruth E., Father, b. 1876, d. 1949
BLACKSON, Ruth E., ssw-Richard C., Mother, b. 1876, d. 1945
BOWEN, Isaac M., Age 32y 10m 1d, b. N/D, d. 01/21/1878
BOYCE, C. Robert, ssw-Doris B., b. 07/24/1922, d. 10/20/1982
BOYCE, Doris B., ssw-C. Robert, b. 06/18/1928, d. N/D
BRADFORD, Effie L., ssw-W. Lee, b. 04/18/1871, d. 02/26/1956
BRADFORD, W. Lee, ssw-Effie L., b. 04/13/1871, d. 01/07/1950
BRYAN, Anna Ada, d/o T. B. & Sarah Bryan, b. 11/06/1880, d. 04/30/1899
BRYAN, Anna H., ssw-William C., b. 03/22/1908, d. 10/18/1985
BRYAN, Anna M., ssw-David J., Mother, b. 04/20/1862, d. 07/10/1954
BRYAN, Annie E., w/o George W. Age 26y 7m 24d, b. N/D, d. 08/01/1881
BRYAN, Arthur B., Jr., b. 1914, d. 1920
BRYAN, Burton, Age 76y 6m 17d, b. N/D, d. 09/21/1902
BRYAN, Charles H., ssw-Miranda J., b. 01/12/1873, d. 12/03/1954
BRYAN, David J., ssw-Anna M., Father, b. 10/27/1863, d. 10/21/1934
BRYAN, Delbert, s/o Chas. H. & M. Jennie, b. 06/26/1905, d. 07/23/1905
BRYAN, Derrick J., Age 9m, b. 11/02/1993, d. 08/22/1994
BRYAN, Edith A., ssw-George F., b. 1880, d. 1969
BRYAN, George F., ssw-Edith A., b. 1879, d. 1950
BRYAN, George F., ssw-Hallie C., Pfc., USA, WWII, b. 10/20/1908, d. 12/02/1978
BRYAN, George W., b. 09/10/1855, d. 02/17/1918
BRYAN, Hallie C., ssw-George F., b. 03/23/1910, d. 08/13/1985
BRYAN, Herbert, s/o Chas. H. & M. Jennie, b. 06/26/1905, d. 04/27/1922
BRYAN, Joseph, ssw-Una V., b. 1918, d. 1918
BRYAN, Lavenia E., b. 09/05/1862, d. 11/02/1935
BRYAN, Louise B. Gray, b. 04/09/1934, d. 04/09/1962
BRYAN, Lula A., ssw-Raymond, b. 03/18/1912, d. N/D
BRYAN, Mary P., w/o George W., b. 09/29/1854, d. 03/01/1934

BRYAN, Minnie B., b. 01/14/1904, d. N/D

BRYAN, Miranda J., ssw-Charles H., b. 09/11/1873, d. 06/07/1955

BRYAN, N. Aubrey, Jr., s/o Norris & Ina Bryan, b. 05/26/1962, d. 05/29/1962

BRYAN, Otto G., b. 03/30/1904, d. 05/25/1904

BRYAN, Rawlins H., b. 1916, d. N/D

BRYAN, Raymond, ssw-Lulu A., b. 07/01/1914, d. N/D

BRYAN, Reece Q., s/o Raymond & Lulu A. Bryan, b. 1944, d. 1944

BRYAN, Sarah J., w/o Burton, b. 10/15/1831, d. 01/23/1906

BRYAN, Sarah L., Mother, b. 1858, d. 1953

BRYAN, Thomas B., Father, b. 1853, d. 1947

BRYAN, Una V., ssw-Joseph, b. 1885, d. 1919

BRYAN, William B., Brother, b. 1879, d. 1962

BRYAN, William C., ssw-Anna H., b. 05/16/1902, d. 12/06/1991

BRYAN, William J., Age 22y 2m 11d, b. N/D, d. 02/25/1875

BURRIS, Mary E., d/o T. L. & Mary H., Age 1y 1m 24d, b. N/D, d. 09/18/1885

CANNON, George W., ssw-Mary, b. 06/29/1851, d. 09/17/1932

CANNON, Johnson W., Age 62y, b. N/D, d. 11/13/1883

CANNON, Johnson W., s/o George & Mary H., b. 03/26/1881, d. 11/13/1883

CANNON, Maranda E., w/o Johnson W., Age 78y 5m 10d, b. N/D, d. 10/05/1898

CANNON, Mary, w/o George W., Age 53y 2m 8d, b. N/D, d. 07/20/1903

CANNON, Sarah, ssw-George W., b. 08/24/1860, d. N/D

CARLISLE, Elizabeth V., b. 12/21/1918, d. 06/08/1970

CARLISLE, George H., b. 05/08/1909, d. 05/02/1988

CARRE, Joseph F., ssw-Julia A., m. 09/07/1935, b. 1908, d. N/D

CARRE, Julia A., ssw-Joseph F., m. 09/07/1935, b. 1914, d. 1995

CONAWAY, Bertha May, d/o Jos. S. & Sarah J., b. 09/05/1901, d. 10/25/1901

CONAWAY, Charles, ssw-Edna Mae, b. 10/14/1901, d. 02/23/1950

CONAWAY, Edna Mae, ssw-Charles, b. 01/12/1912, d. 06/27/1973

CONAWAY, John W., ssw-Mary E., b. 05/29/1842, d. 12/04/1910

CONAWAY, Mary E., w/o John W., ssw-John W., b. 01/04/1844, d. 06/06/1923

CONAWAY, Olin, ssw-Olivette, b. 04/07/1900, d. 01/11/1987

CONAWAY, Olivette, ssw-Olin, b. 09/13/1900, d. 06/08/1987

CONAWAY, Orlando W., s/o Jos. S. & Sarah J., b. N/D, d. 03/09/1891

CONAWAY, Oscar B., ssw-Walter L., b. 1896, d. 1991

CONAWAY, Sarah Jane, ssw-Bertha May & Orlando W., b. 1867, d. 1939

CONAWAY, Walter L., ssw-Oscar B., b. 1895, d. 1981

CONAWAY, William C., b. 10/22/1835, d. 09/08/1918

CONLEY, Bernice L., ssw-Robert E., b. 11/04/1946, d. N/D

CONLEY, Robert E., ssw-Bernice L., Sgt., USMC, Vietnam, b. 05/12/1944, d. 11/22/1982

CONOWAY, Donna L., ssw-Patricia A., b. 1961, d. 1961

CONOWAY, Elsie, ssw-Ollie, b. 12/11/1911, d. 02/02/1996

CONOWAY, Ollie, ssw-Elsie, b. 01/19/1909, d. 07/06/1970

CONOWAY, Patricia A., ssw-Donna L., b. 1959, d. 1960

DAVIS, Anna Mae, ssw-Arthur P., b. 1910, d. N/D

DAVIS, Arthur P., ssw-Anna Mae, b. 1898, d. 1973

DAVIS, William H., b. 02/09/1885, d. 03/11/1960

DAY, Frank L., ssw-Mollie T., b. 1875, d. 1946

DAY, Mollie T., ssw-Frank L., b. 1879, d. 1969

DICKERSON, Blanche R., ssw-Ernest, b. 1895, d. 1970

DICKERSON, Catherine P., b. 12/25/1907, d. 07/18/1981

DICKERSON, Ernest, ssw-Blanche R., b. 1896, d. 1965

DICKERSON, George P., b. 05/01/1898, d. 06/20/1965

DILL, James A., Age 25y 7m 16d, b. N/D, d. 08/02/1880

DILL, Samuel P., Rev. Age 29y 1m 11d, b. N/D, d. 08/24/1880

DOLBY, Armenia J., ssw-William J., Lina A., Jennie S. & Harvey L. Dolby and Lina A. Lyons, b. 1900,
    d. 1903

DOLBY, Harvey L., ssw-William J., Lina A., Jennie S. & Armenia J. Dolby and Lina A. Lyons, b. 1890,
    d. 1894

DOLBY, Jennie S., ssw-William J., Lina A., Harvey L. & Armenia J. Dolby and Lina A. Lyons, b. 1876,
    d. 1900

DOLBY, John C., Age 66y 2m 16d, b. N/D, d. 12/13/1881

DOLBY, John M., b. 03/06/1855, d. 06/02/1896

DOLBY, Lina A., ssw-William J., Armenia L., Harvey L. & Jennie S. Dolby and Lina A. Lyons, b. 1856,
    d. 1935

DOLBY, Mary S., w/o John C., Age 50y 4m 5d, b. N/D, d. 05/08/1864

DOLBY, William J., ssw-Lina A., Armenia J., Harvey L. & Jennie S. Dolby and Lina A. Lyons, b. 1850,
    d. N/D

DOUGLASS, Dorothy M., ssw-W. Ross, b. 05/25/1917, d. N/D

DOUGLASS, W. Ross, ssw-Dorothy M., SSgt., USA, WWII, b. 04/28/1914, d. 02/13/1994

DUKES, Alton P., ssw-Pauline R., b. 1905, d. 1972

DUKES, Flora A., d/o T. P. & M. E., b. 03/03/1877, d. 10/16/1878

DUKES, John H., ssw-Martha J., b. 11/14/1844, d. 12/07/1916

DUKES, M. Flora, b. 12/04/1890, d. 01/26/1978

DUKES, Martha J., ssw-John H., b. 11/28/1852, d. 09/14/1927

DUKES, Pauline R., ssw-Alton P., b. 1917, d. 1989

ELLIOTT, Benjamin T., b. 1892, d. 1982

ELLIOTT, Bessie H., b. 1904, d. 1991

ELLIOTT, Calhoun, b. 1919, d. 1942

ELLIOTT, Clifford N., b. 03/26/1926, d. 01/27/1943

ELLIOTT, Elizabeth Gibbons, w/o Norval Elliott, b. 1913, d. 1942

ELLIOTT, Elva, b. 09/24/1903, d. 08/17/1937

ELLIOTT, Hannah R., ssw-John M., b. 1864, d. 1945

ELLIOTT, John H., b. 09/27/1819, d. 02/13/1889

ELLIOTT, John M., ssw-Hannah R., b. 1860, d. 1948

ELLIOTT, Louisa, w/o John H., b. 02/19/1827, d. 05/11/1865

ELLIOTT, Maranda, w/o Wingate, Age 38y 7m 19d, b. N/D, d. 11/29/1868

ELLIOTT, Mary A., w/o Wingate B., b. 11/04/1833, d. 01/03/1916

ELLIOTT, Norval E., b. 01/27/1903, d. 12/28/1983

ELLIOTT, Sarah A. Conaway, w/o James H., b. 01/04/1843, d. 12/01/1920

ELLIOTT, Thomas L., b. 08/11/1866, d. 08/23/1919

ELLIOTT, Wingate, ssw-Maranda, b. 12/12/1824, d. 06/10/1900

ENGLISH, Willie E., s/o Edgar, b. 10/17/1880, d. 08/02/1881

EVANS, Charles R., Sr., AB, USAF, Vietnam, b. 05/12/1946, d. 04/02/1995

EVANS, John W., Jr., F1, USN, WWII, b. 1920, d. 1990

FISHER, Frances A., ssw-Norman C., b. 10/08/1917, d. N/D

FISHER, Norman C., ssw-Frances A., b. 10/13/1912, d. 07/05/1986

FLEETWOOD, Almyra E., ssw-William T. & Mary E., b. 1892, d. 1893

FLEETWOOD, Catherine E., ssw-William T., b. 07/02/1916, d. 04/15/1996

FLEETWOOD, Mary E., w/o William T., ssw-Almyra E. & William T., Age 38y 11m 7d, b. N/D, d. 11/23/1903

FLEETWOOD, William T., ssw-Catherine E., b. 09/12/1911, d. 10/30/1981

FLEETWOOD, William T., ssw-Mary E. & Almyra E., b. 1859, d. 1932

FOSKEY, Evelyn, ssw-Leroy, b. 1927, d. 1961

FOSKEY, Leroy, ssw-Evelyn, b. 1924, d. 1990

FRAMPTON, Billy, ssw-Charles T. & Mary E., Baby, b. 1954, d. 1954

FRAMPTON, Charles T., ssw-Mary E., b. 08/20/1917, d. 12/05/1989

FRAMPTON, Mary E., ssw-Charles T., b. 11/28/1917, d. 07/02/1974

GERMAN, Anna Mae, ssw-Harold W. G., Sr., b. 08/20/1932, d. N/D

GERMAN, Harold W. G., Sr., ssw-Anna Mae, Sgt., USA, WWII, b. 03/31/1923, d. 11/15/1993

GILES, Mary, w/o William Age 79y 6m, b. N/D, d. 02/22/1892

GILES, William, Age 77y 8m 16d, b. N/D, d. 06/02/1887

GILMORE, Elizabeth F., ssw-George R., b. 11/07/1919, d. N/D

GILMORE, George R., ssw-Elizabeth F., b. 01/04/1913, d. N/D

GIVENS, Arley, ssw-Mary E. & Thomas W., b. 1894, d. 1915

GIVENS, Bessie E., b. 03/25/1903, d. 07/06/1978

GIVENS, Caldwell Quell, ssw-Caroline, b. 05/19/1855, d. 05/30/1902

GIVENS, Caroline, ssw-Caldwell Quell, b. 08/26/1860, d. 08/26/1934

GIVENS, Catheline, ssw-Pearl V., b. 1928, d. 1928

GIVENS, Cora V., b. 09/08/1877, d. 12/07/1974

GIVENS, Eliza W., ssw-Fred, b. 1856, d. 1924

GIVENS, Ethel C., ssw-Catheline, b. 1907, d. 1961

GIVENS, Fred, ssw-Eliza W., b. 1864, d. 1949

GIVENS, Glenn W., b. 10/06/1916, d. 05/20/1992

GIVENS, Herschel, b. 1932, d. 1932

GIVENS, Linden E., b. 11/28/1897, d. 05/12/1981

GIVENS, Mary E., ssw-Thomas W. & Arley, b. 1873, d. 1952

GIVENS, Norman C., Age 8wks, b. N/D, d. 1903

GIVENS, Pearl V., ssw-Catheline, b. 1931, d. 1940

GIVENS, Raymond T., ssw-Catheline, b. 1901, d. 1975

GIVENS, Robert S., b. 07/27/1874, d. 10/28/1957

GIVENS, Robert S., ssw-Sarah E., b. 03/19/1866, d. 12/16/1951

GIVENS, Sarah E., ssw-Robert S., b. 08/30/1862, d. 01/08/1906

GIVENS, Sarrie A., Age 11wk, b. N/D, d. 1904

GIVENS, Thomas W., ssw-Mary E. & Arley, b. 1872, d. 1963

HARRINGTON, Elva M., ssw-Frank, b. N/D, d. N/D

HARRINGTON, Frank, ssw-Elva M., b. 1890, d. 1932

HASTINGS, Annie E., w/o Jas. T. Age 29y 4m 4d, b. N/D, d. 04/01/1884

HASTINGS, Christine E., ssw-Joseph W. b. 01/14/1919, d. 07/23/1979

HASTINGS, James H., ssw-Mary E., b. 02/09/1843, d. 10/12/1917

HASTINGS, James T., ssw-Annie E., b. N/D, d. N/D

HASTINGS, Joseph W., ssw-Christine E., Sgt., USA, WWII, b. 03/01/1908, d. 05/17/1980

HASTINGS, Lola F., ssw-Thos. H., Mother, b. 1873, d. 1931

HASTINGS, Mary E., ssw-James H., b. 11/17/1853, d. 07/21/1926

HASTINGS, Samuel J., b. 10/31/1823, d. 11/20/1911

HASTINGS, Sarah A., b. 01/12/1837, d. 10/16/1900

HASTINGS, Sarah J., w/o Jas. H., b. 09/30/1839, d. 09/20/1875

HASTINGS, Thos. H., ssw-Lola F., Father, b. 1863, d. 1948

HATFIELD, Elijah, Age 65y, b. N/D, d. 02/14/1853

HATFIELD, Sally, w/o Elijah, Age 66y 7m, b. N/D, d. 09/19/1856

HEARN, Benjamin B., Father, b. 04/02/1820, d. 07/30/1909

HEARN, Benjamin M., s/o Wm. H. & Sarah E., Age 22y 11m 18d, b. N/D, d. 11/01/1904

HEARN, Charles, ssw-Estella J., b. 1891, d. 1959

HEARN, Estella J., ssw-Charles, Mother, b. 1890, d. 1942

HEARN, Hazel C., b. N/D, d. N/D

HEARN, Mary J., w/o Benjamin B., Age 75y 6m 27d, b. N/D, d. 02/23/1897

HEARN, Sarah E., ssw-William H., Mother, b. 1858, d. 1938

HEARN, William H., ssw-Sarah E., Father, b. 1851, d. 1929

HEARN, Wm. Brinkley, b. 02/25/1889, d. 04/13/1997

HEARNE, Levator W., s/o William H. & Sarah E., Age 1y 1m 21d, b. N/D, d. 07/22/1902

HENDRICKSON, Arthur P., b. 01/31/1927, d. 02/10/1951

HENDRICKSON, Lillian M., b. 07/10/1889, d. 05/09/1943

HIGGINS, Arnold L., b. 02/03/1942, d. 04/30/1984

HITCH, Harley H., ssw-Mae L., b. 08/08/1874, d. 03/19/1960

HITCH, Mae L., ssw-Harley H., b. 04/08/1883, d. 03/21/1942

HOWARD, Mildred H., b. 11/10/1908, d. N/D

HOWARD, Walters Sammons, b. 08/20/1908, d. 08/24/1977

ISAAC, Norman, b. 10/04/1931, d. 08/02/1934

JACOBS, Susie, b. 1879, d. 1943

JAMES, Anna G., ssw-Earl C., b. 05/14/1914, d. N/D

JAMES, Annie E., Mother, b. 02/07/1872, d. 03/01/1944

JAMES, Arthur I., b. 02/11/1902, d. 07/11/1970

JAMES, Caldwell W., ssw-Nettie E., b. 1854, d. 1939

JAMES, Carlton G., Jr., b. 10/20/1967, d. 12/02/1992

JAMES, Catharine W., w/o Noah H., b. 07/05/1852, d. 12/19/1906

JAMES, Clarence T., b. 02/19/1878, d. 05/27/1965

JAMES, Earl C., ssw-Anna G., b. 05/19/1901, d. 10/29/1969

JAMES, Edna, b. 1915, d. 1933

JAMES, Emma M., ssw-Thomas C., Mother, b. 1873, d. 1956

JAMES, Florence E., b. 02/18/1886, d. 05/27/1966

JAMES, Granville H., b. 01/13/1908, d. 10/31/1986

JAMES, Grover C., ssw-Lizzie W., b. 07/31/1884, d. 01/19/1968

JAMES, Inf. d/o J. Alvin & Lillie M., b. 1926, d. 1926

JAMES, Iva Ruth, b. 05/31/1919, d. N/D

JAMES, Laura E., ssw-Raymond W., b. 12/08/1903, d. 09/04/1977

JAMES, Lizzie W., ssw-Grover C., b. 03/30/1893, d. 02/13/1964

JAMES, Mary V., b. 07/10/1879, d. 03/03/1970

JAMES, Nettie E., ssw-Caldwell W., b. 1864, d. 1909

JAMES, Noah H., ssw-Catharine W., b. 06/27/1840, d. 01/26/1920

JAMES, Phillip E., b. 03/11/1882, d. 02/26/1958

JAMES, Raymond W., ssw-Laura E., b. 05/10/1896, d. 07/28/1962

JAMES, Thomas C., ssw-Emma M., Father, b. 1873, d. 1935

JEFFERSON, Howard C., b. 1881, d. 1993

JEFFERSON, Jennie P., b. 1884, d. 1972

JONES, Alfred H., Son, b. 1876, d. 1885

JONES, Charles H., Son, b. 1872, d. 1952

JONES, Charles H., ssw-Mary Ann, b. 09/01/1827, d. 01/31/1903

JONES, Cora B., Daughter, b. 1860, d. 1864

JONES, Eliza J., ssw-Thomas F., Mother, b. 1843, d. 1915

JONES, Mary Ann, w/o Charles H. Jones, b. 08/04/1832, d. 05/27/1896

JONES, Minus, Son, b. 1874, d. 1875

JONES, Thomas F., ssw-Eliza J., Father, b. 1824, d. 1910

JONES, Wilson M., s/o James H. & Ida A., b. 04/03/1878, d. 09/29/1878

JOSEPH, C. Donald, ssw-Edith, b. 01/07/1928, d. N/D

JOSEPH, Edith T., ssw-C. Donald, b. 05/10/1929, d. N/D

JOSEPH, Frederick B., b. 1858, d. 1937

JOSEPH, Hattie A., b. 1878, d. 1930

JOSEPH, Senary B., w/o Frederick B., b. 1864, d. 1905

KAY, Gurney V., ssw-Lillian W., b. 01/10/1901, d. 12/10/1981

KAY, Lillian W., ssw-Gurney V., b. 10/08/1900, d. 04/01/1987

KING, Frances M., ssw-Wilbure J., b. 1885, d. 1940

KING, Wilbure J., ssw-Frances M., b. 1877, d. 1941

KYTTLE, Charles R., ssw-Mary J., S1, USN, WWII, b. 10/27/1926, d. 07/26/1993

KYTTLE, Mary J., ssw-Charles R., b. 03/08/1931, d. N/D

LAKE, Lula O., w/o James P., b. 01/07/1891, d. 07/16/1914

LAMBDEN, Ella M., b. 04/12/1861, d. 09/01/1933

LENTZ, Anna M., ssw-Edward W., b. 1888, d. 1966

LENTZ, Edward W., ssw-Anna M., b. 1881, d. 1964

LINGO, Annie, ssw-Henry, Robert & Margori, b. 1878, d. 1879

LINGO, Henry, ssw-Annie, Robert & Margori, b. 1851, d. 1885

LINGO, Margori, ssw-Henry, Annie & Robert, b. 1888, d. 1888

LINGO, Robert, ssw-Henry, Annie & Margori, b. 1879, d. 1880

LINGO, William E., ssw-Mary J. Lingo Workman, b. 02/23/1849, d. 08/25/1882

LOPER, Anna Raughley, ssw-Emma R. Raughley, b. 06/27/1892, d. 01/25/1978

LYONS, Lina A., ssw-William J., Lina A., Jennie S., Harvey L. & Armenia J. Dolby, b. 1887, d. 1906

MAXWELL, Elias, Age 49y 4m 24d, b. 10/18/1825, d. 02/10/1875

MAXWELL, Isiah T., b. 01/26/1863, d. 06/30/1940

MAXWELL, John M., Age 78y 3d, b. 07/15/1851, d. 03/18/1921

MAXWELL, Mary A., Age 61y 5m 2d, b. 09/06/1869, d. 01/08/1930

MAXWELL, Naoma A., w/o Elias, Age 79y 9m 2d, b. 03/18/1825, d. 01/12/1904

MCALISTER, Bertha M., ssw-Carl N., b. 12/28/1890, d. 09/08/1972

MCALISTER, Carl N., ssw-Bertha M., b. 09/05/1891, d. 02/07/1981

MCALLISTER, Barkley T., ssw-Sallie A. & Mae R., b. 1861, d. 1938

MCALLISTER, Clara E., ssw-Dennard H., b. 1892, d. 1972

MCALLISTER, Dennard H., ssw-Clara E., b. 1885, d. 1966

MCALLISTER, Helen L., ssw-Rowland H., b. 1917, d. N/D

MCALLISTER, Mae R., ssw-Barkley T. & Sallie A., b. 1894, d. 1895

MCALLISTER, Rowland H., ssw-Helen L., b. 1913, d. 1974

MCALLISTER, Sallie A., ssw-Barkley T. & Mae R., b. 1863, d. 1896

MCALLISTER, Sarah H., w/o James H., b. 03/12/1855, d. 04/21/1890

MCDONALD, Mary Elizabeth, w/o James T., b. 10/25/1884, d. 02/16/1914

MEARS, Harvey, s/o Wm. & Sarah E. Mears, b. 10/12/1893, d. 05/20/1894

MEARS, Larrie Irvan, s/o Ananias D. & Sabrina, Age 3y 2m 21d, b. N/D, d. 11/10/1886

MEARS, Myrtle E., b. 03/13/1904, d. 04/20/1984

MEARS, Sally Jane, d/o Sabra & A. D., Age 3y 5m 7d, b. N/D, d. 03/22/1879

MEARS, Sarah E., ssw-William M., Mother, b. 03/15/1860, d. 01/25/1937

MEARS, William M., ssw-Sarah E., Father, b. 11/12/1853, d. 03/03/1938

MESSICK, Alice May, d/o Phillip S. & Annie, b. 10/25/1867, d. 07/27/1872

MESSICK, Alvernon, ssw-Willie May, b. 1864, d. 1956

MESSICK, Angelina D., d/o Nathaniel & Sarah A., b. 09/25/1860, d. 02/01/1901

MESSICK, Annie L., d/o Phillip & Annie, b. 12/14/1878, d. 07/18/1900

MESSICK, Annie M., w/o Phillip S., b. 06/09/1843, d. 12/18/1878

MESSICK, Arthur M., b. 12/29/1875, d. 10/16/1909

MESSICK, Aura T., s/o Aura & Gertie, b. 06/17/1915, d. 01/23/1916

MESSICK, Bessie G., ssw-Creston E., b. 1885, d. 1977

MESSICK, Clayton C., b. 09/27/1818, d. 11/23/1894

MESSICK, Clayton H., b. 1841, d. 1913

MESSICK, Creston E., ssw-Elsie F. & Bessie G., b. 1909, d. 1981

MESSICK, Elsie F., ssw-Creston E., b. 1911, d. N/D

MESSICK, J. Gertrude, d/o Aura C. & Gertie, b. 09/24/1917, d. 01/03/1919

MESSICK, Martha A., w/o Clayton C., b. 06/1830, d. 03/28/1879

MESSICK, Minnie J., ssw-Roy C., b. 09/26/1891, d. 05/10/1963

MESSICK, Norval A., s/o Alvernon & Willie, b. 05/07/1905, d. 05/09/1905

MESSICK, Phillip S., ssw-Annie M., DE, Pvt., Civil War Cav., b. 05/31/1845, d. 06/18/1931

MESSICK, Robert T., ssw-Anna Raughley Loper, Age 71y, b. N/D, d. 09/19/1917

MESSICK, Roy C., ssw-Minnie J., b. 08/25/1885, d. 07/12/1953

MESSICK, Sarah A., w/o Clayton H. Messick, b. 03/12/1846, d. 07/20/1893

MESSICK, Willie May, ssw-Alvernon, b. 1875, d. 1962

MILLS, Dwight Morrison, Tec5, USA, WWII, b. 07/22/1917, d. 12/06/1981

MINTER, Linda P., ssw-Wade H., b. 01/28/1918, d. 08/18/1991

MINTER, Wade H., ssw-Linda P., Cpl., USA, WWII, b. 06/24/1919, d. 10/21/1987

MOORE, Mary E., Inf. d/o Charles C. & Louise, b. 05/15/1904, d. 05/12/1908

MORRIS, Sallie W., w/o W. J., Age 45y 2m 28d, b. N/D, d. 10/01/1886

MUMFORD, Julia A., b. 11/22/1852, d. 10/07/1938

MUMFORD, Lydia, w/o Robert H., ssw-Robert H., Mother, b. 02/07/1857, d. 07/30/1893

MUMFORD, Robert H., ssw-Lydia A., Father, b. 09/07/1853, d. 09/04/1927

MUMFORD, Walter k., b. 09/24/1920, d. 12/09/1987

MURPHY, Blanche M. Tyndall, b. 01/06/1888, d. 09/20/1961

O'NEAL, Joseph A., ssw-Mattie M., b. 08/02/1888, d. 10/07/1969

O'NEAL, Mattie M., ssw-Joseph A., b. 09/27/1897, d. 10/10/1978

OLIVER, Anne C., b. 02/17/1844, d. 09/21/1859

OTT, Jacob, b. N/D, d. 09/18/1942

PARKER, Carl E., ssw-Jennie Lee, b. 1879, d. 1948

PARKER, Edith M., b. 1913, d. 1913

PARKER, Jennie Lee, ssw-Carl E., b. 1887, d. 1973

PIANKA, Charlotte A., b. 1936, d. 1963

POORE, James B., Pfc., USA, WWII, b. 1921, d. 1995

PRETTYMAN, Elizabeth A., Age 37y 21d, b. N/D, d. 03/28/1874

PUSEY, Delema E., ssw-William C., b. 05/12/1898, d. 12/16/1987

PUSEY, Dora F., b. 11/06/1888, d. 04/24/1974
PUSEY, J. Lester, ssw-William C., b. 12/23/1895, d. 03/17/1971
PUSEY, Rebecca, ssw-William C., b. 12/14/1922, d. 06/12/1983
PUSEY, Robert L., b. 12/08/1890, d. 09/06/1978
PUSEY, William C., ssw-Delema E., b. 01/20/1928, d. 03/08/1971
RAUGHLEY, Emma R., ssw-Anna Raughley Loper, Age 33y, b. N/D, d. 02/1902
REMENTER, Alyce V., ssw-Roland J., Sr., b. 09/22/1917, d. N/D
REMENTER, Baby, b. 1946, d. 1946
REMENTER, Blanche, b. 1918, d. 1918
REMENTER, Carol C., ssw-R. James, Jr., b. 06/30/1941, d. N/D
REMENTER, Charles E., b. 1895, d. 1939
REMENTER, Clara L., b. 1897, d. 1982
REMENTER, Clarence A., b. 1890, d. 1944
REMENTER, Emira F., ssw-Harry J., b. 04/21/1895, d. 01/25/1955
REMENTER, Esther E., b. 10/25/1919, d. 10/18/1983
REMENTER, Harry J., ssw-Emira F., b. 10/23/1886, d. 11/10/1967
REMENTER, James M., b. 1909, d. 1910
REMENTER, James, Father, b. 1857, d. 1925
REMENTER, Jannie A., b. 1900, d. 1985
REMENTER, Martin T., b. 1911, d. 1970
REMENTER, Mary L., b. 1885, d. 1899
REMENTER, Michael J., b. 12/15/1965, d. 09/27/1986
REMENTER, Orla J., b. 1917, d. 1917
REMENTER, R. James, Jr., ssw-Carol C., b. 02/18/1939, d. 08/25/1991
REMENTER, Roland J., Sr., ssw-Alyce V., b. 12/13/1915, d. N/D
REMENTER, Sarah E., Mother, b. 1857, d. 1938
RICHARDSON, Etta Mae, ssw-Howard D. b. 09/10/1914, d. N/D
RICHARDSON, Howard D., ssw-Etta Mae, b. 01/28/1911, d. 10/31/1976
RIGGIN, Alice, b. N/D, d. N/D
RIGGIN, Milan, b. N/D, d. N/D
ROGERS, Albert C., b. 06/21/1901, d. 03/17/1959
ROGERS, Allen W., ssw-Elsie C., b. 08/10/1912, d. 01/29/1983
ROGERS, Curtis S., ssw-Mary E., b. 1855, d. 1937
ROGERS, Elsie C., ssw-Allen W., b. 06/16/1912, d. N/D
ROGERS, Emma S., b. 1868, d. 1936
ROGERS, Ira B., ssw-Mary E., b. 1890, d. 1966
ROGERS, Jennie C., b. 03/21/1897, d. 08/28/1976
ROGERS, John E., b. 01/24/1895, d. 06/21/1910
ROGERS, Mary E., ssw-Curtis S., b. 1858, d. 1937
ROGERS, Mary E., ssw-Ira B., b. 1888, d. 1917
ROGERS, Minos R., b. 10/10/1880, d. 08/15/1900
ROGERS, Stephen H., b. 1864, d. 1936
ROGERS, Thomas O., b. 05/14/1895, d. 12/01/1959
SALMONS, Asbury, ssw-Elizabeth, b. 1855, d. 1920
SALMONS, Elizabeth, ssw-Asbury, b. 1856, d. 1934
SCOTT, Charles W., Father, b. 05/29/1918, d. N/D
SCOTT, Donald C., Father & Son, b. 02/26/1946, d. 05/19/1991
SCOTT, Edith E., Mother, b. 11/03/1920, d. 07/29/1982

SEARLS, Helen J., ssw-Norman E., b. 05/04/1917, d. 08/23/1994

SEARLS, Norman E., ssw-Helen J., b. 10/10/1920, d. N/D

SHOCKLEY, Oliver R., ssw-Violet L., b. 1910, d. 1978

SHOCKLEY, Violet L., ssw-Oliver R., b. 1913, d. N/D

SHORT, Annie M., w/o Horace G., b. 08/27/1868, d. 06/29/1905

SHORT, Thedoshia E., ssw-Thomas E., Grandmother, b. 1865, d. 1941

SHORT, Thomas E., ssw-Thedoshia E., Grandfather, b. 1860, d. 1930

SIMPSON, Margaret, Age 70y, b. N/D, d. 08/15/1893

SMITH, Agnes M., ssw-Albert E., b. 01/26/1898, d. 04/18/1993

SMITH, Albert E., ssw-Agnes m., b. 05/02/1904, d. 08/31/1985

SPICER, Anna M., ssw-Thomas B., b. 1834, d. 1913

SPICER, Edward W., ssw-Mary J., b. 01/03/1838, d. 06/06/1908

SPICER, Elmo M., b. 1885, d. 1928

SPICER, Ezra, s/o Mary J. & E. W., Age 29d, b. N/D, d. 09/20/1873

SPICER, John W., b. 03/16/1875, d. 01/08/1921

SPICER, Laura D., w/o John W., b. 08/31/1873, d. 07/19/1898

SPICER, Martha A., b. 1852, d. 1938

SPICER, Mary J., w/o Edw. W., b. 02/12/1848, d. 11/23/1890

SPICER, Sophrona J., d/o E. W. & Mary J., Age 1y 3m 29d, b. N/D, d. 11/05/1863

SPICER, Thomas B., ssw-Anna M., b. 1837, d. 1911

SPICER, William J., b. 04/16/1837, d. 06/30/1890

SULLIVAN, Donald K., b. 05/28/1963, d. 03/14/1991

SWAIN, Nancy, Age 73y 7m, b. N/D, d. 07/19/1887

TAYLOR, Elias D., Age 83y 6m 16d, b. N/D, d. 02/05/1885

TAYLOR, Jane, w/o Wm. E., Age Abt. 72y, b. N/D, d. 04/15/1893

TAYLOR, Wm. E., Age 65y 3m 11d, b. N/D, d. 04/15/1888

TAYLOR, Woody, s/o Elias & Levia E., Age 2y 6m 10d, b. N/D, d. 04/03/1861

THOMPSON, Anna L., ssw-Anna Raughley Loper, Age 22y 5m 20d, b. N/D, d. 02/18/1898

TINDAL, Anner, w/o Joseph B., b. 04/28/1853, d. 12/12/1923

TINDAL, Annie M., d/o James H. & Mary A., Age 5m 12d, b. N/D, d. 03/23/1875

TINDAL, B. H., ssw-M. D. b. 1815, d. 1894

TINDAL, Caleb C., b. 1851, d. 1923

TINDAL, Carl K., b. 04/24/1918, d. 08/26/1918

TINDAL, Charles A., Civil War, Age 22y 11m 27d, b. N/D, d. 09/21/1864

TINDAL, Inf. o/ J. H. & Clara Tindal, b. N/D, d. N/D

TINDAL, Jacob M., Age 19y 2m 11d, b. N/D, d. 05/23/1866

TINDAL, James H., b. 07/04/1846, d. 07/23/1917

TINDAL, James R., Father, b. 04/14/1822, d.06/11/1878

TINDAL, Jonathan A., ssw-Martha P., b. 05/10/1841, d. 05/25/1912

TINDAL, Joseph B., b. 05/16/1860, d. 12/31/1929

TINDAL, Julia A., w/o A. Tindal, b. 10/18/1818, d. 06/10/1889

TINDAL, M. D., ssw-B. H., b. 1817, d. 1895

TINDAL, Margaret H., w/o George P., Age 32y 4m 26d, b. N/D, d. 08/09/1864

TINDAL, Martha L., d/o A. & Julia A., Age 28y 3m 14d, b. N/D, d. 03/23/1884

TINDAL, Martha P., w/o Jonathan A., b. 03/24/1855, d. 03/30/1899

TINDAL, Mary A., w/o James H., b. 06/01/1854, d. 05/15/1903

TINDAL, Mary Ann, d/o Benton H. & Mathilda, Age 14y 2m 8d, b. 1849, d. 08/19/1863

TINDAL, Minos, s/o A. & Julia A., Age 27y 4m 4d, b. N/D, d. 04/04/1886

TINDAL, Sarah A., w/o James R., b. 10/25/1829, d. 09/26/1880

TINDALL, Alberta, b. 1914, d. 1914

TINDALL, Alice R., b. 02/17/1914, d. 0/01/1979

TINDALL, Bessie E., ssw-William W., b. 1883, d. 1975

TINDALL, C. Marshall, ssw-Infant sons, b. 1903, d. 1982

TINDALL, Delbert R., b. 04/30/1909, d. 09/22/1983

TINDALL, Edith, b. 1866, d. 1904

TINDALL, Essie C., b. 1885, d. 1946

TINDALL, Harry C., b. 06/20/1900, d. 11/10/1981

TINDALL, Helen, d/o Shepard & Hester G., b. 02/21/1891, d. 03/02/1891

TINDALL, Herman, s/o Shepard & Hester G., b. 02/21/1891, d. 03/02/1891

TINDALL, Hester G., w/o Shepard, b. 03/30/1855, d. 05/29/1911

TINDALL, Inf. Sons, ssw-C. Marshall, b. N/D, d. N/D

TINDALL, Jincie E., ssw-Rev. William J., b. 06/23/1845, d. 04/22/1933

TINDALL, John M., b. 1866, d. 1950

TINDALL, Myrtle, d/o Shepard & Hester G., Age 1y 5m, b. N/D, d. 06/18/1877

TINDALL, Shepard, ssw-Hester G., b. 06/17/1853, d. 09/10/1919

TINDALL, William J., Rev., ssw-Jincie E., b. 08/09/1842, d. 06/01/1922

TINDALL, William W., ssw-Bessie E., b. 1878, d. 1952

TONGE, Grace G., ssw-Walter Harvey, b. 03/06/1927, d. N/D

TONGE, Walter Harvey, ssw-Grace G., PHM3, USN, WWII, b. 05/16/1923, d. 12/03/1975

TRICE, Herbert T., b. 1885, d. 1948

TRUITT, Eliza A., b. 08/17/1836, d. 02/06/1921

TURNER, James H., b. 03/01/1899, d. 11/21/1980

TYNDALL, Agnes C., ssw-Joseph T., b. 07/29/1923, d. N/D

TYNDALL, Carl S., ssw-Florence W., b. 1883, d. 1945

TYNDALL, Charles James, ssw-Esther L., Sgt., USA, b. 04/07/1917, d. 04/17/1977

TYNDALL, Charles R., Brother, b. 1875, d. 1952

TYNDALL, Edward W., b. 1878, d. 1952

TYNDALL, Estella M., b. 09/27/1890, d. 04/18/1980

TYNDALL, Esther L., ssw-Charles James, b. 11/16/1914, d. 03/15/1992

TYNDALL, Florence W., ssw-Carl S., b. 1889, d. 1969

TYNDALL, J. Ermyl, b. 06/09/1899, d. 01/16/1985

TYNDALL, Jennie C., b. 12/10/1905, d. 02/23/1976

TYNDALL, Joseph T., ssw-Agnes C., b. 03/25/1921, d. N/D

TYNDALL, Joshua C., s/o Peter & Sarah Jane, Father, b. 01/24/1886, d. 02/22/1963

TYNDALL, Julia J., ssw-Wm. Ernest & Wm. Caleb, Mother, b. 1877, d. 1968

TYNDALL, Mabel Helen, b. 03/09/1932, d. N/D

TYNDALL, Mamie B., w/o Harvey W., b. 05/28/1886, d. 10/09/1910

TYNDALL, Mary C., b. 12/14/1892, d. 04/19/1925

TYNDALL, Medford I., b. 1912, d. 1912

TYNDALL, Melvin M., b. 07/22/1912, d. 10/16/1978

TYNDALL, Peter, ssw-Sarah J. Short, b. 09/08/1843, d. 01/22/1926

TYNDALL, Sarah J. Short, w/o Peter, b. 01/15/1850, d. 10/31/1920

TYNDALL, Vesta L., b. 1882, d. 1937

TYNDALL, Walter M., b. 02/02/1885, d. 08/19/1956

TYNDALL, Willise Burnice, b. 1915, d. 1915

TYNDALL, Wm. Caleb, ssw-Julia J. & Wm. Ernest, Son, b. 1913, d. 1935

TYNDALL, Wm. Ernest, ssw-Julia J., & Wm. Caleb, Father, b. 1877, d. 1966

WALLER, Archie J., ssw-Blanche H., b. 12/31/1896, d. 05/13/1988

WALLER, Blanche H., ssw-Archie J., b. 05/23/1897, d. 04/21/1986

WARREN, Elizabeth, w/o Samuel, b. 09/31/1789, d. 10/01/1831

WARREN, Hester, Age 38y 8d, b. N/D, d. 05/27/1867 [Note: stone broken]

WARREN, Samuel, s/o Kendal & Hester, b. 03/05/1791, d. 11/24/1835

WEBB, Arthur, b. 04/30/1909, d. 08/26/1976

WEBB, Mabel L., b. 06/02/1906, d. 11/09/1980

WEST, Annie L. Messick, d/o Philips & Annie M., b. 12/14/1878, d. 07/18/1900

WEST, Berth J., ssw-Rowland T., b. 01/29/1912, d. N/D

WEST, Charlotte, ssw-Samuel P., Mother, b. 02/16/1852, d. 01/24/1923

WEST, Dorothy E., ssw-Paul H., b. 10/11/1908, d. 06/19/1986

WEST, Madison P., b. 01/27/1931, d. 10/28/1994

WEST, Paul H., ssw-Dorothy E., b. 03/24/1904, d. 09/03/1985

WEST, Rowland T., ssw-Berth J., b. 05/26/1911, d. 11/21/1982

WEST, Sallie L., b. 03/14/1878, d. 10/31/1967

WEST, Samuel P., ssw-Charlotte A., Father, b. 09/23/1858, d. 03/14/1922

WEST, Sarah A., Mother, b. 02/03/1835, d. 10/13/1905

WEST, Thomas P., b. 02/20/1878, d. 01/11/1953

WEST, William B., s/o D. W. & Pearl West, b. 11/28/1916, d. 01/22/1917

WEST, William S., Father, b. 12/08/1829, d. 07/18/1905

WHARTON, Sarah Tyndall, b. 11/06/1919, d. 06/05/1995

WHISLER, John E., b. 03/29/1865, d. 12/06/1933

WILKINS, Sarah L., Mother, b. 08/27/1848, d. 04/21/1920

WILLIAMS, Benjamin Age 77y 11m 7d, b. N/D, d. 11/07/1916

WILLIAMS, Harry L., S1, USN, WWII, b. 1913, d. 1975

WILLIAMS, Harvey S., DE, Pfc., USA, WWII, b. 03/21/1905, d. 08/02/1968

WILLIAMS, Isaac H., ssw-Virginia, b. 04/09/1872, d. 07/11/1939

WILLIAMS, Mary E., w/o Benjamin, Age 24y 2m 16d, b. N/D, d. 06/03/1867

WILLIAMS, T. Elizabeth, w/o Benjamin J., b. 02/03/1836, d. 11/25/1913

WILLIAMS, Virginia, ssw-Isaac H., b. 08/30/1874, d. 10/16/1944

WOLFE, Howard M., Jr., b. 01/29/1958, d. 06/13/1986

WORKMAN, Elizabeth, w/o William S., b. 01/27/1840, d. 11/18/1892

WORKMAN, Mary J. Lingo, ssw-William E. Lingo, b. 04/10/1850, d. 05/06/1934

WORKMAN, William S., b. 01/31/1838, d. 12/23/1908

(NA-003 & HU-274) GREENWOOD MENNONITE CHURCH CEMETERY

Located North East of Greenwood on the south east side of Shawnee Rd. (Rt. 36) 0.6 miles north east of Ellendale-Greenwood Highway (Rt. 16)

Recorded: April 19, 1995

BACHMANN, Johanna Graul, b. 11/05/1867, d. 07/19/1956

BACHMANN, Max, b. 03/17/1871, d. 03/21/1932

BAWEL, Anna Mae, ssw-Orrie, b. 1919, d. 1970

BAWEL, Fannie R., b. 08/13/1862, d. 12/05/1932

BAWEL, Joseph, b. 10/11/1866, d. 02/20/1955

BAWEL, Lizzie, Age 28y 9m 10d, b. 01/12/1890, d. 10/22/1918

BAWEL, Orrie, ssw-Anna Mae, b. 1902, d. 1991

BAWEL, Urrie, b. 1911, d. 1974

BEACHY, Alvin D., ssw-Pauline, b. 11/06/1906, d. 12/30/1983

BEACHY, Pauline, ssw-Alvin D., b. 12/29/1909, d. 02/22/1969

BEALMAN, Mary M., Mother, Age 67y 1m 9d, b. 10/10/1859, d. 11/19/1926

BENDER, Caroline G., ssw-Valentine W., b. 1869, d. 1954

BENDER, Clayton M., ssw-Mary, b. 05/21/1918, d. N/D

BENDER, Esther M., ssw-Nevin V., b. 06/04/1898, d. 10/09/1967

BENDER, Hilda, Age 12y 7m 23d, b. N/D, d. 12/01/1920

BENDER, Inf. s/o Nevin & Esther, b. 09/20/1941, d. 09/20/1941

BENDER, Mary, ssw-Clayton M., b. 06/27/1920, d. 03/16/1992

BENDER, Nevin V., ssw-Esther M., b. 10/27/1892, d. 06/09/1975

BENDER, Valentine W., ssw-Caroline G., b. 1865, d. 1934

BYLER, Elsie, b. 1912, d. 1968

BYLER, Raymond R., b. 07/07/1929, d. 03/21/1963

CHAFFINCH, Bertha L., b. 06/22/1905, d. 02/17/1925

CHRISTNER, Anna M., ssw-Benedict J., b. 1889, d. 1975

CHRISTNER, Benedict J., ssw- Anna M., b. 1888, d. 1957

EDGAR, Dawn E., b. N/D, d. 10/11/1960

EMBLETON, Bertha, Baby, b. 10/24/1939, d. 11/21/1939

EMBLETON, John L., ssw-Martha L., b. 1904, d. 1978

EMBLETON, Martha L., ssw-John L., b. 1906, d. N/D

EMBLETON, Paula M., b. 03/25/1927, d. 03/11/1992

FITZGERALD, Magnus E., ssw-Mary M., b. 1916, d. 1979

FITZGERALD, Mary M., ssw-Magnus E., b. 1921, d. 1984

FRIES, John E., b. 10/05/1865, d. 07/22/1937

GINGERICH, Eli, b. 12/01/1858, d. 08/26/1932

GINGERICH, Lydia, b. 12/06/1854, d. 07/05/1931

GRAUL, Harry Karl, b. 07/15/1899, d. 02/13/1977

GRAUL, Herman O., b. 02/16/1871, d. 08/03/1920

GUENGERICH, Arlene Mae, b. 09/11/1954, d. 12/12/1954

GUENGERICH, Lulu L., ssw-Willis V., b. 02/10/1903, d. N/D

GUENGERICH, Willis V., ssw-Lulu L., b. 05/22/1900, d. 06/04/1980

HERSHBERGER, Allen S., Age 22y 26d, b. 04/21/1919, d. 05/17/1941

HERSHBERGER, Edward, b. 05/28/1835, d. 10/03/1922

HERSHBERGER, Gideon E., Age 71y 8m 7d, b. 02/17/1863, d. 10/26/1935

HERSHBERGER, Susanna, Age 75y 3m 15d, b. 09/18/1865, d. 01/03/1941

HERTZLER, Mary M., b. 01/22/1891, d. 02/18/1990

HOCHSTEDLER, Catherine, ssw-David, b. 1850, d. 1937

HOCHSTEDLER, David, ssw-Catherine, b. 1846, d. 1927

HOSTETLER, Eugene E., b. 12/21/1961, d. 08/25/1979

HOSTETLER, Joseph H., ssw-Nancy D., b. 04/10/1880, d. 04/23/1966

HOSTETLER, Nancy D., ssw-Joseph H., b. 04/18/1882, d. 07/30/1972

HOSTETTER, J. Virgil, Sr., ssw-Lois G., b. 02/02/1912, d. N/D

HOSTETTER, Lois G., ssw-J. Virgil, Sr., b. 04/15/1913, d. N/D

HUSSEY, Edith A., b. 12/05/1876, d. 06/18/1957

JONES, Clara E., d/o Abraham & Arminlie, b. N/D, d. 04/17/1922

JONES, E., Baby, b. N/D, d. N/D [located next to Elwood]

JONES, Elwood, b. N/D, d. N/D

JONES, Rosamund Curtis Victoria, ssw-Saltus C., Age 77y, Died in Scotland, b. N/D, d. 12/29/1963
JONES, Saltus C., ssw-Rosamund Curtis, b. 11/15/1888, d. 01/11/1958
MACKELL, Edward J, ssw-Mabel W., b. 02/24/1908, d. 12/26/1968
MACKELL, Mabel W., ssw-Edward J., b. 05/24/1909, d. N/D
MACKELL, Thomas J., SSgt, USA, WWII, b. 07/04/1917, d. 10/02/1978
MAST, Alvin, ssw-Cora, b. 05/07/1905, d. 12/20/1900
MAST, Amanda S., b. 1879, d. 1964
MAST, Clarence, ssw-Sylvia B., b. 10/21/1909, d. 08/23/1963
MAST, Cora, ssw-Alvin, b. 08/14/1908, d. 03/06/1987
MAST, Dale J., b. 10/03/1961, d. 03/12/1982
MAST, Elia D., b. 1874, d. 1966
MAST, Fred, ssw-Sara, b. 08/08/1915, d. 08/18/1960
MAST, Gladys Arlene, d/o Alvin & Cora, Age 5m 14d, b. N/D, d. 04/14/1944
MAST, Ralph Allen, Inf. s/o Alvin & Cora, b. 01/08/1935, d. 01/08/1935
MAST, Sara, ssw-Fred, "Sally," b. 01/05/1919, d. 10/19/1994
MAST, Sylvia B., ssw-Clarence, b. 05/09/1909, d. 10/11/1984
MILLER, Ada K., b. 07/15/1880-, d. 01/01/1948
MILLER, Annie S., ssw-Eli D., b. 02/10/1892, d. 11/01/1977
MILLER, Eli D., ssw-Annie S., b. 08/21/1899, d. 10/25/1974
MILLER, Ellen Louise, Mother, b. 01/19/1919, d. 01/31/1955
MILLER, Henry, b. 01/19/1934, d. 09/06/1976
MILLER, Jerry S., Father, b. 1884, d. 1967
MILLER, Laura E., ssw-Roy R., b. 1917, d. N/D
MILLER, Nancy S., Mother, b. 1883, d. 1936
MILLER, Roy R., ssw-Laura E., b. 1911, d. 1982
MILLER, s/o J. S. & Nancy, b. 01/15/1928, d. 03/15/1928
MILLER, s/o J. S. & Nancy, b. 08/14/1925, d. 08/14/1925
MULLETT, Benedict B., ssw-Fannie M., b. 09/14/1906, d. N/D
MULLETT, Fannie M., ssw-Benedict B., b. 03/08/1912, d. N/D
NLN, Baby, b. N/D, d. N/D [located next to E. Jones] 2 stones with same information
NLN, Tracy, b. 1965, d. 1965 [located between Clayton M. Wisseman & Laura E. Miller]
ORENDORF, Anna E., ssw-Jonas, b. 1881, d. 1952
ORENDORF, Clara Amelia, Mother, b. 02/27/1873, d. 03/28/1958
ORENDORF, Edna E., b. 05/02/190, d. 07/03/1921
ORENDORF, Elias, ssw-Lydia, Father, Age 76y 7m 11d, b. 09/26/1844, d. 05/07/1920
ORENDORF, Jonas, ssw-Anna E., b. 1873, d. 1931
ORENDORF, Lewis, Father, Age 52y 6m 24d, b. 11/17/1870, d. 05/11/1923
ORENDORF, Lydia, ssw-Elias, Mother, Age 74y 11m 1d, b. 06/08/1846, d. 05/09/1920
ORTH, Martha Graul, b. 12/04/1900, d. 09/07/1940
PAULEY, Ellen, b. 11/28/1915, d. 02/19/1964
RUSSELL, Clinton B., ssw-Elsie L., b. 1923, d. 1985
RUSSELL, Elsie L., ssw-Clinton B., b. 1924, d. N/D
SCHLABACH, Dorothy Ellen, d/o Elias & Minnie, b. 02/19/1937, d. 02/08/1939
SCHLABACH, Edna A., ssw-Loyd E., b. 1917, d. 1976
SCHLABACH, Lorenzo, ssw-Polly M., b. 03/17/1890, d. 04/13/1971
SCHLABACH, Loyd E., ssw-Edna A., b. 1916, d. N/D
SCHLABACH, Mary E., b. 12/08/1924, d. N/D
SCHLABACH, Polly M., ssw-Lorenzo, b. 07/23/1894, d. 06/12/1989

SCHLABACH, Timothy, b. 11/20/1925, d. N/D
SCHROCK, Christian, ssw-Sarah Ovendarf, b. 08/25/1863, d. 03/24/1948
SCHROCK, Donald Ray, b. 06/07/1950, d. 06/12/1977
SCHROCK, Doris Arlene, d/o Eli & Lucy, b. 01/16/1941, d. 03/05/1941
SCHROCK, Eli C., ssw-Lucy B., b. 09/29/1902, d. 06/22/1968
SCHROCK, Enos, b. 11/17/1898, d. 02/08/1982
SCHROCK, Harvey C., ssw-Violet L., b. 1910, d. 1978
SCHROCK, Lewis J., b. 1883, d. 1962
SCHROCK, Lucy B., ssw-Eli C., b. 07/18/1902, d. 07/25/1989
SCHROCK, Mary, b. 1874, d. 1953
SCHROCK, Sarah Ovendarf, ssw-Christian, b. 01/01/1868, d. 10/22/1918
SCHROCK, Violet L., ssw-Harvey C., b. 1915, d. 1989
SHETLER, Ella, b. 1885, d. 1977
SHOWALTER, Carol Ann, b. 1950, d. 1955
SMITH, Lillian E., b. 08/23/1942, d. 10/18/1990
SMITH, Norman S., Jr., ssw-Pauline F., b. 1906, d. 1982
SMITH, Pauline F., ssw-Norman S., Jr., b. 1913, d. 1976
SPEICHER, Daniel E., Loving Father & Husband, b. 05/11/1962, d. 11/11/1987
SPEICHER, Jacob Daniel, Jr., b. 1955, d. 1956
SPEICHER, Martha J., b. 08/01/1958, d. 08/02/1958
SPEICHER, Mary C., b. 08/01/1958, d. 08/14/1958
STOLTZFUS, Anna Elizabeth, ssw-Llewellyn Roy, b. 03/26/1925, d. 09/20/1988
STOLTZFUS, Grace, b. 07/20/1962, d. 07/20/1962
STOLTZFUS, Hiram J., b. 1923, d. 1985
STOLTZFUS, Llewellyn Roy, ssw-Anna Elizabeth, b. 11/26/1921, d. 09/20/1988
STOLTZFUS, Sadie A., b. 1886, d. 1963
STOLTZFUS, William L., b. 1887, d. 1978
SWARTZENTRUBER, Amelia, ssw-Eli, b. 11/27/1894, d. 02/10/1985
SWARTZENTRUBER, Christian L., b. 01/16/1904, d. 08/04/1933
SWARTZENTRUBER, Eli, ssw-Amelia, b. 07/25/1893, d. 12/01/1973
SWARTZENTRUBER, Elizabeth L., b. 06/26/1874, d. 04/13/1925
SWARTZENTRUBER, Laban, ssw-Nanna, b. 12/03/1900, d. N/D
SWARTZENTRUBER, Milton, ssw-Savanna, b. 09/29/1898, d. 03/28/1976
SWARTZENTRUBER, Nanna, ssw-Laban, b. 06/09/1900, d. 05/23/1981
SWARTZENTRUBER, Savanna, ssw-Milton, b. 05/23/1898, d. 05/26/1973
SWARTZENTRUBER, Valentine M., Age 15y 9m 22d, b. 05/24/1922, d. 03/16/1938
TROYER, Ammon P., ssw-Huldah B., b. 06/05/1896, d. 11/11/1979
TROYER, Harry, b. 06/29/1916, d. 08/27/1983
TROYER, Hulda B., ssw-Ammon P., b. 01/12/1895, d. 05/25/1978
TUCKER, Atwood, ssw-Hilda, b. 03/31/1912, d. 01/29/1985
TUCKER, Hilda, ssw-Atwood, b. 06/07/1913, d. 05/30/1991
TUCKER, Inf. s/o Duaue & Miriam, b. 02/22/1959, d. 02/22/1959
WARNICK, Baby, b. N/D, d. N/D
WARNICK, Sue L., Mother, b. 04/05/1915, d. 10/18/1956
WARREN, Jessie M., "Mickey," b. 10/28/1923, d. 01/25/1987
WARRINGTON, Charles W., b. N/D, d. N/D
WELFREY, Hester V., ssw-P. William, b. 1920, d. 1993
WELFREY, P. William, ssw-Hester V., b. 1913, d. 1973

WILLEY, David E., b. 1937, d. 1952
WILLIAMSON, Bessie L., b. 01/28/1900, d. 10/1944
WILLIAMSON, Irene, b. 10/22/1938, d. 10/22/1938
WILLIAMSON, W. W., Age 75y 6m 3d, b. 1855, d. 1931
WISSEMAN, Clark H., Age 31y 11m 15d, b. 01/07/1903, d. 12/22/1934
WISSEMAN, Clayton M., b. 03/25/1931, d. 03/29/1931
WISSEMAN, Cora E., b. 05/22/1880, d. 02/07/1962
WISSEMAN, George, b. 05/01/1874, d. 09/23/1936
WISSEMAN, Henry C., Age 59y 6m, b. 06/02/1875, d. 12/22/1934
WISSEMAN, Twins, b. N/D, d. N/D
YODER, Bert, ssw-Susie, b. 03/31/1901, d. 05/16/1991
YODER, Caroline S., ssw-Paul Daniel, b. 09/29/1925, d. N/D
YODER, Clara Mae, ssw-Davis S., Jr., b. 02/06/1917, d. N/D
YODER, Davis S., ssw-Savilla B., b. 07/14/1890, d. 07/17/1966
YODER, Davis S., Jr., ssw-Clara Mae, b. 11/18/1919, d. N/D
YODER, Delbert D., b. 01/26/1939, d. 09/22/1982
YODER, Lee, ssw-Lena, b. 1905, d. 1974
YODER, Lena, ssw-Lee, b. 1913, d. 1988
YODER, Mary E., d/o Lee, b. 02/06/1934, d. 02/27/1934
YODER, Paul Daniel, ssw-Caroline S., b. 04/23/1918, d. 11/19/1983
YODER, Paul M., b. 04/02/1925, d. 06/07/1942
YODER, Rhoda A., d/o Monroe & Naomi, b. 08/21/1944, d. 12/03/1944
YODER, Rhoda S., Age 19y b. 02/01/1937, d. 07/28/1956
YODER, Savilla B., ssw-David S., b. 04/10/1889, d. 12/14/1968
YODER, Susie, ssw-Bert, b. 03/06/1900, d. 03/27/1993
YUTZY, Joseph R., b. 03/24/1951, d. 11/16/1981
ZEHR, Ralph, s/o Vernon & Verna, b. 10/09/1947, d. 10/09/1947
ZEHR, Verna Schrock, ssw-Vernon, b. 11/18/1905, d. 12/29/1971
ZEHR, Vernon, ssw-Verna Schrock, b. 06/05/1907, d. 09/14/1994
ZOOK, Amelia M., w/o S. Y., b. 1877, d. 1927
ZOOK, Fanny, Age 65y, b. N/D, d. 09/14/1935
ZOOK, Irence M., b. 02/03/1901, d. 03/20/1984
ZOOK, Lena I., b. 07/16/1900, d. 08/07/1956
ZOOK, Milt, Age 67y, b. N/D, d. 12/21/1932
ZOOK, Sylvia M., b. 01/15/1889, d. 04/10/1919

(NA-004 & HU-NR) MACEDONIA A. M. E. CHURCH CEMETERY

Located East of Greenwood on the N. W. side of Shawnee Rd. (Rt. 36) approximately 300 yards N. E. of Ellendale-Greenwood Highway (Rt. 16)
Recorded: January 6, 1998

ANCRUM, Harold, SC, Pvt., USA, Korea, b. 10/29/1932, d. 10/05/1960
AUSTIN, William K., NJ, Pvt., 35 Field Arty., 92nd Divn., b. N/D, d. 03/13/1945
BAGBY, Milford H., NJ, Pvt., USA, WWI, b. 01/16/1896, d. 01/10/1966
BAILEY, Mary, b. N/D, d. N/D [Given by Co. workers at Libby McNeil 1955]
BATSON, Carl G., ssw-Marie H., b. 09/10/1932, d. 04/14/1982
BATSON, Curtis b. 1955, d. 1985

BATSON, Marie H., ssw-Carl G., b. 04/03/1931, d. N/D
CANNON, Carrie, Age 90y, b. N/D, d. 12/11/1990
CANNON, Sarah, Grandmother, b. N/D, d. 08/24/1945
CANNON, William R., b. 05/10/1973, d. 05/10/1973
COLLINS, Alberta, b. 1938, d. 1990
COVERDALE, Alice M., b. 02/01/1910, d. 07/23/1987
COVERDALE, Alvin J., b. 1927, d. 1988
COVERDALE, Annie E., b. 1895, d. 1986
COVERDALE, Geraldine, b. N/D, d. N/D
COVERDALE, Willis Bider, b. N/D, d. 04/1945
COVERDALE, Wilson W., b. 05/17/1911, d. 07/14/1989
CROMWELL, Weston, b. 1893, d. 1960
DIXON, Alonzo J., Pvt., USA, WWII, b. 11/04/1919, d. 04/24/1993
DIXON, Elfreda R., b. 03/31/1923, d. 01/31/1967
DIXON, Rosella R., b. 1919, d. 1991
DUKER, Lorenzo, b. 02/16/1862, d. 1954
ELLEGOOD, Emory J., b. 03/20/1898, d. 12/08/1979
FISHER, James W., b. 1903, d. 1974
FISHER, William T., DE, Pvt., USA, WWII, b. 04/26/1906, d. 01/28/1971
FOUNTAIN, Edith H., b. 1898, d. 1978
FRISBY, Ronald R., b. 1945, d. 1974
HAINES, William W., USA, b. 12/22/1913, d. 03/11/1991
HAMPTON, James, Pvt., USA, WWII, b. 03/08/1915, d. 06/06/1979
HARMON, Elva M., ssw-Morris E., b. 09/06/1900, d. 10/06/1967
HARMON, Morris E., Rev., ssw-Elva M., b. 04/02/1880, d. 10/31/1966
HARVEY, Ella, b. N/D, d. 02/28/1946
HAYES, Annie W., ssw-Leola, b. 02/25/1891, d. 12/11/1983
HAYES, Jean D., b. 01/20/1934, d. 11/16/1969
HAYES, Leola, ssw-Annie W., b. 10/12/1894, d. 03/22/1979
HAYES, Marl, ssw-Shirley, m. 07/28/1956, b. 01/15/1933, d. N/D
HAYES, Shirley, ssw-Marl, m. 07/28/1956, d. 07/31/1937, d. 08/16/1989
HAYNES, John W., b. 07/19/1888, d. 12/22/1958
HAYNES, Olivia Elsie, b. 01/04/1889, d. 01/30/1966
HEATH, George W., Sr., ssw-Lettie S., b. 1911, d. 1980
HEATH, Lettie S., ssw-George W., Sr., b. 1908, d. 1961
HEATH, Queen, b. 1914, d. 1995
HENDERSON, Irvin, b. 04/06/1966, d. 04/06/1966
HENRY, Alice L., ssw-William S., b. 03/23/1929, d. 03/09/1995
HENRY, Titus M., DE, Pfc., 3782 QM Truck Co., WWII, b. 12/28/1906, d. 04/17/1971
HENRY, William S., ssw-Alice L., b. 10/22/1921, d. 01/07/1994
HIGGINS, Beatrice D., ssw-James J., Sr., b. 05/30/1915, d. 04/02/1995
HIGGINS, Edmond R., DE, Co. I, 813 Pioneer Inf., WWI, b. 02/29/1892, d. 07/14/1969
HIGGINS, Estella M., b. 06/17/1896, d. 03/28/1978
HIGGINS, James J., Sr., ssw-Beatrice D., b. 06/12/1915, d. N/D
HIGGINS, Stanley, A1C, USAF, Korea, b. 1924, d. 1978
HINES, Isaac A., b. 1903, d. 1994
HUGHES, Irvin Andrew, DE, Cpl., 68 Trans Hv. Truck Co., TG., b. 05/25/1929, d. 10/17/1954
HUGHES, Larry D., b. 1950, d. 1996

HUTSON, Constance B., ssw-Joseph E., b. 03/08/1931, d. 06/01/1985
HUTSON, Joseph E., ssw-Constance B., b. 09/17/1922, d. N/D
JOHNSON, Queen, b. 1935, d. 1982
JONES, Alice, b. 09/17/1900, d. 12/02/1975
KENJYATTA, Udomo T., b. 10/25/1973, d. 12/05/1955
LOWERY, Mary J., b. 04/18/1911, d. 12/23/1970
MATTHEWS, Florence M., b. 01/06/1888, d. 08/11/1972
MAY, Ola M., b. 01/08/1909, d. 11/23/1978
MAY, Will, FL, Pvt., Co. G, 69 Pioneer Inf., WWI, b. 04/19/1893, d. 07/08/1966
MENNINGALL, Bead__, b. 03/16/1892, d. 09/19/1959
MENNINGALL, Gertrude, b. 05/06/1909, d. 04/10/1971
MITCHELL, Emma J., b. 08/03/1913, d. 03/24/1997
MITCHELL, Orlando C., Pvt., USA, WWII, b. 12/25/1915, d. 01/19/1988
PASKINS, Ethel, b. N/D, d. 06/28/1958
PASKINS, Florence M., ssw-Florine M. Powell, b. 08/18/1911, d. 07/22/1949
PASKINS, Leon, b. 08/28/1909, d. 02/08/1995
PASKINS, Mary E. Goldie, b. 10/23/1909, d. 02/26/1980
PASKINS, Wayman E., DE, Sp4, USA, Vietnam, b. 04/25/1947, d. 02/14/1968
PATTON, Phillip E., b. 1947, d. 1990
PEPPER, Phyllis, b. 1936, d. 1997
POWELL, Florine M., ssw-Florence M. Paskins, b. 01/26/1930, d. 03/09/1951
PRATTIS, Wanda A., b. 10/04/1950, d. 12/05/1986
PURNELL, John, b. 03/11/1888, d. 02/15/1973
SMITH, Clay, DE [Balance of information unreadable]
SMITH, Ike, b. N/D, d. N/D
TAYLOR, Alonzo L., Father, b. 1892, d. 1969
TAYLOR, Arlie F., b. 04/04/1900, d. 01/08/1983
TAYLOR, Ella S., Wife, b. 1892, d. 1914
TAYLOR, Emma C., Wife, b. 1893, d. 1964
TAYLOR, Lorenzo, ssw-Martha A., b. 04/19/1904, d. 12/17/1972
TAYLOR, Martha A., ssw-Lorenzo, b. 12/14/1905, d. 02/04/1993
THOMAS, Isaac H., MD, Pvt., 417 Res. Labor Bn., b. N/D, d. 07/29/1936
TRADER, Helen V., ssw-Robert L., b. 08/10/1914, d. 08/25/1996
TRADER, Robert L., ssw-Helen V., b. 08/06/1918, d. 06/05/1981
WARD, Latoya L., b. 10/26/1973, d. 01/07/1975
WATSON, Alice, ssw-Louis, b. 1910, d. N/D
WATSON, Louis, ssw-Alice, b. 1909, d. 1988
WRIGHT, Alphonsa, b. 1931, d. 1990
WRIGHT, Robert S., Pfc., USA, b. 1928, d. 1989
WYNN, [Balance of information unreadable]

(NA-005 & HU-45) CHAPLAINS CHAPEL CEMETERY
Located N. W. of Georgetown at the N. W. corner of Chaplains Chapel Rd. (Rd. 42) and Deer Forest Rd. (Rd. 565)

EVANS, Charlie, s/o James A. & Maggie J., Age 1y 2m 28d, b. N/D, d. 12/25/1872
EVANS, D. Douglass, s/o James A. & Annie T., b. 09/22/1895, d. 06/16/1896
EVANS, Delaware, s/o James A. & Annie T., Age 1y 4m 28d, b. N/D, d. 04/17/1884

EVANS, James A., b. 10/16/1840, d. 11/08/1898
EVANS, Maggie J., w/o James, Age 34y 8m 9d, b. N/D, d. 01/25/1876
EVANS, Maggie M., d/o James A. & Maggie, Age 2y 8m, b. N/D, d. 01/17/1873
EVANS, Mary Wolfe, d/o Annie T., Age 5y 11m 3d, b. N/D, d. 09/19/1891
MACKLIN, Charles, Age 65y 2m 15d, b. N/D, d. 04/09/1870
MACKLIN, Eli H., b. 09/29/1830, d. 07/18/1904
MACKLIN, Jonathan, b. 11/14/1835, d. 05/14/1902
MACKLIN, Margaret A., w/o Charles, b. 11/09/1811, d. 01/28/1885

(NA-006 & HU-248) COKESBURY METHODIST CHURCH CEMETERY
Located West of Georgetown on the North Side of Seashore Highway (Rt. 404) at the junction with Cokesbury Rd. (Rd. 529)
Recorded: June 1993

ADAMS, Connie Jane, b. 02/10/1953, d. 04/28/1973
ADAMS, Derek Karl, b. 10/31/1954, d. 02/09/1992
ADAMS, Etha Mae, b. 01/12/1874, d. 01/24/1957
ADAMS, Florence P. F., w/o John C., b. 03/12/1932, d. N/D
ADAMS, Howard Allan, b. 03/30/1943, d. 04/09/1989
ADAMS, Isaac, b. 07/17/1833, d. 03/24/1875
ADAMS, Isaac John, b. 04/25/1904, d. 03/31/1971
ADAMS, Jean, w/o Howard A., b. 03/26/1945, d. N/D
ADAMS, John C., b. 08/17/1928, d. 01/17/1983
ADAMS, Margaret, w/o Isaac, Age 73y 9m b. N/D, d. 07/14/1914
ADAMS, Noah G., b. 07/03/1882, d. 10/24/1900
ADAMS, Wilber L., b. 06/27/1875, d. 01/05/1918
BAILEY, Joshua B., b. 02/02/1900, d. 06/01/1927
BAILEY, Sadie Lillian Sammons, b. 11/08/1888, d. 09/21/1970
BAILEY, Sina A., b. 1871, d. 1922
BAKER, Delema Waples Isaacs, b. 12/03/1894, d. 01/03/1978]
BAKER, Frank N., 1st Sgt., b. 11/13/1894, d. 08/18/1954
BAKER, Cinda S., b. 04/06/1900, d. 03/11/1963
BAKER, John E., b. 05/12/1888, d. 09/30/1970
BARNES, John, b. N/D, d. N/D
BETTS, James E., b. 1935, d. N/D
BETTS, Virgie L., b. 1926, d. 1979
BILLEY, George W., b. 1864, d. 1950
BLADES, Betty Jane, w/o R. O., b. 06/05/1937, d. N/D
BLADES, Joseph A., b. 11/06/1865, d. 08/17/1907
BLADES, Richard Outten, USAF, Ko9rea, b. 05/02/1932, d. 01/14/1988
BLAKE, Arthur Everett, b. 11/11/1887, d. 06/27/1960
BLAKE, Evelyn C., b. 1917, d. 1981
BLAKE, Everett B., b. 1862, d. 1938
BLAKE, Louella O., b. 1870, d. 1958
BLAKE, William A., b. 1898, d. 1989
BRADFORD, Helen C., b. 1909, d. 1939
BRADFORD, Paul John, b. 1906, d. 1988
BRITTINGHAM, Howard S., b. 1892, d. 1962

BRITTINGHAM, Leva J., b. 1907, d. 1991
BRITTINGHAM, Lucy, b. 1936, d. 1944
CALLAWAY, Anna J., b. 1844, d. 1925
CALLAWAY, Annie J., b. 01/15/1874, d. 10/26/1930
CALLAWAY, Elmer J., b. 12/19/1884, d. 08/07/1973
CALLAWAY, Harry J., b. 08/17/1891, d. 02/01/1969
CALLAWAY, Joshua W., b. 01/05/1870, d. 06/02/1953
CALLAWAY, Lettie G., b. 03/31/1890, d. 02/04/1982
CALLAWAY, William, b. 1841, d. 1891
CALLOWAY, Emma, (Mrs.), b. 02/16/187_, d. 04/11/1965
CALLOWAY, Henry L., b. 09/02/1917, d. 10/13/1918
CALLOWAY, William, b. 07/29/1850, d. 10/02/____
CANNON, Alice M., b. N/D, d. N/D
CANNON, Sarah, b. N/D, d. N/D
CARPENTER, Robert M., b. 03/08/1863, d. 10/22/1934
CARRIER, Amy K., b. 08/23/1935, d. 06/17/1980
CARRIER, Donald N., Jr., b. 1932, d. N/D
COFFIN, Helen (Hudson), b. 1928, d. N/D
COFFIN, Sheddy W., b. 1909, d. 1982
COLLINS, Elijah J., b. 09/10/1902, d. 10/12/1926
COLLINS, Ida E., w/o Joseph, b. 12/01/1877, d. 03/29/1904
CONAWAY, Martha J., w/o Peter W., b. 04/29/1875, d. 06/12/1908
CONAWAY, Peter W., b. 1855, d. 1935
COREY, Alfred R., b. 1892, d. 1968
COREY, Mary Thomas (Palmer), b. 1892, d. 1969
DAY, James Alfred, s/o J. R. & S. A., Age 5y 2m 25d, b. N/D, d. 03/09/1861
DAY, John, Age 76y 3d, b. N/D, d. 03/26/1872
DAY, John S., b. 1895, d. 1962
DAY, Lovey, w/o John, Age 69y 2m 6d, b. N/D, d. 02/03/1865
DAY, Mariah L., w/o John, b. 08/20/1853, d. 05/14/1910
DICKERSON, Ida M., b. 1888, d. 1973
DICKERSON, Inf. s/o Gary, b. N/D, d. N/D
DICKERSON, Inf. d/o Gary, b. N/D, d. N/D
DICKERSON, James Edgar, b. 1882, d. 02/06/1949
DICKERSON, Medford Franklin, b. 06/26/1909, d. 08/19/1910
DICKERSON, Thelma Rae, b. 06/06/1915, d. 08/07/1915
DILTZ, Brenda Joyce, b. N/D, d. N/D
DILTZ, Ona Beatrice, b. 12/10/1915, d. 06/28/1989
DILTZ, Robert J., b. 05/31/1915, d. N/D
DONOVAN, Annie Mary, w/o William H., b. 02/11/1885, d. 02/25/1911
DONOVAN, Catherine Hudson, b. 1908, d. 1990
ELLIOTT, Dollie Moore, b. 1894, d. 1959
ELLIOTT, Dorothy, b. 1919, d. 1944
ELLIOTT, Elisha H., b. 1886, d. 1953
ELLIOTT, Essa, d/o J. P. & Laura, b. 02/13/1894, d. 02/18/1894
ELLIOTT, John P., Father, b. 1854, d. 1942
ELLIOTT, Laura J., Mother, b. 1861, d. 1943
ELLIOTT, Linnen, s/o J. P. & Laura J., Age 28d, b. N/D, d. 04/16/1896

ELLIOTT, Linwood, s/o W. H. & Naomi, b. 11/11/1907, d. 06/10/1912
ELLIOTT, Naomi C., b. 1888, d. 1943
ELLIOTT, William Herman, b. 1881, d. 1979
ELZEY, Sarah S., b. 10/05/1845, d. 02/29/1896
ELZEY, Wilson, b. 12/28/1845, d. 01/26/1919
FITZGERALD, Viola B., d/o P. W. Conaway, b. 01/17/1899, d. 01/13/1980
FLEETWOOD, Amanda L., b. 07/06/1903, d. 01/17/1904
FLEETWOOD, Arthur Lee, b. 08/01/1899, d. 10/27/1971
FLEETWOOD, Betty L., b. 05/06/1928, d. 09/09/1928
FLEETWOOD, Charles N., b. 02/28/1900, d. 08/12/1992
FLEETWOOD, Charles W. F., b. 06/20/1880, d. 03/26/1900
FLEETWOOD, Covington, b. 07/12/1907, d. 01/10/1908
FLEETWOOD, Edna E., b. 09/07/1908, d. N/D
FLEETWOOD, Edney, d/o H. E. & R. E., b. 07/28/1915, d. 09/09/1915
FLEETWOOD, Elva Mae, b. 06/27/1919, d. 07/19/1921
FLEETWOOD, Frances Mae, w/o Charles, b. 10/26/1908, d. 05/02/1986
FLEETWOOD, Francis W., s/o H. E. & R. E., b. 10/28/1897, d. 07/17/1921
FLEETWOOD, George Delbert, USA, WWII, b. 09/09/1907, d. 05/29/1987
FLEETWOOD, George W., b. 03/05/1926, d. N/D
FLEETWOOD, Hattie T., b. 10/24/1880, d. 02/11/1962
FLEETWOOD, Helen E., b. 04/03/1915, d. 04/07/1915
FLEETWOOD, Horace E., b. 1868, d. 1934
FLEETWOOD, Katherine Frances, b. 05/27/1927, d. N/D
FLEETWOOD, Mary E., w/o William E., b. 04/04/1842, d. 10/17/1931
FLEETWOOD, Mildred C., b. 04/22/1913, d. 06/03/1978
FLEETWOOD, Nobel C., b. 09/01/1904, d. 02/05/1984
FLEETWOOD, Rebecca E., b. 1871, d. 1966
FLEETWOOD, Roland H., b. 03/25/1903, d. 10/22/1976
FLEETWOOD, Ryla C., b. 1910, d. 1926
FLEETWOOD, Sarah E., b. 11/09/1909, d. 12/30/1909
FLEETWOOD, William Cyus, b. 10/12/1875, d. 10/01/1959
FLEETWOOD, William E., b. 01/16/1837, d. 09/18/1910
FLEMING, Helen M. F., b. 1907, d. 1983
FLEMING, William H., b. 1905, d. 1984
GARDNER, John Levi, USA, Korea, b. 09/12/1929, d. 09/18/1987 [Cremated]
GREEN, Charity S., w/o James B., b. 10/15/1892, d. 02/06/1916
HARRIS, Alta, b. 1904, d. 1905
HARRIS, Alvin, b. 1904, d. 1905
HARRIS, Laura H., b. 1874, d. 1951
HARRIS, Laurence C., b. 1870, d. 1946
HEADLEY, Elva M., b. 1914, d. N/D
HEADLEY, George W., b. 1899, d. 1974
HILL, Catherine Blades, b. 11/16/1865, d. 04/22/1949
HILL, Joseph A., b. 11/06/1865, d. 04/17/1907
HILL, Mildred C. Fleetwood, b. N/D, d. N/D
HITCHENS, Harold G., Son, b. 12/25/1908, d. 08/09/1925
HITCHENS, Isaac, Father, b. 1865, d. 1955
HITCHENS, Lillie M., Mother, b. 1876, d. 1941

HOBBS, John R., b. 12/22/1903, d. 01/13/1971

HOPKINS, Lockwood, b. 1904, d. 1981

HUDSON, Clara F., b. 1913, d. 1936

HUDSON, George W., b. 04/10/1906, d. 06/02/1993

HUDSON, George W., b. 1870, d. 1948

HUDSON, Ida J., b. 1877, d. 1965

HUDSON, John L., b. 1894, d. 1971

HUDSON, Joseph W., Pvt., WWII, b. 09/12/1920, d. 12/09/1944

HUDSON, Joseph W., s/o Ida & George, b. 02/12/1945, d. 04/20/1945

HUDSON, Michelle R., [Reinterred Seaford Odd Fellows Cemetery]

HUDSON, Mildred Elizabeth, b. 11/29/1912, d. 09/08/1987

HURD, Hanna M., b. N/D, d. N/D

ISAACS, Alton B., b. 04/28/1903, d. 04/04/1980

ISAACS, Amelia, b. 1857, d. 1938

ISAACS, Catherine J., b. 1860, d. 1939

ISAACS, Charles H., b. 09/17/1861, d. 09/29/1932

ISAACS, Charles T., b. 1855, d. 1929

ISAACS, Clark, b. 10/02/1901, d. 10/17/1901

ISAACS, Cordelia R., b. N/D, d. 03/09/1950

ISAACS, Delma, d/o Chas. & Cordelia, b. 07/25/1897, d. 08/01/1897

ISAACS, Edna M., d/o Chas. & Cordelia, b. 09/12/1906, d. 03/23/1907

ISAACS, Elizabeth, Age 82y, b. N/D, d. 03/30/1930

ISAACS, George W., b. 1859, d. 1948

ISAACS, Harry, Age 21d, b. 03/18/1891, d. 04/08/1891

ISAACS, Harvey, s/o Wm. B. & Martha, Age 2m 27d, b. N/D, d. 05/18/1874

ISAACS, Hiram J., b. 12/16/1840, d. 04/17/1921

ISAACS, Infant, b. 09/17/1913, d. 09/17/1913

ISAACS, J. Elwood, s/o John E. & Missouri, b. 12/06/1899, d. 04/03/1921

ISAACS, James D., Age 1y 5m, b. N/D, d. 05/1828

ISAACS, James O., b. 03/28/1848, d. 08/31/1898

ISAACS, John E., b. 1875, d. 1938

ISAACS, Julia A., d/o Lewis & Lizzie, b. 06/01/1881, d. 11/06/1889

ISAACS, Julia A., w/o Noah, Sr., b. 10/20/1839, d. 05/30/1893

ISAACS, Katie, d/o T. W. & S. C., b. N/D, d. N/D

ISAACS, Leah S., b. 03/28/1903, d. N/D

ISAACS, Lettie, d/o Luther & Martha, Age 16d, b. N/D, d. 06/08/1896

ISAACS, Lewis S., Age 60y 9m 28d, b. 09/29/1842, d. 07/27/1908

ISAACS, Maggie, d/o Chas. & Cordelia, b. 10/26/1902, d. 01/16/1903

ISAACS, Maggie P., b. 1859, d. 1933

ISAACS, Mariah H., b. 02/14/1832, d. 02/26/1922

ISAACS, Martha J., w/o Wm. L., b. 08/07/1870, d. 03/25/1917

ISAACS, Mary A., w/o Noah Sr., Age 62y 11m 2d, b. N/D, d. 03/25/1880

ISAACS, Mary B., d/o Lewis & Lizzie, b. 09/01/1877, d. 10/30/1889

ISAACS, Mary Emily, d/o Noah & Mary, Age 13y 10d, b. N/D, d. 08/27/1863

ISAACS, Minos, b. 07/16/1839, d. 03/19/1914

ISAACS, Missouri B., b. 1881, d. 1956

ISAACS, Newel F., b. 06/30/1908, d. 09/19/1991 [Cremated]

ISAACS, Noah, Jr., b. 1883, d. 1926

ISAACS, Noah, Sr., Age 98y, b. 06/14/1807, d. 11/20/1906
ISAACS, Rhoda E., d/o B. J. & M., Age 29y 3m 14d, b. N/D, d. 01/01/1900
ISAACS, U. Sidney, Pvt., Died in France, b. 12/24/1839, d. 12/01/1918
ISAACS, W. Herman, s/o J. W. & Lovey, Age 8y 8m 26d, b. N/D, d. 09/19/1878
ISAACS, William L., b. 10/23/1867, d. 04/30/1936
JESTER, Arthur Burton, b. 03/22/1908, d. 09/26/1934
JESTER, Eleanor E., b. 08/03/1937, d. 02/07/1938
JESTER, Meddie Evelyn, b. 04/01/1912, d. 09/10/1989
JESTER, William H., b. 08/10/1902, d. 02/12/1981
JEWELL, Belle, b. 1881, d. N/D
JEWELL, Earl Henry, b. 08/22/1908, d. 12/18/1971
JEWELL, Elmer, b. 05/02/1902, d. 01/24/1970
JEWELL, Harry, b. 1881, d. 1960
JOHNSON, Raymond, Age 77y 7m 9d, b. 1881, d. 1960
KENNEDY, Emma M., b. N/D, d. 1931
KING, Evelyn Ida, b. 09/26/1930, d. 03/30/1991
KING, George, b. 1852, d. 1927
KING, Laura, b. 1894, d. 1982
KING, Leonard, b. 1890, d. 1962
KING, Matilda, b. 1858, d. 1926
LAMBDEN, Granville A., b. 1898, d. 1958
LAMBDEN, Joshua J., Sr., b. 1859, d. 1948
LAMBDEN, Lena, b. 1875, d. 1929
LAMBDEN, Mabel K. Wilkins, b. 1906, d. 1980
LANKFORD, Baby, b. N/D, d. 1930
LANKFORD, Maggie E., b. 06/11/1906, d. N/D
LANKFORD, Norman E., b. 12/24/1903, d. 01/14/1974
LEAGER, Mary White, b. 11/12/1899, d. 09/15/1987
LEFKOVITZ, Margaret, b. 1894, d. 1989
LITTLETON, Benjamin F., b. 1918, d. 1941
LITTLETON, James N., b. 1878, d. 1952
LITTLETON, Lola, b. 1876, d. 1956
LOCKWOOD, Hopkins, b. 1904, d. 1981
LUBINIECKI, Inf. s/o J. & Emma B., b. 04/10/1941, d. 06/13/1941
MARVIL, Annie, w/o Wm., Age 22y, b. N/D, d. 05/12/1907
MARVIL, William, b. 05/18/1951, d. N/D
MARVIL, William, s/o Wm. & Annie, b. 05/10/1907, d. 07/15/1907
MCALLISTER, Ethel May, w/o Carl N., b. 01/14/1893, d. 10/10/1918
MCDOWELL, Benjamin F., b. 06/12/1875, d. 10/17/1948
MCDOWELL, Benjamin R. C., b. 02/08/1839, d. 04/16/1904
MCDOWELL, Lavenia E. P., w/o Z. W., b. 04/07/1847, d. 11/24/1907
MCDOWELL, Mary E., b. 07/01/1875, d. 07/24/1938
MCDOWELL, Sarah E., b. 04/07/1847, d. 06/21/1922
MCDOWELL, Z. James, b. 06/03/1873, d. 09/12/1939
MCDOWELL, Zachariah W., b. 11/26/1842, d. 02/05/1922
MEARS, Capitolia, w/o Noah C., b. 03/25/1882, d. 01/14/1906
MESSICK, Albert H., b. 1879, d. 1954
MESSICK, Alfred P., b. 1904, d. 1983

MESSICK, Alice M. Willey, b. 06/21/1917, d. 01/07/1973

MESSICK, Amanda C., w/o George H., b. 10/18/1849, d. 02/02/1913

MESSICK, Arthur H., b. 1904, d. 1974

MESSICK, Carroll, b. 1911, d. 1976

MESSICK, Dorcus, b. 1957, d. 1960

MESSICK, Elizabeth P., w/o W. S., b. 05/31/1872, d. 07/02/1958

MESSICK, George H., b. 05/31/1852, d. 09/15/1933

MESSICK, Isaiah H., b. 1878, d. 1961

MESSICK, Jacob, b. 1877, d. 1951

MESSICK, Leroy, b. 1903, d. 1981

MESSICK, Mary B., b. 1872, d. 1961

MESSICK, Mary S., b. 1888, d. 1972

MESSICK, Mary Swain, b. 1883, d. 1972

MESSICK, Myrtle D., b. 1908, d. N/D

MESSICK, Willard S., b. 10/11/1861, d. 03/16/1928

MOORE, Henry C., b. 1883, d. 1932

MUNSELL, Ervin W., b. 12/05/1916, d. 06/11/1985

NEVENS, Ella M., b. 1910, d. 1931

O'DAY, Daisey M., b. 1928, d. 1929

O'DAY, Elizabeth E., w/o George E., b. 01/11/1916, d. N/D

O'DAY, Emma R., b. 1876, d. 1936

O'DAY, George E., USA, WWII, b. 06/17/1911, d. 05/18/1981

O'DAY, James E., b. 1880, d. 1951

O'DAY, Lillie D., b. 1896, d. 1919

O'DAY, Louise W., b. 1888, d. 1960

O'DAY, Zebedee T., b. 1856, d. 1917

OWENS, Edward, b. 10/29/1842, d. 06/03/1925

OWENS, Julia A., w/o Edward, b. 07/02/1848, d. 06/18/1898

PALMER, Letitia E. Penuel, w/o Philatus H. Palmer, b. 10/10/1853, d. 07/27/1938

PALMER, Philetus H., b. 10/27/1853, d. 07/27/1938

PENNYWELL, Lemuel H., b. 08/17/1828, d. 08/11/1922

PENNYWELL, Sarah E. Cannon, w/o Lemuel, b. 11/26/1829, d. 02/26/1914

PESTRIDGE, Willie M., w/o George, b. 02/05/1897, d. 10/15/1918

REYNOLDS, Minnie M. Ward, b. 06/26/1877, d. 01/03/1899

SALMONS, Belitha L., b. N/D, d. N/D

SAMMONS, Bernice, d/o Clara & Edmund, b. 1903, d. 1903

SAMMONS, Cornell, b. 12/03/1915, d. N/D

SAMMONS, Edward F., b. 01/20/1834, d. 10/17/1897

SAMMONS, Edward T., s/o Wm. & Tabatha H., Age 26y 5m 15d, b. N/D. d. 03/21/1891

SAMMONS, Emeline F., b. 11/30/1837, d. 01/14/1898

SAMMONS, Helen T., b. 10/12/1910

SAMMONS, Lou Ann, d/o Helen & Cornell, b. 1954, d. 1954

SAMMONS, Sara A., w/o Belitha L., b. 09/15/1802, d. 07/18/1892

SAMMONS, Willard P., b. 10/02/1880, d. 01/25/1919

SAMUELS, Joseph P., b. 02/11/1840, d. 12/02/1911

SAMUELS, Mary Ann, w/o J. P., b. 02/11/1844, d. 08/30/1930

SAVAGE, A. Kenneth, b. 05/03/1926, d. 05/05/1926

SAVAGE, Alice M., b. 1895, d. 1989

SAVAGE, Annie E., w/o John W., b. 10/05/1848, d. 04/01/1946
SAVAGE, Arthur H., b. 07/30/1905, d. 05/06/1929
SAVAGE, Charles Franklin, b. N/D, d. N/D
SAVAGE, John W., b. 4/05/1848, d. 05/14/1918
SAVAGE, Lemuel W., Rev., 1891, d. 1958
SAVAGE, Lizzie, b. 06/01/1881, d. 11/01/1961
SAVAGE, Mae West, b. 11/03/1884, d. 03/19/1973
SAVAGE, Robert J., b. 02/14/1879, d. 02/05/1931
SAVAGE, Ruben, b. 08/27/1877, d. 03/25/1956
SAVAGE, William P., Sr., b. 10/05/1869, d. 05/15/1950
SHORT, Birdie M., b. 1884, d. 1962
SHORT, Caldwell, b. 05/13/1846, d. 04/06/1911
SHORT, Clarence E., b. 1904, d. 1946
SHORT, Clarence E., s/o Chas. C. & Sarah, b. 07/27/1897, d. 06/28/1899
SHORT, Daniel J., b. 1879, d. 1965
SHORT, Edith Mae, b. 02/11/1875, d. 03/09/1967
SHORT, Ellen, b. 10/14/1841, d. 06/05/1918
SHORT, Elmer Cannon, s/o John S. & Sarah, Age 14y 4m 11d, b. N/D, d. 12/27/1875
SHORT, Florence R., d/o Chas. & Sarah, b. 04/14/1901, d. 10/25/1901
SHORT, George W., b. 05/07/1872, d. 10/26/1944
SHORT, Georgie Ellen, w/o John W., b. 08/12/1849, d. 08/15/1889
SHORT, Herman J., b. 07/31/1898, d. 03/24/1969
SHORT, James E., b. 03/21/1846, d. 04/08/1908
SHORT, John Cannon, b. 09/29/1829, d. 09/11/1916
SHORT, John W., b. 11/08/1847, b. 09/15/1914
SHORT, Johnnie, s/o John S. & Sarah, Age 1y 8m 6d, b. N/D, d. 01/12/1872
SHORT, Lillie O., d/o John & Sarah, Age 5y 9m 10d, b. N/D, d. 11/16/1872
SHORT, Mary, b. 1885, d. 1955
SHORT, Mary E., b. 08/24/1866, d. 10/31/1944 [On backside of Calloway stone]
SHORT, Millie, b. 05/16/1902, d. 11/1902 [On backside of Calloway stone]
SHORT, Sarah Elizabeth Day, w/o Jno C., b. 03/22/1829, d. 09/11/1916
SHORT, Sarah Elizabeth Day, w/o John, b. 03/22/1868, d. 05/23/1908
SHORT, Willie D., d/o John & Sarah, Age 1y 6d, b. N/D, d. 05/25/1880
SINGLETON, Beulah, b. 03/30/1921, d. 12/23/1990
SMITH, Asa J., b. 08/29/1884, d. 02/12/1945
SMITH, Carlton R., b. 07/22/1913, d. 01/25/1922
SMITH, Charity E., b. 07/27/1882, d. 10/15/1970
SMITH, Ethel V., b. 07/03/1915, d. 01/06/1984
SMITH, Hannah M. b. 03/11/1895, d. 12/16/1977
SMITH, Helen G., b. 07/30/1911, d. 12/22/1970
SMITH, Hilda M., b. 04/27/1904, d. 01/10/1992
SMITH, Infant o/Irvin & Charity, b. 01/02/1904, d. 01/07/1904
SMITH, Irvin M., b. 06/21/1877, d. 01/11/1935
SMITH, John Alvin, b. 03/11/1924, d. 03/29/1984
SMITH, Joseph F., b. 03/31/1854, d. 04/17/1930
SMITH, Lavinia W., b. 01/03/1847, d. 02/01/1930
SMITH, Liza Issach, b. 1870, d. 1910
SMITH, Margaret A., w/o Wm. C., b. 10/29/1835, d. 05/12/1895

SMITH, Marvel A., b. 11/08/1867, d. 08/02/1905

SMITH, May Rena, b. 08/27/1889, d. 12/24/1972

SMITH, Philip H., b. 1867, d. 1919

SMITH, Raymond, b. 03/28/1897, d. 06/04/1932

SMITH, Robert E., b. 10/03/1854, d. 01/03/1911

SMITH, William C., b. 07/16/1831, d. 02/15/1911

SPICER, Anna M., b. 1873, d. 1941

SPICER, C. Maurice, b. 1893, d. 1917

SPICER, Charles J., Age 67y 6m 18d, b. 04/23/1844, d. 11/11/1911

SPICER, Clara, b. 1875, d. N/D

SPICER, Della J., b. 02/08/1909, d. 08/09/1925

SPICER, Edna, b. 1905, d. 1925

SPICER, Ella Mae, b. 01/11/1926, d. 06/21/1942

SPICER, Frank J., b. 1868, d. 1934

SPICER, Harry J., b. 10/31/1878, d. 01/09/1911

SPICER, Infant Daughter, b. 08/12/1925, d. 08/12/1925

SPICER, Infant Son, b. 08/01/1927, d. 08/01/1927

SPICER, James Edward, b. 07/29/1954, d. 09/16/1982 [Cremated]

SPICER, John, Sr., b. 05/24/1909, d. 10/14/1987

SPICER, John H., b. 1870, d. 1934

SPICER, Lawrence C., b. 05/01/1929, d. N/D

SPICER, Lawrence D., b. 01/28/1899, d. 08/27/1933

SPICER, Mary E., w/o Chas. J., b. 01/05/1847, d. 07/07/1899

SPICER, Minnie, b. 1903, d. 1927

SPICER, Norman E., h/o Susie, b. 06/25/1915, d. N/D

SPICER, Olive, b. 1883, d. 1957

SPICER, Pearl F., b. 08/27/1901, d. 12/24/1980

SPICER, Raymond J., USA, WWII, b. 09/16/1918, d. 09/22/1984

SPICER, Susie, b. 01/09/1925, d. 08/04/1991

SPICER, William L., b. 05/22/1919, d. 09/13/1984

SWAIN, Byard, b. N/D, d. N/D

SWAIN, Daniel B., b. 09/17/1863, d. 06/18/1954

SWAIN, Effie E., b. 07/17/1873, d. 05/29/1949

SWAIN, Ethel M., Daughter, b. 1900, d. 1950

SWAIN, George F., b. 1871, d. 1946

SWAIN, Hannah Jane, d/o Uriah & Abi, b. 03/24/1833, d. 07/08/1905

SWAIN, Hester J., w/o Thomas W., b. 08/31/1846, d. 01/08/1921

SWAIN, John B., b. 09/20/1823, d. 12/03/1902

SWAIN, John H., b. 1823, d. 1921

SWAIN, Julia A., w/o Theophilus, b. 04/09/1851, d. 11/03/1927

SWAIN, Lavinia A., w/o John B., b. 03/11/1825, d. 09/29/1899

SWAIN, Lemuel W., h/o Willie W., b. 10/05/1856, d. 02/18/1936

SWAIN, Lizzie R., b. 1878, d. 1961

SWAIN, Maggie B., b. 1876, d. 1959

SWAIN, Martha L., w/o John B., b. 03/15/1820, d. 11/04/1867

SWAIN, Mary Mae, d/o Geo. F. & M. B., Age 5y 1m 17d, b. N/D, d. 10/28/1901

SWAIN, Mary P., w/o John H., b. 1836, d. 1922

SWAIN, Mary P., b. 1911, d. 1960

SWAIN, Priscilla, w/o John B., b. 09/06/1818, d. 06/29/1906
SWAIN, Roy H., b. 1886, d. 1966
SWAIN, Theophilus, b. 06/07/1840, d. 04/07/1921
SWAIN, Thomas W., b. 06/19/1833, d. 06/21/1929
SWAIN, Willie W., w/o L. W., b. 08/12/1868, d. 02/10/1900
TAYLOR, Berthie, d/o Cyrus & Elizabeth, b. 08/19/1892, d. 07/17/1893
TAYLOR, Charity H. Hudson, b. 09/16/1903, d. 10/07/1970
TAYLOR, Clara E., Mother, b. 1899, d. 1932
TAYLOR, Effie W., d/o Cryus & Elizabeth, b. 12/06/1883, d. 06/06/1885
TAYLOR, John H., b. 1854, d. 1932
TAYLOR, Oliver B., Father, b. 1895, d. 1948
TAYLOR, William T., b. 1859, d. 1932
TINKER, No other information
TRUITT, A. L., b. 1848, d. 1927
TUCKER, Elmer, b. N/D, d. N/D
WARD, Alma Ellen, d/o James, b. 1857, d. 1945
WARD, Annie E., b. 07/03/1842, d. 06/25/1930
WARD, James H., b. 11/30/1829, d. 07/21/1909
WARRINGTON, Alfred M., b. 10/08/1847, d. 09/09/1919
WARRINGTON, Cartha F., b. 1879, d. 1950
WARRINGTON, Cora E., b. 01/02/1895, d. 05/08/1918
WARRINGTON, Cordia W., b. 1874, d. 1940
WARRINGTON, Cordia W., b. 1901, d. 1962
WARRINGTON, Edna E., b. 03/24/1904, d. 08/02/1904
WARRINGTON, Edna M., b. 1906, d. 1985
WARRINGTON, Emma K., b. 09/18/1852, d. 01/20/1920
WARRINGTON, Henry W., b. 05/18/1917, d. 05/20/1917
WARRINGTON, Jennifer Lynn, b. 10/01/1980, d. 10/11/1988
WARRINGTON, Joseph A., b. 01/20/1851, d. 02/03/1974
WARRINGTON, Joseph M., Interred 09/12/1972
WARRINGTON, Larry Lee, b. 06/12/1957, d. 06/10/1979
WARRINGTON, Leonard S., b. 09/21/1880, d. 12/01/1955
WARRINGTON, Lovie A., b. 01/21/1852, d. 07/28/1924
WARRINGTON, Mary B., b. 10/03/1914, d. 12/20/1914
WARRINGTON, Sara Emma Palmer, w/o Leonard S., b. 10/10/1883, d. 10/10/1919
WATSON, Howard W., Sr., b. 1927, d. 1986
WEST, Abraham, b. N/D, d. N/D
WHARTON, Ida E., b. 05/08/1915, d. N/D
WHARTON, Infant, b. N/D, d. 08/14/1967
WHARTON, Walter Hunter, Sr., b. 03/06/1908, d. 03/06/986
WHITE, E., Inf. o/Lewis, b. 12/25/1978, d. 12/25/1978
WHITE, Edith Mae, b. 03/14/1906, d. 08/19/1984
WHITE, Elizabeth J. b. 12/03/1947, d. 05/06/1987
WHITE, Julius, b. 12/28/1911, d. N/D
WHITE, Kazuyo, b. 05/10/1945, d. 01/05/1970
WHITE, Malia J., d/o Philip & Mary J., b. 01/06/1897, d. 02/02/1897
WHITE, Mary J., w/o P. D., b. 1873, d. 1951
WHITE, Nellie E., b. 10/21/1921, d. 10/17/1985

WHITE, Pauline M., b. 07/02/1924, d. 10/25/1992
WHITE, Philip D., b. 1867, d. 1941
WHITE, Robert Dalton, Sr., b. 12/20/1943, d. 05/06/1987
WHITE, Robert J., Jr., b. N/D, d. 11/16/1978
WHITE, S. Elizabeth, w/o Wm. B., b. 04/20/1828, d. 08/30/1910
WHITE, William B., b. 11/08/1818, d. 04/30/1905
WHITE, William D., b. 02/07/1898, d. 12/18/1980
WHITE, William P., b. N/D, d. 01/26/1984
WILKINS, Anna Mae, b. N/D, d. 07/22/1989
WILKINS, Isaac T., b. 03/14/1840, d. 01/15/1916
WILLEY, Asbury, b. 10/01/1885, d. 06/0/1950
WILLEY, Atles R., b. 12/19/1922, d. 09/23/1990
WILLEY, Elsie M., b. 02/17/1895, d. 03/28/1953
WILLEY, George H., s/o T. L. & Rebecca, Age 26y 18d, b. N/D, d. 01/19/1888
WILLEY, Glennie B., b. 04/30/1920, d. N/D
WILLEY, Pandora, b. 1943, d. 1943
WILLEY, Rebecca J., b. 12/09/1839, d. 01/03/1917
WILLEY, T. L., b. 07/12/1828, d. 08/05/1903
WILSON, A. Estella, b. 1879, d. 1961
WILSON, Bertha, Mother, b. 1878, d. 1944
WILSON, Edward R., b. 1885, d. 1964
WILSON, Elijah J., b. 09/10/1902, d. 11/12/1926
WILSON, Elzey, b. 12/28/1845, d. 01/20/1918
WILSON, George, b. 1847, d. 1924
WILSON, Helen L., b. 07/25/1913, d. N/D
WILSON, Inf. s/o M. W. & Bertha, b. 02/1912, d. 02/1912
WILSON, Inf. s/o Minos J., b. N/D, d. 02/22/1975
WILSON, Inf. s/o M. W. & Bertha, Age 3d, b. N/D, d. 03/21/1899
WILSON, Jean E., b. 1937, d. 1949
WILSON, Mary Elizabeth, b. 1910, d. 1992
WILSON, Minos W., Father, b. 1872, d. 1938
WILSON, Minos Woodrow, b. 12/10/1912, d. 08/22/1975
WILSON, Polly W., b. 1851, d. 1930
WILSON, Samuel R., Sr., b. 1897, d. 1974
WILSON, Sarah J., b. 12/23/1917, d. 02/04/1934
WILSON, Sarah J., b. 1917, d. 1932
WILSON, Sarah S., b. 10/15/1845, d. 02/29/1896
WILSON, William T., b. N/D, d. 09/10/1968
WINGATE, Charles L., DE, Pvt., 897 Engineer Avn. Bn., WWII, b. 08/14/1925, d. 04/06/1972
WINGATE, Charles Lorenzo, b. 08/14/1928, d. 04/06/1972
WINGATE, Craten, s/o J. C. & Susie K., b. 04/21/1921, d. 04/11/1922
WINGATE, Emma, w/o Willard S., b. 07/28/1869, d. 12/10/1920
WINGATE, Jesse Andrew, b. 10/06/1923, d. 10/06/1923
WINGATE, John Gorton, b. 02/02/1896, d. 01/31/1960
WINGATE, John Willard, b. 10/06/1923, d. 08/14/1924
WRIGHT, June Alice, b. 1943, d. 1964
ZIEGLER, Danielle, Jeanne, Infant, b. N/D, d. 07/24/1988

The following stones were recorded by the Hudson Survey but are now missing or unreadable:
JOHNSON, Bayard, Age 77y 7m 9d, b. N/D, d. 10/20/1900
SAMMONS, Ethel May, w/o Willard P., b. 12/19/1890, d. 07/26/1908

BEIDEMAN, 47, 137, 165, 201, 202, 270
BELL, 9, 13, 47, 100, 180, 183
BENDER, 47, 305
BENNETT, 47, 79, 100, 117, 147, 148, 164, 200, 202, 222, 251
BENNUM, 117
BENSON, 148, 165, 168, 171, 189, 202, 218
BENTLEY, 183
BERINGER, 47
BERKES, 202
BERNHART, 47
BERNHEIMER, 47
BERNSTEIN, 85
BERWICK, 202
BESENFELDER, 47
BEST, 11, 241
BETTS, 10, 16, 47, 100, 137, 148, 168, 198, 202, 231, 311
BEUTER, 47
BEVIS, 270
BICKELHAUPT, 47
BIDDLE, 202
BIGLEY, 47
BILLEY, 311
BILLINGS, 47, 148
BINGHAM, 270
BINYON, 47
BIRD, 47
BISHOP, 251
BISTER, 48
BIVENS, 183
BLACK, 48, 79, 117
BLACKSON, 294
BLACKWELL, 183
BLADES, 311
BLAINE, 48
BLAKE, 48, 100, 311
BLAKELEY, 16
BLANDON, 16

BLANER, 270
BLANKENSHIP, 85
BLEW, 117
BLIGHT, 251
BLIZZARD, 16, 17, 85, 100, 137
BLOCKSOM, 117, 137
BLOTH, 48
BLUGERMAN, 251
BLUNT, 189
BOHN, 85
BOKAN, 223
BOLAND, 270
BOLLES, 117
BOLTZ, 48
BONE, 85
BOONE, 183, 189
BORGESE, 270
BOSMAN, 117
BOSTON, 48
BOSWELL, 148
BOTJER, 220
BOUNDS, 48
BOWDEN, 17, 48, 100, 265
BOWE, 189
BOWEN, 294
BOWER, 17, 202
BOWERS, 17
BOWLES, 137
BOWMAN, 251
BOWSER, 48
BOYCE, 17, 48, 148, 149, 200, 270, 294
BOYD, 202
BOYER, 202
BOYKIN, 183, 263
BOYLE, 17
BOYLEN, 48
BRADFORD, 294, 311
BRADLEY, 13, 17, 117, 149, 230, 251, 288
BRADY, 202
BRANDT, 149, 270

BRANFORD, 270
BRASUR, 232
BRASURE, 17
BRATTEN, 183
BRERETON, 262
BREWSTER, 202
BREZINA, 48
BRICKNER, 100
BRIDGHAM, 200
BRIGGS, 183
BRILLANTE, 48
BRIMER, 231
BRINKLEY, 13, 251
BRITTIAN, 100
BRITTINGHAM, 17, 48, 79, 85, 100, 149, 165, 183, 189, 202, 220, 223, 265, 311, 312
BROCKETT, 183
BROCKINGTON, 117
BROCKMAN, 48
BROCKWAY, 48, 251
BROOKFIELD, 183
BROOKS, 48, 183
BROUTON, 189
BROWN, 13, 48, 117, 183, 189, 202, 265, 270, 271
BRUMBY, 241
BRUNDGE, 189
BRYAN, 48, 79, 85, 117, 118, 223, 271, 294, 295
BRYN, 251
BUCHANAN, 149
BUCK, 49, 251
BUCKLEY, 49, 180
BUCKMASTER, 251
BUCKSON, 149
BUCKWALTER, 271
BULINSKI, 49
BULLOCK, 17
BUMBRAY, 236
BUNCH, 189
BUNDICK, 265
BUNTING, 49, 79

BURBANK, 49
BURCIK, 49
BURKE, 251
BURKHART, 49
BURLINGAME, 149
BURNELL, 49
BURNHAM, 17, 271
BURNS, 118, 223, 265
BURNSIDE, 261
BURRIS, 49, 118, 189, 202, 271, 295
BURROUGHS, 17
BURROUS, 118
BURTELLE, 137, 138
BURTON, 13, 17, 115, 118, 183, 189, 231, 234, 241, 242, 265, 271
BUSH, 49, 242
BUSHEY, 17, 18, 49
BUTLER, 49, 183, 189
BUTTON, 271
BYERS, 149
BYLER, 305
BYNES, 189
BYRD, 183
CACKIER, 265
CADE, 118
CAGLE, 49
CAHALL, 79
CAHN, 171
CAIN, 202, 271
CALDWELL, 171, 251, 271
CALHOON, 18, 118, 149, 202
CALHOUN, 18, 49, 149, 202, 271
CALLAWAY, 202, 288, 312
CALLOWAY, 312
CAMEAN, 18
CAMP, 118
CAMPBELL, 18, 49, 50, 85, 149, 168, 169, 171, 189, 203, 251, 265, 288
CAMPER, 79

CANFIELD, 18
CANNON, 9, 18, 118, 180, 189, 265, 295, 309, 312
CAPEHART, 50
CARBIN, 189
CARD, 85, 251
CAREY, 18, 50, 80, 86, 100, 101, 118, 119, 136, 138, 149, 171, 203, 234
CARLISLE, 145, 203, 271, 295
CARMEAN, 50, 101, 149, 150, 271
CARMICHAEL, 189
CAROW, 18
CARPENTER, 18, 19, 50, 86, 101, 115, 119, 138, 150, 171, 198, 200, 203, 251, 312
CARRE, 295
CARRIER, 312
CARROLL, 50, 150, 189, 198
CARTER, 19, 50, 101, 183, 189, 265
CARTWRIGHT, 271
CASE, 252
CATCHELL, 101
CAULK, 189
CECIL, 138
CEPHAS, 183, 190
CHACONAS, 252
CHADWICK, 138
CHAFFINCH, 305
CHALABALA, 50
CHALLENGER, 252
CHALOVPKA, 19
CHAMBERLAIN, 7, 101
CHAMBERS, 50
CHANCE, 198
CHANDLER, 19, 50, 119, 183
CHANEY, 19
CHAPPEL, 86

CHASE, 222
CHERKOWSKY, 222
CHING, 271
CHIPMAN, 203
CHORMAN, 86
CHORMANN, 86
CHRISTIAN, 236
CHRISTNER, 305
CHURCH, 183, 190
CIABATTONE, 19
CIRWITHAN, 13
CIRWITHEN, 150
CIRWITHIAN, 183, 190
CISLER, 50
CLAPPER, 190
CLARK, 11, 19, 50, 203, 236, 242, 252, 265
CLARKS, 12
CLAVETTE, 101
CLAYVILLE, 203, 204
CLEAVER, 150
CLEMENTS, 119
CLEMONS, 150
CLENDANIEL, 19, 50, 80, 101, 138, 150, 165, 168, 169, 171, 198, 204, 271
CLIFFORD, 86
CLIFTON, 19, 20, 80, 86, 119, 138, 145, 150, 151, 204, 223, 271
CLOGG, 204
CLULEY, 271
CLYMER, 50
COATES, 145
COATS, 151
COBBS, 190
COCHRANE, 50
COCKRAN, 190
COFFEN, 151
COFFIN, 20, 50, 138, 151, 312
COHAN, 252
COLATRIANO, 50
COLBOURN, 9

ELLEGOOD, 309

ELLINGSWORTH, 23, 80, 87, 102, 122, 139, 166, 169, 172, 173, 206, 273

ELLIOTT, 54, 173, 290, 296, 312, 313

ELLIS, 191, 273, 290

ELLISON, 263

ELMER, 13

ELSASSER, 273

ELZEY, 313

EMBLETON, 305

EMICK, 54

EMMERT, 23, 253

EMORY, 87

ENFIELD, 181

ENGLISH, 296

ENNIS,, 102, 154, 173, 253

ERICKSON, 54

ESHAM, 232, 233

ESPERON, 23

EVANS, 54, 87, 123, 191, 200, 206, 231, 242, 266, 273, 290, 296, 310, 311

EWING, 123, 273, 274

EXLEY, 154

EYE, 54

FAILING, 206

FAILOR, 54

FAIRCLOTH, 191

FAIVRE, 253

FAMBRO, 13

FARENS, 154

FARIES, 23, 274

FARLEY, 88

FARLOW, 184, 191

FARRELL, 54

FARRINGTON, 23, 266

FARROW, 54

FASSEL, 154

FAUCETT, 123, 230

FAUST, 54

FAWLKES, 191

FEARING, 123

FENNER, 206

FENTERS, 54

FERGUSON, 54

FERL, 123

FERRARI, 253

FICHTER, 274

FIELDS, 123

FILLIUS, 253

FINCH, 191

FINK, 54

FINNITY, 154

FIORITTI, 23

FISHER, 23, 54, 88, 102, 123, 136, 166, 173, 184, 253, 274, 296, 309

FITCH, 54

FITHEN, 23

FITZCHARLES, 55

FITZGERALD, 200, 206, 305, 313

FLAHERTY, 253

FLATT, 253

FLEETWOOD, 224, 225, 296, 297, 313

FLEMING, 313

FLETCHER, 23, 266

FLOUNDERS, 55

FLUHARTY, 88

FOLTZ, 55

FOOKS, 219

FORAKER, 55

FORDYCE, 55

FOREMAN, 184, 191, 266

FORKUM, 206

FORMICHELLA, 253

FORST, 23, 24, 102

FORSYTH, 253

FOSKEY, 55, 88, 231, 297

FOSQUE, 24

FOSTER, 55, 206

FOUCHE, 139

FOUNTAIN, 55, 154, 191, 309

FOWLER, 24, 123, 136, 139, 154, 166

FOX, 55, 123

FRAESDORF, 55

FRAIZER, 184

FRAME, 13, 230, 262, 266, 274

FRAMPTON, 297

FRANCIS, 184

FRANK, 154

FRANKLIN, 88, 206

FRANTZ, 123

FRASER, 55

FRAZER, 274

FRAZIER, 24, 191, 243

FREAR, 253

FREEMAN, 55, 191

FREISCHMIDT, 55

FRENCH, 253

FRESE, 274

FREUND, 55

FRIED, 55

FRIEND, 55

FRIES, 305

FRISBY, 309

FRITCHMAN, 274

FRYE, 55, 274

FRYLING, 274

FULLER, 55, 266

FULLMAN, 184

FURLOW, 266

FURROUGHS, 24

FUSSELL, 237

FUTCHER, 88

GADOW, 274

GADSON, 184

GAGE, 55

GAGNON, 274

GALBRAITH, 55

GALE, 253

GALLAGHER, 253

GALLANT, 55

GALLASHAW, 184

GALLO, 55
GAMBLE, 191
GANRUDE, 88
GANTT, 274
GANTZ, 243
GARDNER, 313
GARRISON, 191
GARY, 55
GASSER, 55
GASVODA, 55
GAUMER, 293
GAYLE, 191
GEISE, 55
GELDER, 253
GERE, 206
GERMAN, 297
GEYER, 24, 56
GIBBONS, 56
GIBBS, 56, 191, 266
GIBSON, 164, 165, 253
GIES, 56
GIESE, 173
GIESS, 56
GIFFORD, 80
GILBERT, 24, 191
GILES, 297
GILGORE, 56
GILL, 191
GILLESPIE, 154
GILLILAND, 88
GILMARTIN, 274
GILMER, 123
GILMORE, 297
GILTENBOTH, 274
GINGERICH, 305
GIOVANNOZZI, 24
GIVAN, 88
GIVENS, 297
GLADDING, 206
GLADYSZ, 56
GLOVER, 266
GOBAS, 274
GOBAY, 154

GOEHRINGER, 222
GOEPEL, 56, 274
GOETZ, 102
GOFF, 56, 102
GOLDEN, 56, 173, 274
GOLDSBOROUGH, 184
GOLDSMITH, 173
GONAZELZ, 191
GOOCH, 184, 266
GOOD, 56, 225
GOODEN, 123
GOODHART, 24
GOODMAN, 263
GOODRICH, 254
GOODWIN, 24, 56, 274
GOODY, 254
GOONER, 154, 155
GOOTEE, 290
GORDEN, 123
GORDON, 56, 144
GORDY, 24
GORECKI, 56
GOSLEE, 123
GOSWELLEN, 231
GOTHARD, 123
GOUGE, 56
GOVATOS, 274
GOWER, 274
GRAHAM, 56, 102, 237, 243, 254, 274
GRAICE, 88
GRANTHAM, 254
GRAUL, 305
GRAVES, 24
GRAVIET, 254
GRAY, 24, 184, 206, 231, 232
GREEN, 24, 56, 88, 102, 165, 184, 219, 220, 225, 266, 274, 313
GREENE, 88, 274
GREENLEE, 56
GREENLY, 225
GRENOBLE, 254

GRIERSON, 103
GRIESBACK, 56
GRIEVES, 254
GRIFFIN, 191, 274
GRIFFITH, 56, 169, 184, 185, 191
GROLLER, 56
GROSH, 56
GROVES, 191
GRUBBS, 274
GUENGERICH, 305
GUENVEUR, 254
GUERIN, 173
GUNBY, 232
GUNDRY, 254
GUTHERIE, 274
GVERIN, 56
HAAS, 56
HAASS, 181
HABIB, 274
HABIG, 254
HACKET, 185
HACKETT, 56, 103
HADDER, 88, 274, 275
HADRICK, 185
HAEHNLE, 56
HAFF, 275
HAFFNER, 173
HAINES, 24, 309
HAIRSTON, 185
HALE, 254
HALEY, 275
HALFEN, 206
HALL, 57, 88, 123, 124, 185, 198, 206, 243, 254, 266, 275
HALLETT, 191, 198
HAMILTON, 57, 191, 254
HAMMOND, 57, 124, 155, 191, 275
HAMPTON, 309
HANBY, 139, 254
HAND, 103
HANDLEY, 57

HANDY, 191
HANLEY, 57
HANNA, 275
HANNAGAN, 254
HANZER, 12, 185, 243
HARDER, 206, 207
HARDING, 207
HARDY, 185
HARIG, 57
HARLEY, 57
HARMAN, 191, 237, 243, 249
HARMON, 12, 13, 57, 165, 185, 191, 192, 235, 237, 238, 243, 244, 245, 263, 275, 309
HARMSTEAD, 275
HARPER, 7, 57, 88, 89, 275
HARPSTER, 57
HARRIMAN, 10
HARRINGTON, 124, 139, 297
HARRIS, 12, 192, 198, 218, 235, 262, 275, 313
HARRISON, 173, 207, 218
HARRISSON, 155
HART, 24
HARTLEY, 173
HARVEY, 309
HASSELL, 266
HASSEMER, 57
HASTING, 89
HASTINGS, 9, 24, 25, 57, 89, 103, 207, 290, 293, 297, 298
HATCH, 57
HATFIELD, 124, 145, 207, 298
HAUGHEY, 57
HAVELKA, 25
HAYDEN, 275
HAYES, 57, 309
HAYNES, 309
HAYS, 275

HAZEL, 103, 155
HAZZARD, 12, 25, 57, 81, 124, 136, 144, 185, 192, 207, 275
HEADLEY, 155, 313
HEARN, 9, 207, 254, 298
HEARNE, 298
HEATH, 57, 309
HEATHER, 81, 155
HEAVELO, 81
HEAVELOW, 13, 166, 192
HEIKEL, 57
HEITMULLER, 207
HELLENS, 173, 207
HELLMANN, 57
HELM, 7
HEMMONDS, 181
HEMMONS, 181
HENDERLONG, 57
HENDERSON, 207, 290, 293, 309
HENDRICKS, 207
HENDRICKSON, 207, 298
HENKEL, 57
HENNING, 254
HENRY, 12, 57, 185, 245, 290, 291, 309
HENSON, 179
HERBER, 169
HERHOLDT, 57, 58
HERMAN, 207
HERMICKE, 58
HERRITY, 58
HERSHBERGER, 305
HERTZLER, 305
HESS, 58
HICKMAN, 25, 58, 103, 155
HIGGINS, 298, 309
HIGMAN, 200
HILDEBRAND, 25
HILL, 7, 25, 58, 81, 155, 192, 198, 207, 275, 276, 291, 313

HINCKLEY, 276
HINES, 309
HINTON, 192
HITCH, 89, 173, 207, 276, 291, 298
HITCHEN, 291
HITCHENS, 9, 25, 58, 103, 219, 220, 235, 266, 276, 291, 313
HOBBS, 58, 192, 198, 313
HOCHSTEDLER, 305
HODGDON, 103
HOEBEE, 276
HOLDING, 58
HOLLAND, 58, 89, 103, 115, 124, 155, 231, 266, 276
HOLLEGER, 58
HOLLINGER, 58
HOLLINGSWORTH, 25
HOLLIS, 207, 266
HOLLOMAN, 235
HOLLOWAY, 25, 58, 103
HOLLOWELL, 58
HOLMES, 58, 266
HOLMGREN, 254
HOLSON, 254, 255
HOLSTEIN, 198
HOLSTON, 25, 145, 198
HONEYVILLE, 185
HOOD, 25, 26, 263
HOOK, 58
HOOPER, 255
HOPKINS, 13, 26, 124, 185, 230, 235, 314
HORN, 255
HORNECK, 58
HORSEY, 89, 291
HORST, 255
HORTON, 207
HOSTEDLER, 207
HOSTETLER, 305
HOSTETTER, 305
HOUCK, 103

KERPER, 60
KERSEY, 208
KERSTIER, 60
KETTERER, 29
KEWLEY, 255
KEY, 277
KEYS, 12
KIBLER, 208
KIDD, 60
KILLEN, 60
KILLIAN, 60
KIMMEY, 126
KING, 29, 60, 61, 81, 90,
    105, 193, 200, 208, 220,
    221, 232, 267, 277, 299,
    315
KINGMAN, 255
KINTER, 255
KIRBY, 208, 246, 277
KIRKER, 277
KIRKPATRICK, 61
KITTRELL, 193
KLETT, 208, 209
KLINE, 61, 291
KLINGER, 61
KNERR, 174
KNOTTS, 255
KNOWLES, 145
KOEPPEL, 105
KOHEL, 61
KOHLENBERG, 29
KOHR, 61
KOLLOCK, 222, 223
KOLODZIEJ, 157
KOMOROWSKI, 209
KOPPLE, 105
KOSTER, 291
KOVAR, 209
KRAJEWSKI, 61
KRAMEDAS, 255
KRAMER, 61, 255
KRAUS, 209
KRILOWICZ, 61

KRING, 29
KROH, 174
KUNSMAN, 277
KUSIK, 255
KUVIK, 61
KUYWESKI, 61
KWACZ, 61
KYTTLE, 299
LACEY, 61, 126, 209, 267
LADD, 209
LAFFERTY, 255, 277
LAKE, 174, 299
LAMBDEN, 29, 299, 315
LAMBDIN, 126
LAMBERT, 61
LAMERE, 256
LAMPIE, 256
LANE, 29, 61, 199
LANGABEE, 174
LANGE, 277
LANK, 29, 61, 90, 91, 126,
    127, 157, 256
LANKFORD, 315
LAPINE, 61
LARE, 61
LARIMORE, 61
LARSEN, 157, 277
LASALLE, 61
LASSELLE, 145
LASSITER, 193
LATHROP, 277
LAVACHIA, 277
LAVENETS, 277
LAVIN, 277
LAWRIE, 61
LAWSON, 29, 61, 62, 91,
    158
LAWTON, 62
LAWVER, 256
LAYFIELD, 7
LAYTON, 62, 256
LEACH, 62, 256
LEAGER, 315

LEAVY, 127
LEBEGERN, 277
LECATES, 62
LECATO, 256
LECOMPTE, 62, 209
LEE, 29, 62, 91, 185, 256,
    263
LEFFLER, 62
LEFKOVITZ, 315
LEGATES, 29, 62, 91
LEGGINS, 185
LEGRAND, 193
LEHMAN, 256
LEHMANN, 29
LEITHMANN, 29
LEITTON, 62
LEKITES, 29, 127
LEMAIRE, 62
LENTZ, 299
LEONARD, 29, 127
LEPPO, 62
LEUTHAUSER, 62
LEVERAGE, 29, 81, 158
LEVERETT, 246
LEWICKI, 278
LEWIS, 29, 115, 193, 256,
    267, 278
LICHTENSTEIN, 256
LIGHTHIPE, 256
LILES, 185
LILLY, 81
LINDALE, 30, 209, 278
LINDLE, 127, 174
LINDSAY, 30, 62
LINE, 105
LINGENFELTER, 278
LINGO, 12, 91, 105, 127,
    225, 250, 256, 299
LINK, 256
LINKER, 174
LINN, 105
LINTHICUM, 209
LIPPINCOTT, 30

MCCRAY, 263
MCCREA, 186, 193
MCCULLOCH, 279
MCDANIEL, 158, 267, 279
MCDERMOTT, 257
MCDONALD, 64, 193, 299
MCDOWELL, 221, 279, 315
MCDOWEN, 158
MCDUFFIE, 193
MCFEE, 128
MCFERRAN, 128
MCFERREN, 129
MCGEE, 31, 64, 92, 106, 129, 225, 230
MCGINNIS, 31, 64
MCGOVERN, 279
MCGRATH, 31
MCHARGUE, 64
MCHENRY, 210, 279
MCILVAIN, 64, 106
MCKENNA, 64
MCKINNEY, 257
MCLAUGHLIN, 64
MCMANUS, 257
MCNATT, 279
MCNEIL, 257
MCNEILLY, 257
MCQUAID, 175
MCQUAY, 64, 279
MCSWEENEY, 64
MCWILLIAMS, 64, 257
MEARS, 31, 32, 299, 300, 315
MEGEE, 32, 106, 129, 225
MEHOLIC, 64
MELLON, 158
MELOTT, 92
MELSON, 279
MELVIN, 158, 175, 279
MENNELLA, 257
MENNINGALL, 310
MENTZINGER, 32

MEREDITH, 32, 175, 210, 221
MEREIDER, 32
MERRILL, 186
MERRITT, 279
MESSICK, 32, 92, 106, 129, 140, 158, 175, 210, 279, 300, 315, 316
METZNER, 92
MEYERS, 257
MICKLE, 193
MIDEL, 106
MIELDS, 129
MIFFLIN, 14, 257
MILBY, 92, 158, 167
MILES, 64, 210
MILLANE, 279
MILLER, 32, 64, 129, 169, 186, 199, 239, 246, 247, 257, 267, 306
MILLIKEN, 82
MILLMAN, 32, 64, 65, 92, 158, 167, 175, 199, 210
MILLS, 32, 65, 159, 199, 200, 210, 257, 300
MILMAN, 175
MILTENBERGER, 65
MINCY, 92
MINNER, 159, 279
MINOR, 267
MINTER, 300
MINTZ, 65
MIQUEL, 193
MIRCH, 106, 129
MISENER, 279
MITCHELL, 9, 32, 65, 92, 93, 106, 159, 175, 188, 230, 231, 233, 279, 280, 310
MOLLOY, 65
MONET, 159
MONIHAN, 65
MONLEY, 193
MONMILLER, 65

MONTE, 257
MONTGOMERY, 106
MOORE, 32, 33, 65, 66, 82, 93, 106, 129, 140, 159, 175, 193, 210, 233, 234, 257, 280, 300, 316
MOOTZ, 257
MORAN, 66
MORENGO, 66
MORGAN, 33, 66, 82, 159, 169, 175, 176, 186, 199, 210, 211, 239, 257, 280
MORLEY, 211
MORRIS, 7, 33, 66, 82, 106, 114, 129, 130, 140, 141, 144, 159, 167, 193, 235, 239, 247, 257, 267, 280, 291, 300
MORRISON, 211
MORROW, 181
MORTON, 66
MOSLEY, 12, 14, 239, 247, 248, 263, 267
MOSS, 66, 93
MOY, 280
MUIR, 66
MULLAHY, 66
MULLANEY, 66
MULLEN, 66, 193
MULLETT, 306
MULVANEY, 66
MUMFORD, 93, 300
MUNCY, 257
MUNSELL, 316
MUNTZ, 235
MURCH, 280
MURK, 66
MURPHY, 66, 159, 169, 170, 186, 193, 211, 257, 300
MURRAY, 33, 221, 280
MUSTARD, 33, 130
MUTTI, 280
MYERS, 239

PERKINS, 12, 194
PERROTT, 68
PERRY, 186, 194, 258
PESTRIDGE, 316
PETERSON, 68, 194
PETTYJOHN, 12, 14, 35, 82, 94, 107, 131, 141, 186, 187, 194, 211, 226, 230
PFISTER, 281
PHELPS, 187
PHILLIPS, 35, 68, 107, 231, 258, 268, 281, 292
PIANKA, 300
PICHILLI, 258
PIERCE, 194, 211
PIERRE, 194
PIERSON, 68, 281, 282
PILIERO, 176
PILKINGTON, 68
PINDER, 12
PINKNEY, 187
PIPER, 12, 14, 187
PITMAN, 159
PITTS, 194
PIZZUTO, 68
PLACK, 68
PLANGGER, 68
PLATT, 68
PLEASANTON, 211
PLOSKON, 68
PLUMMER, 35, 68, 159, 176
POE, 268
POLITE, 68
POLK, 9, 131, 248, 263
PONDER, 131, 159, 258
POOL, 131
POOLE, 115, 211
POORE, 211, 300
POPE, 194
PORST, 68
PORTER, 35, 68, 181
POSTLES, 35, 36, 176, 211
POTTER, 36, 199

POULSON, 194
POULTERER, 258
POUPARD, 282
POWELL, 68, 187, 194, 282, 310
POWERS, 36, 107
PRATTIS, 310
PRENGER, 258
PREOLE, 199
PRETTYMAN, 94, 107, 131, 159, 160, 167, 176, 194, 200, 248, 250, 300
PRICE, 12, 68, 69, 187, 263, 282
PRIDE, 36, 107, 211, 212, 226
PRIDEOUX, 194
PRIMROSE, 131
PRINGLE, 69
PRITCHET, 263
PRITCHETT, 36, 69
PROCTOR, 258
PROKO, 69
PRUITT, 69
PURCELL, 94
PURDY, 282
PURKS, 160
PURNELL, 69, 141, 160, 194, 310
PUSEY, 9, 69, 107, 292, 300, 301
QUACKENBOSS, 282
QUIG, 36
QUIGLEY, 69
QUIL, 170
QUILLEN, 36, 199, 221, 258, 282
QUIMBY, 258
QUINN, 282
QUINONES, 194
RADIS, 232
RADKE, 131
RAEA, 94
RALPH, 292

RANDER, 69
RANDOLPH, 187
RANSON, 268
RASH, 292
RASPE, 176
RATHBUN, 212
RATLEDGE, 160, 164, 258
RAUGHLEY, 301
RAYFIELD, 194
RAYNE, 226
REARDON, 69
RECORDS, 69
REDDEN, 199
REDHEFFER, 107
REED, 11, 36, 37, 46, 69, 82, 83, 107, 108, 131, 137, 141, 167, 168, 176, 177, 187, 212, 226, 248, 268, 282
REEDER, 69
REGISTER, 94
REICHHOLD, 282
REID, 194
REIDER, 239
REMENTER, 301
REMINGTON, 69
RENDFREY, 226
RENTZ, 69
REVEL, 233
REVELL, 233
REVELLE, 160, 170
REYNOLDS, 11, 37, 69, 83, 94, 95, 108, 132, 141, 160, 164, 165, 187, 194, 212, 221, 282, 316
RHOADES, 258
RHODES, 37, 187, 292
RICE, 37, 69, 95, 212
RICHARD, 194
RICHARDS, 37, 69, 95, 144, 232
RICHARDSON, 14, 69, 194, 301
RICHESON, 258

SEBRING, 283
SEELEY, 283
SEESMAN, 71
SEIBERT, 71
SEIDLE, 259
SELBY, 213
SELDEN, 259
SEMPLE, 71
SENNETT, 213
SEUTTER, 95
SEYMOUR, 268
SEYMOURE, 268
SHAFER, 71
SHAFFER, 71, 109
SHANE, 222
SHANER, 292
SHANNON, 195
SHARP, 39, 71, 95, 96, 132, 187, 195, 218, 227, 230
SHARPE, 187
SHARPER, 248
SHARY, 71
SHAUD, 72
SHAW, 259
SHAY, 72
SHELDON, 213, 283
SHELTON, 187, 248
SHENKLE, 177
SHEPARD, 161
SHEPHERD, 39
SHEPPARD, 161, 187, 195
SHERMAN, 72, 109, 161
SHETLER, 307
SHEW, 213
SHIELDS, 213
SHIVELHOOD, 132
SHOCKLEY, 39, 72, 96, 109, 141, 161, 167, 195, 201, 213, 214, 283, 292, 302
SHOEMAKER, 221
SHOOP, 72
SHORT, 39, 72, 84, 96, 109, 132, 141, 142, 161, 167,

177, 181, 219, 223, 227, 230, 232, 233, 259, 268, 283, 302, 317
SHORTS, 187
SHOURDS, 214
SHOWALTER, 307
SHOWELL, 72, 263, 264, 268
SHUPARD, 259
SHUTE, 72
SHUTT, 72
SIMMONS, 39, 72, 259
SIMMS, 72
SIMONS, 72
SIMPERS, 72
SIMPLER, 84, 96, 109, 283
SIMPSON, 161, 227, 283, 302
SIMS, 187
SINGLETON, 268, 317
SIPPLE, 72, 259
SIZEMORE, 181
SKELLY, 9
SKIDMORE, 132
SLATER, 284
SLAUGHTER, 214
SLAW, 39
SLENCZKA, 284
SMACK, 96
SMALL, 214, 218, 284
SMIDTH, 39
SMITH, 7, 39, 40, 72, 73, 96, 109, 161, 164, 177, 181, 182, 187, 188, 195, 196, 214, 221, 233, 239, 248, 259, 302, 307, 310, 317, 318
SMITHERS, 132
SMOCK, 259
SMOOT, 199
SMYK, 73
SNAVELY, 73
SNELL, 73
SNYDER, 40, 73, 284

SOCKOLOSKY, 73
SOCKOM, 14
SOCKRIDER, 214
SOCKRITER, 109
SOCKUM, 12, 248
SOCKUME, 239
SOMERS, 14
SOOKIASIAN, 73
SOUCEK, 284
SOUDER, 73
SOUTHARD, 214
SPARKS, 109
SPEICHER, 307
SPELLMAN, 196
SPENCE, 188, 268
SPENCER, 40, 115, 161, 214
SPICER, 73, 177, 214, 227, 228, 302, 318
SPIEGEL, 284
SPOSATO, 73
STACY, 284
STAFFEL, 264
STAIB, 40, 73
STALLINGS, 284
STANISZEWSKI, 259
STANLEY, 73, 188, 268
STANNART, 284
STANSBURY, 73
STANTON, 214, 228
STARKEY, 132
STAUFFER, 73
STAYTON, 145, 201, 214
STEAD, 73
STEEDLE, 284
STEELE, 40, 73, 96, 109, 110, 233, 284
STEELMAN, 40, 73, 132, 142, 284
STEEN, 142, 161, 162, 214, 219
STEGEMAN, 259
STEIN, 259
STEINER, 110

STENGER, 40
STEPHENS, 40, 96, 284
STEPHENSON, 132
STERBUTZL, 228
STERRETT, 239
STERRITT, 214
STEVENS, 188, 200, 214
STEVENSON, 40, 73, 110, 142, 144, 162, 196, 248, 284
STEVERSON, 73
STEWART, 73, 96, 110, 259, 268
STOCKLEY, 248, 268, 284
STODDART, 284
STOETZEL, 40
STOLTING, 284
STOLTZFUS, 307
STONEBERGER, 177
STONESIFER, 260
STOOMS, 110
STOREY, 199
STORMER, 162
STOTT, 74
STOUT, 142, 215
STRAIT, 215
STRAND, 165
STREET, 239, 240, 248, 249, 264
STRICKLAND, 284, 285
STRICKROTH, 260
STUART, 145, 177
STUCHLIK, 40, 110
STURGIS, 115, 230
STURMFELZ, 285
SUAREZ, 188
SULLIVAN, 74, 285, 302
SUNKETT, 268
SUPPLES, 40
SUTER, 285
SUTHERLAND, 260
SUTTON, 196
SUYDAM, 199

SWAIN, 177, 215, 228, 302, 318, 319
SWANN, 285
SWARTZENTRUBER, 307
SWEET, 40, 41
SWIFT, 162
SWINZOW, 74
SWISHER, 96
SYMONDS, 215
SZEG, 74
T., 228
TABOR, 74
TACARR, 14
TALLENT, 221
TAPPAN, 285, 288
TARR, 110
TATTERSAIL, 115
TAYLOR, 12, 74, 96, 110, 132, 162, 177, 188, 196, 215, 228, 235, 236, 240, 292, 302, 310, 319
TEAS, 96, 162
TEES, 96
TEWELOW, 285
THACKERY, 41
THARP, 41
THAWLEY, 285
THAYER, 132, 177
THOMAS, 41, 74, 84, 110, 188, 196, 215, 221, 230, 260, 268, 285, 310
THOMLINSON, 96
THOMPSON, 14, 74, 110, 132, 196, 219, 236, 240, 249, 260, 268, 285, 302
THOROUGHGOOD, 250, 260
THORTON, 228
TIKOB, 260
TILLEY, 196
TILLMAN, 196
TILNEY, 132, 133
TIMMONS, 268
TINDAL, 302

TINDALL, 303
TINGLE, 74, 110, 196, 215, 249
TINKER, 319
TITTERMARY, 96
TITUS, 199, 200
TOBIN, 41, 260
TODD, 41, 162
TOLBERT, 74
TOLMIE, 74
TOLSON, 12, 14
TOMLINSON, 133
TONGE, 303
TOOMEY, 285
TOPPIN, 285
TORBERT, 74, 260
TORRACK, 74
TORREY, 260
TOWERY, 74
TOWLSON, 285
TOWNSEND, 7, 9, 162, 196, 260
TOYER, 285
TRACY, 215
TRADER, 196, 310
TRANSEAU, 215
TRAVIS, 215, 285
TRAYLOR, 215
TRENCH, 74
TRIBBITT, 74
TRICE, 303
TRIFILLIS, 285
TRIMBLE, 7, 8
TRIPLETT, 215
TROTTER, 196
TROYER, 307
TRUITT, 41, 74, 75, 96, 97, 162, 182, 188, 215, 233, 285, 286, 303, 319
TRUMBALL, 75
TSELIOS, 260
TUBBS, 260
TUCKER, 75, 110, 177, 182, 188, 196, 216, 307, 319